The Student Edition of Lotus® 1-2-3® Release 2.2

Limited Warranty

Addison-Wesley warrants that the Student Edition of 1-2-3 (''the program'') will substantially conform to the published specifications and to the documentation during the period of 90 days from the date of original purchase, provided that it is used on the computer hardware and with the operating system for which it was designed. Addison-Wesley also warrants that the magnetic media on which the program is distributed and the documentation are free from defects in materials and workmanship during the period of 90 days from the date of original purchase. Addison-Wesley will replace defective media or documentation or correct substantial program errors at no charge, provided you return the item with dated proof of purchase to Addison-Wesley within 90 days of the date of original purchase. If Addison-Wesley is unable to replace defective media or documentation or correct substantial program errors, your license fee will be refunded. These are your sole remedies for any breach of warranty.

Except as specifically provided above, Addison-Wesley makes no warranty or representation, either express or implied, with respect to this program, documentation or media, including their quality, performance, merchantability, or fitness for a particular purpose. Lotus makes no warranty or representation, either express or implied, with respect to this program, documentation or media, including their quality, performance, merchantability or fitness for a particular purpose.

Because programs are inherently complex and may not be completely free of errors, you are advised to verify your work. **In no event will Addison-Wesley or Lotus be liable for direct, indirect, special, incidental, or consequential damages arising out of the use of or inability to use the program, documentation or media,** even if advised of the possibility of such damages. Specifically, neither Addison-Wesley nor Lotus is responsible for any costs including, but not limited to, those incurred as result of lost profits or revenue (in any case, the program must be used only for educational purposes, as required by your license), loss of use of the computer program, loss of data, the costs of recovering such programs or data, the cost of any substitute program, claims by third parties, or for other similar costs. In no case shall the liability of Addison-Wesley exceed the amount of the license fee and in no case shall Lotus have any liability.

The warranty and remedies set forth above are exclusive and in lieu of all others, oral or written, express or implied. No Addison-Wesley dealer, distributor, agent, or employee is authorized to make any modification or addition to this warranty.

Some statutes do not allow the exclusion of implied warranties; if any implied warranties are found to exist, they are hereby limited in duration to the 90-day life of the express warranties given above. Some states do not allow the exclusion or limitation of incidental or consequential damages, nor any limitation on how long implied warranties last, so these limitations may not apply to you. This warranty gives you specific legal rights and you may also have other rights which vary from state to state.

To obtain performance of this warranty, return the item with dated proof of purchase within 90 days of the purchase date to: Addison-Wesley Publishing Company, Inc., Educational Software Division, Jacob Way, Reading, MA 01867.

The Student Edition of Lotus® 1-2-3® RELEASE 2.2

The spreadsheet software integrating worksheet, database, and graphics... adapted for education

Timothy J. O'Leary
Arizona State University

Linda I. O'Leary

Addison-Wesley Publishing Company, Inc.
Benjamin/Cummings Publishing Company, Inc.

Reading, Massachusetts • Menlo Park, California • New York
Don Mills, Ontario • Wokingham, England • Amsterdam • Bonn
Sydney • Singapore • Tokyo • Madrid • San Juan

Dedicated to our parents

Charles D. O'Leary   Jean Larson O'Leary   Irene A. Perley Coats

and in memory of

Albert Lawrence Perley

The Student Edition of Lotus 1-2-3, Release 2.2 is published by Addison Wesley Publishing Company, Inc. and Benjamin/Cummings Publishing Company, Inc.

Contributors include:
Alan Jacobs, Executive Editor
Dana Degenhardt, Senior Product Development Manager
Rachel Bunin, Project Manager
Karen Wernholm, Software Production Supervisor
Nancy Benjamin, Development Editor and Production Coordinator
Martha White Tenney, Text Designer
Jean Seal, Cover Designer
Gex, Inc., Compositor

ISBN 0-201-90772-0 Manual

CDEFGHIJ-HA-99876543210

Preface

Lotus 1-2-3 is one of the most widely used and most powerful software products on the market today. It combines a superior spreadsheet with excellent graphics and an efficient database. Its power and flexibility have made it an industry standard. Therefore, it is not surprising that the educational version of Lotus 1-2-3 has become the spreadsheet of choice for education. It is used in the educational setting in microcomputing applications ranging from engineering and biology to accounting and finance.

The new Lotus 1-2-3 Release 2.2 has built upon and expanded Release 2.01 to offer you more speed and analytical power. It is a high-performance spreadsheet for analyzing, managing, and presenting information. And now the Student Edition of Lotus 1-2-3 Release 2.2 lets students keep up with the latest version of this industry standard, preparing them to step right into the business world.

The Student Edition of Lotus 1-2-3 Release 2.2 continues to be fully file compatible with the professional version. It also reads any files that are 1-2-3 compatible and its files can be easily imported into other programs, such as most popular word processing programs.

The Differences Between the Student Edition of Lotus 1-2-3 Release 2.2 and the Professional Version

The Student Edition is fully functioning and identical to the professional version of Release 2.2, except:

- The Translate utility has been removed
- Allways has been removed
- A header, "The Student Edition of Lotus 1-2-3" and the student's name, automatically prints at the top of all printed worksheets

New Features

The Student Edition of Lotus 1-2-3 Release 2.2 has a full-size spreadsheet (256 columns by 8192 rows), and includes the Access system. All of the printer and graphics drivers provided in Lotus 1-2-3 are included in this package. The hands-on interactive labs have been revised and expanded to demonstrate many of the new Release 2.2 features, such as file linking, Undo, minimal recalculation, and a macro LEARN mode. It also has an expanded reference section.

Objectives

The Student Edition of Lotus 1-2-3 Release 2.2 is designed to introduce students to the powerful capabilities of the most popular electronic spreadsheet available. The primary objectives of this book are:

- To provide a complete educational environment for learning 1-2-3
- To provide a powerful and flexible tool for teachers and students
- To teach the fundamentals of spreadsheets, graphics, and databases
- To establish good problem-solving techniques

To accomplish these objectives, this book has the following features:

- One resource. The material contained in two separate 1-2-3 manuals has been combined into one complete text, including initializing and installing 1-2-3, tutorial lab exercises, and reference.
- Interactive labs. A comprehensive Overview and nine topic-specific hands-on labs have been developed to teach 1-2-3 concepts, commands, and applications in a problem-solving environment.
- Cross-references. Extensive cross-referencing between the Reference section and the interactive labs supports the expansion and clarification of key concepts and commands.
- Teaching aids. Numerous teaching aids throughout the book reinforce important concepts, build a powerful vocabulary, and promote the development of critical problem-solving skills.
- Logical design. The organization of the text allows students to master complex ideas in small, easily assimilated steps.

- Flexible design. The text has been developed in modular fashion to allow students at various levels of computer expertise to learn 1-2-3 efficiently. This design also allows instructors to develop courses using all or selected parts of the manual.

Organization

The Student Edition of Lotus 1-2-3 Release 2.2 presents the fundamentals of 1-2-3 in clear, simple language that encourages learning. Each topic is developed systematically, with the assumption that the student's total knowledge of a subject area is based on the reading of a previous section.

The manual is divided into three sections.

Section 1, ''Getting Started,'' introduces 1-2-3 by explaining the basic skills required to install, start, run, and end the program.

The section begins by detailing the contents of the Student Edition package. The student is then provided with a concise explanation of the conventions used throughout the manual. The fundamentals of working with the computer and the software are discussed in detail. Next, complete, easy-to-follow instructions for initializing 1-2-3, formatting disks, backing up the original disks, copying 1-2-3 to a hard disk, and starting, using, and exiting the Install program are provided.

This section then provides step-by-step instructions on how to start 1-2-3 from a two-disk or hard-disk system, how to change the default directory for 1-2-3, and how to start 1-2-3 from the Access system. Finally, it provides a comprehensive chapter on starting, setting up, and leaving the PrintGraph program, as well as a chapter on 1-2-3's Help facility.

Section 2, ''An Overview to 1-2-3 and Lab Activities,'' starts with the Overview, a hands-on interactive lab designed to familiarize the student with the power and scope of the 1-2-3 program. The Overview introduces students to the spreadsheet and use of the keyboard in the worksheet, to the graphics and database capabilities, and to the macro features of 1-2-3. This broad presentation demonstrates the total 1-2-3 program in a nonthreatening environment; it provides a meaningful foundation upon which to build.

The nine interactive lab activities follow. Through the use of carefully developed case studies supported by numerous data files, students learn 1-2-3 by solving problems.

Each lab begins with a list of objectives, followed by a brief description of the case study used throughout the lab. The case studies present real-world problems and situations across a variety of settings. The student becomes involved in the case itself as well as the application of 1-2-3 commands.

The student follows the case study while completing the activities in each lab. As the student performs each step in the lab, a screen print is presented in the manual to keep the student on track and to reinforce key concepts. At the end of the lab, a list of key terms and definitions is presented along with several practice problems.

Each lab requires approximately 45 minutes to complete (not including practice problems). The actual time to complete any one lab will vary somewhat from lab to lab, student to student, and instructor to instructor.

The labs have been designed in a modular fashion, to allow instructors the greatest flexibility in course development. After students have mastered the basic spreadsheet commands in Labs 1 and 2, they may proceed directly to graphics, database, macros, or advanced spreadsheet labs. The numerous alternative paths that are available are detailed in the Instructor's Manual.

Labs 1 and 2 have one continuing case study and should be presented as a unit. Labs 3 and 4 introduce the graphics capability of 1-2-3. Labs 5 and 6 introduce advanced spreadsheet techniques such as linking files, freezing titles, creating windows, hiding columns, and naming ranges. Labs 5 and 6 have a continuing case study and should be presented as a unit. Lab 7 introduces creating and using databases, and explores the search and replace feature. Lab 8 presents advanced database concepts, such as extracting information, creating a frequency distribution, and using a data table. Lab 9 presents an introduction to macros, including the use of the STEP and LEARN modes.

Students completing all nine labs will be able to organize and analyze information in a spreadsheet effectively and efficiently. In addition, they will be able to display information in charts and graphs, enter and extract information from databases, and create and use macros.

Section 3, "Reference," contains comprehensive descriptions of the 1-2-3 commands, menus, and functions. The main areas of this section include basic spreadsheet skills, commands, macros, @functions, and the PrintGraph program. This section is extensively cross-referenced to the Lab Activities in Section 2.

Acknowledgments

The development of the Student Edition of Lotus 1-2-3 Release 2.2 has required a tremendous team effort from many individuals, and we would like to thank all those who have contributed to it. Through their combined efforts, we have built upon and improved the previous student editions of Lotus 1-2-3.

We are particularly grateful for the contributions of many people at Addison-Wesley. In particular, we thank Alan Jacobs, Executive Editor, and Dana Degenhardt, Senior Product Development Manager, for their continued support of the project. Also, thanks to Karen Wernholm for contributing to the smooth production of this book.

For the day-to-day coordination of the development of this book, we would like to thank Rachel Bunin, Project Manager, for her good humor, persistence, and organizational skills. It has been a pleasure working with her. Credit also needs to be given to Nancy Benjamin for her conscientious editing skills and production coordination. Without their combined efforts and pleasant natures, this project would not have been the success it is.

Our thanks to the staff and programmers of Lotus Development Corporation, who provided us with their technical expertise and created the software for this package.

We are also indebted to the reviewers for their valuable insights, criticisms, and suggestions. Included among them are: Mark Hale, University of Florida, Gainesville; Phillip A. Jones, University of Richmond; and Lloyd Rosenberg, Baruch College, City University of New York. In addition, we are grateful to Mary Koonmen and the students at the John Jay College of Criminal Justice for their Student Field Test, which provided many helpful suggestions.

Timothy J. O'Leary
Linda I. O'Leary

Contents

One Getting Started

Two Overview and Lab Activities

Getting Started

1

Before You Begin

This chapter describes the contents of the Student Edition of Lotus 1-2-3 Release 2.2 package and the typographical conventions used in this manual. You should read this introduction before you use or install 1-2-3.

Checking Your Package

Your package for the Student Edition of Lotus 1-2-3 Release 2.2 should contain the following:

- The User's Manual (this book)
- Five disks for the 5¼″ version; two disks for the 3½″ version
- License Agreement (printed on the disk box)
- Registration Card
- Keyboard templates

The User's Manual

The User's Manual consists of three sections.

Getting Started	This section includes instructions on how to initialize and install 1-2-3, how to start and end 1-2-3, how to start and end PrintGraph, and how to use the Help facility.
An Overview to 1-2-3 and Lab Activities	The Overview is a short hands-on interactive lab designed to introduce you to 1-2-3's worksheet, graphics, and database capabilities. The Lab Activities are nine hands-on, interactive labs covering worksheets, graphics, databases, and macros.
Reference	The reference section is a comprehensive discussion of 1-2-3 commands and procedures.

Disks

The 5¼″ version of the Student Edition of Lotus 1-2-3 Release 2.2 contains five disks.

System disk	The System disk contains the complete 1-2-3 program—Worksheet, Graphics, Database—as well as the Access system, which lets you start 1-2-3, PrintGraph, or Install from a menu.

PrintGraph disk	The PrintGraph disk contains PrintGraph, a separate program that lets you print the graphs you create with 1-2-3, and a copy of the Access system.
Utilities disk	The Utilities disk contains the Install program, which you must run to use a printer or to display graphs, and a copy of the Access system. This disk also contains the Macro Library Manager.
Install Library disk	The Install Library disk contains a library of programs, called drivers, that let 1-2-3 run with your equipment.
Help and Sample Files disk	The Help and Sample Files disk has several files used in Section 2, ''An Overview to 1-2-3 and Lab Activities.'' The on-line Help facility is also included on this disk.

The 3½″ version contains two disks.

System disk with PrintGraph	The System disk with PrintGraph has the 1-2-3 System, as well as the Access system, which lets you start 1-2-3, or PrintGraph from a menu, the PrintGraph program, the Macro Library Manager, and the on-line Help facility.
Utilities disk	The Utilities disk contains the Install program, the Install Library, the Sample files, and a copy of the Access system.

Two Keyboard Templates

The keyboard templates are the guides that you place on your keyboard to remind you what each function key or special key combination does in 1-2-3. If the function keys on your keyboard are in two columns on the left of the typewriter key section (IBM PC or PC/XT or compatibles), use the rectangular template. If you have an IBM PS/2 or another keyboard in which the function keys lie across the top, use the horizontal template. You will find the templates in the box that holds the 1-2-3 disks.

Product Support

Neither Addison-Wesley nor Lotus Development Corporation provides phone assistance to students for the Student Edition of Lotus 1-2-3 Release 2.2. Phone assistance is provided to *registered* instructors adopting the Student Edition.

If you encounter difficulty using the Student Edition software:

- Consult the reference section of the User's Manual for information on the commands or procedures you are trying to perform.
- Use the Help screens to locate specific program or error message information.

If you have to ask your instructor for assistance, describe your question or problem in detail. Write down what you were doing (the steps or procedures you followed) when the problem occurred. Also write down the exact error message (if any).

Typographical Conventions

You issue 1-2-3 commands and instructions by pressing particular keys or sequences of keys. These keys are designated either by symbols (for arrow keys, function keys, and the return, or enter key) or by small caps (for example, ESC). This manual uses the following terminology:

Press: This tells you to strike or press a key. It is used primarily with the arrow keys, the special keys, the function keys, and the ENTER key, ↵, to perform an operation. For example, the instruction to press the ↵ key would appear as:

Press: ↵

Type: This also tells you to strike or press a key. It is used primarily with the standard typewriter keys to enter information into a worksheet. Keys you type are printed in boldface. For example, the instructions to type the word TOTAL would appear as:

Type: **TOTAL**

Move to: This tells you to move the cell pointer to a particular location in the worksheet, usually with the arrow keys. For example, the instruction to move the cell pointer to cell D10 would appear as:

Move to: D10

Combinations

When two keys are separated by a - (hyphen), such as CTRL-(→), you must press and hold down the first key, press the second key, and then release both keys. For example, you would press and hold down CTRL, press (→), and then release both keys.

When two keys are separated by only a space, such as END HOME, press the first key, release it, press the second key, and release it. For example, press END and release it, and then press HOME and release it.

Command Sequences

Command sequences in the Lab Activities are offset and indented. The first letter of each command option is printed in boldface, indicating that it should be typed or selected. Any other parts of the command sequence to be typed are also in boldface. For example, the command to retrieve the file LABELS would be shown as:

/ **F**ile **R**etrieve **LABELS** (↵)

In this case, you would type /**FRLABELS** and then press (↵).

2

Initializing and Installing 1-2-3

This chapter leads you through the steps you should follow before you can use the Student Edition of Lotus 1-2-3 Release 2.2: using the Initialization program, preparing disks, making backup copies of the original disks, and installing 1-2-3 so that it will work with your equipment. The procedures vary depending on the type of system you have: two-disk or hard-disk. The following pictures will appear in the left margin to help you find the sections relevant to your type of system:

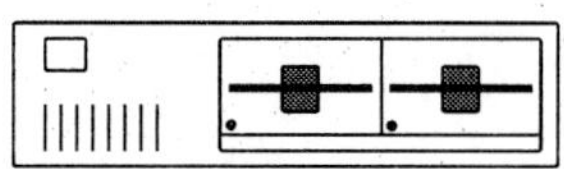

Two-disk system

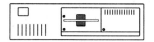

Hard-disk system

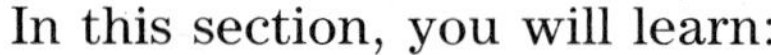

Preliminaries

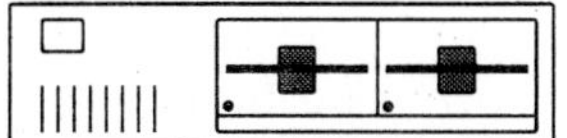

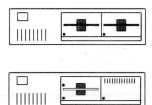

In this section, you will learn:

- How to start your computer
- The fundamentals of working with disks
- How to run the Initialization program
- How to prepare disks for use
- How to make backup copies of your original disks
- How to create data disks
- How to copy 1-2-3 to your hard disk (if you have one)
- How to install 1-2-3

You will need the following items:

- The five 1-2-3 disks if you are using the 5¼″ version; the two 1-2-3 disks if you are using the 3½″ version
- The DOS system disk (version 2.0 or higher), or DOS installed on your hard disk (see system requirements on back cover)
- If you are using a two-disk system, six blank disks with sleeves and labels for the 5¼″ version and three disks with labels for the 3½″ version (to make backup copies of your program disks and to create a data disk)
- If you are using a hard-disk system, one blank disk with sleeve and label for the 5¼″ version and one blank disk with label for the 3½″ version (to create a data disk)
- Write-protect tabs for the 5¼″ disks only

Working with Disks

Your computer has one or two disk drives that use either 5¼″ or 3½″ removable disks.

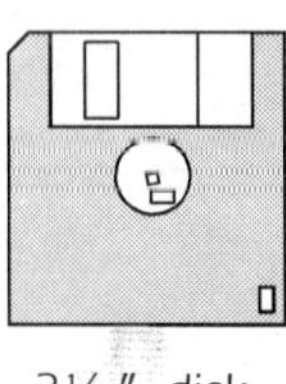

3½″ disk

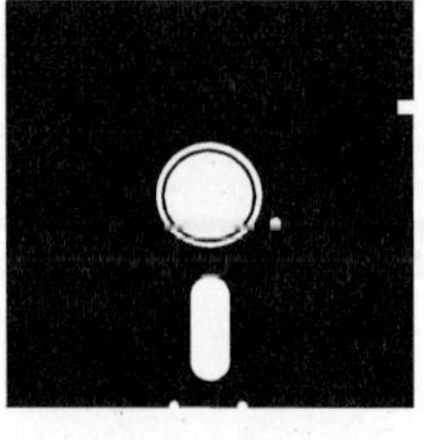

5¼″ disk

In addition, your computer may have a fixed, or hard, disk. This is usually a nonremovable unit built into the computer that can store the contents of many disks.

The Student Edition of Lotus 1-2-3 Release 2.2 is packaged on disks in either 5¼″ or 3½″ format. Even if you have a hard disk, you will be using the disks to load the program and to store copies of the worksheets, databases, and graphs you create.

Whenever you work with disks, keep the following in mind:

- Do not touch the exposed areas of the disk. If you are using 3½″ disks, do not handle a disk with the shutter (the sliding metal door at the bottom center of the disk) open.
- If you are using 5¼″ disks, take care when you write on the disk label; a sharp point or hard pressure may damage the disk. Use a felt-tip pen to write on a label that is already on the disk.
- Always replace the 5¼″ disk back in the sleeve after using it.
- Keep the disk away from heat, sunlight, smoke, and magnetic fields, such as telephones, televisions, and transformers.
- If the drive slot is horizontal, slide the disk into the drive with the label facing up. The notch on a 5¼″ disk should be on the left; for 3½″ disks, the metal shutter should be inserted first. If the drive is vertically mounted, the label should face left and the notch should be at the bottom.

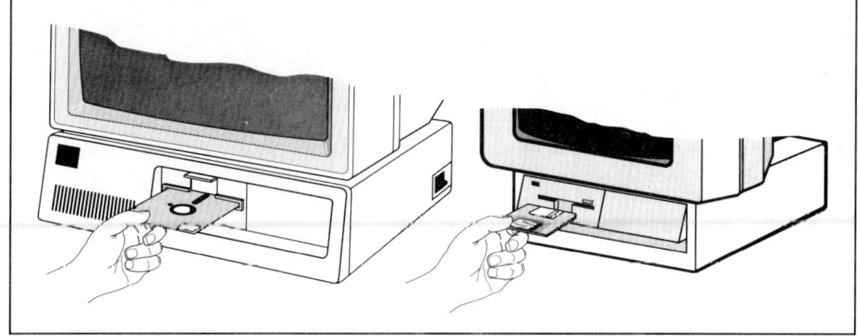

- Put the disk in the drive as far as it will go, but do not force it. If you are using 5¼″ disks, you must close the drive door after you insert the disk.
- Do not remove a disk while the drive access light is on.

Write-Protecting Disks

In addition to environmental hazards, disks are also vulnerable to human error. Whenever you are working with a disk, you can avoid some accidents by "write-protecting" it. This ensures that you do not accidentally alter or erase any information on the disk. Write-protecting it does not prevent you from running a program from the disk or retrieving information from it.

The procedure for write-protecting a disk depends on what kind of disk you have.

- For 5¼″ disks, cover the notch on the side of the disk with a write-protect tab. Put half of the tab over the notch and fold the tab over so it sticks to the other side.
- For 3½″ disks, there is a small write-protect window in the upper right corner of the disk. When the window is open, the disk is protected. If necessary, slide the small plastic tab over to uncover the window.

Starting Your Computer

Before you can prepare disks or make copies of your 1-2-3 disks, you must load DOS, the *D*isk *O*perating *S*ystem that lets the computer do basic tasks such as copying and formatting disks. Your computer should be off when you start this section. If you make a typing error, use BACKSPACE to erase the letters and then type the entry correctly.

1. This step is for two-disk systems only; skip to step 2 if you are using a hard disk.

   Insert your DOS disk in drive A (the upper or left drive). If you are using 5¼″ disks, close the drive door.

2. Turn on the computer.

   Some computers also have a separate switch for the monitor; if so, turn it on.

   It may take up to one minute for the small blinking underscore, or the *cursor*, to appear in the upper left corner of the screen. When the computer is ready, it either displays the date or asks you to enter it.

3. Enter the date (if necessary) in the form MM-DD-YY and press ↵.

   For example, if the date is September 9, 1990, type 09-09-90 and press ↵.

4. Enter the time (if necessary) in HH:MM twenty-four hour format and press ↵.

   For example, if the time is 1:45 p.m., type 13:45 and press ↵.

If you enter the date or time incorrectly, DOS lets you try again. When you have finished entering the date and time, the operating system prompt appears. This book uses A> for two-disk systems and C> for hard-disk systems; your prompt may look somewhat different.

Initializing 1-2-3

Before you can install and start the Student Edition of Lotus 1-2-3 Release 2.2 or make backup copies of the disks, you must run the Initialization program. This program records your name and school name on your copy of 1-2-3, identifying you as the licensee. You need to complete this procedure only once.

Note This is a very important step and it is crucial that you enter the information accurately. Your name will print on your worksheets exactly as you enter it during the Initialization procedure.

The following directions assume that if you have a hard-disk system your hard disk is drive C, your first disk drive is drive A, and your second (if present) is drive B. If you have a two-disk system, these instructions assume that your disk drives are A and B. If this is not the case, substitute the correct drive letters. If you are unsure, ask your technical resource person for assistance.

The system prompt (A> for a two-disk system, C> for a hard-disk system, or something similar) should be on the screen.

Note The Initialization program cannot be run with RAM-resident programs or from the OS/2 window. If you have either, reboot your computer with your DOS disk.

Note Low-density drives (360K 5¼″ or 720K 3½″) often cannot read disks that were created on high-density drives (1.2 MB 5¼″ drive or 1.44 MB 3½″). If you use a high-density floppy drive to initialize 1-2-3, you may no longer be able to use your System disk in a low-density drive. If you have low-density drives, use them for the following steps. Or ask your technical resource person for assistance.

Note At any time during the Initialization procedure, you can press CTRL-BREAK to quit the program without saving any entries. The BREAK key is at the upper right of your keyboard. On some keyboards, it is the SCROLL LOCK key; on PS/2 keyboards, it is the PAUSE key.

1. Insert the System disk (System disk with PrintGraph for 3½″ users) in drive A and, if necessary, close the door. (The disk should not be write-protected.)

2. Make drive A the current drive; if the A> prompt is not on the screen,

   Type: **A:**
   Press: ↵

3. To begin the Initialization program,

   Type: **INIT**
   Press: ↵

   The copyright screen appears.

4. To see the next screen,

   Press: ↵

The following informational screen appears:

```
During initialization, you will be asked to enter your name and
your school's name.  Enter your full name at the 'Student Name'
prompt and your school's name at the 'School Name' prompt.

If you make a typing error, use the BACKSPACE key to erase
characters to the left of the cursor.  Or to insert new characters,
use ← and → to move the cursor to the appropriate place and then
type the new characters.

Press ENTER to continue or press CTRL-BREAK to end this program.
```

It describes the Initialization program and explains how to correct typing errors.

5. After reading the screen,

Press: ↵

The name screen appears (see page 15).

6. The program wants you to enter your name.

You can type up to 30 characters. If you make a typing error, use BACKSPACE to erase the letters, then retype the entry correctly. To insert characters, use ← and → to move the cursor to the desired position, then type the new characters.

Type: Your first and last names
Press: ↵

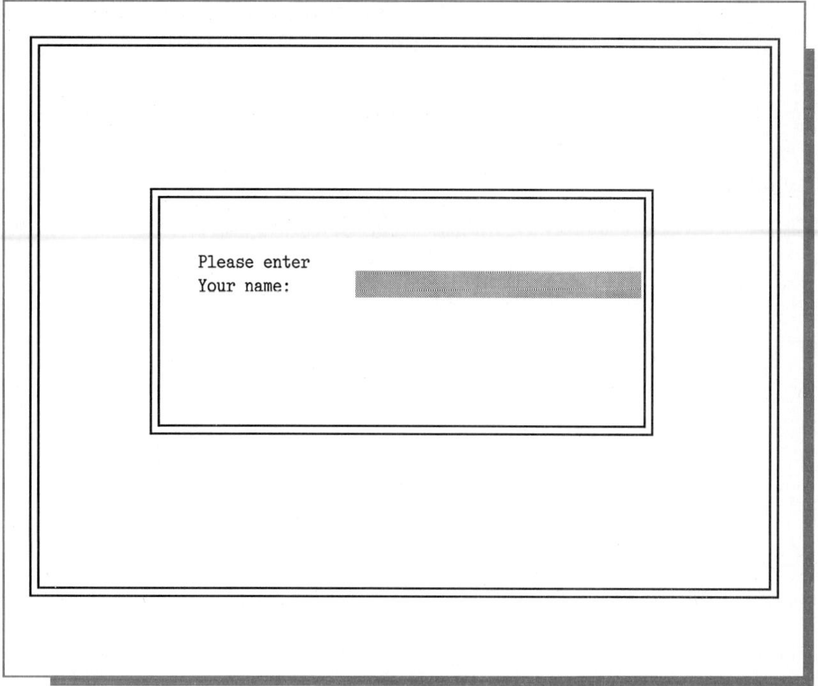

7. Next, the program asks if your entry is correct.

   If you have made a typing error, and wish to re-enter your name,

   Type: **N**
   Press: ↵

   Type the new name or make any corrections and press ↵. Remember, it is very important that your name appears accurately on this screen.

   To confirm that you have entered your name correctly,

   Type: **Y**
   Press: ↵

8. The school name screen appears. At the prompt for your school name,

   Type: Your school name
   Press: ↵

   The school name can be a maximum of 30 characters.

9. The program asks if your entry is correct. Again, it is very important that your school name is spelled correctly on this screen.

If you have made an error and wish to re-enter the school name,

Type: **N**
Press: ↵

Type the new name or make any corrections and press ↵.

To confirm that you have entered your school name correctly,

Type: **Y**
Press: ↵

10. The final confirmation screen appears. It shows the information that will be recorded on your System disk.

```
FINAL CONFIRMATION SCREEN
The following information will be recorded on your System Disk:

Product: 1-2-3

Release: 2.2 Student Edition

Serial Number:
        RR00000-1116144
Your name:
        Linda O'Leary
Your school's name:
        Arizona State University


   Press ENTER to continue or press CTRL-BREAK to end this program.
```

This is your last chance to correct your name and school name that will be recorded, making you the licensee of record. Once recorded, you cannot change this information; it will be used in the program and your name will appear on your printed worksheets.

If you are not sure that this is the information you want to record, to leave the Initialization program without recording this information:

Press: CTRL-BREAK

Any information you typed will be deleted and you must run the Initialization program again.

If you are sure that the information on the final confirmation screen is correct,

Press: ↵

11. After a short pause, 1-2-3 tells you that the Initialization program is now complete. To leave the program and return to the operating system prompt,

Press: ↵

Remove the System disk from drive A.

Preparing Your Disks

You are now ready to make backup copies of the original program disks (if you are using a two-disk system) or copy 1-2-3 to your hard disk (if you are using a hard-disk system). You will then create the data disk that you will use in the Lab Activities.

Formatting Blank Disks

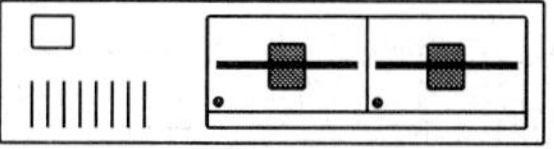

Note If you are using a hard-disk system, skip this section and continue at "Copying 1-2-3 to a Hard Disk" on page 20.

In this section, you will prepare, or format, six blank 5¼″ disks or three blank 3½″ disks so that they can hold information. You should format only blank disks (or disks that contain files you do not want, since formatting erases whatever is on the disk).

Be sure that your Lotus disks are not in the drive. If you already know how to format disks, do so, then skip to the next section, "Backing Up the 1-2-3 Disks."

Before you begin, make sure that the new blank disks are not write-protected. If necessary, remove the write-protect tabs or close the write-protect windows on the disks.

Note If you make a typing error, use BACKSPACE to erase the letters, then retype the entry correctly.

1. Make sure your computer is turned on and the operating system prompt (A>) is displayed on the screen.

2. Insert the DOS disk in drive A and close the drive door.

3. If the A:> prompt is not on the screen, to make A the current drive,

   Type: **A:**
   Press: ↵

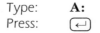

4. Insert one of the blank disks in drive B and close the drive door.

5. Type: **FORMAT B:**
   Press: ↵

   Your screen will display a message saying, "Insert new diskette for drive B: and strike any key when ready."

6. To begin formatting,

   Press: ↵

   The message "Formatting..." appears on the screen and the lights next to the drive doors go on. Formatting can take as long as a minute. When the process is finished, the lights go out, and the message "Format complete" appears. DOS displays information about available space on the disk and asks "Format another (Y/N)?"

7. To tell DOS that you want to format another disk,

   Type: **Y**

   With some versions of DOS, you then have to press ↵.

8. Remove the formatted disk from drive B, and put a label on it to show that it is formatted.

9. Repeat steps 4 through 8 to format the other blank new disks.

10. To stop formatting after the last disk, in response to the question "Format another (Y/N)?,"

    Type: **N**

    With some versions of DOS, you have to press ↵.

    The system prompt should appear on the screen.

You can now use the formatted disks to make backup copies of your original 1-2-3 disks and to create a data disk.

Backing Up the 1-2-3 Disks

A backup disk is a copy of an original disk. If anything happens to the backup copy you are using, you can make another copy from the original.

To follow the steps in this section, you will need:

- Your DOS system disk
- Six formatted, labelled 5¼″ disks or three formatted, labelled 3½″ disks
- The original 1-2-3 disks
- Write-protect tabs for the 5¼″ disks only

Before you begin, make sure that the original 1-2-3 disks are write-protected so that you cannot accidentally alter or erase any information on them. If necessary, attach write-protect tabs or open the write-protect windows on the original disks. Also check that the disks you will use for backup copies are *not* write-protected.

1. Insert the original System disk in drive A.
2. Insert a formatted blank disk in drive B.
3. If the A:> prompt is not on the screen, to make drive A the current drive,

   Type: **A:**
   Press: ↵

4. To copy the contents of the original System disk to the backup disk,

   Type: **COPY *.* B:**
   Press: ↵

   The asterisks in the command tell DOS to copy every file on the disk in drive A to the disk in drive B.

   The lights next to the drive doors go on and DOS lists the files it is copying. When it is done copying files, the lights go out and DOS displays a message telling you the number of files it copied.

5. Remove the original System disk from drive A and store it in a safe place.

6. Remove the backup disk from drive B and label it to indicate that it is a backup copy, for example, "1-2-3 Release 2.2 System disk: backup." If you are using 5¼" disks, use a felt-tip pen to write on the label.
7. Repeat steps 1 through 6 to back up each of the remaining program disks.
8. When you are done copying disks, proceed to the section "Creating a Data Disk" on page 23.

You should put your original program disks in a safe place, and use your backup disks in the rest of the installation procedures and whenever you start 1-2-3 or PrintGraph.

Copying 1-2-3 to a Hard Disk

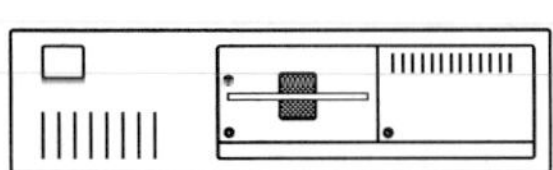

If you have a hard-disk system, you should copy 1-2-3 to the hard disk. Running 1-2-3 directly from your hard disk lets you start the program quickly and run any companion programs without changing disks.

Note If you already have 1-2-3 Release *2.01* on your hard disk, and wish to replace it with Release 2.2, see Appendix A on page R-180. Release 2.2 will not run unless you remove certain copy protected Release 2.01 files from your hard drive.

You can also store your work on the hard disk (or on a separate data disk), although you will still want to make a backup disk of your data files.

Copying 1-2-3 to your hard disk involves two separate procedures:

- Creating a 1-2-3 directory
- Copying files to that directory

The following instructions assume that DOS has been installed on your hard disk on drive C. If your hard disk is called by some other letter, for example, D, substitute that letter in the instructions. For further assistance, ask your dealer or the technical resource person at your school.

Creating a Directory for 1-2-3 Because hard disks can store so many files, it is a good idea to group similar files in separate *directories* or subdivisions. This section tells you how to create a directory for all your 1-2-3 files, then how to copy those files to the new directory. For more information about directories, see your DOS manual.

To create a directory for your 1-2-3 files, follow the directions below. If you make a typing error, use BACKSPACE to erase the letters, then retype the entry correctly.

1. At the C> prompt,

   Type: **PROMPT PG**
   Press: ↵

   The PROMPT PG command changes the DOS prompt to display the current drive and directory, in this case, C:\>.

2. To create a directory (**M**ake **D**irectory),

   Type: **MD\123**
   Press: ↵

   A directory named 123 is created for the 1-2-3 files.

   Note You can give your directory any name. If you do use a different name, substitute the name of your 1-2-3 directory for 123 in the following directions.

3. Now, to move into the new 123 directory (**C**hange **D**irectory),

   Type: **CD\123**
   Press: ↵

   You are now in the 123 directory and your DOS prompt should be C:\123>.

Copying the 1-2-3 Files

1. Make sure you are in the 123 directory and the DOS prompt is displayed on the screen. Place the System disk (5¼″ version) or the System disk with PrintGraph (3½″ version) in drive A.

2. At the DOS prompt, C:\123>,

   Type: **COPY A:*.***
   Press: ↵

   The asterisks in the command tell DOS to copy every file on the disk in drive A. DOS lists the files as it copies them to the hard disk. After all the files have been copied, a message tells you the number of files copied, and the C:\123> prompt appears on the screen.

3. Remove the disk from drive A.

4. Insert another 1-2-3 disk into drive A and repeat steps 2 and 3 to copy the four other 5¼″ disks or one other 3½″ disk to your hard disk.

Formatting a Disk Before you create your data disk, you need to format a disk.

Note If your system is an IBM AT or compatible and you have a high-density drive, you might want to use the 360K drive rather than the high-density drive for these procedures. Refer to your DOS manual or ask your technical resource person.

1. Make sure the C:\> prompt is on your screen, then,

Type: **FORMAT A:**

Note You *must* include the drive name (A:) in the command or you can accidentally reformat your hard disk.

Press: ↵

Your screen should say "Insert new diskette for drive A: and strike any key when ready."

2. Insert a new blank disk in drive A.

3. To start formatting,

Press: ↵

The message "Formatting..." appears on the screen. The drive indicator light next to the drive door goes on, and the drive makes a whirring noise. Formatting can take as long as one minute. When the process is finished, the light goes out, and the message "Format complete" appears. DOS displays information about available space on the disk and asks "Format another (Y/N)?"

4. If you want to make backup copies of your original program disks in case something happens to one of the original disks, you will want to format six disks altogether (for 5¼″ users) or three disks altogether (for 3½″ users). (You can follow the instructions in the previous section, "Backing Up the 1-2-3 Disks." If you need help, ask your instructor.) In response to the prompt,

Type: **Y**

With some versions of DOS, you have to press ↵.

Remove the formatted disk and put a label on it to show that it is formatted.

When you have finished formatting all the disks you want to format, in response to the prompt,

Type: **N**

Creating a Data Disk

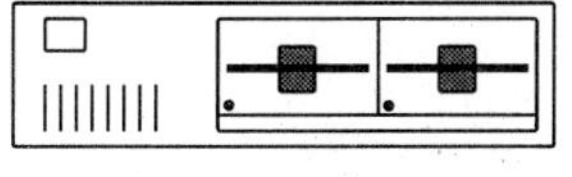

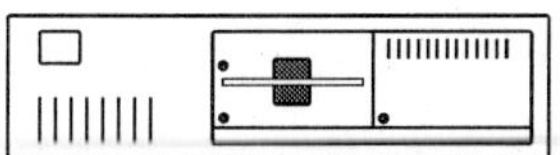

In this section, you will use the Copy command to copy the Sample files to a formatted blank disk. This disk will be your data disk. It will hold the files to be used in Section 2, "An Overview to 1-2-3 and Lab Activities."

The next step, creating the data disk, is the same for hard-disk and two-disk systems. If you are using a hard-disk system with only one drive, you will have to swap disks.

1. Insert the Help and Sample Files disk (for 5¼″ users) or the Utilities disk (for 3½″ users) in drive A.

   If you are using a two-disk system, insert the formatted blank disk in drive B. This disk will become your data disk.

2. At the DOS prompt,

   Type: **COPY A:*.WK1 B:**
   Press: 

   This command tells DOS to copy every file (indicated by the asterisk) that ends with the file extension .WK1.

3. If you are using a hard-disk system, when the screen prompts you, remove the Help and Sample Files disk (for 5¼″ users) or the Utilities disk (for 3½″ users). Insert the formatted blank disk in the drive. This disk will become your data disk.

   Press: 

   Each drive lights alternately as DOS copies files from the disk with the Sample files to the data disk. As the files are copied, you may need to insert the disk with the Sample files every time DOS prompts you for a disk in drive A. Some versions of DOS will list the name of the first file on the disk with the Sample files and tell you to "Insert diskette for drive B: and strike any key when ready." Insert the data disk when you are asked for a disk in drive B. When all .WK1 files have been copied, DOS tells you the total number of files copied, and the A> prompt reappears.

4. Label the disk "1-2-3 Data Disk." If you are using 5¼″ disks, make sure you use a felt-tip pen.

Store the original disks in a cool, dry place away from direct sunlight, magnets, and static electricity. From now on, you should use the backup copies of these disks if you are using a two-drive system.

Problems with Disks

If one of your 1-2-3 disks is defective or if you damage or erase an original 1-2-3 disk, see the limited warranty for instructions on returning it for a replacement.

You are now ready to use the Install program.

Installing 1-2-3 Release 2.2

The Install program tells 1-2-3 what type of equipment you are using. You could start 1-2-3 without first using the Install program; however, you would not be able to display graphs or use your printer.

The Hardware Chart

The Install program asks a number of questions about what type of equipment you have. Before you use the Install program, fill in the following hardware chart so you will have the required information at your fingertips. If you are unsure of how to do this, consult your dealer or the technical resource person at your school. Be sure to include the brand name and model for each piece of equipment. If your computer does not have a graphics card and monitor with graphics capability, you will not be able to view graphs on your monitor.

Hardware Chart

Item	Manufacturer	Model
Computer:	______	______
Monitor:	______	______
Screen display card(s):	______	______
Printer:	______	______
Type of interface:	______	______
Plotter:	______	______
Type of interface:	______	______
	Amount	Manufacturer
Conventional memory:	______ KB	______
Expanded memory:	______ MB	______
Hard disk capacity:	______ MB	______
Math coprocessor: yes or no		

Hardware Chart continued

Item	Amount	Manufacturer
Disk drive size (check all that apply)		
5¼″ High density (1.2 MB)	________	
5¼″ Low density (360K)	________	
3½″ High density (1.44 MB)	________	
3½″ Low density (720K)	________	
Operating system		
DOS version: ________		
Network		
Network software: ________		
Network version: ________		
Network adapter: ________		
Memory-resident programs: ________		

Starting the Install Program: Two-Disk System

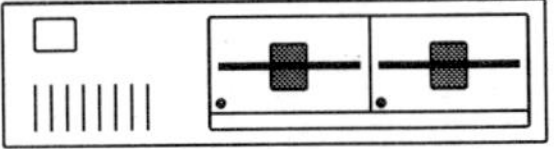

This section describes how to start the Install program with a two-disk system. If you have a hard disk, see the next section, "Starting the Install Program: Hard-Disk System."

Before you start the Install program, make sure you have:

- Completed the Initialization program
- Completed the hardware chart
- The set of 1-2-3 backup disks (they should *not* be write-protected)

CAUTION If you have a file facility program that searches DOS paths, do not use it with the Install program.

1. Make sure the computer is on and the A> prompt (or the appropriate system prompt) is on the screen.

   If it is not, follow the instructions in the section "Starting Your Computer" on page 11.

2. Place the backup Utilities disk in drive A.

3. At the DOS prompt,

   Type: **INSTALL**
   Press: ↵

It may take up to 30 seconds for the Install program to start. If the screen says "Bad command or filename,"

- Make sure the backup Utilities disk (*not* the Install Library disk) is in drive A. If it is not, insert it and repeat step 3.
- Check that you spelled "INSTALL" correctly. If you did not, repeat step 3.

If the screen says "Abort, Retry, Ignore?,"

- If you have the 5¼″ version, check that the drive door is closed. If it is open, close it, then type **R** and press ↵.
- Otherwise, type **A** and start again from step 1. If that does not solve the problem, make another backup copy of your Utilities disk and start this section again.

4. The introductory screen appears. After reading the introduction, to continue,

   Press: ↵

5. Following the directions on the next screen, replace the Utilities disk in drive A with the Install Library disk.

   Press: ↵

6. Following the instructions on the screen, replace the Install Library disk with the System disk.

   Press: ↵

7. The Install main menu appears. You can now follow the instructions in the section, "The Install Program," on page 27.

Starting the Install Program: Hard-Disk System

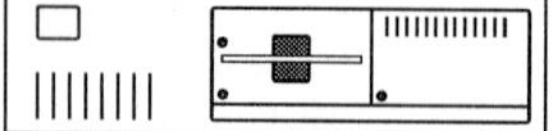

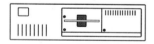

Before you start the Install program, make sure you have:

- Completed the Initialization program
- Copied the program disks to your hard disk
- Completed the hardware chart

CAUTION If you have a file facility program that searches DOS paths, do not use it with the Install program.

1. Make sure the computer is on and the operating system prompt is displayed.

2. If you are not in the 123 directory, C:\123>, which has your 1-2-3 files,

   Type: **CD\123**
   Press: ↵

Note If you already have 1-2-3 Release *2.01* on your hard disk, and wish to replace it with Release 2.2, see Appendix A on page R-180. Release 2.2 will not run unless you remove certain copy protected Release 2.01 files from your hard drive.

3. At the C:\123> prompt,

   Type: **INSTALL**
   Press: ↵

   The introductory screen should appear in about 15 seconds. If the screen says "Bad command or filename,"

   - Check that you spelled "INSTALL" correctly. If you did not, repeat step 3.
   - Make sure you are in the directory containing your 1-2-3 files. If you do not know what directory you are in, type **DIR**, press ↵, and look for the 1-2-3 files. If you are in the wrong directory, type **CD\123** (substitute the name you have used for the directory if it is different) to change the directory.
   - Make sure that all the 1-2-3 files are in the directory. If you do not think they are, return to the section on "Copying 1-2-3 to a Hard Disk" on page 20 and copy them again.

4. After reading the introductory screen, to continue,

   Press: ↵

   The Install main menu appears (see page 28). You can now follow the instructions in the next section to run the Install program.

The Install Program

The Install program consists of a series of *menus*, from which you make selections. As you go through the Install program, you specify the equipment you will use with 1-2-3. Each time you make a choice, you are selecting a special program, known as a *driver*, that tells 1-2-3 how to work with the equipment you choose. When you finish selecting your equipment, Install stores your choices in a file with a .SET extension, called a driver set. Unless you name the file differently, 1-2-3 will save the driver set in a file called 123.SET. A driver set is like any file: you can copy it from one disk to another. The driver set

```
                              M A I N   M E N U

                                          First-Time Installation
Use ↓ or ↑ to move menu pointer.          provides step-by-step
                                          instructions for completing
 First-Time Installation                  the installation procedure.
 Change Selected Equipment                You will select drivers
 Advanced Options                         that allow 1-2-3 to display
 Exit Install Program                     graphs and print your 1-2-3
                                          worksheets and graphs.

                                          Press ENTER to select
                                          First-Time Installation.

↓ and ↑ move menu pointer                 F1  displays a Help screen
ENTER selects highlighted choice          F9  takes you to main menu
ESC   returns to previous screen          F10 displays current selections
```

will work with other copies of 1-2-3, as long as they are all the same release. If other people in your school have the same release and equipment, you can create a driver set file once and then copy it to other disks.

Keys Used in the Install Program When you use the Install program, you will use some or all of the keys listed in the following table. Some of the keys, such as ESC, may be in different positions on different keyboards.

Key Name	Action	Key
Down	Moves menu pointer down	↓
Up	Moves menu pointer up	↑
Enter	Selects highlighted choice	↵
Escape	Takes you to previous screen	ESC
Home	Moves menu pointer to top of menu	HOME
End	Moves menu pointer to bottom of menu	END
Delete	Removes selection from driver set	DEL
F1	Displays a Help screen for the current selection	F1
F9	Takes you to main menu	F9
F10	Shows current selections	F10

Using the Install Menus Each menu screen is divided into three sections:

- The left portion of the screen lists the menu choices. The current selection is highlighted by the menu pointer. Use the up and down arrow keys to move the menu pointer. When the menu choice you want is highlighted, press ↵ to select it.
- The box at the right side of the screen describes the menu item that is highlighted. As you highlight different choices, the description changes.
- The bottom section of the screen provides instructions for moving around the screen within the Install program.

When you make a menu choice, the Install program usually displays a screen of explanations or instructions. If you want to go back to the previous screen, press ESC.

Help The Install program includes Help screens to further explain choices on the menu. If you have read the box at the right of the screen that explains the highlighted choice and you still need more information, press F1 to display the related Help screen. Press ESC to return to the menu.

First-Time Installation If you are installing 1-2-3 for the first time, highlight "First-Time Installation" with the menu pointer, then press ↵. (If you decide that you do not want to install 1-2-3 right now, select "Exit Install Program.")

After reading the informational screen on creating driver sets, to continue,

Press: ↵

The next series of screens will ask you to specify your hardware for:

- Screen display
- Text printer
- Graphics printer

To answer these questions, refer to the hardware chart you filled in on pages 24-25. Menus for text and graphics printers from which you have already made choices will display a triangle (▶) next to the selected driver.

If you want more information than the box at the right side of the screen provides, press (F1) to see a Help screen.

Screen Display Selection You can display graphs if you have a graphics monitor (monochrome or color) or if you have a graphics display card (such as a Hercules card or an enhanced graphics adapter) for a monochrome monitor. If you are not sure whether your computer can display graphs, check your hardware chart or ask your dealer or the technical resource person at your school.

The first question Install asks is ''Can your computer display graphs?'' Select ''Yes'' if your computer contains a graphics screen display card and you want to be able to display the graphs you create in 1-2-3. You will be prompted to specify the number of monitors you have connected to your computer system and to select a graphic screen display from a list of available display drivers. To make this selection, highlight your choice and press (↵).

Select ''No'' if your monitor is capable of displaying only text or if you do not need to display graphs; Install will proceed to the Text Printer selection screen. Even if you select ''No,'' you will be able to use 1-2-3 to create worksheets and print your work (if you have a printer). You will not, however, be able to display graphs on your monitor.

Text Printer(s) Selection The Install program uses the term ''text printer'' for the printer you use to print numbers and letters, as well as many special characters that 1-2-3 lets you produce.

Install asks ''Do you have a text printer?'' Select ''Yes'' if you have a printer connected to your computer system and you want to use it to print your work in 1-2-3, or if you currently do not have a printer but know which one you will eventually be using. Select ''No'' if you do not have a printer or if you do not want to print in 1-2-3; Install will proceed to the Graphics Printer selection screen.

If you select ''Yes,'' you will be prompted to complete two steps to select a text printer: select the name of the printer manufacturer, and select the specific printer model series or model. Follow the instructions on your screen.

If your printer is not listed in the Install program, and if you do not know whether it is compatible with any of the printers you see, select ''Unlisted,'' then choose one from the following list.

- ''Complete Capability'' if you can disable automatic line feed and the printer has a backspace capability

- ''Forced Auto-LF'' if you cannot disable automatic line feed, but the printer has a backspace capability
- ''No Backspace'' if you can disable automatic line feed, but the printer does not have a backspace capability
- ''No Backspace, Forced Auto-LF'' if you cannot disable automatic line feed and the printer does not have a backspace capability

If you do not know which option to choose, consult your printer manual or call your dealer.

The appendix provides a complete list of printer and display drivers for 1-2-3.

Graphics Printer Selection The Install program uses the term ''graphics printer'' for the printer you use to print graphs. Even if you plan to use the same printer for graphs that you have already selected for text, you must still make a selection from the Graphics Printer(s) menu.

Install asks, ''Do you want to print graphs?'' Select ''Yes'' if you have a printer connected to your computer system that is capable of printing graphs and you want to use PrintGraph to print the graphs you create in 1-2-3. Select ''No'' if you do not have a printer capable of printing graphs or if you do not want to use PrintGraph to print graphs; Install will proceed to the Naming Your Driver Set screen.

If you select ''Yes,'' you will be prompted to complete two steps to select a graphics printer: select the name of the printer manufacturer, and select the specific printer model series or model. Follow the instructions on your screen.

If your printer does not have graphics capability, you will not be able to print out graphs even though they are displayed on the screen.

For information on using First-Time Installation to create additional driver sets, see the section ''Creating More Than One Driver Set'' on page 33.

Naming Driver Sets When you have completed the description of your hardware, the Install program asks, ''Do you want to name your driver set?''

Unless you plan to create more than one driver set, you may want to use the default name 123.SET. 1-2-3 automatically looks for this driver set when you start 1-2-3 or any of its companion programs. To use the default name, select ''No.''

If you want to use 1-2-3 with more than one type of computer (for instance, a personal computer at school and a portable computer at home), you must create a different driver set for each computer system. Select ''Yes'' if you need to create a new name for the driver set.

Each driver set you create must have a different name. Besides the name 123.SET, you can use more descriptive names, such as HOME.SET and SCHOOL.SET. The name you give your driver set can contain up to eight characters, but may not contain any of the following symbols: [ ] ; , . / ? : + = < > \ '.

Do not type the extension .SET after the name of the driver set, since the Install program adds that automatically. See the section ''Starting 1-2-3'' on page 36 for instructions for starting 1-2-3 with a driver set other than 123.SET.

Saving Your Driver Set If you have a hard-disk system, Install will copy the driver set to the 1-2-3 program immediately after you enter the driver set name.

If you have a two-disk system, after you name the driver set, Install will display screens that prompt you to switch disks so the program can copy the driver set to the appropriate Release 2.2. disks.

If you are using a two-disk system and creating a variety of driver sets, you may not have enough space on your System disk for the driver set files. You can save extra driver sets on a blank formatted disk. When the Install program asks for the System disk, put in the disk you are using to hold the driver sets. The Install program will save the driver set on the blank formatted disk instead of on the System disk. See the section ''Starting 1-2-3'' on page 36 for instructions for starting 1-2-3 with a driver set on another disk. If you do not need to make any other changes, you are finished with the Installation procedure.

Exit the Install Program After Install has finished copying the driver set you created, it displays a screen saying that you have finished the installation procedure. At this point, you can:

Press: ↵ to leave the Install program. (Install will display an Exit screen, where you can choose to end the program or return to the Install main menu.)

Press: (F9) to return directly to the Install main menu
Press: (F10) to display a list of the the drivers in the driver set you created or to create another driver set.

You can also exit Install by returning to the 1-2-3 main menu and selecting "Exit Install Program."

If you are using a two-disk system, replace the write-protect tab or close the write-protect window on the System disk to prevent yourself from accidentally saving files on it.

If you need to create additional driver sets, change a screen display, text printer, or graphics printer driver in your driver set, or find out more information about the Install program, read the following section.

Creating More Than One Driver Set To create additional driver sets, return to the 1-2-3 main menu (select "No" when the Install program asks, "Do you want to leave Install?"). Select "First-Time Installation" again and make your selections for the second driver set. You must go through all the installation menus even if most of the choices are the same as in the first driver set you created.

If you need to change only one or two selections to make the second driver set (perhaps only your screen display is different), you can use "Change Selected Equipment" on the 1-2-3 main menu. This choice allows you to make whatever changes you want without having to repeat the selections you want to keep. You must give each successive driver set a different name so that the previous ones remain on the disk unchanged.

Change Selected Equipment In addition to its function in creating additional driver sets, the option "Change Selected Equipment" lets you choose the equipment (or options) you want to change. If you have already chosen a printer, a triangle (▶) appears in front of the current selection.

If you make any changes to a driver set, select "Save Changes" from the menu. Install will ask you for a name for the revised driver set. If you do not plan to create more than one driver set, press (↵); your driver set will be called 123.SET. If you use a name other than 123.SET, you will have to type that name whenever you start 1-2-3 or any of its companion programs. For further details, see the section on "Starting 1-2-3" on page 36. (If you select "Exit Install Program" before you save your changes, the Install program asks if you want to save them. Select "Yes" unless you do not want to save the changes you made.)

Advanced Options Advanced Options lets you do many things you cannot do elsewhere in the Install program.

Select "Make Another Driver Set Current" to enter the name of another driver set so you can make changes in it with "Change Selected Equipment" or "Modify Current Driver Set." If you do not use this option, the Install program assumes you want to make changes in 123.SET.

Select "Add New Drivers to Library" if you have new equipment that came with its own driver programs. These separate drivers should have a .DRV file extension. This option creates a library (SINGLE.LBR) from all the separate drivers. You can then select the new drivers from the Install menus.

Select "Modify Current Driver Set" to make changes in the current driver set (123.SET, unless you have made another driver set current). Some text-display and graph-display driver combinations are not available through the Screen Display option in the other Install menus; the "Modify Current Driver Set" option lets you select from the Graph Display, then from the Text Display menu. There are also drivers (for example, for collating sequence) that you can change only through this menu. You must also use this option to select a new driver that you add to the library.

If you make any changes in your driver set, select "Save Changes" from the menu. Install will ask you for a name for the revised driver set. If you do not plan to create more than one driver set, press ↵; your driver set will be called 123.SET. To use another name, type the new name and press ↵. (If you select "Exit Install Program" before you save your changes, the Install program asks if you want to save them. Select "Yes" unless you do not want to save the changes you made.)

If You Do Not Find What You Are Looking For You can set some options from within the 1-2-3 program after you complete the installation procedure:

- If you use a serial printer, select the baud rate from within 1-2-3 by using the / **W**orksheet **G**lobal **D**efault **P**rinter **I**nterface command.
- If your printer can use both a serial and a parallel interface, you select the one you want to use from within 1-2-3. (The default is a parallel interface.)
- If you have a math coprocessor, 1-2-3 automatically uses it.

3

Starting and Ending 1-2-3

This chapter provides step-by-step instructions for starting and ending 1-2-3. It also describes how to change the drive or directory where 1-2-3 stores the files you create.

Starting 1-2-3

1-2-3 is a single program that combines three capabilities: Worksheet, Database, and Graphics. (Section 2, ''An Overview to 1-2-3 and Lab Activities'' and Section 3, ''Reference,'' describe how to use the specific features you need.)

The procedure you use to start 1-2-3 depends on the kind of system you have: two-disk or hard-disk. Read the section that applies to your type of computer system for starting 1-2-3.

Two-Disk System

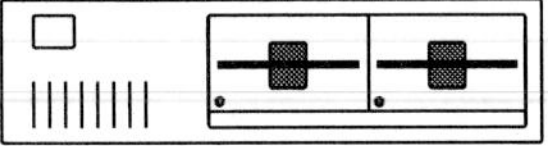

1. Make sure your computer is on and the operating system prompt (A>) is displayed.
2. Remove the DOS disk from drive A.
3. Insert the System disk in drive A. Place a formatted disk in drive B. Use the data disk if you plan to use ''An Overview to 1-2-3 and Lab Activities.'' If the driver set you are using is on another disk, use that disk in drive B. Otherwise, use any blank formatted disk. Always have a disk in each drive; the operating system may display an error message if a drive is empty.

   If you are using 5¼″ disks, remember to close the drive door(s).

4. At the A> prompt,

   Type: **123**
   Press: ↵

   Note To use a driver set with a name other than 123.SET, type **123** followed by a space and the name of the driver set, then press ↵. It is not necessary to type the extension .SET. For example, to start 1-2-3 with a driver set called COMPAQ.SET, type **123 COMPAQ**. If the driver set is on another disk (see the section ''Saving Driver Sets'' in Chapter 2, ''Initializing and Installing 1-2-3'') include the path of the driver set. For example, type **123 B:\COMPAQ** and press ↵ to use a driver set named COMPAQ that is stored on a disk in drive B.

First, the 1-2-3 logo screen is displayed. It contains information you entered with the Initialization program. Next, a blank 1-2-3 worksheet should appear on the screen. If the screen says "Bad command or filename,"

- Make sure that the System disk is in drive A. If it is not, insert it and repeat step 4.
- Check that you typed 123 correctly. If you did not, repeat step 4.

If the screen says "Abort, Retry, Ignore?,"

- Check that the disk is fully inserted in the drive. If you are using 5¼″ disks, make sure the drive door is closed. Insert the disk properly and type **R**.
- Otherwise, type **A** and repeat step 4.

If the 1-2-3 logo stays on the screen,

- Check that you installed 1-2-3 correctly for your equipment.

5. 1-2-3 will automatically save files on drive A. If you want to change this, read the section "Changing the Default Directory" on page 39.

Hard-Disk System

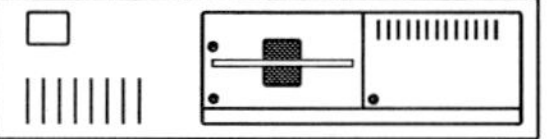

These instructions assume DOS has been installed on your hard disk on drive C. If your hard disk is called by some other letter, for example, D, substitute that letter in the instructions. For further assistance, ask your dealer or the technical resource person at your school.

CAUTION Network Users Do not use 1-2-3 if your computer is the server in a local area network.

If your computer is on and you see the C> prompt, skip to step 2. If your computer is off, start from step 1.

1. Make sure the disk drive is empty and turn the computer on. Make sure the DOS prompt C:\> is on your screen.
2. To change to the 123 directory you created,

   Type: **CD\123**
   Press: ↵

If you used a different name for the directory, substitute that name.

3. To start the program,

   Type: **123**
   Press: ↵

   Note To use a driver set with a name other than 123.SET, type **123** followed by a space and the name of the driver set, then press ↵. It is not necessary to type the extension .SET. For example, to start 1-2-3 with a driver set called COMPAQ.SET, type **123 COMPAQ**. If the driver set is on another disk (see the section ''Saving Driver Sets'' in Chapter 2, ''Initializing and Installing 1-2-3''), include the path of the driver set, for example, **123 A:\COMPAQ**.

   First, the 1-2-3 logo screen (including information entered with the Initialization program) is displayed. Next, a blank 1-2-3 worksheet should appear on the screen. If the screen says ''Bad command or filename,''

   - Check that you typed 123 correctly. If you did not, repeat step 3.
   - Make sure that you are in the directory with your 1-2-3 files.

   If the name of your directory does not appear beside the C> prompt, type **CD** and press ↵; DOS displays the complete prompt, including the directory, on the screen. If you are in the wrong directory, start again from step 2.

   Make sure that all the 1-2-3 files are in the directory. If you do not think they are, return to the section ''Copying 1-2-3 to a Hard Disk'' in Chapter 2, ''Initializing and Installing 1-2-3,'' and copy them again. Then repeat step 3.

   1-2-3 will automatically save files on the directory from which you started the program, in this case, the 123 directory. If you want to change this, read the next section. Otherwise, go to the section ''Ending a 1-2-3 Session'' on page 41 to learn how to exit from the program.

The Default Directory

When you start 1-2-3 for the first time, the program automatically retrieves files from and saves files to the drive or directory from which you started the program. This is called the *default directory*. For example, if you start 1-2-3 from drive A, 1-2-3 will save files on drive A. If you start 1-2-3 directly from your hard disk's C:\123 directory, 1-2-3 will automatically designate that drive as the default directory. In order to run the labs and retrieve files from and save files to the data disk, it is suggested that you make the B drive the default drive if you are using a two-disk system. If you are using a hard-disk system, you may want to make drive A the default.

Changing the Default Directory

If you want to save your work on a disk in a drive or a directory other than the one from which you start 1-2-3, you can do so from within the program. Once you change the default drive or directory, you will not need to do so again unless you want to make further changes.

The instructions that follow assume you are familiar with choosing commands from 1-2-3 menus. You might first want to read about using menus in Chapter 2 of the Reference section.

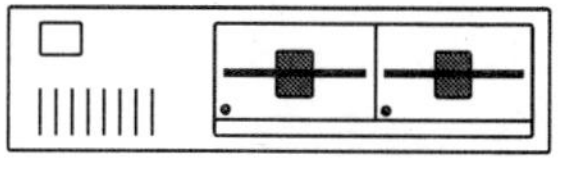

1. A blank worksheet should be on the screen. To access the 1-2-3 main menu,

   Type: / (slash)

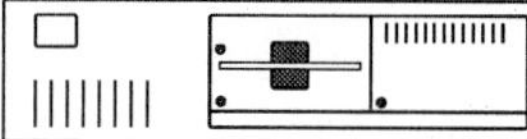

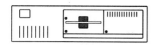

2. To select **W**orksheet **G**lobal **D**efault **D**irectory,

   Type: **W**
   Type: **G**
   Type: **D**
   Type: **D**

3. The Default settings sheet is on your screen. The default directory is listed at the top of the second column. On the second line of the screen, 1-2-3 also displays the current directory at startup, which will be A:\ unless you started the program directly from your hard disk, in which case it will probably be C:\123. To change the default directory,

   Press: ESC

The steps you follow next depend on the type of computer system you have: two-disk or hard-disk. Follow the instructions that are applicable to your computer system.

Two-Disk System

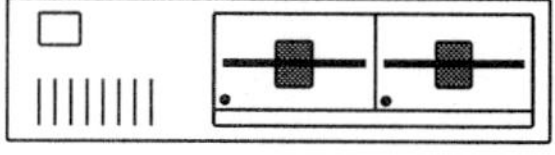

4. If you have two disk drives, you should store your work on the disk in the second, or B, drive. Be sure you have a formatted disk in that drive.

   Type: **B:**
   Press: ↵

5. Remove the write-protect tab or close the write-protect window on the System disk. To save the new directory designation, select **U**pdate:

   Type: **U**

6. To leave the 1-2-3 main menu, select **Q**uit:

   Type: **Q**

Replace the write-protect tab or open the write-protect window on the System disk. You have now changed the default directory for a two-disk system. To learn how to leave the program, go to the section "Ending a 1-2-3 Session" on page 41.

Hard-Disk System

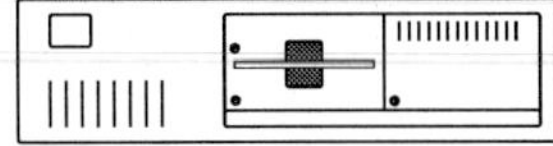

If you have a hard disk, you can change the directory where you want 1-2-3 to store your data.

4. Type the name of the directory where you want 1-2-3 to store files. For example, if your hard disk is C and you have no directories,

   Type: **C:**
   Press: ↵

   If your hard disk drive is C and you have already created a subdirectory named DATA in your 123 directory, to change the 1-2-3 default directory to DATA,

   Type: **C:\123\DATA**
   Press: ↵

   If necessary, substitute the name of your directory in the command. Be sure you correctly specify both drive and directory path.

5. To save the directory designation, select **U**pdate:

   Type: **U**

6. To leave the 1-2-3 main menu, select **Q**uit:

   Type: **Q**

This completes changing the default directory for a hard-disk system. To learn how to leave the program, go to the next section "Ending a 1-2-3 Session."

Ending a 1-2-3 Session

Follow the instructions in this section to end a 1-2-3 session.

1. To access the 1-2-3 main menu,

   Press: /

2. To select **Q**uit,

   Type: **Q**

3. To leave 1-2-3, select **Y**es:

   Type: **Y**

   1-2-3 returns you to the operating system prompt.

Starting 1-2-3 from the Access System

The Access system lets you start 1-2-3 by choosing the program's name from a menu. Access makes it easy to switch back and forth between 1-2-3 and the 1-2-3 utility programs. When you start 1-2-3 from the Access system, you return to the Access system when you end 1-2-3.

To start 1-2-3 from the Access system:

1. Make sure your computer is turned on and the operating system prompt is displayed. Remove any disks from the disk drives.

2. At the operating system prompt, do one of the following:

   - If you have a hard-disk system,

     Type: **CD\123**
     Press: ↵ to make the 1-2-3 Release 2.2 program directory the current directory

   - If you have a two-disk system, insert the System disk in drive A. Then,

     Type: **A:**
     Press: ↵ to make drive A the current drive

3. Type: **LOTUS**
   Press: ↵

   The Access menu appears at the top of the screen.

4. Select 1-2-3 from the menu by doing one of the following:

   - Use (←) or (→) to highlight the 1-2-3 menu item and then press (↵) to select it.
   - Type **1**, the first character of the 1-2-3 menu item.

1-2-3 displays a logo screen, which contains the information you entered with the Initialization program, and then displays the worksheet.

4

Starting and Ending PrintGraph

You use 1-2-3's Print command to print text and numbers, but you use a separate program, PrintGraph, to print or plot graphs you have created or saved during a 1-2-3 session. This chapter introduces PrintGraph.

PrintGraph lets you select colors (if you have a color graphics printer or plotter), fonts (type styles), density (number of dots per character), and the graph's position on the paper.

If you are using the 5¼″ version, the PrintGraph program is on a separate PrintGraph disk; in the 3½″ version, PrintGraph is on the System disk with PrintGraph.

If you have a hard disk, the steps that follow assume that the hard disk is called C and that you have created a directory called 123 for the 1-2-3 program files. If your drive or directory is named differently, substitute those names in the following procedures.

CAUTION Network Users Do not use PrintGraph if your computer is the server in a local area network. You can run the program if you are using a local computer on the IBM PC network.

Starting PrintGraph

1. Make sure your computer is turned on and the operating system prompt is displayed.
2. *Two-disk systems only:* Remove the DOS disk and insert the backup PrintGraph disk in drive A. If you are using the 3½″ version, this will be the backup System disk with PrintGraph.

   Hard-disk systems only: To change the directory,

   Type: **CD\123**
   Press: ↵
3. To access the PrintGraph program,

   Type: **PGRAPH**
   Press: ↵

   Note PrintGraph uses the driver sets you created when you used the Install program. To use a driver set with a name other than 123.SET, type **PGRAPH** followed by a space and the name of the driver set, then press ↵. It is not necessary to type the extension .SET. For example, to start PrintGraph with a driver set called COMPAQ.SET, type **PGRAPH COMPAQ**. If you do not type the name of the driver set, PrintGraph will use 123.SET to start the program.

The PrintGraph menu and settings sheet should appear on the screen.

If the screen says ''Bad command or filename,''

- Check that you typed PGRAPH correctly. If you did not, repeat step 3.
- *Two-disk systems only:* Make sure the PrintGraph disk is in the drive. If it is not, insert it and repeat step 3.
- *Hard-disk systems only:* Make sure that you are in the directory with your 1-2-3 files. If the name of your directory does not appear beside the C> prompt, type **CD** and press ↵. DOS displays the complete prompt, including the directory, on the screen. If you are in the wrong directory, return to step 2 and change the directory. Then repeat step 3. Make sure all the 1-2-3 files are in the directory. If you do not think they are, return to the section ''Copying 1-2-3 to the Hard Disk'' in Chapter 2, ''Initializing and Installing 1-2-3,'' and copy them again. Then repeat step 3.

Customizing the Hardware Setup

You will probably want to change two hardware settings: the type of graphics printer and the default directory.

When you ran the Install program, you chose one or more printers to use for printing graphs. When you start PrintGraph, you must ''remind'' the program of your choice. If you chose more than one graphics printer, you must tell PrintGraph which one to use.

When you start PrintGraph for the first time, the program automatically retrieves files from and saves files to the A drive, the default drive and directory. If this arrangement is satisfactory, you do not need to change it. If you want to change the default drive and directory, follow the directions in the section ''Changing the Default Directory'' in Chapter 3, ''Starting and Ending 1-2-3.''

This section details the procedures for changing the default directory and setting printer type. Once you make the changes, you will not need to do so again, unless you want to make further changes.

Note Any changes you make to the PrintGraph settings are effective immediately but will be ''forgotten'' as soon as you leave the PrintGraph program unless you save them.

The instructions that follow assume you are familiar with choosing commands from 1-2-3 menus. You might want to read about using menus in Chapter 2 of the Reference section. If you are using disks, remove the write-protect tab or close the write-protect window before proceeding. When you have finished customizing the settings, write-protect the disks again.

Setting Printer Type

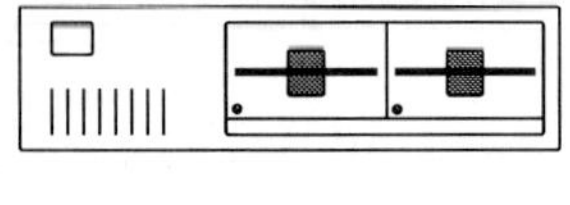

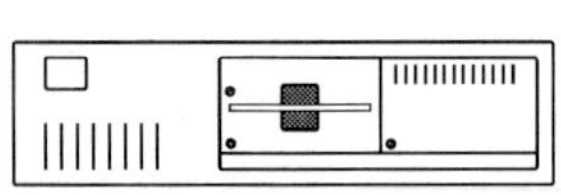

1. From the main PrintGraph menu, to select **S**ettings **H**ardware **P**rinter:

   Type: **S**
   Type: **H**
   Type: **P**

2. The printers you selected during Installation are displayed. To select the printer you want to use, move the highlight bar to the appropriate printer and press SPACEBAR to mark or unmark a selection. A # symbol marks the selected printer or plotter. Then, to select the marked device,

   Press: ↵

   Hard-disk systems: You should tell PrintGraph where print fonts are stored. To select **F**onts-Directory,

   Type: **F**

   The default directory A: is displayed.

   Enter the name of the directory that holds all your PrintGraph program files. For example, if you copied all the files from the PrintGraph disk to C:\123,

   Type: **C:\123**
   Press: ↵

3. To save the printer and font directory settings,

   Type: **Q**
   Type: **S**

   The main PrintGraph menu reappears. Follow the procedure in the next section to change the default directory or go on to the section "Ending a PrintGraph Session" on page 46.

Changing the Default Directory

You can designate the drive or directory where you want to store .PIC files. 1-2-3 stores all the graph "picture" files with a .PIC extension. These are the graph files you create in 1-2-3 and print using the PrintGraph program. To store them on a data disk in drive B, follow the directions for two-disk systems. To store the files in a directory on your hard disk, follow the directions for a hard-disk system. To change the default directory, follow the steps below.

1. From the main PrintGraph menu, to select **S**ettings **H**ardware **G**raphs-Directory:

   Type: **S**
   Type: **H**
   Type: **G**

   PrintGraph displays the default directory, A:\.

2. *For two-disk systems:* You will probably want to store your graph picture files on a data disk in drive B. To change the graphs directory from A:\ to B:\:

   Type: **B:**
   Press: ↵

   For hard-disk systems: Enter the directory's path. For example, if you want to store .PIC files in an existing subdirectory in your 123 directory on your hard disk named DATA,

   Type: **C:\123\DATA**
   Press: ↵

3. To save the new startup directory,

   Type: **Q**
   Type: **S**

   The main PrintGraph menu reappears.

Ending a PrintGraph Session

Follow the instructions in this section to leave the PrintGraph program and return to DOS.

1. To select **E**xit:

   Type: **E**

2. To confirm that you want to exit:

   Type: **Y**

   The DOS prompt should appear on the screen.

Starting PrintGraph from the Access System

To start PrintGraph from the Access system:

1. Make sure your computer is turned on and the operating system prompt is displayed. Remove any disks from the disk drives.

2. At the operating system prompt, do one of the following:

   If you have a hard-disk system,

   Type: **CD \ 123** (to make the 1-2-3 Release 2.2 program directory the current directory)

   Press: ↵

   If you have a two-disk system, insert the PrintGraph disk in drive A. Then,

   Type: **A:** (to make drive A the current drive)

3. Type: **LOTUS**

   Press: ↵

   The Access menu appears at the top of the screen.

4. Select PrintGraph from the menu.

   The PrintGraph logo screen appears, and then the main PrintGraph menu appears.

5

The Help Facility

1-2-3's Help facility is an on-line reference manual. When you press the Help function key, (F1), a screen appears with information about what you are doing. You can get help at any point in your work with 1-2-3 — between commands or even in the middle of a command. Help is also available in PrintGraph.

Each Help screen includes a menu of additional Help topics so that you can move to another screen easily. Help does not affect the program you are using; when you leave Help, the screen appears exactly as it did before you pressed (F1).

Starting Help

For two-disk systems: Be sure that you have changed your startup directory. (See "Changing Your Startup Directory" in Chapter 3, "Starting and Ending 1-2-3.")

After starting 1-2-3 or PrintGraph, the appropriate program disk must be in drive A before you use the Help facility. For 5¼" users, the Help and Sample Files disk is used for Help in 1-2-3 and the PrintGraph disk is used for PrintGraph Help. For 3½" users, the System disk with PrintGraph includes the Help files for both 1-2-3 and PrintGraph.

If you are using 5¼" disks, remove the System disk from drive A and insert the Help and Sample Files disk in that drive. You can run the 1-2-3 program without having the System disk in drive A; however, you cannot use Help without having the Help disk in the drive. If you are using 3½" disks, you do not need to change disks since the System disk contains all the files you need. Your data disk should be in drive B.

For Help about any 1-2-3 or PrintGraph commands, with the appropriate disk in drive A,

Press: (F1)

For hard-disk systems: After starting 1-2-3 or PrintGraph, for Help about any 1-2-3 or PrintGraph commands,

Press: (F1)

Using Help

To view related Help screens, use the pointer-movement keys ((→), (←), (↑), (↓)) to highlight the Help topic you want to select and then press (↵). To view an unrelated Help screen, select the Help Index, then select a topic from the list that appears.

Several keys have special functions within Help:

- (F1) displays the first Help screen you viewed during a session.
- ESC exits Help and returns the cursor to the screen where it was before you pressed (F1).
- BACKSPACE displays previous Help screens. You can press the key up to fifteen times to review Help screens you saw in a particular Help session. You cannot use the key to review a Help screen you viewed during an earlier Help session.

Speeding Access to Help

You can get Help faster by changing your configuration file to provide Instant Help instead of Removable Help. (See Chapter 2 in the Reference section for information on changing your configuration file using the / **W**orksheet **G**lobal **D**efault **O**ther **H**elp command.)

Leaving Help

Press ESC to leave Help. When you leave Help, you return to exactly where you were when you pressed (F1).

If you are using a two-disk system, leave the Help and Sample Files disk in drive A so that you can get Help at any time.

Help for Error Messages

If 1-2-3 displays an error message, you can press (F1) to learn what caused the error and how you can correct it. To clear the error message, press ESC.

If you clear the error message before pressing (F1), you can still see the error message's Help screen by following this procedure:

1. Press (F1).
2. Highlight "Help Index" and press (↵).
3. Select "Error Message Index."

   Help displays the first of five screens that list all error messages alphabetically.
4. Highlight the error message for which you want help and press (↵).

   If the message you want is not listed on the screen, select "Continued" at the lower left of the screen to view the next screen in the error message list.

If, after 1-2-3 displays an error message, your computer locks up (that is, if 1-2-3 does not respond to any keystrokes), write down the error message and restart your computer. Start 1-2-3 and follow the above procedure to look up the error message to see what caused the error.

Overview and Lab Activities

This section contains an introductory lab and a series of nine interactive, hands-on labs that introduce 1-2-3 concepts, commands, and techniques.

''An Overview to 1-2-3'' introduces the four major parts of 1-2-3: worksheets, graphics, databases, and macros. The intent of the overview is not for you to learn specific commands, but rather to become familiar with the capabilities of the program. The overview begins with a list of objectives, followed by an introduction to the case study that is the background to the lab. It continues by briefly demonstrating the four major areas of 1-2-3.

The remaining nine labs teach specific 1-2-3 commands and procedures. Each lab begins with a list of objectives and an introduction to the case study used throughout the lab. The 1-2-3 commands and procedures are introduced in a step-by-step fashion with the case study as the background. Each lab concludes with a list of key terms, a matching exercise, and several practice problems.

Before you begin this section, you must have properly installed the System disk and created the data disk. See Chapter 2, ''Initializing and Installing 1-2-3,'' in Section 1, ''Getting Started,'' for details.

You begin every lab by loading 1-2-3. Remember that the 1-2-3 System disk must always be in drive A when you start the program, unless you have completed the procedure that allows you to start 1-2-3 directly from the hard disk. See Chapter 3, ''Starting and Ending 1-2-3'' in Section 1, ''Getting Started,'' for details.

As you work through the labs, you will be retrieving, creating, and saving a number of files. For a computer with two disk drives, set up 1-2-3 to save files on the data disk in drive B. For a hard-disk system, 1-2-3 can save files either in a subdirectory on the hard disk or in your data disk in drive A. In either case, set up 1-2-3 to save the files to the correct drive. See ''Starting and Ending 1-2-3'' in Section 1 for details.

An Overview to 1-2-3

Objectives

In this overview, you will explore:

- Worksheets
- Graphics
- Databases
- Macros

Case Study

Tom Larson is a member of Trackers, a stock club that meets once a month. Each member of the club has been assigned three stocks to follow and analyze. Tom's responsibility is to track ISA, MCP, and TWS.

Tom recently acquired the Student Edition of Lotus 1-2-3 Release 2.2 and has been using it to record and analyze the data. We will use the file Tom created to track his stock prices to explore 1-2-3's worksheet, graphics, database, and macro capabilities.

Turn the computer on and load 1-2-3. Your screen should be similar to Figure 1.

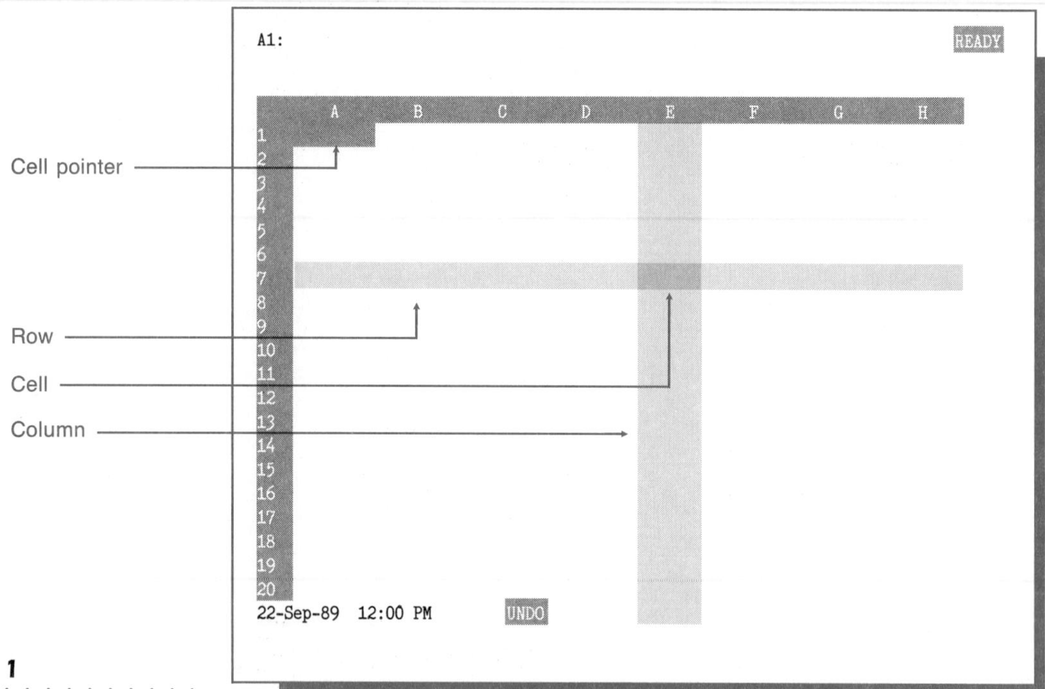

Figure 1

This is a blank 1-2-3 **worksheet**. A worksheet is an electronic representation of a spreadsheet used to enter and analyze data. The worksheet consists of cells that are created by the intersection of a numbered row and a lettered column. The highlight bar inside the worksheet is the **cell pointer**. The cell pointer displays your cell location in the worksheet. It is currently in cell A1 (column A, row 1).

The parts of a worksheet will be described in detail in Lab 1.

Moving Around the Worksheet

The keyboard allows you to communicate with 1-2-3. For example, you use the pointer-movement keys to move the cell pointer around the worksheet. The keyboard is described in detail in Lab 1. Watch the movement of the cell pointer as you do the following:

Press: (↓) three times
Press: (→) two times

Your screen should now look similar to Figure 2.

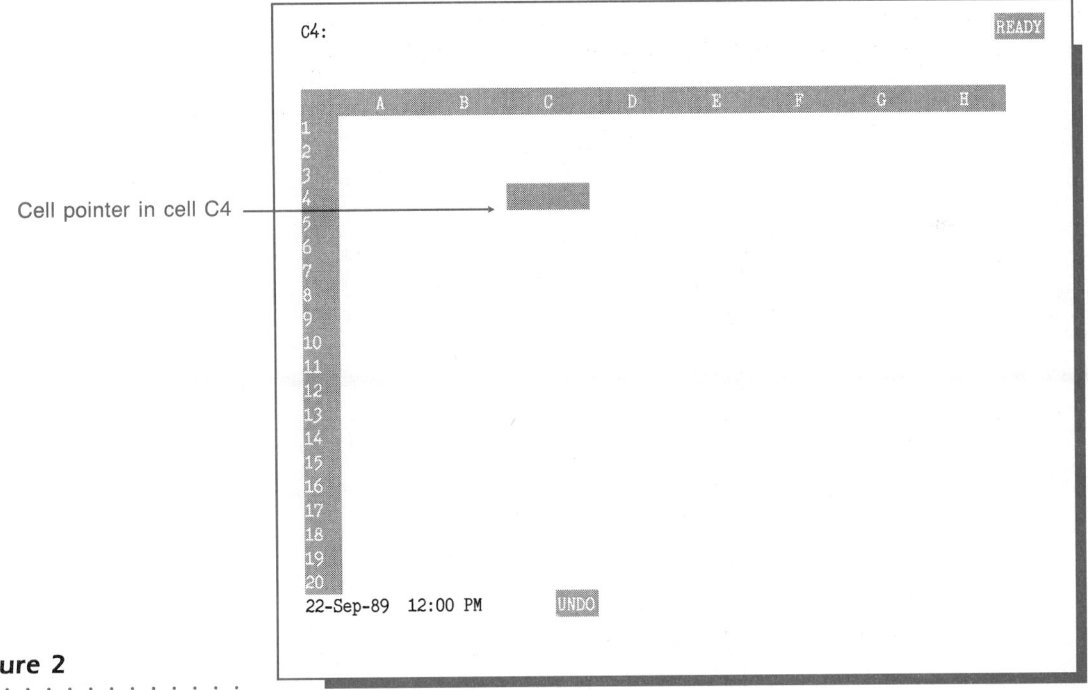

Figure 2

The cell pointer is now in cell C4. Next, use the pointer-movement keys to move the cell pointer to cell D15, then to cell E12.

Many other keys also control the cell pointer. You will learn about them in Lab 1.

Tom has created a worksheet file that contains the data for the stocks he is tracking. To see this worksheet file,

Press: / (slash)

Notice the two lines of new information displayed in the second and third lines of the screen. This is the 1-2-3 **main menu**. Pressing / accesses this menu. You use the main menu to enter all commands to 1-2-3.

Tom has entered his stock data into a file named STOCKS. To retrieve this file, issue the command **F**ile **R**etrieve **STOCKS** by doing the following:

Press:	**F**
Press:	**R**
Type:	**STOCKS**
Press:	↵

Your screen should now look similar to Figure 3.

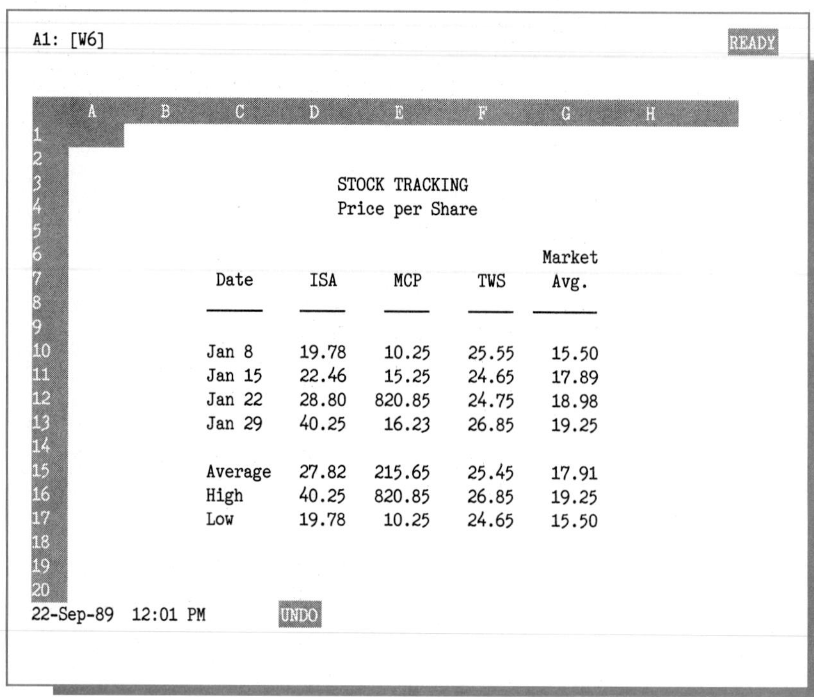

A1: [W6] READY

STOCK TRACKING
Price per Share

Date	ISA	MCP	TWS	Market Avg.
Jan 8	19.78	10.25	25.55	15.50
Jan 15	22.46	15.25	24.65	17.89
Jan 22	28.80	820.85	24.75	18.98
Jan 29	40.25	16.23	26.85	19.25
Average	27.82	215.65	25.45	17.91
High	40.25	820.85	26.85	19.25
Low	19.78	10.25	24.65	15.50

22-Sep-89 12:01 PM UNDO

Figure 3

Tom created this worksheet to track the weekly performance of three stocks, ISA, MCP, and TWS, and the market average. The average, high, and low values for each stock have also been calculated using a 1-2-3 @function. In Labs 1 and 2, you will learn how to enter data, formulas, and @functions into a worksheet.

Now look at cell E12. The price per share of MCP stock for January 22 should be 20.85, not 820.85. To correct this error, using the right (→) and down (↓) pointer-movement keys,

Move to: E12
Type: **20.85**

To enter the new value, you need to press (↵). Watch your screen carefully and notice how the average and high values for MCP automatically change to reflect the new value.

Press: (↵)

Your screen should now look similar to Figure 4.

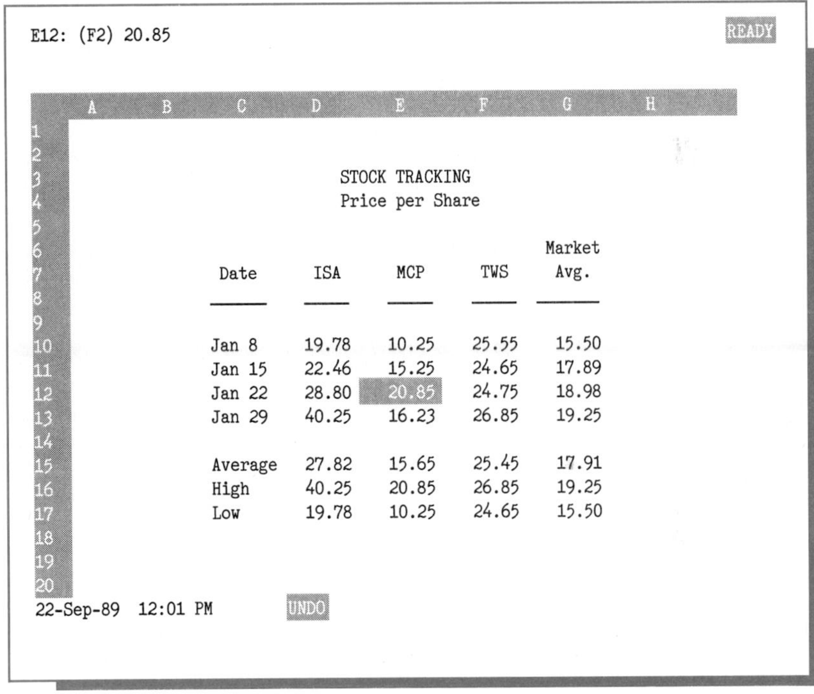

Figure 4

The formulas in the worksheet have been recalculated to reflect the new value in cell E12. This recalculation feature allows 1-2-3 to perform what-if analysis. What-if analysis and many worksheet commands are presented in Labs 1, 2, 5, and 6.

Exploring Graphics

Looking at the data in the worksheet, you can see that the stock prices change each week. However, it is not easy to visualize trends and changes. The graphics capabilities of 1-2-3 allow you to see a visual representation of the data in the worksheet.

Note In the following section, you will be viewing graphs. You must have a computer system that supports graphics. If you do not, skip to the next section on Exploring Databases.

Tom has created both a line and a bar graph of the data. To view the line graph, we will issue the command / **Graph Name Use**, followed by the name of the graph. To do this,

Press: /
Press: **G**
Press: **N**
Press: **U**

If you have a color monitor, to enter the name of the graph,

Type: **LINE-C**
Press: ↵

If you have a monochrome monitor, to enter the name of the graph,

Type: **LINE**
Press: ↵

Your screen should look similar to Figure 5.

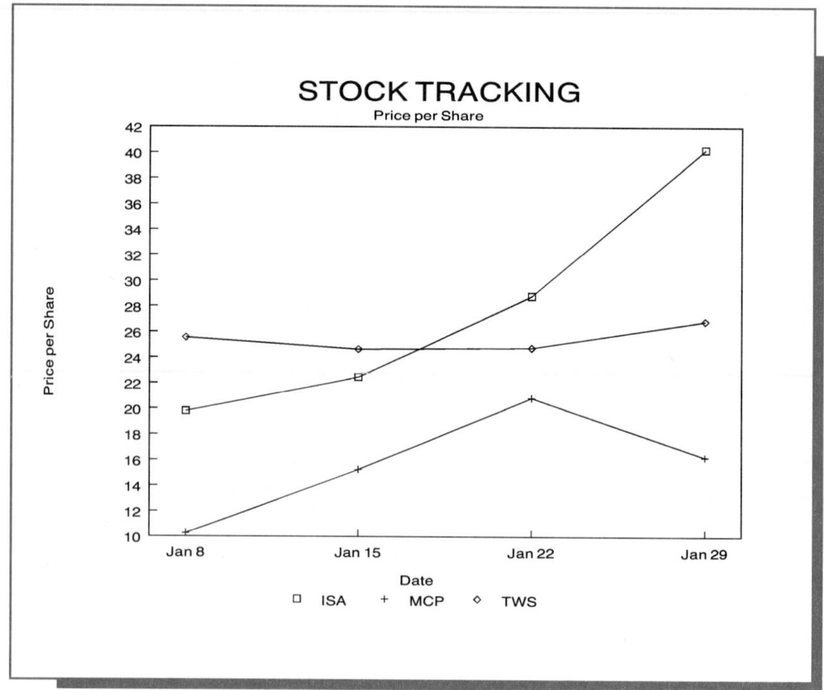

Figure 5

The line graph clearly shows the trend for the three stocks over the four-week period.

To clear the graph from the screen, press any key, for example, the SPACEBAR.

Press: SPACEBAR

To see the same data represented as a bar graph,

Press: **N**
Press: **U**

If you have a color monitor, to enter the name of the graph,

Type: **BAR-C**
Press: ↵

If you have a monochrome monitor, to enter the name of the graph,

Type: **BAR**
Press: ↵

Your screen should look similar to Figure 6.

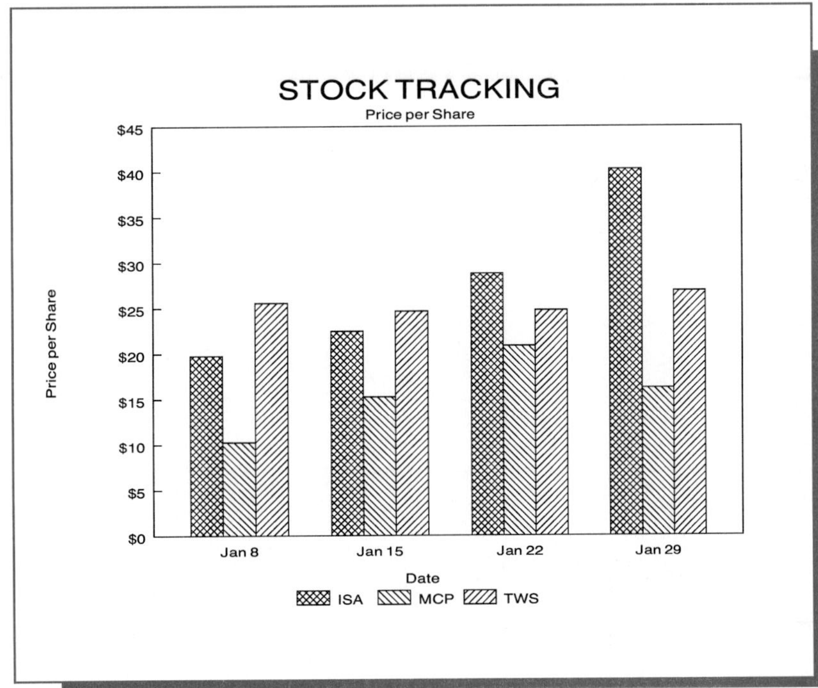

Figure 6

As you can see, the use of graphs to display the data in a worksheet helps you to visualize trends and patterns of change. To clear the graph from the screen,

Press: SPACEBAR

To leave the Graph menu,

Press: **Q**

Creating and printing graphs are presented in Labs 3 and 4.

Exploring Databases

After tracking his stocks' performance for several more weeks, Tom expanded his worksheet to include a database of stock prices.

The 1-2-3 worksheet is much larger than the area you can view on your display screen at one time. The area of the worksheet that you can see on your screen at one time is called a **window**. To see the area of the worksheet where Tom entered the data for his database of stock prices,

Press: PGDN

Your screen should look similar to Figure 7.

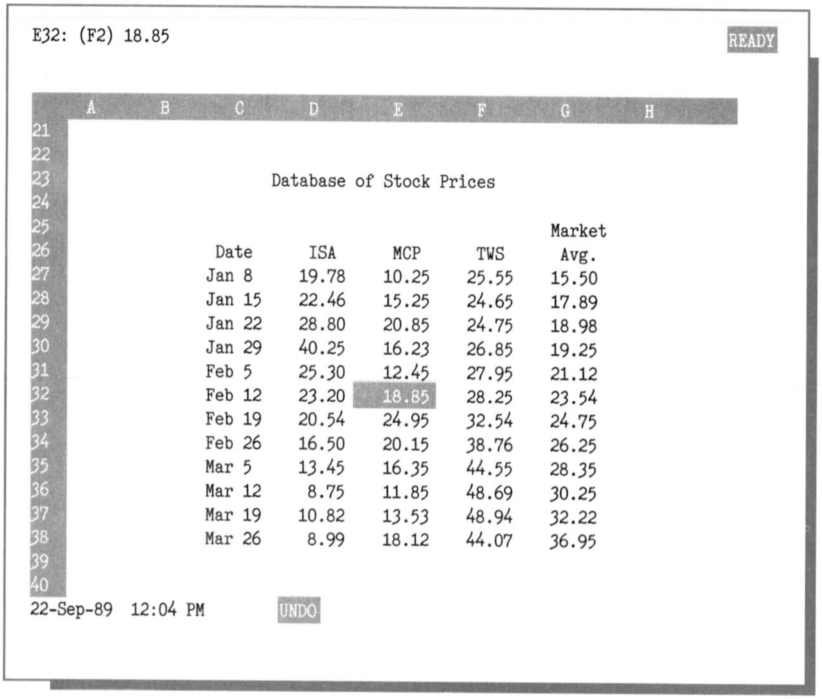

Figure 7

E32: (F2) 18.85 READY

A B C D E F G H

Database of Stock Prices

Date	ISA	MCP	TWS	Market Avg.
Jan 8	19.78	10.25	25.55	15.50
Jan 15	22.46	15.25	24.65	17.89
Jan 22	28.80	20.85	24.75	18.98
Jan 29	40.25	16.23	26.85	19.25
Feb 5	25.30	12.45	27.95	21.12
Feb 12	23.20	18.85	28.25	23.54
Feb 19	20.54	24.95	32.54	24.75
Feb 26	16.50	20.15	38.76	26.25
Mar 5	13.45	16.35	44.55	28.35
Mar 12	8.75	11.85	48.69	30.25
Mar 19	10.82	13.53	48.94	32.22
Mar 26	8.99	18.12	44.07	36.95

22-Sep-89 12:04 PM UNDO

The area of the worksheet that contains the database of stock prices is now visible in the window. A database simply contains information that is organized in a specific way. Tom's database contains the weekly stock prices for the three stocks and the market average for January 8 through March 26.

The information in a database can be sorted or arranged alphabetically or numerically by 1-2-3. It can also be searched to locate specific information, much as you would search through a filing cabinet to locate a specific record. Creating and using databases are described in detail in Labs 7 and 8.

Using a Macro

At the end of each month, Tom prepares a report and a graph of the month's stock prices for the Trackers Club meeting. To prepare the monthly reports, he copies the appropriate data from the database area of the worksheet to the analysis area. Figure 8 shows these two areas of the worksheet.

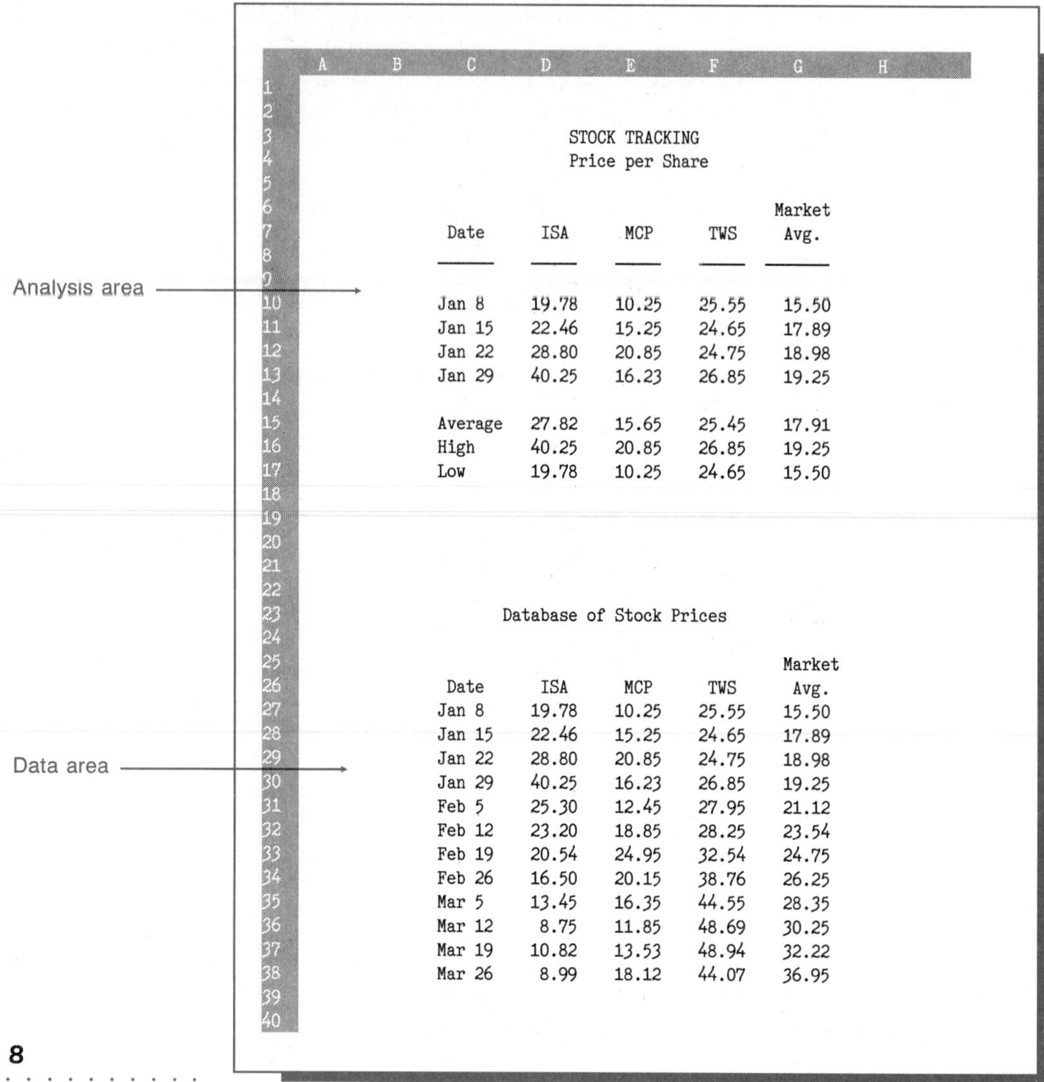

STOCK TRACKING
Price per Share

Date	ISA	MCP	TWS	Market Avg.
Jan 8	19.78	10.25	25.55	15.50
Jan 15	22.46	15.25	24.65	17.89
Jan 22	28.80	20.85	24.75	18.98
Jan 29	40.25	16.23	26.85	19.25
Average	27.82	15.65	25.45	17.91
High	40.25	20.85	26.85	19.25
Low	19.78	10.25	24.65	15.50

Database of Stock Prices

Date	ISA	MCP	TWS	Market Avg.
Jan 8	19.78	10.25	25.55	15.50
Jan 15	22.46	15.25	24.65	17.89
Jan 22	28.80	20.85	24.75	18.98
Jan 29	40.25	16.23	26.85	19.25
Feb 5	25.30	12.45	27.95	21.12
Feb 12	23.20	18.85	28.25	23.54
Feb 19	20.54	24.95	32.54	24.75
Feb 26	16.50	20.15	38.76	26.25
Mar 5	13.45	16.35	44.55	28.35
Mar 12	8.75	11.85	48.69	30.25
Mar 19	10.82	13.53	48.94	32.22
Mar 26	8.99	18.12	44.07	36.95

Figure 8

To prepare the report of the March stock data, Tom needs to copy the March data in cells C35 through G38 of the database into cells C10 through G13 of the analysis area.

To copy the March data, Tom could use the main menu and issue the command to copy (you will learn how to use the Copy command in Lab 2). However, because he plans to copy from the data area to the analysis area frequently, Tom created a **macro** to perform the command sequence for him. A macro is a set of commands and instructions that are stored in a worksheet. The commands are executed whenever you run (invoke) the macro.

To see the macro Tom entered in the worksheet,

Press: CTRL-(→) (hold down CTRL and press (→))

Your screen should look similar to Figure 9.

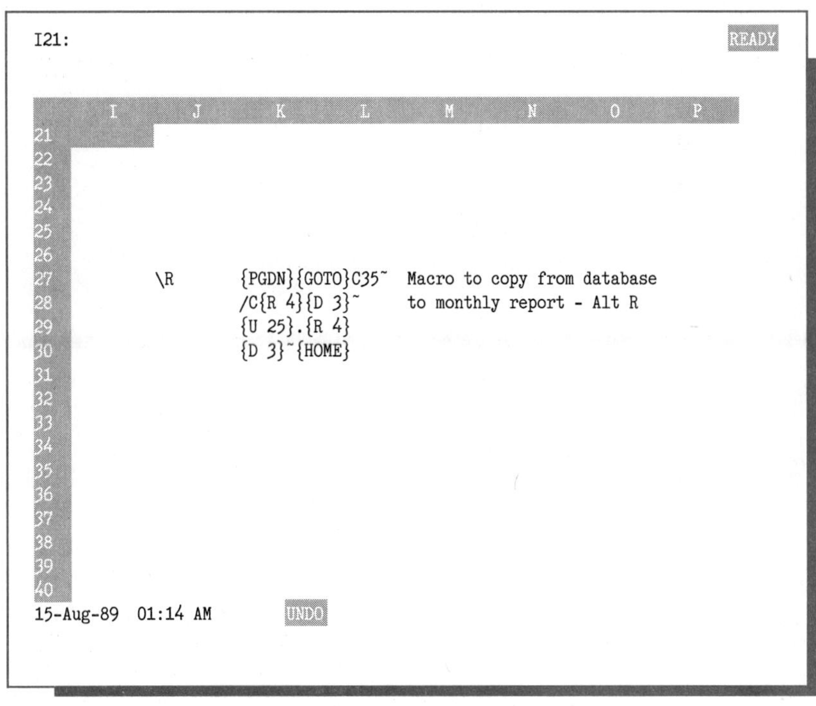

Figure 9

You are now viewing another window on the worksheet. The macro is displayed in cells K27 through K30. A description of what the macro does is located in cells M27 and M28. You will learn more about how to write and use macros in Lab 9.

Before issuing the command to execute the macro, move to the top of the worksheet:

Press: HOME

Watch your screen closely as you execute the macro commands to copy the data for March 5 through March 26 from the database area to the analysis area.

Press: ALT-**R** (hold down ALT and press the letter R)

Your screen should look similar to Figure 10.

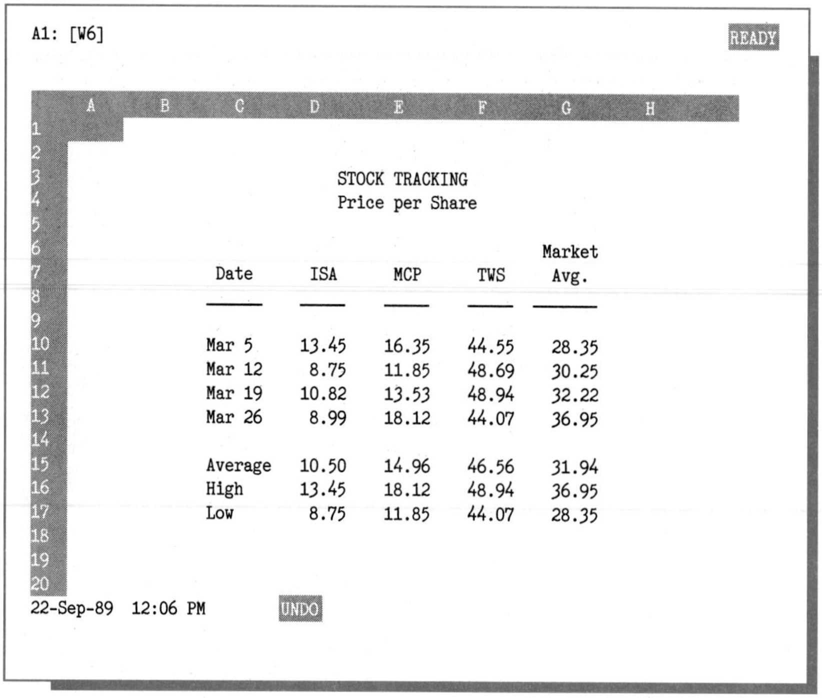

```
A1: [W6]                                                      READY

     A    B    C    D    E    F    G    H
 1
 2
 3                      STOCK TRACKING
 4                      Price per Share
 5
 6                                              Market
 7               Date     ISA     MCP     TWS     Avg.
 8               ____     ___     ___     ___     ____
 9
10               Mar 5    13.45   16.35   44.55   28.35
11               Mar 12    8.75   11.85   48.69   30.25
12               Mar 19   10.82   13.53   48.94   32.22
13               Mar 26    8.99   18.12   44.07   36.95
14
15               Average  10.50   14.96   46.56   31.94
16               High     13.45   18.12   48.94   36.95
17               Low       8.75   11.85   44.07   28.35
18
19
20
22-Sep-89  12:06 PM        UNDO
```

Figure 10

The January stock data have been replaced by the March data. The average, high, and low values have been recalculated using the new data. To see the same macro executed again but more slowly,

Press: ALT-**S**

The bar graph Tom created to view the January data will now display the data for March. Tom has written another macro to display this graph.

If you have a color monitor, to view the graph,

Press: ALT-**C**

If you have a monochrome monitor, to view the graph,

Press: ALT-**B**

Your screen should look similar to Figure 11.

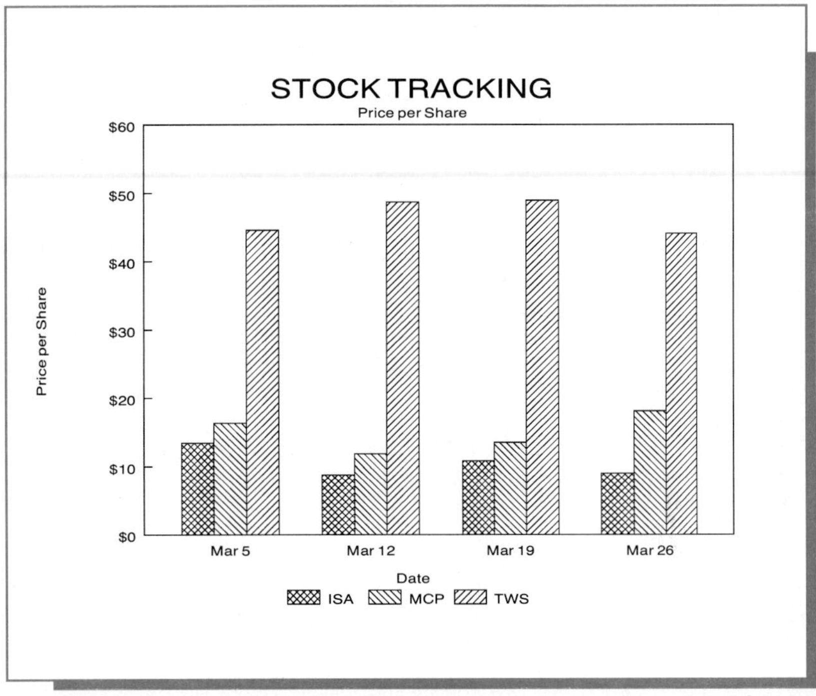

Figure 11

Using macros to perform 1-2-3 commands makes producing Tom's monthly report and graph easy.

To clear the graph from the screen,

Press: SPACEBAR

The command to leave 1-2-3 is / **Q**uit **Y**es. To issue this command,

Press: /
Press: **Q**
Press: **Y**

1-2-3 reminds you that you have made changes to your worksheet and have not saved these changes on your data disk. At this point, you do not want to save your changes and you do want to exit from 1-2-3.

Press: **Y**

1

Creating a Worksheet

Objectives

In Lab 1, you will learn how to:

- Move around the worksheet
- Enter labels and values
- Edit entries
- Use the 1-2-3 menus
- Enter formulas
- Save a worksheet

Case Study

In Labs 1 and 2, you will create the worksheet shown in Figure 1.1. You will learn how to enter information into the worksheet and how to edit those entries.

	Six-Month Budget for Chris Kent						
	JAN	FEB	MAR	APR	MAY	JUN	TOTAL
WAGES:	2000	2000	2000	2000	2000	2000	12000
EXPENSES:							
RENT	475	475	475	475	475	475	2850
FOOD	362	362	362	362	362	362	2172
CLOTHING	150	150	150	150	150	150	900
CAR INSURANCE	357						357
CAR EXPENSES	94	94	94	94	94	94	564
LIFE INSURANCE	277						277
LOAN PAYMENT						731	731
LEISURE	300	300	300	300	300	300	1800
SAVINGS	350	350	350	350	350	350	2100
TOTAL EXPENSES:	2365	1731	1731	1731	1731	2462	11751
BALANCE:	–365	269	269	269	269	–462	249

Figure 1.1

This worksheet is a six-month budget for Chris Kent, the activities director of a local athletic club. He recently purchased the 1-2-3 program and wants to use it to set up a monthly budget.

Chris Kent's monthly wage is $2,000. Some of his estimated expenses are the same each month and others are not. Rent, food, clothing, car expenses, leisure, and savings are the same each month. Periodic expenses include car insurance, life insurance, and loan payments. Total expenses are the sum of all expenses, and the balance is calculated by subtracting his total expenses from his wages.

Exploring 1-2-3's Worksheet

After you load 1-2-3, your screen should look similar to Figure 1.2. (If you need help loading, see Chapter 3, ''Starting and Ending 1-2-3'' in Section 1, ''Getting Started.'')

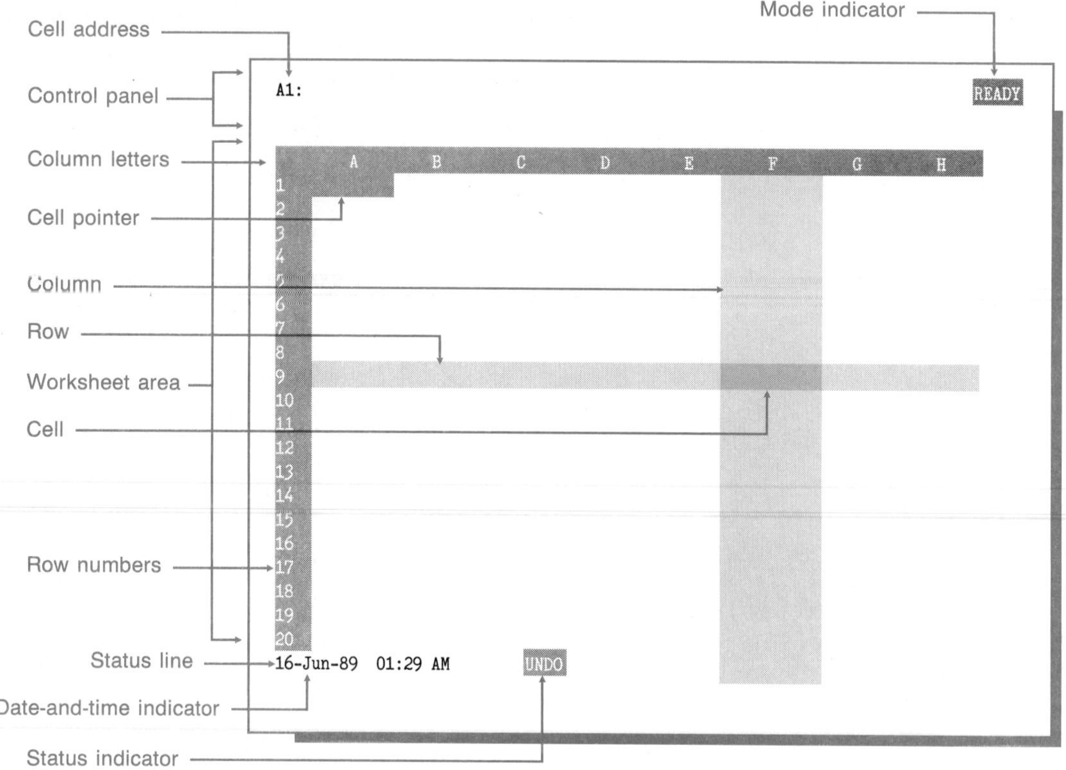

Figure 1.2

Figure 1.2 shows a blank 1-2-3 display screen. It is divided into three areas: the worksheet area, the control panel, and the status line.

The **worksheet area** is located in the center of the display screen and occupies the largest amount of space on the screen. The **worksheet** consists of a rectangular grid of **rows** and **columns**. The border of **row numbers** down the left side of the worksheet area identifies each row in the worksheet. The border of **column letters** across the top of the worksheet area identifies each column in the worksheet.

The part of the worksheet you see on your screen is called a **window**, which displays only a portion of the entire worksheet area. The entire worksheet has a total of 256 columns, labeled A through IV, and 8,192 rows, numbered 1 through 8192.

The basic unit of a worksheet is a **cell**, which is formed by the intersection of a column and a row. For example, cell A1 is the intersection of column A and row 1.

The highlight bar shown in cell A1 is the **cell pointer**. It identifies the cell you are using. The cell containing the cell pointer is the **current cell**.

The **control panel** is located above the worksheet area. It consists of three lines that display information, command choices, and prompts. The first line currently displays two pieces of information. On the left side of the first line, the **cell address** of the current cell is displayed. The cell address always consists of the column letter followed by the row number of the current cell. Because the cell pointer is now located in cell A1, the cell address displays ''A1:''.

The highlighted box on the right side of the first line is the **mode indicator**. It indicates the current **mode**, or state, the 1-2-3 program is in. Here, the current mode is READY. There are fourteen different modes of operation. As you use the program, the mode indicator will change to display the current mode. Modes will be discussed as they appear throughout the labs.

The bottom line of the display screen contains the **status line**. This line displays the date-and-time indicator, status indicators, and error messages. Currently it displays the **date-and-time indicator** on the left side. This indicator displays the date and time as maintained by DOS. As you use the program, **error messages** may replace the date-and-time indicator to tell you that the program detects an error or cannot perform a task. The highlighted box containing the word ''UNDO'' is a **status indicator**. Status indicators tell you that a certain key or program condition is in effect. Currently, the Undo feature is in effect. You will learn about this feature in Lab 2. Other status indicators will be displayed as they are activated and will be discussed as they appear throughout the labs.

Examining the Keyboard

The keyboard allows you to communicate with 1-2-3. Figure 1.3 shows two typical keyboards.

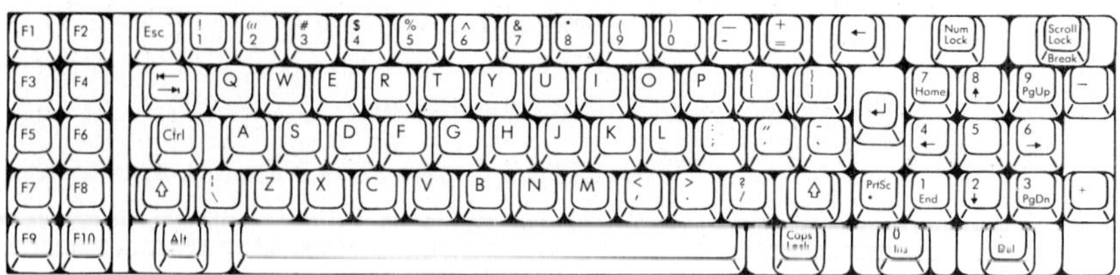

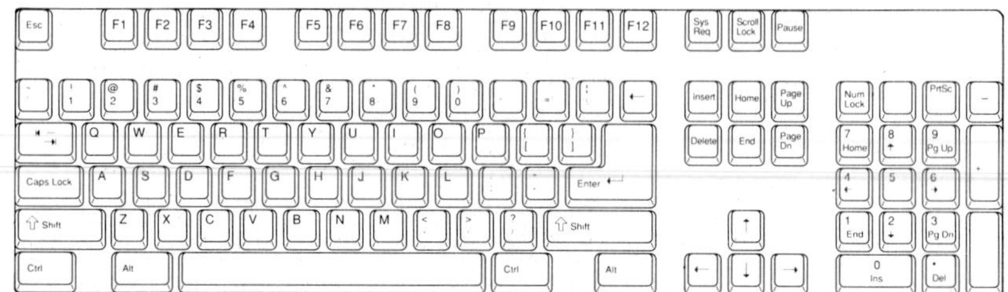

Figure 1.3

The keyboard has three general areas: the typewriter section, the function keys, and the numeric keypad.

The typewriter section is arranged like a standard typewriter keyboard. Letter and number keys are in their usual places, and holding the shift key down and typing a letter key produces a capital letter.

In addition to the standard operations, the typewriter section has keys for special operations. Table 1.1 lists these special keys and their operations.

Table 1.1

Key	Description
ESC	Cancels a command
CTRL	Causes keys to take on new meanings
ALT	Causes keys to take on new meanings
INS	Switches between inserting and typing over existing characters
DEL	Deletes a character
TAB	Moves the cursor to the next tab setting
↵	Allows the user to enter data or command sequences

Table 1.1 Continued

Key	Description
NUM LOCK	Changes the cursor movement keys to number keys, or vice versa
CAPS LOCK	Switches the letters to uppercase or lowercase
BACKSPACE	Moves the cursor back one space and deletes the character
SCROLL LOCK	Switches between moving the cell pointer and scrolling the entire worksheet
CTRL-BREAK	Cancels current procedure

The function keys execute special 1-2-3 commands. The function keys are labeled F1 through F10 (or F12 on some keyboards).

The numeric keypad, which is to the right of the typewriter section, can be used for moving around a worksheet and for entering numeric data. To use the keypad to enter numbers, you must first press the NUM LOCK key. If NUM LOCK is not on, pressing these keys moves the cell pointer around the worksheet.

Typically, you use the numeric keypad to move the cell pointer around the worksheet; you use the numbers in the typewriter section to enter numeric data.

Some keyboards have a separate keypad for the four directional arrow keys. Use of these keys moves the cell pointer in the direction of the arrow on the key.

Moving Around the Worksheet

The arrow keys in the numeric keypad are used to move the cell pointer around the worksheet in the direction of the arrow. Note the changes in the control panel and the movement of the cell pointer as you

Press: [↓] three times
Press: [→] two times

Your screen should look similar to Figure 1.4.

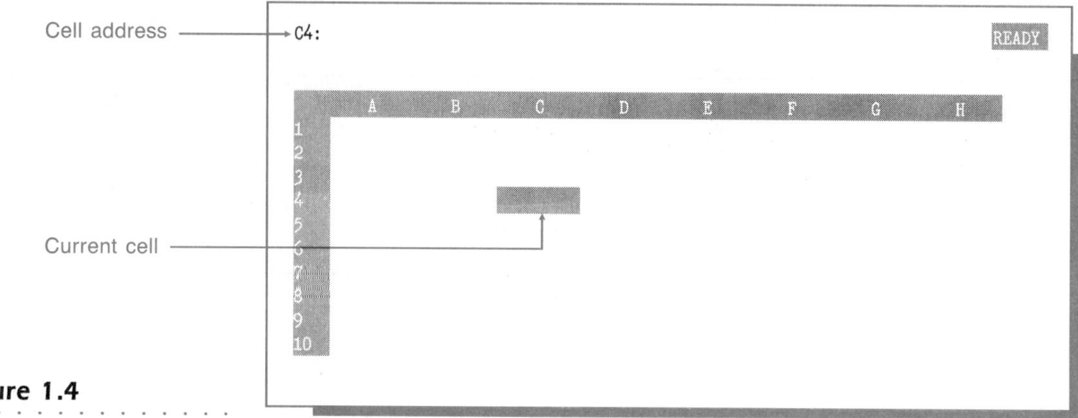

Figure 1.4

The cell pointer should now be in cell C4, making this cell the current cell. The cell address in the control panel reflects the new location of the cell pointer.

Practice moving around the worksheet by using the four arrow keys, ↓, ↑, →, and ←, to move the cell pointer to cells D9, F18, and B12.

The HOME key will return you to the top left corner of the worksheet. This position in the worksheet is also called the **home position**.

Press: HOME

The cell pointer should now be back in cell A1.

The worksheet has more columns than those you can see on your screen at one time. To view the next full window of the worksheet, you would hold down the CTRL key and press either → to move right one full screen or ← to move left one full screen.

To move right one full screen:

Press: CTRL-→

Note When two keys are separated by a hyphen (-), you must hold down the first key while pressing the second key.

Your screen should show columns I through P, as shown in Figure 1.5.

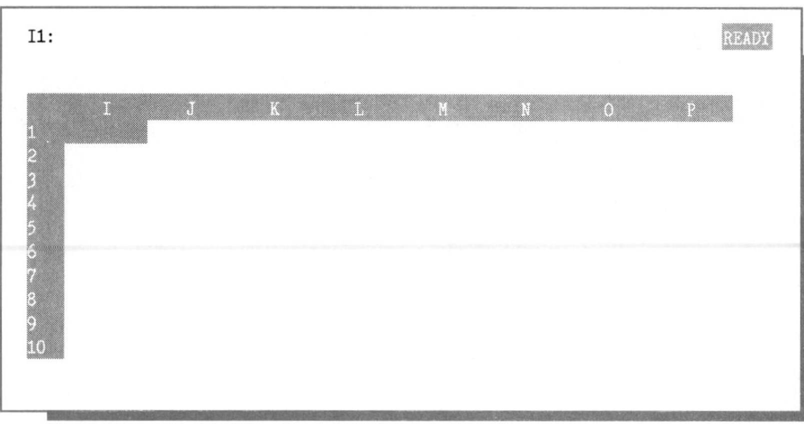

Figure 1.5

To return to the previous window,

Press: CTRL-(←)

The screen should again show columns A through H.

By holding down the CTRL key while pressing either (→) or (←), you can quickly move horizontally through the worksheet. This is called **scrolling**.

Pressing the PGDN key allows you to move down one full screen (20 rows) at a time.

Press: PGDN

Your screen should now look similar to Figure 1.6.

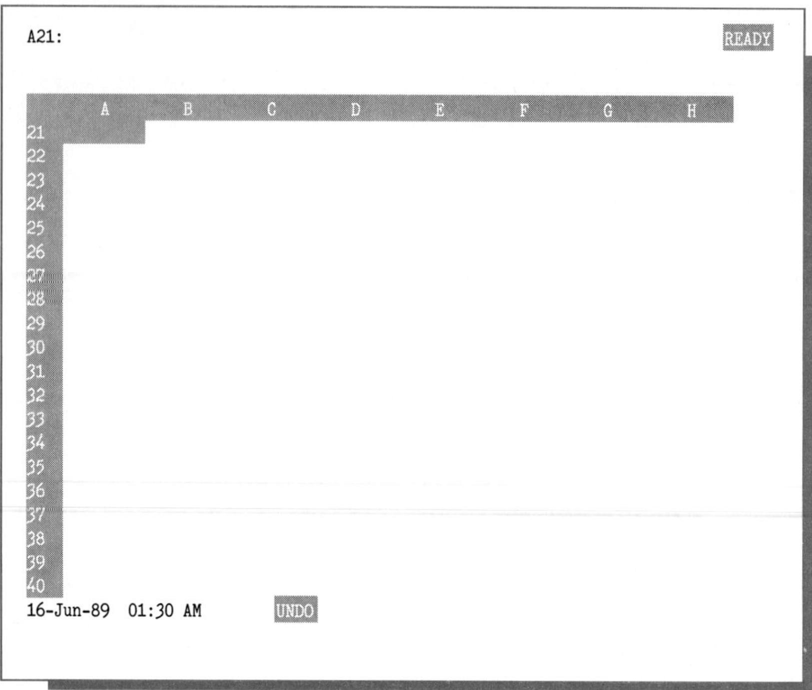

Figure 1.6

You have moved down one full screen, and rows 21 through 40 are now displayed in the window. Similarly, pressing the PGUP key allows you to move up one full screen.

Press: PGUP

Your screen has moved up one full window on the worksheet, returning you to the screen that displays rows 1 through 20. By holding down the PGUP or PGDN key, you can quickly scroll vertically through the worksheet.

To move to the last row of the worksheet,

Press: END

Notice the status indicator, END, displayed in the status line. This tells you the END key is being used.

Press: ↓

The cell pointer moved to cell A8192. Your screen should look similar to Figure 1.7.

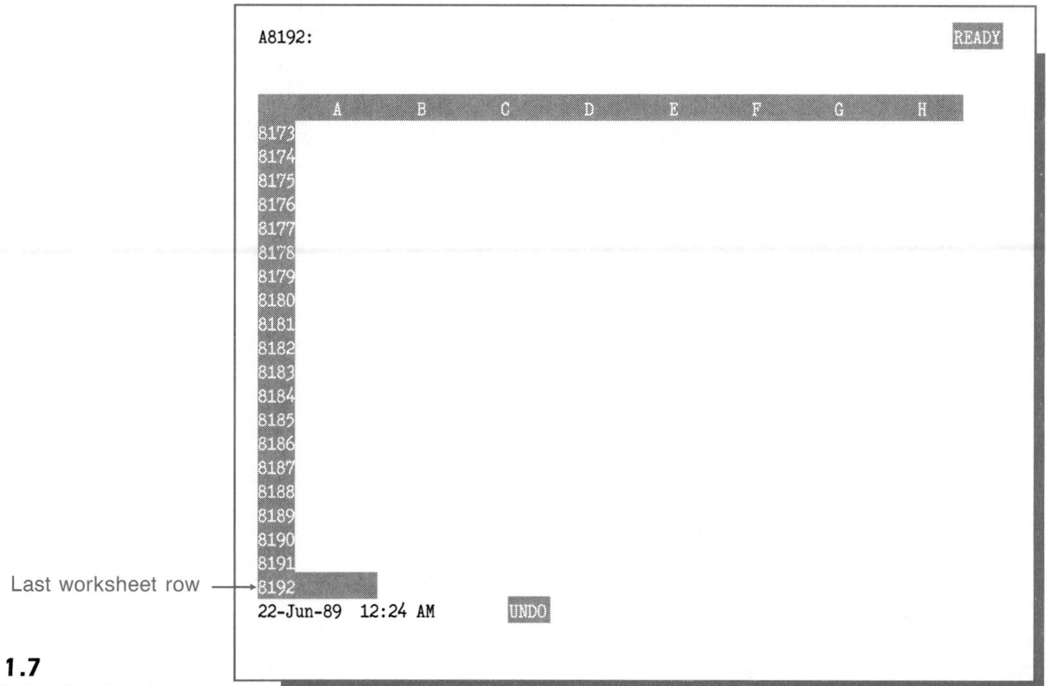

Figure 1.7

Columns are sequenced first from A to Z, then from AA to AZ, and then from BA to IV. To move to the last column of the worksheet,

Press: END
Press: (→)

The cell pointer moved to cell IV8192. Your screen should look similar to Figure 1.8.

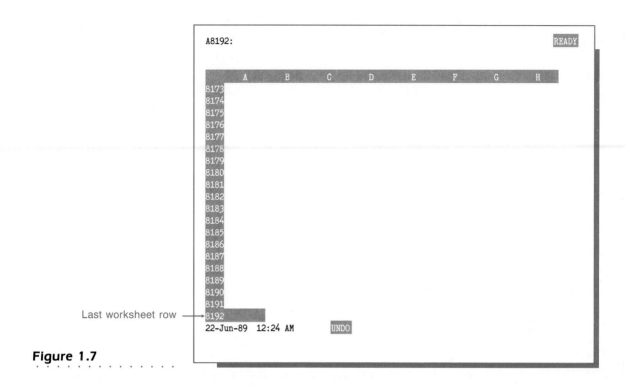

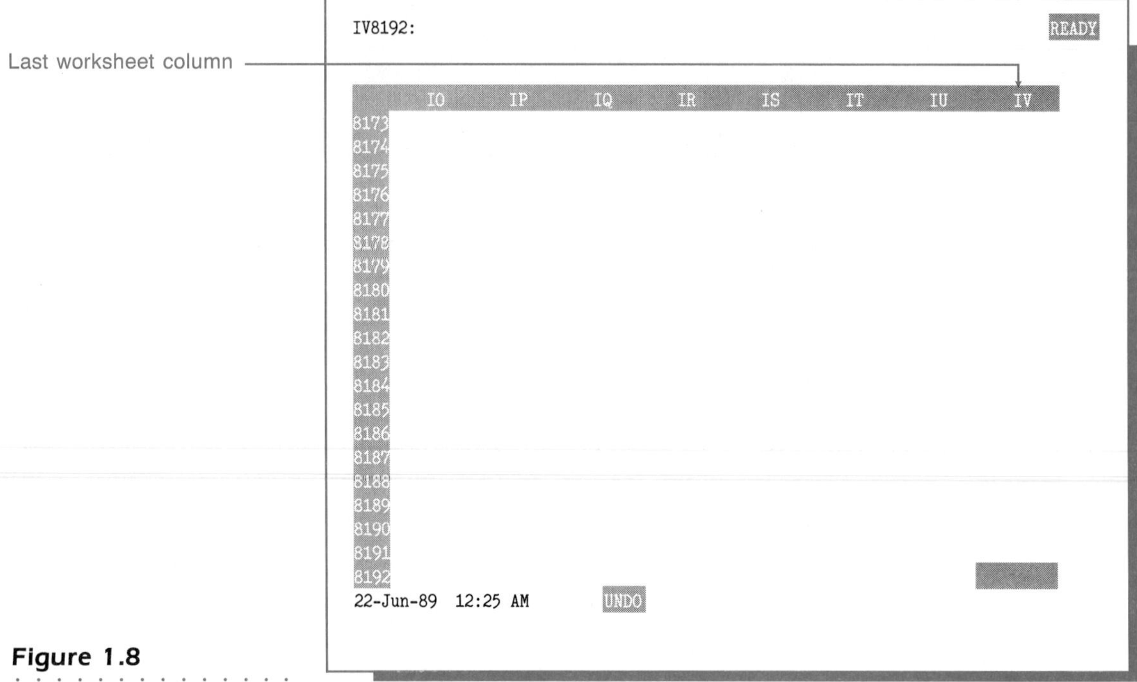

Figure 1.8

Cell IV8192 is the bottom right corner of the worksheet.

Sometimes a faster method of moving around the worksheet is to use the Goto function key, (F5). For example, to go to cell H128, first

Press: (F5)

Look at the second line of the control panel. The message, or **prompt**, ''Enter address to go to:'' is displayed. The current location of the cell pointer follows the prompt. A prompt is how 1-2-3 communicates with you. It is prompting you to enter the new cell address to move to. 1-2-3 automatically entered the current location of the cell pointer in response to the prompt. Since this is not the address you want to move to, you need to enter the correct cell address. You can enter the cell address in lowercase or uppercase characters.

Type: **H128**

To tell 1-2-3 that your response to the prompt is complete,

Press: (↵)

Your screen should look similar to Figure 1.9.

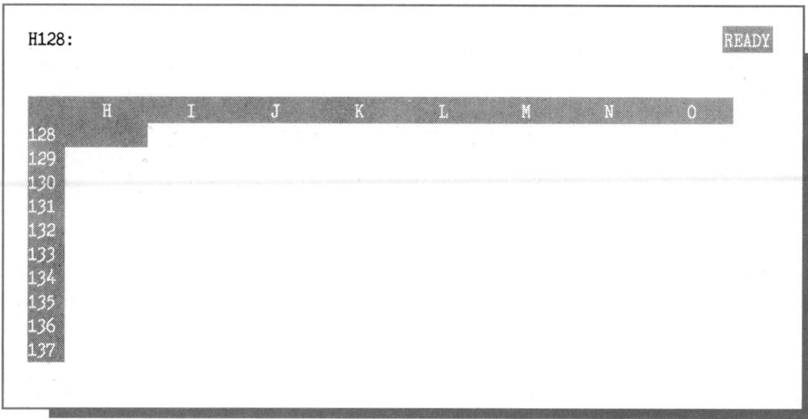

Figure 1.9

Cell H128 is placed in the upper left corner of the window and the cell pointer is positioned in that cell.

To return quickly to cell A1,

Press: HOME

Now move the cell pointer to cell A45 using the ↓ key. The row numbers on the screen now go from 26 to 45. You have moved the window down the worksheet by individual rows rather than by a full screen.

Practice each of the following key sequences, and watch how your screen changes.

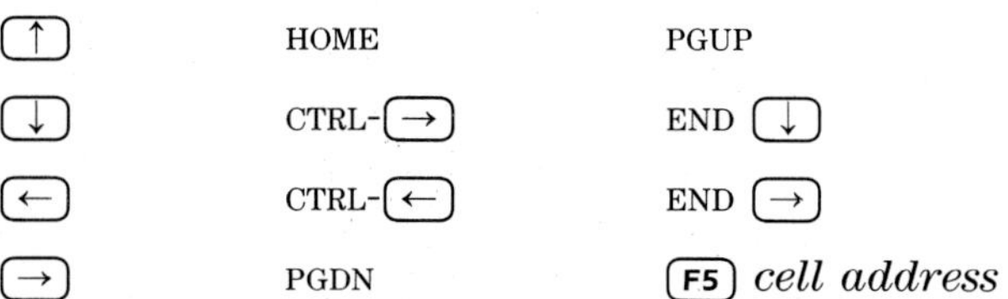

↑	HOME	PGUP
↓	CTRL-→	END ↓
←	CTRL-←	END →
→	PGDN	F5 *cell address*

When you are ready to go on,

Press: HOME

Entering Labels

Now it is time to work on Chris Kent's budget. You will learn how to enter information into the worksheet and how to correct, or **edit**, entries.

Entries into the worksheet are either labels or values. **Labels** are text entries, such as words and symbols that describe other worksheet entries. They cannot be used for arithmetic calculations. **Values** are numbers and formula entries.

The first character you enter in a cell determines how 1-2-3 will define the cell contents. Cell entries that begin with a number from 0 through 9 or any of the **numeric symbols** +, −, ., (, @, #, and $ are values. Cell entries that begin with an alpha character (A through Z), ', '', ^, or any other character are defined as labels.

For example, if you entered the number 14 into a cell, it would be a value and could be used to calculate other values. However, if you preceded the number 14 with an apostrophe ('14), 1-2-3 would interpret it as a label and could not use it to calculate other arithmetic values.

To show how the first character of a cell entry is interpreted, the mode indicator displays either LABEL or VALUE. When the cell entry is complete, the mode indicator returns to READY.

You will begin creating Chris Kent's worksheet by entering the labels for the months in row 2.

Move to: B2

Check the cell address in the control panel to be sure that the cell pointer is in cell B2.

Type: **january**

Your screen should now look similar to Figure 1.10.

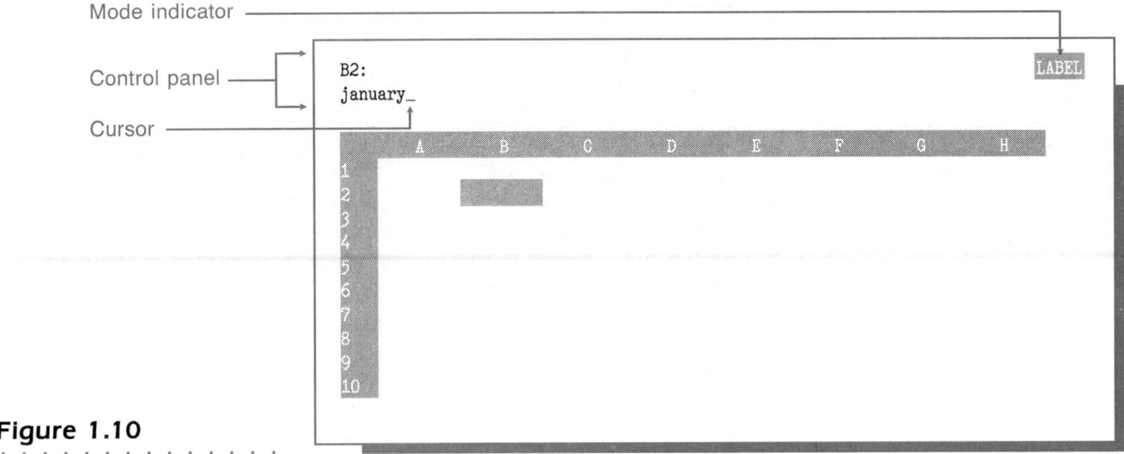

Figure 1.10

If you make a typing error, use the BACKSPACE key to erase the letters back to your mistake and then type the entry correctly.

The mode indicator changed from READY to LABEL. The second line of the control panel displays the label **january** followed by a blinking underscore, or **cursor**. The cursor shows you where each character will appear as you type. Notice, however, that the label has not yet been entered into cell B2 of the worksheet.

To enter the label into cell B2,

Press: ↵

Your screen should now look similar to Figure 1.11.

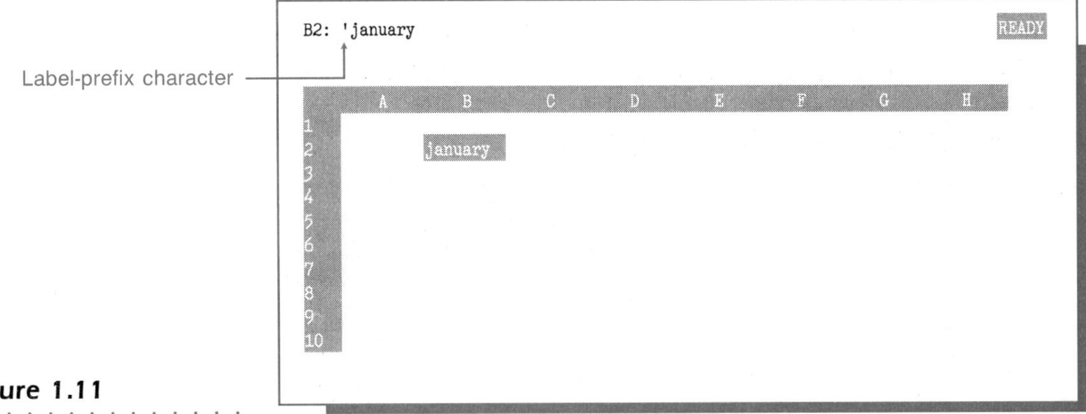

Figure 1.11

The label, **january**, is displayed in cell B2. (If you entered the label in the wrong cell location, move the cell pointer to the entry and type **/RE** (↵). The cell entry will be erased. This command sequence is discussed in more detail in Lab 2.)

Also notice that, following the cell address in the control panel, the contents of the current cell are displayed as **'january**. The apostrophe (') before the label is a **label-prefix character**. This character is automatically entered before all label entries (in the control panel, but not in the current cell). It controls the placement or alignment of the label within the cell space. The apostrophe aligns a label at the left side of the cell space. You will see how label alignment can be changed shortly.

Next, we want to change **january** to **jan**. This can be accomplished in either READY mode or EDIT mode.

To use READY mode, with the cell pointer in cell B2,

Type: **jan**
Press: (↵)

When you press (↵), **jan** is entered in the worksheet. Another way to enter information in the worksheet is to move the cell pointer to another cell. For example, with the cell pointer still in cell B2,

Type: **Jan**
Press: (→)

The label is entered in cell B2, and the cell pointer is moved to cell C2.

The second method of changing entries uses EDIT mode, which is accessed by using the Edit function key, (F2). To change **Jan** to **JAN** using EDIT mode,

Move to: B2
Press: (F2)

Your screen should look similar to Figure 1.12.

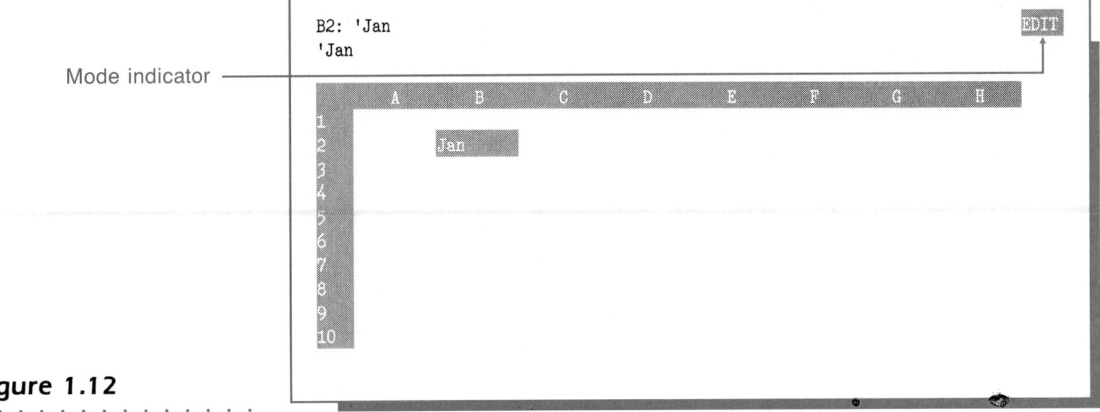

Figure 1.12

The second line of the control panel now displays **'Jan**, and the mode indicator has changed from READY to EDIT. In EDIT mode, you can use the keys in Table 1.2 for specific tasks.

Table 1.2

Key	Action
←	Moves the cursor one space left in the entry
→	Moves the cursor one space right in the entry
HOME	Moves the cursor to the first character in the entry
END	Moves the cursor to the space after the last character
CTRL-→ or TAB	Moves the cursor five spaces to the right
CTRL-← or SHIFT-TAB	Moves the cursor five spaces to the left
BACKSPACE	Deletes characters to the left of the cursor
INS	Overwrites text
DEL	Deletes characters at the cursor
ESC	Erases all characters in the entry

To delete the **an** from **Jan** in the second line of the control panel,

Press: ← two times
Press: DEL two times

To complete the edit,

Type: **AN**
Press: ↵

Your screen should look similar to Figure 1.13.

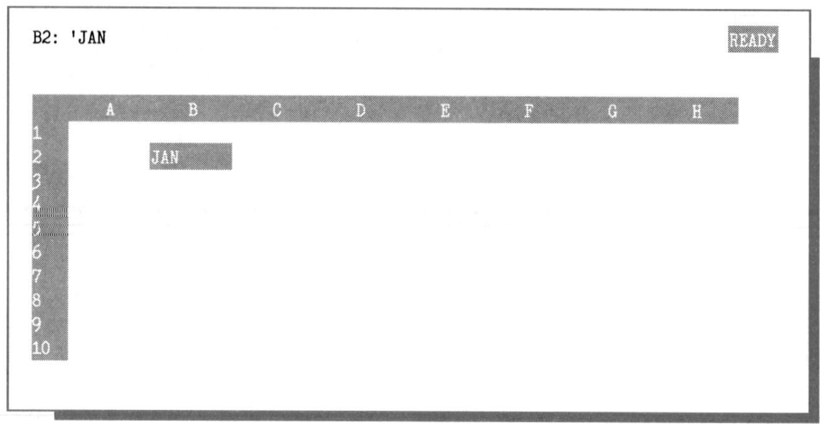

Figure 1.13

You have returned to READY mode, and **JAN** is now entered into cell B2.

As you can see, editing would be particularly useful for changing long or complicated entries.

Next, you will practice using READY and EDIT modes to enter the column label for cell C2.

Move to: C2
Type: **february**
Press: ↵

To change **february** to **Feb** in READY mode,

Type: **Feb**
Press: ↵

To change **Feb** to **FEB** using EDIT mode,

Press: F2
Press: BACKSPACE two times
Type: **EB**
Press: ↵

Your screen should look similar to Figure 1.14.

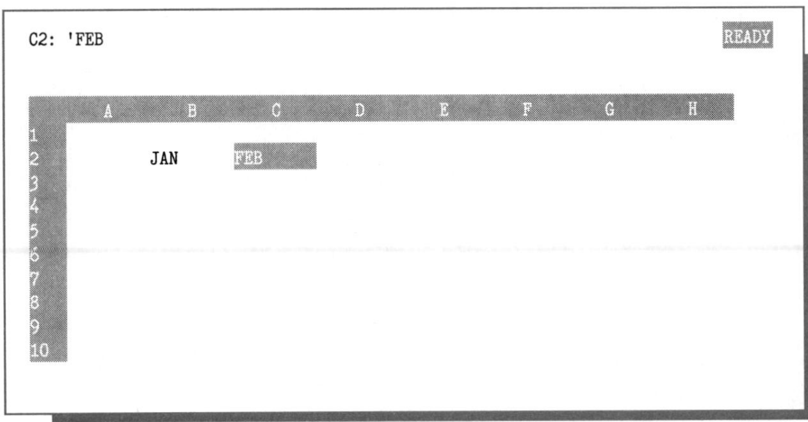

Figure 1.14

Notice that both **JAN** and **FEB** are displayed to the left side of their cell space. This is because the default label-prefix character (') was automatically entered by 1-2-3. Labels can be displayed in their cell space as left-aligned, centered, or right-aligned. You can specify the alignment of a label within the cell space by entering the following label-prefix characters before the label:

Label-prefix character	*Effect*
' (apostrophe)	left-aligned
^ (caret)	centered
'' (quote)	right-aligned

If no label-prefix character is specified, 1-2-3 automatically enters an apostrophe and the label is left-aligned.

To change **JAN** to right alignment,

Move to: B2
Type: **''JAN**
Press: ↵

Your screen should now look similar to Figure 1.15.

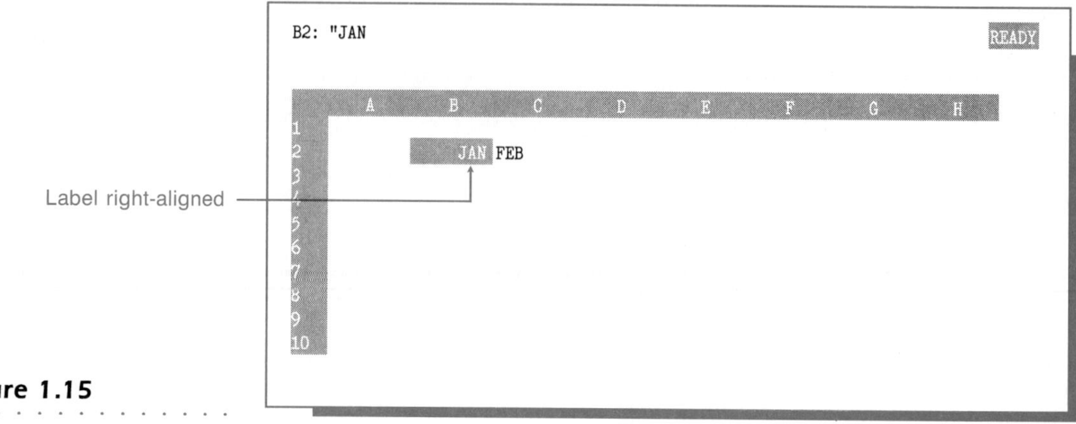

Figure 1.15

JAN is displayed right-aligned in the cell space. Notice there is a blank space to the right of the label. 1-2-3 reserves this space for special characters, such as an end parenthesis or a percent sign, used in numeric entries.

Now, change **FEB** to right alignment in either EDIT or READY mode.

You are ready to enter the labels for the other months. Because we want the months entered as all capital letters,

Press: CAPS LOCK

The status indicator, CAPS, appears in the status line to tell you the CAPS LOCK key is on. The CAPS LOCK key affects only the letter keys, not the number or punctuation keys.

Now enter and right-align the labels **MAR**, **APR**, **MAY**, **JUN**, and **TOTAL** in cells D2 through H2. Use ↵ to enter the last label in cell H2. Your screen should look similar to Figure 1.16.

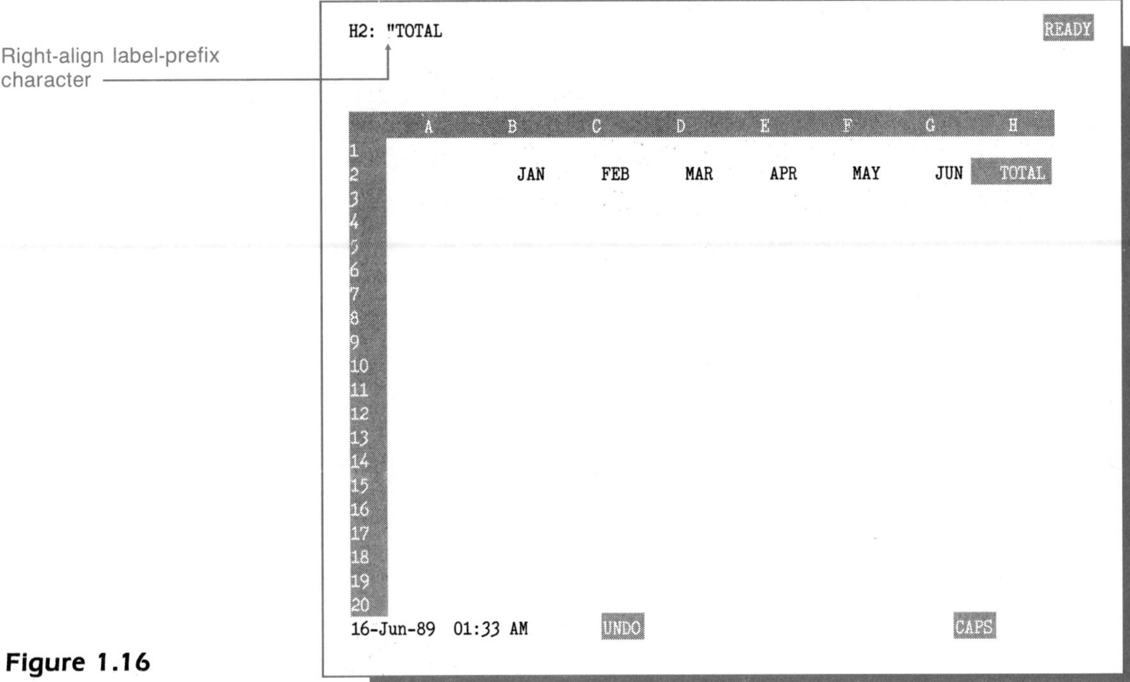

Figure 1.16

To turn off CAPS LOCK,

Press: CAPS LOCK

Next, you want to underline the column title for **JAN**. To do this, you will enter nine hyphen characters in the cell.

Move to: B3
Type: '---------
Press: ↵

The apostrophe preceding the entry defines the entry as a label. Without it, the first character in the entry (-) would have been interpreted as a value (a negative sign) and an error would have resulted.

Cell B3 should be completely filled with a series of hyphens.

An easier way to fill a cell with repeated characters is to begin the entry with another label-prefix character, the backslash (\). This label-prefix character tells 1-2-3 to fill the cell with the character(s) following the backslash.

Move to: C3
Type: \-
Press: ↵

Your screen should look similar to Figure 1.17.

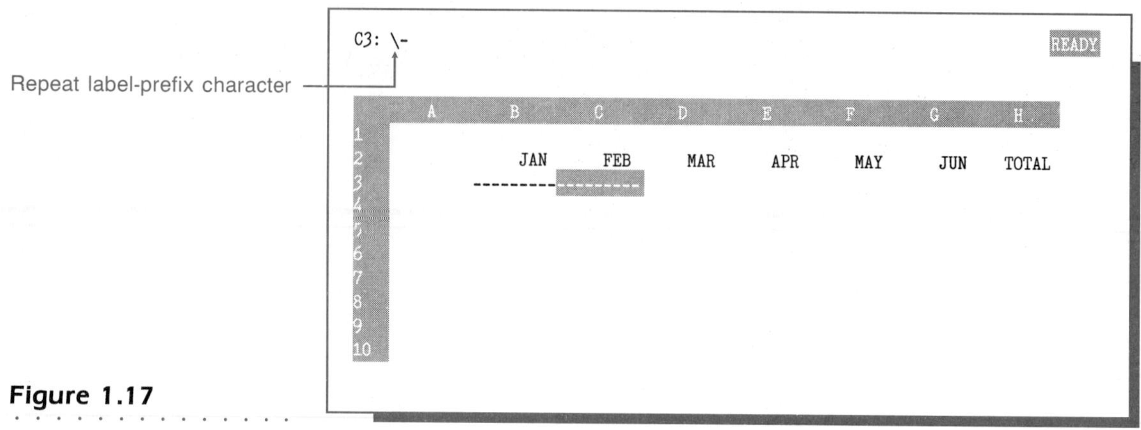

Figure 1.17

You can use the backslash character to fill a cell with any repeated character. For example, if you want all asterisks in a cell, type *.

Now, underline the other column titles.

To enter a title for the worksheet,

Move to: C1
Type: **Six-Month Budget for Chris Kent**
Press: ↵

Although the title is longer than the nine spaces in cell C1, it is fully displayed in the worksheet. A label that is longer than the cell width is called a long label. As long as the cells to the right of C1 are empty, the long label in cell C1 can be fully displayed. If cell D1, E1, or F1 contained data, the long label in C1 would be cut off at that point.

The row labels for Chris Kent's worksheet are entered in the same manner as the column labels. This has already been done for you and saved in a file on your data disk.

As you retrieve this file, we will explore the structure of the 1-2-3 menus.

Examining the 1-2-3 Menus

You access the 1-2-3 menus by pressing the slash key, /, located on the bottom right of the typewriter section of your keyboard.

Press: /

Your screen should look similar to Figure 1.18.

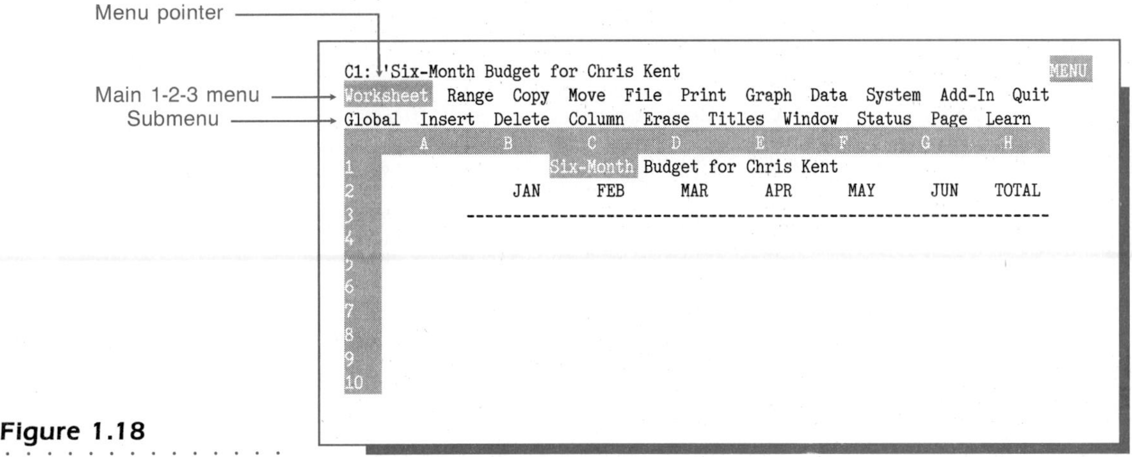

Figure 1.18

Look at the control panel. The first line has not changed. The second line, however, now shows the main 1-2-3 **menu**, or list, of eleven different **commands**, beginning with Worksheet and ending with Quit.

The highlight bar that is currently on Worksheet is the **menu pointer**. The third line shows the submenu of commands associated with the highlighted main menu command, and the mode indicator displays MENU.

1-2-3 provides a context-sensitive Help facility for all commands. To obtain help (information) on a particular command, begin the command and then press the Help function key, F1. For example, you have begun a command by typing the slash key, /. To obtain help on the commands shown in the control panel,

Press: F1

Note If you are using a two-disk system, and need more information on obtaining help, see Chapter 5, "The Help Facility," in Section 1, "Getting Started."

Your screen should look similar to Figure 1.19.

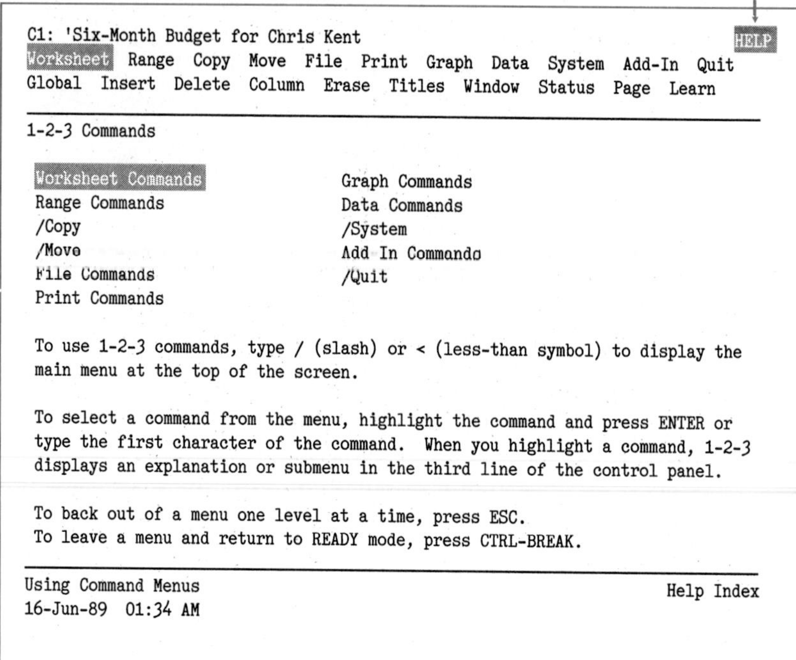

Mode indicator
C1: 'Six-Month Budget for Chris Kent
HELP
Worksheet Range Copy Move File Print Graph Data System Add-In Quit
Global Insert Delete Column Erase Titles Window Status Page Learn
1-2-3 Commands
Worksheet Commands
Range Commands
/Copy
/Move
File Commands
Print Commands
Graph Commands
Data Commands
/System
Add In Commands
/Quit
To use 1-2-3 commands, type / (slash) or < (less-than symbol) to display the main menu at the top of the screen.
To select a command from the menu, highlight the command and press ENTER or type the first character of the command. When you highlight a command, 1-2-3 displays an explanation or submenu in the third line of the control panel.
To back out of a menu one level at a time, press ESC.
To leave a menu and return to READY mode, press CTRL-BREAK.
Using Command Menus
Help Index
16-Jun-89 01:34 AM

Figure 1.19

The mode indicator now displays HELP, and the screen provides information on the main menu commands.

You can get more information by using the arrow keys to move the highlight bar to any of the Help topics displayed in reverse video and pressing ↵.

For information on the File command,

Move to: File Commands
Press: ↵

Your screen should look similar to Figure 1.20.

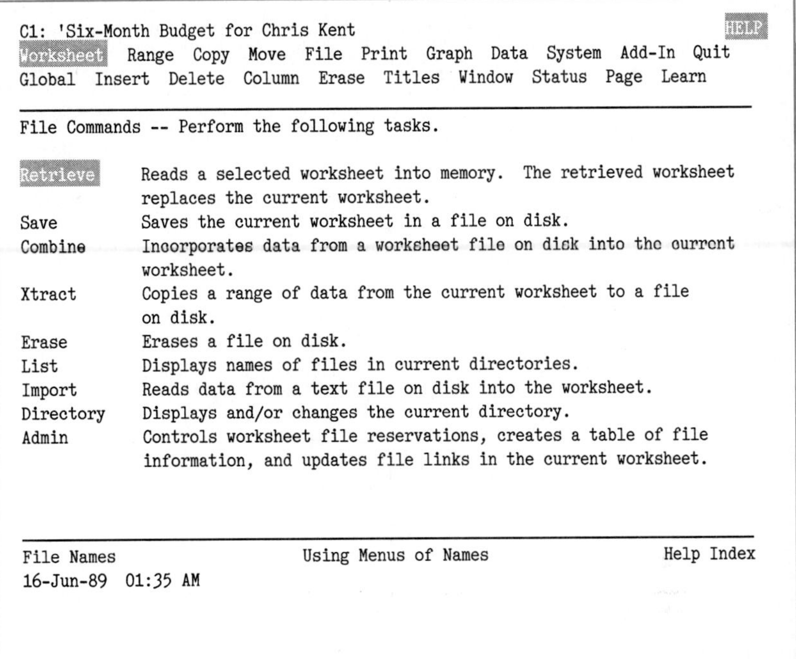
```
C1: 'Six-Month Budget for Chris Kent                                    HELP
Worksheet  Range  Copy  Move  File  Print  Graph  Data  System  Add-In  Quit
Global  Insert  Delete  Column  Erase  Titles  Window  Status  Page  Learn

File Commands -- Perform the following tasks.

Retrieve     Reads a selected worksheet into memory.  The retrieved worksheet
             replaces the current worksheet.
Save         Saves the current worksheet in a file on disk.
Combine      Incorporates data from a worksheet file on disk into the current
             worksheet.
Xtract       Copies a range of data from the current worksheet to a file
             on disk.
Erase        Erases a file on disk.
List         Displays names of files in current directories.
Import       Reads data from a text file on disk into the worksheet.
Directory    Displays and/or changes the current directory.
Admin        Controls worksheet file reservations, creates a table of file
             information, and updates file links in the current worksheet.

File Names                    Using Menus of Names                  Help Index
16-Jun-89  01:35 AM
```

Figure 1.20

You now have information about the submenu commands associated with the main menu command, File. These commands allow you to work with files stored on a disk. Since we want to retrieve a file, to see more Help information about the highlighted Retrieve command,

Press: ↵

Your screen should look similar to Figure 1.21.

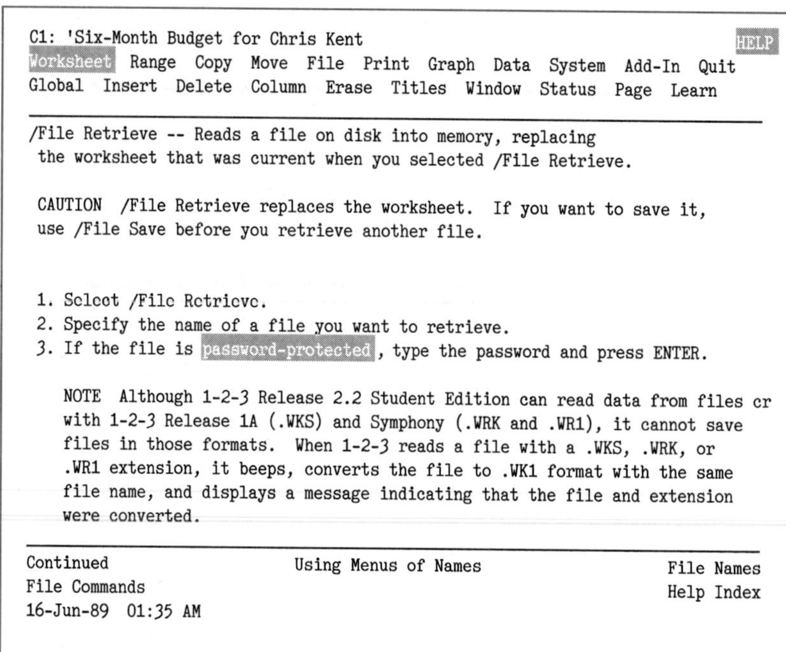

C1: 'Six-Month Budget for Chris Kent
HELP
Worksheet Range Copy Move File Print Graph Data System Add-In Quit
Global Insert Delete Column Erase Titles Window Status Page Learn
/File Retrieve -- Reads a file on disk into memory, replacing
the worksheet that was current when you selected /File Retrieve.
CAUTION /File Retrieve replaces the worksheet. If you want to save it,
use /File Save before you retrieve another file.
1. Select /File Retrieve.
2. Specify the name of a file you want to retrieve.
3. If the file is password-protected, type the password and press ENTER.
NOTE Although 1-2-3 Release 2.2 Student Edition can read data from files cr
with 1-2-3 Release 1A (.WKS) and Symphony (.WRK and .WR1), it cannot save
files in those formats. When 1-2-3 reads a file with a .WKS, .WRK, or
.WR1 extension, it beeps, converts the file to .WK1 format with the same
file name, and displays a message indicating that the file and extension
were converted.
Continued
Using Menus of Names
File Names
File Commands
Help Index
16-Jun-89 01:35 AM

Figure 1.21

The screen now shows information on the File Retrieve command. Notice the "CAUTION" statement in this Help screen. It tells you that / **F**ile **R**etrieve replaces the worksheet. If you want to save the worksheet, use the / **F**ile **S**ave command before you retrieve another file. Caution statements are included in many Help screens to advise you of potential problems and to help you avoid errors.

To turn off the Help menu and return to your original position in the worksheet,

Press: ESC

To review, you access the main menu by pressing /, ask for help by pressing F1, and then select the desired Help topic for more detailed information. By using the Help system, you can obtain an explanation of each command. This is a good way to find out about 1-2-3. You can access the Help menu at any time by pressing F1.

You will now retrieve a file. Make sure that the data disk containing the Sample Files is in drive B if you are using a two-drive system.

You can select a command in one of three different ways:

1. Type the first letter (in uppercase or lowercase) of the command.
2. Use the (→) and (←) keys to move the menu pointer to highlight the command and then press (↵) (this is called menu pointing).
3. Use a combination of methods 1 and 2.

The third line of the control panel lists the various submenu commands associated with the highlighted command. To move the menu pointer to File,

Press: (→) four times

Your screen should now look similar to Figure 1.22.

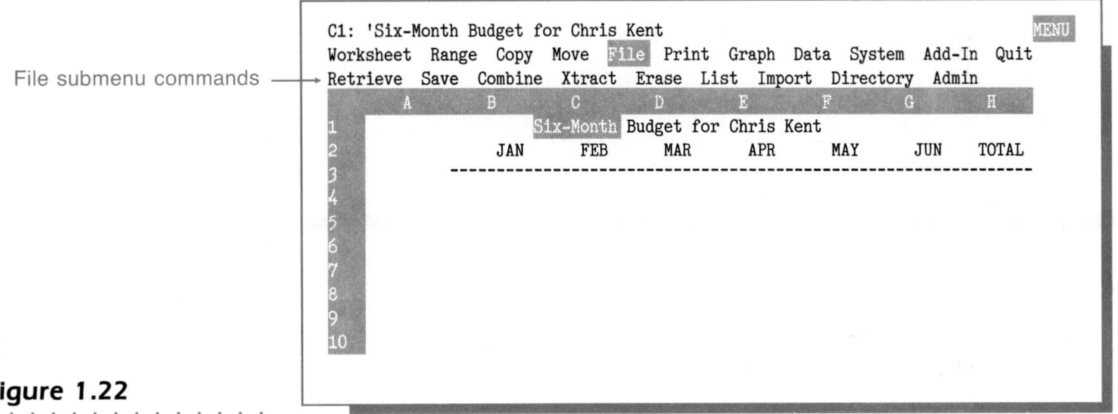

Figure 1.22

Now the third line of the control panel displays a submenu of nine commands associated with the highlighted File command.

You want to retrieve a file. Because the File command is already highlighted, you can either press (↵) or type F to select this command. Select:

File

Your screen should now look similar to Figure 1.23.

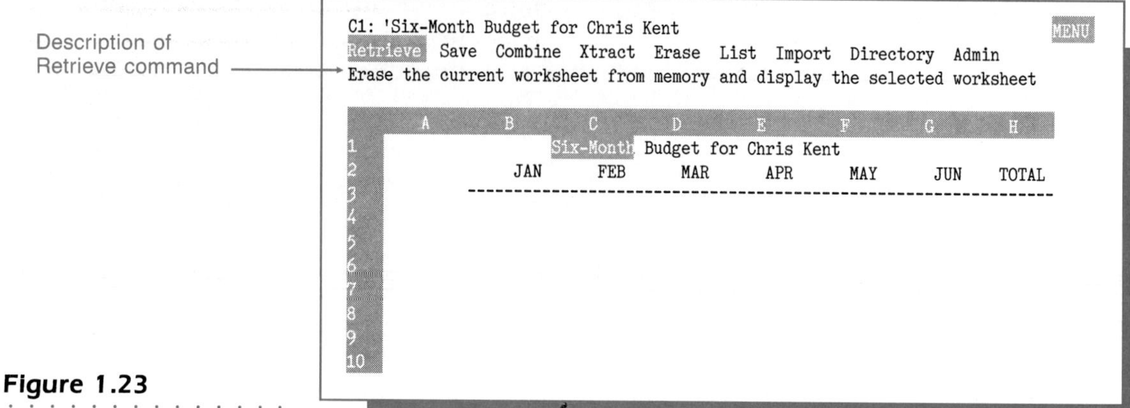

Figure 1.23

The File submenu commands, which were on the third line of the control panel, are now on the second line. The third line now presents a brief description of the highlighted Retrieve command. You now want to retrieve a file, so select:

Retrieve

Your screen should look similar to Figure 1.24.

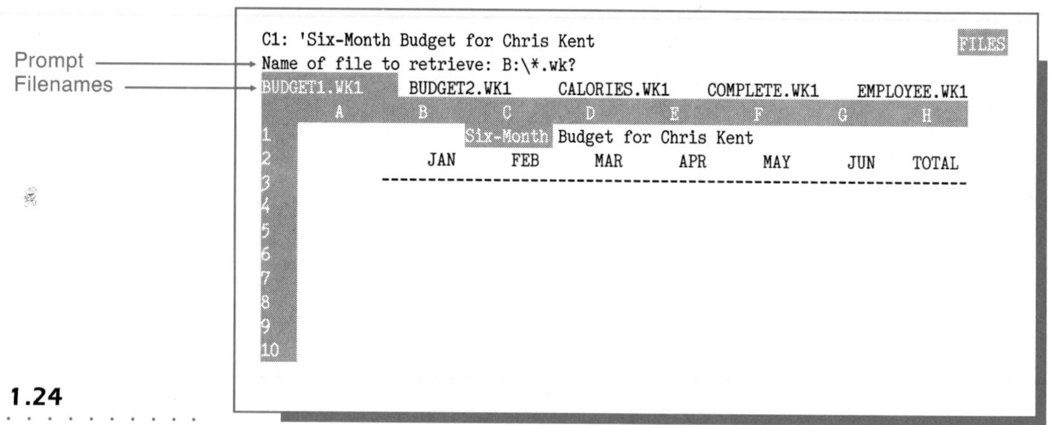

Figure 1.24

The second line of the control panel prompts you to specify the name of the file you want to retrieve. Following the prompt, the drive (B:) that 1-2-3 is using is displayed. (If you are using a hard-disk system, your prompt will probably display C:.) The third line lists worksheet files on your data disk. The mode indicator displays FILES.

You can select the name of the file to be retrieved by typing the filename or by using the menu pointer. Besides using the → and ← keys, you can move the menu pointer even more quickly through the list of files by using the following keys:

END	Takes you to the last file
HOME	Takes you to the first file
↑	Takes you to the previous list of files
↓	Takes you to the next list of files

These keys are especially helpful when you have a disk that contains many files.

Move the menu pointer by using the arrow keys to highlight the file named LABELS.WK1.

Then, to select this file,

Press: ↵

Your screen should now look similar to Figure 1.25.

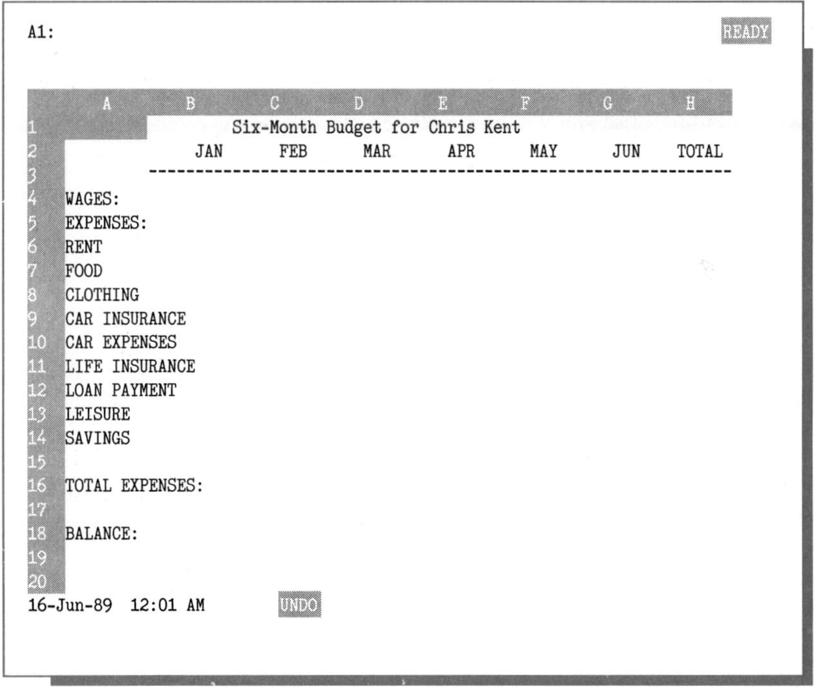

Figure 1.25

The worksheet that contains the column and row labels is now displayed on your screen, and the mode indicator displays READY.

To review, the command sequence used to retrieve the file LABELS.WK1 was:

/ File **R**etrieve **LABELS.WK1** ↵

You can issue a command by typing the first letter of each command, by using the menu pointer, or by a combination of the two methods. The most efficient way (fewest keystrokes) is to type the first letter of the command.

Entering Values

We are now ready to enter some values into the worksheet. Values are numbers or the results of formulas. All values begin with a number from 0 through 9 or one of the following numeric symbols: +, −, ., (, @, #, or $.

You will begin by entering the value of Chris Kent's monthly wages.

Move to: B4
Type: **2000**
Press: ↵

Continue to enter 2000 into the cells for February through May, but not June, and observe the mode indicator as it changes from READY to VALUE.

Your screen should look similar to Figure 1.26.

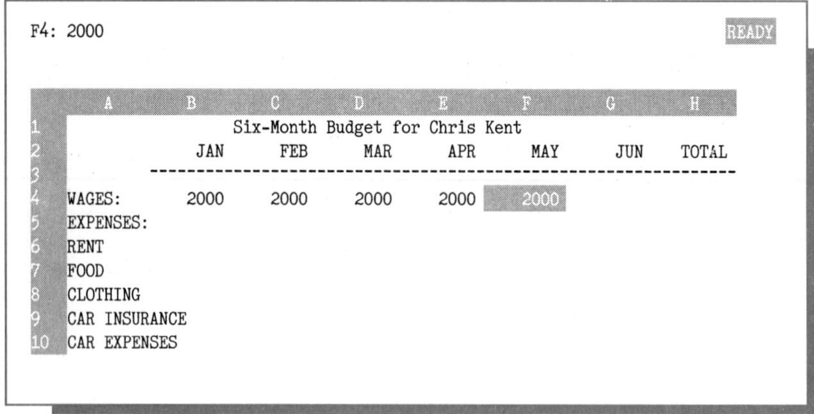

Figure 1.26

The values are all right-aligned in their cells. Unlike labels, which can be left-aligned ('), right-aligned (''), or centered (ˆ), values can only be right-aligned.

If you insert a ', '', or ˆ before a value, the entry is defined as a label and will have a numeric value of zero if used in arithmetic operations. For example, to enter the wages for June as ''2000,

Move to: G4
Type: **''2000**

The mode indicator displays LABEL, because the first character in the entry is a nonnumeric character.

Press: ↵

The number appears correct in cell G4; however, because the number is a label, calculations using the data in this cell will be incorrect, as you will soon see.

Entering a Formula

You are now ready to enter a formula to calculate Chris Kent's total wages. A **formula** is an entry that performs a calculation and displays the results of the calculation in the cell containing the formula. You can use either numeric values or cell addresses in a formula. If you use cell addresses, 1-2-3 performs the calculation using the values contained in the cells referenced in the formula.

There are three types of formulas: numeric, string, and logical. The most common type, numeric, calculates numeric values using the following **arithmetic operators**:

ˆ for exponentiation

* for multiplication

/ for division

+ for addition

– for subtraction

A numeric formula can begin with a number or with one of the numeric symbols that defines an entry as a value. When the first entry in a formula is a cell address (which begins with a letter), begin the formula with a plus (+) symbol. This is necessary to define the cell entry as a value. The letter of the cell address can be typed in either uppercase or lowercase. A numeric formula cannot contain any spaces.

To add the entries in cells B4, C4, D4, E4, F4, and G4 and have the sum displayed in cell H4,

Move to: H4
Type: **+B4+C4+D4+E4+F4+G4**
Press: ↵

Your screen should look similar to Figure 1.27.

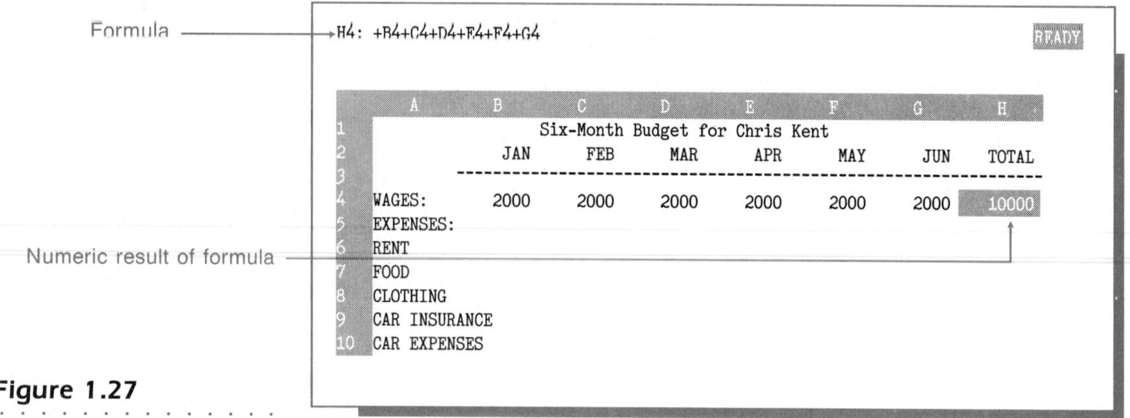

Formula
H4: +B4+C4+D4+E4+F4+G4
READY
A B C D E F G H
Six-Month Budget for Chris Kent
JAN FEB MAR APR MAY JUN TOTAL
WAGES: 2000 2000 2000 2000 2000 2000 10000
EXPENSES:
RENT
FOOD
CLOTHING
CAR INSURANCE
CAR EXPENSES
Numeric result of formula

Figure 1.27

The formula appears in the control panel, and the numeric result appears in the worksheet cell.

But the total value displayed in cell H4 is incorrect; it should be 12000. The error occurs because the entry in cell G4 is a label and so has a value of zero.

To correct the error,

Move to: G4
Press: F2
Press: HOME
Press: DEL
Press: ↵

Your screen should look similar to Figure 1.28.

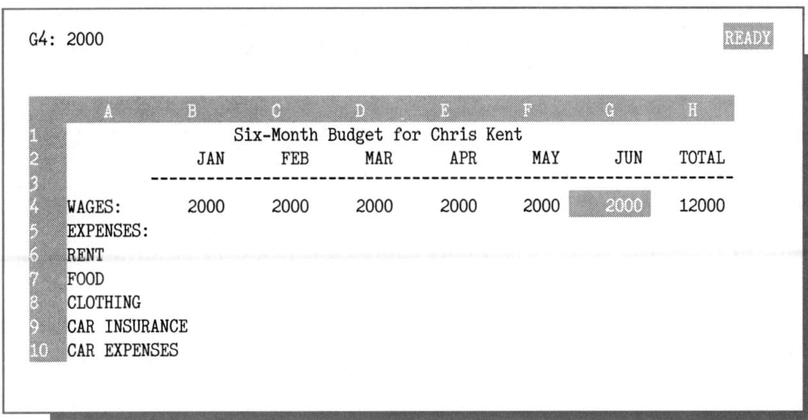

G4: 2000
READY
A B C D E F G H
1 Six-Month Budget for Chris Kent
2 JAN FEB MAR APR MAY JUN TOTAL
3 --
4 WAGES: 2000 2000 2000 2000 2000 2000 12000
5 EXPENSES:
6 RENT
7 FOOD
8 CLOTHING
9 CAR INSURANCE
10 CAR EXPENSES

Figure 1.28

Now that the entry in cell G4 is a value it can be used in calculations. The formula in cell H4 has been recalculated using the new data in cell G4. The **automatic recalculation** of formulas as data is changed is one of the most powerful features of electronic worksheets.

Saving the Worksheet

Before you save the worksheet, your instructor may want to have you enter your name in cell A1.

If you exit the 1-2-3 program without saving the current worksheet, the changes you made to it would be lost. To save the current version of the worksheet, issue the following command sequence:

/ **F**ile **S**ave

The prompt ''Enter name of file to save:'' appears in the control panel. The current drive and the name of the file you retrieved, LABELS.WK1, is displayed following the prompt. You could save the current worksheet as it appears on the screen using this filename, or you can save it using a new filename. In case you want to use the original file LABELS.WK1 again to repeat the exercises, you will name the current worksheet BUDGET.WK1. A 1-2-3 filename should be no longer than eight characters and can include any combination of letters, numbers, underscores, and hyphens. It cannot include any blank spaces. To enter the new filename, in either uppercase or lowercase characters,

Type: **BUDGET**
Press: ↵

The current version of the worksheet has been saved on your disk as BUDGET.WK1. Lotus 1-2-3 automatically adds the file extension, .WK1, to all files created using the program unless you enter a filename extension of your own when saving the file. The file LABELS.WK1 is still on your data disk, unchanged.

To verify that the current worksheet has been saved on the disk, erase the screen and the current worksheet from memory by issuing the following command sequence:

/ **W**orksheet **E**rase

In response to the prompt to confirm that you want to erase the worksheet, select:

Yes

This prompt is a safety precaution to prevent the accidental loss of a worksheet file that might not have been saved.

Your screen should now display a blank worksheet. Retrieve the file BUDGET by issuing the following command sequence:

/ **F**ile **R**etrieve **BUDGET** ↵

Your screen should now look similar to Figure 1.29.

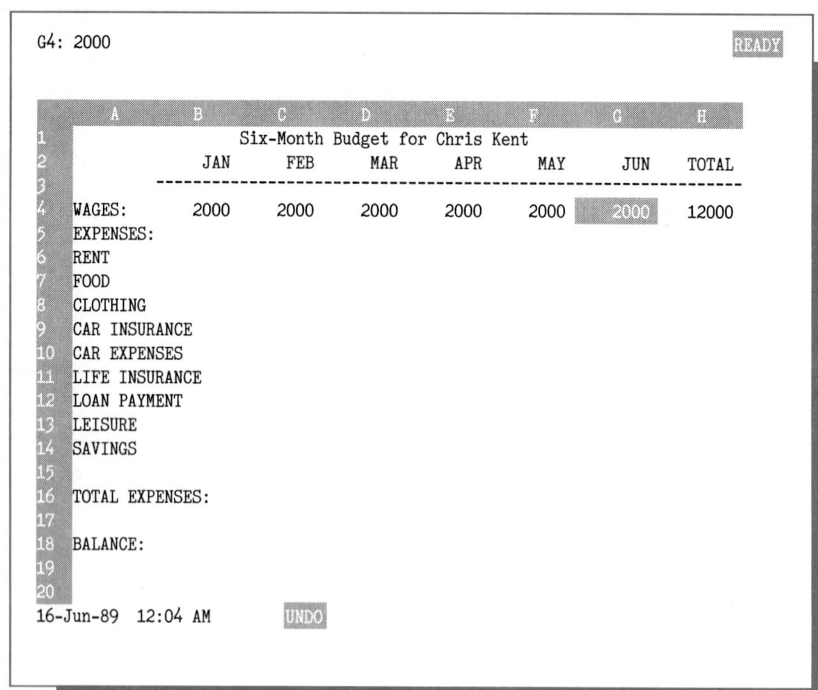

Figure 1.29

The worksheet is displayed as you saved it. Even the cell pointer is in the same cell as it was at the time the file was saved.

Whenever a file is retrieved, the current worksheet is automatically erased from the screen and memory and replaced by the retrieved worksheet file. Therefore, it is not necessary to use the / **W**orksheet **E**rase command before you retrieve a file.

Printing a Worksheet Screen

If you have printer capability, a quick way to print a copy of what you see on your display screen is to use the PrintScreen (PRTSC) key (you must hold down SHIFT while pressing PRTSC).

To print your display screen,

Press: SHIFT-PRTSC

Leaving 1-2-3

Always be careful before you retrieve a file, erase a worksheet, or end a 1-2-3 session that you save the current worksheet if you want to use it again. If you do not save it, you will lose it.

If you want to leave 1-2-3 at this time, issue the following command:

/ **Q**uit **Y**es

If you are using a two-disk system, you may see the message "Insert disk with COMMAND.COM in drive A and strike any key when ready." To exit properly and return to the DOS prompt, follow these instructions. (*Note:* COMMAND.COM is on your DOS disk.)

Glossary of Key Terms

Arithmetic operator	The symbols used in a formula that control the type of calculation to be performed: +, −, /, *, ^.
Automatic recalculation	The recalculation of all formulas in a worksheet when data in cells referenced by the formula change.
Cell	The basic unit of a worksheet formed by the intersection of a row and a column.
Cell address	The column letter and row number of the current cell displayed in the first line of the control panel.
Cell pointer	The highlight bar that identifies the current cell location in the worksheet.
Column	A vertical line of cells down the worksheet.
Column letter	The border of letters across the top of the worksheet area that labels the columns in the worksheet.
Command	An instruction you give 1-2-3 by selecting from the menu that appears when you press /.
Control panel	The top three lines of the screen, which display information about the current cell, command choices, and prompts.
Current cell	The cell that the cell pointer is on.
Cursor	A blinking underscore that shows you where each character will appear as you type.
Date-and-time indicator	The date and time displayed in the status line.
Edit	Correcting entries made in a worksheet.
Error message	A program message displayed in the status line when a program error is detected.
Formula	A mathematical expression that defines the relationship among two or more cells in a worksheet.
Home position	The upper left corner cell of the worksheet. Usually cell A1.

Label	An entry beginning with an alpha character, ', '', ^, or any other character not considered a value.
Label-prefix character	Special characters entered before a label that control the display of the label: ', '', ^, or \.
Menu	The series of choices that appear on the control panel after you access the main 1-2-3 menu.
Menu pointer	The highlight bar that identifies the current menu selection.
Mode	The current state of operation of the program.
Mode indicator	A highlighted word in the top right line of the control panel that indicates the current mode of operation of the worksheet.
Numeric symbol	The characters +, −, ., (, @, #, and $ that define an entry as a value.
Prompt	A program response displayed in the control panel that requires a user response.
Row	A horizontal line of cells across the worksheet.
Row number	The row of numbers down the left side of the worksheet area that labels the rows in the worksheet.
Scrolling	The process of moving several rows or columns or full screens horizontally or vertically through the worksheet.
Status indicator	A highlighted word displayed in the status line that describes a program or special key condition.
Status line	The bottom line of the screen, which displays the date-and-time indicator, status indicators, and error messages.
Value	A number (0 through 9) or the result of a formula.
Window	The part of the worksheet displayed on the screen.
Worksheet	The electronic representation of a financial spreadsheet created from a rectangular grid of rows and columns.
Worksheet area	The center area of the screen, which contains the worksheet.

Practice Problems

1. Matching

1. F5	______	a. retrieves a worksheet
2. F2	______	b. enters EDIT mode
3. \	______	c. aligns labels to the right
4. HOME	______	d. saves a worksheet
5. /FR	______	e. moves the cell pointer to the upper left corner of the worksheet
6. ''	______	f. moves down one screen
7. PGDN	______	g. accesses the 1-2-3 main menu
8. +B6–F4	______	h. moves the cell pointer to a specified cell
9. /FS	______	i. simple formula
10. /	______	j. fills a cell with repeated characters

2. In the following worksheet, several items are identified by letters. In the space below the worksheet, enter the correct term for each item. The first one has been completed for you. (Hint: Use the Glossary of Key Terms for this lab.)

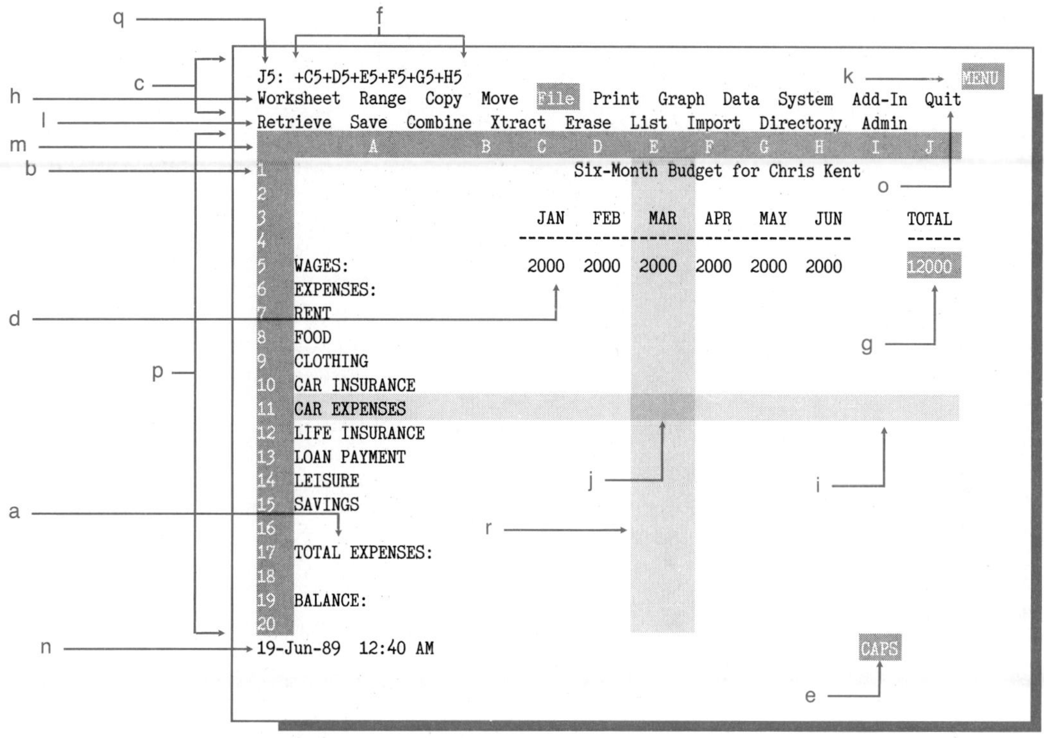
q
f
c
h
l
m
b
k
J5: +C5+D5+E5+F5+G5+H5
MENU
Worksheet Range Copy Move File Print Graph Data System Add-In Quit
Retrieve Save Combine Xtract Erase List Import Directory Admin
A B C D E F G H I J
1 Six-Month Budget for Chris Kent
2
3 JAN FEB MAR APR MAY JUN TOTAL
4
5 WAGES: 2000 2000 2000 2000 2000 2000 12000
6 EXPENSES:
7 RENT
8 FOOD
9 CLOTHING
10 CAR INSURANCE
11 CAR EXPENSES
12 LIFE INSURANCE
13 LOAN PAYMENT
14 LEISURE
15 SAVINGS
16
17 TOTAL EXPENSES:
18
19 BALANCE:
20
19-Jun-89 12:40 AM
CAPS
o
d
g
p
j
i
a
r
n
e

a.	label	**j.**	______
b.	______	**k.**	______
c.	______	**l.**	______
d.	______	**m.**	______
e.	______	**n.**	______
f.	______	**o.**	______
g.	______	**p.**	______
h.	______	**q.**	______
i.	______	**r.**	______

3. Retrieve the file BUDGET2. This is a worksheet file similar to the budget we started in this lab. However, it contains several errors. Follow these steps to locate and correct the errors:

   a. The column and row labels have both uppercase and lowercase characters intermixed. Also, they are not aligned properly. Change the column labels so that they are all capital letters and are right-aligned. Change the row labels so that only the first letter of each word is capitalized and they are left-aligned.

   b. Look at the values in the TOTAL column (H) and the Total Expense row (19). Some of the totals are incorrect. Determine the reason for the incorrect values and make the necessary corrections.

   c. Use the repeat label-prefix character to underline the column headings (row 4).

   d. Enter your name in cell A1 and the current date in cell A2.

   e. Print a copy of your display screen.

   f. Save the corrected version of the file as BUDGET3.

4. Marty Brown earns $1,800 a month and has budgeted the following fixed monthly expenses:

Rent	450
Food	355
Clothing	100
Phone	45
Car loan	275

He also has two periodic expenses. In January, he must pay $328 for a course he is taking at the university. In April, his automobile license registration of $125 is due. Create a worksheet using the following steps:

   a. Enter the labels JAN, FEB, MAR, APR, MAY, JUN, and TOTAL in cells B3 through H3. Enter them in all capital letters and right-aligned.

   b. Use the repeat label-prefix character to underline the column headings.

c. Enter the row labels so that only the first letter of each word is capitalized and the labels are left-aligned. The labels should all be entered in column A as follows:

Row 5	Wages:
Row 7	Expenses:
Row 8	Rent
Row 9	Food
Row 10	Clothing
Row 11	Tuition
Row 12	Phone
Row 13	Car Loan
Row 14	License
Row 16	Total Exp:
Row 18	Balance:

d. Enter the values for wages in cells B5 through G5.

e. Enter the fixed monthly expenses for January only.

f. Enter the two periodic expenses.

g. Enter the formula to calculate the total for wages in cell H5.

h. Enter your name in cell A1 and the current date in cell A2.

i. Print a copy of your display screen.

j. Save the worksheet using the filename BROWN.

You will complete this worksheet in a practice problem in Lab 2.

5. Alice Sloan has just started a marketing research firm called Sloan Research. Her first and only client to date has agreed to pay her $42,000 to conduct a national survey for a new product.

   Alice will receive payments (revenues) each month for six months: January, $5,000; February, $6,000; March, $7,000; April, $7,000; May, $8,000; and June, $9,000. She has estimated that her monthly expenses during this time period will be:

Salaries	2900
Rent	735
Telephone	475
Supplies	275
Miscellaneous	110

   She also has two periodic expenses. In January, Alice has to prepay a six-month insurance premium of $736. In June, she has a $4,200 small-business loan payment due.

   Create a worksheet using the following steps:

   a. Enter your name in cell A1 and the current date in cell A2.

   b. Enter the worksheet title, Six-Month Budget for Sloan Research, in cell C2.

   c. Enter the labels JAN, FEB, MAR, APR, MAY, JUN, and TOTAL in cells B3 through H3. They should all be capital letters and right-aligned.

   d. Underline the column headings using the repeat label-prefix character. The underline should extend from cell B4 through cell H4.

e. Enter the labels in column A as follows:

Row 5	REVENUES:
Row 7	EXPENSES:
Row 8	Salaries
Row 9	Rent
Row 10	Telephone
Row 11	Insurance
Row 12	Loan
Row 13	Supplies
Row 14	Misc.
Row 16	TOTAL EXP:
Row 18	NET

f. Enter the values for the monthly revenues (payments) in cells B5 through G5.

g. Enter the fixed monthly expenses for January only.

h. Enter the two periodic expenses.

i. Enter the formula to calculate the Total Revenues in cell H5.

j. Save the worksheet using the filename SLOAN.

k. Print a copy of your display screen.

You will complete this worksheet in a practice problem in Lab 2.

2

Enhancing a Worksheet

Objectives

In Lab 2, you will learn how to:

- Change column widths
- Insert and delete rows and columns
- Point a range
- Copy formulas
- Copy cell entries
- Use absolute cell references
- Use @functions
- Erase cell entries
- Use the Undo feature
- Print a worksheet
- Save and replace files

Case Study

In Lab 1, you defined the column and row titles of Chris Kent's budget worksheet and entered the monthly wage values. You also entered a simple formula to compute the total for his wages. You will continue working on the budget for Chris Kent in Lab 2.

To complete the worksheet, you will enter the values for Chris's expenses and enter two new formulas to calculate his total expenses and balance. You will also redefine the column widths and insert and delete columns and rows to improve the appearance of the worksheet.

Changing Column Widths

After loading 1-2-3, retrieve the worksheet file BUDGET1.WK1 by issuing the following command sequence:

/ **F**ile **R**etrieve **BUDGET1.WK1** ↵

Your screen should look similar to Figure 2.1.

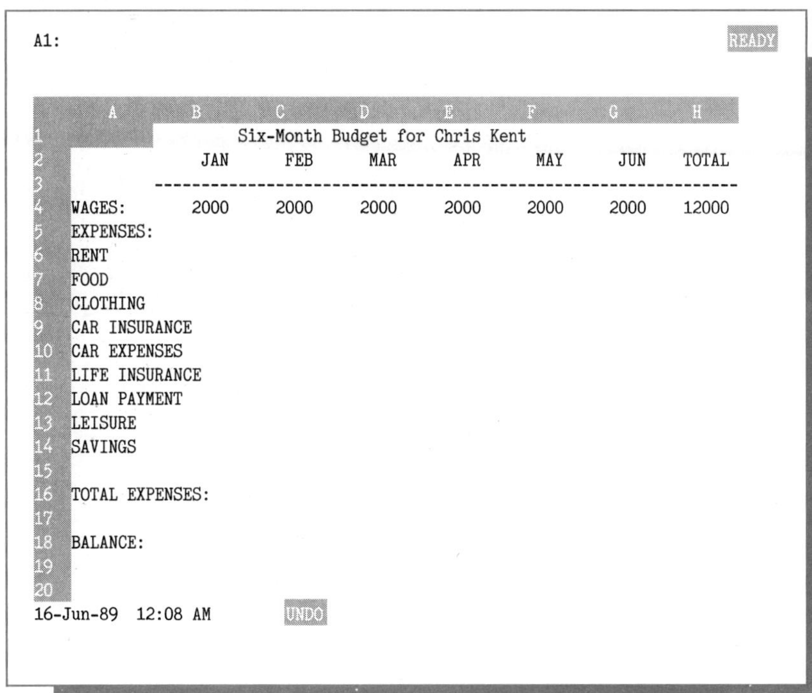

A1:
READY
A B C D E F G H
Six-Month Budget for Chris Kent
JAN FEB MAR APR MAY JUN TOTAL
WAGES: 2000 2000 2000 2000 2000 2000 12000
EXPENSES:
RENT
FOOD
CLOTHING
CAR INSURANCE
CAR EXPENSES
LIFE INSURANCE
LOAN PAYMENT
LEISURE
SAVINGS
TOTAL EXPENSES:
BALANCE:
16-Jun-89 12:08 AM
UNDO

Figure 2.1

This worksheet should be virtually the same as the one you created in Lab 1 and saved as BUDGET.WK1. Before you insert more data into the worksheet, you will improve its appearance by adjusting **column widths** and inserting rows and columns.

Some of the row labels in column A are longer than the initial or **default** column width setting of nine spaces and overflow into column B. For example, the label ''TOTAL EXPENSES'' in cell A16 overlaps into cell B16.

Move to: A16

Although the label is fifteen characters long, it is fully displayed in the worksheet because the cell to the right (B16) is empty. If cell B16 contained data, the long label in cell A16 would be truncated or cut off so that it fit in cell A16. Since we will be entering data in column B, we will increase the width of column A so that the labels will not be truncated.

To change the width of a single column, with the cell pointer anywhere within the column you want to change, issue the following command sequence:

/ **W**orksheet **C**olumn **S**et-Width

The prompt ''Enter column width (1..240):'' is displayed in the control panel. The column width can be set between 1 and 240 spaces. The current column width, 9, is displayed following the prompt. To increase the column width to 15, continue the command sequence as follows:

15 ↵

Your screen should now look similar to Figure 2.2.

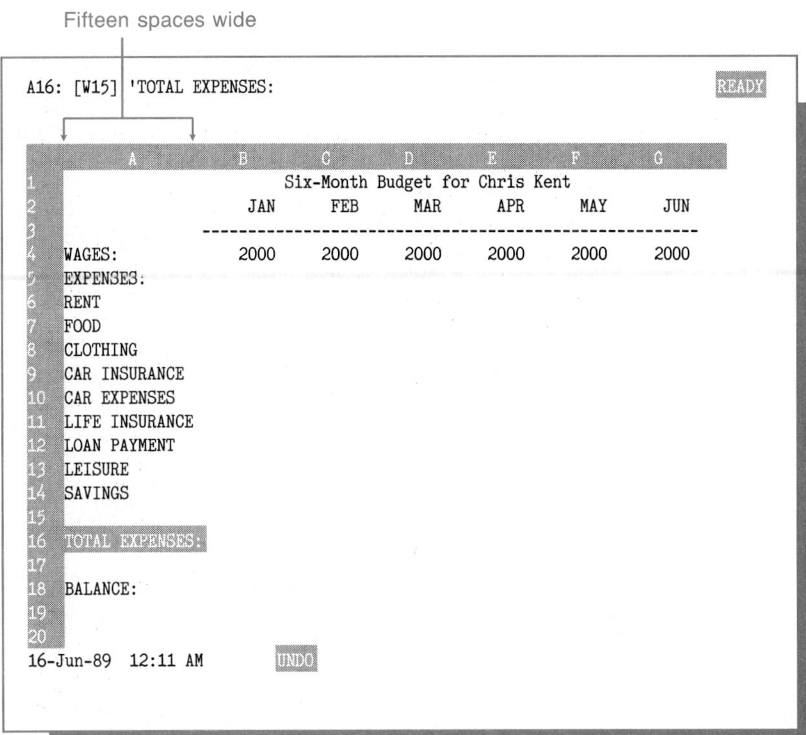

Figure 2.2

Column A has expanded to fifteen spaces wide and the label is fully displayed within the cell space. The new column width is displayed in the control panel in brackets following the cell address [W15]. When the cell pointer is anywhere within a column whose column width has been changed using the Worksheet Column command, the control panel will display the column width setting.

As a result of increasing the width of column A, the TOTAL column (H) was pushed to the right and is no longer visible in the window. To provide space in the window for the TOTAL column, we will decrease the width of all other columns in the worksheet to 5 spaces. To do this, we will use the Worksheet Global command. Select:

/ **W**orksheet **G**lobal

Your screen should look similar to Figure 2.3.

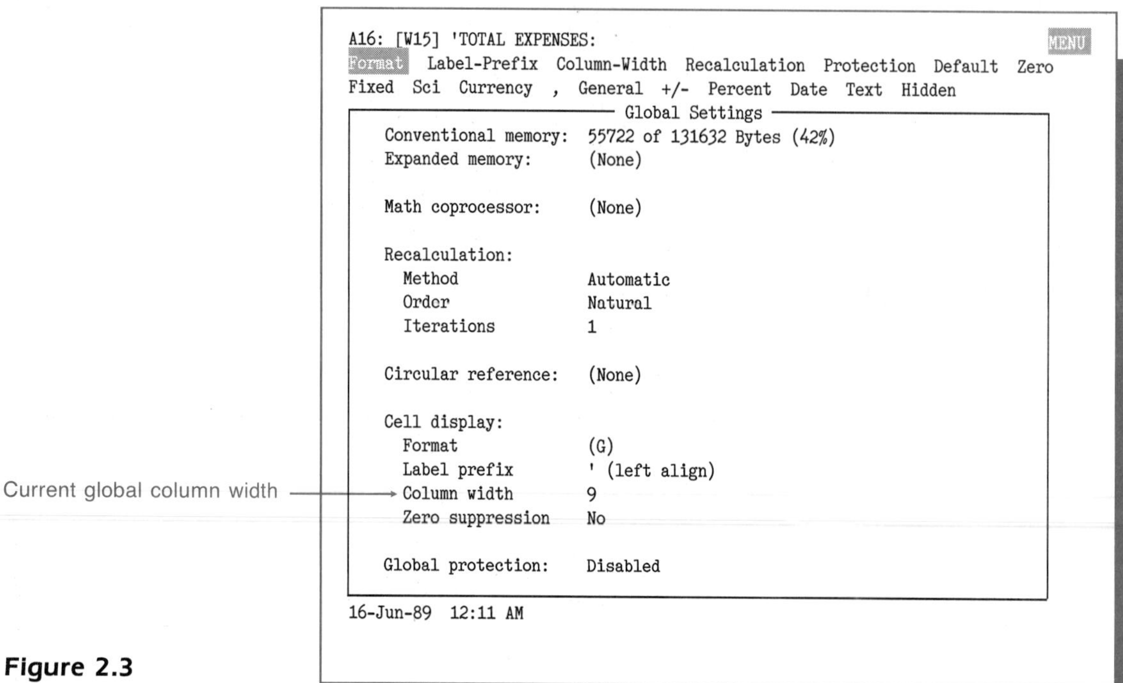

Figure 2.3

The worksheet has been replaced by the Global settings sheet. As a part of many commands, 1-2-3 will display a **settings sheet** to help you keep track of the current settings for the options associated with the command you are using. You do not make changes directly on the sheet. Your changes are made by selecting the appropriate command displayed above the settings sheet in the control panel.

The Global settings sheet displays the current global settings for the worksheet. **Global** settings are settings that affect the entire worksheet. The setting we want to change is the column width. The Global settings sheet shows that the current setting for all columns in the worksheet (except the column set individually using the Worksheet Column command) is 9.

To make the new global column width setting 5 spaces, continue the command sequence as follows:

Column-Width **5** (↵)

All column widths are now changed to 5 spaces except column A, which was individually set. Changes made using the Worksheet Column command always override global settings.

To see the change in the Global settings sheet, select:

/ **W**orksheet **G**lobal

The Global settings sheet shows the new global column width of 5.

To cancel this command and return to READY mode,

Press: CTRL-BREAK

Although the TOTAL column is now visible, a series of asterisks (*****) appears in cell H4.

Move to: H4

Your screen should now look similar to Figure 2.4.

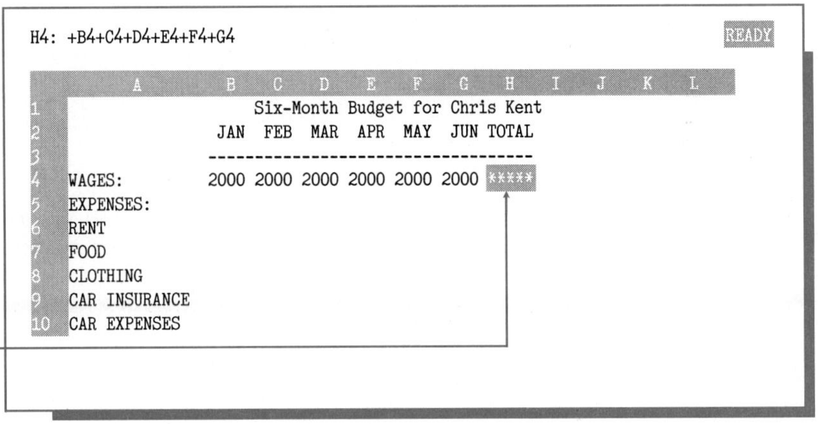

```
H4: +B4+C4+D4+E4+F4+G4                                        READY

         A          B    C    D    E    F    G    H    I    J    K    L
1                       Six-Month Budget for Chris Kent
2                   JAN  FEB  MAR  APR  MAY  JUN TOTAL
3                   -----------------------------------
4   WAGES:          2000 2000 2000 2000 2000 2000 *****
5   EXPENSES:
6   RENT
7   FOOD
8   CLOTHING
9   CAR INSURANCE
10  CAR EXPENSES
```

Column width too small

Figure 2.4

The correct formula is displayed in the control panel. However, the value 12000 does not appear in the worksheet because the cell is not wide enough. Whenever the width of a cell containing a value is too small to display the entry fully, asterisks are displayed. The cell's width has to be at least one space larger than the value. (1-2-3 reserves one extra space for special numeric displays, such as a percent sign.)

Individual cells cannot be expanded in 1-2-3. To correct the problem, you could change the width of column H (individually) or change the width of all columns in the worksheet (globally) or change the width of several adjacent columns. Since the values for the months look crowded, we will increase the column width for columns B through H. To change the width of several adjacent columns, select:

/ **W**orksheet **C**olumn **C**olumn-Range **S**et-Width

In response to the prompt in the control panel, you must specify the range of columns whose width you want to change. A **range** is a cell or rectangular group of adjoining cells in the worksheet. Figure 2.5 shows possible ranges.

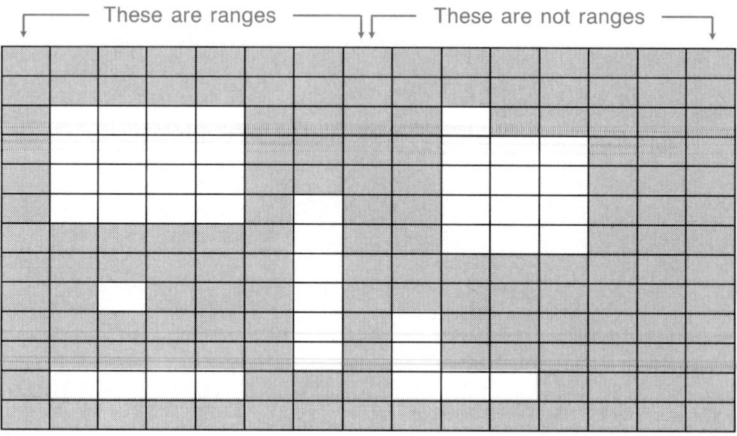
These are ranges
These are not ranges

Figure 2.5

A range is entered using the beginning cell address and ending cell address separated by two periods. In response to the prompt, 1-2-3 displays the cell address of the current cell as the default response. To specify the range of columns, any row can be used. Since the cell pointer is already on row 4, we will enter the range as B4..H4.

Type: **B4..H4**

The default response is cleared and the new range is displayed following the prompt. You can type one or two periods in the range, but 1-2-3 will always display a range with two periods.

Press: ↵

To enter the new width,

Type: **6**
Press: ↵

Your screen should look similar to Figure 2.6.

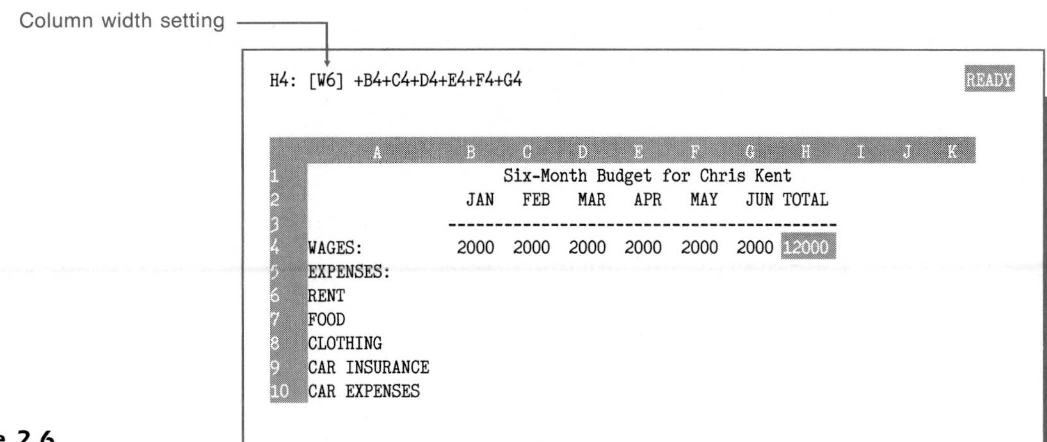

Figure 2.6

The width of columns B through H changed to 6 spaces each and the value in cell H4 is fully displayed. The column width setting is displayed in the control panel because the width of these columns was changed using the Worksheet Column command.

Inserting and Deleting Columns

You can further improve the worksheet's appearance by inserting a blank column after column A. Move the cell pointer to any cell in column B and issue the command sequence:

/ **W**orksheet **I**nsert **C**olumn ↵

Your screen should now look similar to Figure 2.7.

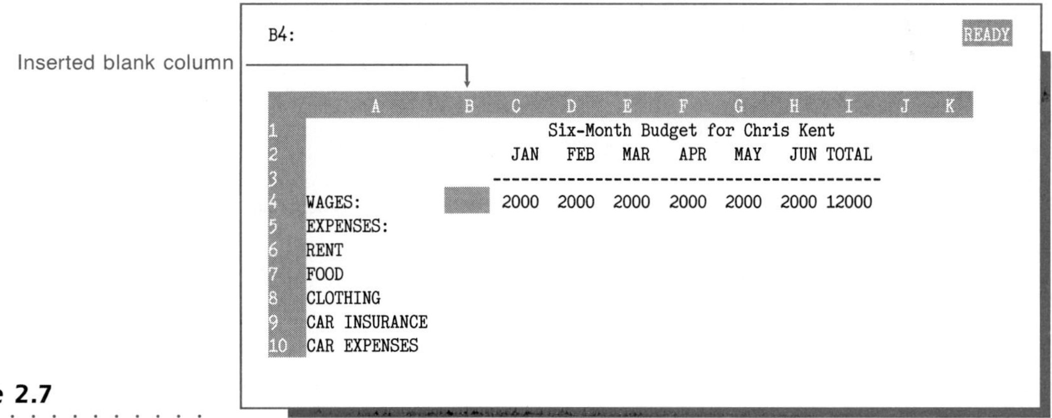

Figure 2.7

A blank column has been inserted into the worksheet, by moving all cell entries to the right one column.

A second blank column between JUN and TOTAL would improve the worksheet's appearance even more. Move the cell pointer to column I and issue the following command sequence:

/ **W**orksheet **I**nsert **C**olumn ↵

To delete a column, follow the same procedure, except select **D**elete instead of **I**nsert. Everything in the column will then be deleted.

Inserting and Deleting Rows

You can insert and delete rows in nearly the same manner that you inserted and deleted columns. The only difference in the command sequence is that you replace **C**olumn with **R**ow.

To insert a row between the worksheet's title and the months, move the cell pointer to any cell in row 2 and issue the following command sequence:

/ **W**orksheet **I**nsert **R**ow ↵

Your screen should now look similar to Figure 2.8.

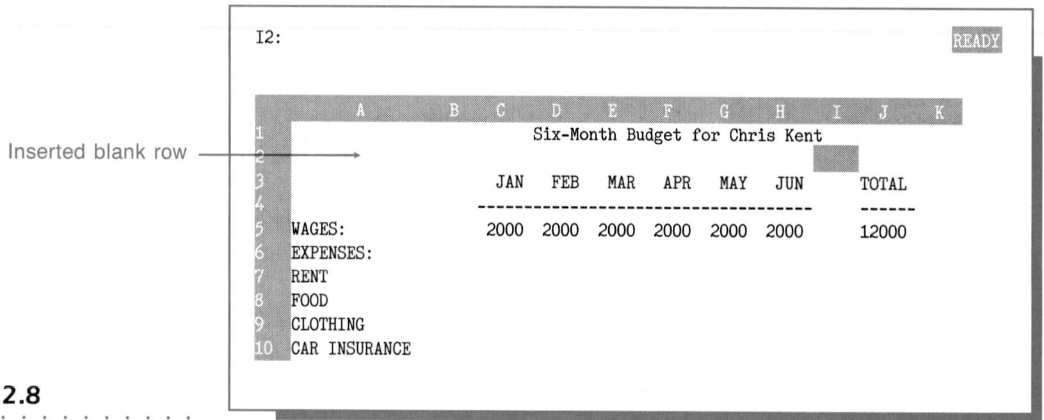

Figure 2.8

A blank row has been inserted (row 2) into the worksheet by moving all cell entries below row 2 down one row.

To insert another row between WAGES and EXPENSES, move the cell pointer to any cell in row 6 and issue the following command sequence:

/ **W**orksheet **I**nsert **R**ow ↵

To delete a row, use the same procedure, except select **D**elete instead of **I**nsert. Be careful when you are deleting rows and columns that you do not accidentally delete any rows or columns of important information.

Using the Copy Command

In Lab 1 you entered the value of 2000 for Chris's wages individually into each cell. A faster way to enter the same data into several cells is to use the Copy command.

Chris's rent expense is $475 per month. You will enter this value into cell C8 for his January rent and then copy this value into cells D8 through H8 for his February through June rent expenses.

Move to: C8
Type: **475**
Press: ↵

To copy the contents of cell C8 to cells D8, E8, F8, G8, and H8, select:

/ **C**opy

Your screen should look similar to Figure 2.9.

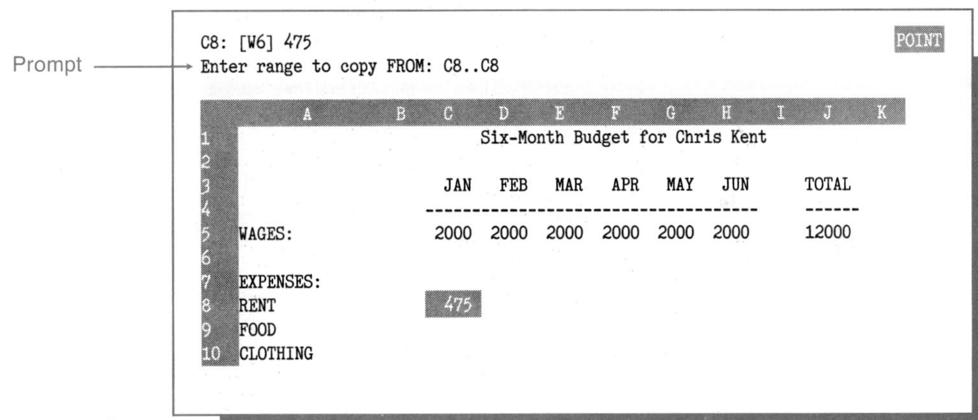

Figure 2.9

The second line of the control panel displays the prompt "Enter range to copy FROM:".

1-2-3 anticipated that the current position of the cell pointer (C8..C8) is the cell you want to copy from.

If you wanted to copy from another cell or range of cells, you would enter that cell location. In this case, however, you do want to copy from cell C8. To confirm this selection,

Press: ↵

The second line of the control panel now displays the prompt "Enter range to copy TO:". Again, 1-2-3 has anticipated your response. This time, however, it is not correct.

To specify the correct range, D8 through H8, continue the command sequence as follows:

D8..H8 ↵

Your screen should now look similar to Figure 2.10.

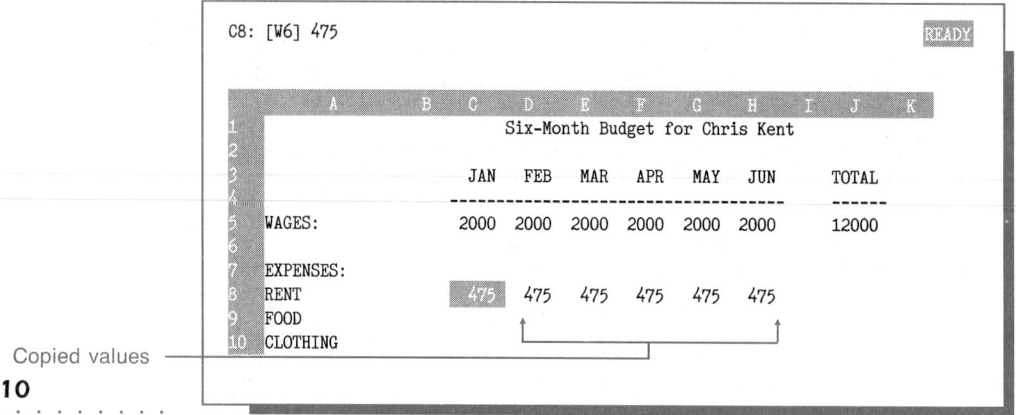

Figure 2.10

The value "475" has been copied to the specified range of cells.

Practice using the Copy command by moving to C9, entering the value **362**, and copying the contents of cell C9 to cells D9 through H9.

You have used the Copy command to copy from a single cell to a range of cells. You can also copy from a range of cells by specifying the beginning and ending cells of the range following the FROM prompt.

Pointing a Range

Another method of defining the data range to be copied is to use the cell pointer to highlight the cell or range of cells. Whenever 1-2-3 displays POINT in the mode indicator, you can use this method to specify a range. To see how this works,

Move to: C10
Type: **150**
Press: ↵

This value needs to be copied to cells D10 through H10. Begin the Copy command as usual:

/ **Copy**

To accept cell C10 as the cell to copy from,

Press: ↵

You are now ready to specify the range to copy to.

Notice that the mode indicator now displays POINT. Instead of typing in the cell range to copy to, you will use the cell pointer to highlight the range. To move the cell pointer to the cell beginning the range,

Move to: D10

To **anchor**, or specify, this cell as the beginning of the range,

Type: . (period)

This cell is now the **anchor cell**. Next, to move the cell pointer to the last cell of the range (H10),

Press: → four times

Your screen should look similar to Figure 2.11.

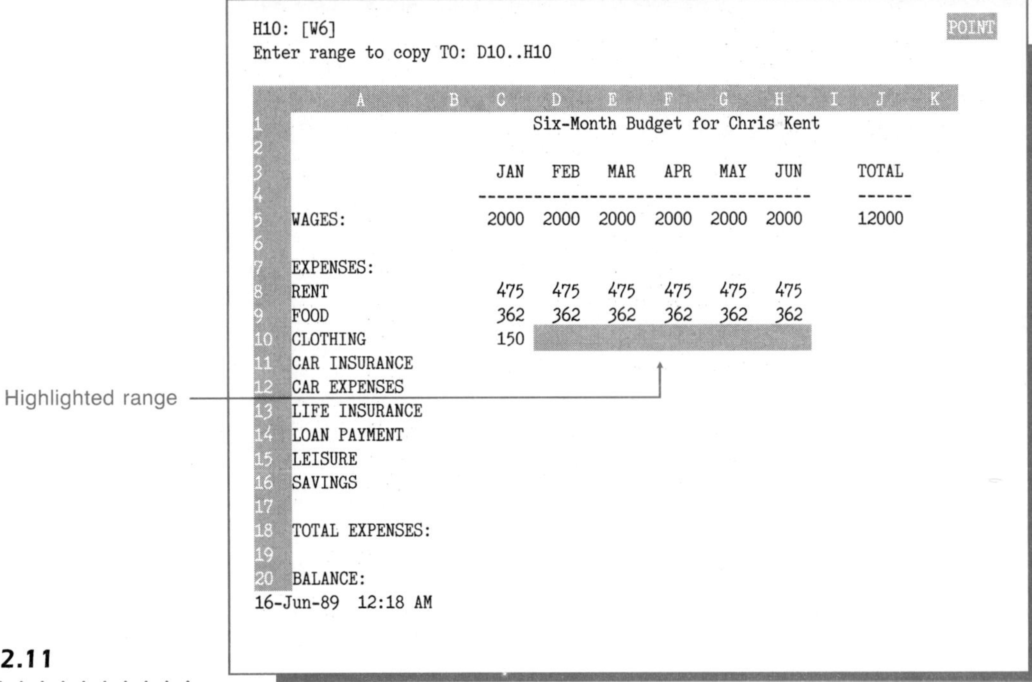

Figure 2.11

The range D10 to H10 is highlighted on the screen. The highlighted range is also displayed as D10..H10 following the prompt in the control panel.

The final step is to tell 1-2-3 that this is the end of the range:

Press: ↵

Your screen should look similar to Figure 2.12.

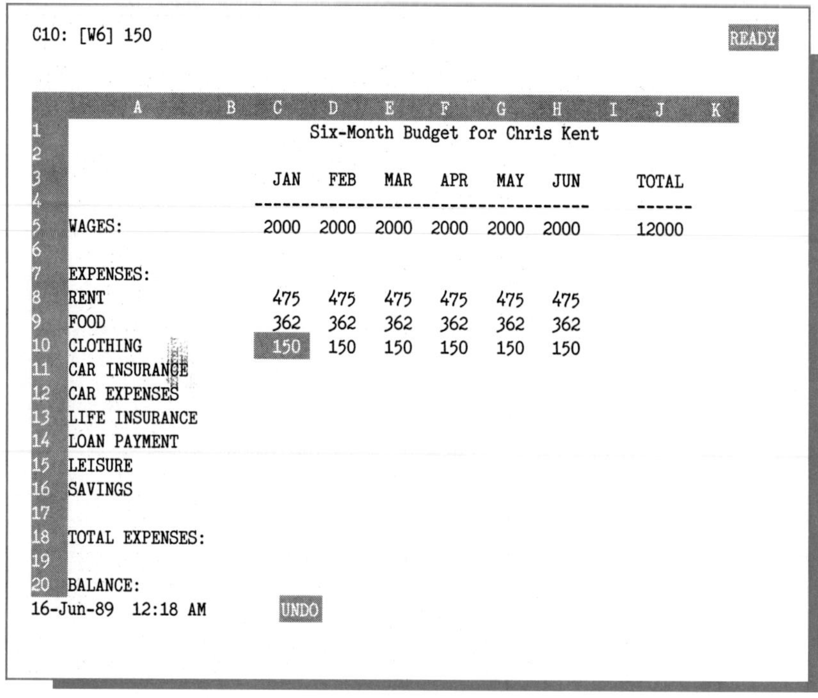

Figure 2.12

The clothing expense is now copied across the range you defined.

POINT mode is available in many command options and can be particularly helpful in a large worksheet.

Now use the Copy command to fill in car expenses (row 12) at 94 a month and savings (row 16) at 250 a month.

Complete the rest of the worksheet by filling in car insurance in January at 357, life insurance in January at 277, and loan payment in June at 731. Your screen should now look similar to Figure 2.13.

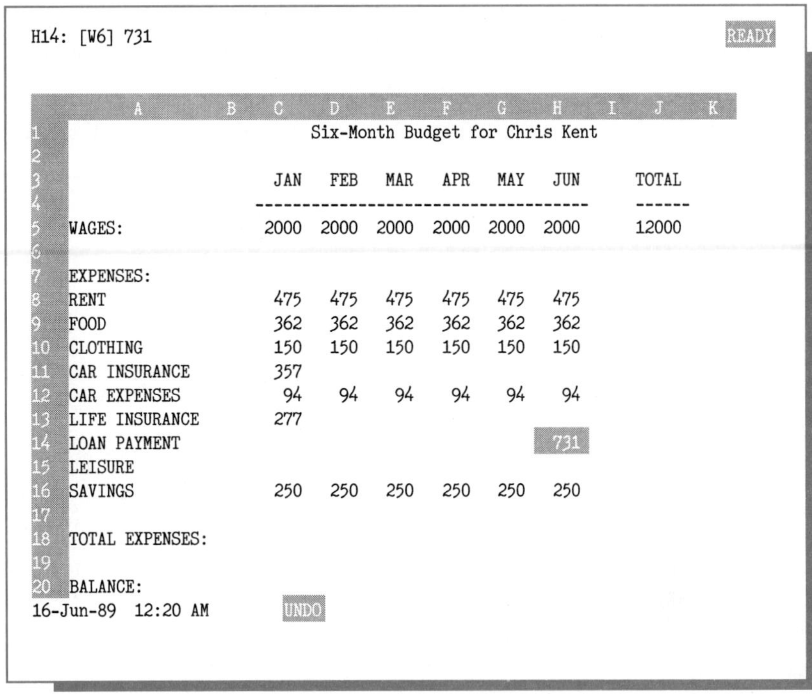
H14: [W6] 731 READY

	A	B	C	D	E	F	G	H	I	J	K
1			Six-Month Budget for Chris Kent								
2											
3			JAN	FEB	MAR	APR	MAY	JUN		TOTAL	
4			------	------	------	------	------	------		------	
5	WAGES:		2000	2000	2000	2000	2000	2000		12000	
6											
7	EXPENSES:										
8	RENT		475	475	475	475	475	475			
9	FOOD		362	362	362	362	362	362			
10	CLOTHING		150	150	150	150	150	150			
11	CAR INSURANCE		357								
12	CAR EXPENSES		94	94	94	94	94	94			
13	LIFE INSURANCE		277								
14	LOAN PAYMENT							731			
15	LEISURE										
16	SAVINGS		250	250	250	250	250	250			
17											
18	TOTAL EXPENSES:										
19											
20	BALANCE:										

16-Jun-89 12:20 AM UNDO

Figure 2.13

Copying a Formula

To complete the worksheet, you need to enter the formulas to calculate Chris Kent's leisure expense, total expenses, and balance. Chris feels he can budget 10 percent of his wages toward leisure.

The formula to calculate January's leisure expense will take the value in cell C5 and multiply it by .10. The arithmetic operator that indicates multiplication is an asterisk (*).

To enter this formula,

Move to: C15
Type: **+C5*.10**
Press: ↵

Notice that 1-2-3 displays the formula in the control panel as +C5*0.1. Although you entered the formula using the multiplier .10, 1-2-3 always displays a decimal with a leading zero followed by the decimal value.

Copy the formula in cell C15 to cells D15 through H15. The calculated value, 200, appears in each cell.

Your screen should look similar to Figure 2.14.

```
D15: [W6] +D5*0.1                                                    READY

       A          B   C     D     E     F     G     H     I    J    K
 1                        Six-Month Budget for Chris Kent
 2
 3                      JAN   FEB   MAR   APR   MAY   JUN       TOTAL
 4                      ------------------------------------    ------
 5   WAGES:             2000  2000  2000  2000  2000  2000      12000
 6
 7   EXPENSES:
 8   RENT                475   475   475   475   475   475
 9   FOOD                362   362   362   362   362   362
10   CLOTHING            150   150   150   150   150   150
11   CAR INSURANCE       357
12   CAR EXPENSES         94    94    94    94    94    94
13   LIFE INSURANCE      277
14   LOAN PAYMENT                                        731
15   LEISURE             200   200   200   200   200   200
16   SAVINGS             250   250   250   250   250   250
17
18   TOTAL EXPENSES:
19
20   BALANCE:
16-Jun-89  12:21 AM      UNDO
```

Figure 2.14

Move to: D15

The formula in this cell is +D5*0.1. The cell address referenced in this formula reflects the new column location of the formula in the worksheet. The formula in cell C15 references the value in cell C5, and the formula in cell D15 references the value in cell D5. This way, the formula appropriately calculates the value based on the wages earned for that month.

When the formula in cell C15 was copied, the cell addresses in the copied formulas were automatically adjusted relative to their new location in the worksheet. This is because the formula in cell C15 contains a **relative cell reference**. Whenever a cell address is entered in a formula using just the column letter and row number, the cell address will change to reflect its new location in the worksheet when the formula is copied. 1-2-3 interprets the formula in cell C15 as ''multiply the contents of the cell ten rows above times 0.1.'' When the formula is copied to cell D15, 1-2-3 still interprets the formula as ''multiply the contents of the cell ten rows above times 0.1.'' To do this, 1-2-3 adjusts the relative cell reference so the formula becomes +D5*.10.

To see how the other formulas adjusted relative to their new location in the worksheet, move the cell pointer to each formula in the range (E5 through H5) and read the formulas in the control panel.

Using @Functions

Next, you need to enter the formula to calculate the total expenses for each month in cell C18 and then copy it across the row through cell H18. The formula to compute the total could be entered as +C8+C9+C10+C11+C12+C13+C14+C15+C16. However, using 1-2-3's @functions is easier.

@Functions are built-in formulas that perform certain types of calculations automatically. To learn more about @functions, use the Help facility.

Press: F1

The Help index is displayed. If the Help index is not on your screen, refer to Chapter 5, "The Help Facility," in Section 1, "Getting Started." To get Help information about @functions,

Move to: @Function Index
Press: ↵
Move to: @@
Press: ↵
Move to: @Function Basics
Press: ↵

Your screen should look similar to Figure 2.15.

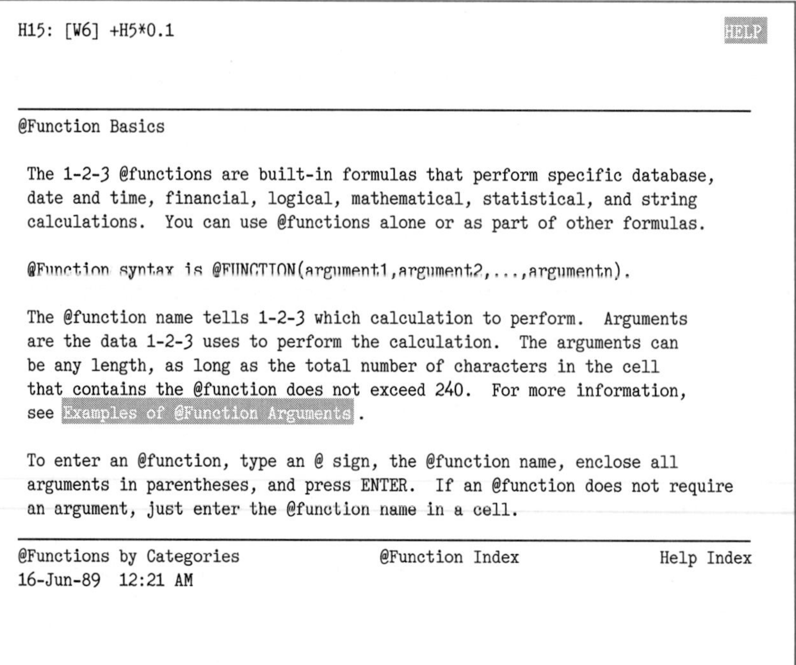
H15: [W6] +H5*0.1 HELP

@Function Basics

The 1-2-3 @functions are built-in formulas that perform specific database, date and time, financial, logical, mathematical, statistical, and string calculations. You can use @functions alone or as part of other formulas.

@Function syntax is @FUNCTION(argument1,argument2,...,argumentn).

The @function name tells 1-2-3 which calculation to perform. Arguments are the data 1-2-3 uses to perform the calculation. The arguments can be any length, as long as the total number of characters in the cell that contains the @function does not exceed 240. For more information, see Examples of @Function Arguments .

To enter an @function, type an @ sign, the @function name, enclose all arguments in parentheses, and press ENTER. If an @function does not require an argument, just enter the @function name in a cell.

@Functions by Categories @Function Index Help Index
16-Jun-89 12:21 AM

Figure 2.15

Read the information about @Function Basics on this screen carefully. The structure or **syntax** of an @function is as follows:

@function name(argument1,argument2, . . .,argumentn)

The arguments are the data that 1-2-3 uses in the calculation of the @function. The @function name tells 1-2-3 which type of calculation to perform. When you enter @functions, be sure to follow these basic rules of syntax:

- Do not leave spaces between the @function name and the arguments.
- Separate multiple arguments in an @function by a comma or a semicolon, not a space.
- Enclose the arguments in parentheses.
- Use either uppercase or lowercase letters to type an @function name.

To leave the Help facility and return to the worksheet,

Press: ESC

You will use the **@SUM** function to calculate the total monthly expenses. This function uses a list of values for the arguments. A list can be a cell, a range, a formula, or any combination of these separated by commas. In this case, the list is the range, C8..C16. To enter this @function,

Move to: C18
Type: **@SUM(C8..C16)**
Press: ↵

Note If the @function contains an error, 1-2-3 will beep and enter EDIT mode when you try to enter the @function. Locate and correct the error and reenter the @function.

Your screen should now look similar to Figure 2.16.

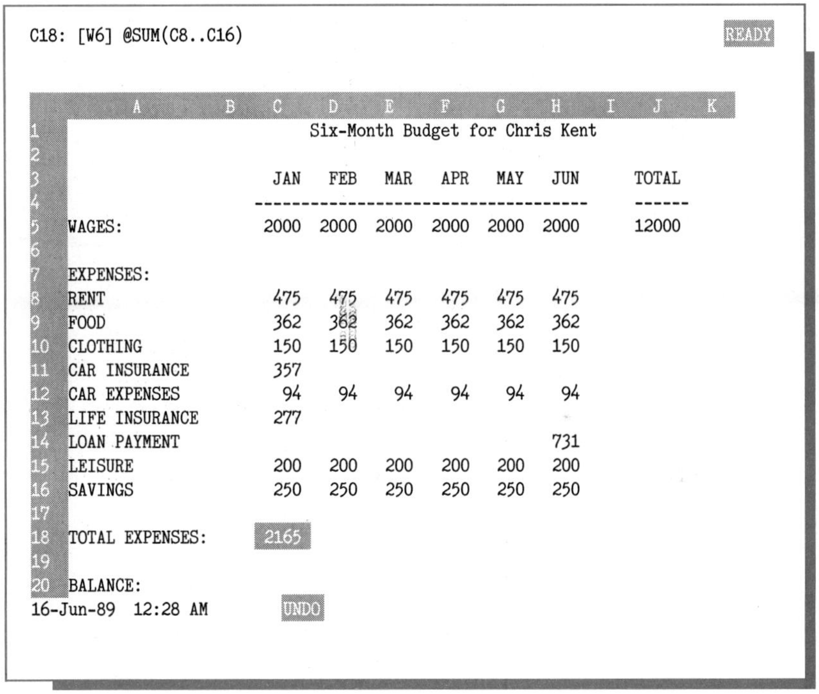

```
C18: [W6] @SUM(C8..C16)                                                 READY

         A          B    C     D     E     F     G     H       I    J    K
 1                            Six-Month Budget for Chris Kent
 2
 3                      JAN   FEB   MAR   APR   MAY   JUN       TOTAL
 4                     -----------------------------------     ------
 5  WAGES:             2000  2000  2000  2000  2000  2000       12000
 6
 7  EXPENSES:
 8  RENT                475   475   475   475   475   475
 9  FOOD                362   362   362   362   362   362
10  CLOTHING            150   150   150   150   150   150
11  CAR INSURANCE       357
12  CAR EXPENSES         94    94    94    94    94    94
13  LIFE INSURANCE      277
14  LOAN PAYMENT                                      731
15  LEISURE             200   200   200   200   200   200
16  SAVINGS             250   250   250   250   250   250
17
18  TOTAL EXPENSES:    2165
19
20  BALANCE:
16-Jun-89  12:28 AM       UNDO
```

Figure 2.16

The calculated value, 2165, is displayed in cell C18.

As you can see, using an @function to calculate this sum was a lot easier than typing in the formula.

Copy the @function in cell C18 to cells D18 through H18. The range specified in the @function is adjusted appropriately because of relative cell referencing.

Next, you need to enter the formula to compute Chris's monthly balance (row 20). The monthly balance is the monthly wages minus monthly total expenses. You can also use the cell pointer to specify cell addresses in a formula or @function. To do this,

Move to: C20
Type: +
Move to: C5

Notice that the mode indicator now displays POINT.

Type: – (minus)
Move to: C18
Press: ↵

The complete formula is displayed in the control panel, and the calculated value, −165, is displayed in cell C20.

Now copy this formula across row 20 through June.

Your screen should look similar to Figure 2.17.

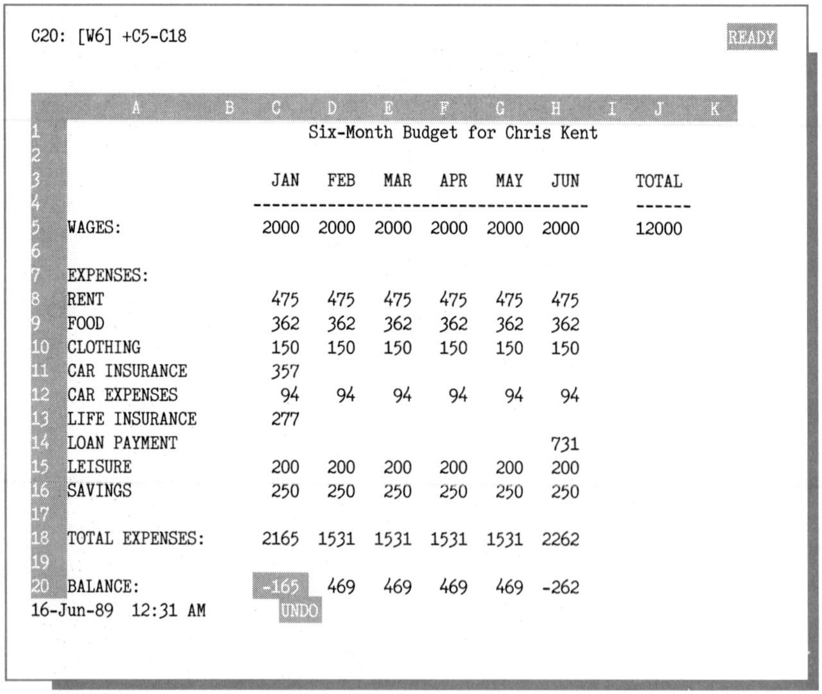

```
C20: [W6] +C5-C18                                                    READY

          A           B    C     D     E     F     G     H     I   J   K
1                              Six-Month Budget for Chris Kent
2
3                         JAN   FEB   MAR   APR   MAY   JUN        TOTAL
4                      ------------------------------------        ------
5   WAGES:                2000  2000  2000  2000  2000  2000        12000
6
7   EXPENSES:
8   RENT                   475   475   475   475   475   475
9   FOOD                   362   362   362   362   362   362
10  CLOTHING               150   150   150   150   150   150
11  CAR INSURANCE          357
12  CAR EXPENSES            94    94    94    94    94    94
13  LIFE INSURANCE         277
14  LOAN PAYMENT                                         731
15  LEISURE                200   200   200   200   200   200
16  SAVINGS                250   250   250   250   250   250
17
18  TOTAL EXPENSES:       2165  1531  1531  1531  1531  2262
19
20  BALANCE:              -165   469   469   469   469  -262
16-Jun-89  12:31 AM        UNDO
```

Figure 2.17

Chris shows a negative balance in January and June because of the car and life insurance and loan payment expenses due during those months.

To complete the worksheet, the formula to calculate the TOTAL in column J needs to be entered. This has already been done for you and saved in the file NUMBERS.WK1. To erase your current worksheet from the screen and the computer's memory and to retrieve the file NUMBERS.WK1, issue the following command sequence:

/ **F**ile **R**etrieve **NUMBERS.WK1** ⏎

Your screen should now look similar to Figure 2.18.

```
A1: [W15]                                                          READY

     A               B    C     D     E     F     G     H      I     J
 1                              Six-Month Budget for Chris Kent
 2
 3                         JAN   FEB   MAR   APR   MAY   JUN        TOTAL
 4                       -----------------------------------        ------
 5   WAGES:               2000  2000  2000  2000  2000  2000        12000
 6
 7   EXPENSES:
 8   RENT                  475   475   475   475   475   475         2850
 9   FOOD                  362   362   362   362   362   362         2172
10   CLOTHING              150   150   150   150   150   150          900
11   CAR INSURANCE         357                                        357
12   CAR EXPENSES           94    94    94    94    94    94          564
13   LIFE INSURANCE        277                                        277
14   LOAN PAYMENT                                          731         731
15   LEISURE               200   200   200   200   200   200         1200
16   SAVINGS               250   250   250   250   250   250         1500
17
18   TOTAL EXPENSES:      2165  1531  1531  1531  1531  2262        10551
19
20   BALANCE:             -165   469   469   469   469  -262         1449
16-Jun-89  12:31 AM        UNDO
```

Figure 2.18

Using an Absolute Cell Reference

Chris now wants to know what proportion of his total wages for 6 months (J5) is allocated to expenses each month. To begin, place a new descriptive label in cell A19.

Move to: A19
Type: **PROPORTION**
Press: ⏎

To enter the formula to make this calculation,

Move to: C19
Type: **+C18/J5**
Press: ⏎

Eighteen percent of his total wages is allocated to January expenses.

Copy this formula to cells D19 through H19.

Although the value in cell C19 appears to have been calculated properly, all the other cells in that row display the message ERR. This is because the formula in cell C19 was entered using a relative cell reference.

Move to: D19

Your screen should look similar to Figure 2.19.

D19: +D18/K5 READY

	A	B	C	D	E	F	G	H	I	J
1				Six-Month Budget for Chris Kent						
2										
3			JAN	FEB	MAR	APR	MAY	JUN		TOTAL
4			------	------	------	------	------	------		------
5	WAGES:		2000	2000	2000	2000	2000	2000		12000
6										
7	EXPENSES:									
8	RENT		475	475	475	475	475	475		2850
9	FOOD		362	362	362	362	362	362		2172
10	CLOTHING		150	150	150	150	150	150		900
11	CAR INSURANCE		357							357
12	CAR EXPENSES		94	94	94	94	94	94		564
13	LIFE INSURANCE		277							277
14	LOAN PAYMENT							731		731
15	LEISURE		200	200	200	200	200	200		1200
16	SAVINGS		250	250	250	250	250	250		1500
17										
18	TOTAL EXPENSES:		2165	1531	1531	1531	1531	2262		10551
19	PROPORTION		0.180	ERR	ERR	ERR	ERR	ERR		
20	BALANCE:		-165	469	469	469	469	-262		1449

16-Jun-89 12:32 AM UNDO

Figure 2.19

The formula in cell D19 now references cell K5, which is a blank cell. Since cell K5 contains nothing, 1-2-3 assumes that its value is zero. The formula in cell D19 requires division by zero, which is impossible. Therefore, ERR is displayed in the worksheet. Look at the other formulas in this row, and you will see the same problem.

The formula in cell C19 should have been entered in such a way that the reference to cell J5 would not be changed when the formula was copied. To do this, you need to use an absolute cell reference in the formula.

An **absolute cell reference** prevents the relative adjustment of a cell address in a formula when it is copied. To maintain the reference to a specific cell address when you are copying formulas, enter a dollar sign ($) before both the column letter and the row number of the cell address in the formula.

It is also possible to enter a formula using a **mixed cell reference**. This is done by entering the dollar sign ($) before either the column letter or the row number of the cell address, but not before both. The result is that either the row or the column will not be adjusted during the copy. For example, the address A$5 would be copied by changing the column letters, but the row number would always be 5.

You can enter the dollar sign directly by typing it or by using F4, the ABS (absolute) key. To edit the formula in cell C19 to have absolute cell referencing and to demonstrate the use of the ABS key,

Move to: C19
Press: F2

We need to change the reference to cell J5 in the formula to an absolute reference. The edit cursor should be positioned on or immediately to the right of the cell address before using the ABS key. This tells 1-2-3 which cell address to alter. Since the edit cursor is in the correct location,

Press: F4

The cell address to the left of the edit cursor now contains a dollar sign before the column letter and the row number, making it absolute. Each time you press F4, the cell address will change from absolute to mixed to relative. To see this change, watch the control panel as you

Press: F4 slowly four times

The cell address cycles through all possible combinations of the different reference types. It should now be absolute. To complete the edit,

Press: ↵

Copy this formula across row 19 through June.

Your screen should now look similar to Figure 2.20.

```
C19: +C18/$J$5                                                  READY

    A            B    C     D     E     F     G     H     I    J
1                          Six-Month Budget for Chris Kent
2
3                      JAN   FEB   MAR   APR   MAY   JUN        TOTAL
4                     ------------------------------------      ------
5   WAGES:            2000  2000  2000  2000  2000  2000        12000
6
7   EXPENSES:
8   RENT               475   475   475   475   475   475         2850
9   FOOD               362   362   362   362   362   362         2172
10  CLOTHING           150   150   150   150   150   150          900
11  CAR INSURANCE      357                                        357
12  CAR EXPENSES        94    94    94    94    94    94          564
13  LIFE INSURANCE     277                                        277
14  LOAN PAYMENT                                     731          731
15  LEISURE            200   200   200   200   200   200         1200
16  SAVINGS            250   250   250   250   250   250         1500
17
18  TOTAL EXPENSES:   2165  1531  1531  1531  1531  2262        10551
19  PROPORTION       0.180 0.127 0.127 0.127 0.127 0.188
20  BALANCE:          -165   469   469   469   469  -262         1449
16-Jun-89  12:32 AM      UNDO
```

Figure 2.20

Move across row 19 to confirm that each formula references cell J5. Using an absolute cell reference easily solved this problem.

Erasing Entries

Chris decides that the PROPORTION row of data does not really belong in his budget, so he wants to clear, or erase, the entire row.

Move to: A19

Issue the following command sequence:

/ **R**ange **E**rase **A19..H19** ↵

Your screen should look similar to Figure 2.21.

```
A19: [W15]                                                   READY

     A            B     C     D     E     F     G     H     I     J
1                          Six-Month Budget for Chris Kent
2
3                        JAN   FEB   MAR   APR   MAY   JUN         TOTAL
4                        -----------------------------------        ------
5   WAGES:               2000  2000  2000  2000  2000  2000         12000
6
7   EXPENSES:
8   RENT                  475   475   475   475   475   475          2850
9   FOOD                  362   362   362   362   362   362          2172
10  CLOTHING              150   150   150   150   150   150           900
11  CAR INSURANCE         357                                         357
12  CAR EXPENSES           94    94    94    94    94    94           564
13  LIFE INSURANCE        277                                         277
14  LOAN PAYMENT                                         731           731
15  LEISURE               200   200   200   200   200   200          1200
16  SAVINGS               250   250   250   250   250   250          1500
17
18  TOTAL EXPENSES:      2165  1531  1531  1531  1531  2262         10551
19
20  BALANCE:             -165   469   469   469   469  -262          1449
16-Jun-89  12:33 AM     UNDO
```

Figure 2.21

The entire row is now erased.

Using the Undo Feature

Chris realizes that he erased the row of data too soon. He wanted to record the values for later use. To cancel the most recent operation that changed worksheet data or settings, Chris can use the Undo (ALT-F4) feature. This feature restores the worksheet to the way it was the last time 1-2-3 was in READY mode.

Press: ALT-F4

The row of data that Chris had erased is redisplayed. It appears exactly as it did before he used the Erase command.

After recording the information, Chris now wants to erase the row again. Rather than using the Erase command, he can press Undo again and 1-2-3 will redo the entry or command.

Press: ALT-F4

The status indicator at the bottom of the screen displays UNDO whenever 1-2-3 can activate the Undo feature. The row is again erased from the worksheet.

This feature is an important safeguard against mistakes that may take a lot of time to fix. However, be careful when you use this command as you may get some unexpected results. Each time you begin a command, start an entry, or use certain function keys that affect the worksheet data, 1-2-3 creates a temporary backup copy of the worksheet as it last appeared in READY mode. The backup copy is stored in memory. Since 1-2-3 does not wait until the command or entry is complete before backing up the worksheet, you must use the Undo feature immediately after executing the command or making the entry that you want to undo. A backup worksheet is not created if the key you press does not cause a change in the worksheet data.

Using the Worksheet

The completed worksheet shows that Chris has a cash flow problem in January, with a negative balance of $165. However, over the six-month period, Chris has a positive balance of $1449.

Chris is not too concerned about the deficit in January because he has a secret vacation fund he can borrow money from. To cover the cost of car insurance, Chris plans to borrow $357 in January from this fund.

Chris would like to buy a new car in July. He estimates the down payment to be $2100. At his current rate of savings, however, Chris will have only $1500 in June. He will have to increase his savings rate.

To see the effect on Chris's budget, change his monthly savings (C16..H16) to $350 ($2100 divided by 6 months). The process of changing selected factors in a worksheet is called **what-if analysis**. What if his savings changed to $350 a month?

After you change the data in row 16, your screen should look similar to Figure 2.22.

C16: 350 READY

	A	B	C	D	E	F	G	H	I	J
1			Six-Month Budget for Chris Kent							
2										
3			JAN	FEB	MAR	APR	MAY	JUN		TOTAL
4			------	------	------	------	------	------		------
5	WAGES:		2000	2000	2000	2000	2000	2000		12000
6										
7	EXPENSES:									
8	RENT		475	475	475	475	475	475		2850
9	FOOD		362	362	362	362	362	362		2172
10	CLOTHING		150	150	150	150	150	150		900
11	CAR INSURANCE		357							357
12	CAR EXPENSES		94	94	94	94	94	94		564
13	LIFE INSURANCE		277							277
14	LOAN PAYMENT							731		731
15	LEISURE		200	200	200	200	200	200		1200
16	SAVINGS		350	350	350	350	350	350		2100
17										
18	TOTAL EXPENSES:		2265	1631	1631	1631	1631	2362		11151
19										
20	BALANCE:		-265	369	369	369	369	-362		849

16-Jun-89 12:35 AM UNDO

Figure 2.22

Chris now has a total balance of $849 and a total savings of $2100.

When 1-2-3 recalculates a worksheet, only those formulas directly affected by a change in the data are recalculated. This is called **minimal recalculation**. Without this feature, in large worksheets the time it takes to recalculate all formulas each time a value is changed could take several minutes. The minimal recalculation feature decreases the recalculation time by only recalculating affected formulas.

Chris feels he can afford a more active social life, so he decides to increase his leisure allowance from 10 to 15 percent of wages. To make this change, use the Edit function key, F2, to change the formula in cell C15 to +C5*0.15, then copy this formula to cells D15 through H15.

Your screen should look similar to Figure 2.23.

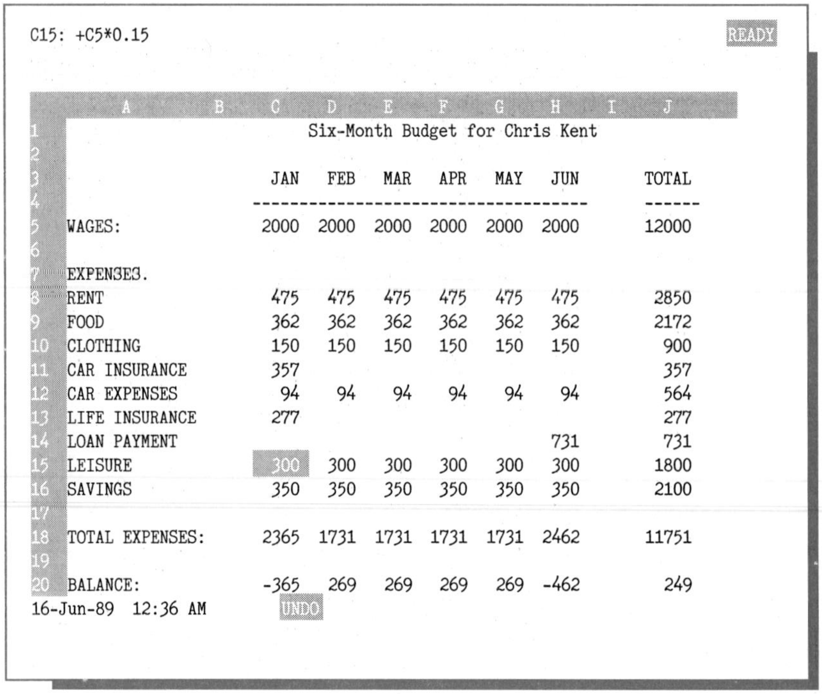

```
C15: +C5*0.15                                                          READY

     A           B      C     D     E     F     G     H     I       J
 1                          Six-Month Budget for Chris Kent
 2
 3                     JAN   FEB   MAR   APR   MAY   JUN          TOTAL
 4                   ------------------------------------        ------
 5   WAGES:           2000  2000  2000  2000  2000  2000          12000
 6
 7   EXPENSES.
 8   RENT              475   475   475   475   475   475           2850
 9   FOOD              362   362   362   362   362   362           2172
10   CLOTHING          150   150   150   150   150   150            900
11   CAR INSURANCE     357                                          357
12   CAR EXPENSES       94    94    94    94    94    94            564
13   LIFE INSURANCE    277                                          277
14   LOAN PAYMENT                                    731            731
15   LEISURE           300   300   300   300   300   300           1800
16   SAVINGS           350   350   350   350   350   350           2100
17
18   TOTAL EXPENSES:  2365  1731  1731  1731  1731  2462          11751
19
20   BALANCE:         -365   269   269   269   269  -462            249
16-Jun-89  12:36 AM     UNDO
```

Figure 2.23

Even by increasing his leisure allowance, Chris still has a positive balance ($249). He feels this balance is enough to cover any unexpected expense.

Next, you will save and print the worksheet.

Saving and Replacing a File

Before 1-2-3 will allow you to save any worksheet, it checks to see if another worksheet with the same name exists on the disk. If one does not exist, the worksheet is automatically saved. If one does exist, 1-2-3 prompts you to select either **C**ancel, **R**eplace, or **B**ackup.

To save the current worksheet by copying it over the partial worksheet saved in Lab 1 as BUDGET.WK1, issue the following command sequence:

/ **F**ile **S**ave **BUDGET.WK1** ↵

The second line of the control panel prompts you to select **C**ancel, **R**eplace, or **B**ackup. If you select **C**ancel, the file will not be saved as BUDGET, and you could reissue the command using another filename. If you select **R**eplace, the current worksheet will be saved as BUDGET, and the previous worksheet will be lost.

If you select **B**ackup, the current worksheet will be saved as BUDGET.WK1 and a backup copy of the existing file on disk would be saved as BUDGET.BAK.

Since you want to replace the old worksheet, select:

Replace

This feature protects against your accidentally saving one file over another with the same name.

Printing a File

You will now print the worksheet using the 1-2-3 Print command. Many print options are available with 1-2-3, but we will look at those most commonly used.

If your printer is off, turn it on. Check to see that it is on line. If your printer uses continuous form paper, adjust the printer paper so that the perforated line is just above the printer's scale. Begin the Print command as follows:

/ **P**rint

The two print options, **P**rinter and **F**ile, displayed in the control panel allow you to send the output directly to the printer for printing or to a file to be printed later. To send the output directly to the printer, select:

Printer

The Print settings sheet is displayed. The only option that you must select is the range. The default settings for the other options are satisfactory for now. To specify the range as the entire worksheet, select:

Range **A1..J20** (↵)

The Print settings sheet is displayed again, reflecting the range you specified.

Finally, to tell the program that the paper is aligned with the top of the printer's scale and to begin printing, select:

Align **G**o

Your printer may take a few moments before it begins to print the worksheet. Do not select **Go** again, because it will result in multiple printouts of the worksheet.

When the printing is finished, issue the following command:

Page

Your printer output should look similar to Figure 2.24.

Your name →

Current data →

The Student Edition of Lotus 1-2-3 Timothy J. O'Leary

Six-Month Budget for Chris Kent

	JAN	FEB	MAR	APR	MAY	JUN	TOTAL
WAGES:	2000	2000	2000	2000	2000	2000	12000
EXPENSES:							
RENT	475	475	475	475	475	475	2850
FOOD	362	362	362	362	362	362	2172
CLOTHING	150	150	150	150	150	150	900
CAR INSURANCE	357						357
CAR EXPENSES	94	94	94	94	94	94	564
LIFE INSURANCE	277						277
LOAN PAYMENT						731	731
LEISURE	300	300	300	300	300	300	1800
SAVINGS	350	350	350	350	350	350	2100
TOTAL EXPENSES:	2365	1731	1731	1731	1731	2462	11751
BALANCE:	−365	269	269	269	269	−462	249

Figure 2.24

The header "The Student Edition of Lotus 1-2-3" and your name are automatically printed at the top of your worksheet.

Return to READY mode by issuing the following command:

Quit

Exit 1-2-3.

Glossary of Key Terms

Absolute cell reference A cell address that always refers to the same cell even if it is copied to a new cell location.

Anchor Defines the cell that begins a range of cells to be highlighted while in POINT mode.

Anchor cell The beginning cell of a range.

Column width The number of spaces that a column contains.

Default A setting that 1-2-3 automatically uses unless another setting is specified.

@function A built-in formula that performs certain types of calculations automatically.

Global A setting that affects the entire worksheet.

Minimal recalculation The recalculation of only those formulas affected by a change in data in the worksheet.

Mixed cell reference A cell address that is part absolute and part relative.

Pointing Using the cell pointer to specify a cell or a range of cells.

Range A cell or a rectangular group of adjoining cells in the worksheet.

Relative cell reference A cell address that refers to a cell's position rather than to the cell itself and adjusts relative to its new position when copied.

Settings sheet Displays the current settings for the options associated with the command in use.

@SUM An @function that calculates the total value of cells in a specified range of cells.

Syntax The structure that must be followed when entering @functions.

What-if analysis A technique used to evaluate the effects of changing selected values or formulas in a worksheet.

Practice Problems

1. Matching

1. /WCS	_______	a. the Undo feature key sequence
2. +D5	_______	b. copies a range of cells
3. F4	_______	c. prints output from a worksheet
4. /RE	_______	d. deletes a column
5. /WIR	_______	e. sets column width
6. ALT-F4	_______	f. erases a range of cells
7. +$D$5	_______	g. switches a cell reference among absolute, mixed, and relative
8. /C	_______	h. inserts a new row
9. /PP	_______	i. absolute cell reference
10. /WDC	_______	j. relative cell reference

2. Linda Fry has been trying to create a worksheet for her personal budget and has been having some problems. Retrieve the worksheet file LINDA.

   a. The entries in rows 4 and 5 represent Linda's monthly rent. These figures should not be there. Use the Erase command to correct this error.

   b. Look at row 19. The month labels should be in row 1. Move the labels in row 19 to row 1. (Hint: Although you could retype all the labels in row 1 and then erase row 19, there is a much easier way using one of 1-2-3's commands.)

   c. You have probably noticed the asterisks in the worksheet. Globally change the column widths to 9 spaces.

   d. Insert two blank rows as rows 1 and 2. Delete row 7 and insert a row at row 4.

   e. In cell B4, use the repeat label-prefix character to enter a series of underline (_) characters and copy this entry from cell B4 to cell C4 through cell H4.

   f. Enter your name in cell A1 and the date in cell A2.

g. Save your corrected version of the worksheet using the filename FRY.

h. Print the worksheet.

3. To complete this problem, you first must have built the worksheet as specified in Practice Problem 4 of Lab 1. If you have already completed that problem, retrieve the file BROWN. Continue to create the budget for Marty Brown by following these steps:

   a. Fill in the monthly expenses for February through June. (Remember, tuition and license registration are periodic expenses.)

   b. Marty would like to add an entry for Savings and to allocate 5 percent of his monthly wages toward this expense. Enter the label Savings in cell A15. Enter a formula to calculate savings in cell B15, then copy it to cells C15 through G15.

   c. Marty forgot to allow for expenses for leisure activities and other miscellaneous items. He feels $115 would be adequate. He would like to enter the label Misc Exp. in the row below License.

      Insert a row in the appropriate space, enter the label Misc Exp., and enter the value 115 for JAN through JUNE.

   d. Enter a blank row below Savings.

   e. Copy the total formula from cell H5 to cells H8 through H16.

   f. Enter the formulas required to calculate the Total expense and Balance. Copy these formulas across through the TOTAL column (H).

   g. Marty realizes he has much more money left over each month (Balance) than he needs to cover unexpected expenses. He decides to increase his monthly savings. The monthly savings is currently calculated as 5 percent of monthly wages. Change the percent used to calculate savings for all months except JAN, so that the balance for each month is as close as possible to, but no more than, $200. (Limit your adjustment to 2 decimal places.) What is the total savings now?

h. Increase the width of column A to 10. Decrease all other column widths to 8.

i. Enter the current date in cell A2.

j. Save your completed version of this worksheet using the filename BROWN1.

k. Print the worksheet.

4. To complete this problem, you first must have built the worksheet as specified in Practice Problem 5 in Lab 1. If you have already completed that problem, retrieve the file SLOAN. Complete this worksheet by following these steps:

   a. Enter the current date in cell A2.

   b. Fill in the monthly expenses for February through June. (Remember, insurance and loan payment expenses are periodic.)

   c. Alice Sloan forgot to include a local 2.3 percent business tax on revenues. She would like to enter this expense in the row just below Telephone. Insert a row in the appropriate space. Enter the label Local Tax in cell A11. Enter the appropriate formula (.023 times monthly revenues) in cell B11. Copy this formula from cell B11 to cells C11 through G11.

   d. Alice has decided that a reserve fund should be created to support the development of new business clients. She thinks that 3 percent of monthly revenues should be put into this fund. Enter the label Reserve in cell A16. Enter the formula to make this calculation in cell B16. Copy this formula across the row through cell G16. Insert a blank row following row 16.

   e. Use an @function to calculate the Total Expenses in cells B18 through G18. Use formulas to calculate the Net (net = revenue − total expenses) values.

   f. After studying the net balances and thinking about the importance of developing new business, Alice decides to increase the percentage allocation to the reserve fund. The current percentage is 3 percent of Revenues. Change the percent used to calculate the reserve fund so that the total Net is as close as possible to, but no less than, $4500.

g. Save your completed version of this worksheet using the filename SLOAN1.

h. Print the worksheet.

5. Create your own personal six-month budget beginning in January and ending in June. Include eight expense items, with some fixed expenses, some periodic expenses, and some calculated by formulas. Complete the worksheet by following these steps:

   a. Enter your name in cell A1 and the current date in cell A2.

   b. Enter an appropriate title for the worksheet in row 1.

   c. Enter labels for the months and the total across row 3.

   d. Enter labels for the income, expenses, total expenses, and balance down column A.

   e. Enter all the appropriate values, formulas, and @functions.

   f. Adjust column widths as needed.

   g. Save the worksheet using the filename PERSONAL.

   h. Print the worksheet.

3

Creating a Line Graph

Objectives

In Lab 3, you will learn how to:

- Create line graphs
- Specify the X axis
- Specify data to be graphed
- Create and edit titles
- Create and edit legends
- Use data labels
- Use grids
- Save current graph settings

Case Study

Nancy Rich, a student at Central State University, is preparing a report on the future population growth for the state. While researching the report, she collected the population estimates of four cities, Newton, South Fork, Century, and Danbury, for the years 1990 through 1994.

Nancy has entered these data into a worksheet file. Although the data are nicely displayed, she feels it is difficult to see the trend of population growth for the cities over the five-year period. She thinks that a line graph may display the data more clearly for her report. We will follow Nancy as she creates this graph.

Previewing Graph Commands

Note To be able to view the graphs in Labs 3 and 4, you will need a computer with graphics capabilities and to have properly installed 1-2-3 to display graphs (see Chapter 4, "Starting and Ending PrintGraph," in Section 1, "Getting Started").

Before loading 1-2-3, you need to load the program GRAPHICS. COM from your disk operating system (DOS). On most computer systems, this program allows you to print a copy of a graph displayed on your screen. To load this file, with the DOS disk in drive A, at the A> prompt:

Type: **GRAPHICS.COM**
Press: ↵

If you are using a hard-disk drive, you do not have to put DOS in drive A. At the C> prompt,

Type: **GRAPHICS.COM**
Press: ↵

The A> prompt (C> prompt for hard-disk users) should be displayed again.

Note If the error message "File not Found" is displayed, either the GRAPHICS.COM file is not on your operating system or you entered the filename incorrectly. If you are unable to load GRAPHICS.COM or if your computer system will not print graphics using GRAPHICS.COM, you can still complete Lab 3 without printing the graphs as directed. Your instructor may have you print the graphs in Lab 3 and in the practice exercises after you complete Lab 4.

Now, load Lotus 1-2-3 in the usual manner.

Nancy has entered the population estimates for the four cities into a worksheet file named POPULATE. To see this worksheet, select:

/ **F**ile **R**etrieve

Although the files to retrieve are listed in the control panel, only one line of filenames can be seen at a time. To display all the files on the screen at once, use the Name function key, F3.

Press: F3

A menu of worksheet files is displayed on the screen. The name of the highlighted file and information about its size and date of creation are displayed on the third line of the control panel. To select a file from the menu, use the pointer-movement keys to highlight the filename of your choice and press ↵. Continue the command sequence by selecting POPULATE.WK1.

Your screen should look similar to Figure 3.1.

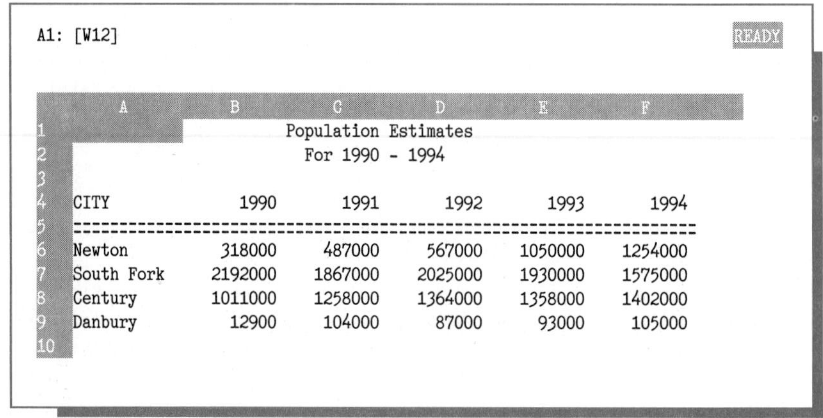
A1: [W12] READY

	A	B	C	D	E	F
1			Population Estimates			
2			For 1990 - 1994			
3						
4	CITY	1990	1991	1992	1993	1994
5	============	==========	==========	==========	==========	==========
6	Newton	318000	487000	567000	1050000	1254000
7	South Fork	2192000	1867000	2025000	1930000	1575000
8	Century	1011000	1258000	1364000	1358000	1402000
9	Danbury	12900	104000	87000	93000	105000
10						

Figure 3.1

This worksheet shows the projected population for Newton, South Fork, Century, and Danbury for the years 1990 through 1994.

Nancy wants to create a line graph to visually display the projected growth for the four cities over the five-year period. A **line graph** represents numeric data as a set of connected points along a line. Line graphs are particularly useful for showing change over time.

Graphs consist of several important parts, which are illustrated in Figure 3.2.

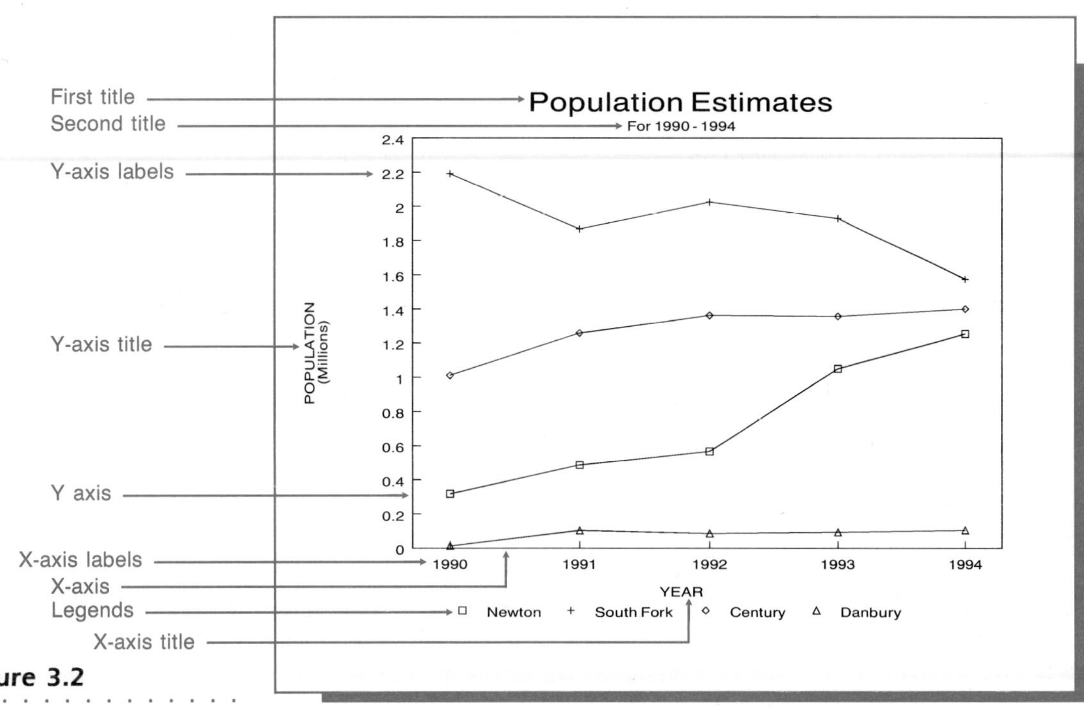

Figure 3.2

Line, bar, and XY graphs have two reference lines, or axes:

X axis	a horizontal line at the bottom of the graph
Y axis	a vertical line at the left edge of the graph

A 1-2-3 graph can have four different **titles**:

first title	a short description of the entire graph
second title	an additional description for the first title
X-axis title	a short description of the X axis
Y-axis title	a short description of the Y axis

At the bottom of the graph, **legends** briefly describe or reference data in the graph.

In 1-2-3, you use the Graph command to create and modify graphs. Issue the following command:

/ **G**raph

Your screen should look similar to Figure 3.3.

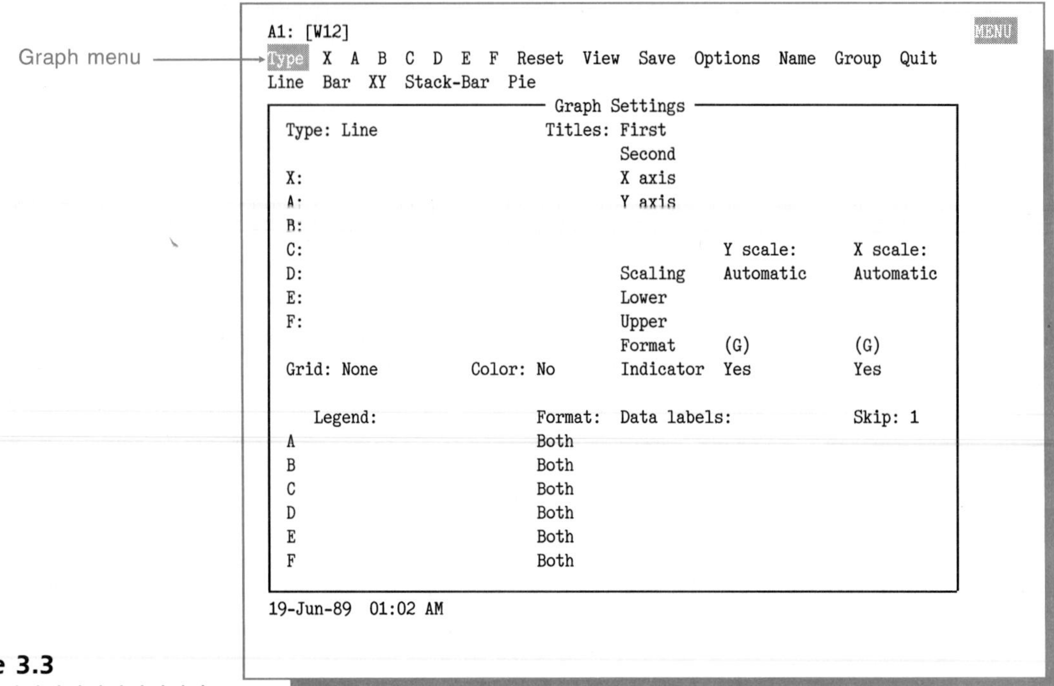

Figure 3.3

The Graph settings sheet is displayed on the screen. Like the Global settings sheet, this settings sheet helps you keep track of the choices you have made. The Graph settings sheet shows you the current graph settings for the Graph commands displayed in the **Graph menu**. Since there are no graph settings specified yet, the settings sheet is empty except for the names of the graph settings and for any default graph settings.

To briefly preview the Graph commands displayed in the second line of the control panel,

Press: F1

Read this screen carefully, as it describes each of the graph commands we will be using in Labs 3 and 4. (If you are using a two-disk system and don't see the Help screen, see Chapter 5, "The Help Facility," in Section 1, "Getting Started.")

The first Graph command we will specify is Type. For further Help information about this command,

Press: ↵

Your screen now shows information on the five types of graphs you can create using 1-2-3. In this lab, you will create a line graph. In Lab 4, you will create bar, stacked bar, XY, and pie graphs.

To leave the Help facility and return to the Graph menu,

Press: ESC

Creating Line Graphs

The first step is to select the type of graph you want to create. Continue the command sequence by selecting:

Type

Your screen should now look similar to Figure 3.4.

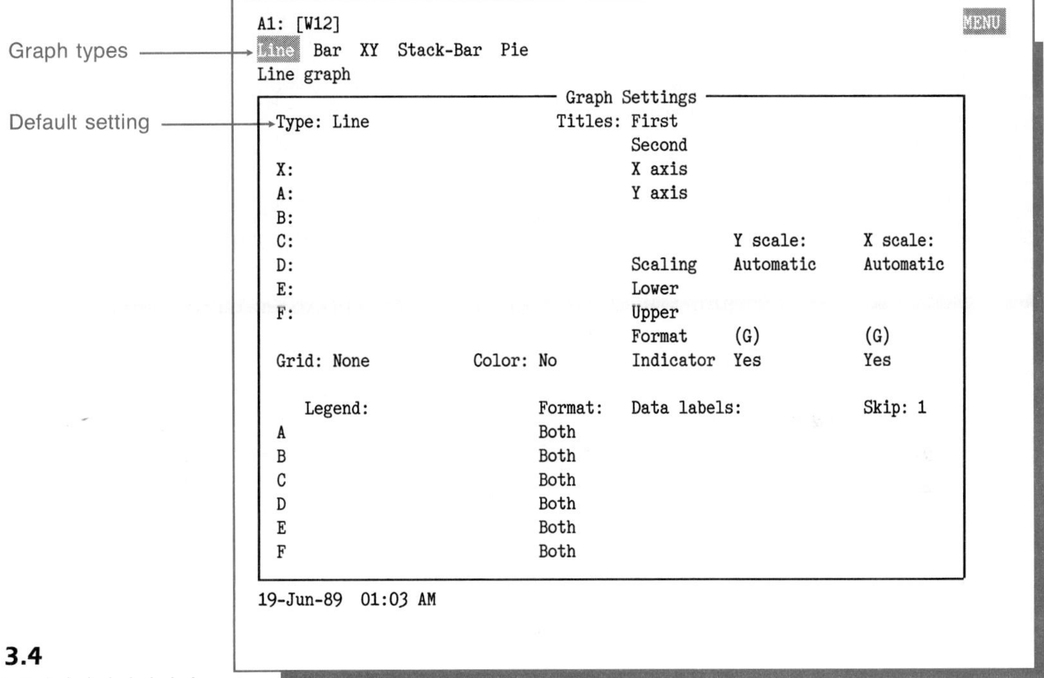

Figure 3.4

The second line of the control panel lists the five types of graphs: line, bar, XY, stacked bar, and pie. The Graph settings sheet is still displayed on the screen. As you can see, the settings sheet shows that the default graph type is a line graph. Since this is the type of graph we want to create, to accept the default,

Press: ↵

You are returned to the Graph menu rather than to READY mode and can continue specifying graph settings. 1-2-3 is now ready to create a line graph.

Defining the X-Axis Labels

In a line graph, the X command on the Graph menu is used to label the horizontal, or X, axis. These labels must be contained in a continuous range of cells in the worksheet. For Nancy's line graph, the X axis will be the years 1990 through 1994, which are in the continuous range of cells B4 through F4.

To set the years as the X-axis labels, continue the command sequence as follows:

X

The Graph settings sheet is cleared from the screen and the worksheet is displayed. This lets you see the range of cells containing the data to be specified as the X data range. In response to the prompt to "Enter x-axis range:", continue the command sequence as follows:

B4..F4 ↵

Did you notice that POINT was displayed in the mode indicator? You can also use pointing to specify the range. This is especially helpful when the range extends beyond the window and you do not know which cell ends the range.

The Graph settings sheet is displayed again. The range of cells you specified for the X data range is displayed in the settings sheet. It is easy to check the range of cells defined as the X-axis labels. Simply reselect the X command from the Graph menu and 1-2-3 will highlight the range.

To see how this works, select:

X

Your screen should look similar to Figure 3.5.

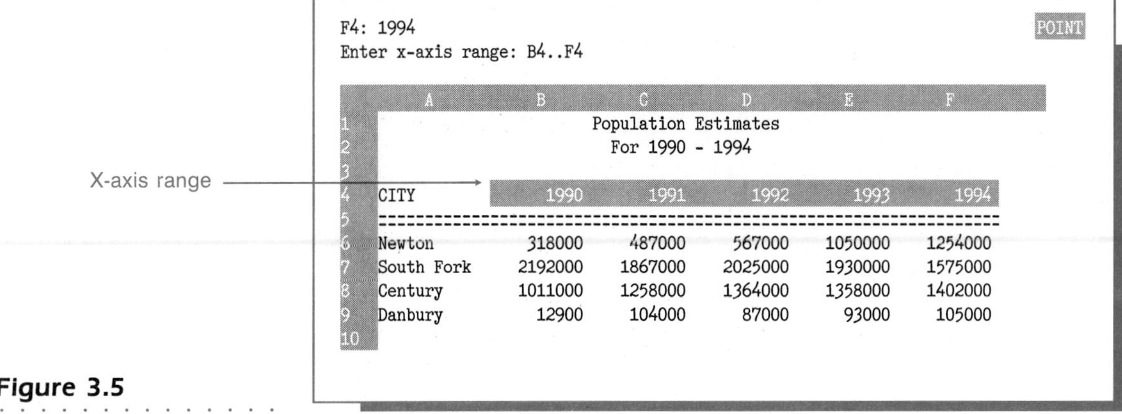

X-axis range
F4: 1994
Enter x-axis range: B4..F4
POINT
A B C D E F
Population Estimates
For 1990 - 1994
CITY 1990 1991 1992 1993 1994
Newton 318000 487000 567000 1050000 1254000
South Fork 2192000 1867000 2025000 1930000 1575000
Century 1011000 1258000 1364000 1358000 1402000
Danbury 12900 104000 87000 93000 105000

Figure 3.5

The range B4..F4 should now be highlighted. If it is not, enter the correct range before continuing.

To accept this range,

Press: ↵

Defining Data Ranges

Now that you have specified the type of graph and the X-axis labels, the next step is to specify the worksheet ranges that contain the numbers to be graphed.

Six different numeric data ranges, represented by the letters A, B, C, D, E, and F displayed in the Graph menu, can be shown on a single graph.

For now, you are going to graph only one data range: the population estimates for Newton, which are located in cells B6 through F6. To specify the data range, you use the same procedure you used to specify the X axis. You can enter the data range by typing or by pointing. To specify cells B6 through F6 as the A data range, continue the command sequence as follows:

A B6..F6 ↵

The A data range setting is displayed in the Graph settings sheet.

To view the graph, select:

View

Your screen should look similar to Figure 3.6.

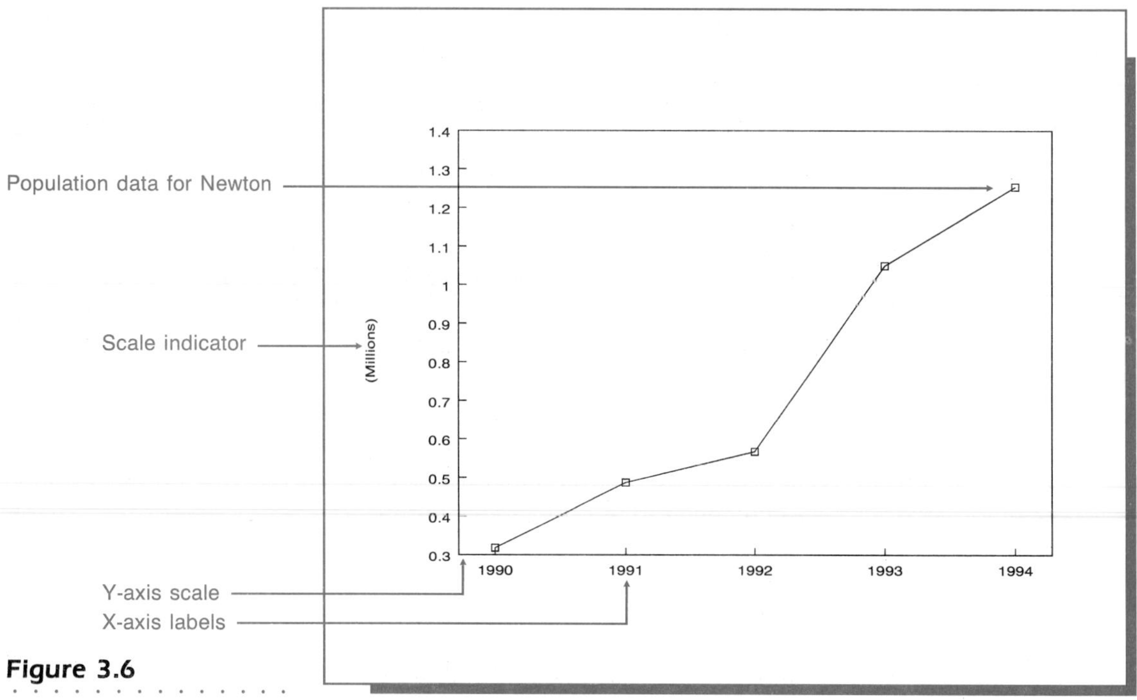

Figure 3.6

The years are displayed on the X axis, and the population data for Newton are plotted in the graph as a series of square symbols connected by a line. 1-2-3 automatically set the scale of values on the Y axis. The Y-axis values were determined by the high and low values in the A range. The notation (Millions) is the **scale indicator** and is automatically displayed by the program.

To clear the graph and return to the Graph menu, you can press any key, for example, SPACEBAR.

Press: SPACEBAR

Adding Titles

You could improve the appearance and clarity of the graph greatly by adding some titles. The command to add titles is found under Options. Select:

Options

Your screen should look similar to Figure 3.7.

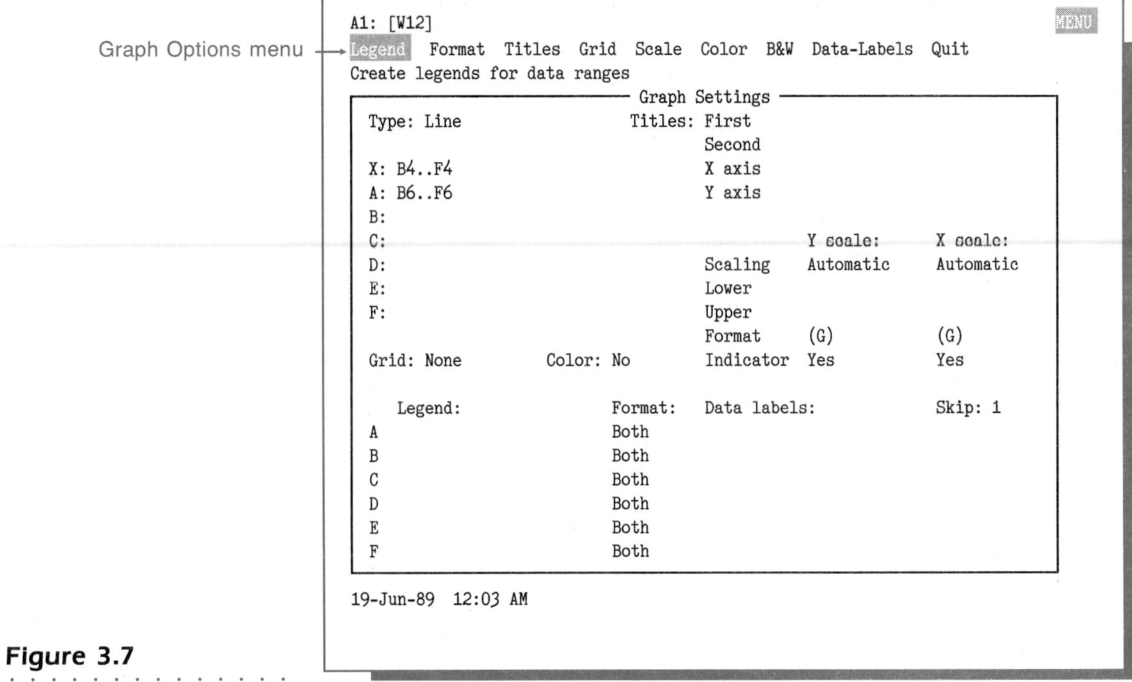

Figure 3.7

The second line of the control panel lists the nine graph options. Select:

Titles

Your screen should look similar to Figure 3.8.

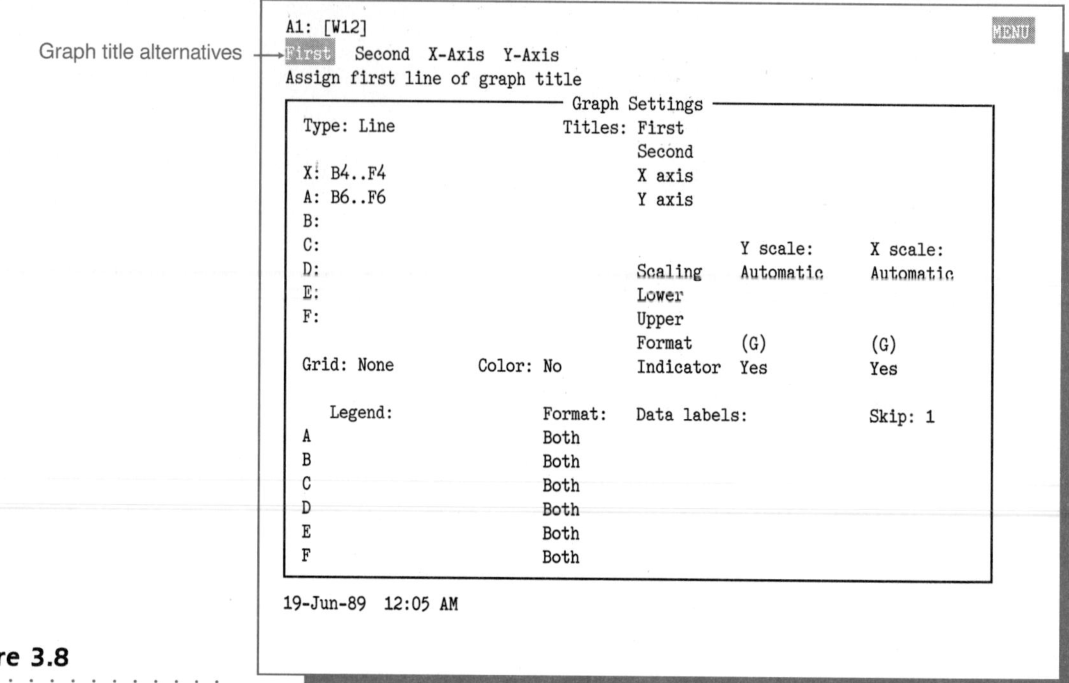

Figure 3.8

The four graph title alternatives listed in the second line of the control panel will allow you to enter titles for the first (main title) and second (subtitle) lines at the top of the graph, as well as titles for the X and Y axes.

To display the worksheet screen so that you can easily refer to cells in the worksheet while specifying the graph title,

Press: F6

Whenever a settings sheet is displayed on the screen, you can use the Window function key, F6, to clear the settings sheet and display the worksheet. The worksheet will continue to be displayed until F6 is pressed again to redisplay the settings sheet.

To enter the first, or main, title, select:

First

You can respond to the prompt for the title in one of two ways. You can type in the title or you can reference a cell in the worksheet containing the label you want to use as the title. In this case, you want to use the title, Population Estimates, displayed in cell C1 of the worksheet as the first title line of the graph. To enter worksheet labels directly into graph titles, use the backslash (\) key followed by the cell address containing the label.

To specify the label in cell C1 as the first graph title line, complete the command sequence as follows:

\C1 ↵

You are now returned to the Options menu.

To leave this menu and view the graph, issue the following command sequence:

Quit **V**iew

Your screen should look similar to Figure 3.9.

First title

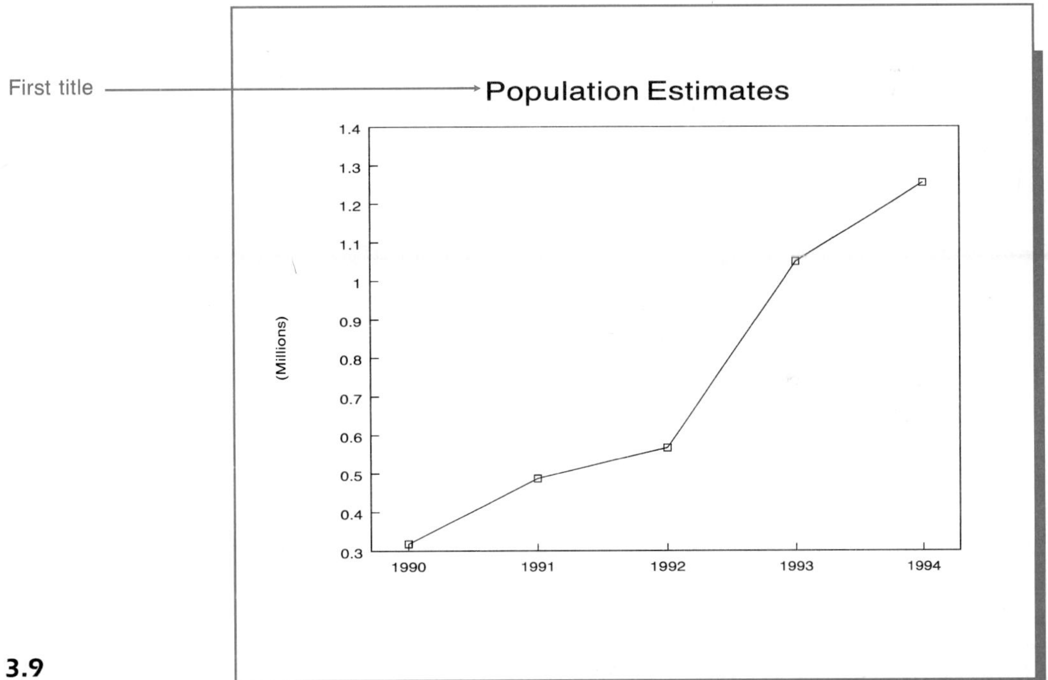

Figure 3.9

The backslash feature inserted the contents of cell C1 from the worksheet into the graph.

1-2-3 automatically centered the title over the graph.

Press any key to return to the Graph menu. Next, you want to add a second title, For Newton, to the graph. Issue the following command sequence:

Options **T**itles **S**econd

Since this title is not a worksheet label that can be copied into the graph, you must enter it directly by typing. Continue the command sequence as follows:

For Newton [↵]

To specify titles for the X axis and the Y axis, issue the following command sequences:

Titles **X**-Axis **YEAR** [↵]
Titles **Y**-Axis **POPULATION** [↵]

To leave the Options menu and see the titles you have added to the graph, select:

Quit **V**iew

Your screen should look similar to Figure 3.10.

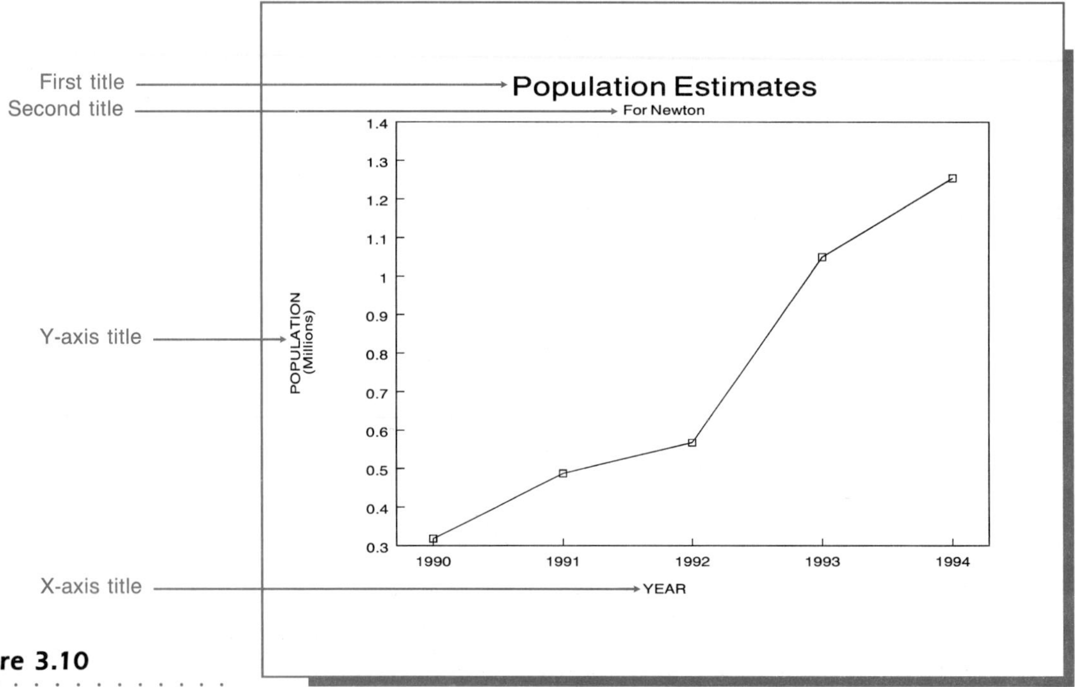

Figure 3.10

Both the first and second titles are centered over the graph. The X-axis title, YEAR, and the Y-axis title, POPULATION, are also centered along their respective axes.

To return to the Graph menu,

Press: SPACEBAR

Adding New Data Ranges

Next, Nancy wants to add the population data for the other three cities to the graph. The population data for South Fork is located in cells B7 through F7. To specify these cells as the B data range, issue the following command sequence:

B B7..F7 ↵

Specify the population figures for Century and Danbury as the third and fourth data ranges (C and D) by issuing the following command sequences:

C B8..F8 ↵
D B9..F9 ↵

View this new graph by selecting:

View

Your screen should now look similar to Figure 3.11.

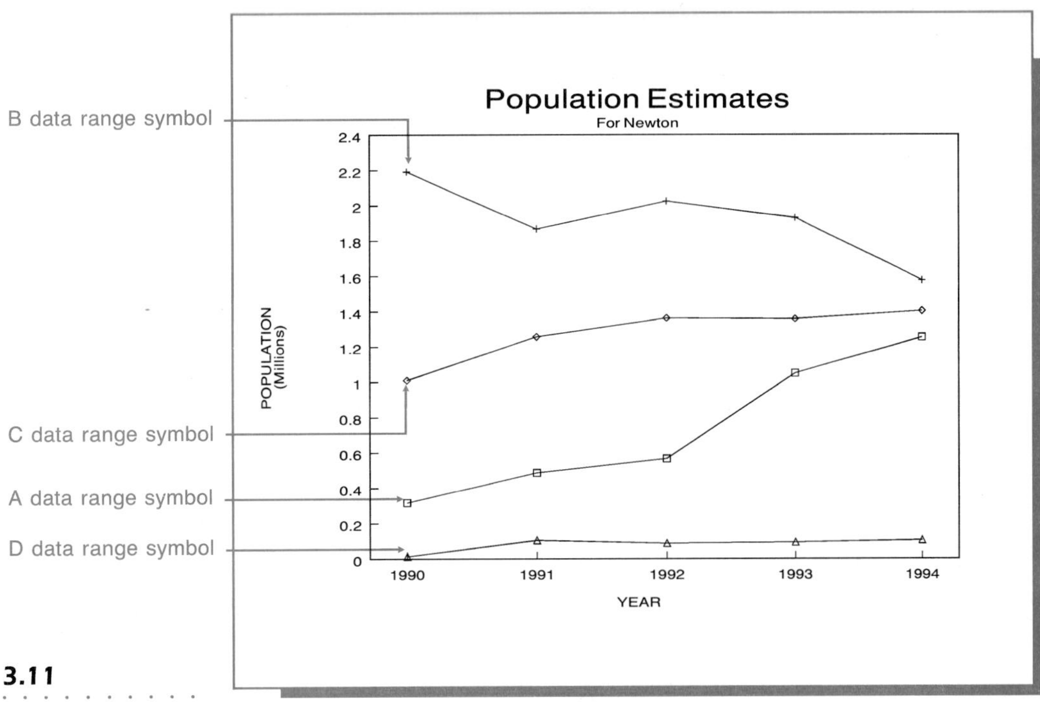

Figure 3.11

The data ranges for all four cities are now displayed in the graph. Notice that each data range is distinguished by a different symbol. Also notice that 1-2-3 automatically redefines the scale of the Y axis based upon the highest and lowest values in the four data ranges.

The graph title is no longer appropriate, since the graph now represents the population estimates for four cities. You will change the title to Population Estimates For 1990–1994.

To return to the Graph menu, press any key. Change the second title line by selecting:

Options **T**itles **S**econd

Your screen should look similar to Figure 3.12.

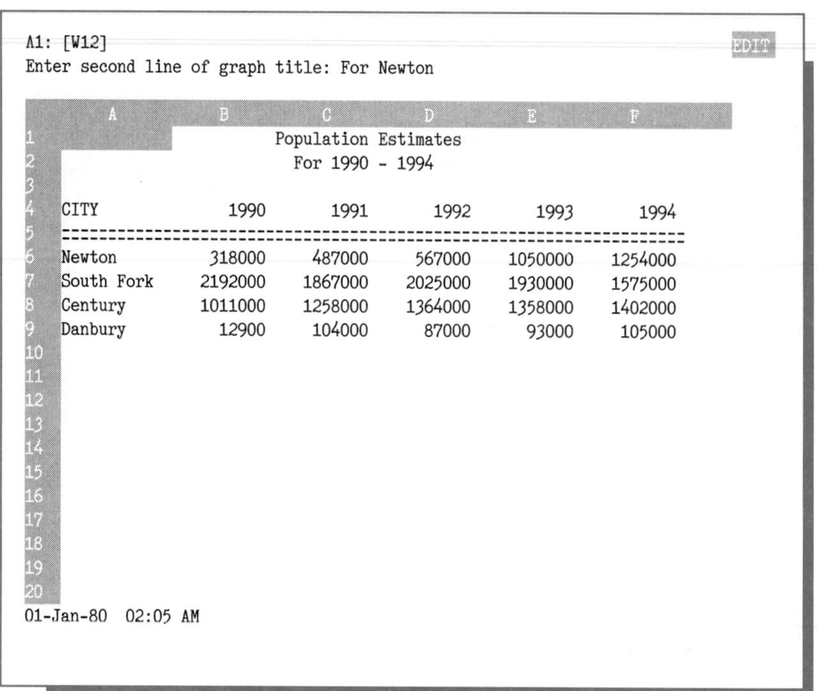

A1: [W12] EDIT

Enter second line of graph title: For Newton

Population Estimates

For 1990 - 1994

CITY	1990	1991	1992	1993	1994
Newton	318000	487000	567000	1050000	1254000
South Fork	2192000	1867000	2025000	1930000	1575000
Century	1011000	1258000	1364000	1358000	1402000
Danbury	12900	104000	87000	93000	105000

01-Jan-80 02:05 AM

Figure 3.12

The current second title line is displayed following the prompt. To erase the title For Newton,

Press: ESC

Cell C2 contains the label For 1990–1994. To specify this label as the new second title in the graph, complete the command sequence as follows:

\C2 ↵

View the graph again by selecting:

Quit **V**iew

Your screen should look similar to Figure 3.13.

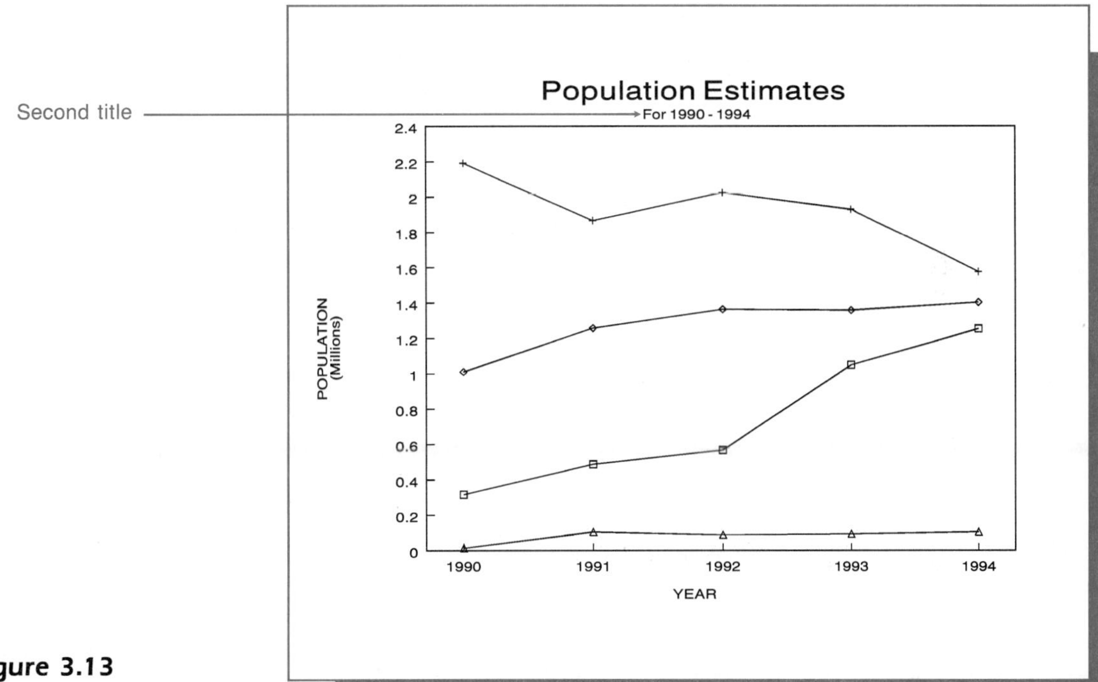

Figure 3.13

The new second graph title line is displayed centered over the graph.

Creating and Editing Legends

The four data ranges in the graph are distinguished from each other by a different symbol placed on each line. It is difficult, however, to know which line goes with which data range. Legends, which are short descriptions of each line, will solve this problem. 1-2-3 will accept long legends (up to nineteen characters), but it will wrap long legends to a second line. For easier readability, it is best to keep legends short.

To clear the graph from the screen,

Press: SPACEBAR

The command to add legends is found under Options. Select:

Options **L**egend

If necessary, press F6 to toggle back to view the settings sheet. Your screen should now look similar to Figure 3.14.

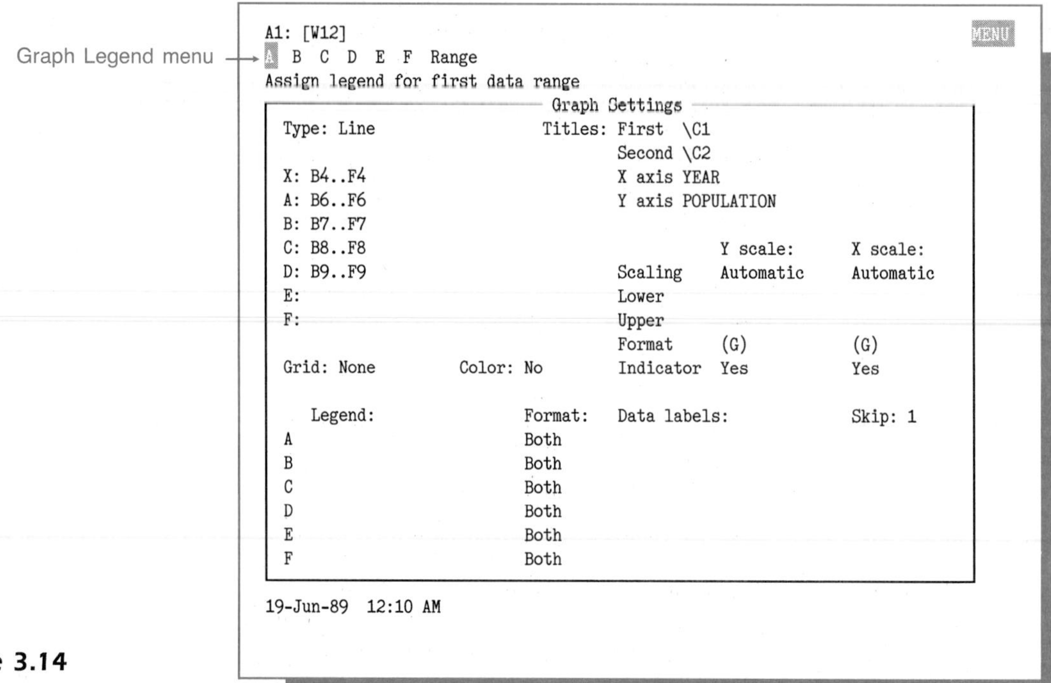

Figure 3.14

Legends are specified using the same procedure as the graph titles: by typing the actual legend or by using the backslash key followed by the cell address of the worksheet entry to be used as the graph legend.

You will begin by entering the label, Newton, from cell A6, for the legend for the A data range. Issue the following command sequence:

F6 **A** \ **A6** ↵

A quicker way to set the legends is to use the Range command in the Graph Legend menu. Select:

Legend **R**ange

The Range command allows you to specify a range of cells in the worksheet that contain entries that you want to be the legends for the graph data ranges. 1-2-3 uses the first entry in the range as the A data range legend, the second entry as the B data range legend, and so forth.

To specify the labels in cells A6 through A9 as the legends for the A through D data ranges, continue the command sequence as follows:

A6..A9 (↵)

To redisplay the Graph settings sheet,

Press: (F6)

The cell addresses are displayed in the settings sheet as if you had entered them individually using the backslash feature.

To view the graph and the legends, select:

Quit **V**iew

Your screen should look similar to Figure 3.15.

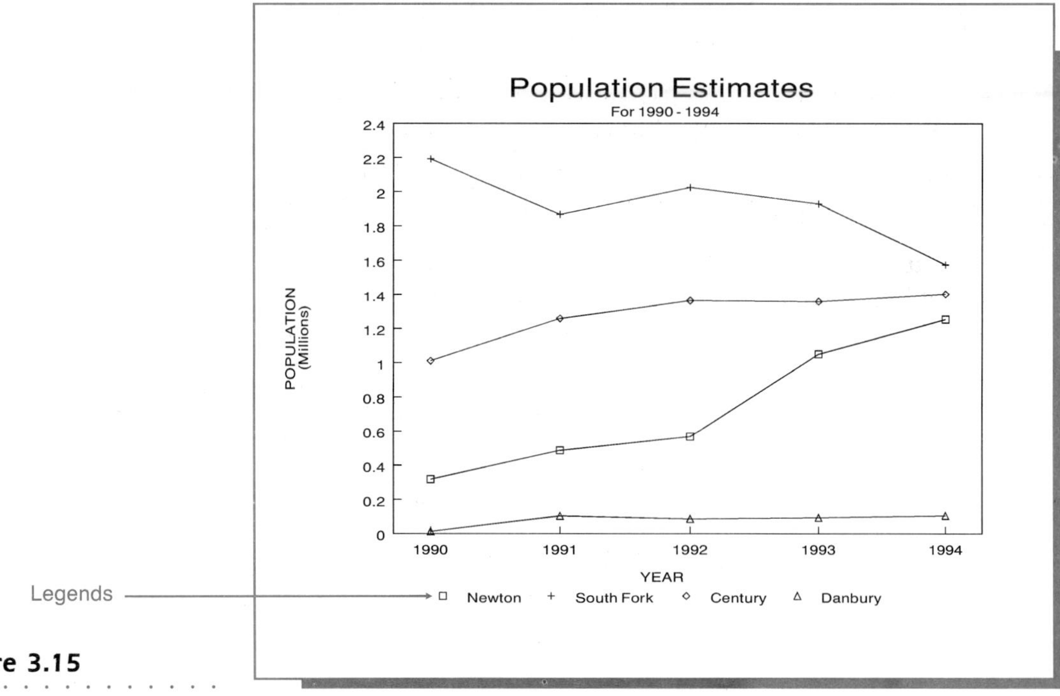

Figure 3.15

The four legends are displayed at the bottom of the graph. If the legends are too long to be fully displayed on one line, they will wrap to a second line.

Using Data Labels

For many graphs, it is important to display the exact value being plotted. To do this, **data labels** are used.

Nancy wants to see if adding data labels to the plotted points for the population estimates for South Fork will improve her graph.

To do this, return to the main Graph menu by pressing SPACEBAR and then issue the following command sequence:

Options **D**ata-Labels

Your screen should look similar to Figure 3.16.

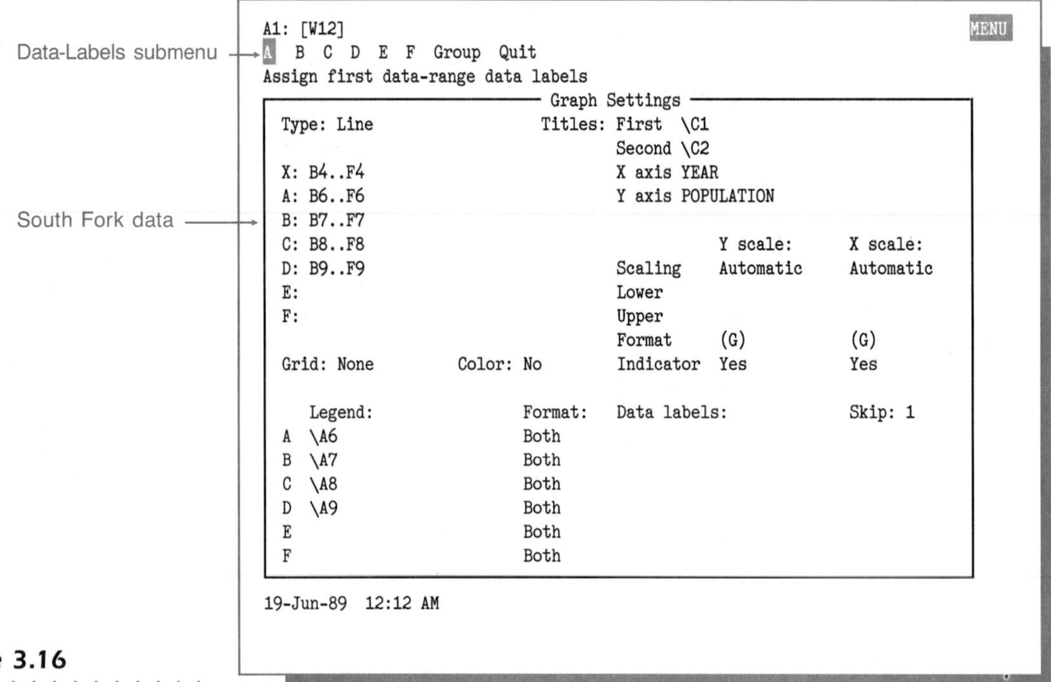

Figure 3.16

The Data-Labels submenu allows you to specify data labels for each individual range of data (A–F) or for all the data ranges at once (Group). Since Nancy wants to see how the data labels would look only for the B data range (South Fork), select

B

To specify the range containing the values to be displayed as the data labels, continue the command sequence,

B7..F7 ⏎

Your screen should look similar to Figure 3.17.

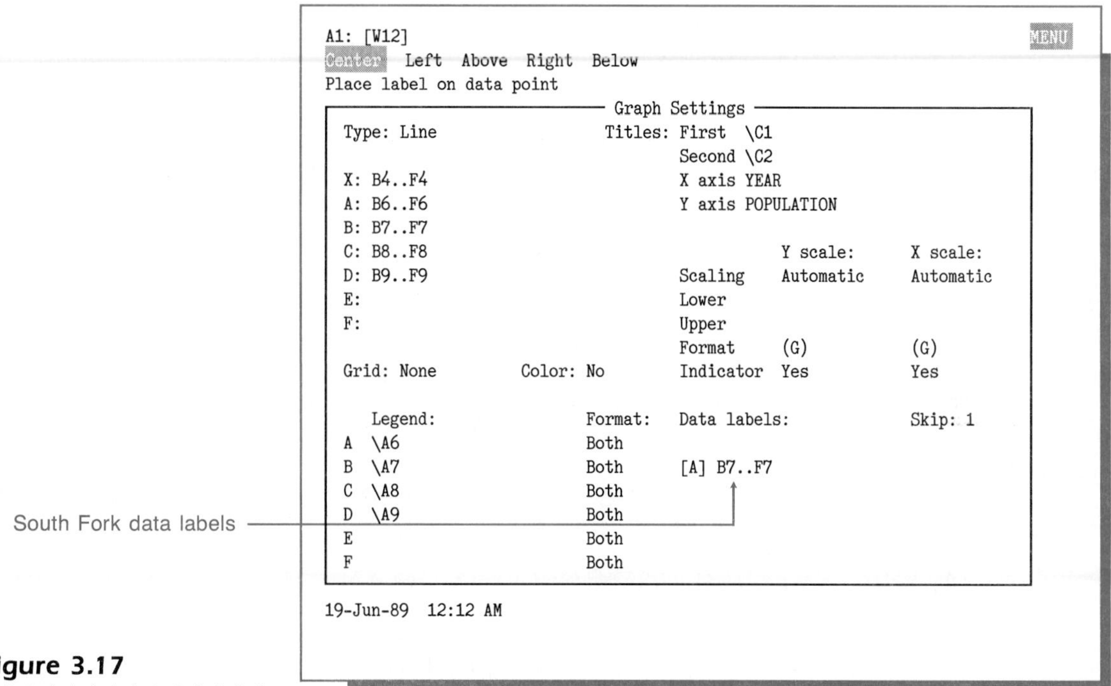

Figure 3.17

Next, the placement of the data labels must be specified. They can be displayed centered, left, above, right, or below each data point.

To place the data labels above the data points, select:

Above

To view the graph, select:

Quit **Q**uit **V**iew

Your screen should look similar to Figure 3.18.

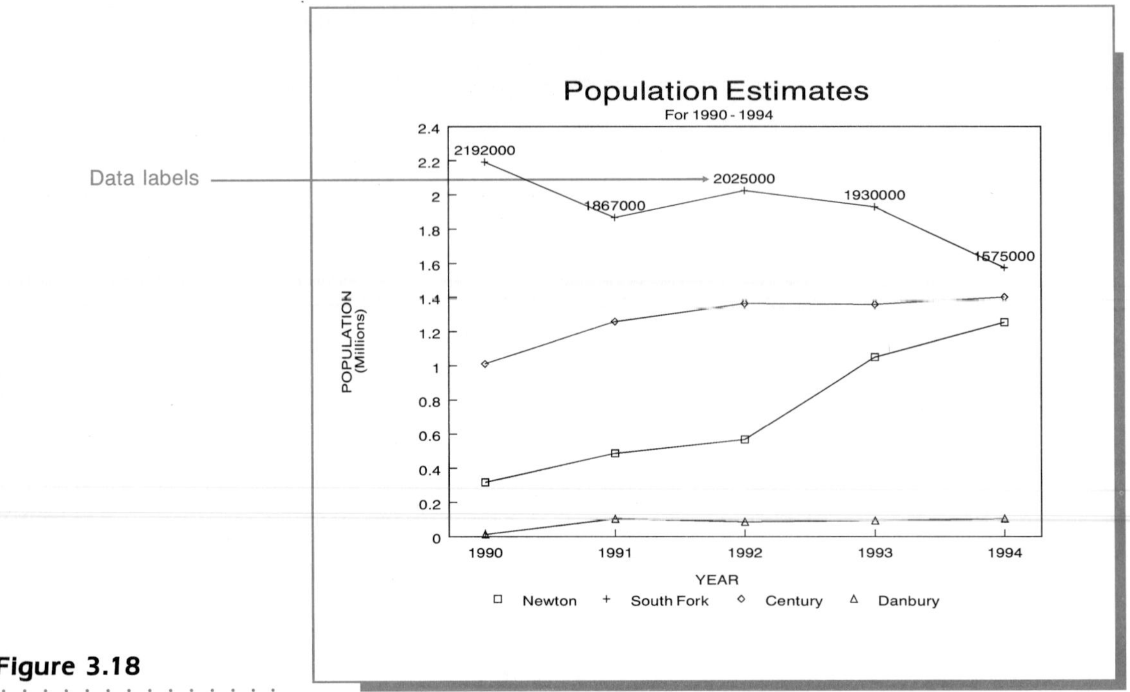

Figure 3.18

The data labels are displayed in the graph above the data points for South Fork.

Nancy feels that a data label over each data point for the four cities may clutter the graph too much. So instead, she decides to add grid lines to try to improve the readability of the graph.

Using Grids

The Grid option allows you to specify horizontal lines, vertical lines, or both to form a **grid** within the graph. A grid makes it easier to read the value of a data point or the height of a bar.

Press SPACEBAR to return to the Graph menu and issue the following command sequence:

Options **G**rid **H**orizontal **Q**uit

To view the graph, select:

View

Your screen should look similar to Figure 3.19.

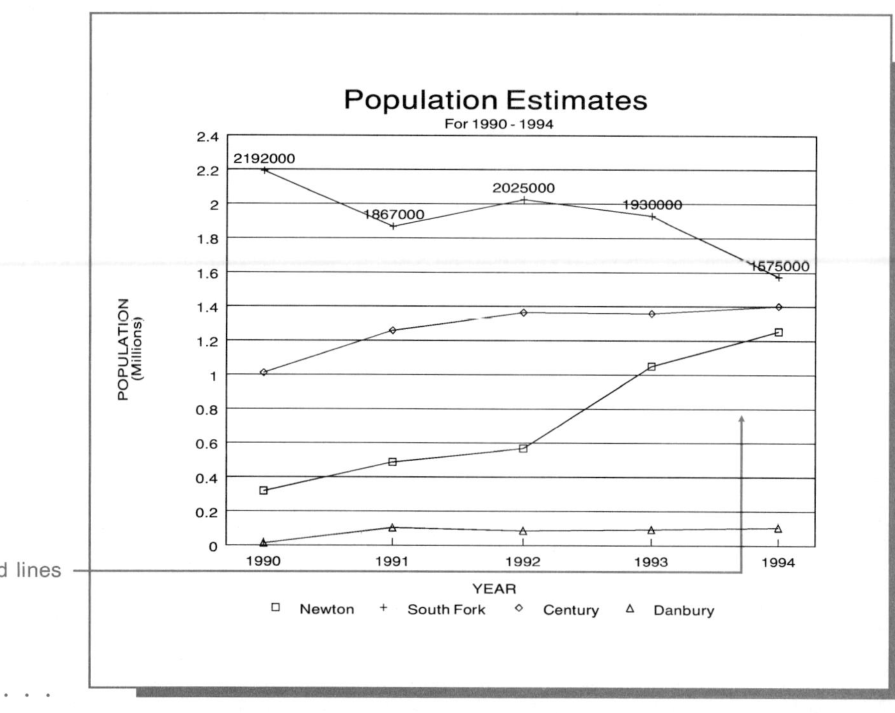

Figure 3.19

It is now easier to tell what the population is at each point on the graph. Use grids and data labels sparingly because they can sometimes clutter a graph, making it more difficult to read.

Cancelling Graph Settings

After looking at the graph, Nancy decides to clear the data labels for South Fork from the graph. To do this, the data range displaying the data label (B) must be cleared, or reset, using the Graph Reset command.

Press SPACEBAR to return to the Graph menu and then select

Reset

The Reset menu lets you cancel all the current graph settings (Graph), individual data ranges (X and A–F), all data ranges (Ranges), or all graph options (Options).

To cancel the South Fork data range (B) and return to the Graph menu, select

B Quit

The Graph settings sheet shows you that the B data range is no longer defined, and the corresponding data-label range is also cleared.

Be very careful when using the Reset command that you select the correct submenu command. Otherwise, you can inadvertently cancel many graph settings that are time consuming to respecify.

Now issue the following command sequence to respecify the South Fork data range:

B B7..F7 ↵

To view the graph, select:

View

Your screen should look similar to Figure 3.20.

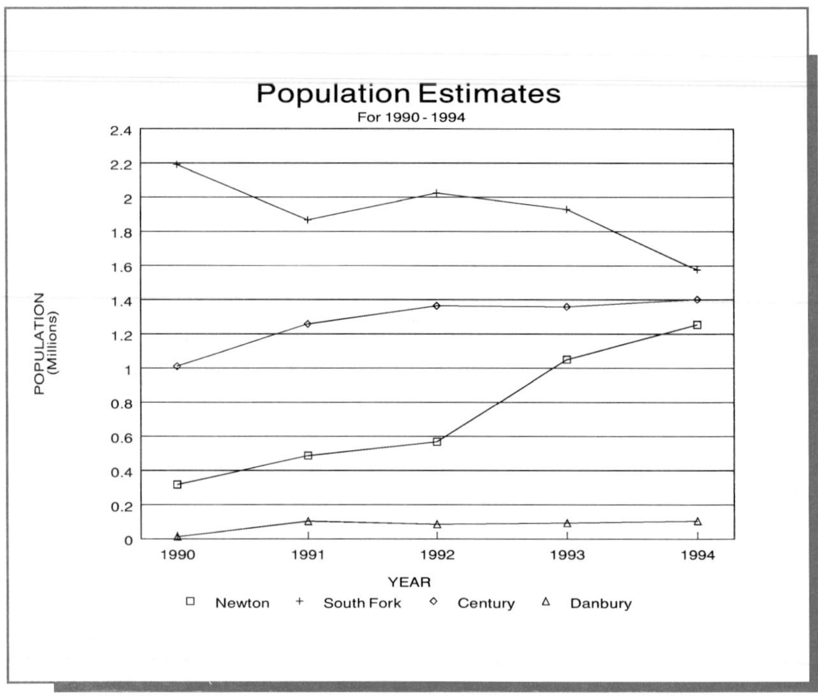

Figure 3.20

This looks better, but Nancy feels the horizontal grid lines also detract from the graph. To clear the horizontal grid from the graph, press any key to return to the Graph menu and then issue the following command sequence:

Options **G**rid **C**lear **Q**uit

To view the graph, select:

View

The graph is now displayed without grid lines.

Printing the Graph

Note To print a graph using the following procedure, you must have loaded the GRAPHICS.COM file as directed at the beginning of this lab. If you were unable to locate the GRAPHICS.COM file, skip to the section ''Saving Current Graph Settings.''

To identify this graph as the one you created, delete the current second title and replace it with your first and last name, for example: By Linda O'Leary. View the line graph.

To print the displayed graph,

Press: SHIFT-PRTSC

Note If your printer does not respond by printing the graph, it is possible that your computer cannot use GRAPHICS.COM to print graphs.

In the next lab, you will learn how to use the PrintGraph program to print your graphs. However, using SHIFT-PRTSC is a quick way to print a copy of a displayed graph.

Saving Current Graph Settings

To save the current graph in the worksheet so you can use it again, all you need to do is save the worksheet. The current graph settings will be saved as well. The next time you retrieve the file, you can view the graph again.

Press SPACEBAR to clear the graph. To return to READY mode, select:

Quit

Save this worksheet and the graph settings in a new file by issuing the following command sequence:

/ **F**ile **S**ave **POPULATG** ↵

Now erase the worksheet from the screen and the computer's memory by issuing the following command sequence:

/ **W**orksheet **E**rase **Y**es

Always save your worksheet before you use the Erase command or you will lose your work.

On your screen, you now should have a blank worksheet that has no current graph settings. Confirm this by issuing the following command:

/ **G**raph **V**iew

The computer should beep and display a blank screen, indicating that the current worksheet has no graph settings.

Return to the Graph settings sheet by pressing SPACEBAR. Then return to READY mode by selecting:

Quit

Retrieve the file POPULATG.

Now try viewing the graph by issuing the following command sequence:

/ **G**raph **V**iew

Your line graph is displayed on your screen just the way you left it.

In this lab, you saved only one graph in the worksheet file. In the next lab, you will learn how to save more than one graph in a single worksheet file.

Exit from 1-2-3.

Glossary of Key Terms

Data labels The labels attached to data points on a graph with the / **G**raph **O**ptions **D**ata-Labels command.

Graph menu The selection of menu items displayed when / **G**raph is selected.

Grid The horizontal, vertical, or intersecting lines that can be specified in a graph with the / **G**raph **O**ptions **G**rid command.

Legends The patterns and symbols used in a graph and the text that defines them.

Line graph A graph that represents numeric data as a set of points along a line.

Scale indicator A label automatically placed along the Y axis by 1-2-3 to describe the numerical scale of the Y axis.

Title A descriptive label placed at the top of a graph or along the X or Y axes.

X axis The horizontal boundary of a graph.

Y axis The vertical boundary of a graph.

Practice Problems

1. Matching

1. /G	______	a. displays values next to the corresponding point on a graph
2. Type	______	b. saves a worksheet, including the current graph settings
3. A,B,C,D,E,F	______	c. erases a data range
4. View	______	d. displays symbols and descriptive labels
5. Title	______	e. adds horizontal or vertical reference lines to the graph
6. Legend	______	f. accesses the Graph menu
7. Data label	______	g. determines the kind of graph
8. Grid	______	h. displays the graph on the screen
9. Reset	______	i. labels and describes a graph
10. /FS	______	j. defines the data range to be graphed

2. The following table presents income by age and education, as published in a recent journal:

	Age				
	25	35	45	55	65
All adults	22000	32000	37500	37000	28000
College graduates	29000	40000	51000	57000	51000

Load GRAPHICS.COM. Display this data as a line graph by completing the following steps:

a. Create a worksheet file of this data. Put your name in cell A1 and the date in cell A2.

b. Specify a line graph.

c. Set the X axis as age.

d. Specify the income data for all adults and college graduates as the two data ranges.

e. Enter a first title line: Income by Age and Education.

f. Enter a second title line that displays your name and the current date.

g. Enter an X-axis title line: Age.

h. Enter a Y-axis title line: Income.

i. Create a legend to identify the two groups of data.

j. Display the graph and print the graph using SHIFT-PRTSC.

k. Save this worksheet with the current graph settings as INCOME. Print the worksheet.

3. The following data, from the Bureau of Labor Statistics, presents statistics for mothers in the workforce. Since 1960, the number of mothers in the workforce has increased dramatically. Show these data in the form of a line graph.

Ages of Children	Mothers in the Workforce (in Millions)		
	1960	1970	1985
Under 3	1.6	2.3	4.6
3–5	1.3	2.3	3.6
6–17	5.1	7.6	11.8

You will need to load GRAPHICS.COM and then complete the following steps:

a. Create a worksheet file of these data. Put your name in cell A1 and the date in cell A2.

b. Specify a line graph.

c. Set the X axis as the years 1960, 1970, and 1985.

d. Specify the number of mothers in the workforce by ages of children as the three data ranges.

e. Enter a first title line: Mothers in the Workforce Since 1960.

f. Enter a second title line that displays your name and the current date.

g. Enter an X-axis title line: Years.

h. Enter a Y-axis title line: Millions.

i. Create a legend to identify the three groups of data.

j. Add horizontal grid lines.

k. Display the graph and print the graph using SHIFT-PRTSC.

l. Save this worksheet with the current graph settings as MOTHERS. Print the worksheet.

4. To complete this problem, you first must have built the worksheet as specified in Practice Problem 4 of Lab 2. If you have completed that problem, load GRAPHICS.COM, retrieve the file SLOAN1, and complete the following steps:

   a. Specify a line graph.

   b. Set the X axis to display the months January through June.

   c. Specify the Revenues, Total Expenses, and Net values as the three data ranges.

   d. Enter the first title line: Six-Month Budget for Sloan Research.

   e. Enter a second title line that displays your name and the current date.

   f. Enter the X-axis title line: Months.

   g. Enter the Y-axis title line: Dollars.

   h. Create a legend to identify the three groups of data.

   i. Display the graph and print the graph using SHIFT-PRTSC.

   j. Save the worksheet with the current graph settings as SLOAN1.

5. To complete this problem, you first must have built the worksheet as specified in Practice Problem 5 of Lab 2. If you have completed that problem, load GRAPHICS.COM and retrieve the file PERSONAL. Complete the following steps:

   a. Specify a line graph.

   b. Set the X axis to display the months January through June.

   c. Specify any three of the expenses as data ranges A, B, and C. Specify Total Expenses and Balance as data ranges D and E.

d. Enter an appropriate first title line.

e. Enter a second title line that displays your name and the current date.

f. Enter appropriate X-axis and Y-axis title lines.

g. Create appropriate legends to identify the five groups of data.

h. Display the graph and print the graph using SHIFT-PRTSC.

i. Save the worksheet with the current graph settings as PERSONAL.

4

Creating and Printing Graphs

Objectives

In Lab 4, you will learn how to:

- Use the Access system
- Name and recall graph settings
- Create bar, stacked bar, and XY graphs
- Create pie and exploded pie charts
- Use the Data Fill command
- Save graphs
- Print graphs

Case Study

Carl Conrad has been on a strict low-calorie diet for the past few weeks. This morning, however, Carl woke up very hungry and splurged on breakfast. Along with what his diet allows for breakfast, Carl had two pieces of bacon, two eggs, two links of sausage, two waffles, and a roll.

As soon as he finished his last bite, Carl felt guilty. He immediately went to his calorie converter and exercise guide to see what he could do to burn off those extra calories. Table 4.1 shows how many minutes of each exercise would be required to burn off Carl's breakfast.

Table 4.1

		Type of Exercise			
Food	Calories	Run	Swim	Bike	Walk
Bacon (2)	85	6	10	13	22
Eggs (2)	235	18	28	36	60
Sausage (2)	123	9	15	19	32
Waffles (2)	420	32	52	64	110
Roll (1)	260	20	32	40	68
Totals:	1123	85	137	172	292

For example, to burn off the 85 calories from the two strips of bacon, Carl would have to run 6 minutes, swim 10 minutes, bike 13 minutes, or walk 22 minutes. To burn off the entire 1123 extra calories, Carl would have to run for 85 minutes, swim for 137 minutes, bike for 172 minutes, or walk for 292 minutes.

Using the Access System

In this lab, you will use 1-2-3 to create graphs and PrintGraph to print graphs. To make it easier to switch between 1-2-3 and PrintGraph, you will begin this lab by using the Access system. To do this with a two-disk system and with the System disk in drive A, at the A> prompt,

Type: **LOTUS**
Press: 

If you have a hard-disk system, instead of typing "1-2-3" at your system prompt,

Type: **LOTUS**
Press: ↵

Your screen should be similar to Figure 4.1.

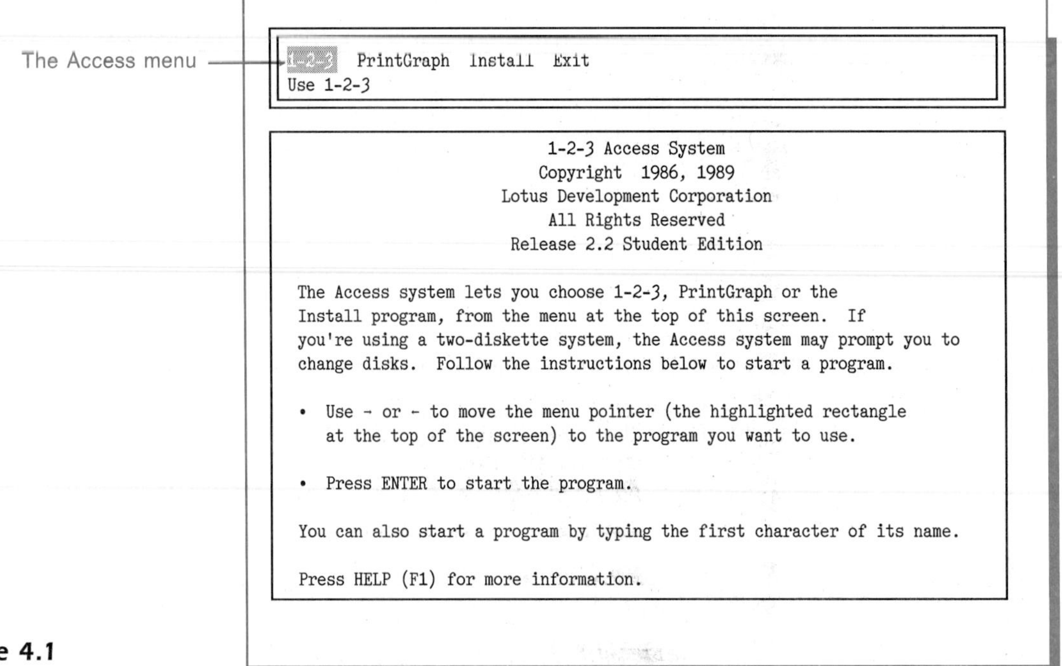

The Access menu
1-2-3 PrintGraph Install Exit
Use 1-2-3
1-2-3 Access System
Copyright 1986, 1989
Lotus Development Corporation
All Rights Reserved
Release 2.2 Student Edition
The Access system lets you choose 1-2-3, PrintGraph or the Install program, from the menu at the top of this screen. If you're using a two-diskette system, the Access system may prompt you to change disks. Follow the instructions below to start a program.
• Use → or ← to move the menu pointer (the highlighted rectangle at the top of the screen) to the program you want to use.
• Press ENTER to start the program.
You can also start a program by typing the first character of its name.
Press HELP (F1) for more information.

Figure 4.1

The Access menu appears at the top of the screen. A description of the highlighted command appears on the second line. Read the information below the menu about how to use the Access system. To load 1-2-3, with the highlight over 1-2-3,

Press: ↵

The 1-2-3 program is loaded in the usual manner.

Creating a Bar Graph

Carl has created a worksheet that contains the calorie data from Table 4.1. To see this worksheet, retrieve the file CALORIES.WK1.

Your screen should look similar to Figure 4.2.

```
A1:                                                              READY

   A     B       C        D        E        F        G        H
1
2                    CALORIE BURN-OFF
3
4        FOOD:   CALORIES:   TYPE OF EXERCISE:
5                             Run     Swim     Bike     Walk
6        Bacon        85        6       10       13       22
7        Eggs        235       18       28       36       60
8        Sausage     123        9       15       19       32
9        Waffles     420       32       52       64      110
10       Roll        260       20       32       40       68
11       ----------------------------------------------------
12       Totals:    1123       85      137      172      292
13       ====================================================
14
```

Figure 4.2

Each food that Carl had for breakfast is listed in column B. The calorie content of each food is listed in column C. Columns D through G list the number of minutes of each type of exercise required to burn off the calories shown in column C.

In Lab 3, you learned about line graphs. There are four other types of graphs: bar, stacked bar, XY, and pie. Bar and stacked bar graphs use data ranges in the same way line graphs do. However, a **bar graph** shows numeric data as a set of evenly spaced bars, each of which represents a value in the range that you are graphing.

The data in Carl's worksheet compare the length of time required by four different forms of exercise to burn off the calories in five different foods. You could create a line graph using this data, but a bar graph would show the difference in exercise time required to burn off the calories for each food more clearly.

To create a bar graph of this data, begin by defining the Type of graph as follows:

/ **G**raph **T**ype **B**ar

Using the Group Command

Next you need to specify the data ranges. The X data range will display the four exercise categories, Run, Swim, Bike, and Walk, as the x-axis labels. The X data range is D5 through G5. The data ranges for the numeric data to be graphed are the number of minutes of each type of exercise needed to burn off the calories for each type of food consumed. The data are located in cells D6 through G10.

1-2-3 has a quick way to define the data range settings for a graph if the data in the worksheet are located in consecutive columns or rows. Since the X data range and the A through E data ranges are in the worksheet range D5 through G10, we can use the Graph Group command to quickly define the graph data ranges. Select:

Group

In response to the prompt to enter the group range, continue the command sequence by highlighting the range in POINT mode as

D5..G10

1-2-3 will automatically divide the group range into all the data ranges for the graph beginning with the X data range and proceeding through the A through E ranges.

Press: ↵

The next menu displays the choices Columnwise or Rowwise. This tells 1-2-3 whether to divide the ranges by columns or rows. Since we want each row of the graph to be a data range for the graph, select:

Rowwise

The X and A through E data ranges have been specified and are displayed in the Graph settings sheet.

To view the graph, select:

View

Your screen should be similar to Figure 4.3.

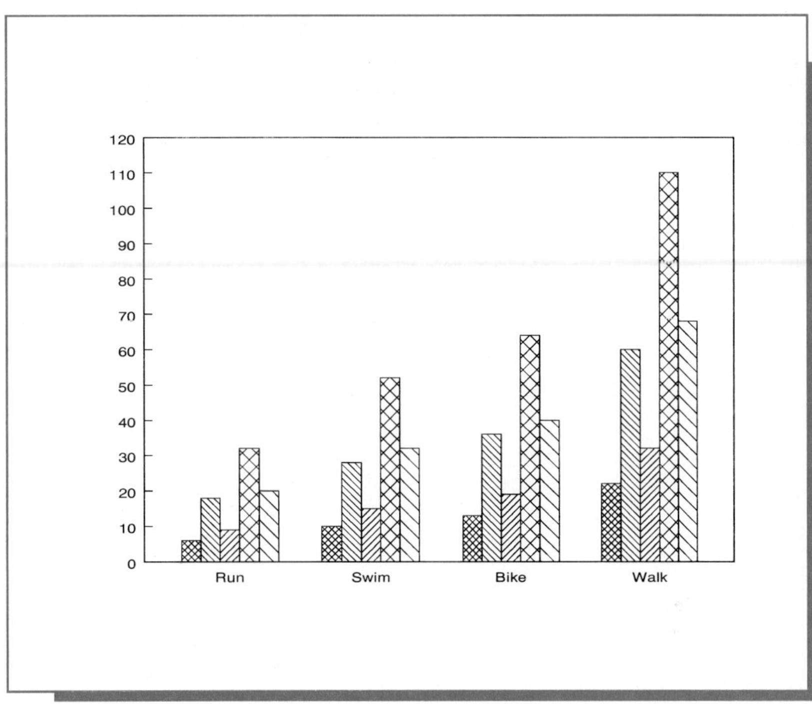

Figure 4.3

The bar graph is displayed. Using the Group command to specify the data ranges can save a lot of time; however, the worksheet must be set up so that the X and A through F data ranges are in a continuous range.

Each group of bars shows how long that exercise would have to be performed to burn off the calories in each food. For example, the first group of bars shows how many minutes Carl would have to run to burn off each food.

The bars in the graph contain five different **hatch patterns** or designs to identify the five different food categories.

If you have a color monitor and want to view the graph in color, press SPACEBAR to clear the graph and then issue the following command sequence:

Options **C**olor **Q**uit **V**iew

You can switch to and from color by using the Options Color command and the Options B&W command. In color, each bar is filled with a solid color. In black and white, each bar contains a different hatch pattern.

Press SPACEBAR to clear the graph and to return to the Graph menu.

To complete the graph, select **O**ptions to add the following:

Legends for the A through E data ranges

First title:	CALORIE BURN-OFF
Second title:	By [Your Name]
X-axis title:	TYPE OF EXERCISE
Y-axis title:	MINUTES

When you have finished, view the graph. Your screen should be similar to Figure 4.4.

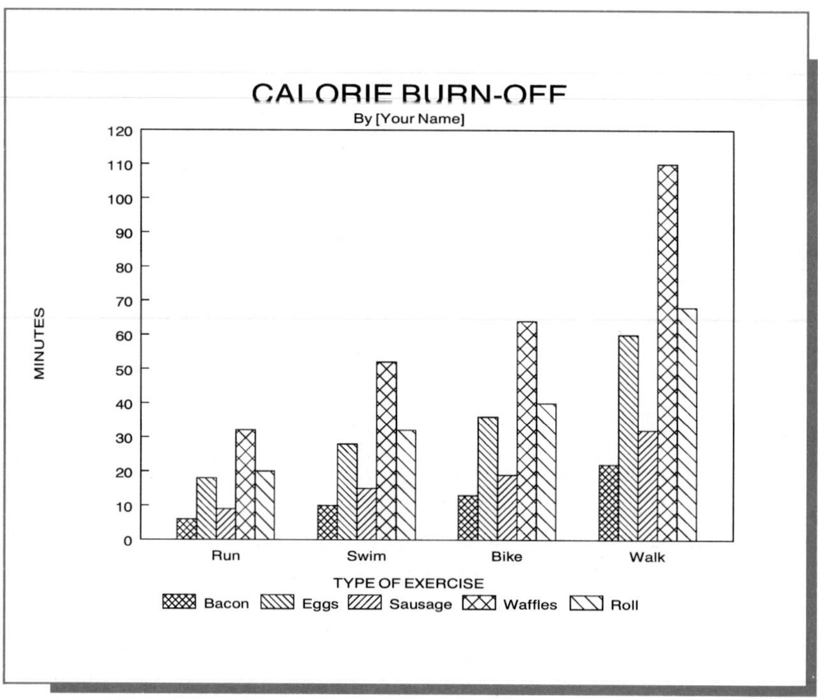

Figure 4.4

Press SPACEBAR to clear the graph and to return to the Graph menu.

Saving Graphs for Printing

To print your graph using the Lotus 1-2-3 PrintGraph program, you must first save the graph settings in a special file. This file is called a **graph file** and has a file extension of .PIC.

To save the current graph settings for printing, you use the Graph Save command. However, if you do not have a color printer and you are viewing your graph in color, you must reset the graph to B&W before you save the graph settings for printing. If you do not reset the graph to B&W, the printed graph will typically appear as solid bars. To reset the graph to B&W, issue the following command sequence:

Options **B**&W **Q**uit

To save the graph for printing, issue the following command sequence:

Save **BAR** ↵

A description of the graph is saved on your data disk in a file called BAR.PIC. 1-2-3 automatically adds the .PIC extension to any graph you save for printing.

A graph filename can have no more than eight characters and must follow the same naming conventions as other 1-2-3 files.

To print the bar graph now, you would leave 1-2-3 and enter the PrintGraph program. Before you do that, let's explore some other features of the Graph command.

Naming Graphs

Carl would like to create another graph using the worksheet data. To create more than one graph in a worksheet, each graph needs to be named. When you name a graph, the graph's specifications are stored with the graph's name. You can view and modify the graph simply by recalling the name of the graph. If the current graph settings are not named, they will be deleted as you specify new graph settings. If you want the **named graph** to display in color, you will have to turn on the color option again before naming the graph.

A graph name can be up to fifteen characters long and should be descriptive of the graph. The name cannot contain spaces, commas, semicolons, or the characters +, −, /, $, >, <, @, *, or #. It can be entered using either uppercase or lowercase characters; 1-2-3 will always display the graph name in uppercase. To save the current graph settings under the name BAR, issue the following command sequence:

Name **C**reate **BAR** ↵

The bar graph settings are named and stored in the computer's memory for later recall. The named graphs are not saved to the disk with the worksheet file until the worksheet is saved.

To demonstrate how to recall named graphs, you will reset, or clear, the current graph settings and then recall the named graph BAR. First, to erase the current graph settings, use the Reset command and then view the current graph as follows:

Reset **G**raph **V**iew

1-2-3 beeps and displays a blank screen. This means that there are no current graph settings in memory. Now, to recall the named graph BAR, press SPACEBAR and issue the following command sequence:

Name **U**se **BAR** (↵)

The bar graph should be displayed on your screen.

Naming graphs is an important feature because it allows you to have more than one set of graph settings in a single worksheet.

It is perfectly acceptable to name the graph specifications and then use the same name to save the graph for printing. The graph settings will be stored in the worksheet with the name BAR, and the graph description will be saved on the disk as BAR.PIC for printing.

Understanding the difference between naming graphs, saving graphs, and saving files is important:

- / **G**raph **N**ame **C**reate names a graph so that it can be recalled later and displayed on your screen.
- / **G**raph **S**ave creates a new file on your data disk with a .PIC extension for printing with the PrintGraph program.
- / **F**ile **S**ave creates a worksheet file with a .WK1 extension. The worksheet file includes all values and labels, along with all named graph settings and current graph settings.

Changing the Graph Type

Carl is interested in how much time it would take to burn off his entire breakfast, not just the waffles or the sausage. To graph this, he can change the current bar graph to a stacked bar graph simply by changing the graph type.

A **stacked bar graph** compares totals as well as individual values. Each part of a stacked bar graph represents a value in one of the data ranges.

Press SPACEBAR to clear the graph and return to the Graph menu.

Change the graph type to stacked bar and view it by issuing the following command sequence:

Type **S**tack-Bar **V**iew

Your screen should look similar to Figure 4.5.

Figure 4.5

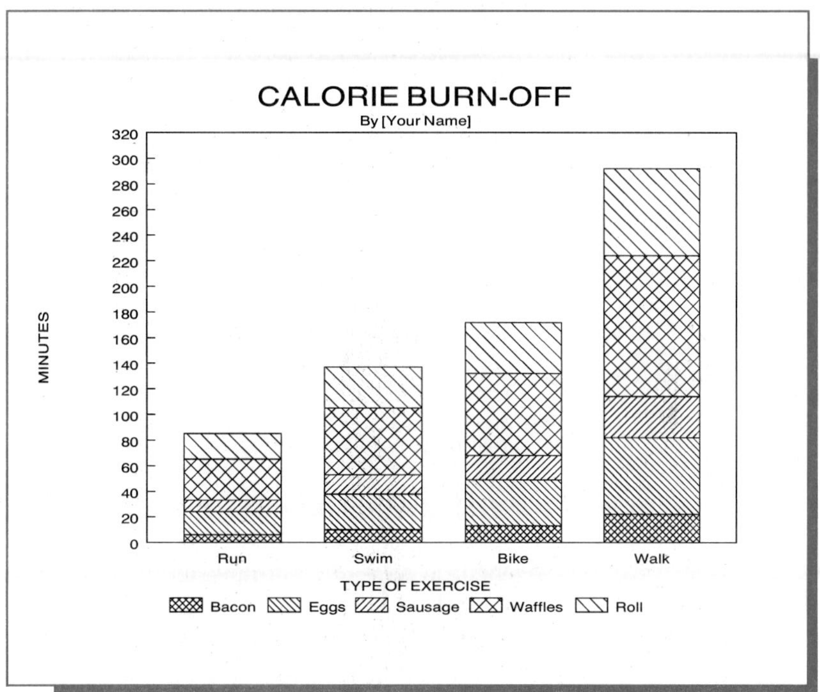

In this graph, the amount of time it would take to burn off each food consumed is stacked one on top of the other in a single bar. The parts of the bar are differentiated by various hatch patterns or colors (if you have a color monitor and use the Options Color command). Each bar represents the total amount of time required to burn off the extra calories from Carl's breakfast for each type of exercise.

To burn off the calories from his breakfast, it will take Carl 292 minutes of walking but less than 90 minutes of running.

Press SPACEBAR to return to the Graph menu. Remember to turn off the color option before you save the graph as a .PIC file. Name the graph settings STACKED. Save the graph for printing as STACKED.PIC.

Creating a Pie Chart

Carl would now like to see what part of the total calories of his breakfast is made up of each of the foods he ate. The best graph for this purpose is a pie chart.

A **pie chart** shows the relationship between a whole and its parts. In a pie chart, each value in a range is a slice of the pie, and the size of each slice corresponds to a percentage of the total.

Graph settings for pie charts are different from line or bar graphs. Before you can create a pie chart, you need to reset the current graph settings.

Issue the following command sequence:

Reset **G**raph

Then specify a pie chart by issuing the following command sequence:

Type **P**ie

In pie charts you use the X data range to label the slices of the pie and the A data range to specify the numeric data to be graphed. The labels for the slices are located in cells B6 through B10. The A data range is the number of calories for each food located in cells C6 through C10. Since the data for this graph is located in a continuous range, you can use the Group command to define the data ranges. To do this, issue the following command sequence:

Group **B6..C10** ↵

To use the columns of data for the graph ranges, select:

Columnwise

To view the pie chart, select:

View

Your screen should look similar to Figure 4.6.

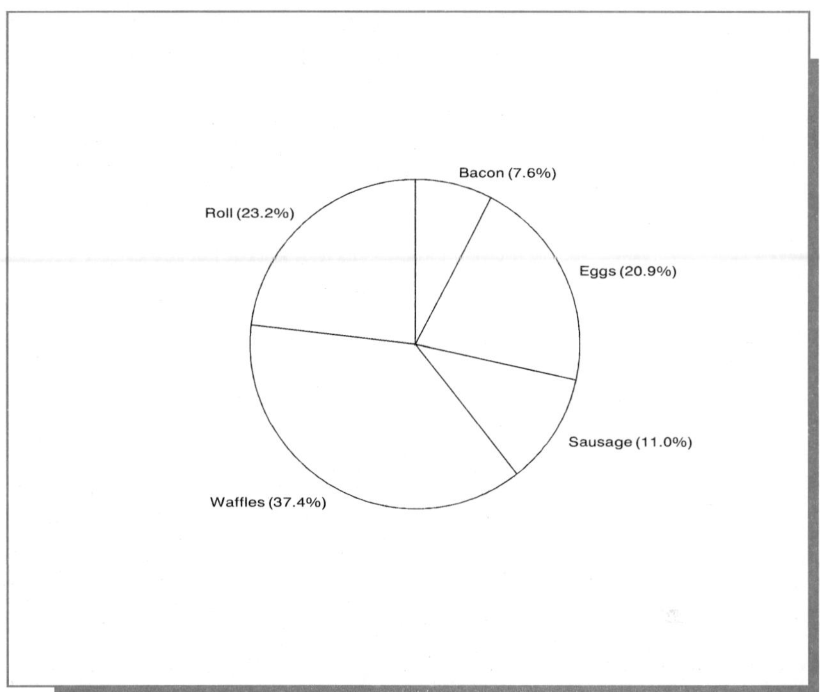

Figure 4.6

Each food item, defined in the X range, labels each slice of the pie. The percentage for each food as a caloric portion of the total breakfast is automatically calculated by 1-2-3; for example, 7.6 percent of the total calories consumed came from the bacon.

Note If you have a color monitor and the graph on your screen is not in color, you may want to use the Options Color command.

Shading the Pie Chart

To further differentiate the pie's slices, you can add shading (color or hatch patterns) to the pie chart. There are eight different hatch patterns. To assign a hatch pattern or color to each of the five slices of the pie, you will fill a worksheet column with the values 1 to 5. The **shading values** are specified as the B data range and can be any number from 1 to 8. Shading values can appear almost anywhere in the worksheet, as long as the cells can be defined in a single range.

Press SPACEBAR to clear the graph and then leave the Graph menu by selecting:

Quit

We will enter the shading values in column A of the worksheet next to the worksheet labels.

Move to: A6

Rather than typing in each number, you can use the Data Fill command to fill the column with a sequence of numbers. To do this, select:

/ **D**ata **F**ill

To specify the range of cells to fill, continue the command sequence as follows:

A6..A10 ↵

To enter the number 1 as the **start value** or the first value 1-2-3 enters in the range,

Type: **1**
Press: ↵

To accept the number 1 as the **step value** or the increment between each of the values,

Press: ↵

The **stop value** is the number 1-2-3 uses as the upper limit for the sequence. Since the range contains only five cells, it will reach the end of the range before the default stop value (8191). You could enter the number 5, or simply accept the default. To accept the default,

Press: ↵

Your screen should look similar to Figure 4.7.

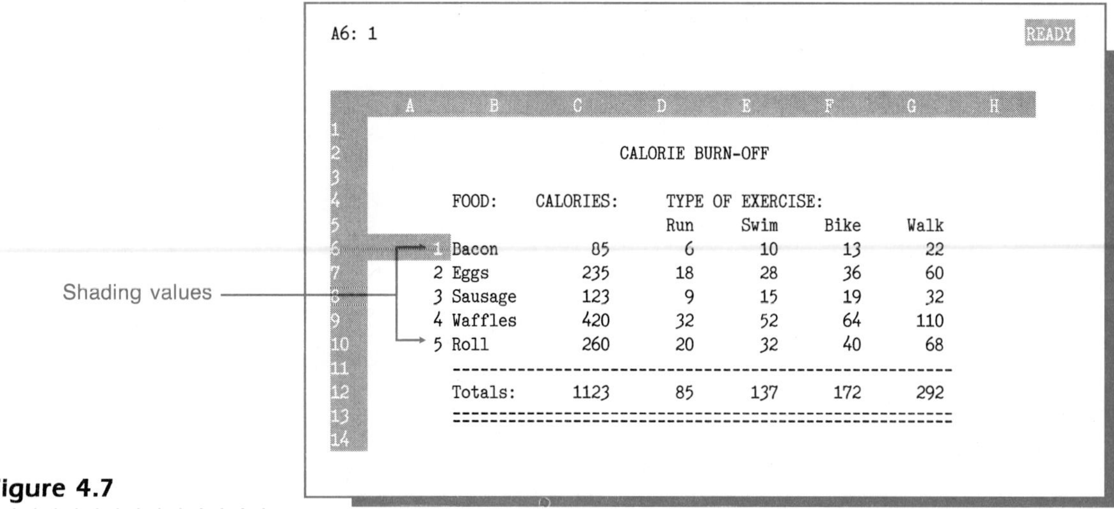

Figure 4.7

The numbers 1 through 5 are entered in the specified range of cells. To define these values as the B data range, issue the following command sequence:

/ **Graph B A6..A10** ↵

To view the graph, select:

View

Your screen should look similar to Figure 4.8.

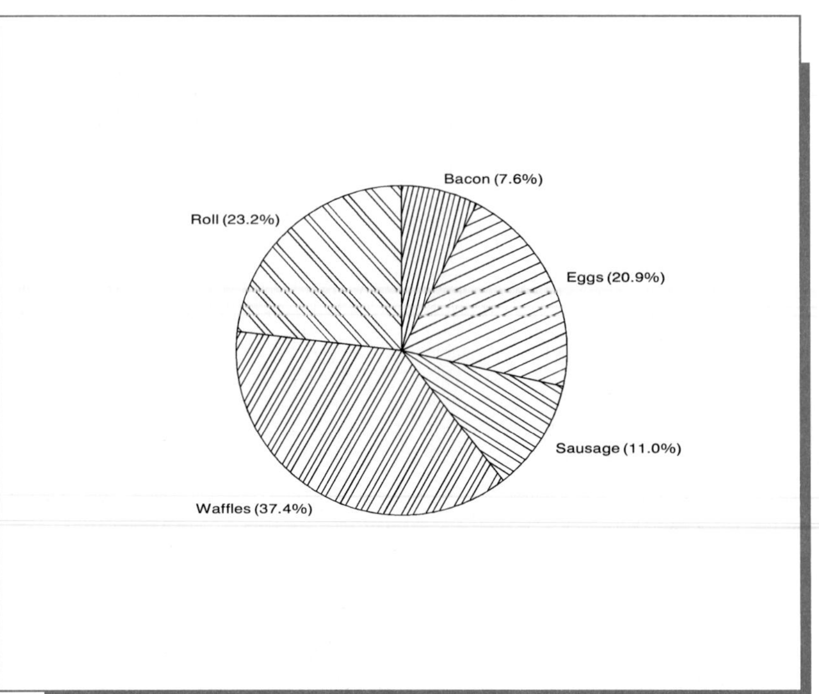

Figure 4.8

The shading values specified in the B range determine the shading for each slice of the pie. If you changed the values in the worksheet, the shading would change correspondingly.

Creating an Exploded Pie Chart

A slice or several slices of the pie can be further emphasized by exploding the slice(s) from the pie. To do this, you add 100 to the value in the B data range of the slice(s) to be exploded.

To return to READY mode, press SPACEBAR to clear the graph. Then, to leave the Graph menu, select:

Quit

To explode the ''Roll'' slice from the pie,

Move to: A10
Type: **105**
Press: ↵

The last digit (in this case, 5) determines the shading for the exploded slice.

You can display the current graph quickly from READY mode by using the Graph function key, F10, rather than / **G**raph **V**iew.

To view the graph,

Press: F10

Your screen should now look similar to Figure 4.9.

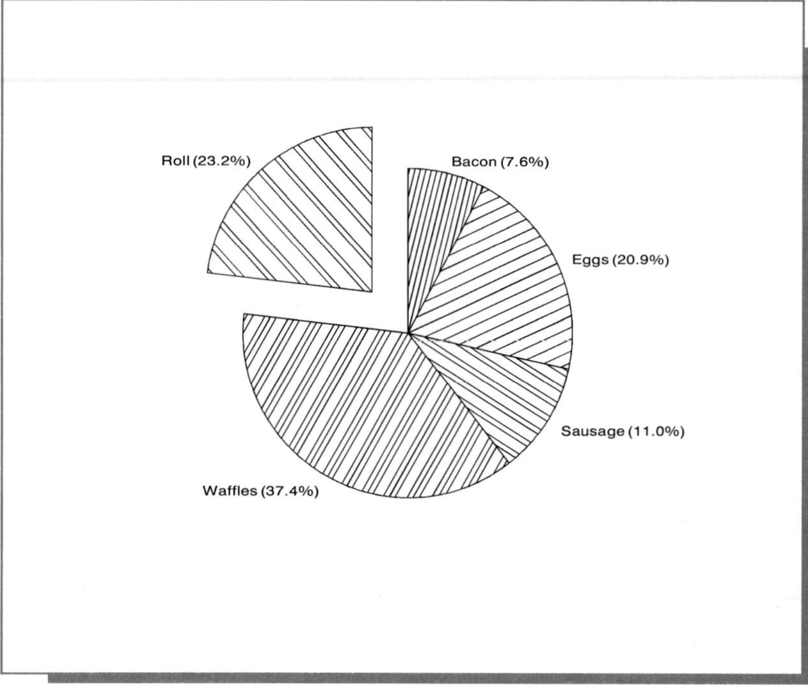

Figure 4.9

The slice of the pie chart representing ''Roll'' is exploded.

Complete the pie chart as follows:

- Set the first graph title: CALORIE CONTENT.
- Enter your name as the second title line.
- View the graph.
- Name the graph: PIE.
- Save the graph: PIE.PIC.

Using What-if Graphing

Now Carl would like to see the effect that eating only one waffle would have had on his total food percentages. To do this, you will use what-if graphing, which shows how changes in the worksheet data affect graphs using those data. To change the worksheet, return to READY mode by selecting:

Quit

To reflect this change, you need to halve the number of calories and exercise time required:

Move to: C9
Type: **210**
Move to: D9
Type: **16**
Move to: E9
Type: **26**
Move to: F9
Type: **32**
Move to: G9
Type: **55**
Press: ↵

Your screen should look similar to Figure 4.10.

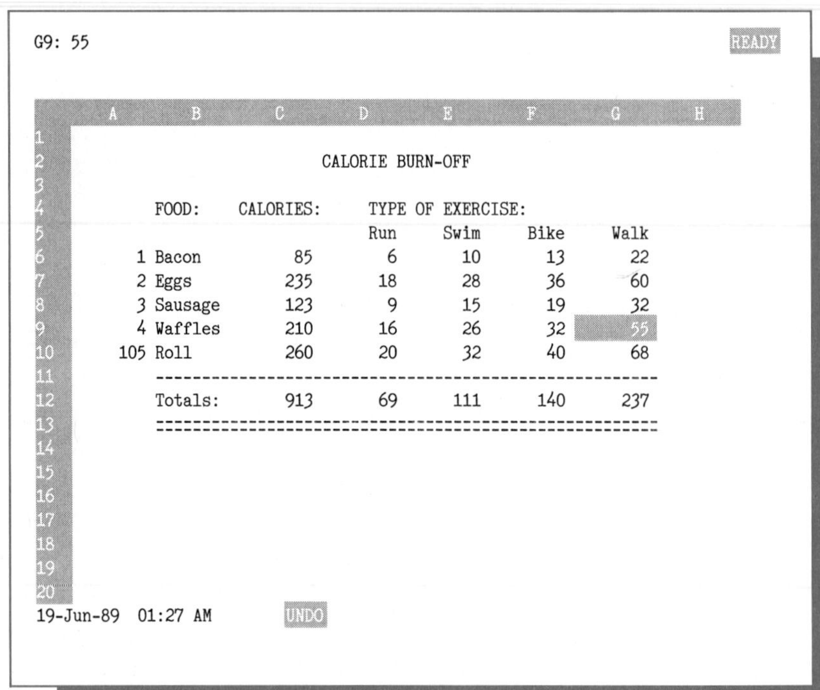
G9: 55 READY

	FOOD:	CALORIES:	TYPE OF EXERCISE:			
			Run	Swim	Bike	Walk
1	Bacon	85	6	10	13	22
2	Eggs	235	18	28	36	60
3	Sausage	123	9	15	19	32
4	Waffles	210	16	26	32	55
105	Roll	260	20	32	40	68
	Totals:	913	69	111	140	237

CALORIE BURN-OFF

19-Jun-89 01:27 AM UNDO

Figure 4.10

To view the pie chart to see how this change has affected the relative percentages of each food,

Press: F10

Your screen should look similar to Figure 4.11.

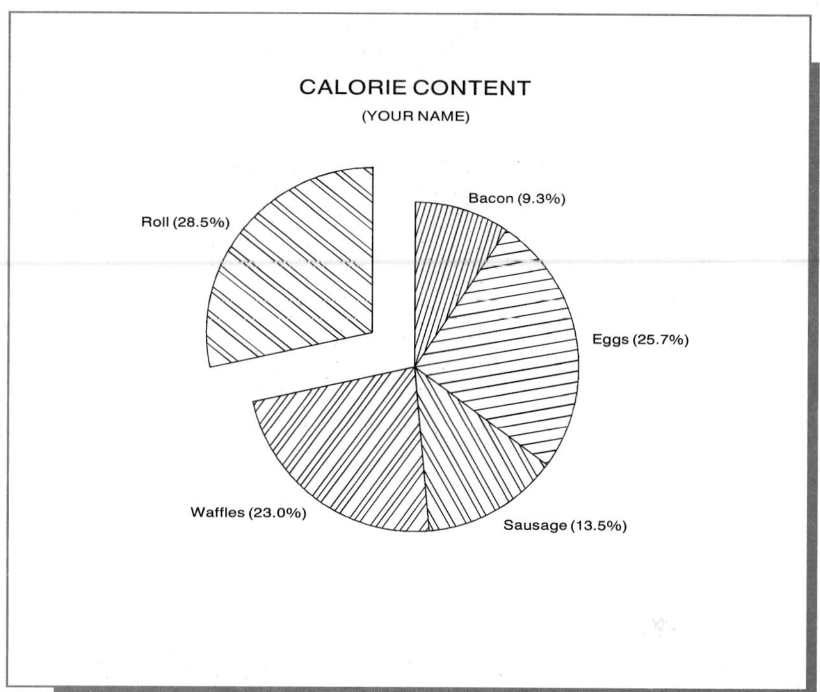

Figure 4.11

One waffle takes up a much smaller percentage of Carl's total caloric intake. Changes in the worksheet data are immediately reflected in the graphs that use those data. Using the Graph function key, F10, allows you to see the results of changes in your data quickly.

Clear the graph by pressing SPACEBAR and reset all graph settings by issuing the following command:

/ **G**raph **R**eset **G**raph

Creating an XY Graph

Carl would like to see the relationship between exercise time and calorie burn-off. The best graph for this is an XY graph.

XY graphs, also called **scatter charts**, typically are used to show the relationships between two variables by plotting pairs of values. One of the pairs is defined in the X range, and the others are defined in one of the remaining data ranges.

The graph will plot the number of calories on the X axis and the number of minutes needed to burn off those calories on the Y axis.

Specify an XY graph by issuing the following command sequence:

Type **XY**

The X data range is used to define the values to be plotted along the X axis. The A data range is used to set the values you want to be plotted on the Y axis in your first line, or on one single line.

Now, using the Group command, define the X range as the number of calories for each food (C6..C10) and the Y axis as the number of minutes of exercise for running (D6..D10).

To view the graph, select:

View

Your screen should look similar to Figure 4.12.

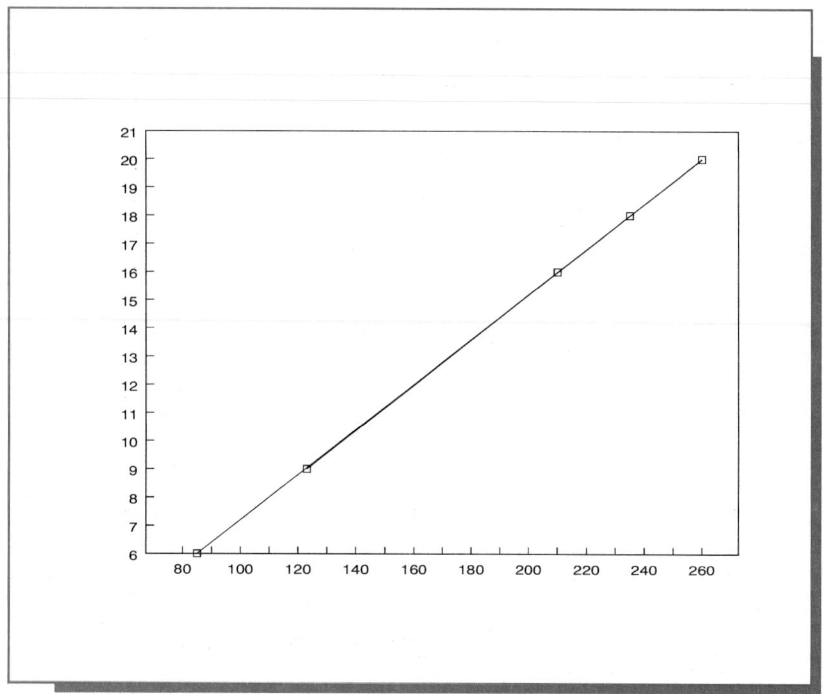

Figure 4.12

The X-axis scale shows the number of calories and the Y-axis scale displays the number of minutes of running. The graph line shows the relationship between the number of minutes of exercise for running and the number of calories burned off. As the number of calories increases, the number of minutes of running needed to burn them off increases.

Press SPACEBAR to return to the Graph menu.

Now add the values for the other forms of exercise so you can see how they compare with one another. To define the number of minutes of exercise for swimming, biking, and walking, expand your group range to C6..G10.

To view the graph again, select:

View

Your screen should look similar to Figure 4.13.

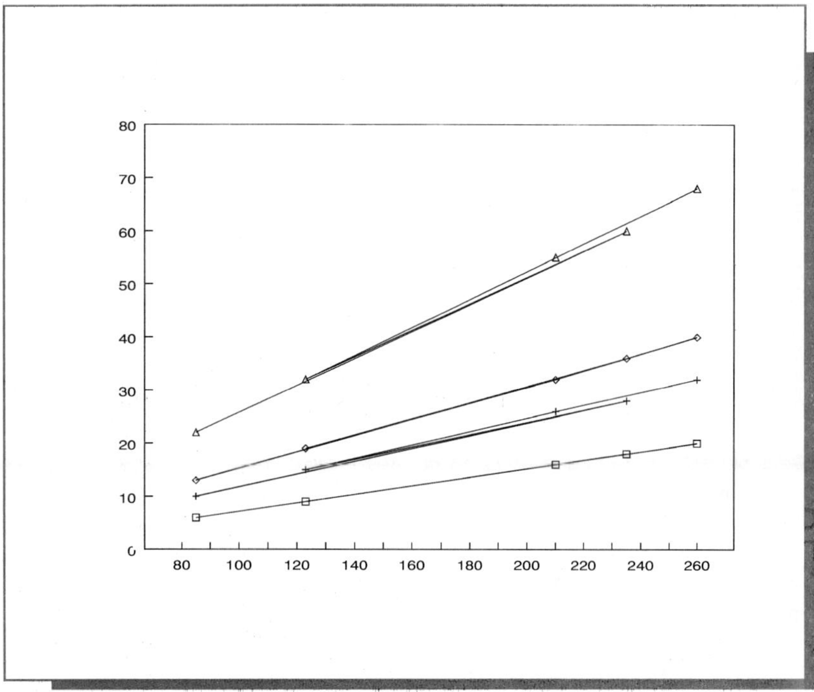

Figure 4.13

The X- and Y-axis scales reflect the range of values in the data ranges. Each line shows the relationship between the number of calories and minutes of exercise for each type of exercise.

Press SPACEBAR to clear the graph.

Complete the XY graph as follows:

- Set the first graph title: EXERCISE EFFICIENCY.
- Enter your name as the second graph title.
- Set the X-axis graph title: Number of Calories.

- Set the Y-axis graph title: Minutes of Exercise.
- Set legends for the four exercises: Run, Swim, Bike, and Walk.
- View the graph.

Your screen should look similar to Figure 4.14.

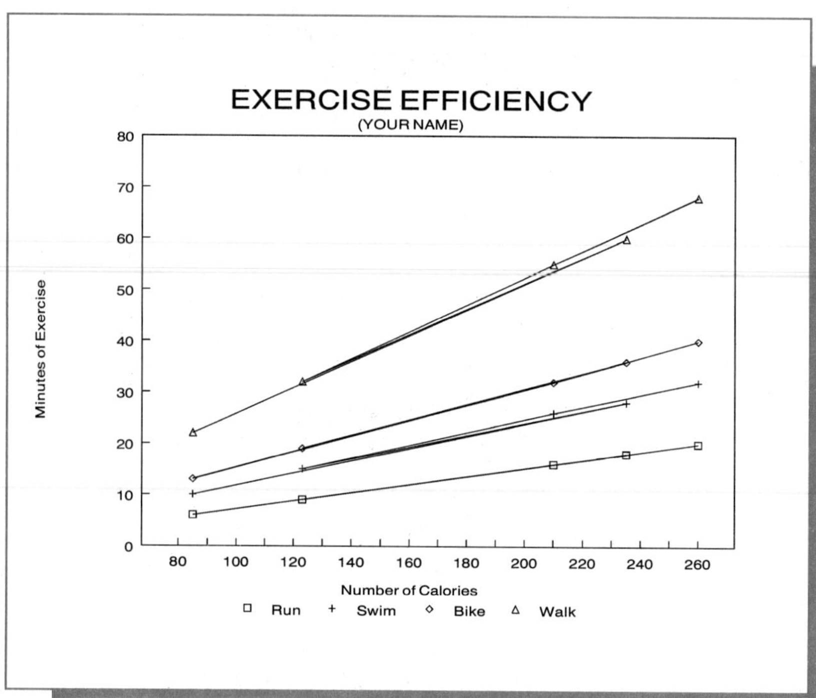

Figure 4.14

This graph shows the relative efficiency of each exercise to burn off calories. The more horizontal the line, the faster the exercise will burn off calories. You can see that running is the most efficient way to burn calories and that walking is the least efficient.

Press SPACEBAR to return to the Graph menu.

- Name the graph: XY.
- Save the graph: XY.PIC.

Recalling Previously Named Graphs

Now view each of the graphs you have named. After viewing a graph, press SPACEBAR before you issue the next command sequence.

Name **U**se **BAR** ↵

Name **U**se **STACKED** ↵

Name **U**se **PIE** ↵

Name **U**se **XY** ↵

Leave the Graph menu by selecting:

Quit

You are now ready to print the graphs you saved using the Graph Save command. To do this, you use the PrintGraph program. Before you can start this program, you must exit 1-2-3. First, save the worksheet containing all thc named graphs as GRAPHS. If you do not save the worksheet, the named graphs will be lost as they are stored in memory only until the worksheet file is saved. After saving the worksheet, exit 1-2-3.

You are returned to the Access menu rather than to the DOS prompt.

Using PrintGraph

To complete this section, you must have properly installed and established your hardware setup for the PrintGraph program. For details, see Chapter 4, ''Starting and Ending PrintGraph,'' in Section 1, ''Getting Started.''

The Access menu lets you select the utility program you want to use. To select PrintGraph,

Type: **P**

If you have a 5¼″ two-disk system, replace the 1-2-3 disk with the PrintGraph disk as directed on the screen and press ↵.

Note To load the PrintGraph program directly from the DOS prompt, insert the PrintGraph disk in the drive, make the drive containing the PrintGraph disk the current drive, and type **PGRAPH**.

In a few minutes, your screen should look similar to Figure 4.15.

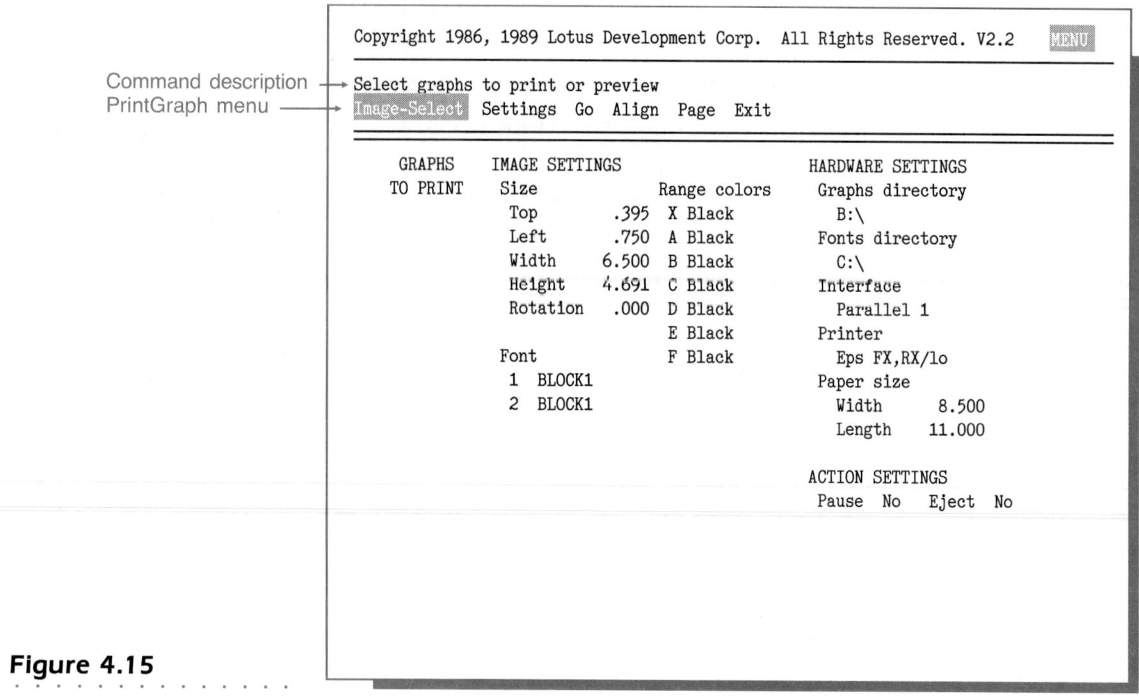

Figure 4.15

Note Your hardware setup settings may differ from those in Figure 4.15, depending on your particular computer system.

The PrintGraph menu is automatically displayed in the third line of the control panel. You do not press / to display the menu. Move the menu pointer to each command and read the short description on the line above the menu. You select commands from the menu just as you do in 1-2-3.

Printing a graph involves three simple steps: selecting the graph to be printed, preparing the printer to print, and printing.

First, to select the graph(s) to be printed, issue the following command:

Image-Select

Your screen should look similar to Figure 4.16.

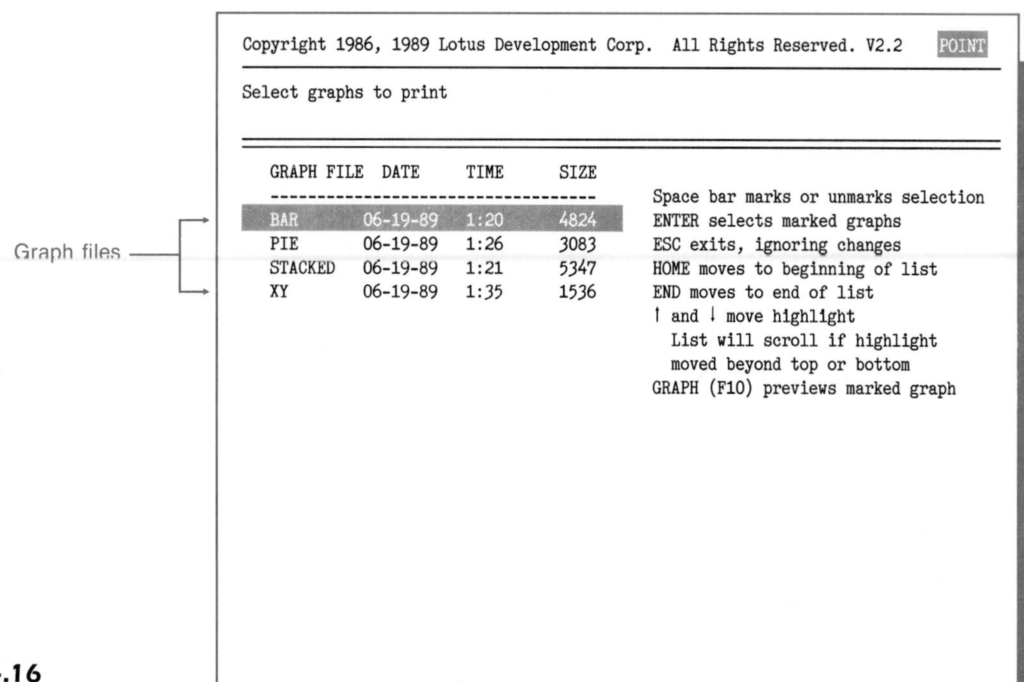
Copyright 1986, 1989 Lotus Development Corp. All Rights Reserved. V2.2
POINT
Select graphs to print
GRAPH FILE DATE TIME SIZE
BAR 06-19-89 1:20 4824
PIE 06-19-89 1:26 3083
STACKED 06-19-89 1:21 5347
XY 06-19-89 1:35 1536
Space bar marks or unmarks selection
ENTER selects marked graphs
ESC exits, ignoring changes
HOME moves to beginning of list
END moves to end of list
↑ and ↓ move highlight
List will scroll if highlight
moved beyond top or bottom
GRAPH (F10) previews marked graph
Graph files

Figure 4.16

Although you cannot change any of the graph settings in the graph files, you can preview them by using the Graph function key, F10.

Move to: XY
Press: F10

Your screen should look similar to Figure 4.17.

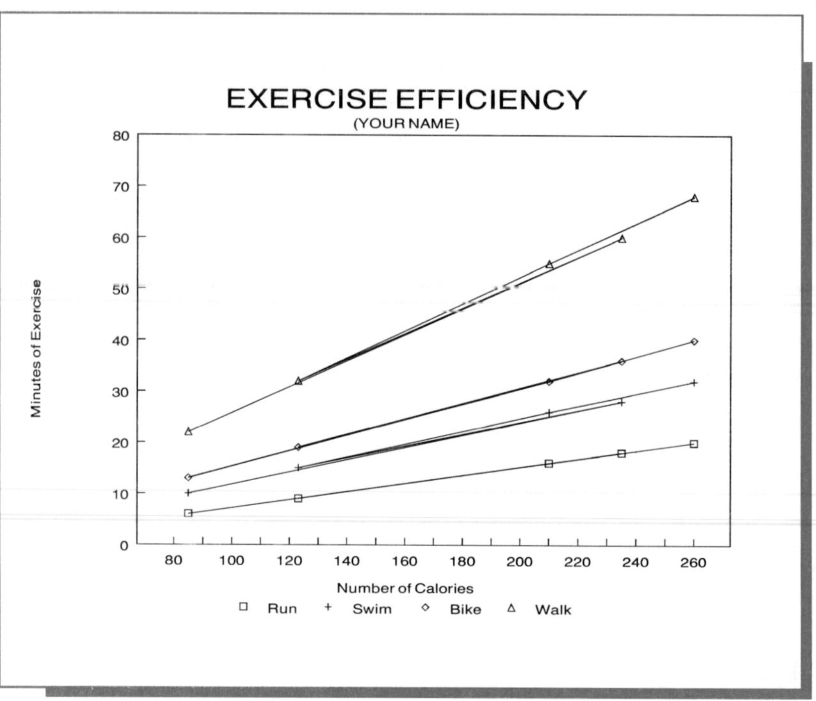

Figure 4.17

Press SPACEBAR to return to the list of graph files.

For now, you will print the BAR and PIE graphs. To select or mark the graphs to be printed:

Move to: BAR
Press: SPACEBAR
Move to: PIE
Press: SPACEBAR

A # sign appears next to the selected graph files. To complete your selections,

Press: ↵

Your screen should look similar to Figure 4.18.

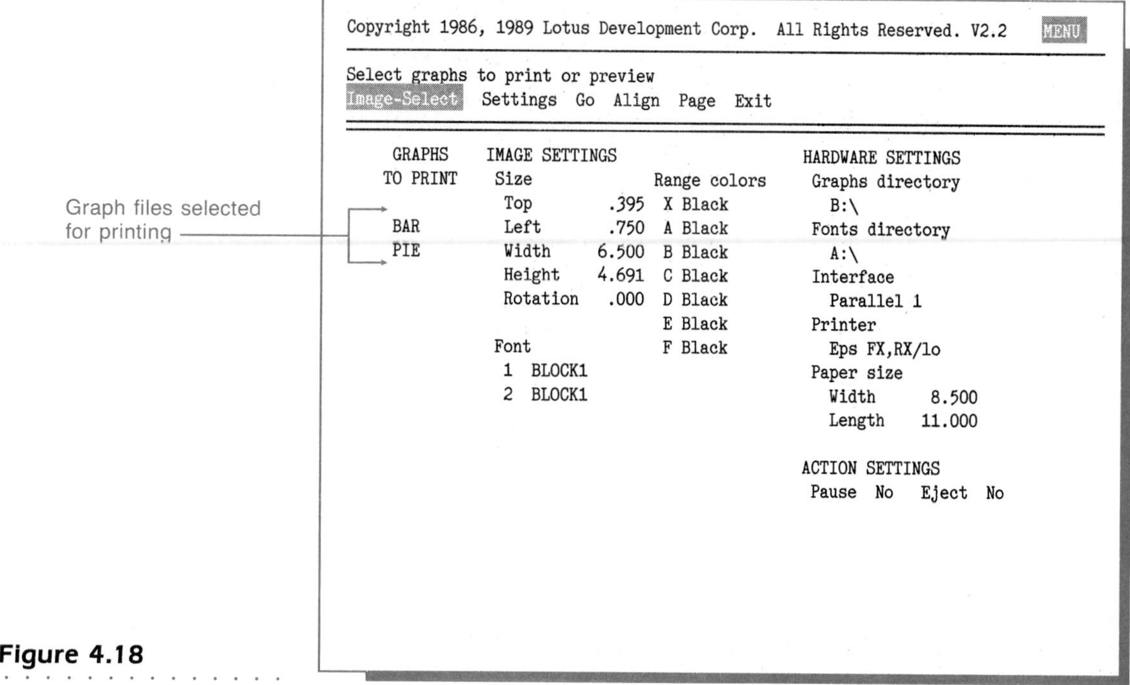

Figure 4.18

The selected graph filenames are displayed in the settings sheet.

Next, prepare the printer by turning it on. If you are using continuous form paper, adjust the page so that the perforation is near the first print position. Make sure the printer is on line.

Finally, issue the following command sequence:

Align **G**o

Align tells the printer that the paper is now at the top of a page. In a few moments, your printer should begin to print the graphs.

To advance the paper to the top of the next page and to leave the PrintGraph program, issue the following command:

Page **E**xit **Y**es

Again, you are returned to the Access menu. To leave the Access system and return to the DOS prompt, select:

Exit

Glossary of Key Terms

Bar graph A graph that shows numeric data as a set of evenly spaced bars, each bar representing a value in the range being graphed.

Exploded pie chart A pie chart with one or more slices exploded to emphasize a particular value or values.

Graph file A file created by the Graph Save command. It has a .PIC file extension. It contains a description of a graph and is used by the PrintGraph program to print a copy of the graph.

Hatch patterns The display pattern 1-2-3 uses to distinguish among data ranges in bar graphs, stacked bar graphs, and pie charts.

Named graph A graph whose settings have been assigned a name so that more than one set of graph settings can be created in a worksheet.

Pie chart A graph that compares parts to the whole, with each value in a range being a slice of the pie.

Scatter chart Another name for an XY graph.

Shading values A range of numbers (1 through 8) that defines the hatch pattern or colors for the corresponding slices of a pie chart.

Stacked bar graph A graph that compares totals as well as individual values, with each part representing a value in one of the data ranges.

Start value The first value 1-2-3 enters in a range during the Data Fill command.

Step value The increment between values in a range that is filled using the Data Fill command.

Stop value The number 1-2-3 uses as the upper limit for the sequence of values entered using the Data Fill command.

XY graph A graph that shows the relationship between two variables by plotting pairs of values.

Practice Problems

1. Matching

1. F10	______	a. a type of graph that shows the relationship between two variables
2. /GN	______	b. the shading value used to explode a slice of a pie chart
3. /GS	______	c. names graphs
4. /FS	______	d. the type of graph that compares the parts to the whole
5. Pie	______	e. displays the current graph
6. 105	______	f. a picture file extension
7. XY	______	g. selects graphs to be printed
8. PrintGraph	______	h. saves a graph file for printing
9. .PIC	______	i. saves a worksheet file
10. Image-Select	______	j. the program that prints saved graphs

2. To complete this problem, you first must have built the worksheet as specified in Practice Problem 3 in Lab 3. If you have already completed that problem, retrieve the file MOTHERS. The employment data on mothers in the workforce can be displayed as a bar graph or a stacked bar graph.

   a. Create a bar graph with the X axis as the years 1960, 1970, and 1985. The Y axis will be the number of mothers (in millions). Do the following:

      (1) Add titles:

      First: Mothers in the Workforce Since 1960

      Second: Your name and the current date

      X axis: Years

      Y axis: Number in Millions

      (2) Add legends to identify the three data groups.

      (3) Name the graph: BAR.

      (4) Save the graph for printing: EMPBAR.PIC.

b. Create a stacked bar graph using the same data ranges specified for the bar graph. The titles and legends will also remain the same. Do the following:

(1) Name the graph: SBAR.

(2) Save the graph for printing: EMPSBAR.PIC.

c. Create a pie chart for the year 1985 that shows the percentage of mothers in the workforce with children in these age groups: under 3 years, 3 to 5 years, and 6 to 17 years. Your pie chart will have three slices. Do the following:

(1) Add titles

First: Mothers in the Workforce in 1985

Second: Your name and the current date

(2) Add shading to the slices and explode the 3 to 5 age group slice.

(3) Name the graph: PIE.

(4) Save the graph for printing: EMPPIE.PIC.

d. Save the worksheet file as MOTHERS2.WK1.

e. Use the PrintGraph program to print the graphs EMPBAR.PIC, EMPSBAR.PIC, and EMPPIE.PIC.

3. Following the return of a midterm exam, a group of six students were discussing their test scores and how hard they had studied. One student complained that it had not helped to study for this exam.

The following table shows the study time in minutes and the test score for each of the six students.

Name	Study Time	Test Score
Mary	180	96
Sue	170	92
Tom	130	91
Mike	85	86
Alice	65	80
Frank	35	65

Create a worksheet of these data. Put your name in cell A1 and the date in cell A2.

Create an XY graph with the X axis as the study time and the Y axis as the test scores. Do the following:

- **a.** Set the first graph title: Study Time vs. Test Scores. Set the second title: Your name and the current date.
- **b.** Set the X-axis title: Study Time.
- **c.** Set the Y-axis title: Test Score.
- **d.** Name the graph: XY.
- **e.** Save the graph: XYSTUDY.PIC.
- **f.** Save the worksheet: STUDY.WK1.

What is the relationship between the amount of study time and the test scores for these students?

4. To complete this problem, you first must have built the worksheet as specified in Practice Problem 4 of Lab 2. If you have already completed that problem, retrieve the file SLOAN1. Complete the following steps:

- **a.** Create a bar graph with the X axis as the months January through June. Each group of bars will show the Revenue, Total Expense, and Net for each month.
  - **(1)** Add titles:

First:	Six-Month Budget for Sloan Research
Second:	Your name and the current date
X axis:	Months
Y axis:	Dollars

  - **(2)** Add legends to identify each of the three data groups.
  - **(3)** Name the graph: SLOANB.
  - **(4)** Save the graph for printing as: SLOANB.PIC.
- **b.** Create a stacked bar graph using the same data ranges specified for the bar graph. The titles and legends will also remain the same.
  - **(1)** Name the graph: SLOANSB.
  - **(2)** Save the graph for printing: SLOANSB.PIC.

c. Save the worksheet as SLOANB.

d. Using the PrintGraph program, print SLOANB and SLOANSB.

5. To complete this problem, you first must have built the worksheet as specified in Practice Problem 4 of Lab 2. If you have already completed that problem, retrieve the file SLOAN1. Complete the following steps:

   a. Create a pie chart for the revenue showing the percentage revenue received for each month for the six month period as follows:

      (1) Add titles:

      First: Sloan Research Monthly Revenue

      Second: Your name and the current date

      (2) Add shading to the pie chart and explode the June slice.

      (3) Name the graph: REVPIE.

      (4) Save the graph for printing: REVPIE.PIC.

   b. Create a second pie chart that shows the percentage for each month's total expenses. Do the following:

      (1) Add titles:

      First: Sloan Research Monthly Expenses

      Second: Your name and the current date

      (2) Add shading to the pie chart and explode the March slice.

      (3) Name the graph: EXPPIE.

      (4) Save the graph for printing: EXPPIE.PIC.

   c. Save the worksheet as SLOANP.

   d. Use the PrintGraph program to print REVPIE.PIC and EXPPIE.PIC.

5

Using Worksheets

Objectives

In Lab 5, you will learn how to:

- Locate and eliminate circular references
- Hide and unhide columns
- Link files
- Name a range of cells
- Use the @MIN, @MAX, and @AVG functions
- Format cells
- Back up a file

Case Study

In Labs 5 and 6 you will follow the use of electronic worksheets by Bynner's Bookshops, a chain of bookstores in the Southwest.

Sam Bynner, the chain's manager, is concerned about his company's finances and has decided to incorporate more long-range planning into company policies and strategies. Sam has recently learned about the worksheet capabilities of 1-2-3 and has decided to use the program to help him with his financial planning.

Displaying the Filename

Sam has just started to use 1-2-3 to create an income statement for Bynner's Bookshops, and he is having some problems.

To see his worksheet, load 1-2-3 and retrieve the file JANUARY.WK1.

This income statement extends beyond row 20. To view the rest of the worksheet, use (↓) to

Move to: A23

Your screen should look similar to Figure 5.1.

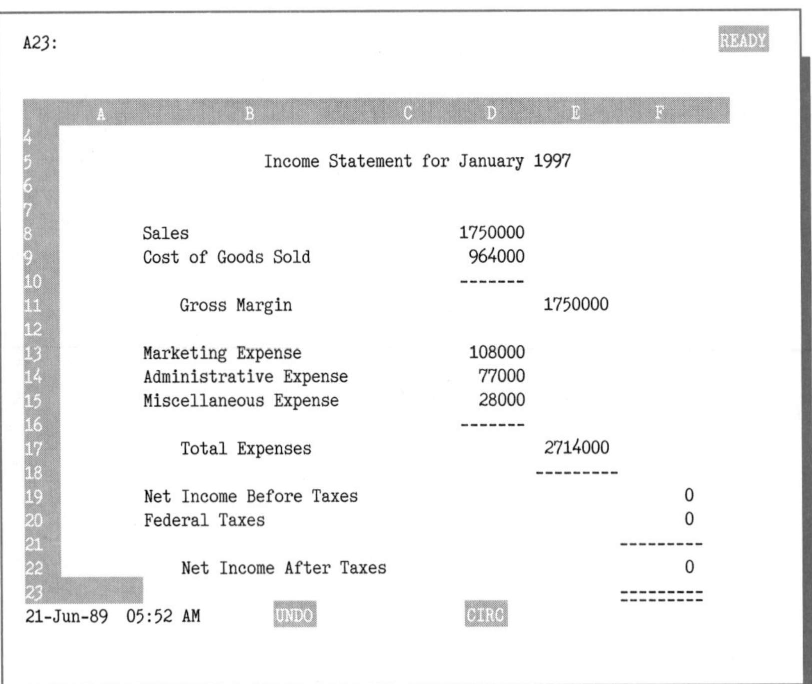

Figure 5.1

In this lab you will be working with several different files. To help keep track of the file you are using, you can display the filename in the status line in place of the date-and-time indicator. To do this, issue the following command sequence:

/ **W**orksheet **G**lobal

The date-and-time indicator is a default 1-2-3 worksheet setting. To change this setting, select:

Default

The Default settings sheet is displayed. To turn off the date display and turn on the filename display, select:

Other **C**lock **F**ilename **Q**uit

Your screen should look similar to Figure 5.2.

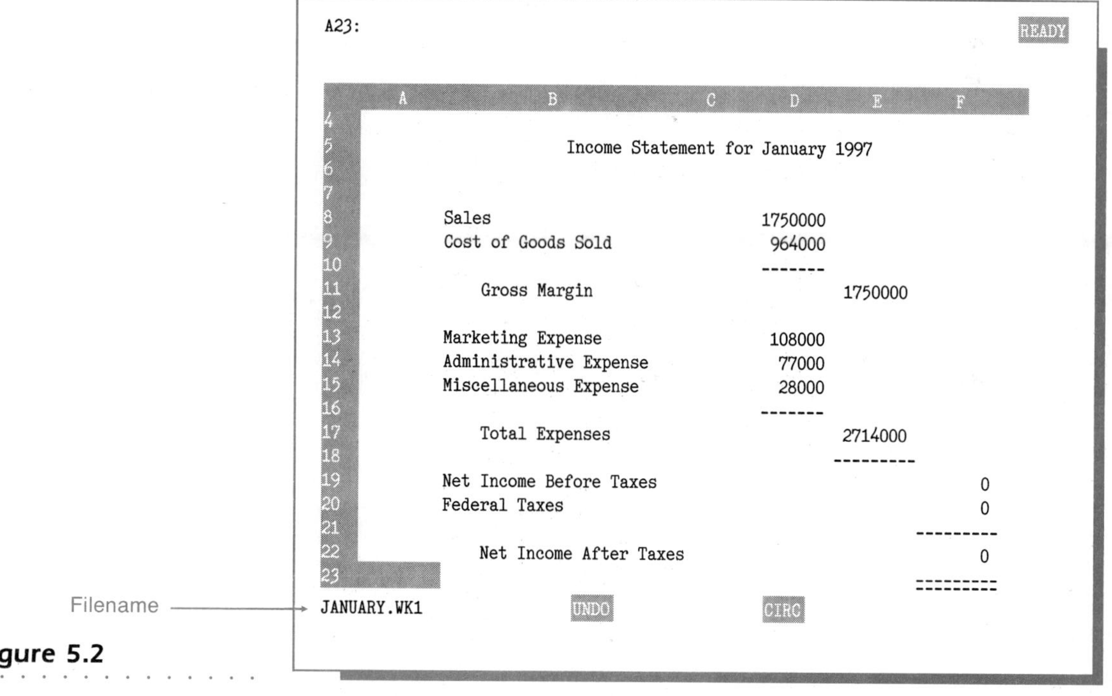

Figure 5.2

The filename JANUARY.WK1 is displayed in the status line.

The worksheet has errors in the formulas used to calculate the Gross Margin and Total Expenses. The correct equations should be:

Gross Margin = Sales − Cost of Goods Sold

Total Expenses = Marketing Expense + Administrative Expense + Miscellaneous Expense (+D13+D14+D15)

Correct the formulas in cells E11 and E17 to calculate Gross Margin and Total Expenses.

Locating a Circular Reference

There is also an error in the formula to calculate Net Income Before Taxes. To see this formula,

Move to: F19

Your screen should look similar to Figure 5.3.

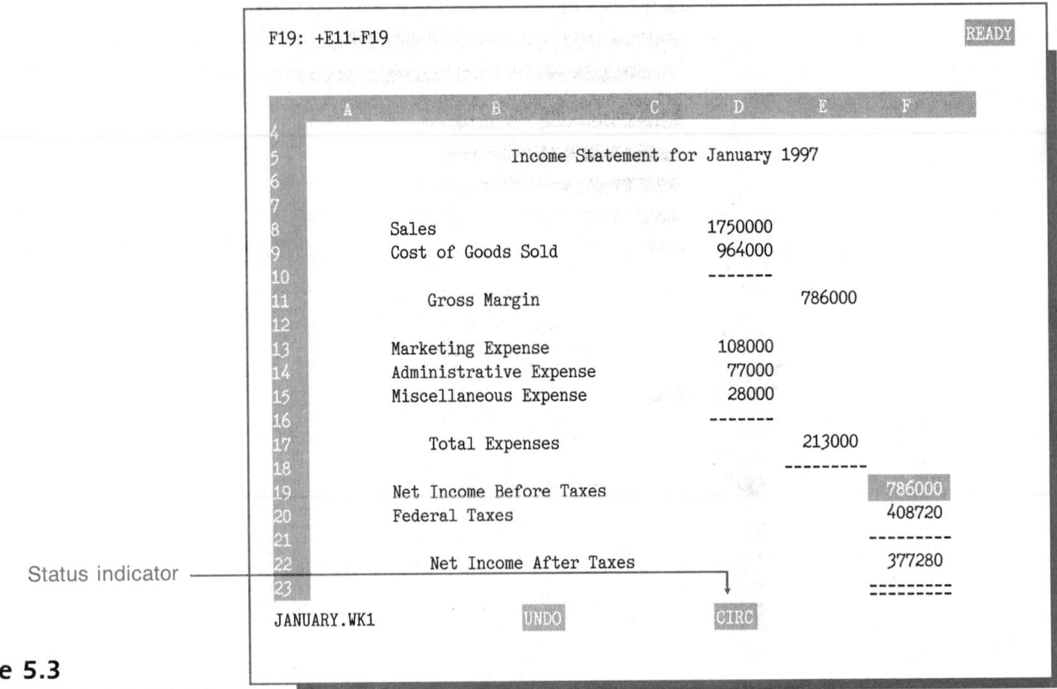

Figure 5.3

The formula in cell F19 is +E11−F19. The formula should be Net Income Before Taxes = Gross Margin − Total Expenses (+E11−E17). Because the incorrect formula in cell F19 references itself as part of the computation, a **circular reference** error occurs, and the status indicator, CIRC, is displayed. A circular reference occurs whenever a cell's formula refers to itself, either directly or indirectly.

For some special applications, you may want to have circular referencing. Such cases, however, are not very common. Generally, whenever CIRC appears, stop and locate the cell or cells causing the circular reference by using the Worksheet Status command sequence.

To see how this works, issue the following command sequence:

/ **W**orksheet **S**tatus

Your screen should look similar to Figure 5.4.

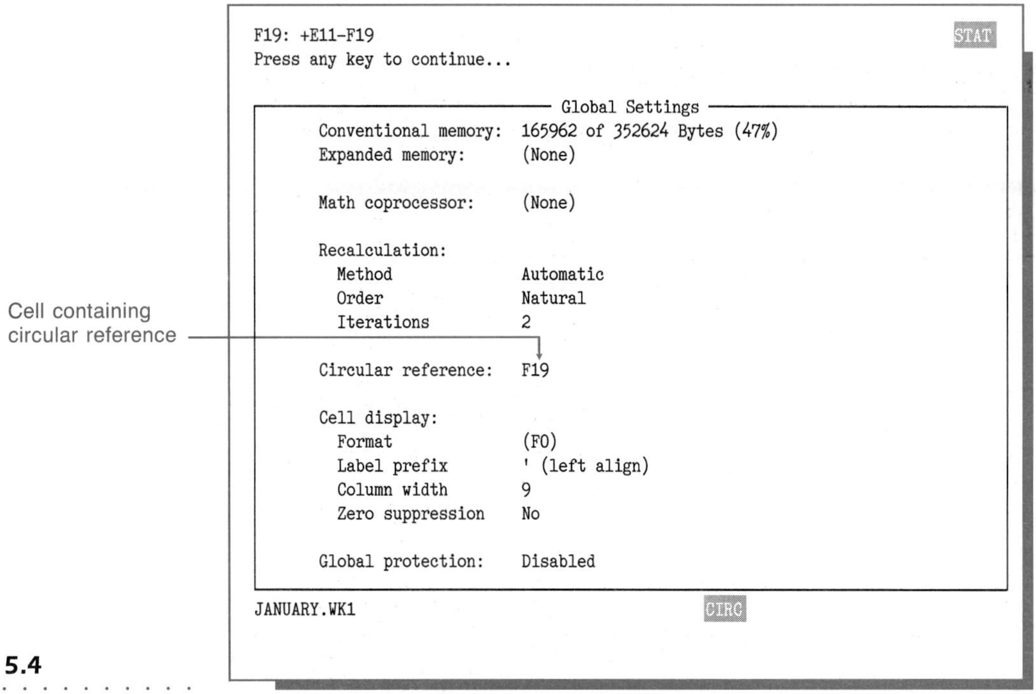

```
F19: +E11-F19                                                          STAT
Press any key to continue...

 ─────────────────────────────── Global Settings ───────────────────────────
      Conventional memory:  165962 of 352624 Bytes (47%)
      Expanded memory:      (None)

      Math coprocessor:     (None)

      Recalculation:
        Method              Automatic
        Order               Natural
        Iterations          2

      Circular reference:   F19

      Cell display:
        Format              (F0)
        Label prefix        ' (left align)
        Column width        9
        Zero suppression    No

      Global protection:    Disabled

JANUARY.WK1                                      CIRC
```

Cell containing circular reference

Figure 5.4

The **status screen** displays the Global settings sheet. It displays information about available memory, recalculation, cell display format, circular references, and global protection. The status screen tells us that the location of the circular reference is in cell F19.

The cell location of only one circular reference can be displayed at a time. If you correct the CIRC cell reference in the worksheet and the message is still displayed in the status indicator, recall the status window to locate the source of another circular reference.

To clear the screen of the status screen and return to the worksheet, press any key.

In this case, solving the problem is easy. The equation in cell F19 to calculate Net Income Before Taxes should be the difference between Gross Margin and Total Expenses. Now correct the formula in cell F19.

Your screen should look similar to Figure 5.5.

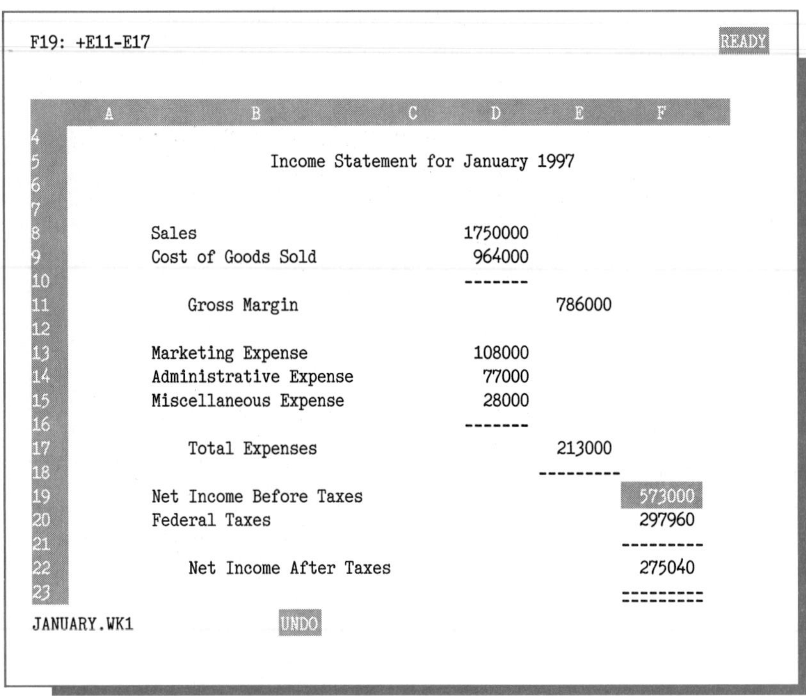

F19: +E11-E17
READY
A B C D E F
Income Statement for January 1997
Sales 1750000
Cost of Goods Sold 964000

Gross Margin 786000
Marketing Expense 108000
Administrative Expense 77000
Miscellaneous Expense 28000

Total Expenses 213000

Net Income Before Taxes 573000
Federal Taxes 297960

Net Income After Taxes 275040
=========
JANUARY.WK1
UNDO

Figure 5.5

The CIRC message has disappeared.

Other circular references may be more complex. For example, as shown in Figure 5.6, a formula in cell B5 could refer to cell B15, which contains a formula referring to cell E15, which contains a formula referring to E5, which refers back to cell B5.

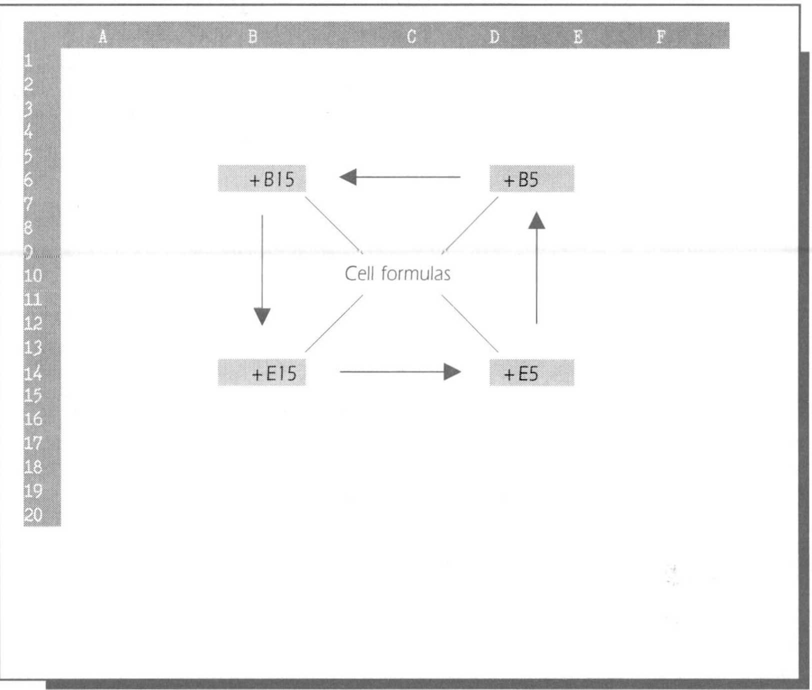

Figure 5.6

Even in complex cases, however, circular references are usually easy to locate and correct with the help of the status screen.

Save the corrected worksheet as JANEXP.

Hiding and Unhiding Columns

Another useful feature of 1-2-3 is its ability to hide a column of information. This is particularly helpful when you want to print a worksheet without displaying all the rows and columns. You will see how this works by hiding column E.

Issue the following command sequence:

/ **W**orksheet **C**olumn **H**ide **E19** ↵

This command sequence uses cell E19 to refer to column E. (You could have used any cell address in column E.)

Your screen should now look similar to Figure 5.7.

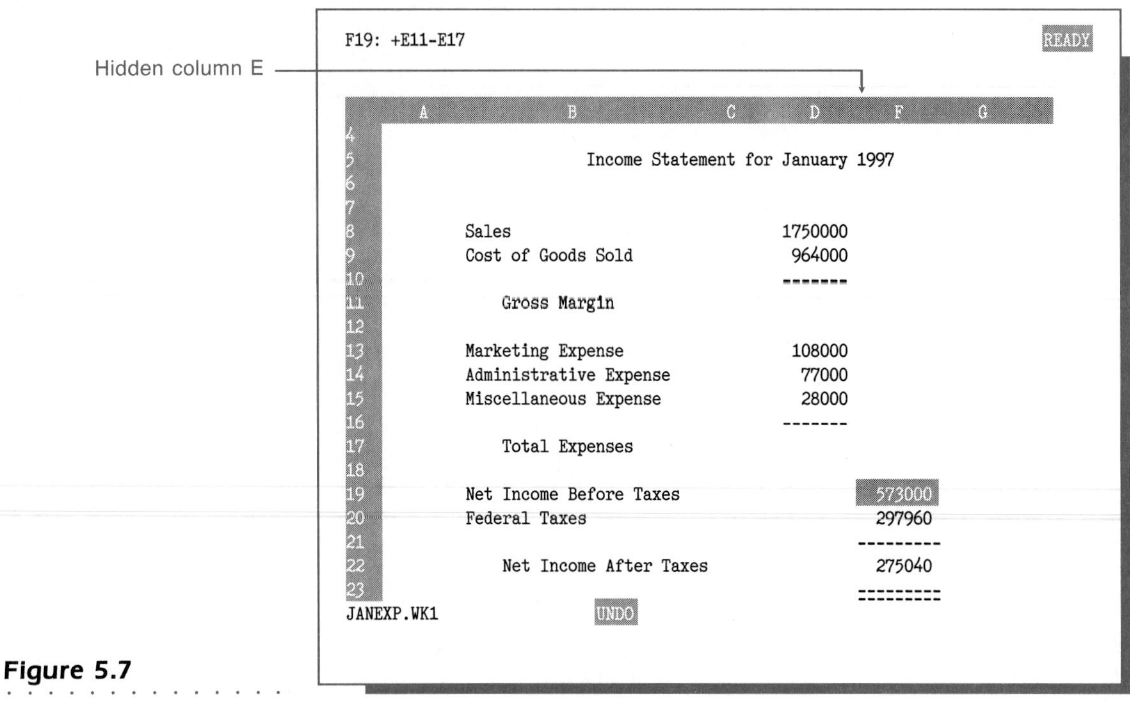

Hidden column E
F19: +E11-E17
READY
A B C D F G
4
5 Income Statement for January 1997
6
7
8 Sales 1750000
9 Cost of Goods Sold 964000
10 -------
11 Gross Margin
12
13 Marketing Expense 108000
14 Administrative Expense 77000
15 Miscellaneous Expense 28000
16 -------
17 Total Expenses
18
19 Net Income Before Taxes 573000
20 Federal Taxes 297960
21 ---------
22 Net Income After Taxes 275040
23 =========
JANEXP.WK1
UNDO

Figure 5.7

Column E is no longer visible in the worksheet; even the column letter has disappeared. When you hide several columns or rows, only those areas of the worksheet that are not hidden will be printed.

To display the hidden column, issue the following command sequence:

/ **W**orksheet **C**olumn **D**isplay

Your screen should now look similar to Figure 5.8.

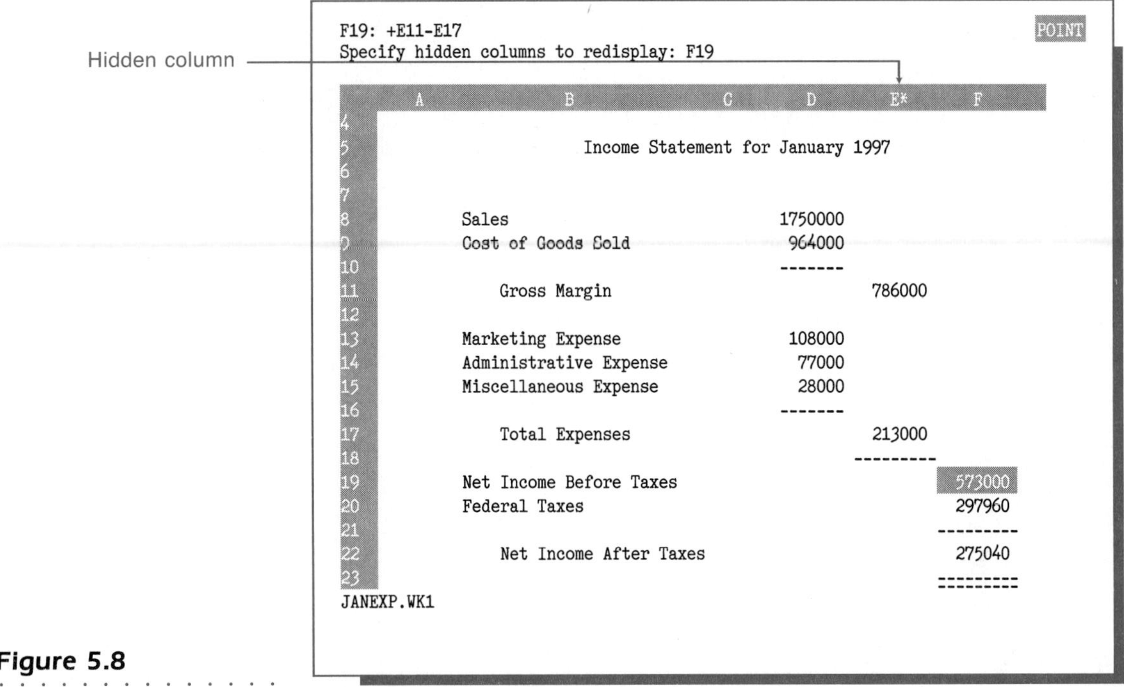

Hidden column
F19: +E11-E17
Specify hidden columns to redisplay: F19
POINT
A B C D E* F
Income Statement for January 1997
Sales 1750000
Cost of Goods Sold 964000
Gross Margin 786000
Marketing Expense 108000
Administrative Expense 77000
Miscellaneous Expense 28000
Total Expenses 213000
Net Income Before Taxes 573000
Federal Taxes 297960
Net Income After Taxes 275040
JANEXP.WK1

Figure 5.8

The hidden column is now displayed and marked with an asterisk (*) to identify the hidden column.

The control panel prompts you to specify which column to unhide. 1-2-3 incorrectly anticipated that the current cell position, F19, was the column to unhide. To unhide column E, complete the command as follows:

E19 ↵

Again, any cell address in column E would be acceptable.

Column E is again displayed on the screen.

File Linking

After looking at the values in the January statement, Sam asks the marketing director to check his January expense figures. Sam thinks the marketing expenses are too high.

The marketing director has created a worksheet of the department's expenses also using Lotus 1-2-3. To see the file containing the marketing expense report, retrieve the file MKTEXP.WK1.

Your screen should be similar to Figure 5.9.

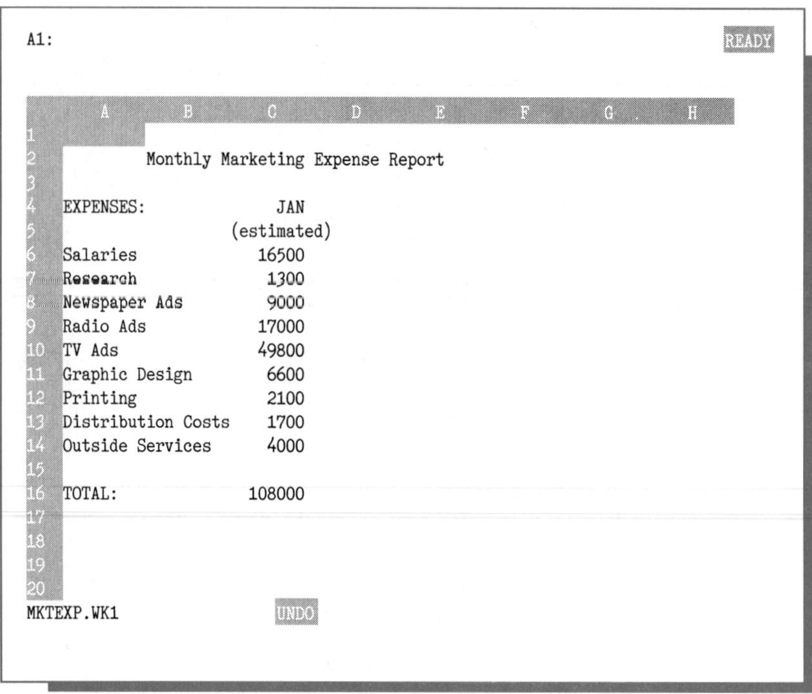

Figure 5.9

The marketing director initially estimated his January monthly expenses for the report. Now he has the actual figures for January and needs to change the worksheet to reflect the new values. First, to change the label in cell C5 to Actual,

Move to: C5
Type: **Actual**
Press: ↵

Next, enter the following new values in the worksheet:

Cell	*Value*
C7	1345
C8	8500
C9	15650
C10	38180
C11	6750
C12	4275
C13	2550
C14	4250

The Total marketing expense (cell C16) is now 98000.

Save the revised worksheet as MKTEXP.WK1, using the Replace option.

Sam decides that this may be a good time to see how the file linking feature of 1-2-3 works. The file linking feature of 1-2-3 allows you to use values from cells in other worksheets in the current worksheet. The file that receives the value is the **target file** and the file that supplies the data is the **source file**. To link files, Sam needs to know the name of the file and the cell in the worksheet containing the January marketing expense total. He is told the filename is MKTEXP and the cell is C16.

The MKTEXP file will be the source file and the JANEXP file will be the target file.

Retrieve the target file, JANEXP.WK1.

To create a link between two files, you enter a **linking formula** in the target file that refers to a cell in the source file. Sam wants the value in cell D13 of the target file to be the same value as in cell C16 of the source file.

Move to: D13

The linking formula uses the following format:

+<<file reference>>cell reference

The file reference is the filename of the source file enclosed in double angle brackets. The cell reference is the cell address of the source file cell containing the value to be copied into the target file.

Type: **+<<MKTEXP>>C16**
Press: ↵

Your screen should be similar to Figure 5.10.

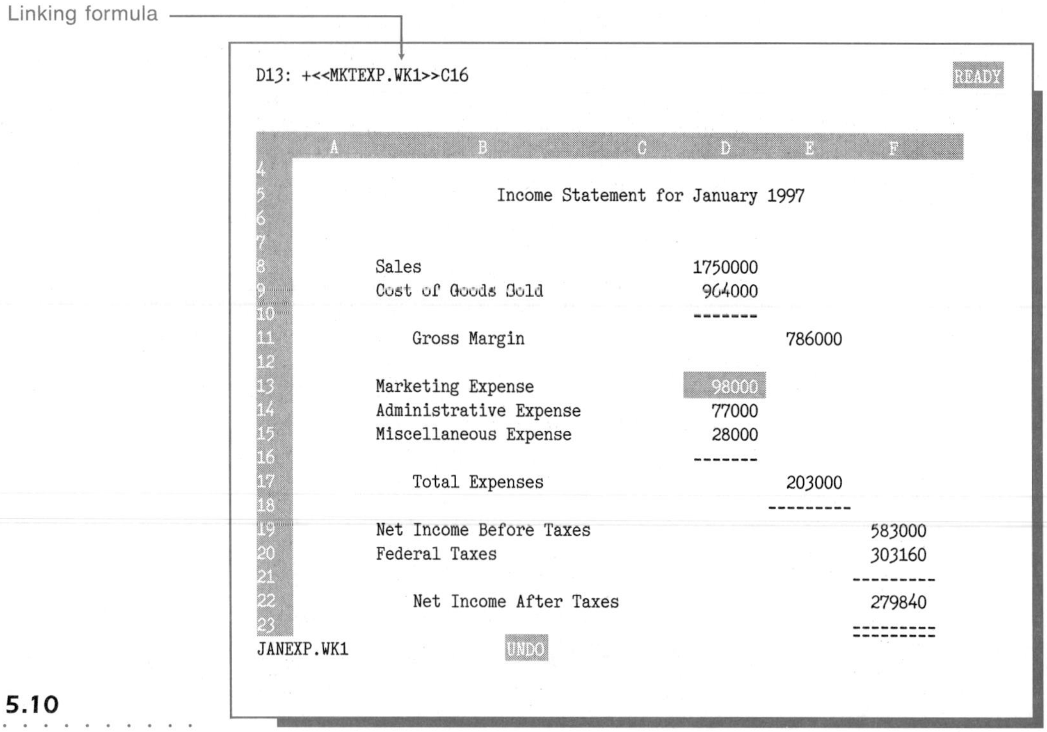

Linking formula

```
D13: +<<MKTEXP.WK1>>C16                                        READY

      A         B          C          D          E          F
 4
 5              Income Statement for January 1997
 6
 7
 8      Sales                          1750000
 9      Cost of Goods Sold              964000
10                                     -------
11         Gross Margin                           786000
12
13      Marketing Expense                98000
14      Administrative Expense           77000
15      Miscellaneous Expense            28000
16                                     -------
17         Total Expenses                         203000
18                                              ---------
19      Net Income Before Taxes                              583000
20      Federal Taxes                                        303160
21                                                        ---------
22         Net Income After Taxes                            279840
23                                                        =========
JANEXP.WK1              UNDO
```

Figure 5.10

The current value in cell C16, 98000, is copied from the source file into the target file. The target file is recalculated using the new data.

Once a linking formula is entered in a worksheet, whenever the value in the cell referenced in the source file changes, the target file is automatically updated when it is retrieved. Another way to update the target file is to use the command / **F**ile **A**dmin **L**ink-Refresh. This command will immediately update the linked cells.

Sam likes how the file linking feature works. Some time in the future, when the corporate income statement is running smoothly, he plans to require that all departments create worksheets for their monthly expense reports and then he will link them directly to the corporate income statement.

Save the revised worksheet using the Replace option with the same filename, JANEXP.

Using @Functions: @SUM, @MIN, @MAX, @AVG

For the next six months, Sam Bynner continues to create monthly income statements similar to the one shown in Figure 5.10.

At the end of six months, Sam wants to summarize the firm's performance. He prepares a combined income statement showing the monthly statements from January through June, along with totals for the first half of the year.

To see the worksheet Sam created for the combined income statement, retrieve the file SIXMONTH. The worksheet title tells you that the values represent thousands of dollars.

The worksheet extends below row 20. To see the rest of the worksheet, use (↓) to

Move to: A24

Your screen should now look similar to Figure 5.11.

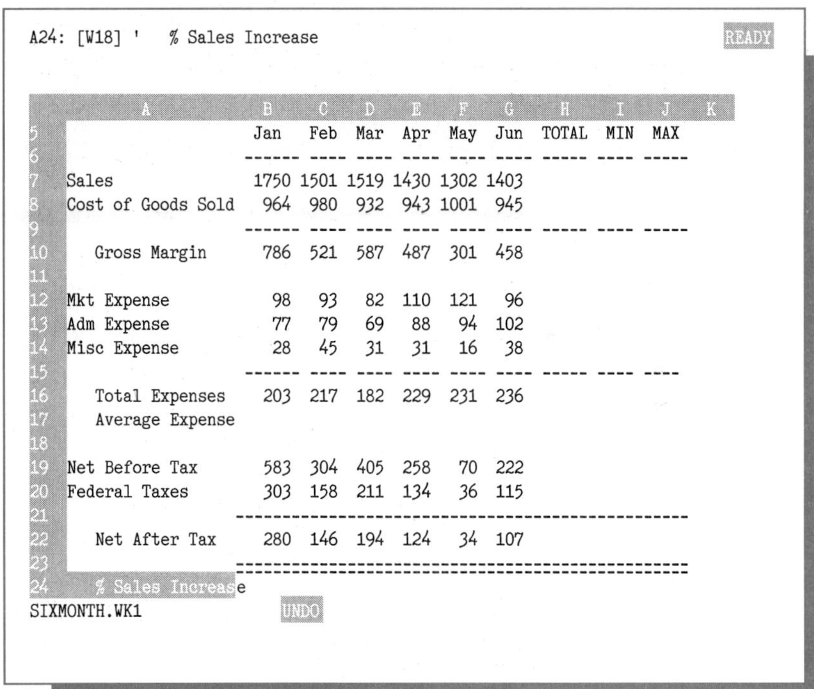

A24: [W18] '   % Sales Increase   READY

	A	B	C	D	E	F	G	H	I	J	K
5		Jan	Feb	Mar	Apr	May	Jun	TOTAL	MIN	MAX	
6		------	----	----	----	----	----	-----	----	-----	
7	Sales	1750	1501	1519	1430	1302	1403				
8	Cost of Goods Sold	964	980	932	943	1001	945				
9		------	----	----	----	----	----	-----	----	-----	
10	Gross Margin	786	521	587	487	301	458				
11											
12	Mkt Expense	98	93	82	110	121	96				
13	Adm Expense	77	79	69	88	94	102				
14	Misc Expense	28	45	31	31	16	38				
15		------	----	----	----	----	----	-----	----	----	
16	Total Expenses	203	217	182	229	231	236				
17	Average Expense										
18											
19	Net Before Tax	583	304	405	258	70	222				
20	Federal Taxes	303	158	211	134	36	115				
21		------	------	------	------	------	------	------	------	------	
22	Net After Tax	280	146	194	124	34	107				
23		======	======	======	======	======	======	======	======	======	
24	% Sales Increase										

SIXMONTH.WK1   UNDO

Figure 5.11

The column labeled Jan is similar to the January Income Statement shown in Figure 5.10. The only difference is that the income figures are now displayed down a single column.

In addition to the income figures for January, this new worksheet shows the figures for February, March, April, May, and June. Sam also plans to calculate totals, as well as the minimums and maximums, for the six months. You will use 1-2-3's @functions to calculate these values.

You will begin by using the @SUM function to calculate the column TOTAL in the worksheet. Cell addresses and ranges can also be pointed in an @function. To see how to use pointing to specify the range B7 through G7 in this @function,

Move to: H7
Type: **@SUM(**
Move to: G7

The mode indicator displays POINT. You can specify a range beginning at either end of the range of cells. To anchor cell G7 as the beginning of the range and to highlight the rest of the range,

Type: **.** (period)
Move to: B7

To complete the @function,

Type: **)**
Press: ↵

Your screen should look similar to Figure 5.12.

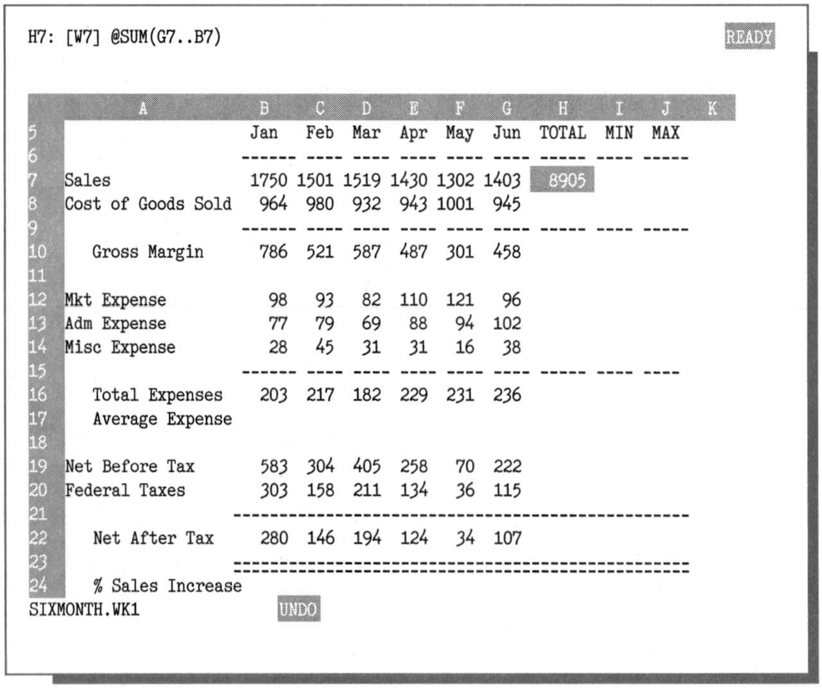

```
H7: [W7] @SUM(G7..B7)                                                READY

            A            B    C    D    E    F    G    H     I    J    K
 5                      Jan  Feb  Mar  Apr  May  Jun  TOTAL  MIN  MAX
 6                    ------ ---- ---- ---- ---- ---- ----- ---- -----
 7  Sales               1750 1501 1519 1430 1302 1403  8905
 8  Cost of Goods Sold   964  980  932  943 1001  945
 9                    ------ ---- ---- ---- ---- ---- ----- ---- -----
10     Gross Margin      786  521  587  487  301  458
11
12  Mkt Expense           98   93   82  110  121   96
13  Adm Expense           77   79   69   88   94  102
14  Misc Expense          28   45   31   31   16   38
15                    ------ ---- ---- ---- ---- ---- ----- ---- ----
16     Total Expenses    203  217  182  229  231  236
17     Average Expense
18
19  Net Before Tax       583  304  405  258   70  222
20  Federal Taxes        303  158  211  134   36  115
21                   -------------------------------------------------
22     Net After Tax     280  146  194  124   34  107
23                   =================================================
24     % Sales Increase
SIXMONTH.WK1                 UNDO
```

Figure 5.12

The total, 8905, is now displayed in cell H7.

Naming a Range

The same range, B7..G7, is needed in the @functions to calculate the minimum and maximum values to be displayed in columns I and J. Rather than respecify the same range over again, you can name the range. The named range is then used in the @function in place of the cell addresses of the range. To use the name SALES for the range of cells B7..G7, select:

/ **R**ange **N**ame

Five Range Name options are displayed in the control panel. They have the following effects:

Create	Assigns or modifies a range name
Delete	Removes a range name
Labels	Creates range names from a range of labels
Reset	Deletes all range names
Table	Creates a list of range names and their range addresses

A range name, which can have up to fifteen characters, should be descriptive of the range contents. The following guidelines should be observed:

- Do not include spaces, semicolons, or numeric symbols in range names.
- Do not create a range name that looks like a cell address, such as B25.
- Do not begin a range name with a number or create a range name that consists entirely of numbers.

To assign the name SALES to cells B7 through G7, complete the command sequence as follows:

Create **SALES** (↵) **B7..G7** (↵)

With the cell pointer in cell H7, look at the @function in the control panel. Your screen should look similar to Figure 5.13.

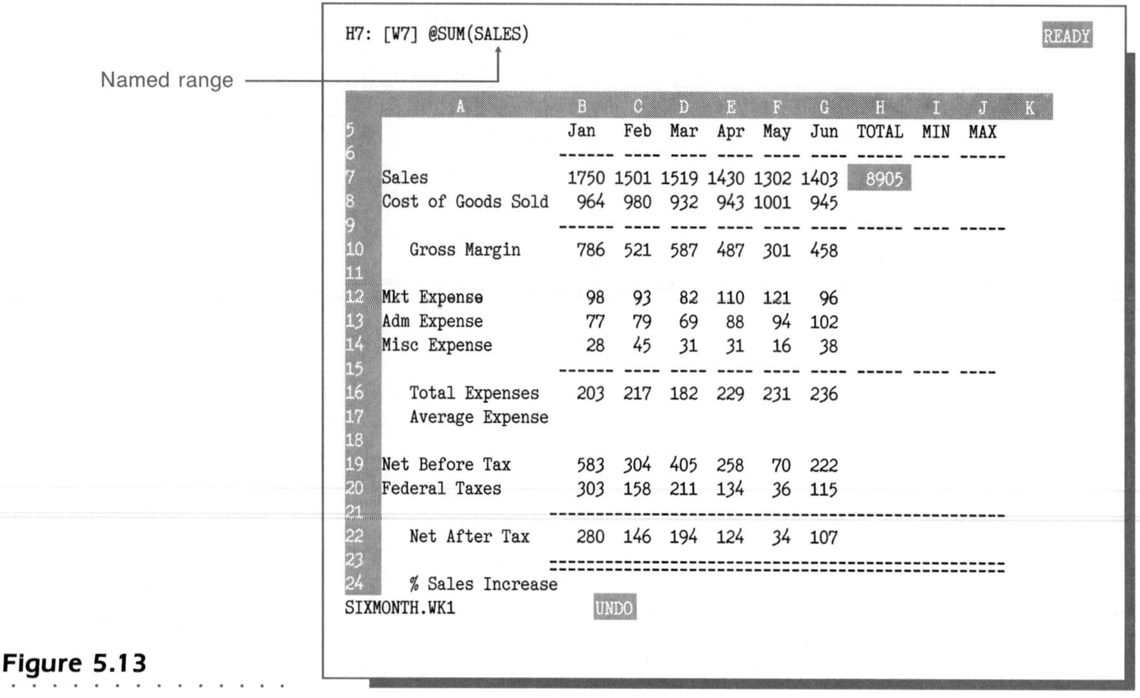

	A	B	C	D	E	F	G	H	I	J	K
5		Jan	Feb	Mar	Apr	May	Jun	TOTAL	MIN	MAX	
6		------	----	----	----	----	----	-----	----	-----	
7	Sales	1750	1501	1519	1430	1302	1403	8905			
8	Cost of Goods Sold	964	980	932	943	1001	945				
9		------	----	----	----	----	----	-----	----	-----	
10	Gross Margin	786	521	587	487	301	458				
11											
12	Mkt Expense	98	93	82	110	121	96				
13	Adm Expense	77	79	69	88	94	102				
14	Misc Expense	28	45	31	31	16	38				
15		------	----	----	----	----	----	-----	----	----	
16	Total Expenses	203	217	182	229	231	236				
17	Average Expense										
18											
19	Net Before Tax	583	304	405	258	70	222				
20	Federal Taxes	303	158	211	134	36	115				
21		------	----	----	----	----	----	-----	----	-----	
22	Net After Tax	280	146	194	124	34	107				
23		======	====	====	====	====	====	=====	====	=====	
24	% Sales Increase										

Figure 5.13

The @function in cell H7 uses the named range, SALES, in place of B7..G7. Naming ranges makes the range easier to enter and the worksheet easier to read and understand.

You will now use this named range with the @MIN function to find the smallest value in the defined range.

Move to: I7
Type: **@MIN(SALES)**
Press: ↵

Your screen should look similar to Figure 5.14.

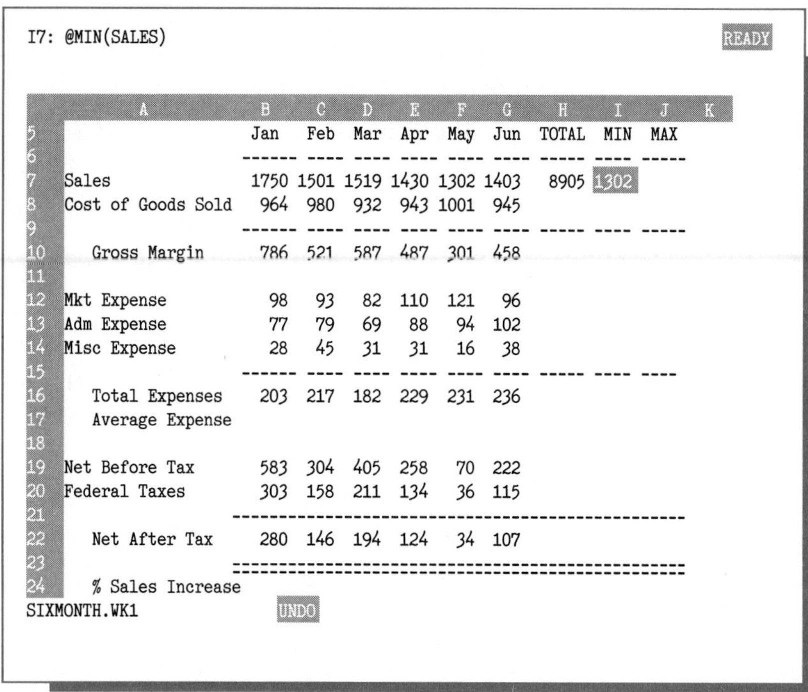

I7: @MIN(SALES) READY

	A	B	C	D	E	F	G	H	I	J
5		Jan	Feb	Mar	Apr	May	Jun	TOTAL	MIN	MAX
6		------	----	----	----	----	----	-----	----	-----
7	Sales	1750	1501	1519	1430	1302	1403	8905	1302	
8	Cost of Goods Sold	964	980	932	943	1001	945			
9		------	----	----	----	----	----	-----	----	-----
10	Gross Margin	786	521	587	487	301	458			
11										
12	Mkt Expense	98	93	82	110	121	96			
13	Adm Expense	77	79	69	88	94	102			
14	Misc Expense	28	45	31	31	16	38			
15		------	----	----	----	----	----	-----	----	----
16	Total Expenses	203	217	182	229	231	236			
17	Average Expense									
18										
19	Net Before Tax	583	304	405	258	70	222			
20	Federal Taxes	303	158	211	134	36	115			
21		------	----	----	----	----	----	-----	----	-----
22	Net After Tax	280	146	194	124	34	107			
23		======	====	====	====	====	====	=====	====	=====
24	% Sales Increase									

SIXMONTH.WK1 UNDO

Figure 5.14

The entry in cell I7, 1302, is the smallest, or minimum, value in the SALES range. The @function is displayed in the control panel using the range name.

Next, to use the @MAX function in cell J7 to find the largest value in the defined range of cells,

Move to: J7
Type: **@MAX(SALES)**
Press: ↵

The maximum value in the SALES range, 1750, has been entered into cell J7.

Now use the Copy command to copy the @functions in cells H7 through J7 to cells H8 through J8.

Move to cells H8, I8, and J8 and look at the @function in each cell. The correct range, B8..G8, is used in the @function, not the named range SALES. A named range, like an unnamed range, adjusts relative to its new location in the worksheet when it is copied. To make a named range absolute, you would enter a dollar sign before the range name (for example, $SALES).

Next, Sam Bynner wants to calculate the average monthly expenses of his chain of bookshops. The @AVG function will calculate the average of a range of cells.

Name the range for January's expenses by issuing the following command sequence:

/ **R**ange **N**ame **C**reate **JANEXP** ↵ **B12..B14** ↵

Then to enter the @function,

Move to: B17
Type: **@AVG(JANEXP)**
Press: ↵

Your screen should look similar to Figure 5.15.

```
B17: [W7] @AVG(JANEXP)                                            READY

           A              B    C    D    E    F    G    H     I    J    K
 5                       Jan  Feb  Mar  Apr  May  Jun  TOTAL  MIN  MAX
 6                      ------ ---- ---- ---- ---- ---- ----- ---- -----
 7  Sales               1750 1501 1519 1430 1302 1403  8905 1302 1750
 8  Cost of Goods Sold   964  980  932  943 1001  945  5765  932 1001
 9                      ------ ---- ---- ---- ---- ---- ----- ---- -----
10     Gross Margin      786  521  587  487  301  458
11
12  Mkt Expense           98   93   82  110  121   96
13  Adm Expense           77   79   69   88   94  102
14  Misc Expense          28   45   31   31   16   38
15                      ------ ---- ---- ---- ---- ---- ----- ---- ----
16     Total Expenses    203  217  182  229  231  236
17     Average Expense    68
18
19  Net Before Tax       583  304  405  258   70  222
20  Federal Taxes        303  158  211  134   36  115
21                     ------------------------------------------------
22     Net After Tax     280  146  194  124   34  107
23                     ================================================
24     % Sales Increase
SIXMONTH.WK1              UNDO
```

Figure 5.15

The average expense for the month of January appears in cell B17.

To complete the worksheet, the next step would be to name the other ranges and to copy the @functions for TOTAL, MIN, and MAX down their respective columns and the @function for the Average Expense across the row. This has already been done for you and saved in the file COMPLETE. Retrieve this file.

To see the rest of the worksheet, use (↓) to

Move to: A24

Setting Cell Formats

Sam would like to determine the percentage increase (or decrease) in each month's sales over the previous month's sales. To enter the formula for this calculation,

Move to: C24
Type: **(C7 – B7)/B7**
Press: (↵)

Your screen should look similar to Figure 5.16.

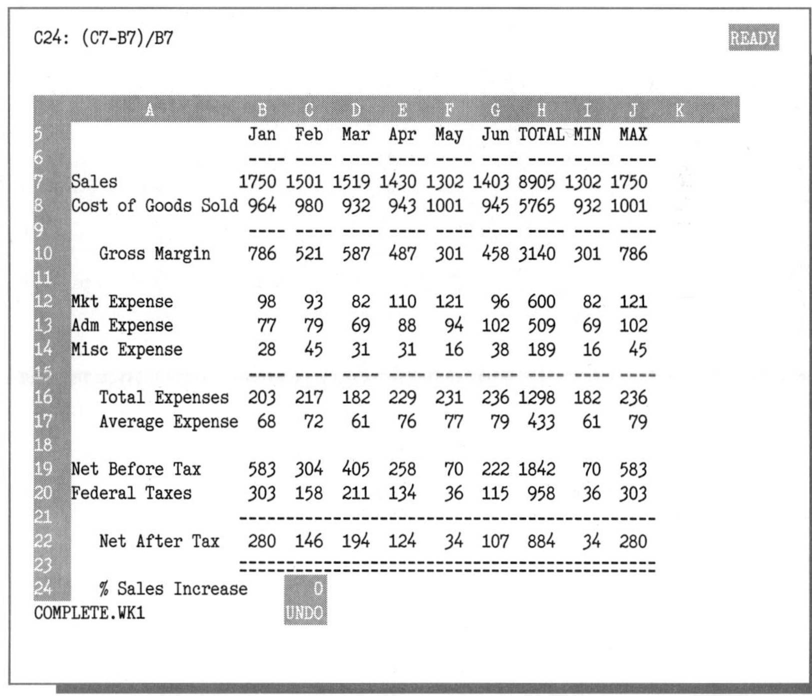

C24: (C7-B7)/B7 READY

	A	B	C	D	E	F	G	H	I	J	K
5		Jan	Feb	Mar	Apr	May	Jun	TOTAL	MIN	MAX	
6		----	----	----	----	----	----	----	----	----	
7	Sales	1750	1501	1519	1430	1302	1403	8905	1302	1750	
8	Cost of Goods Sold	964	980	932	943	1001	945	5765	932	1001	
9		----	----	----	----	----	----	----	----	----	
10	Gross Margin	786	521	587	487	301	458	3140	301	786	
11											
12	Mkt Expense	98	93	82	110	121	96	600	82	121	
13	Adm Expense	77	79	69	88	94	102	509	69	102	
14	Misc Expense	28	45	31	31	16	38	189	16	45	
15		----	----	----	----	----	----	----	----	----	
16	Total Expenses	203	217	182	229	231	236	1298	182	236	
17	Average Expense	68	72	61	76	77	79	433	61	79	
18											
19	Net Before Tax	583	304	405	258	70	222	1842	70	583	
20	Federal Taxes	303	158	211	134	36	115	958	36	303	
21		----	----	----	----	----	----	----	----	----	
22	Net After Tax	280	146	194	124	34	107	884	34	280	
23		====	====	====	====	====	====	====	====	====	
24	% Sales Increase		0								

COMPLETE.WK1 UNDO

Figure 5.16

The calculated value, 0, does not seem correct. If you manually evaluated the formula in cell C24, you would find that the value should be approximately –14 percent.

To find the problem, access the Global settings sheet by issuing the following command:

/ **W**orksheet **S**tatus

Your screen should look similar to Figure 5.17.

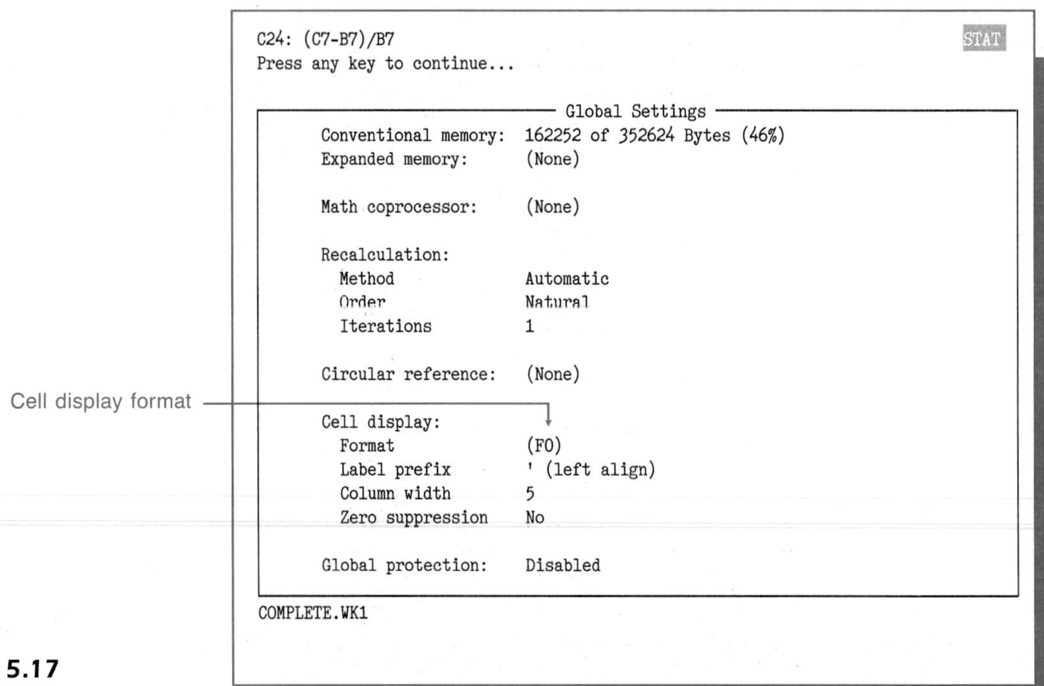

Figure 5.17

The cell display format is (F0). This tells you that the worksheet has been formatted to display numbers without decimals (zero decimal places). This is the default setting.

To change the cell display format to Percent, press any key to return to the worksheet and issue the following command sequence:

/ **R**ange **F**ormat

Your screen should look similar to Figure 5.18.

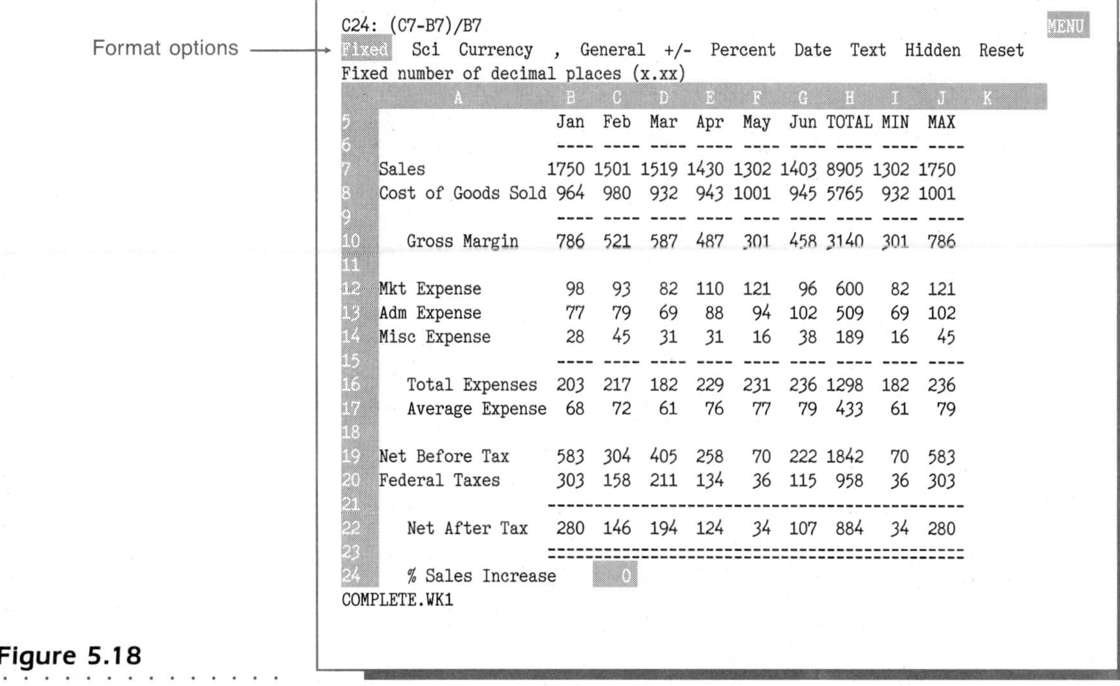

Figure 5.18

The Format command lists eleven options in the control panel. From these, you can specify how numeric values are to be displayed in the worksheet. Since you want to convert the value in cell C24 to a percentage, select:

Percent

The control panel prompts you to specify the number of decimal places you want displayed. The default setting for decimal places is 2, but you want 0. Continue the command sequence as follows:

0 ↵

The next prompt asks you to define the range of cells to be formatted. To accept the displayed range (C24..C24),

Press: ↵

Your screen should look similar to Figure 5.19.

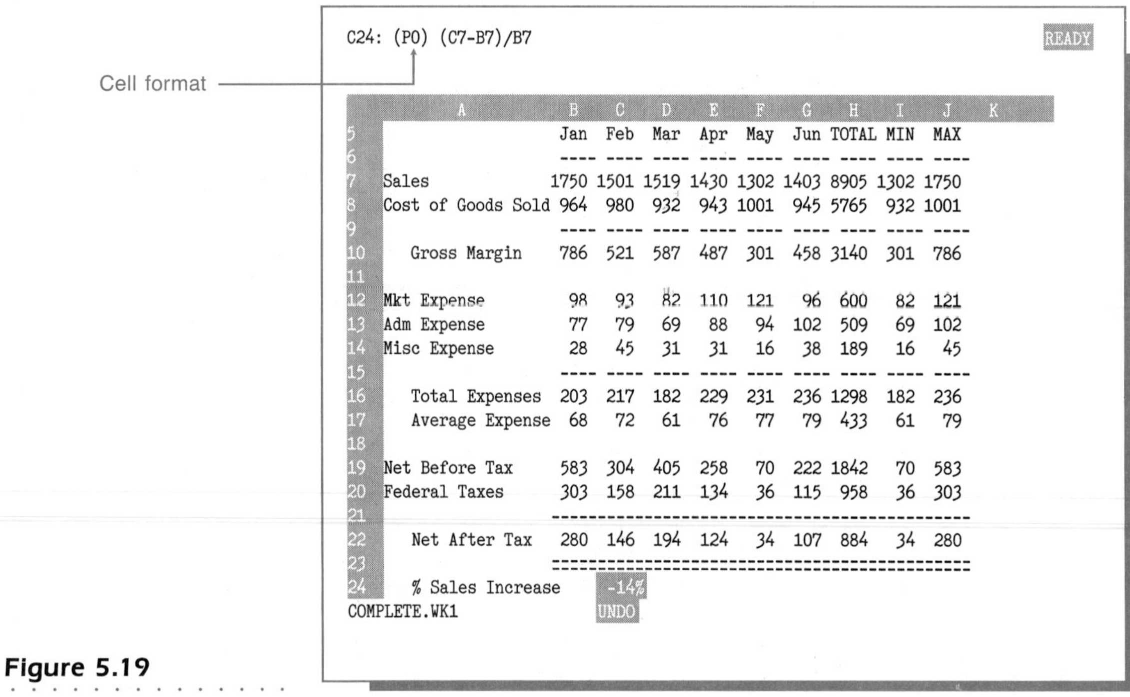

	A	B	C	D	E	F	G	H	I	J
5		Jan	Feb	Mar	Apr	May	Jun	TOTAL	MIN	MAX
6		----	----	----	----	----	----	----	----	----
7	Sales	1750	1501	1519	1430	1302	1403	8905	1302	1750
8	Cost of Goods Sold	964	980	932	943	1001	945	5765	932	1001
9		----	----	----	----	----	----	----	----	----
10	Gross Margin	786	521	587	487	301	458	3140	301	786
11										
12	Mkt Expense	98	93	82	110	121	96	600	82	121
13	Adm Expense	77	79	69	88	94	102	509	69	102
14	Misc Expense	28	45	31	31	16	38	189	16	45
15		----	----	----	----	----	----	----	----	----
16	Total Expenses	203	217	182	229	231	236	1298	182	236
17	Average Expense	68	72	61	76	77	79	433	61	79
18										
19	Net Before Tax	583	304	405	258	70	222	1842	70	583
20	Federal Taxes	303	158	211	134	36	115	958	36	303
21		----	----	----	----	----	----	----	----	----
22	Net After Tax	280	146	194	124	34	107	884	34	280
23		====	====	====	====	====	====	====	====	====
24	% Sales Increase		-14%							

Figure 5.19

The Format Percent command took the calculated value in cell C24 and multiplied it by 100. It also displays a percent sign (%) after the value. The result, –14%, shows Sam that his sales declined by 14 percent from the previous month.

The first line in the control panel now displays the cell format as (P0). The P tells you the cell format is Percent; the zero shows the number of decimal places.

Copy the formula in cell C24 to cells D24 through G24.

The Copy command not only copied the formula, it also copied the cell format.

Next Sam wants to add dollar signs and commas to the worksheet. You just used the Range Format command to format the values in a selected range of cells. Now you will use the Worksheet Global Format command to format the values in all worksheet cells, except those previously formatted with the Range Format command.

To format the worksheet globally to display values with dollar signs and zero decimal places, issue the following command sequence:

/ **W**orksheet **G**lobal **F**ormat **C**urrency **0** ↵

Your screen should look similar to Figure 5.20.

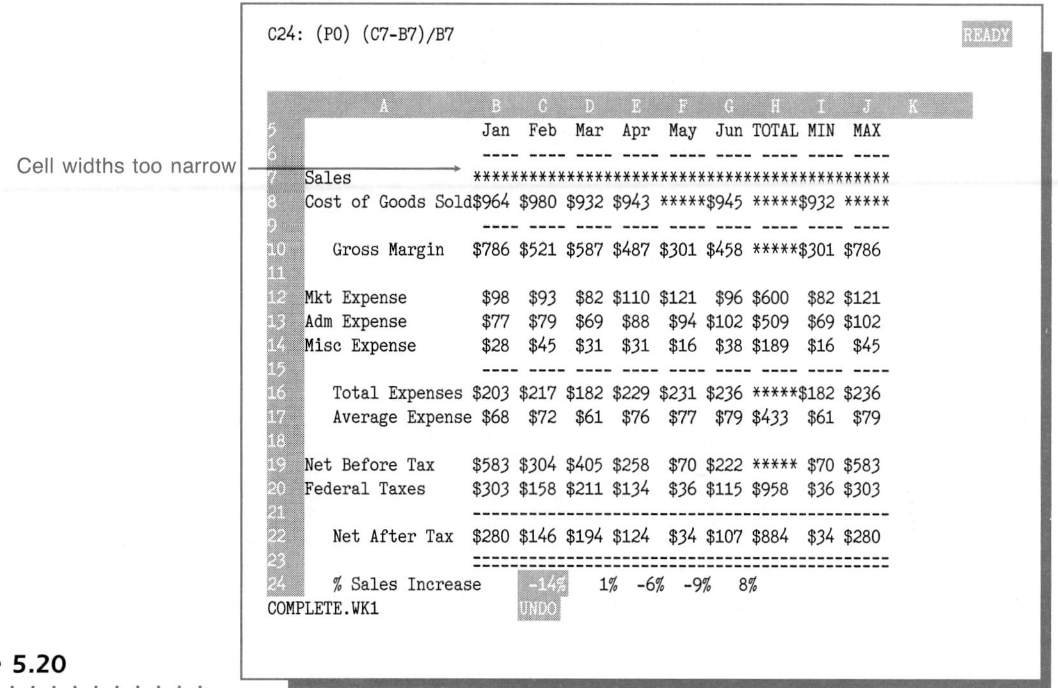

Figure 5.20

All the values in the worksheet now display dollar signs and commas except the values in cells B24 through G24, which were formatted with the Range Format command.

As indicated by the asterisks, some cells are not large enough to display the cell contents including the dollar sign and commas.

To increase the column widths of columns B through J, issue the following command sequence:

/ **W**orksheet **C**olumn **C**olumn-Range **S**et-Width **B24..J24** (↵)

Since you cannot be sure how wide the column widths need to be to display the values, you can increase the width space by space and see how the worksheet adjusts at the same time. To do this,

Press: (→)

The column width increased to six spaces, but that is still not enough to display the values.

Press: (→)

All the values are displayed with the column width set at seven spaces. To complete the command sequence,

Press: (↵)

Your screen should look similar to Figure 5.21.

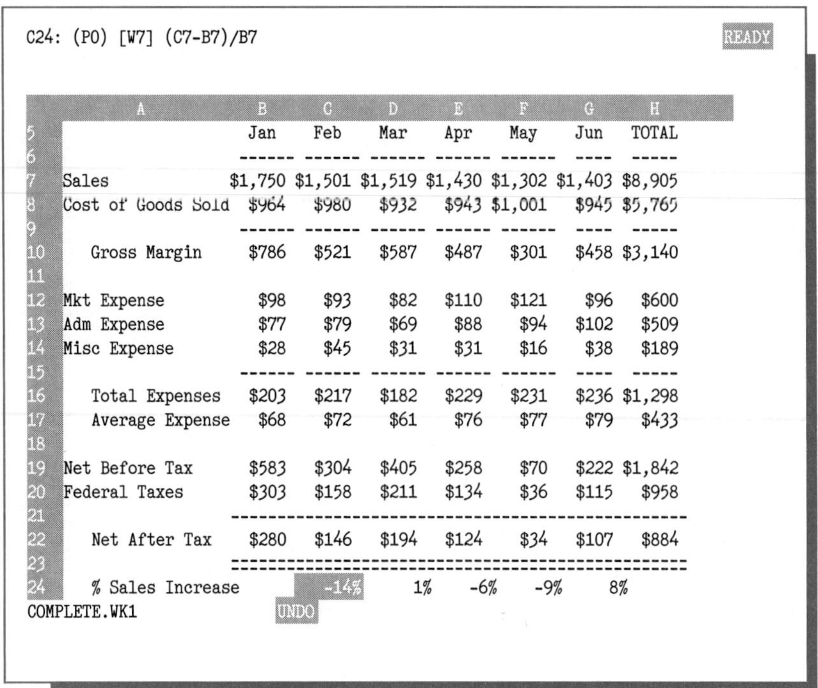

C24: (P0) [W7] (C7-B7)/B7 READY

	A	B	C	D	E	F	G	H
5		Jan	Feb	Mar	Apr	May	Jun	TOTAL
6		------	------	------	------	------	----	-----
7	Sales	$1,750	$1,501	$1,519	$1,430	$1,302	$1,403	$8,905
8	Cost of Goods Sold	$964	$980	$932	$943	$1,001	$945	$5,765
9		------	------	------	------	------	----	-----
10	Gross Margin	$786	$521	$587	$487	$301	$458	$3,140
11								
12	Mkt Expense	$98	$93	$82	$110	$121	$96	$600
13	Adm Expense	$77	$79	$69	$88	$94	$102	$509
14	Misc Expense	$28	$45	$31	$31	$16	$38	$189
15		------	------	------	------	------	----	-----
16	Total Expenses	$203	$217	$182	$229	$231	$236	$1,298
17	Average Expense	$68	$72	$61	$76	$77	$79	$433
18								
19	Net Before Tax	$583	$304	$405	$258	$70	$222	$1,842
20	Federal Taxes	$303	$158	$211	$134	$36	$115	$958
21		-------	-------	-------	-------	-------	-------	-------
22	Net After Tax	$280	$146	$194	$124	$34	$107	$884
23		=======	=======	=======	=======	=======	=======	=======
24	% Sales Increase		-14%	1%	-6%	-9%	8%	

COMPLETE.WK1 UNDO

Figure 5.21

The asterisks have been replaced by the values in the cells. However, because you increased the column widths, the MIN and MAX columns are no longer displayed in the window.

To see the MIN and MAX columns, use (→) to

Move to: J24

Your screen should look similar to Figure 5.22.

Row labels in column A not visible

```
J24: [W7]                                                        READY

    B      C      D      E      F      G     H      I      J     K
5    Jan    Feb    Mar    Apr    May    Jun   TOTAL   MIN    MAX
6   ------ ------ ------ ------ ------ ----  -----   ----   ----
7  $1,750 $1,501 $1,519 $1,430 $1,302 $1,403 $8,905 $1,302 $1,750
8    $964   $980   $932   $943 $1,001   $945 $5,765   $932 $1,001
9   ------ ------ ------ ------ ------ ----  -----   ----   ----
10   $786   $521   $587   $487   $301   $458 $3,140   $301   $786
11
12    $98    $93    $82   $110   $121    $96   $600    $82   $121
13    $77    $79    $69    $88    $94   $102   $509    $69   $102
14    $28    $45    $31    $31    $16    $38   $189    $16    $45
15  ------ ------ ------ ------ ------ ----  -----   ----   ----
16   $203   $217   $182   $229   $231   $236 $1,298   $182   $236
17    $68    $72    $61    $76    $77    $79   $433    $61    $79
18
19   $583   $304   $405   $258    $70   $222 $1,842    $70   $583
20   $303   $158   $211   $134    $36   $115   $958    $36   $303
21 ----------------------------------------------------------------
22   $280   $146   $194   $124    $34   $107   $884    $34   $280
23 ================================================================
24 e        -14%     1%    -6%    -9%     8%
COMPLETE.WK1               UNDO
```

Figure 5.22

Although you can now see the MIN and MAX columns, you cannot see the row labels in column A. This makes it difficult to understand the information displayed in the window. Lab 6 deals with this problem.

Before you print the worksheet, put your name in cell A1 and the current date in cell A2. Print this worksheet.

Creating a Backup File

Many times you may want to use the same filename when you save a file but you also want to keep a copy of the last version of the file on the disk. You can do this by creating a backup file when you save the worksheet. Issue the following command sequence:

/ **F**ile **S**ave ↵ **B**ackup

The last version of the worksheet has been saved as COMPLETE.BAK and the edited version as COMPLETE.WK1. To retrieve a backup file, you must enter the filename with the .BAK file extension. The backup file will not be displayed in the list of .WK1 files. Alternatively, you could rename the backup file and change the file extension to .WK1. Then you could retrieve it like any other worksheet file.

Exit 1-2-3.

Glossary of Key Terms

@AVG Calculates the average in a range of cells.

Circular reference Occurs when a formula refers directly or indirectly to the cell that contains that formula. The status indicator displays CIRC whenever 1-2-3 detects a circular reference.

Linking formula A formula entered in the target file that creates a link to a cell in the source file.

@MAX Calculates the highest value in a range of cells.

@MIN Calculates the lowest value in a range of cells.

Source file The file that supplies the data when files are linked.

Status screen Displays the current worksheet settings.

@SUM Calculates the total value in a range of cells.

Target file The file that retrieves the data when files are linked.

Practice Problems

1. Matching

1. CIRC
2. /WCH
3. +<<FINEXP>>B7
4. @MIN
5. /RNC
6. /RF
7. ******
8. /WS
9. 10.35%
10. $10.35

_______ **a.** hides a column
_______ **b.** returns the smallest value in a range
_______ **c.** indicates insufficient cell width to display a value
_______ **d.** status indicator for circular reference
_______ **e.** formats a range of cells
_______ **f.** names a range of cells
_______ **g.** a number in currency format
_______ **h.** a number in percent format
_______ **i.** linking formula
_______ **j.** displays a Worksheet Status window

2. Four roommates have challenged one another to a weight loss competition. The following table shows their weights after five weeks.

		Weight (lbs.)					
Name	Beg. wt.	Week 1	Week 2	Week 3	Week 4	Avg	% Diff
Joe	202	198	192	190	189		
Tom	180	177	177	175	172		
Phil	229	225	223	220	215		
Larry	212	208	205	203	200		

Use these data to create a worksheet. Enter your name in cell A1 and the current date in cell A2.

a. Appropriately name each person's weight range.

b. Use the @AVG function and the named ranges to calculate each person's average weight.

c. Calculate the percent differences for each person by subtracting the weight in week 4 from the beginning weight and then dividing by the beginning weight. Who had the largest percent difference?

d. Set the format for the percent-difference column to display as a percent with two decimal places.

e. Save the complete worksheet with the filename WEIGHT.

f. Print the worksheet.

3. Robert Dobber has been working on a six-month income statement for his chain of pet shops. He has been having some problems. Retrieve the file ROBERT1 to see the worksheet Robert has created.

a. Put your name in cell A1 and the current date in cell A2.

b. Locate the source of the CIRC reference and correct the formula or @function causing the reference. Does the CIRC message disappear? If not, again locate the source of the CIRC reference and correct it.

c. Complete the MIN and MAX columns by entering the @functions to calculate the minimum and maximum values in columns B through G.

d. Hide columns B through G. Print the worksheet. Unhide columns B through G.

e. Globally change the worksheet to display currency with zero decimal places. Increase the column widths to display the values. What is the new column width?

f. Save the new version of the worksheet as ROBERT2.

g. Print the worksheet.

6

Managing a Large Worksheet

Objectives

In Lab 6, you will learn how to:

- Freeze horizontal and vertical titles
- Create, scroll, and use windows
- Extract and combine worksheets
- Enter and justify text
- Restrict file access using passwords

Case Study

You will continue to follow the case introduced in Lab 5 as Sam Bynner develops and expands the income statement for his chain of bookstores.

At the end of Lab 5, Sam had completed an income statement for a six-month period. Once the income statement was formatted to display currency, however, it could no longer be contained in one window. In Lab 6, Sam has expanded the income statement to cover a one-year period. The increased size of the worksheet has made it increasingly difficult to handle. You will follow Sam as he learns how to manage a large worksheet and uses what-if analysis to help with long-range financial planning for his company.

Freezing Titles

Sam Bynner has extended the six-month statement for Bynner's Bookshops to a full year. To see this worksheet, load 1-2-3 and retrieve the file YEAR.

This worksheet contains income statement figures for twelve months. The worksheet extends beyond column F and below row 20. Although there are quicker ways to move around the worksheet for this lab, use the arrow keys as directed. You need to do this so that your display screen will appear the same as the figures in this lab.

To view the rest of the worksheet, use (↓) and (→) to:

Move to: P24

Your screen should look similar to Figure 6.1.

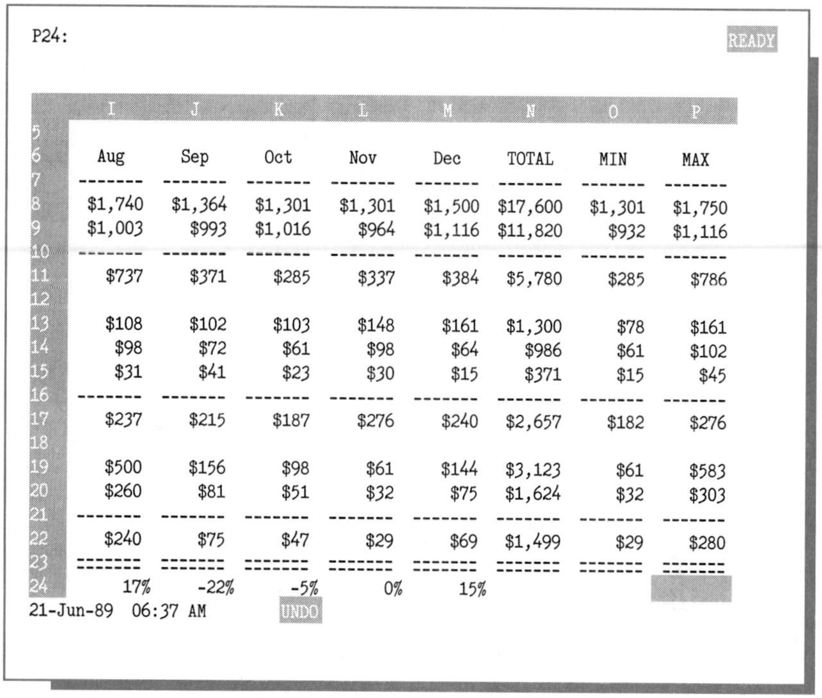

P24: READY

	I	J	K	L	M	N	O	P
5								
6	Aug	Sep	Oct	Nov	Dec	TOTAL	MIN	MAX
7	-------	-------	-------	-------	-------	-------	-------	-------
8	$1,740	$1,364	$1,301	$1,301	$1,500	$17,600	$1,301	$1,750
9	$1,003	$993	$1,016	$964	$1,116	$11,820	$932	$1,116
10	-------	-------	-------	-------	-------	-------	-------	-------
11	$737	$371	$285	$337	$384	$5,780	$285	$786
12								
13	$108	$102	$103	$148	$161	$1,300	$78	$161
14	$98	$72	$61	$98	$64	$986	$61	$102
15	$31	$41	$23	$30	$15	$371	$15	$45
16	-------	-------	-------	-------	-------	-------	-------	-------
17	$237	$215	$187	$276	$240	$2,657	$182	$276
18								
19	$500	$156	$98	$61	$144	$3,123	$61	$583
20	$260	$81	$51	$32	$75	$1,624	$32	$303
21	-------	-------	-------	-------	-------	-------	-------	-------
22	$240	$75	$47	$29	$69	$1,499	$29	$280
23	=======	=======	=======	=======	=======	=======	=======	=======
24	17%	-22%	-5%	0%	15%			

21-Jun-89 06:37 AM UNDO

Figure 6.1

This worksheet provides a convenient way for Bynner's management team to summarize the company's annual financial performance and to analyze its monthly performance. However, the worksheet is difficult to read.

Look, for example, at the entry $737 in cell I11. It is difficult to remember what that figure represents. Is it income, an expense, a total, or a tax?

To see the row labels in column A, use (←) to

Move to: A24

You can now see that the figures in row 11 are for gross margin.

Whenever a worksheet extends beyond a single window and the row labels are no longer visible, understanding the worksheet is difficult. It would be much more convenient if you could keep the titles in column A in the window all the time. **Freezing titles** keeps row and column headings on the screen even when you scroll the windows.

To freeze a vertical column of titles, locate the cell pointer one column to the right of the column you want to freeze. To freeze column A,

Move to: B24

Then issue the following command sequence:

/ **W**orksheet **T**itles **V**ertical

Nothing appears to have happened.

Press: (←)

The program beeps and does not allow the cell pointer to move into the frozen column.

Now watch the monthly figures scroll as you use (→) to

Move to: P24

Your screen should look similar to Figure 6.2.

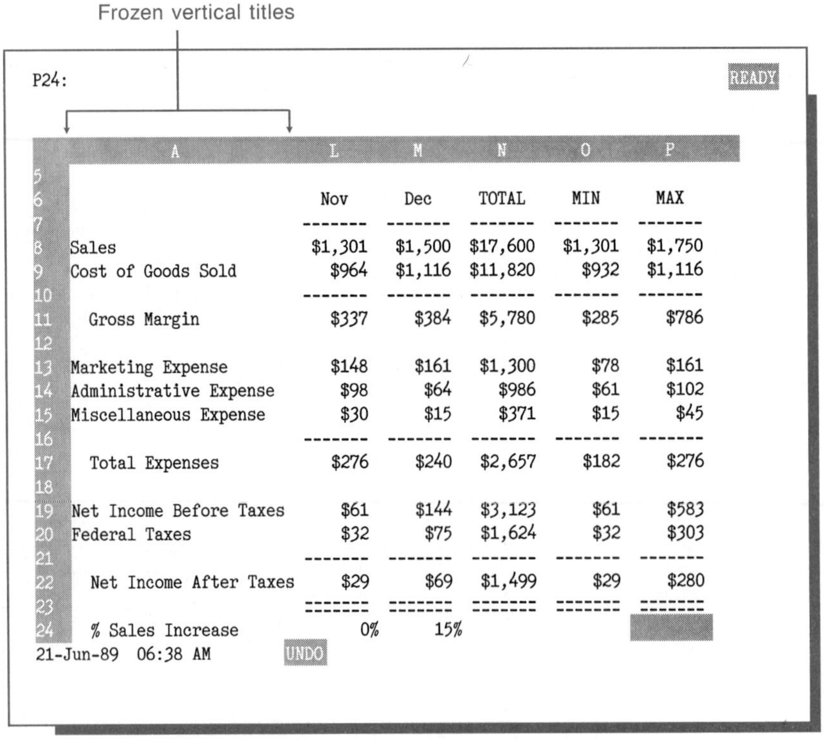

Frozen vertical titles

```
P24:                                                              READY

      A                       L        M        N        O        P
 5
 6                            Nov      Dec      TOTAL    MIN      MAX
 7                            -------  -------  -------  -------  -------
 8  Sales                     $1,301   $1,500  $17,600   $1,301   $1,750
 9  Cost of Goods Sold          $964   $1,116  $11,820     $932   $1,116
10                            -------  -------  -------  -------  -------
11    Gross Margin              $337     $384   $5,780     $285     $786
12
13  Marketing Expense           $148     $161   $1,300      $78     $161
14  Administrative Expense       $98      $64     $986      $61     $102
15  Miscellaneous Expense        $30      $15     $371      $15      $45
16                            -------  -------  -------  -------  -------
17    Total Expenses            $276     $240   $2,657     $182     $276
18
19  Net Income Before Taxes      $61     $144   $3,123      $61     $583
20  Federal Taxes                $32      $75   $1,624      $32     $303
21                            -------  -------  -------  -------  -------
22    Net Income After Taxes     $29      $69   $1,499      $29     $280
23                            =======  =======  =======  =======  =======
24    % Sales Increase            0%      15%
21-Jun-89  06:38 AM   UNDO
```

Figure 6.2

Column A does not move. You have frozen column A so that the row labels always appear in the window. This makes the worksheet much easier to read and to use.

To unfreeze, or clear, the frozen titles, issue the following command sequence:

/ **W**orksheet **T**itles **C**lear

Your screen should now look similar to Figure 6.3.

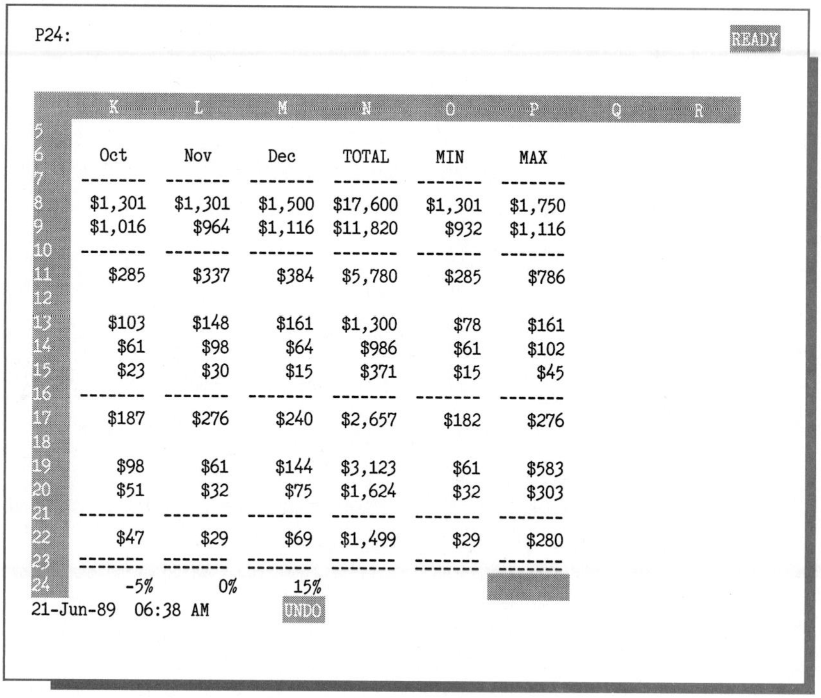

P24: READY

	K	L	M	N	O	P	Q	R
5								
6	Oct	Nov	Dec	TOTAL	MIN	MAX		
7	-------	-------	-------	-------	-------	-------		
8	$1,301	$1,301	$1,500	$17,600	$1,301	$1,750		
9	$1,016	$964	$1,116	$11,820	$932	$1,116		
10	-------	-------	-------	-------	-------	-------		
11	$285	$337	$384	$5,780	$285	$786		
12								
13	$103	$148	$161	$1,300	$78	$161		
14	$61	$98	$64	$986	$61	$102		
15	$23	$30	$15	$371	$15	$45		
16	-------	-------	-------	-------	-------	-------		
17	$187	$276	$240	$2,657	$182	$276		
18								
19	$98	$61	$144	$3,123	$61	$583		
20	$51	$32	$75	$1,624	$32	$303		
21	-------	-------	-------	-------	-------	-------		
22	$47	$29	$69	$1,499	$29	$280		
23	=======	=======	=======	=======	=======	=======		
24	-5%	0%	15%					

21-Jun-89 06:38 AM UNDO

Figure 6.3

Column A no longer appears in the window.

To confirm that the titles are unfrozen, use (←) to

Move to: A24

The cell pointer can now be moved into column A.

Freezing and unfreezing titles horizontally across a row is just as easy as freezing and unfreezing them vertically down a column. To do so, position the cell pointer one row below the row to be frozen. Everything above that row will remain stationary on your screen.

To freeze the rows above row 8, use (↑) to

Move to: A8

Then issue the following command sequence:

/ **W**orksheet **T**itles **H**orizontal

To confirm that the titles are frozen,

Press: (↑)

Next, use (↓) to

Move to: A28

Your screen should now look similar to Figure 6.4.

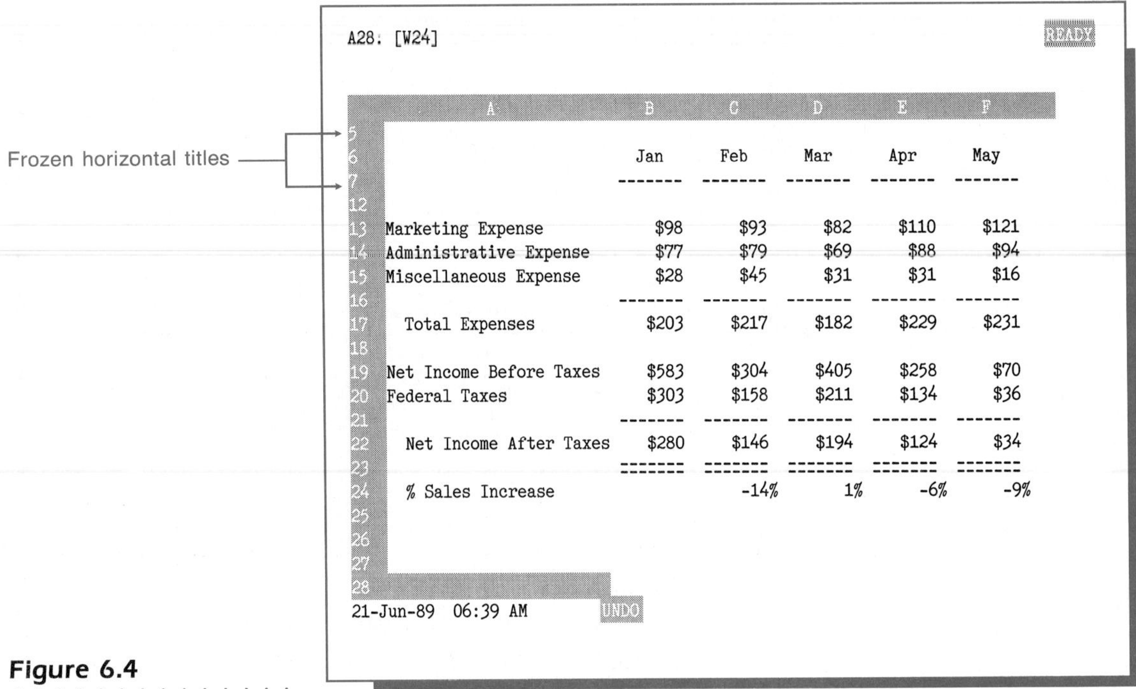

Frozen horizontal titles
A28: [W24]
READY
A B C D E F
Jan Feb Mar Apr May
Marketing Expense $98 $93 $82 $110 $121
Administrative Expense $77 $79 $69 $88 $94
Miscellaneous Expense $28 $45 $31 $31 $16
Total Expenses $203 $217 $182 $229 $231
Net Income Before Taxes $583 $304 $405 $258 $70
Federal Taxes $303 $158 $211 $134 $36
Net Income After Taxes $280 $146 $194 $124 $34
% Sales Increase -14% 1% -6% -9%
21-Jun-89 06:39 AM
UNDO

Figure 6.4

As you scroll the worksheet, rows 5, 6, and 7 remain fixed on the screen.

There may be times when you will want to move the cell pointer to a cell that is within a frozen row or column, such as cell A5 in this worksheet. To do this, the GOTO feature, (F5), is used.

Press: (F5)
Type: **A5**
Press: (↵)

Your screen should be similar to Figure 6.5.

Second set of titles

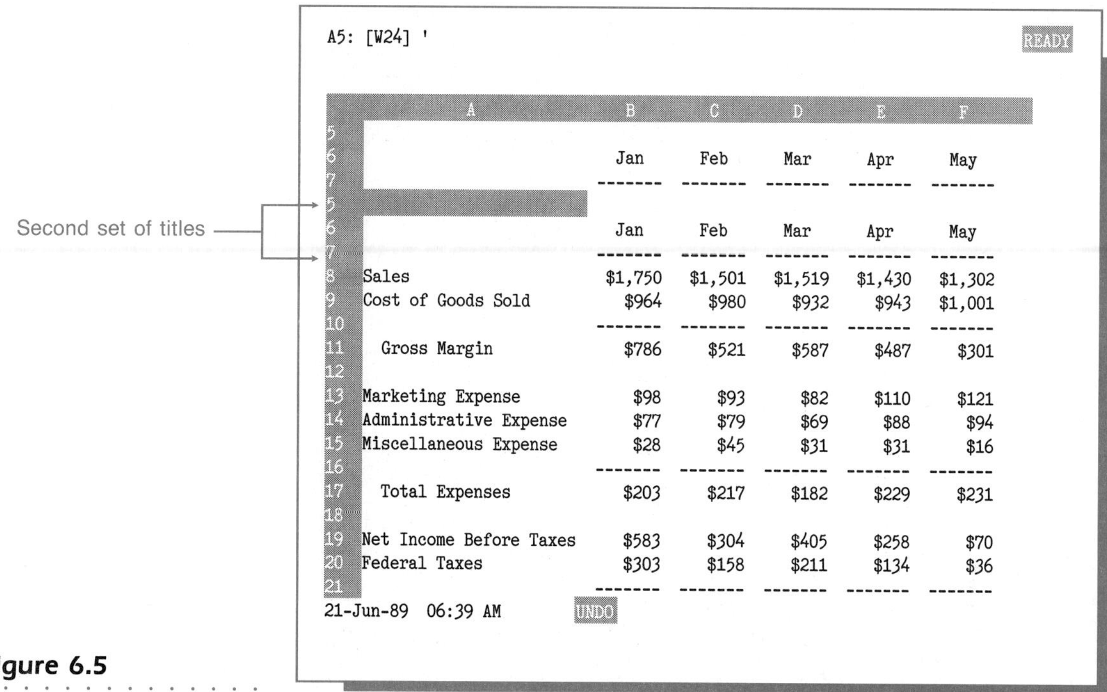

```
A5: [W24] '                                                        READY

      A                           B        C        D        E        F
 5
 6                               Jan      Feb      Mar      Apr      May
 7                           -------  -------  -------  -------  -------
 5
 6                               Jan      Feb      Mar      Apr      May
 7                           -------  -------  -------  -------  -------
 8  Sales                     $1,750   $1,501   $1,519   $1,430   $1,302
 9  Cost of Goods Sold          $964     $980     $932     $943   $1,001
10                           -------  -------  -------  -------  -------
11    Gross Margin              $786     $521     $587     $487     $301
12
13  Marketing Expense            $98      $93      $82     $110     $121
14  Administrative Expense       $77      $79      $69      $88      $94
15  Miscellaneous Expense        $28      $45      $31      $31      $16
16                           -------  -------  -------  -------  -------
17    Total Expenses            $203     $217     $182     $229     $231
18
19  Net Income Before Taxes     $583     $304     $405     $258      $70
20  Federal Taxes               $303     $158     $211     $134      $36
21                           -------  -------  -------  -------  -------
21-Jun-89  06:39 AM        UNDO
```

Figure 6.5

A second set of frozen horizontal titles is displayed immediately below the first set. The cell pointer is positioned in a previously frozen cell.

Press: (↑) four times

You can now move into and use any of the previously frozen rows. To clear the second set of frozen titles:

Press: PGDN
Press: PGUP

To verify that the original frozen horizontal titles are again in effect,

Press: (↑)

The computer beeped and the cell pointer cannot be moved above row 8.

Note To clear a second set of frozen vertical titles, you would use the CTRL-(→) and CTRL-(←) sequence.

Clear the frozen titles by issuing the following command sequence:

/ **W**orksheet **T**itles **C**lear

As you have probably already guessed, you can also freeze titles horizontally and vertically at the same time. To do this, you must position the cell pointer one column to the right of the column to be frozen and one row below the row to be frozen. Everything to the left and above that cell will be frozen.

Move to: B8

Freeze the titles to the left and above the cell pointer by issuing the following command sequence:

/ **W**orksheet **T**itles **B**oth

Press: ↑
Press: ←

The rows above row 8 and the column to the left of column B are frozen. Now, watch your screen closely as you use → and ↓ to

Move to: P8
Move to: P28

Your screen should look similar to Figure 6.6.

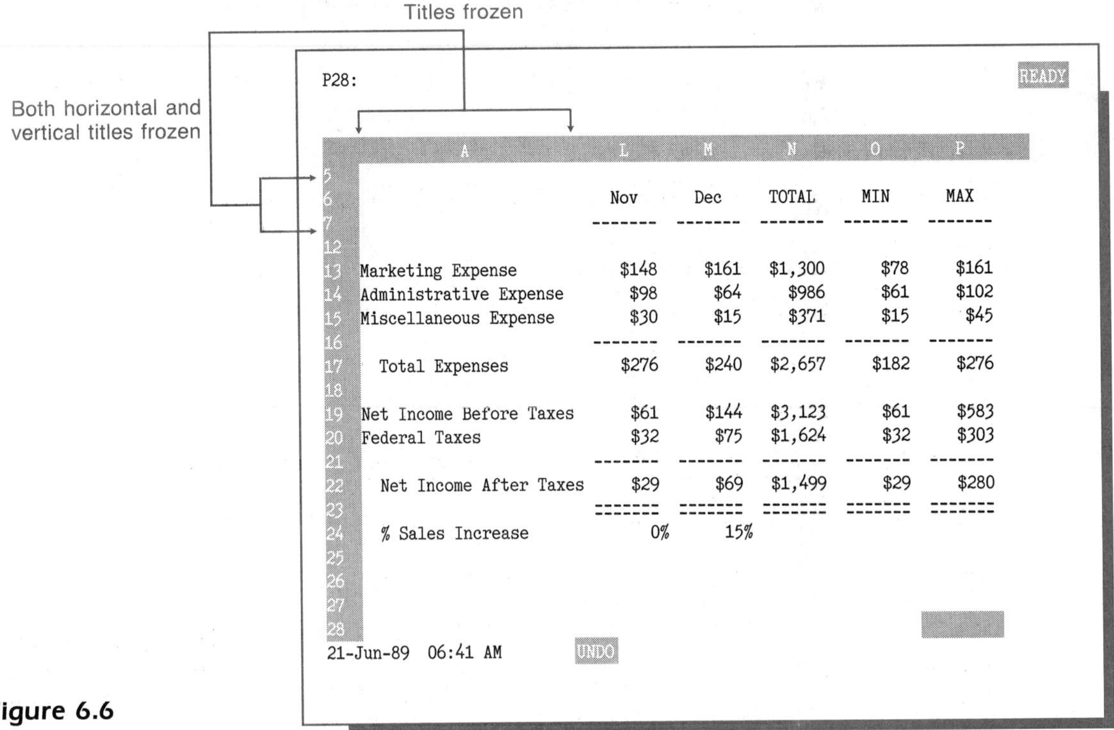

Titles frozen
Both horizontal and vertical titles frozen
P28:
READY
A L M N O P
Nov Dec TOTAL MIN MAX
Marketing Expense $148 $161 $1,300 $78 $161
Administrative Expense $98 $64 $986 $61 $102
Miscellaneous Expense $30 $15 $371 $15 $45
Total Expenses $276 $240 $2,657 $182 $276
Net Income Before Taxes $61 $144 $3,123 $61 $583
Federal Taxes $32 $75 $1,624 $32 $303
Net Income After Taxes $29 $69 $1,499 $29 $280
% Sales Increase 0% 15%
21-Jun-89 06:41 AM
UNDO

Figure 6.6

The vertical titles (column A) and the horizontal titles (above row 8) remain frozen on the screen as you scroll through the worksheet. To return to the upper left position of the worksheet,

Press: HOME

The HOME key returns the cell pointer to cell B8 rather than to cell A1 because all cells above and to the left of cell B8 are frozen.

Creating and Scrolling Windows

The frozen titles greatly improve the readability of the worksheet, but it is still awkward for Bynner's management team to make certain types of comparisons.

Sam Bynner wants to compare his monthly income figures to the annual totals. For example, he wants to compare the income figures for the month of April, located in column E, with the annual totals, located in column N. Because of the size of the worksheet, however, these two columns cannot be displayed at the same time in a single window.

Worksheets are viewed through windows. So far, you have used only one window at a time. You will now use the Worksheet Window command to create two windows on your screen at the same time.

To create a vertical window between columns M and N, move the cell pointer anywhere in column N. Using →,

Move to: N8

Issue the following command sequence:

/ **W**orksheet **W**indow **V**ertical

Your screen should look similar to Figure 6.7.

Row numbers for second window

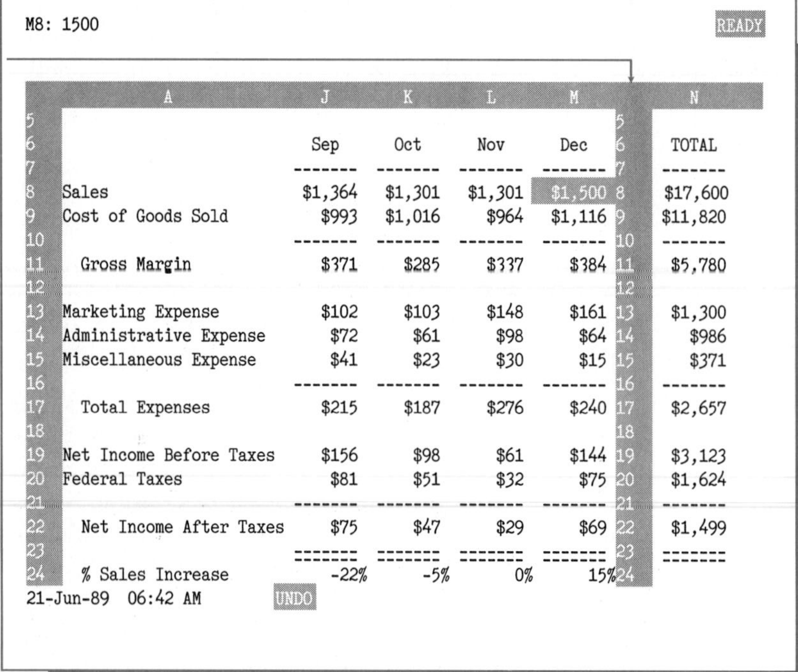

M8: 1500 READY

	A	J	K	L	M		N
5						5	
6		Sep	Oct	Nov	Dec	6	TOTAL
7		-------	-------	-------	-------	7	-------
8	Sales	$1,364	$1,301	$1,301	$1,500	8	$17,600
9	Cost of Goods Sold	$993	$1,016	$964	$1,116	9	$11,820
10		-------	-------	-------	-------	10	-------
11	Gross Margin	$371	$285	$337	$384	11	$5,780
12						12	
13	Marketing Expense	$102	$103	$148	$161	13	$1,300
14	Administrative Expense	$72	$61	$98	$64	14	$986
15	Miscellaneous Expense	$41	$23	$30	$15	15	$371
16		-------	-------	-------	-------	16	-------
17	Total Expenses	$215	$187	$276	$240	17	$2,657
18						18	
19	Net Income Before Taxes	$156	$98	$61	$144	19	$3,123
20	Federal Taxes	$81	$51	$32	$75	20	$1,624
21		-------	-------	-------	-------	21	-------
22	Net Income After Taxes	$75	$47	$29	$69	22	$1,499
23		=======	=======	=======	=======	23	=======
24	% Sales Increase	-22%	-5%	0%	15%	24	

21-Jun-89 06:42 AM UNDO

Figure 6.7

A new column of row numbers appears between columns M and N, separating the two windows. The cell pointer is currently in the left window. Now watch your screen closely as you use (←) to

Move to: B8

Your screen should look similar to Figure 6.8.

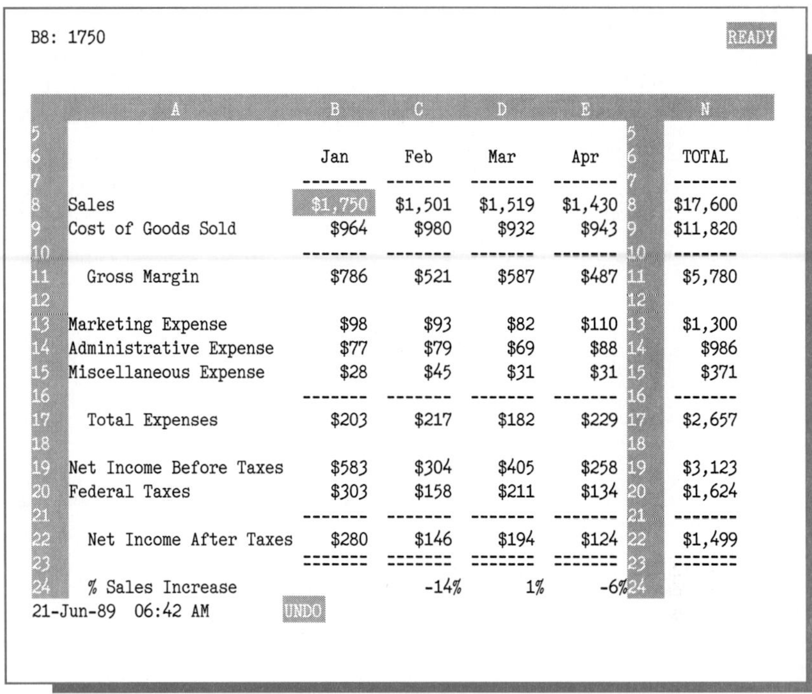
B8: 1750 READY

	A	B	C	D	E		N
5						5	
6		Jan	Feb	Mar	Apr	6	TOTAL
7		-------	-------	-------	-------	7	-------
8	Sales	$1,750	$1,501	$1,519	$1,430	8	$17,600
9	Cost of Goods Sold	$964	$980	$932	$943	9	$11,820
10		-------	-------	-------	-------	10	-------
11	Gross Margin	$786	$521	$587	$487	11	$5,780
12						12	
13	Marketing Expense	$98	$93	$82	$110	13	$1,300
14	Administrative Expense	$77	$79	$69	$88	14	$986
15	Miscellaneous Expense	$28	$45	$31	$31	15	$371
16		-------	-------	-------	-------	16	-------
17	Total Expenses	$203	$217	$182	$229	17	$2,657
18						18	
19	Net Income Before Taxes	$583	$304	$405	$258	19	$3,123
20	Federal Taxes	$303	$158	$211	$134	20	$1,624
21		-------	-------	-------	-------	21	-------
22	Net Income After Taxes	$280	$146	$194	$124	22	$1,499
23		=======	=======	=======	=======	23	=======
24	% Sales Increase		-14%	1%	-6%	24	

21-Jun-89 06:42 AM UNDO

Figure 6.8

The columns in the left window move as the cell pointer moves, but the columns in the right window remain stationary. Now Sam can easily compare the income figures for April in column E to the annual total in column N.

Now watch your screen again as you use ↓ to

Move to: B28

The rows in both windows move together. This is called **synchronized scrolling**.

You can move the cell pointer from one window to the other with the Window function key, F6.

To move the cell pointer to the right window,

Press: F6

F6 is simply a switch that makes the cell pointer jump from one window to the other. Try pressing it a few times.

If the cell pointer is not in the right window, put it there. Now watch your screen as you use ↑ to

Move to: N8

Again, the windows scroll together, synchronized. The windows can also operate independently. This is called **unsynchronized scrolling**. To change to unsynchronized scrolling, issue the following command sequence:

/ **W**orksheet **W**indow **U**nsync

No difference is immediately visible. However, watch your screen as you use (↓) to

Move to: N28

Your screen should look similar to Figure 6.9.

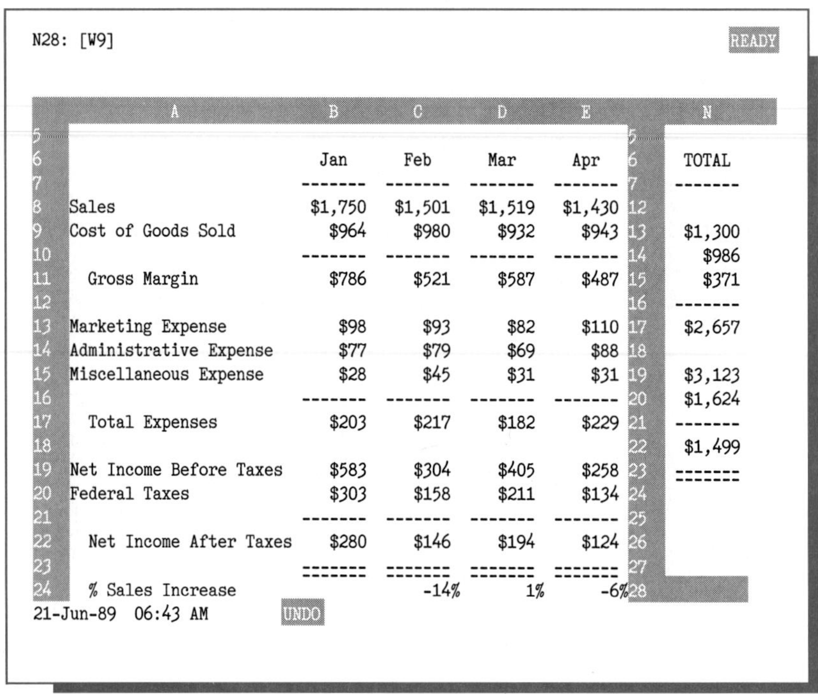

Figure 6.9

The left window remains stationary, while the rows in the right window scroll.

Switch to the left window and scroll down to B28. The rows in both windows should now be lined up.

You can create a horizontal window as easily as you made a vertical window. The command sequence is identical, except that you select **H**orizontal rather than **V**ertical.

Before continuing, remove the window and clear the frozen titles by issuing the following command sequences:

/ **W**orksheet **W**indows **C**lear
/ **W**orksheet **T**itles **C**lear

Extracting and Combining Files

Sam Bynner has reviewed his company's financial statements and is pleased with the company's performance. He is also pleased with the worksheet analysis, particularly with the basic design of the worksheet.

Sam decides to create a new worksheet to help him develop a five-year financial plan. This new worksheet will contain some of the current worksheet's information, such as the row titles and the values in the TOTAL column.

To set up the framework for this new file, you will use the Extract and the Combine commands.

The Extract command takes a portion of the current worksheet and saves it as a new file. First, you will extract the labels in column A to the file FRAME.

Press: HOME
Move to: A6

Issue the following command sequence:

/ **F**ile **X**tract

Your screen should look similar to Figure 6.10.

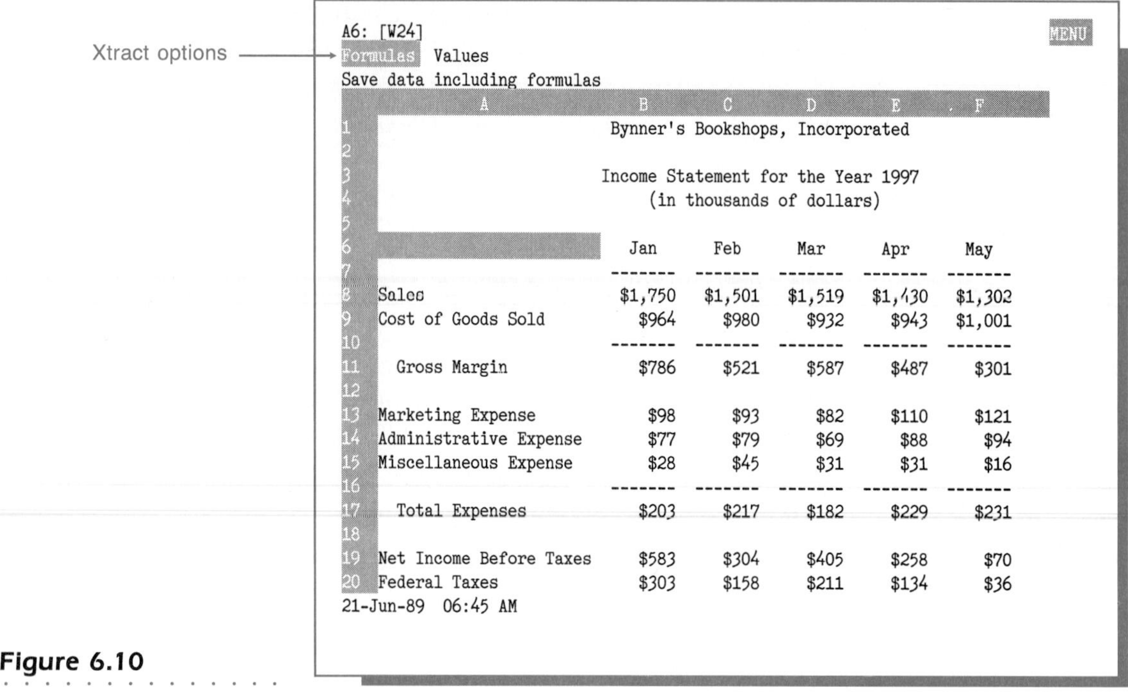

A6: [W24] MENU
Formulas Values
Save data including formulas

	A	B	C	D	E	F
1		Bynner's Bookshops, Incorporated				
2						
3		Income Statement for the Year 1997				
4		(in thousands of dollars)				
5						
6		Jan	Feb	Mar	Apr	May
7		-------	-------	-------	-------	-------
8	Sales	$1,750	$1,501	$1,519	$1,430	$1,302
9	Cost of Goods Sold	$964	$980	$932	$943	$1,001
10		-------	-------	-------	-------	-------
11	Gross Margin	$786	$521	$587	$487	$301
12						
13	Marketing Expense	$98	$93	$82	$110	$121
14	Administrative Expense	$77	$79	$69	$88	$94
15	Miscellaneous Expense	$28	$45	$31	$31	$16
16		-------	-------	-------	-------	-------
17	Total Expenses	$203	$217	$182	$229	$231
18						
19	Net Income Before Taxes	$583	$304	$405	$258	$70
20	Federal Taxes	$303	$158	$211	$134	$36

21-Jun-89 06:45 AM

Figure 6.10

The control panel prompts you to select either formulas or values. If the cells you are extracting contain formulas, you can extract either the values displayed in the worksheet or the formulas used to calculate the values; however, you cannot extract both.

In this case, all the entries in column A are labels; therefore, either response is acceptable. To continue the command sequence,

Press: ↵

The next prompt is to assign a name to the extracted file. Continue the command sequence as follows:

FRAME ↵

To complete the command sequence, define the range to be extracted as

A6..A24 ↵

After a few moments, the defined range is copied into the new file.

Next, you will extract the values in the TOTAL column to another file. Using (→),

Move to: N6

To extract the label and values in cells N6 through N23 to the file TOTAL, issue the following command sequence:

/ **F**ile **X**tract

In this command sequence you need to select values rather than formulas. This is because the new worksheet will not contain the monthly income figures used in the formulas and @functions in column N. If the formulas were copied, they would reference blank cells and the calculated value would be zero. Continue the command sequence as follows:

Values **TOTAL** (↵) **N6..N23** (↵)

Next, you will combine the two files to create a new worksheet file. Begin by retrieving the file FRAME.

Your screen should look similar to Figure 6.11.

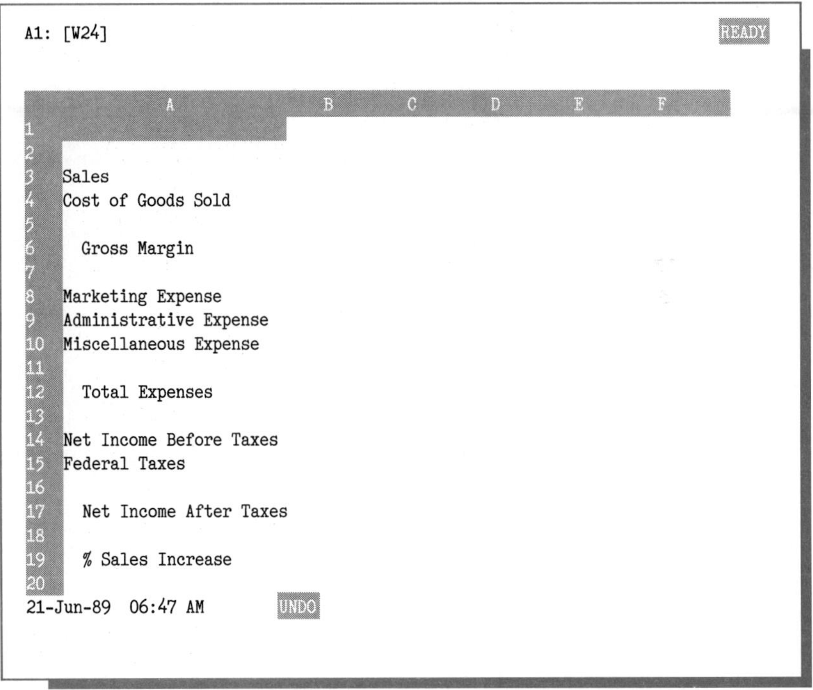

Figure 6.11

The file FRAME contains the labels in column A extracted from the file YEAR.

The Combine command incorporates all or part of a file into the current worksheet. You will use the Combine command to copy the file TOTAL into the file FRAME. Before you use this command, however, the cell pointer must be positioned in the upper left corner of the area in the worksheet where the file is to be inserted.

Move to: B1

Then issue the following command sequence:

/ **F**ile **C**ombine **C**opy

The control panel prompts you to select either the Entire-File or a Named/Specified-Range to be copied.

You want the entire contents of the file TOTAL to be copied, so complete the command sequence as follows:

Entire-File **TOTAL** ↵

Your screen should look similar to Figure 6.12.

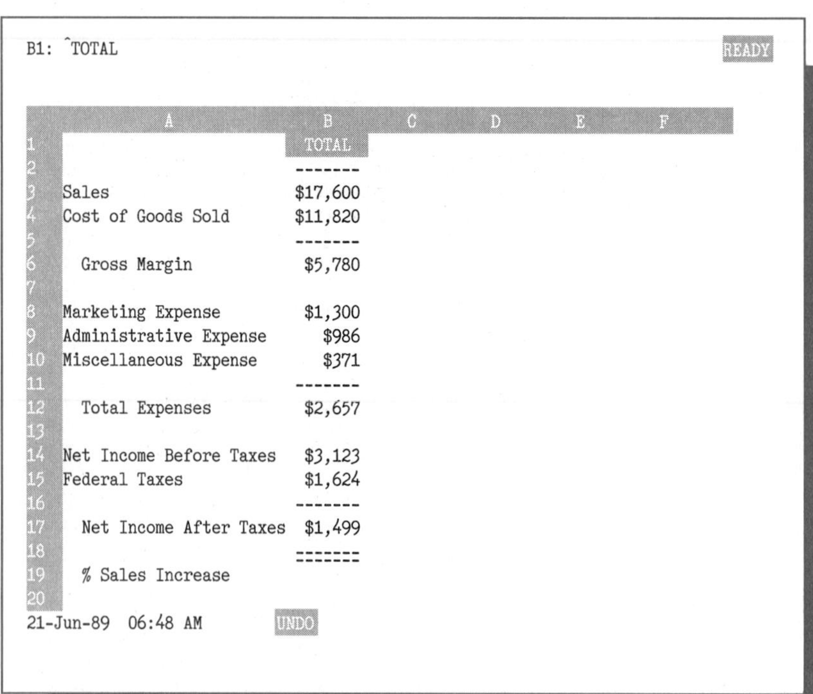

B1: ^TOTAL
READY
A B C D E F
1 TOTAL
2 -------
3 Sales $17,600
4 Cost of Goods Sold $11,820
5 -------
6 Gross Margin $5,780
7
8 Marketing Expense $1,300
9 Administrative Expense $986
10 Miscellaneous Expense $371
11 -------
12 Total Expenses $2,657
13
14 Net Income Before Taxes $3,123
15 Federal Taxes $1,624
16 -------
17 Net Income After Taxes $1,499
18 =======
19 % Sales Increase
20
21-Jun-89 06:48 AM
UNDO

Figure 6.12

The TOTAL column has been copied into the file FRAME. Sam Bynner wants to develop a five-year financial plan using this basic worksheet. The data in the TOTAL column will become the data for the year 1997. He asks his management team to prepare an income statement for the following year (1998) and to project this statement another five years (1999 through 2003).

After hours of discussion and analysis, the management team develops a projected income statement. To see this statement, retrieve the file PROJECT.

To see the rest of the worksheet, use (→) and (↓) to

Move to: G27

Your screen should now look similar to Figure 6.13.

G27: (P2) (G11-F11)/F11 READY

	B	C	D	E	F	G	H	I
8	Actual	Budget	x============	====Projections	=========	=========	=======x	
9	1997	1998	1999	2000	2001	2002	2003	TOTAL
10	-------	-------	-------	-------	-------	-------	-------	-------
11 (Sales →)	17600	23100	28600	34100	39000	44500	50000	236900
12	11820	13000	15000	18000	19412	21000	23000	121232
13	-------	-------	-------	-------	-------	-------	-------	-------
14	5780	10100	13600	16100	19588	23500	27000	115668
15								
16	1300	1900	2600	3800	4131	4900	5250	23881
17	986	1100	1300	1400	1500	1750	1980	10016
18	371	480	560	640	700	790	810	4351
19	-------	-------	-------	-------	-------	-------	-------	-------
20	2657	3480	4460	5840	6331	7440	8040	38248
21								
22	3123	6620	9140	10260	13257	16060	18960	77420
23	1624	3442	4753	5335	6894	8351	9859	40258
24	-------	-------	-------	-------	-------	-------	-------	-------
25	1499	3178	4387	4925	6363	7709	9101	37162
26	=======	=======	=======	=======	=======	=======	=======	=======
27		31.25%	23.81%	19.23%	14.37%	14.10%	12.36%	

21-Jun-89 06:49 AM UNDO

Figure 6.13

Sam Bynner evaluates this worksheet by first looking at the projected growth in sales (row 11).

Future sales are increasing from \$23,100 in 1998 (cell C11) to \$50,000 in 2003 (cell H11). Although dollar sales are increasing each year, the percent of the increase varies from a high of 31.25 percent in 1998 (cell C27) to a low of 12.36 percent in 2003 (cell H27). Sam would prefer to see a steady rate of growth over these years.

Using What-if Analysis

Sam decides to revise this five-year plan based on a constant annual sales increase of 20 percent. He wants to know what effect this revision would have on his firm's growth; that is, what if sales increased at a constant rate of 20 percent a year? As previously discussed, **what-if analysis** is a technique that evaluates the effects of changing selected factors in a worksheet.

Begin by entering a formula to calculate the projected sales in 1998 (cell C11) as 20 percent more than the previous year's sales (cell B11). To do this,

Move to: C11
Type: **+B11*1.2**
Press: ↵

For a better view of the worksheet, use ← to

Move to: A11

The Gross Margin (C14), Net Income Before Taxes (C22), Federal Taxes (C23), and Net Income After Taxes (C25) for 1998 have all been instantaneously recalculated. The % Sales Increase (C27) now reflects the 20 percent increase as calculated by the formula.

Copy the formula to calculate projected sales from 1998 (C11) to 1999 (D11) through 2003 (H11). Then move the cell pointer to cell G11 for a better view of the worksheet.

Your screen should look similar to Figure 6.14.

G11: +F11*1.2 READY

	B	C	D	E	F	G	H	I
8	Actual	Budget	x============	====Projections	=========	========	======x	
9	1997	1998	1999	2000	2001	2002	2003	TOTAL
10	-------	-------	-------	-------	-------	-------	-------	-------
11	17600	21120	25344	30413	36495	43794	52553	227320
12	11820	13000	15000	18000	19412	21000	23000	121232
13	-------	-------	-------	-------	-------	-------	-------	-------
14	5780	8120	10344	12413	17083	22794	29553	106088
15								
16	1300	1900	2600	3800	4131	4900	5250	23881
17	986	1100	1300	1400	1500	1750	1980	10016
18	371	480	560	640	700	790	810	4351
19	-------	-------	-------	-------	-------	-------	-------	-------
20	2657	3480	4460	5840	6331	7440	8040	38248
21								
22	3123	4640	5884	6573	10752	15354	21513	67840
23	1624	2413	3060	3418	5591	7984	11187	35277
24	-------	-------	-------	-------	-------	-------	-------	-------
25	1499	2227	2824	3155	5161	7370	10326	32563
26	========	========	========	========	========	========	========	========
27		20.00%	20.00%	20.00%	20.00%	20.00%	20.00%	

21-Jun-89 06:50 AM UNDO

Figure 6.14

The entire worksheet has been recalculated.

Sam discusses his plans for constant growth at 20 percent a year with his management team. The purchasing director notes that the cost of goods sold will, of course, change whenever sales change. He suggests that the annual cost-of-goods-sold expense be calculated at 67 percent of sales.

The marketing director points out that if sales are to increase 20 percent a year, marketing expenses will have to increase 25 percent a year.

The financial director suggests that the worksheet be modified to compute annual profit margins, which are calculated as follows:

$$\textit{Profit margins} = \frac{\textit{Net income before taxes}}{\textit{Gross margin}} \times 100\%$$

He comments that it would be interesting to see how Bynner's compares with the industry average of 56 percent.

The worksheet has been modified to reflect all these suggestions. To see the modified worksheet, retrieve the file REVISED.

To get a better view of the worksheet, use (↓) to

Move to: A28

To freeze the titles above row 11 and in column A, use (↑) and (→) to

Move to: B11

Then issue the command sequence to freeze both titles.

Your screen should now look similar to Figure 6.15.

B11: 17600 READY

	A	B	C	D	E	F
9		1997	1998	1999	2000	2001
10		-------	-------	-------	-------	-------
11	Sales	17600	21120	25344	30413	36495
12	Cost of Goods Sold	11820	14150	16980	20377	24452
13		-------	-------	-------	-------	-------
14	Gross Margin	5780	6970	8364	10036	12043
15						
16	Marketing Expense	1300	1625	2031	2539	3174
17	Administrative Expense	986	1100	1300	1400	1500
18	Miscellaneous Expense	371	480	560	640	700
19		-------	-------	-------	-------	-------
20	Total Expenses	2657	3205	3891	4579	5374
21						
22	Net Income Before Taxes	3123	3765	4472	5457	6670
23	Federal Taxes	1624	1958	2326	2838	3468
24		-------	-------	-------	-------	-------
25	Net Income After Taxes	1499	1807	2147	2619	3201
26		=======	=======	=======	=======	=======
27	% Sales Increase		20.00%	20.00%	20.00%	20.00%
28	Profit Margins		54.01%	53.47%	54.37%	55.38%

21-Jun-89 06:51 AM UNDO

Figure 6.15

Confirm that the cost-of-goods-sold entries have been changed to 67 percent of sales by examining the formulas in cells C12 through H12. Confirm that the marketing expenses have been increased 25 percent annually by examining the formulas in cells C16 through H16. Confirm that the correct equations have been used to calculate profit margins in cells C28 through H28.

Bynner's profit margins, shown in row 28, are below the industry average of 56 percent. Sam decides that the financial plan should have profit margins that at least equal the industry average.

After talking with his management team, he concludes that the only way for Bynner's to increase profit margins is to reduce expenses and that only administrative expenses can realistically be cut. The goal is to achieve a profit margin of 56 percent by reducing administrative expenses.

To see what happens when you reduce administrative expenses for 1998 from $1100 to $1000,

Move to: C17
Type: **1000**
Press: ↵

Your screen should look similar to Figure 6.16.

```
C17: 1000                                                         READY

              A                    B        C        D        E        F
 9                              1997     1998     1999     2000     2001
10                           -------  -------  -------  -------  -------
11  Sales                       17600    21120    25344    30413    36495
12  Cost of Goods Sold          11820    14150    16980    20377    24452
13                           -------  -------  -------  -------  -------
14    Gross Margin               5780     6970     8364    10036    12043
15
16  Marketing Expense            1300     1625     2031     2539     3174
17  Administrative Expense        986     1000     1300     1400     1500
18  Miscellaneous Expense         371      480      560      640      700
19                           -------  -------  -------  -------  -------
20    Total Expenses             2657     3105     3891     4579     5374
21
22  Net Income Before Taxes      3123     3865     4472     5457     6670
23  Federal Taxes                1624     2010     2326     2838     3468
24                           -------  -------  -------  -------  -------
25    Net Income After Taxes     1499     1855     2147     2619     3201
26                           ============================================
27    % Sales Increase                  20.00%   20.00%   20.00%   20.00%
28    Profit Margins                    55.45%   53.47%   54.37%   55.38%
21-Jun-89  06:52 AM         UNDO
```

Revised profit margin

Figure 6.16

The profit margin increased from 54.01 percent to 55.45 percent, which is not enough.

Try decreasing the administrative expense to $900. The profit margin increases from 55.45 percent to 56.88 percent, which is too much.

You now know that the appropriate level is between $900 and $1000. You need to refine the figures further. Try $950.

The profit margin decreases to 56.17 percent.

Now try $960.

How about $962?

The profit margin is now 55.99 percent.

How about $961?

Your screen should look similar to Figure 6.17.

C17: 961 READY

	A	B	C	D	E	F
9		1997	1998	1999	2000	2001
10		-------	-------	-------	-------	-------
11	Sales	17600	21120	25344	30413	36495
12	Cost of Goods Sold	11820	14150	16980	20377	24452
13		-------	-------	-------	-------	-------
14	Gross Margin	5780	6970	8364	10036	12043
15						
16	Marketing Expense	1300	1625	2031	2539	3174
17	Administrative Expense	986	961	1300	1400	1500
18	Miscellaneous Expense	371	480	560	640	700
19		-------	-------	-------	-------	-------
20	Total Expenses	2657	3066	3891	4579	5374
21						
22	Net Income Before Taxes	3123	3904	4472	5457	6670
23	Federal Taxes	1624	2030	2326	2838	3468
24		-------	-------	-------	-------	-------
25	Net Income After Taxes	1499	1874	2147	2619	3201
26		=======	=======	=======	=======	=======
27	% Sales Increase		20.00%	20.00%	20.00%	20.00%
28	Profit Margins		56.01%	53.47%	54.37%	55.38%

21-Jun-89 06:53 AM UNDO

Revised profit margin

Figure 6.17

This is about as close as you can get. The budget for 1998 will have administrative expenses set at $961.

Determine the administrative expenses for the years 1999 to 2003 in the same way.

When you are done,

Press: HOME

Unfreeze the worksheet titles.

Preparing a Memo

Sam Bynner wants to send a copy of this worksheet, along with a brief, explanatory message, to his father, the president of Bynner's Bookshops, Inc.

Move to: B31
Type: **TO:**
Move to: C31
Type: **President, Sam Bynner Sr.**
Move to: B32
Type: **FROM:**
Move to: C32
Type: **Manager, Sam Bynner Jr.**
Move to: B33
Type: **DATE:**
Move to: C33

Entering the Date

You can enter the current date into a worksheet using the @NOW function. This @function calculates the date using the DOS system date by assigning an integer to each of the 73,050 days from January 1, 1900 through December 31, 2099. The integers are assigned consecutively beginning with 1 and ending with 73,050. They are called **date numbers**.

Type: **@NOW**
Press: ↵

Your screen should be similar to Figure 6.18.

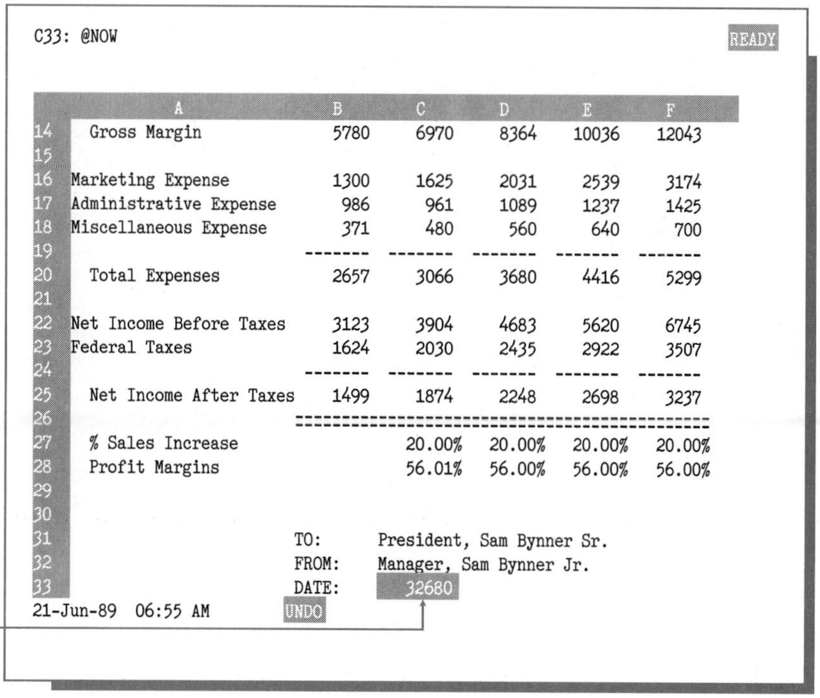

```
C33: @NOW                                                          READY

            A                  B       C       D       E       F
14   Gross Margin            5780    6970    8364   10036   12043
15
16  Marketing Expense        1300    1625    2031    2539    3174
17  Administrative Expense    986     961    1089    1237    1425
18  Miscellaneous Expense     371     480     560     640     700
19                        ------- ------- ------- ------- -------
20   Total Expenses          2657    3066    3680    4416    5299
21
22  Net Income Before Taxes  3123    3904    4683    5620    6745
23  Federal Taxes            1624    2030    2435    2922    3507
24                        ------- ------- ------- ------- -------
25   Net Income After Taxes  1499    1874    2248    2698    3237
26                        ============================================
27   % Sales Increase               20.00%  20.00%  20.00%  20.00%
28   Profit Margins                 56.01%  56.00%  56.00%  56.00%
29
30
31                        TO:      President, Sam Bynner Sr.
32                        FROM:    Manager, Sam Bynner Jr.
33                        DATE:      32680
21-Jun-89  06:55 AM      UNDO
```

Date number

Figure 6.18

The value displayed in cell C33 is the date number for the system date on your computer system. (Of course, this value will be different from the number in Figure 6.18).

To change the display of the date number to a date, use the Range Format Date command, as follows:

/ **R**ange **F**ormat **D**ate

Five date format options are displayed in the control panel. Use the Help system for information on the date formats. You want to display the date as month/day/year. The option that displays the date in this manner is 4 (Long Intn'l). Continue the command sequence as follows:

4 ↵

Your screen should be similar to Figure 6.19.

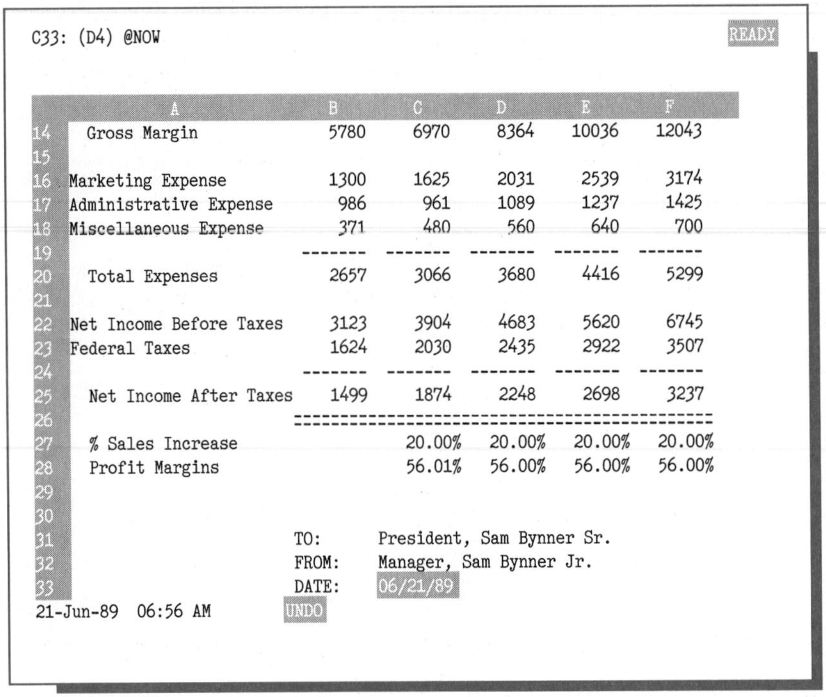

```
C33: (D4) @NOW                                                    READY

         A                      B        C        D        E        F
14    Gross Margin             5780     6970     8364    10036    12043
15
16 Marketing Expense           1300     1625     2031     2539     3174
17 Administrative Expense       986      961     1089     1237     1425
18 Miscellaneous Expense        371      480      560      640      700
19                          -------  -------  -------  -------  -------
20    Total Expenses           2657     3066     3680     4416     5299
21
22 Net Income Before Taxes     3123     3904     4683     5620     6745
23 Federal Taxes               1624     2030     2435     2922     3507
24                          -------  -------  -------  -------  -------
25    Net Income After Taxes   1499     1874     2248     2698     3237
26                          =============================================
27    % Sales Increase                20.00%   20.00%   20.00%   20.00%
28    Profit Margins                  56.01%   56.00%   56.00%   56.00%
29
30
31                          TO:      President, Sam Bynner Sr.
32                          FROM:    Manager, Sam Bynner Jr.
33                          DATE:    06/21/89
21-Jun-89  06:56 AM         UNDO
```

Figure 6.19

Your current date should be displayed in cell C33. If you did not enter a date at the DOS date prompt, the DOS default date is displayed.

Justifying Text

You are now ready to enter the body of the memo.

Move to: B35

Without pressing ↵ until directed, enter the following message as one long label in cell B35.

Type: **I have been working with our management group to develop a projected income statement for the next five years. I think you will be pleased with the results.**

Press: ↵

The two sentences are entered as a long label in cell B35. To change this long label into a paragraph, 1-2-3 lets you rearrange or **justify** the long label to fit within a specified width. Issue the following command:

/ **R**ange **J**ustify **B35..F35** ↵

Move to: B40

Your screen should look similar to Figure 6.20.

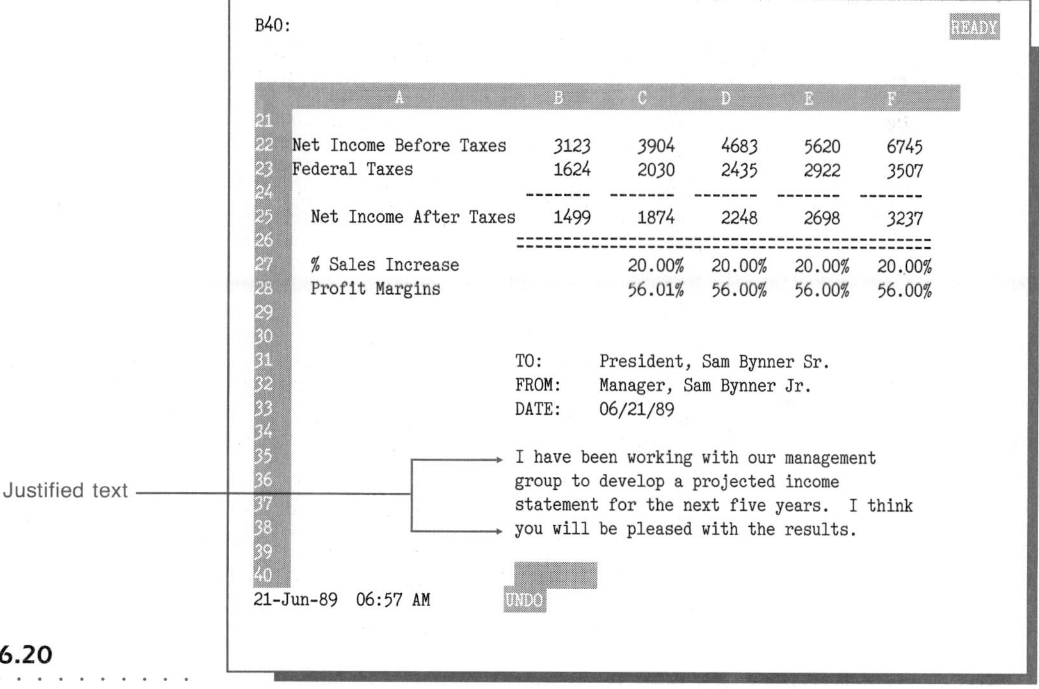

Figure 6.20

The long label in cell B35 has been broken into four long labels contained in cells B35 through B38. The long labels do not exceed the specified width and look like a paragraph.

Enter the following text in cell B40 as one long label, without pressing (↵) until directed.

Type: **To meet the industry standard of a 56 percent profit margin, we decreased the administrative expenses. As you can see, we will need to watch the administrative expenses closely if we want to attain our goal.**

Press: (↵)

Justify the text in cell B40 in the same manner. For a better view of the memo,

Move to: B46

Your screen should now look similar to Figure 6.21.

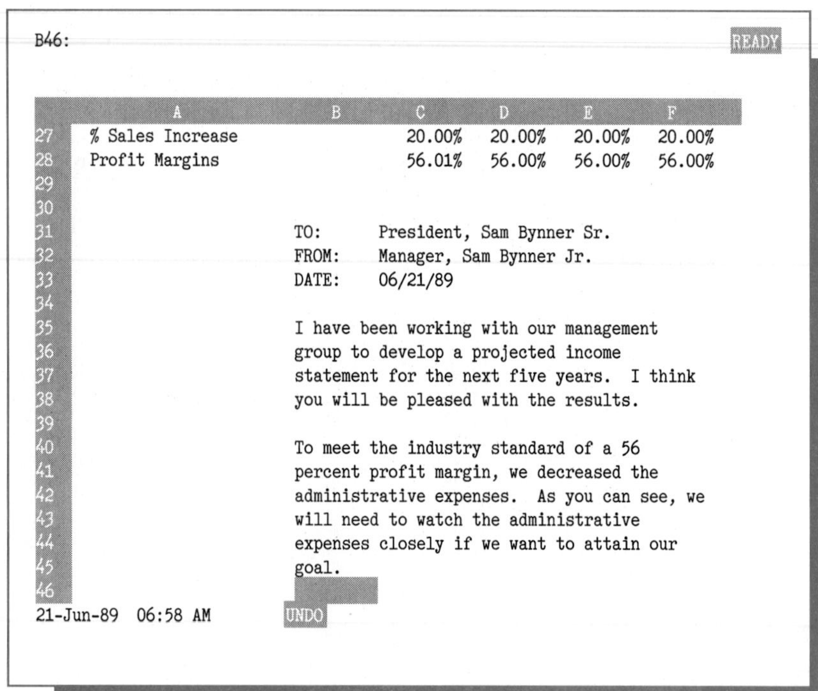

B46:
READY
A B C D E F
27 % Sales Increase 20.00% 20.00% 20.00% 20.00%
28 Profit Margins 56.01% 56.00% 56.00% 56.00%
31 TO: President, Sam Bynner Sr.
32 FROM: Manager, Sam Bynner Jr.
33 DATE: 06/21/89
35 I have been working with our management
36 group to develop a projected income
37 statement for the next five years. I think
38 you will be pleased with the results.
40 To meet the industry standard of a 56
41 percent profit margin, we decreased the
42 administrative expenses. As you can see, we
43 will need to watch the administrative
44 expenses closely if we want to attain our
45 goal.
21-Jun-89 06:58 AM
UNDO

Figure 6.21

The worksheet is ready to be printed.

Printing in Compressed Mode

To print the entire worksheet on a single page, Sam decides to use compressed printing. **Compressed printing** reduces the size and space between characters, increasing the amount of text that can be printed across the width of a page.

Note The following procedure works for most printers, but it may not work for your particular printer. You may need to consult your printer manual before proceeding.

Issue the following command sequence:

/ **P**rint **P**rinter **R**ange **A1..I46** (↵) **O**ptions

The print options are as follows:

Header	Prints a line of text just below the top margin of every page
Footer	Prints a line of text just above the bottom margin of every page
Margins	Sets margins for the printed page
Borders	Prints specified rows or columns on every page
Setup	Specifies font size and style
Pg-Length	Indicates the number of printed lines on the page
Other	Selects other printing procedures
Quit	Returns to the Print menu

To compress the print size, select:

Setup

Now, turn on the compressed print option by entering

\015(↵)

Note The setup string \015 creates compressed printing on many, but not all, printers. Consult your printer manual if you need alternative setup values.

The maximum margin size you can use with compressed print is 132 spaces. To increase the right margin to that number of spaces, continue the command sequence:

Margin **R**ight **132** (↵)

Check to see that the printer is on. If you are using continuous form paper, make sure that the top of the paper is aligned with the top of the printer's scale.

To print the worksheet, select:

Quit Align Go

When the printer stops printing, advance the page and return to READY mode by completing the command sequence:

Page Quit

The printed document should look similar to Figure 6.22. The Student Edition header and your name are automatically printed at the top of the page.

The Student Edition of Lotus 1-2-3 — Timothy J. O'Leary

Bynner's Bookshops, Incorporated

Five Year Financial Plan
(in thousands of dollars)

Income Statement for the Year Ending:

	Actual	Budget	x------	------	Projections	------	------x	
	1997	1998	1999	2000	2001	2002	2003	TOTAL
Sales	17600	21120	25344	30413	36495	43794	52553	227320
Cost of Goods Sold	11820	14150	16980	20377	24452	29342	35211	152332
Gross Margin	5780	6970	8364	10036	12043	14452	17343	74988
Marketing Expense	1300	1625	2031	2539	3174	3967	4959	19596
Administrative Expense	986	961	1089	1237	1425	1601	1861	9160
Miscellaneous Expense	371	480	560	640	700	790	810	4351
Total Expenses	2657	3066	3680	4416	5299	6358	7630	33107
Net Income Before Taxes	3123	3904	4683	5620	6745	8094	9712	41881
Federal Taxes	1624	2030	2435	2922	3507	4209	5050	21778
Net Income After Taxes	1499	1874	2248	2698	3237	3885	4662	20103
% Sales Increase		20.00%	20.00%	20.00%	20.00%	20.00%	20.00%	
Profit Margins		56.01%	56.00%	56.00%	56.00%	56.00%	56.00%	

TO: President, Sam Bynner Sr.
FROM: Manager, Sam Bynner Jr.
DATE: 06/21/89

I have been working with our management group to develop a projected income statement for the next five years. I think you will be pleased with the results.

To meet the industry standard of a 56 percent profit margin, we decreased the administrative expenses. As you can see, we will need to watch the administrative expenses closely if we want to attain our goal.

Figure 6.22

Using Passwords to Restrict Access to Files

The data contained in this worksheet file are confidential. To restrict access to it, Sam decides to save the file with a password. To tell 1-2-3 that you want to save a file with a password, following the filename in the Save command, press SPACEBAR and the letter P.

To save this worksheet as FUTURE with a password, issue the following command sequence:

/ File **S**ave **FUTURE P** ⏎

The prompt, "Enter Password," is displayed in the control panel. A password can be up to 15 characters long. However, it cannot contain any spaces. To enter the password RESTRICT, type:

RESTRICT ⏎

The password is not displayed following the prompt. Instead, for each letter of the password you type, a blank is displayed (or, possibly, a solid block or underscore). This feature further insures the privacy of the password as it is entered.

Your screen should look similar to Figure 6.23.

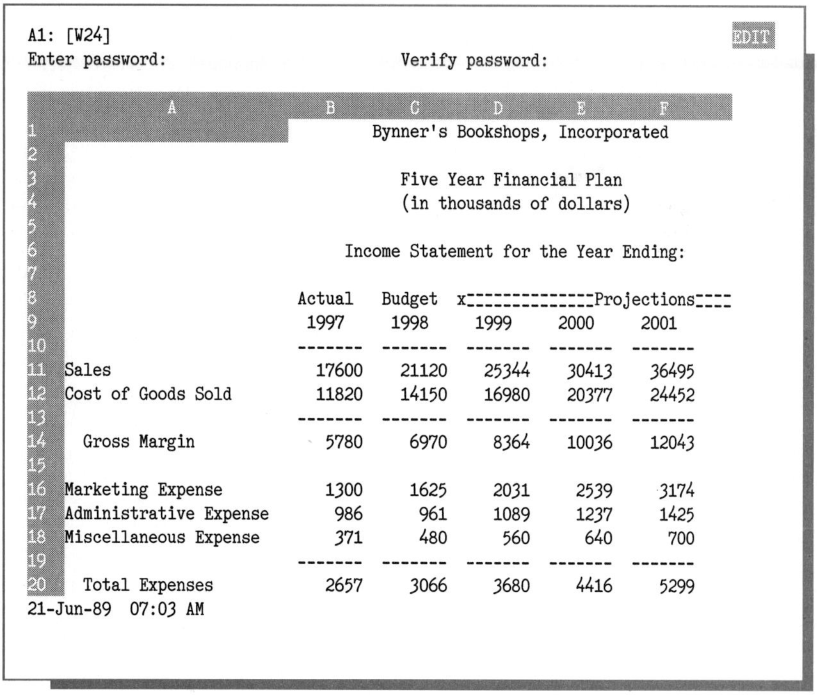

```
A1: [W24]                                                          EDIT
Enter password:                        Verify password:

   A                         B        C        D        E        F
1                                   Bynner's Bookshops, Incorporated
2
3                                      Five Year Financial Plan
4                                      (in thousands of dollars)
5
6                                 Income Statement for the Year Ending:
7
8                          Actual   Budget  x=============Projections====
9                           1997     1998     1999     2000     2001
10                        -------  -------  -------  -------  -------
11 Sales                    17600    21120    25344    30413    36495
12 Cost of Goods Sold       11820    14150    16980    20377    24452
13                        -------  -------  -------  -------  -------
14   Gross Margin            5780     6970     8364    10036    12043
15
16 Marketing Expense         1300     1625     2031     2539     3174
17 Administrative Expense     986      961     1089     1237     1425
18 Miscellaneous Expense      371      480      560      640      700
19                        -------  -------  -------  -------  -------
20   Total Expenses          2657     3066     3680     4416     5299
21-Jun-89  07:03 AM
```

Figure 6.23

In response to the prompt to verify the password, type

RESTRICT ↵

You have now saved this file under the filename FUTURE with the password RESTRICT.

Erase the worksheet from your screen and the computer's memory by issuing the following command sequence:

/ **W**orksheet **E**rase **Y**es

To retrieve the password-restricted file, issue the following command sequence:

/ **F**ile **R**etrieve **FUTURE** ↵

Your screen should look similar to Figure 6.24.

```
A1:                                                                    EDIT
Enter password:
```

Figure 6.24

To respond to the prompt in the control panel, you must enter the password exactly as you entered it during the Save command. Since password protection is case sensitive, you must enter the password so that it matches exactly, including uppercase and lowercase letters. To complete the command, type:

RESTRICT ↵

The file FUTURE is loaded into your computer's memory and displayed on your screen. If you enter the password incorrectly, the error message ''Incorrect password'' is displayed. Press ESC to clear the message and try again.

You can retrieve a password-protected file only if you enter the correct password. If you forget the password, there is no way of retrieving the file.

Exit from 1-2-3.

Glossary of Key Terms

Compressed printing A print option that reduces the space between characters and the size of characters to create a smaller (compressed) type.

Date numbers An integer from 1 to 73,050 assigned to each day from January 1, 1900 through December 31, 2099.

Freezing titles Fixes row and column titles on the screen.

Justify Converts a long label of text in a cell so that none of the lines is longer than a specified width.

Synchronized scrolling The simultaneous scrolling of rows or columns in two windows.

Unsynchronized scrolling The independent scrolling of rows or columns in two windows.

What-if analysis A technique that evaluates the effects of changing selected factors in a worksheet.

Practice Problems

1. Matching

1. /WTV	______	**a.**	writes a part of the worksheet to a file
2. Windows	______	**b.**	moves cell pointer to another window
3. /WWS	______	**c.**	clears frozen titles
4. /FX	______	**d.**	freezes titles vertically
5. /FC	______	**e.**	saves a file with a password
6. /WTC	______	**f.**	synchronizes two windows
7. /FS filename P	______	**g.**	allows display of distant parts of the worksheet at the same time
8. /RJ	______	**h.**	sets the margin for the printed page
9. /PPOM	______	**i.**	justifies text in a range
10. F6	______	**j.**	reads a part of a file into the worksheet

2. In this problem, you will practice many of the 1-2-3 commands you learned for managing a large worksheet. Retrieve the file REVISED. Put your name in cell A1.

   a. Move to cell C28 and create a vertical window at this location.

   b. Switch to the right window and move to cell C11. Freeze the titles above row 11. While moving the cell pointer to column I, compare the sales figures for the projected years to the 1997 figures. What is the first year that sales are more than double the 1997 sales figure?

   c. Move to cell I32. What happened in the left window?

   d. Switch to the left window. Change the window scrolling to unsynchronized. Move to cell B9 and observe the movement of the screen.

   e. Freeze the titles in the left window above row 11.

   f. Switch to the right window. Line up the rows in the two windows.

   g. Use the Global command to display currency with 0 decimal places. What happens in the left window?

   h. Print a copy of your display screen using SHIFT-PRTSC.

   i. Clear the window. Clear the titles. What happens to the format?

3. Sam Bynner is planning a meeting with the department directors next week. The purpose of the meeting is to plan the budget for the following quarter. He wants to generate a report that shows the first-quarter 1997 income statement figures. He feels this information should help the directors plan for the next quarter.

   a. Retrieve the file YEAR. Use this file to extract the row labels and the first three months of income figures to a new file, FIRSTQTR.

   b. Retrieve the file FIRSTQTR and add a new column to calculate the row totals. Label this column TOTAL. Make adjustments to improve the appearance of the new worksheet (insert/delete rows/columns, adjust column widths). Add the title: Bynner's Bookshops, Incorporated, First Quarter 1997 Income Statement.

c. Add the following memo to the worksheet below the report. Use the @NOW function to calculate the date and format the date to display as month/day/year. Enter the body of the memo in one row and then justify it.

   TO: Department Directors

   FROM: (your name)

   DATE: (enter current date using the @NOW function)

   I am distributing this first-quarter 1997 income statement for your information and reference. Please have your comments prepared for the meeting scheduled for next Tuesday.

d. Save this worksheet using the same filename, FIRSTQTR.

e. Print the entire worksheet.

7

Creating a Database

Objectives

In Lab 7 you will learn how to:

- Create, format, and modify a database
- Insert, edit, and delete records
- Sort a database
- Find selected records
- Use the Search and Replace command

Case Study

Starways Film Company is a small, newly formed motion picture firm. Lens Miller, Starway's director, has used 1-2-3 to evaluate several prospective ventures. He is impressed with 1-2-3's ease of use and ability to perform what-if analysis. Lens recently learned that 1-2-3 can also be used as a database.

This lab will follow Starways Film Company as it creates and uses the database of employee records shown in Figure 7.1.

Creating a Database

A **database** is a collection of data that consists of fields and records. A **field** is a collection of related characters, such as a person's name. A **record** is a collection of related fields, such as a person's name, address, Social Security number, and rate of pay. In a 1-2-3 database, each record is a row and each field is a column. There can be more than one database within a worksheet.

The first row of information in the database contains **field names**. The field name is a label that identifies the contents of each column or field of data. Figure 7.1 identifies the parts of a database.

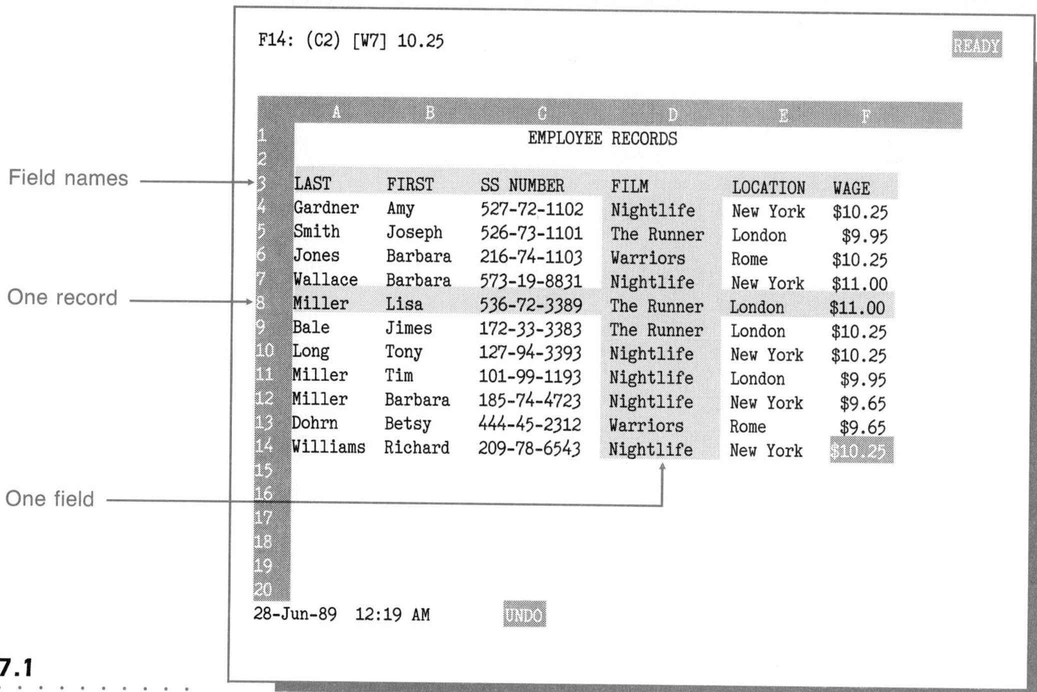

F14: (C2) [W7] 10.25 READY

EMPLOYEE RECORDS

LAST	FIRST	SS NUMBER	FILM	LOCATION	WAGE
Gardner	Amy	527-72-1102	Nightlife	New York	$10.25
Smith	Joseph	526-73-1101	The Runner	London	$9.95
Jones	Barbara	216-74-1103	Warriors	Rome	$10.25
Wallace	Barbara	573-19-8831	Nightlife	New York	$11.00
Miller	Lisa	536-72-3389	The Runner	London	$11.00
Bale	Jimes	172-33-3383	The Runner	London	$10.25
Long	Tony	127-94-3393	Nightlife	New York	$10.25
Miller	Tim	101-99-1193	Nightlife	London	$9.95
Miller	Barbara	185-74-4723	Nightlife	New York	$9.65
Dohrn	Betsy	444-45-2312	Warriors	Rome	$9.65
Williams	Richard	209-78-6543	Nightlife	New York	$10.25

28-Jun-89 12:19 AM UNDO

Figure 7.1

The first step in creating a database is to determine the field names and column widths for each field of data. Each column should be large enough to fully display both the field name and the largest possible entry into that field.

Observe these rules when you are constructing field names. Field names:

- Must be entered in the first row of the database.
- Must be entered as a label in a single cell.
- Must be unique within the database.
- Should be descriptive of the contents of the field.
- Should not begin or end with a blank space.
- Must not exceed 240 characters.

After reviewing his records, Lens decides to use the field names and column widths shown in Table 7.1.

Table 7.1

Field Contents	Field Name	Column Width
Employee's last name	LAST	10
Employee's first name	FIRST	10
Employee's Social Security number	SS NUMBER	14
Name of film	FILM	13
Location of filming	LOCATION	11
Hourly pay	WAGE	7

To create the database of employee records for Starways Film Company, load 1-2-3.

First, enter a title for the database in the first row of the worksheet.

Move to: C1
Type: **EMPLOYEE RECORDS**
Press: ↵

Next, to enter the field names specified in Table 7.1 in row 3,

Move to: A3

The first field of data, the employee's last name, requires a column width of 10 spaces. Increase the column width to 10 spaces by issuing the following command sequence:

/ **W**orksheet **C**olumn **S**et-Width **10** ↵

To enter the first field name,

Type: **LAST**
Press: ↵

Beginning in cell B3, complete the other field names by first setting the appropriate column widths and then entering the field names as specified in Table 7.1. If you make an error entering the field names, correct it just like any other worksheet entry.

When you have finished, your screen should look similar to Figure 7.2.

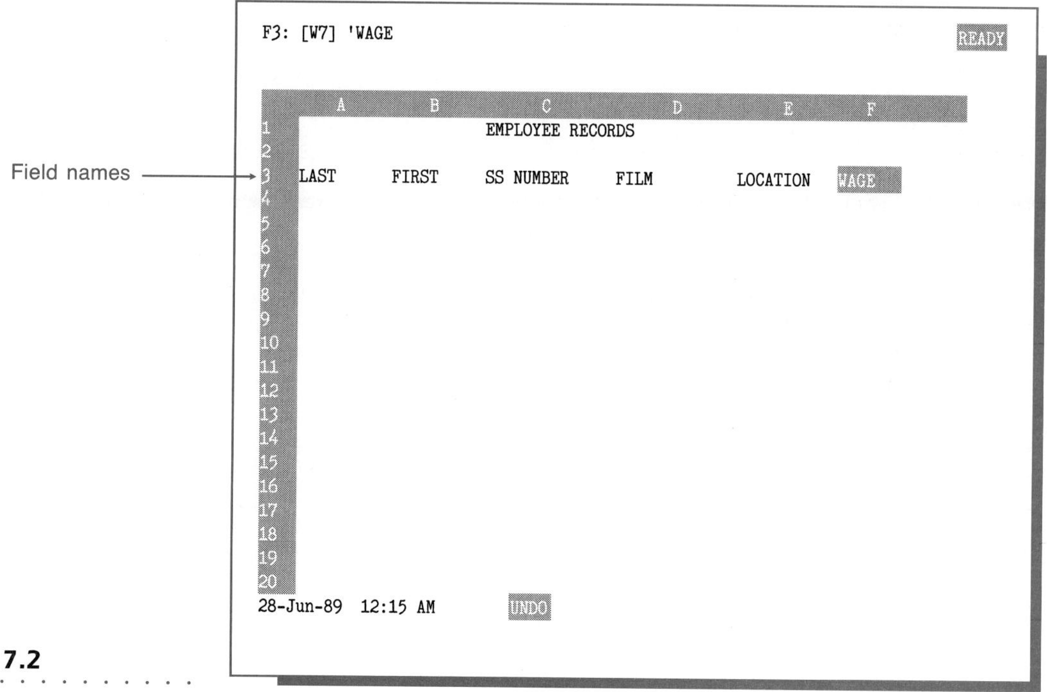

Figure 7.2

Now you are ready to enter the data into the database. Always enter the first record of the database in the row immediately below the field names. Do not leave a blank row below the field names. The data for the first database record are as follows:

LAST	:	Gardner
FIRST	:	Amy
SS NUMBER	:	527-72-1102
FILM	:	Nightlife
LOCATION	:	New York
WAGE	:	10.25

To enter the first record into the database,

Move to: A4
Type: **Gardner**
Move to: B4
Type: **Amy**
Move to: C4
Type: **'527-72-1102**
Press: ↵

Notice that you must precede the Social Security number with an apostrophe, making it a label. If you omitted the apostrophe, the entry would be treated as a formula (527 minus 72 minus 1102), and the value −647 would appear in the worksheet.

To complete the entry of the first record,

Move to: D4
Type: **Nightlife**
Move to: E4
Type: **New York**
Move to: F4
Type: **10.25**
Press: ↵

Your screen should now look similar to Figure 7.3.

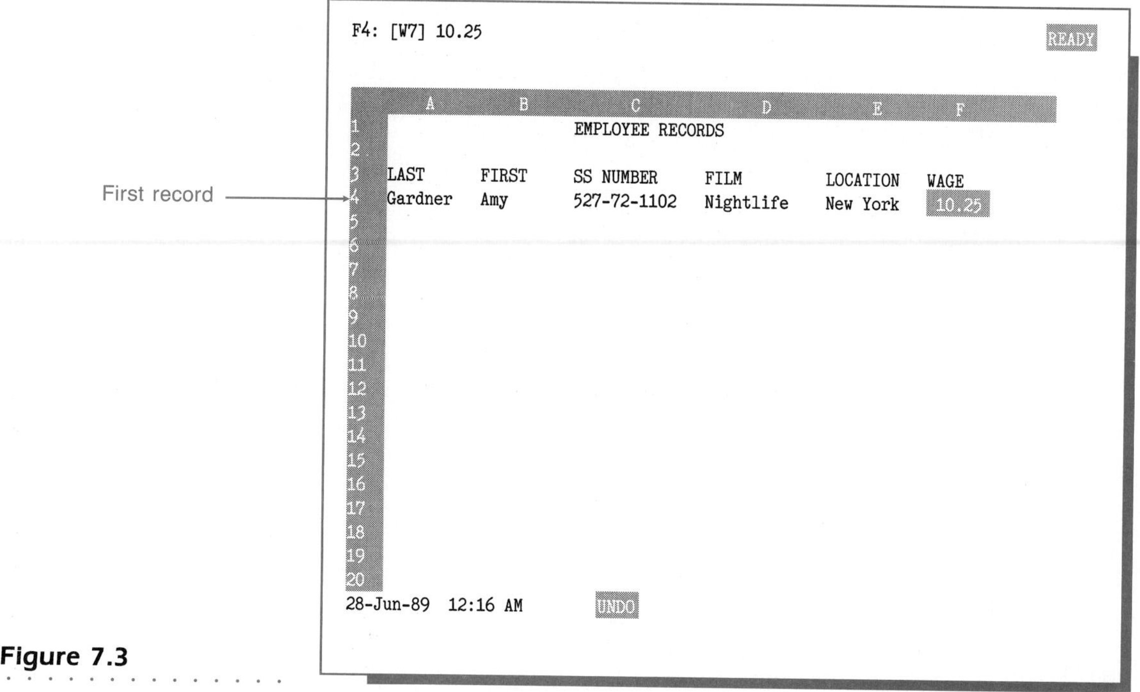

Figure 7.3

The data in a field can be a label, a value, or a formula. However, each field should contain the same type of data (all values or all labels) for each record. It is important to be consistent when you enter data into a database. If a number in a field is defined as a label (for example, the Social Security number), all numbers in that field should be entered as labels. If certain words are abbreviated (for example, St. and Ave.), always abbreviate them the same way. Do not use extra spaces before or after an entry in a field.

Beginning in cell A5, enter the second record into the database.

LAST	:	Smith
FIRST	:	Joseph
SS NUMBER	:	526-73-1101
FILM	:	The Runner
LOCATION	:	London
WAGE	:	9.95

Your screen should look similar to Figure 7.4.

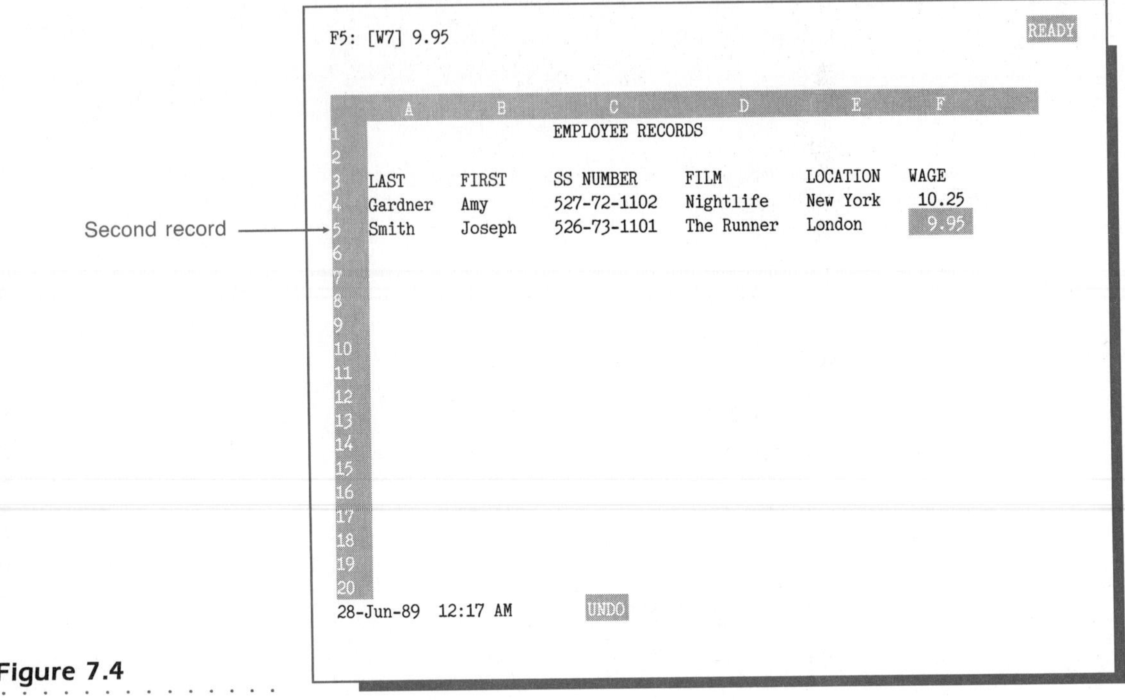

Figure 7.4

The second record is now entered into row 5 in the database.

The appearance of the database can be improved by centering the title over the database and formatting the wage field to display as currency.

First, to center the title over the database,

Move to: C1
Press: F2
Press: HOME
Press: →
Press: SPACEBAR four times
Press: ↵

Next, to format the wage field, column F, to display dollar signs, issue the following command sequence:

/ **R**ange **F**ormat **C**urrency **2** ↵ **F4..F5** ↵

Your screen should now look similar to Figure 7.5.

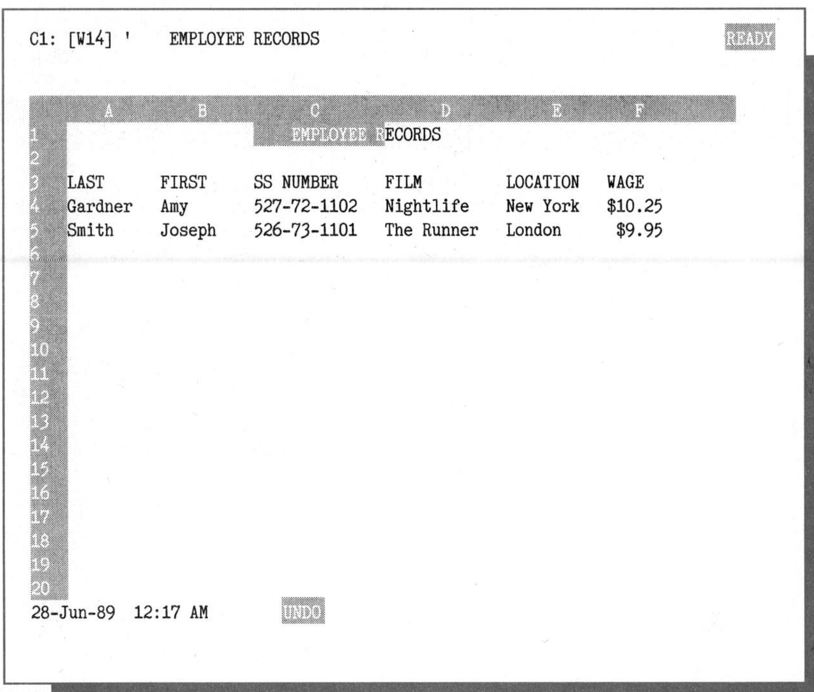

Figure 7.5

After setting up the database and entering the two records, Lens asks his secretary to continue entering more records. To see what has been completed so far, retrieve the file EMPLOYEE.WK1.

Your screen should look similar to Figure 7.6.

```
A1: [W10]                                                          READY

       A         B          C            D            E          F
 1                            EMPLOYEE RECORDS
 2
 3   LAST      FIRST      SS NUMBER    FILM         LOCATION   WAGE
 4   Gardner   Amy        527-72-1102  Nightlife    New York   $10.25
 5   Smith     Joseph     526-73-1101  The Runner   London      $9.95
 6   Jones     Barbara    216-74-1103  Warriors     Rome       $10.25
 7   Wallace   Barbara    573-19-8831  Nightlife    New York   $11.00
 8   Miller    Lisa       536-72-3389  The Runner   London     $11.00
 9   Bale      Jimes      172-33-3383  The Runner   London     $10.25
10   Long      Tony       127-94-3393  Nightlife    New York   $10.25
11   Miller    Tim        101-99-1193  Nightlife    London      $9.95
12   Miller    Barbara    185-74-4723  Nightlife    New York    $9.65
13   Stieen3   Willy      %**+##       Nightlife    New York
14   Dohrn     Betsy      444-45-2312  Warriors     Rome        $9.65
15
16
17
18
19
20
28-Jun-89  12:02 AM          UNDO
```

Figure 7.6

Modifying a Database

There seem to be a few problems in the database. James Bale's first name is misspelled in row 9. Correct it. The record in row 13 should be deleted from the database. Move the cell pointer to any cell in row 13 and use the **W**orksheet **D**elete command to delete row 13.

To add another employee's record to the database, simply move to the last row of the database and type the data. Insert the record shown below into row 14. Remember to enter an apostrophe before the Social Security number.

LAST	:	Williams
FIRST	:	Richard
SS NUMBER	:	209-78-6543
FILM	:	Nightlife
LOCATION	:	New York
WAGE	:	10.25

Your screen should look similar to Figure 7.7.

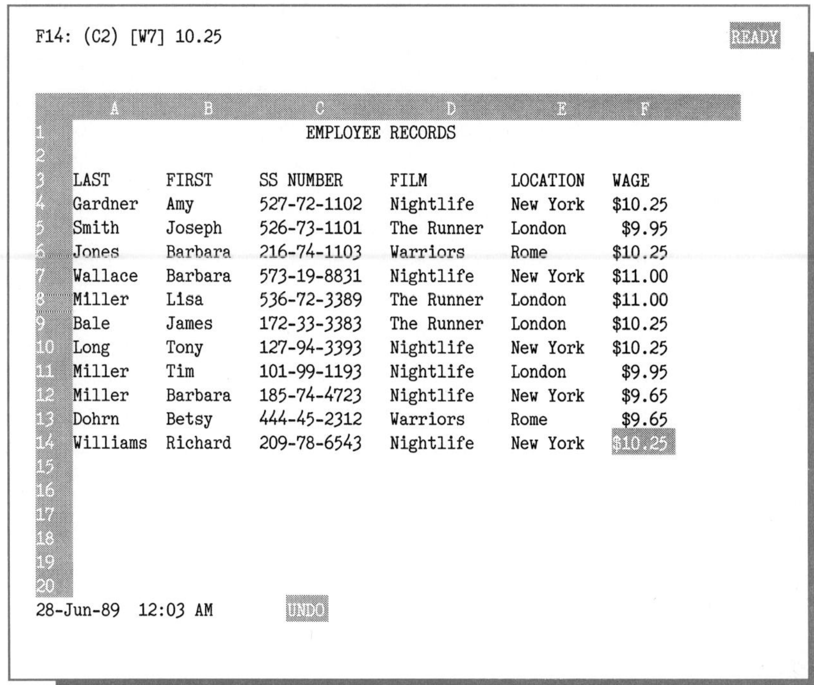

F14: (C2) [W7] 10.25 READY

EMPLOYEE RECORDS

	LAST	FIRST	SS NUMBER	FILM	LOCATION	WAGE
4	Gardner	Amy	527-72-1102	Nightlife	New York	$10.25
5	Smith	Joseph	526-73-1101	The Runner	London	$9.95
6	Jones	Barbara	216-74-1103	Warriors	Rome	$10.25
7	Wallace	Barbara	573-19-8831	Nightlife	New York	$11.00
8	Miller	Lisa	536-72-3389	The Runner	London	$11.00
9	Bale	James	172-33-3383	The Runner	London	$10.25
10	Long	Tony	127-94-3393	Nightlife	New York	$10.25
11	Miller	Tim	101-99-1193	Nightlife	London	$9.95
12	Miller	Barbara	185-74-4723	Nightlife	New York	$9.65
13	Dohrn	Betsy	444-45-2312	Warriors	Rome	$9.65
14	Williams	Richard	209-78-6543	Nightlife	New York	$10.25

28-Jun-89 12:03 AM UNDO

Figure 7.7

Sorting a Database

After looking at the database of records, Lens wants to change the order of the records. The records currently appear in the order they were entered into the database. 1-2-3 has a sorting feature that lets you rearrange the order of records alphabetically, numerically, or chronologically. The records can be sorted either in ascending (low to high) or descending (high to low) order.

Lens wants the records arranged in ascending alphabetical order according to the employee's last name. All database operations are executed using the Data menu. To see this menu, select:

/ **D**ata

There are eight Data menu commands. The command to rearrange the records in a database is **S**ort. Continue the command sequence by selecting:

Sort

Your screen should look similar to Figure 7.8.

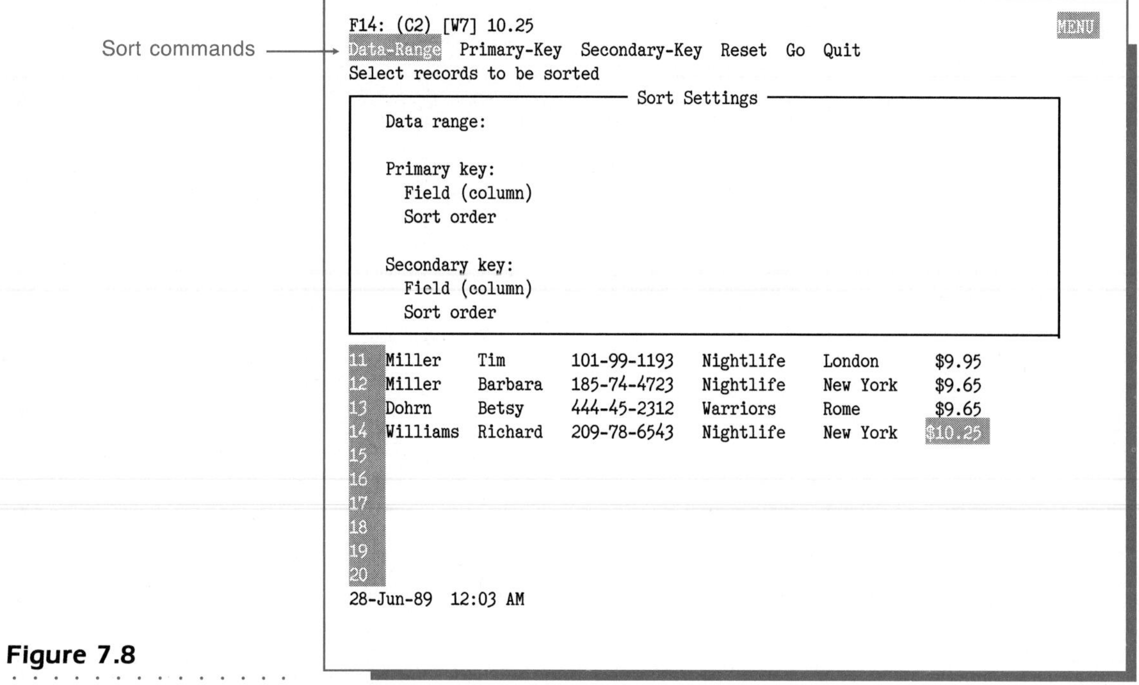

Figure 7.8

The Sort settings sheet is displayed on the screen. The Sort command requires that you specify three items: the range to sort, the field to sort by, and the order of the sort. The settings sheet will help you keep track of the settings you specify.

The Sort commands are displayed in the control panel. For information about these commands,

Press: F1

Your screen should now look similar to Figure 7.9.

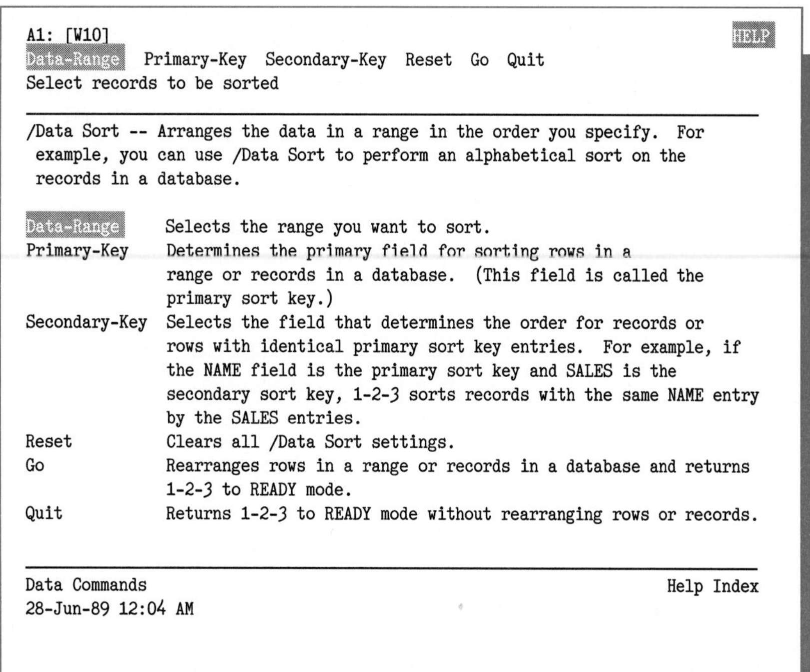

```
A1: [W10]                                                          HELP
Data-Range  Primary-Key  Secondary-Key  Reset  Go  Quit
Select records to be sorted

/Data Sort -- Arranges the data in a range in the order you specify.  For
 example, you can use /Data Sort to perform an alphabetical sort on the
 records in a database.

Data-Range     Selects the range you want to sort.
Primary-Key    Determines the primary field for sorting rows in a
               range or records in a database.  (This field is called the
               primary sort key.)
Secondary-Key  Selects the field that determines the order for records or
               rows with identical primary sort key entries.  For example, if
               the NAME field is the primary sort key and SALES is the
               secondary sort key, 1-2-3 sorts records with the same NAME entry
               by the SALES entries.
Reset          Clears all /Data Sort settings.
Go             Rearranges rows in a range or records in a database and returns
               1-2-3 to READY mode.
Quit           Returns 1-2-3 to READY mode without rearranging rows or records.

Data Commands                                                    Help Index
28-Jun-89 12:04 AM
```

Figure 7.9

The Help screen briefly describes the six Data Sort commands. After you have carefully read the Help information, press ESC to return to the Sort settings sheet.

The first setting you must specify is the range of data to be sorted. Select:

Data-Range

The Sort settings sheet is cleared from the screen to allow you to view the worksheet while you enter the data range. The data range should include all records and fields in the database.

The database records begin in cell A4 (the first field of the first record) and end in cell F14 (the last field of the last record). The field names in row 3 are not included in the data range. If they were included, the field names would be sorted alphabetically within the database records.

Respond to the prompt for the data range as follows:

A4..F14 ↵

You are returned to the Sort settings sheet and the data range you specified is displayed.

Next you must specify the field to sort by. This is called the **sort key.** The sort key determines the new order for the database records. Two sort keys can be specified, a primary key and a secondary key. Continue the command sequence by selecting:

Primary-Key

The **primary key** is the field in the database that will determine the new order of the records. Lens wants the records arranged by last names.

To specify the LAST name field as the primary key, you can enter any cell address in the column. For this database, use cell A4. In response to the prompt,

Type: **A4**
Press: ↵

You are returned to the Sort settings sheet and the specified primary key field is displayed. Immediately below this, the settings sheet also tells you that the **sort order** is descending. This is the default setting. The sort order determines whether the records are listed in **descending order** (Z through A or 9 through 0) or **ascending order** (A through Z or 0 through 9). Since Lens wants the records organized in ascending alphabetical order, in response to the prompt in the control panel,

Type: **A**
Press: ↵

The change is reflected in the settings sheet. To remove the settings sheet and see the worksheet,

Press: F6

Notice that the database contains three records with the same last name (Miller). Lens wants these records sorted by first name within the last name fields, like a telephone directory. To do this, you will specify a **secondary key**. The secondary key determines the order of records with identical primary key entries. Here, the secondary key will be the FIRST name field (column B). Continue the command as follows:

Secondary-Key **B4** ↵ **A**scending ↵

To redisplay the settings sheet,

Press: F6

Your screen should look similar to Figure 7.10.

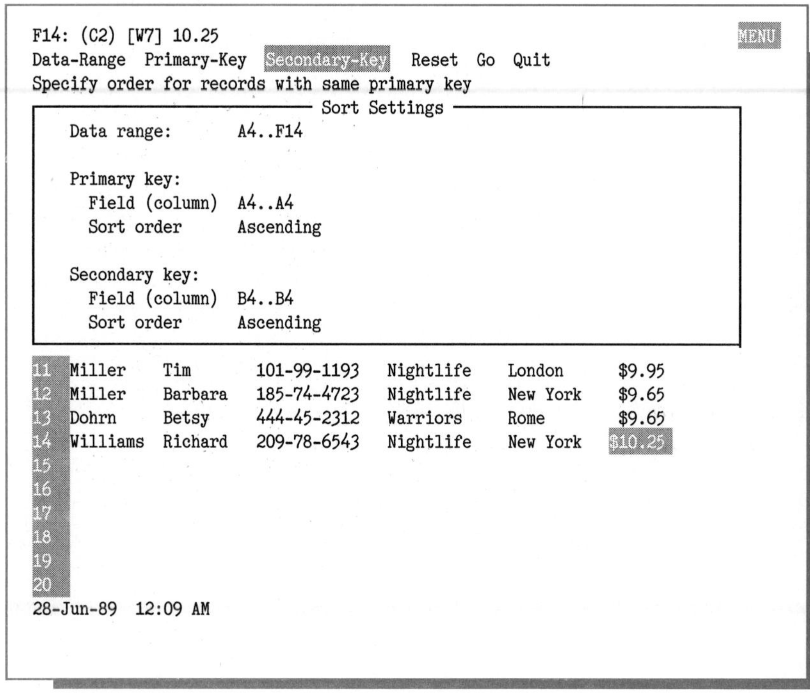
```
F14: (C2) [W7] 10.25                                                  MENU
Data-Range  Primary-Key  Secondary-Key  Reset  Go  Quit
Specify order for records with same primary key
                               Sort Settings
    Data range:          A4..F14

    Primary key:
      Field (column)     A4..A4
      Sort order         Ascending

    Secondary key:
      Field (column)     B4..B4
      Sort order         Ascending

11  Miller    Tim       101-99-1193  Nightlife   London    $9.95
12  Miller    Barbara   185-74-4723  Nightlife   New York  $9.65
13  Dohrn     Betsy     444-45-2312  Warriors    Rome      $9.65
14  Williams  Richard   209-78-6543  Nightlife   New York  $10.25
15
16
17
18
19
20
28-Jun-89  12:09 AM
```

Figure 7.10

The secondary key is an optional sort setting. However, you must specify the data range and primary key settings.

Finally, to perform the sort, select:

Go

Your screen should now look similar to Figure 7.11.

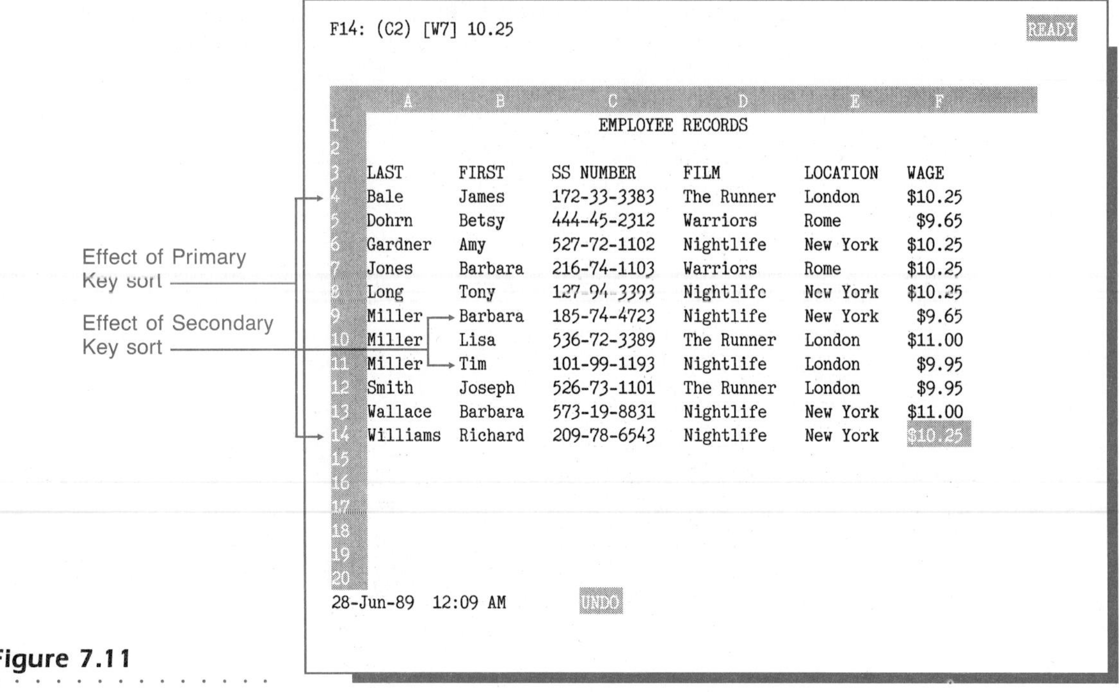

F14: (C2) [W7] 10.25
READY
EMPLOYEE RECORDS
LAST FIRST SS NUMBER FILM LOCATION WAGE
Bale James 172-33-3383 The Runner London $10.25
Dohrn Betsy 444-45-2312 Warriors Rome $9.65
Gardner Amy 527-72-1102 Nightlife New York $10.25
Jones Barbara 216-74-1103 Warriors Rome $10.25
Long Tony 127-94-3393 Nightlife New York $10.25
Miller Barbara 185-74-4723 Nightlife New York $9.65
Miller Lisa 536-72-3389 The Runner London $11.00
Miller Tim 101-99-1193 Nightlife London $9.95
Smith Joseph 526-73-1101 The Runner London $9.95
Wallace Barbara 573-19-8831 Nightlife New York $11.00
Williams Richard 209-78-6543 Nightlife New York $10.25
28-Jun-89 12:09 AM
UNDO
Effect of Primary Key sort
Effect of Secondary Key sort

Figure 7.11

The database is now sorted alphabetically by last name. The three Millers are further sorted by first name, as specified by the secondary key.

Once a database is sorted, if any new records are added to the end of the database then the database must be resorted to maintain the correct order. If, in the meantime, no other sorts have been performed, all you need to do after entering the new records is to redefine the data range to include the new records. 1-2-3 stores the most recent sort settings in memory and as part of the worksheet file when you save the file. To clear previous sort settings, use **S**ort **R**eset.

It is always a good idea to save a copy of the worksheet before you sort a file. Then, if you incorrectly specify the sort settings, you can retrieve the original file and try again.

Finding Records in a Database

Lens comes into the office and says, ''Barbara did a super job on *Warriors*. I want her salary raised to $18.00 an hour.''

You need to find Barbara's record and change her wage to $18.00 an hour. Because the Starways database is small, you can find Barbara's record just by looking at the database. But what if the database were much larger?

Locating a particular item in a database is a common database operation. The 1-2-3 command that **queries** or searches a database to locate records quickly according to specified requirements or **criteria** is Data Query. You will use this command to search the database for Barbara's record.

Before you can use this command, you must enter in any open area of the worksheet the selection criteria for the command to use. This area is called the **criteria range** and consists of at least two rows of information. The first row of the criteria range contains the field name exactly as it appears in the database. You need to locate a record using the data in the FIRST name field.

Move to: A17

To ensure that the criteria field name is an exact duplicate of the field name in the database, copy the field name label (FIRST) in cell B3 to cell A17. To do this, issue the following command sequence:

/ Copy **B3** ↵ ↵

The second row of the criteria range contains the record selection criteria or the entries that you want 1-2-3 to match. In this case, the criteria is Barbara. The criteria can be entered in uppercase or lowercase letters, as 1-2-3 is not case sensitive when searching the database for matches. The criteria must, however, be spelled exactly as it is entered in the database. To enter the criteria,

Move to: A18
Type: **Barbara**
Press: ↵

Your screen should look similar to Figure 7.12.

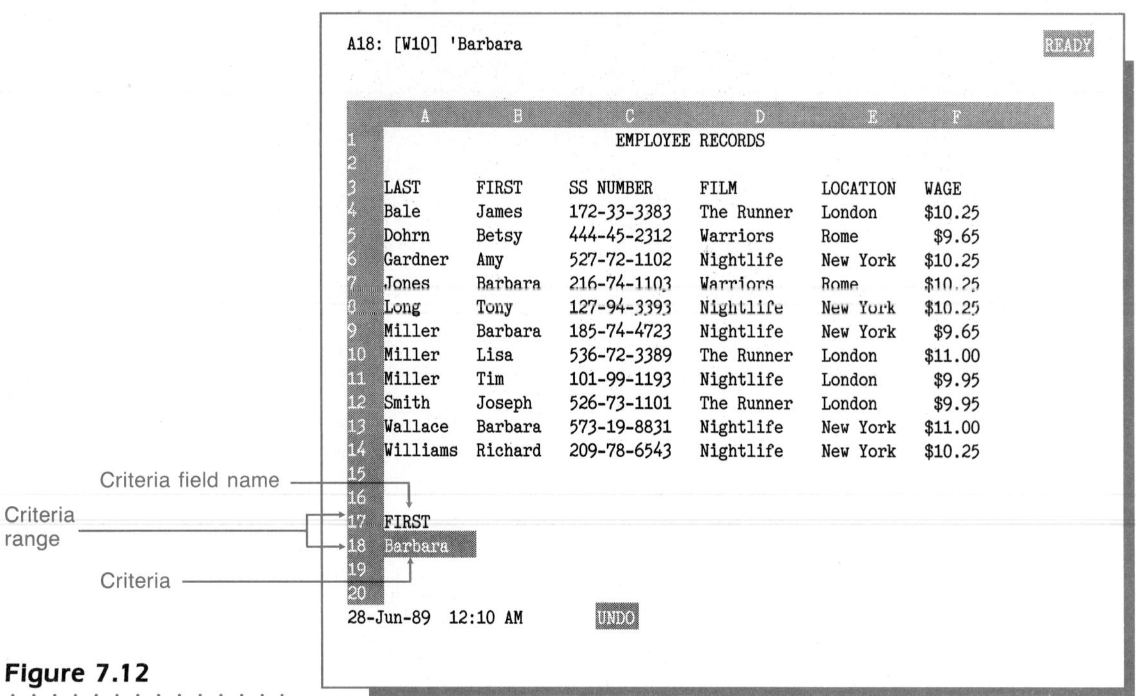

A18: [W10] 'Barbara
READY
EMPLOYEE RECORDS
LAST FIRST SS NUMBER FILM LOCATION WAGE
Bale James 172-33-3383 The Runner London $10.25
Dohrn Betsy 444-45-2312 Warriors Rome $9.65
Gardner Amy 527-72-1102 Nightlife New York $10.25
Jones Barbara 216-74-1103 Warriors Rome $10.25
Long Tony 127-94-3393 Nightlife New York $10.25
Miller Barbara 185-74-4723 Nightlife New York $9.65
Miller Lisa 536-72-3389 The Runner London $11.00
Miller Tim 101-99-1193 Nightlife London $9.95
Smith Joseph 526-73-1101 The Runner London $9.95
Wallace Barbara 573-19-8831 Nightlife New York $11.00
Williams Richard 209-78-6543 Nightlife New York $10.25
FIRST
Barbara
28-Jun-89 12:10 AM
UNDO
Criteria field name
Criteria range
Criteria

Figure 7.12

The field name and criteria have been entered into the criteria range A17 through A18, with the field name in the first row of the range and the criteria to search for in the second row of the range.

Once the selection criteria are entered in the criteria range, you are ready to use the Data Query command. Select:

/ **D**ata **Q**uery

The Query settings sheet is displayed and the second line of the control panel shows the nine Data Query commands. For more information on these commands,

Press: F1

Your screen should look similar to Figure 7.13.

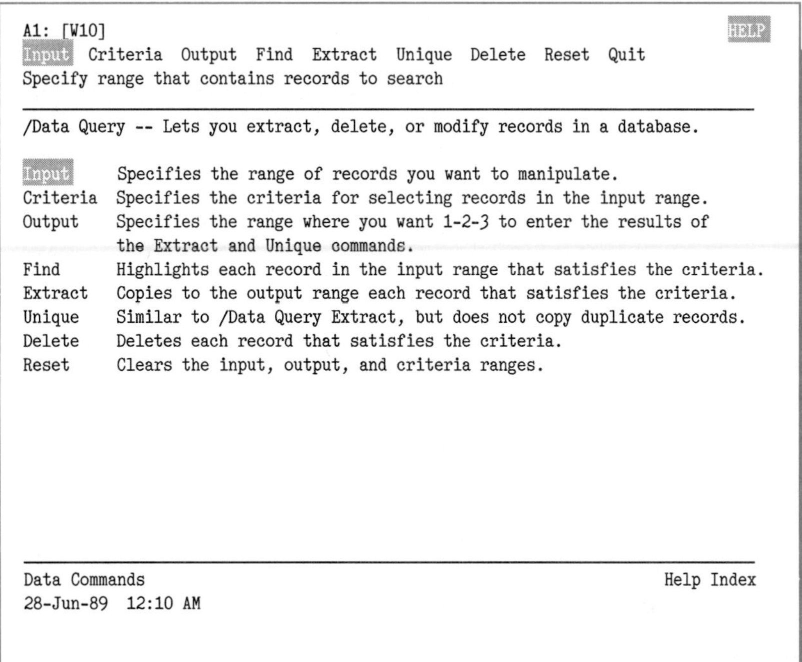
A1: [W10] HELP
Input Criteria Output Find Extract Unique Delete Reset Quit
Specify range that contains records to search

/Data Query -- Lets you extract, delete, or modify records in a database.

Input Specifies the range of records you want to manipulate.
Criteria Specifies the criteria for selecting records in the input range.
Output Specifies the range where you want 1-2-3 to enter the results of the Extract and Unique commands.
Find Highlights each record in the input range that satisfies the criteria.
Extract Copies to the output range each record that satisfies the criteria.
Unique Similar to /Data Query Extract, but does not copy duplicate records.
Delete Deletes each record that satisfies the criteria.
Reset Clears the input, output, and criteria ranges.

Data Commands Help Index
28-Jun-89 12:10 AM

Figure 7.13

The first three commands, Input, Criteria, and Output, are the range settings that are required by the Query command. The next four commands, Find, Extract, Unique, and Delete, are the four different Data Query operations that can be selected.

After you have carefully read the Help menu, press ESC to return to the worksheet.

You will use the Find command to locate the record in the database. The Find command requires that you specify a criteria range and an input range.

Since you just finished entering the criteria, you will specify the criteria range first. This is the range of cells that contains the criteria field name and the selection criteria (A17..A18). To enter the range, continue the command sequence as follows:

Criteria **A17..A18** ↵

Next, you need to specify the **input range**, which is the range of cells in the database to be queried. In this case, it is all database records. This range must include the field names in the first row of the database. To specify the range, continue the command sequence as follows:

Input **A3..F14** ↵

The Query settings sheet reflects the settings you specified for the input and criteria ranges.

Finally, to locate and highlight records in the database that match the selection criteria, select:

Find

Your screen should now look similar to Figure 7.14

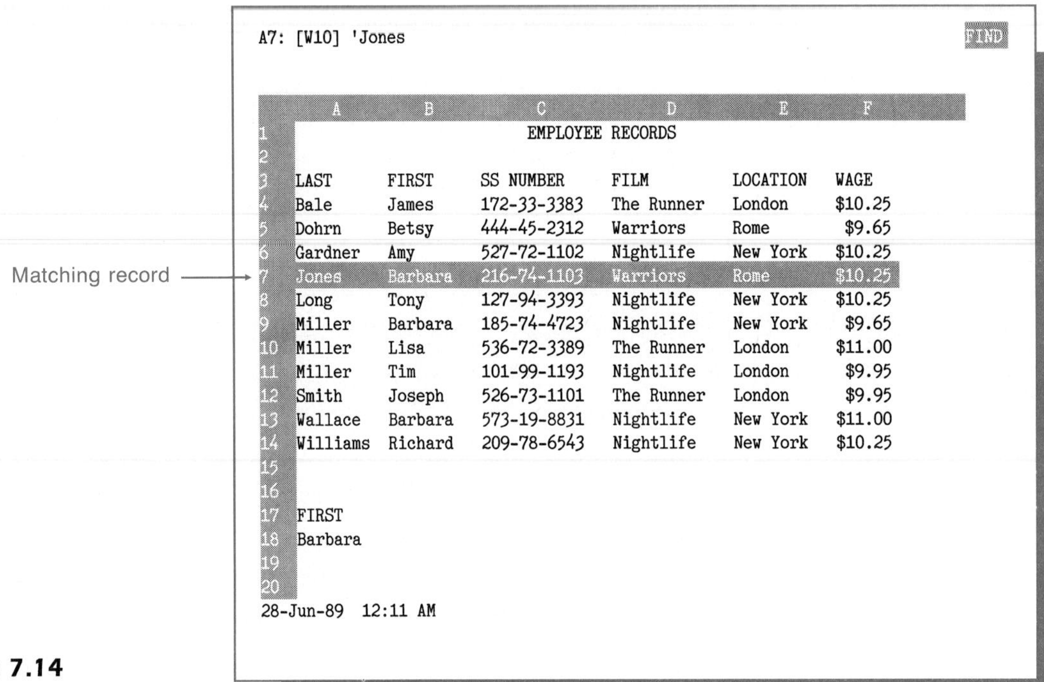
A7: [W10] 'Jones   FIND

	A	B	C	D	E	F
1			EMPLOYEE RECORDS			
2						
3	LAST	FIRST	SS NUMBER	FILM	LOCATION	WAGE
4	Bale	James	172-33-3383	The Runner	London	$10.25
5	Dohrn	Betsy	444-45-2312	Warriors	Rome	$9.65
6	Gardner	Amy	527-72-1102	Nightlife	New York	$10.25
7	Jones	Barbara	216-74-1103	Warriors	Rome	$10.25
8	Long	Tony	127-94-3393	Nightlife	New York	$10.25
9	Miller	Barbara	185-74-4723	Nightlife	New York	$9.65
10	Miller	Lisa	536-72-3389	The Runner	London	$11.00
11	Miller	Tim	101-99-1193	Nightlife	London	$9.95
12	Smith	Joseph	526-73-1101	The Runner	London	$9.95
13	Wallace	Barbara	573-19-8831	Nightlife	New York	$11.00
14	Williams	Richard	209-78-6543	Nightlife	New York	$10.25
15						
16						
17	FIRST					
18	Barbara					
19						
20						

28-Jun-89 12:11 AM

Figure 7.14

The mode indicator has changed from READY to FIND. The cell pointer highlights the record for Barbara Jones. This is the first record in the database that matches the criteria.

Press: ↑

The computer beeps and the cell pointer does not move, indicating there are no other records before Barbara Jones in the database that match the criteria.

Press: ↓

The cell pointer is now highlighting Barbara Miller, the second record that matches the criteria. Each time you press ↓ the cell pointer moves to the next record meeting the criteria.

Press: ↓

Now the record for Barbara Wallace is highlighted. Try to move the cell pointer down again. Again, the computer beeps and the cell pointer does not move. This is because this is the last record in the database that matches the criteria.

You can return to the other records by pressing (↑).

To leave FIND mode,

Press: (↵)

Return to READY mode by selecting:

Quit

You have found three Barbaras in the database, but you do not know which one should be given the raise. However, you remember Lens mentioned that she worked on the film *Warriors*.

To increase the accuracy of the Find command, multiple criteria for different fields can be entered in the criteria range. By entering the criteria in the same row, you tell 1-2-3 to search for records that match all the criteria in the row. 1-2-3 treats the criteria as if they were connected by the word *and*.

To modify the criteria range to include two criteria, FIRST name of Barbara *and* FILM of Warriors,

Move to: B17

Copy the field name, FILM, in cell D3 to cell B17.

Move to: B18
Type: **Warriors**
Press: (↵)

Your screen should look similar to Figure 7.15.

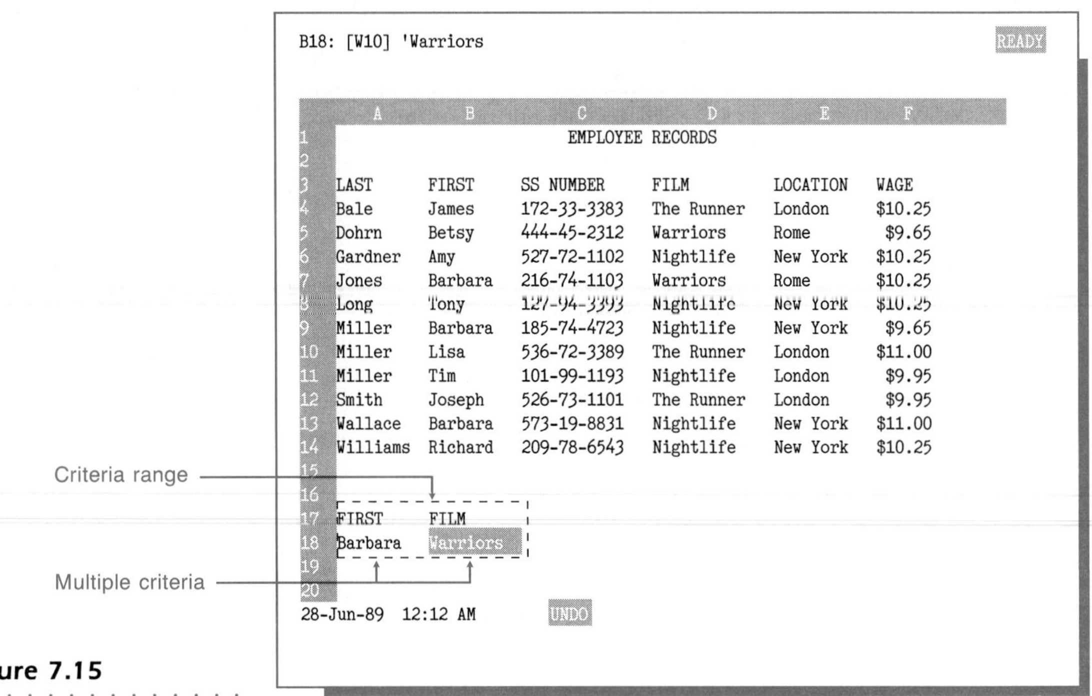

Figure 7.15

The criteria range now contains the field names FIRST and FILM, along with the selection criteria, Barbara and Warriors.

To define the new criteria range, issue the following command sequence:

/ **D**ata **Q**uery **C**riteria **A17..B18** ↵

The Query settings sheet is displayed again. You do not need to specify the input range again because 1-2-3 remembers the range last specified.

To find all the records in the database with FIRST name Barbara *and* FILM Warriors, select:

Find

Your screen should look similar to Figure 7.16.

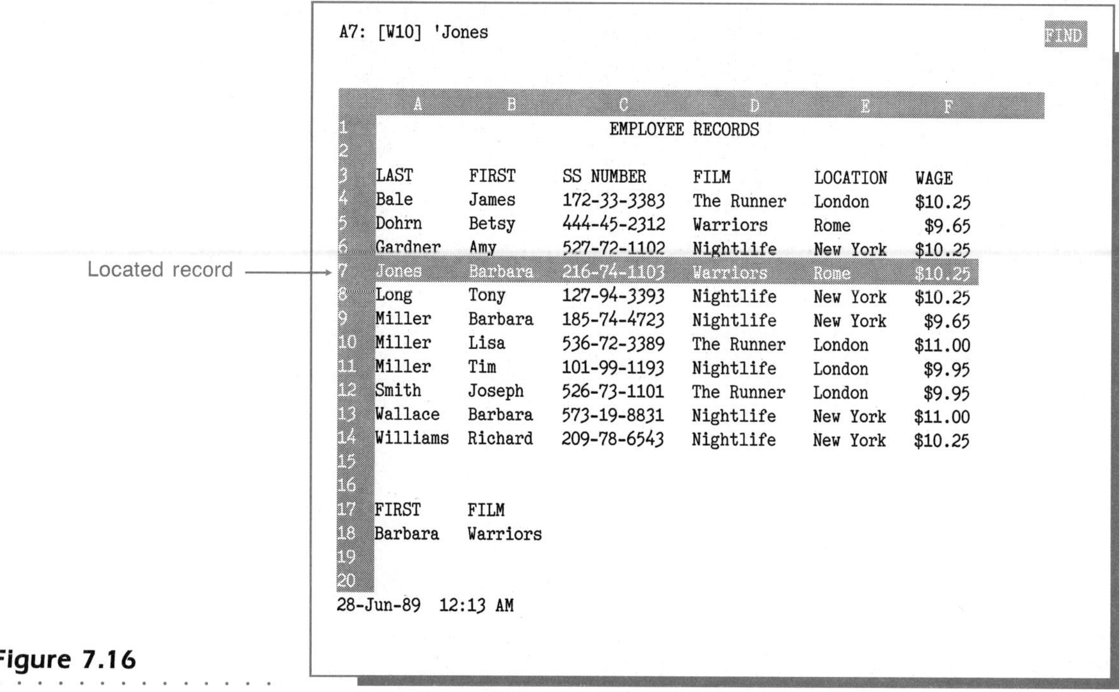

A7: [W10] 'Jones FIND

	A	B	C	D	E	F
1			EMPLOYEE RECORDS			
2						
3	LAST	FIRST	SS NUMBER	FILM	LOCATION	WAGE
4	Bale	James	172-33-3383	The Runner	London	$10.25
5	Dohrn	Betsy	444-45-2312	Warriors	Rome	$9.65
6	Gardner	Amy	527-72-1102	Nightlife	New York	$10.25
7	Jones	Barbara	216-74-1103	Warriors	Rome	$10.25
8	Long	Tony	127-94-3393	Nightlife	New York	$10.25
9	Miller	Barbara	185-74-4723	Nightlife	New York	$9.65
10	Miller	Lisa	536-72-3389	The Runner	London	$11.00
11	Miller	Tim	101-99-1193	Nightlife	London	$9.95
12	Smith	Joseph	526-73-1101	The Runner	London	$9.95
13	Wallace	Barbara	573-19-8831	Nightlife	New York	$11.00
14	Williams	Richard	209-78-6543	Nightlife	New York	$10.25
15						
16						
17	FIRST	FILM				
18	Barbara	Warriors				
19						
20						

28-Jun-89 12:13 AM

Figure 7.16

The cell pointer now highlights Barbara Jones's record. Try to move the cell pointer up or down. 1-2-3 will not move the cell pointer, because only one record meets the criteria.

While in FIND mode, you can edit the contents of the current record. The blinking cursor within the cell pointer identifies the field. To move the cursor, use (→) and (←). As the cursor moves, the cell contents are displayed in the control panel.

To change Barbara's rate of pay to $18.00, use (→) to move the cursor to the WAGE field.

Move to: F7

To change the value in this cell to $18.00, either type in the new data and press (↵) or use the Edit function key, (F2), to modify the cell contents and press (↵).

To leave FIND mode and return to READY mode, issue the following command:

(↵) **Quit**

Whenever multiple criteria are entered in the same row of the criteria range, 1-2-3 searches for only those records that match all the criteria. If the criteria are entered on separate rows, 1-2-3 searches for all records that match any of the criteria. 1-2-3 treats these criteria as if they were connected by the word *or*.

To demonstrate this, you will find all records that have FIRST name of Barbara *or* FILM of Warriors.

To move the criteria in cell B18 to B19, issue the following command sequence:

/ **M**ove **B18** ↵ **B19** ↵

Your screen should look similar to Figure 7.17.

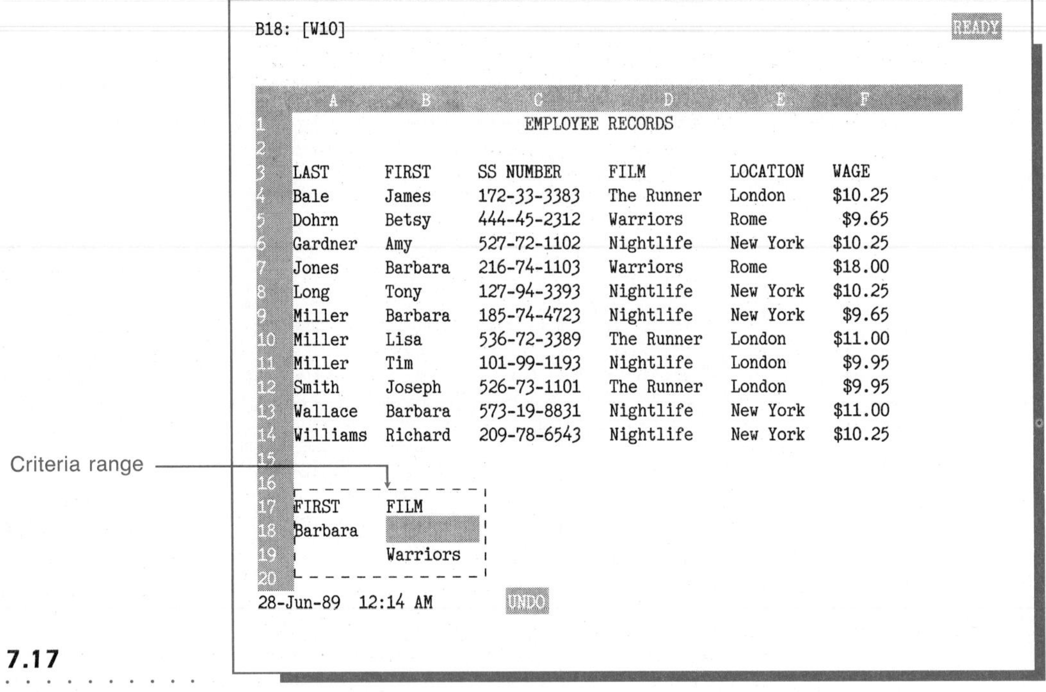

Figure 7.17

Next, to find all records that meet either *or* both of the criteria, issue the following command sequence:

/ **D**ata **Q**uery

Notice in the Query settings sheet that 1-2-3 automatically adjusted the criteria range to A17..B19 when you used the Move command. To complete the command sequence, select:

Find

The first record that meets either of the criteria is highlighted. Use (↓) to find other records that meet the criteria. All records with FIRST name Barbara *or* FILM Warriors are highlighted.

To return to READY mode, complete the command sequence:

(↵) **Q**uit

Finally, change the film to *Nightlife* in cell B19.

Move to: B19
Type: **Nightlife**
Press: (↵)

Because the criteria and input ranges have not changed, you can use the Query function key, (F7), from READY mode to quickly locate all records in the database that match the criteria.

Press: (F7)

The first record that meets the new criteria should be highlighted. Use (↓) to locate all the records that match the criteria.

Another way to end the Data Query Find command is to use (F7). When you use this method, the cell pointer remains in the current cell.

Press: (F7)

Using Search and Replace

Lens has decided to change the name of the film "The Runner" to "The Marathon." To do this, you could use the Data Query Find command to locate all records in the database that have a FILM of "The Runner" and then individually edit each record to change the film title to "The Marathon." However, a quicker way is to use the Range Search command. This command will quickly locate any **string** (combination of characters) within formulas or labels in the worksheet. It will not locate numbers unless they are part of a formula. Select:

/ **R**ange **S**earch

The prompt to enter the range to search is displayed in the control panel. The range will be the column containing the FILM field data. Select:

D4..D14 ↵

Next, you must locate the search string to be specified. It can be entered in either uppercase or lowercase characters, as the search string is not case sensitive. To search for all cell entries of ''The Runner,''

Type: **The Runner**
Press: ↵

Next, you must select **F**ormulas, **L**abels, or **B**oth from the menu. These options have the following meanings:

Formulas	looks for string in formulas only
Labels	looks for string in labels only
Both	looks for string in both formulas and labels

Because the search string is used only as a label entry, select:

Label

Your choice from the next menu lets you Find (locate only) or Replace (locate and replace) matches in the search range. Since Lens wants to change all the entries containing the film title of ''The Runner'' to ''The Marathon,'' the Replace option will be used. Select:

Replace

The final piece of information needed is the replacement string. You must enter this exactly as you want it to appear in the worksheet. To enter the replacement string,

Type: **The Marathon**
Press: ↵

Your screen should be similar to Figure 7.18.

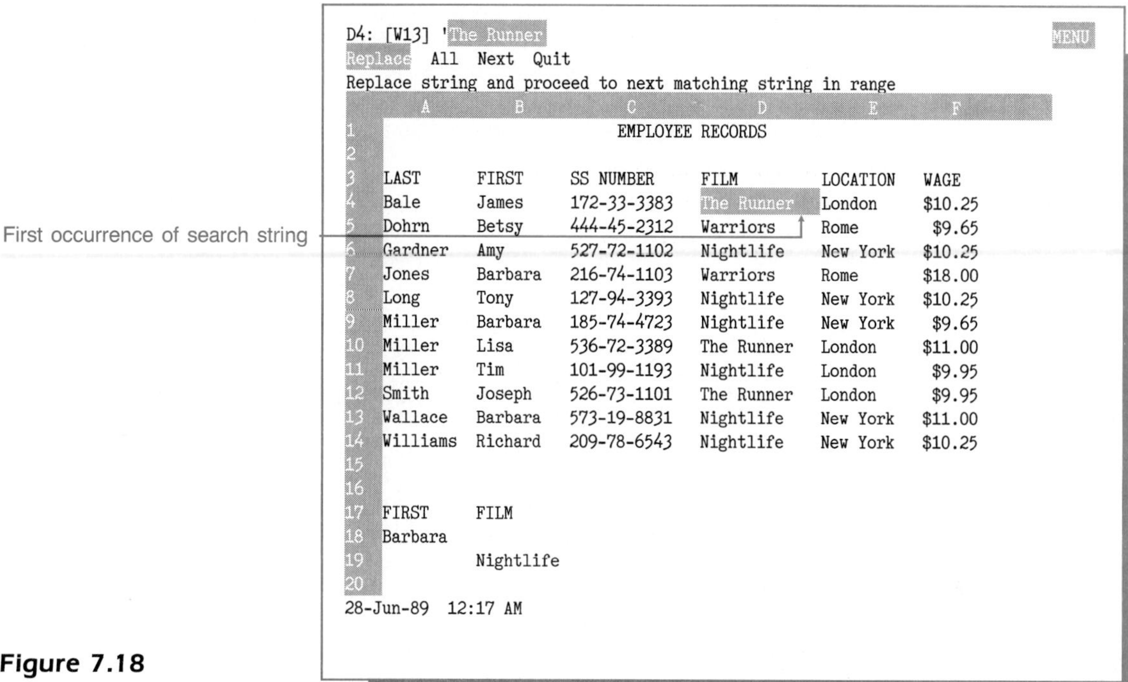

	A	B	C	D	E	F
1			EMPLOYEE RECORDS			
2						
3	LAST	FIRST	SS NUMBER	FILM	LOCATION	WAGE
4	Bale	James	172-33-3383	The Runner	London	$10.25
5	Dohrn	Betsy	444-45-2312	Warriors	Rome	$9.65
6	Gardner	Amy	527-72-1102	Nightlife	New York	$10.25
7	Jones	Barbara	216-74-1103	Warriors	Rome	$18.00
8	Long	Tony	127-94-3393	Nightlife	New York	$10.25
9	Miller	Barbara	185-74-4723	Nightlife	New York	$9.65
10	Miller	Lisa	536-72-3389	The Runner	London	$11.00
11	Miller	Tim	101-99-1193	Nightlife	London	$9.95
12	Smith	Joseph	526-73-1101	The Runner	London	$9.95
13	Wallace	Barbara	573-19-8831	Nightlife	New York	$11.00
14	Williams	Richard	209-78-6543	Nightlife	New York	$10.25
15						
16						
17	FIRST	FILM				
18	Barbara					
19		Nightlife				
20						

28-Jun-89 12:17 AM

Figure 7.18

The cell pointer highlights the first occurrence of the search string in the search range. The menu offers the following options:

Replace replaces the current string with the replacement string and searches for the next matching string in the range

All replaces all matching strings in the search range with the replacement string

Next does not replace the current string but searches for the next matching string

Quit returns 1-2-3 to READY mode

To replace all occurrences of the original film title with the new film title, select:

All

Your screen should be similar to Figure 7.19.

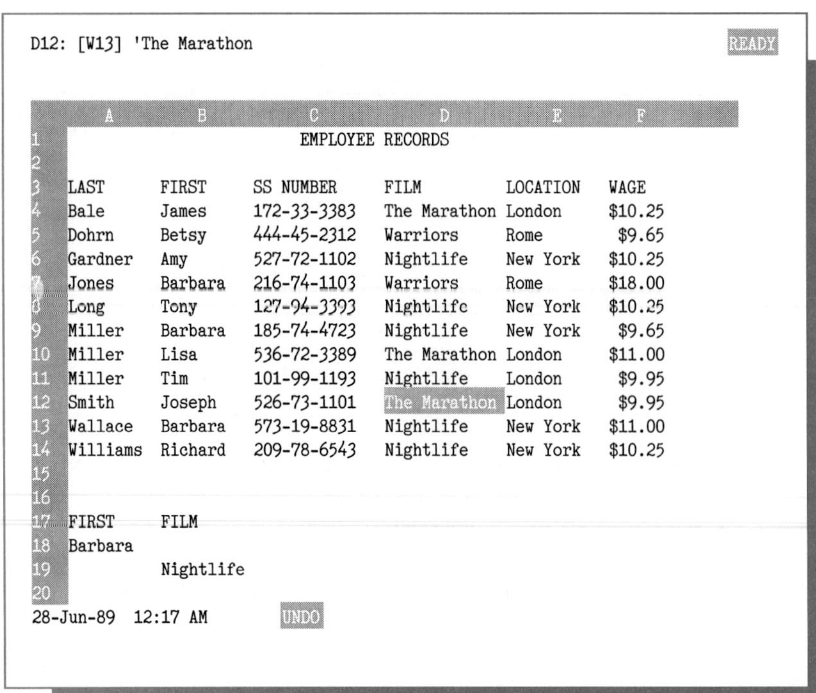

D12: [W13] 'The Marathon READY

	A	B	C	D	E	F
1			EMPLOYEE RECORDS			
2						
3	LAST	FIRST	SS NUMBER	FILM	LOCATION	WAGE
4	Bale	James	172-33-3383	The Marathon	London	$10.25
5	Dohrn	Betsy	444-45-2312	Warriors	Rome	$9.65
6	Gardner	Amy	527-72-1102	Nightlife	New York	$10.25
7	Jones	Barbara	216-74-1103	Warriors	Rome	$18.00
8	Long	Tony	127-94-3393	Nightlife	New York	$10.25
9	Miller	Barbara	185-74-4723	Nightlife	New York	$9.65
10	Miller	Lisa	536-72-3389	The Marathon	London	$11.00
11	Miller	Tim	101-99-1193	Nightlife	London	$9.95
12	Smith	Joseph	526-73-1101	The Marathon	London	$9.95
13	Wallace	Barbara	573-19-8831	Nightlife	New York	$11.00
14	Williams	Richard	209-78-6543	Nightlife	New York	$10.25
15						
16						
17	FIRST	FILM				
18	Barbara					
19		Nightlife				
20						

28-Jun-89 12:17 AM UNDO

Figure 7.19

The new film title quickly replaced all occurrences of the original film title. 1-2-3 automatically returns to READY mode when no more occurrences are found.

Be careful when you use the All command to replace character strings as you may get some unexpected results. You might want to test how this command is working by selecting Replace for the first few occurrences and then changing to All. If you do get unexpected results and the Undo feature is on, you can undo the error if you immediately press ALT-F4 (UNDO) after returning to READY mode.

Print the worksheet, including the criteria range.

Save the worksheet under the filename EMPREC and then exit from 1-2-3.

Glossary of Key Terms

Ascending order Records are sorted in A through Z or 0 through 9 order.

Criteria The cell entries that 1-2-3 interprets as the tests or requirements for the query.

Criteria range The range of cells that contains the field names and criteria to be located in a query.

Database A collection of related information that consists of fields and records.

Data range The range of cells that contains the data records to be sorted.

Descending order Records are sorted in Z through A or 9 through 0 order.

Field A collection of related characters, such as a person's name.

Field name A label that identifies the contents of each column or field of data.

Input range The range of cells that contains the field names and the data records to be queried.

Primary key The column in the data range whose values determine the sort order.

Query The process of searching the database to locate specific records.

Record A collection of related fields, such as a person's name, address, Social Security number, and rate of pay.

Secondary key The field whose entries determine the sort order of records with identical primary key entries.

Sort key The field that determines the order of the sort.

Sort order Determines whether records are sorted in ascending or descending order.

String Any combination of characters.

Practice Problems

1. Matching

1. Field	______	**a.**	a label in the first row of a database
2. F7	______	**b.**	the Query key
3. Field name	______	**c.**	sorts a database
4. /DS	______	**d.**	range in the worksheet that contains the criteria
5. /DQF	______	**e.**	an organized collection of related information
6. Criteria range	______	**f.**	arranges records in a specified order
7. Database	______	**g.**	finds a record in a database
8. Sort	______	**h.**	a collection of related fields
9. Record	______	**i.**	field used to break ties in a sort
10. Secondary key	______	**j.**	a collection of related characters

2. Fran Matthews runs a small job service that supplies temporary clerical workers to local corporations.

   a. Create a database for Fran with the field names and column widths shown below. Enter the database field names in row 4. Put your name in cell A1 and the current date in cell A2.

Field name	*Column width*
LAST NAME	12
FIRST NAME	12
JOB TITLE	12
STREET	17
CITY	14
STATE	6
ZIP CODE	8
TELEPHONE	10

b. Insert the following records into the database.

LAST NAME :	Long
FIRST NAME :	Vera
JOB TITLE :	data entry
STREET :	3145 Pearl St
CITY :	Cranesville
STATE :	PA
ZIP CODE :	16453
TELEPHONE :	927-3815

LAST NAME :	Jones
FIRST NAME :	William
JOB TITLE :	file clerk
STREET :	1349 West Ave
CITY :	Girard
STATE :	PA
ZIP CODE :	16457
TELEPHONE :	935-4198

LAST NAME :	Williams
FIRST NAME :	Daniel
JOB TITLE :	data entry
STREET :	1978 August Ave
CITY :	Little Silver
STATE :	PA
ZIP CODE :	17739
TELEPHONE :	741-2621

LAST NAME :	Jones
FIRST NAME :	Shirley
JOB TITLE :	secretary
STREET :	3842 Glenn St

CITY :	Albion
STATE :	PA
ZIP CODE :	16458
TELEPHONE :	838-7015

c. Sort the records alphabetically by last name as the primary key and by first name as the secondary key. The sort order is ascending.

d. Enter a fifth record using your name and address information. Your job title is data entry.

e. Sort the records again using the same settings as in step c. Print a copy of your display using SHIFT-PRTSC.

f. Sort the records by job title as the primary key and by last name as the secondary key. The order for both keys is ascending.

g. Save the worksheet under the filename TEMPS. Print the worksheet.

3. Retrieve the database file EMPLOYEE. Enter your name in cell A1.

   a. Correct James Bale's first name.

   b. Sort the database by LAST name in ascending order.

   c. Sort the database again by FILM as the primary key in descending order and by WAGE as the secondary key in ascending order. Print a copy of your display using SHIFT-PRTSC.

   d. Find all records in the database for people who worked on location in New York. How many are there?

   e. Find all records in the database for employees who earned $10.25 an hour *and* worked on location in New York. How many are there?

   f. Find all records in the database for employees who earned $11.00 an hour *or* worked on location in London. How many are there?

   g. Save the worksheet using the filename EMPREC2. Print your worksheet, including the criteria range.

8

Using a Database

Objectives

In Lab 8, you will learn how to:

- Use database @functions
- Create a frequency distribution table
- Extract records from the database
- Create a data table

Case Study

Lynne Tellez has just been promoted to employment administrator for MidCon TeleEquip Corporation. Her first assignment is to analyze employee pay rate data.

Before leaving the firm, Lynne's predecessor had created a 1-2-3 database of employee records. Unfortunately, there is no written documentation for the database. You will follow Lynne as she familiarizes herself with an existing file of database records and as she uses the database.

Documenting a Database

After searching through the files and other records left by the previous employment administrator, Lynne found a disk containing a 1-2-3 database worksheet of employee records. Unfortunately, little is known about the database except that it is in the file RECORDS. To see the database, retrieve the file RECORDS.WK1.

Your screen should look similar to Figure 8.1.

A1: [W10] READY

	A	B	C	D	E	F	G	H
1								
2								
3				EMPLOYEE RECORDS				
4								
5	LAST	FIRST	SEX	SS NUMBER	TITLE	PAY	YEARS	CLASS
6	Ludwig	Patrick	M	777-98-8080	Pres.	$29.00	20	1
7	Pratt	Cindy	F	333-46-7838	Vice Pres.	$25.00	19	1
8	Anderson	Dorothy	F	687-18-7920	Designer	$18.50	18	1
9	Tellez	Lynne	F	499-98-9090	Emp. Adm.	$15.00	17	1
10	Bennett	Phillip	M	111-23-6576	Engineer	$13.89	18	1
11	Gale	James	M	172-33-3383	Asst. Mgr.	$14.75	8	1
12	Jones	Calvin	M	216-74-1103	Analyst	$9.25	7	2
13	Walters	Phyllis	F	908-56-4356	Designer	$13.25	15	2
14	Klink	Hugh	M	545-34-1290	Engineer	$9.48	9	2
15	Lane	Marianne	F	543-98-6735	Engineer	$12.29	10	2
16	Altman	Harold	M	565-56-5665	Sales	$9.02	5	2
17	Murillo	Anthony	M	556-87-8839	Tech. Dev.	$7.25	6	2
18	Travers	Steven	M	101-50-5090	Tech. Dev.	$14.00	12	2
19	Owens	Shirley	F	456-45-5678	Admin. Asst.	$8.45	13	3
20	Larson	Connie	F	676-45-3211	Clerk 1	$3.95	3	3

28-Jun-89 12:43 AM UNDO

Figure 8.1

Most of the field names in row 5 seem to make sense: LAST, FIRST, and so forth. Others, such as the label CLASS, are not so obvious.

After reviewing other personnel documents and making a few telephone calls, Lynne determined the meanings of the field names. To record her findings and to document the structure of the file RECORDS, Lynne prepared Table 8.1.

Table 8.1

Field Name	Column Width	Definition	Label (L) or Value (V)
LAST	10	Employee's last name	L
FIRST	10	Employee's first name	L
SEX	5	Male (M) or female (F)	L
SS NUMBER	13	Social Security number	L
TITLE	13	Job title	L
PAY	7	Hourly rate of pay	V
YEARS	6	Length of employment	V
CLASS	6	Job classification	
		Class 1 – Professional	L
		Class 2 – Sales/Tech	L
		Class 3 – Clerical	L
		Class 4 – Maintenance	L

Lynne has filed a copy of Table 8.1 in the Personnel Department's central file, along with a disk containing a copy of the database. You will continue to document the worksheet throughout this lab.

To see the rest of the records in the database,

Press: PGDN

There are 25 employee records.

Press: HOME

Using the Database @Functions

To begin her analysis of the employee pay rate data, Lynne wants to compare pay rates for male and female employees in the database.

Specifically, she wants to calculate the average, the minimum, and the maximum pay for each group. She also wants to determine the total number of males and females in the database.

To obtain these comparisons, you will use some of 1-2-3's database statistical @functions.

You will begin by calculating the average rate of pay for males using the @DAVG function. The syntax for this @function is

@DAVG(input,field,criteria)

To use this @function, you must specify three arguments: input, field, and criteria. You specify the input and criteria ranges the same as in the Data Query command.

The first step is to enter the criteria in any open area of the worksheet. You will use the area to the right of the database of records. To move to this area,

Press: CTRL-→

Because this worksheet will contain many different items, it is good procedure to document the different areas of the worksheet with descriptive labels. These labels identify the contents of each area of the worksheet. This area of the worksheet will contain the criteria for the @functions. To enter a descriptive label to document this area of the worksheet,

Move to: J1
Type: **CRITERIA: Males**
Press: ↵

To enter the criteria field name, SEX,

Move to: K3

Copy the field name SEX from cell C5 to cell K3.

To enter the selection criteria, M, for male,

Move to: K4
Type: **M**
Press: ↵

Your screen should look similar to Figure 8.2.

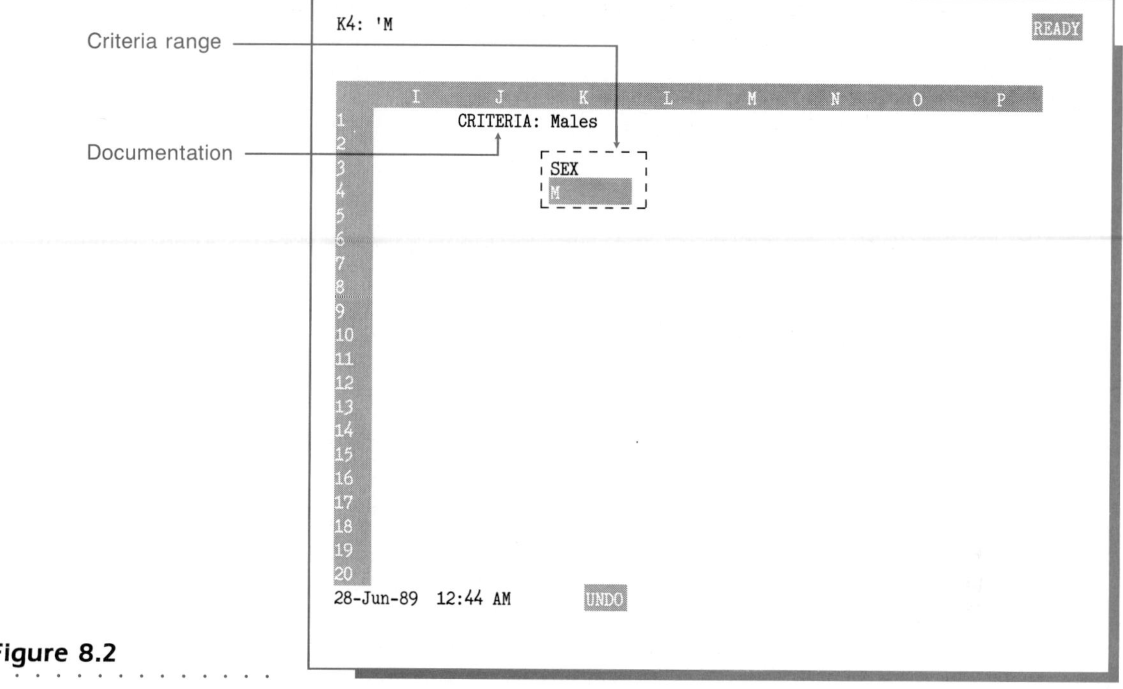

Figure 8.2

You are now ready to enter the database @functions to calculate the pay rate for males.

Move to: J6

Again, document this area of the worksheet by adding a descriptive label.

Type: **STATISTICS: Males**
Press: ↵

To enter the @function to calculate the average pay rate for males,

Move to: L8
Type: **@DAVG(**

The first argument you need to enter is the input range. This range specifies the records in the database to be used in the calculation. It must include the field names. To specify all records,

Type: **A5..H30**

To separate this argument from the next,

Type: , (comma)

The second argument you enter is the field. The field is identified by an **offset number**, which corresponds to the position of the column that contains the field in the input range that the @function will operate on. You determine the offset number by assigning the leftmost column in the input range the value 0, the second column the value 1, the third column the value 2, and so forth.

The offset number specifying the field PAY is 5, as shown in Figure 8.3.

A1: [W10] READY

Offset numbers →

	0	1	2	3	4	5	6	7
	A	B	C	D	E	F	G	H
1								
2								
3				EMPLOYEE RECORDS				
4								
5	LAST	FIRST	SEX	SS NUMBER	TITLE	PAY	YEARS	CLASS
6	Ludwig	Patrick	M	777-98-8080	Pres.	$29.00	20	1
7	Pratt	Cindy	F	333-46-7838	Vice Pres.	$25.00	19	1
8	Anderson	Dorothy	F	687-18-7920	Designer	$18.50	18	1
9	Tellez	Lynne	F	499-98-9090	Emp. Adm.	$15.00	17	1
10	Bennett	Phillip	M	111-23-6576	Engineer	$13.89	18	1
11	Gale	James	M	172-33-3383	Asst. Mgr.	$14.75	8	1
12	Jones	Calvin	M	216-74-1103	Analyst	$9.25	7	2
13	Walters	Phyllis	F	908-56-4356	Designer	$13.25	15	2
14	Klink	Hugh	M	545-34-1290	Engineer	$9.48	9	2
15	Lane	Marianne	F	543-98-6735	Engineer	$12.29	10	2
16	Altman	Harold	M	565-56-5665	Sales	$9.02	5	2
17	Murillo	Anthony	M	556-87-8839	Tech. Dev.	$7.25	6	2
18	Travers	Steven	M	101-50-5090	Tech. Dev.	$14.00	12	2
19	Owens	Shirley	F	456-45-5678	Admin. Asst.	$8.45	13	3
20	Larson	Connie	F	676-45-3211	Clerk 1	$3.95	3	3

22-Sep-89 11:47 AM UNDO

Figure 8.3

Type: **5,**

The last argument you need to enter is the criteria range.

Type: **K3..K4)**
Press: ↵

The value 10.98 generated by the @DAVG function is displayed in cell L8. To document the meaning of this value,

Move to: K8
Type: **AVG. PAY**
Press: ↵

Your screen should look similar to Figure 8.4.

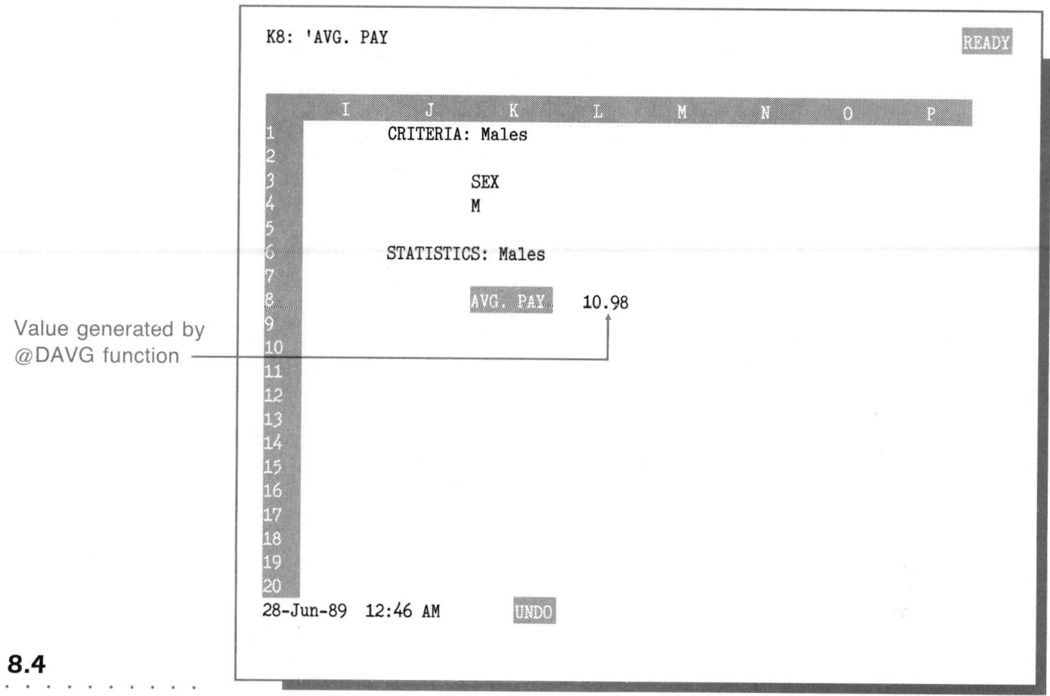

Figure 8.4

You will use the @DMAX, @DMIN, and @DCOUNT @functions to calculate the maximum and minimum rates of pay for males and the number of males in the database. The input, field, and criteria for each of these @functions are identical to those specified in the @DAVG function.

To document the worksheet,

Move to: K9
Type: **MIN. PAY**
Move to: K10
Type: **MAX. PAY**
Move to: K11
Type: **NUMBER**
Press: ↵

To enter the @functions,

Move to: L9
Type: **@DMIN(A5..H30,5,K3..K4)**
Move to: L10
Type: **@DMAX(A5..H30,5,K3..K4)**
Move to: L11
Type: **@DCOUNT(A5..H30,5,K3..K4)**
Press: ↵

Your screen should look similar to Figure 8.5.

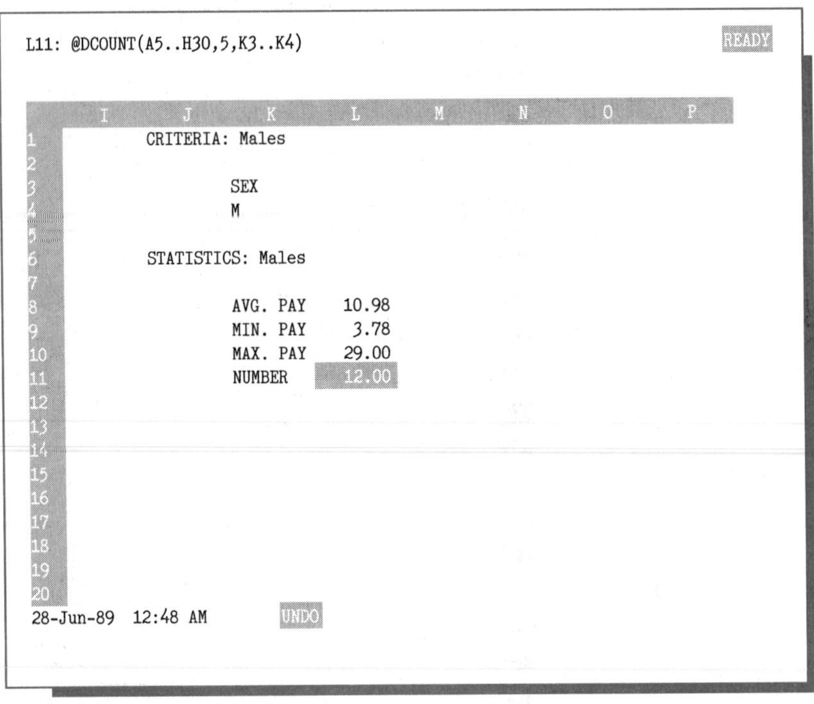

Figure 8.5

The average, minimum, and maximum rates of pay for males and the number of males employed are now calculated. Format the values in L8..L10 to be displayed as currency with two decimal places. Format the value for count in cell L11 as general.

Next, Lynne wants to generate the same statistics for females in the database. To enter a new criteria range for females,

Move to: M1
Type: **CRITERIA: Females**
Move to: N3

Copy the field name SEX from cell K3 to N3.

Move to: N4
Type: **F**
Press: ↵

You are now ready to enter the @functions to calculate the statistics for females.

Move to: M6

To document this area of the worksheet,

Type: **STATISTICS: Females**
Move to: N8

Copy the descriptive labels from K8..K11 to N8..N11.

To enter the appropriate database statistical @functions,

Move to: O8
Type: **@DAVG(A5..H30,5,N3..N4)**
Press: ↵

Enter the remaining @functions to calculate the minimum and maximum pay rates and the count of females in cells O9, O10, and O11, respectively.

Format the calculated pay rates for females to be displayed as currency with two decimal places and the number (count) as general.

Note A quicker way to do this is to copy the @functions in cells L8..L11 to cells O8..O11. First change the input range in each @function in cells L8..L11 to absolute cell references. (Leave the criteria range as relative cell references.) Then copy the @function. The appropriate cell format will also be copied.

Your screen should look similar to Figure 8.6.

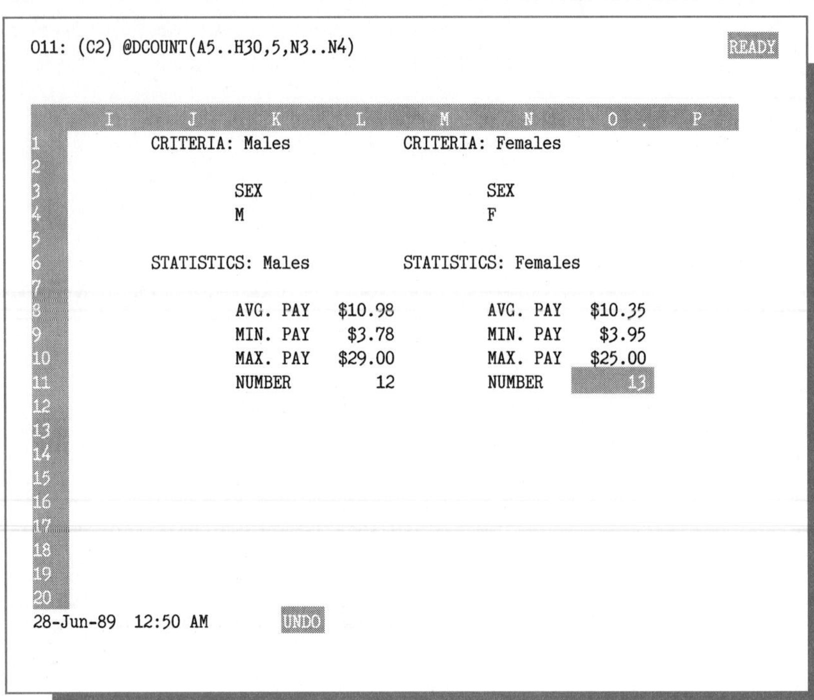

Figure 8.6

Lynne can now easily compare the average, minimum, and maximum pay rates and the number of male and female employees in the database.

Using the Data Distribution Command

Next, Lynne wants to analyze the data further by preparing a **frequency distribution table**, which will calculate the number of employees whose rates of pay fall within specified categories.

Specifically, she wants to find out how many employees earn $4.00 or less, between $4.01 and $6.50, between $6.51 and $9.00, between $9.01 and $13.00, between $13.01 and $18.50, and greater than $18.50 per hour. The Data Distribution command will generate this table for her.

To document this area of the worksheet,

Move to: J13
Type: **PAY RATE DISTRIBUTION**
Press: ↵

Before you use the Data Distribution command, you must enter the upper value in each category in the worksheet as a column of ascending values. To do this,

Move to: K15
Type: **4**
Move to: K16
Type: **6.5**
Move to: K17
Type: **9**
Move to: K18
Type: **13**
Move to: K19
Type: **18.5**
Press: ↵

These values would look better if they were formatted to be displayed as currency. Format the range K15..K19 to display as currency with two decimal places.

Your screen should look similar to Figure 8.7.

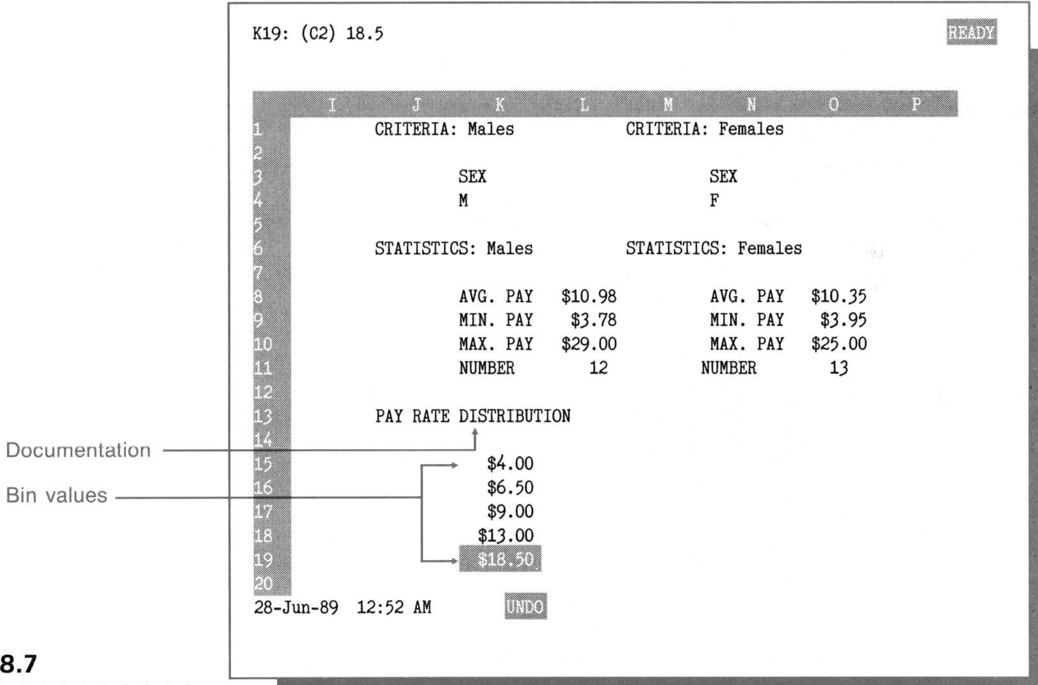

Figure 8.7

The values are called bin values. 1-2-3 interprets each value as the upper limit of each category. The cell to the right of each bin value will display the count value, or number of records whose pay rate falls within the range of each category.

You are now ready to use the Data Distribution command. Select:

/ **D**ata **D**istribution

The prompt "Enter values range:" is displayed. In response to this prompt, you must specify the location of the values to be distributed into bins.

The column of data in the PAY field is the data to be used to generate the frequency distribution table. The values range does not include the field names. To enter this range,

Type: **F6..F30**
Press: ↵

The next prompt requires that you specify the **bin range**, the range of cells containing the bin values.

Type: **K15..K19**
Press: ↵

After a few seconds, the number of records whose PAY falls within each specified category is displayed in the column to the right of the bin values.

To display the count values as integer, format the range L15..L20 as general.

Your screen should look similar to Figure 8.8.

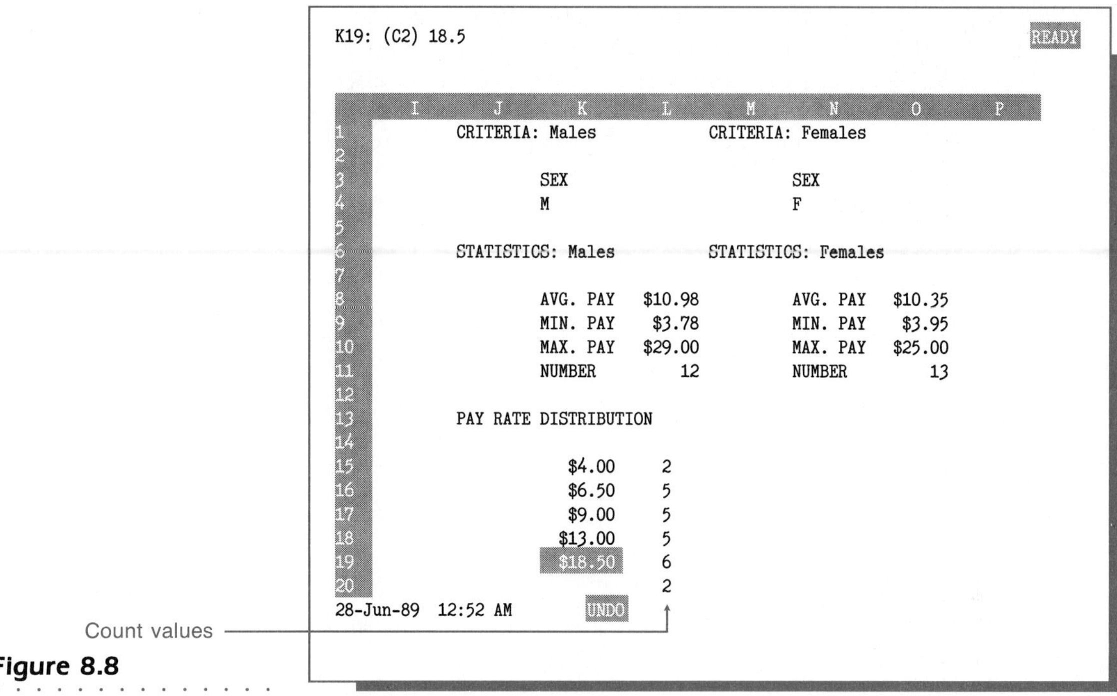

Figure 8.8

The distribution shows that two employees earn $4.00 or less, five earn between $4.01 and $6.50, five earn between $6.51 and $9.00, and so forth. Notice the count value displayed in cell L20. 1-2-3 uses one cell more than there are bins to display the count value for any numbers greater than the last specified bin value. In this database, two employees earn more than $18.50 per hour.

Using the Data Query Extract Command

Finally, Lynne wants to create two separate lists that show the CLASS, TITLE, and PAY data for males and females. To do this, you will use the Data Query Extract command. This command requires a criteria range, an input range, and an **output range**. The only new range that you need to specify is output.

The output range is where the specified fields of data meeting the criteria will be displayed. You will use the worksheet space below the frequency table for the output range. To document this area of the worksheet,

Move to: J22
Type: **OUTPUT: Males**
Press: ↵

The first row of the output range must contain the field names from the database of each field you want to be displayed. Lynne wants only the data in the CLASS, TITLE, and PAY fields to appear in the list. Like the criteria range, the field names in the output range must be exact duplicates of the field names in the database.

Move to: J24

To enter the first output field name, copy the field name CLASS from cell H5 of the database to cell J24. Then copy the field names TITLE and PAY from cells E5 and F5 to cells K24 and L24, respectively.

Your screen should be similar to Figure 8.9.

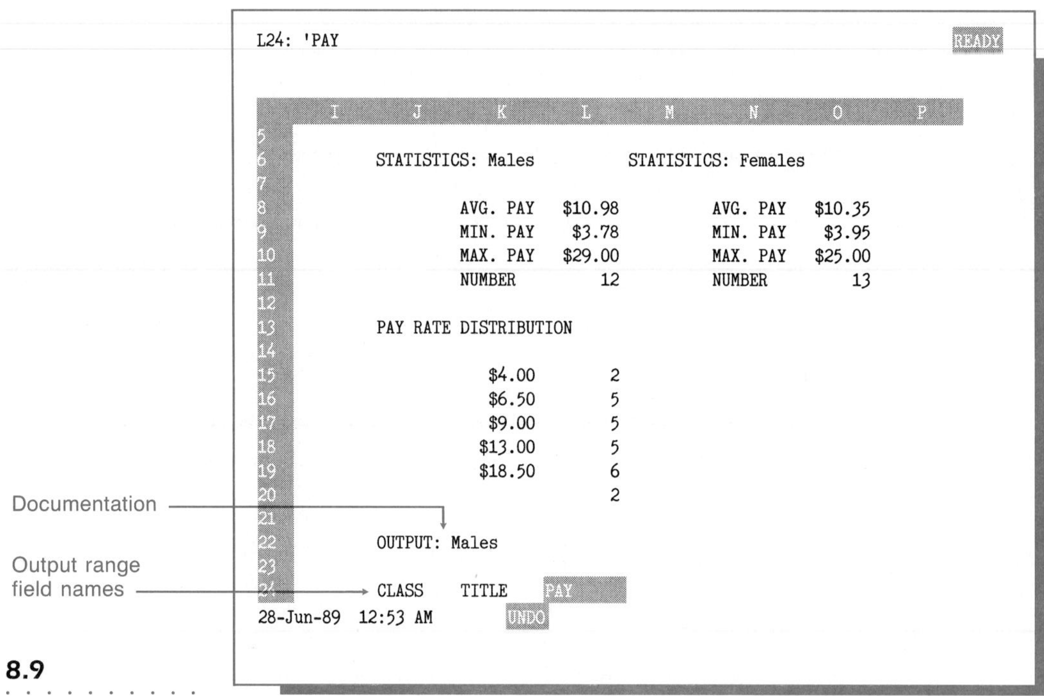

Figure 8.9

You are now ready to use the Data Query command to **extract** the data for males to the output range. Select:

/ **D**ata **Q**uery

The Query settings sheet is displayed.

First, specify the input range. The input range must begin with the row of field names in the database and end with the last record to be queried.

To specify the input range as the entire database from cell A5 through cell H30, continue the command sequence as follows:

Input **A5..H30** (↵)

Next, to specify the criteria range for males as K3 through K4, select:

Criteria **K3..K4** (↵)

The final setting to specify is the output range, where the records meeting the criteria will be displayed.

You can specify the output range in two different ways. One way is to specify a single row ouput range. The output range would consist of only the row containing the output field names. When the data meeting the criteria are copied from the database, they will be displayed below the appropriate field names. 1-2-3 will use as many rows as it needs below the output field names to display the data meeting the criteria. If necessary, it will copy over any existing data.

The other way is to specify a multiple row output range consisting of the field names in the first row and a number of rows below the field names to display the extracted data. 1-2-3 will display as many rows of data below the field names as there are rows in the specified range. However, if the range is not large enough, the error message "Too many records for Output range" will appear, and you must respecify the output range.

You will specify a single row output range, because there is nothing below this area in the worksheet that you do not want copied over. Issue the following command sequence:

Output **J24..L24** (↵)

Now you are ready to extract the job classifications, job titles, and pay for all males in the database. Issue the following command:

Extract **Q**uit

Using (↓),

Move to: L40

Your screen should look similar to Figure 8.10.

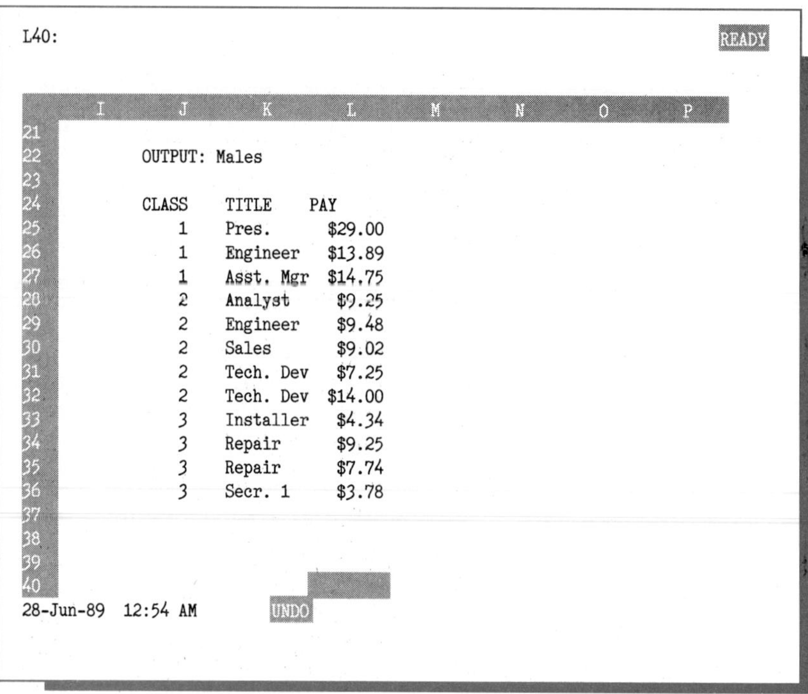

L40:
READY
I
J
K
L
M
N
O
P
OUTPUT: Males
CLASS TITLE PAY
1 Pres. $29.00
1 Engineer $13.89
1 Asst. Mgr $14.75
2 Analyst $9.25
2 Engineer $9.48
2 Sales $9.02
2 Tech. Dev $7.25
2 Tech. Dev $14.00
3 Installer $4.34
3 Repair $9.25
3 Repair $7.74
3 Secr. 1 $3.78
28-Jun-89 12:54 AM
UNDO

Figure 8.10

Look at the contents of cells J25 through L36. The selected field data, CLASS, TITLE, and PAY, for all records meeting the criteria have been copied into these cells.

Next, you need to extract the same fields of information from the database for females.

To extract this information, enter the descriptive label ''OUTPUT: Females'' in cell N22. Then copy the field names from cells J24 through L24 to cells N24 through P24.

Issue the following command sequence:

/ **D**ata **Q**uery **C**riteria **N3..N4** ↵

To specify the new output range, select:

Output **N24..P24** ↵

To copy the selected data into the output range and return to READY mode, issue the following command sequence:

Extract **Q**uit

Your screen should now look similar to Figure 8.11.

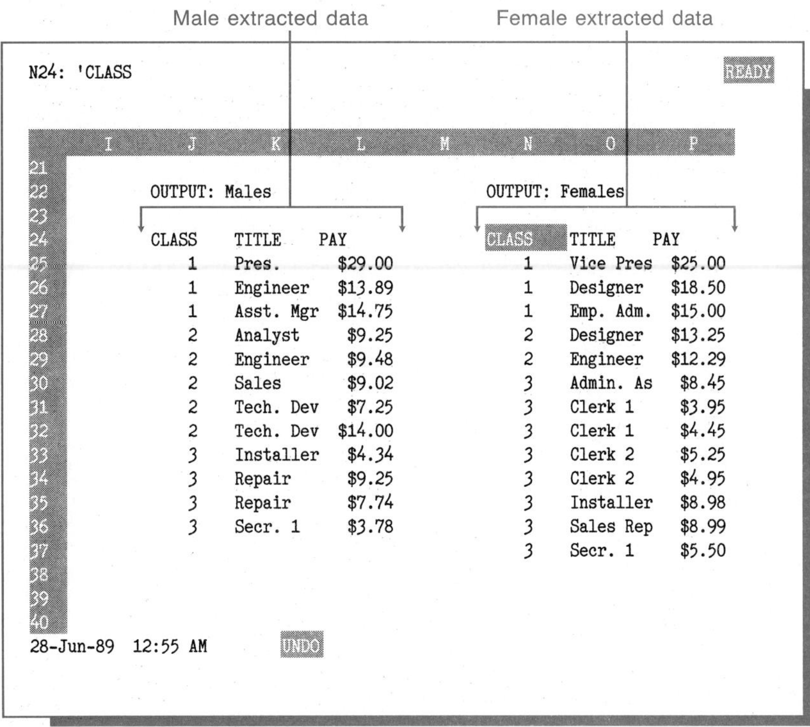

Male extracted data
Female extracted data
N24: 'CLASS
READY
I J K L M N O P
21
22 OUTPUT: Males OUTPUT: Females
23
24 CLASS TITLE PAY CLASS TITLE PAY
25 1 Pres. $29.00 1 Vice Pres $25.00
26 1 Engineer $13.89 1 Designer $18.50
27 1 Asst. Mgr $14.75 1 Emp. Adm. $15.00
28 2 Analyst $9.25 2 Designer $13.25
29 2 Engineer $9.48 2 Engineer $12.29
30 2 Sales $9.02 3 Admin. As $8.45
31 2 Tech. Dev $7.25 3 Clerk 1 $3.95
32 2 Tech. Dev $14.00 3 Clerk 1 $4.45
33 3 Installer $4.34 3 Clerk 2 $5.25
34 3 Repair $9.25 3 Clerk 2 $4.95
35 3 Repair $7.74 3 Installer $8.98
36 3 Secr. 1 $3.78 3 Sales Rep $8.99
37 3 Secr. 1 $5.50
38
39
40
28-Jun-89 12:55 AM
UNDO

Figure 8.11

Lynne presents the pay-rate analysis to her supervisor, who feels that the data will be useful in employment planning. Next, Lynne is assigned a high-priority project relating to labor negotiations.

Using the Data Table Command

The employees in job class 3 are negotiating a new contract and have proposed a 12-percent pay increase. Before responding to this proposal or offering a counter proposal, Lynne's supervisor wants to analyze various alternatives.

Lynne needs to find out what the average pay rate would be for employees in job class 3 if they received a 3-percent, 5-percent, 7-percent, 9-percent, or 12-percent pay increase. The Data Table command will quickly calculate the effect of changing the percent increase on the average pay rate.

First, Lynne needs to calculate the average rate of pay for employees in job class 3. To do this, she will use the @DAVG function once again.

To enter the criteria to specify employees in class 3,

Move to: K44

Copy the field name label CLASS from cell J24 to cell K44.

Move to: K45
Type: **'3**
Press: ↵

Note The entry in cell K45 must be entered as a label because all the CLASS entries in the database are labels.

To document this area of the worksheet, enter the following descriptive label in cell J42:

Move to: J42
Type: **CRITERIA: Class 3**
Press: ↵

Next, to calculate the average rate of pay for all employees in class 3,

Move to: O44
Type: **@DAVG(A5..H30,5,K44..K45)**
Press: ↵

To identify the contents of this area of the worksheet,

Move to: N42
Type: **STATISTIC: Avg. Pay Class 3**
Press: ↵

Your screen should now look similar to Figure 8.12.

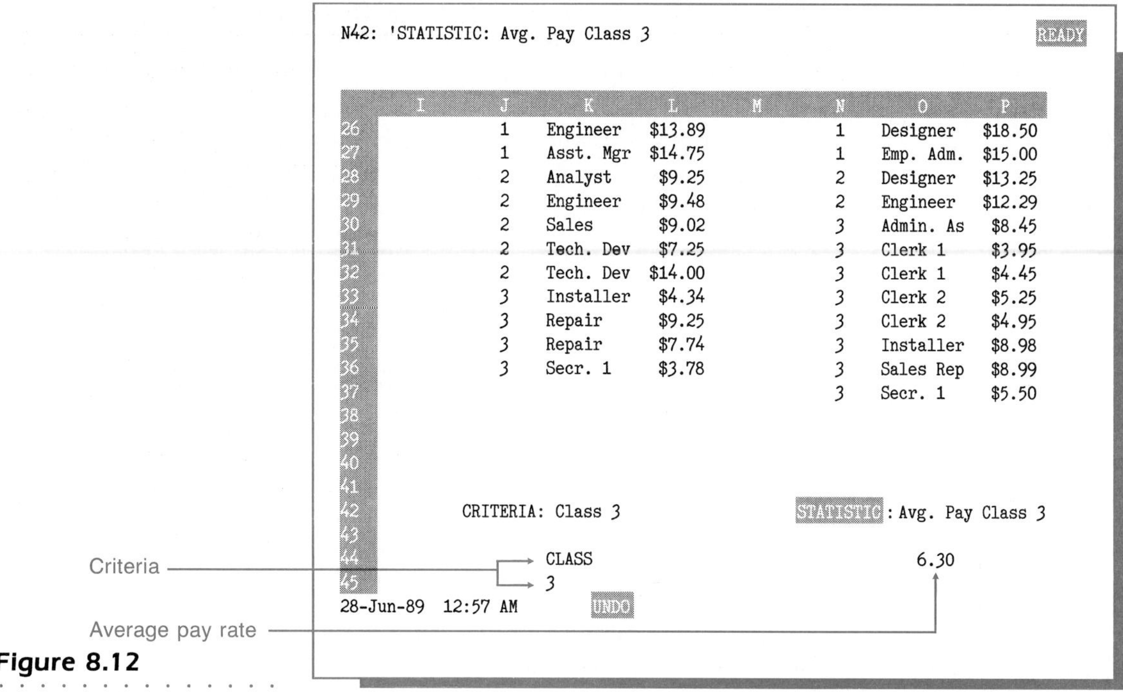

N42: 'STATISTIC: Avg. Pay Class 3
READY
I J K L M N O P
26 1 Engineer $13.89 1 Designer $18.50
27 1 Asst. Mgr $14.75 1 Emp. Adm. $15.00
28 2 Analyst $9.25 2 Designer $13.25
29 2 Engineer $9.48 2 Engineer $12.29
30 2 Sales $9.02 3 Admin. As $8.45
31 2 Tech. Dev $7.25 3 Clerk 1 $3.95
32 2 Tech. Dev $14.00 3 Clerk 1 $4.45
33 3 Installer $4.34 3 Clerk 2 $5.25
34 3 Repair $9.25 3 Clerk 2 $4.95
35 3 Repair $7.74 3 Installer $8.98
36 3 Secr. 1 $3.78 3 Sales Rep $8.99
37 3 Secr. 1 $5.50
38
39
40
41
42 CRITERIA: Class 3 STATISTIC: Avg. Pay Class 3
43
44 CLASS 6.30
45 3
28-Jun-89 12:57 AM UNDO
Criteria
Average pay rate

Figure 8.12

The average rate of pay for employees in class 3 is $6.30.

Lynne now wants to evaluate the effect of the proposed 12-percent wage increase, as well as increases of 3, 5, 7, and 9 percent on the average rate of pay for employees in class 3.

The formula to calculate the new average pay rate based on the current average pay rate and the percent pay increase is:

$$\textit{New average pay rate} = \textit{Current average pay rate} \times (1 + \textit{Percent pay increase})$$

For example, to calculate the effect of a 3-percent pay increase,

$$\textit{New average pay rate} = \$6.30 \times (1 + .03) = \$6.48$$

Lynne can use this equation several times, each time substituting a different percent increase. A faster way, however, is to use 1-2-3's Data Table command. This command is an excellent tool for evaluating what-if situations. Because you want to test the effect of changing one variable, you will use Data Table 1.

Data Table 1 shows the different values generated by a formula each time a single variable is changed in the formula. The data table can be located in any open area of the worksheet. The data table consists of the input values, the formula, and the results of the calculations. The left column of the data table contains the **input values**. These are the values 1-2-3 will substitute for a variable when it performs the calculation. In this case, the input values are the different percent increases. The upper left cell of the table must be blank. The formula(s) being evaluated must be entered into the first cell of the remaining columns.

The data table will occupy cells L52 through M57. First, to document this area,

Move to: J50
Type: **DATA TABLE:**
Move to: K54
Type: **% Inc.**
Press: ↵

To enter the input values of 3, 5, 7, 9, and 12 percent into the first column of the table,

Move to: L52
Type: **3%**
Move to: L53
Type: **5%**
Move to: L54
Type: **7%**
Move to: L55
Type: **9%**
Move to: L56
Type: **12%**
Press: ↓

Your screen should look similar to Figure 8.13.

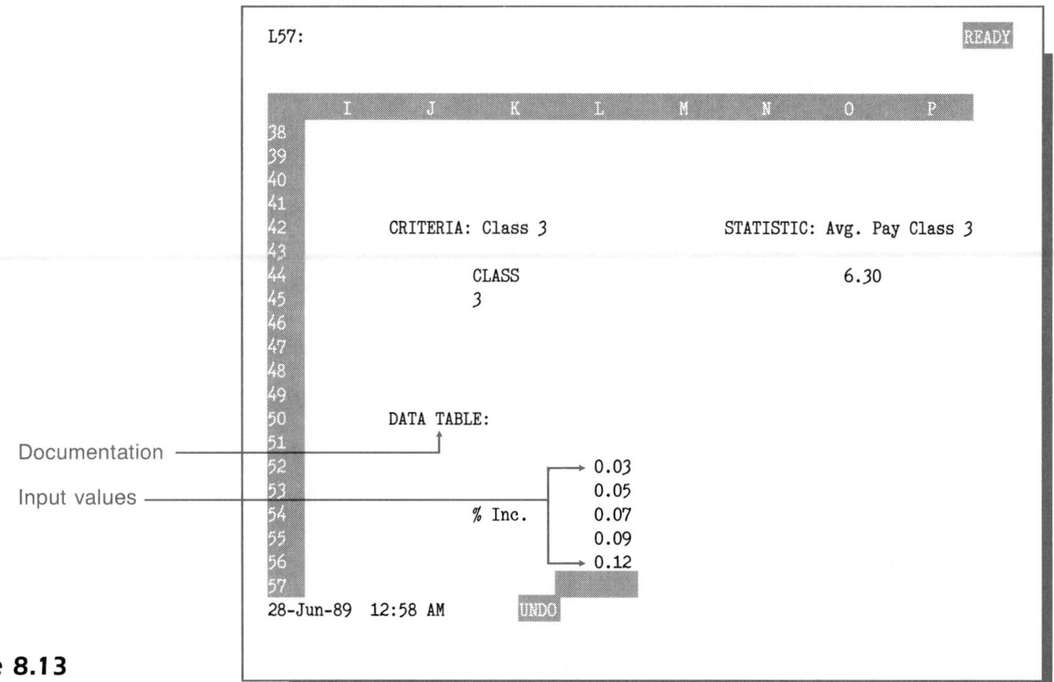

Figure 8.13

The entries in cells L52 through L56 appear in the worksheet as decimals rather than percentages.

The next step is to specify an **input cell**. 1-2-3 uses an input cell, which can be any empty cell in the worksheet, as a temporary storage area for the different values of the variable being tested.

You will use cell O48 as the input cell. To document the location of this cell,

Move to: N46
Type: **INPUT CELL: % Pay**
Press: ↵

Your screen should now look similar to Figure 8.14.

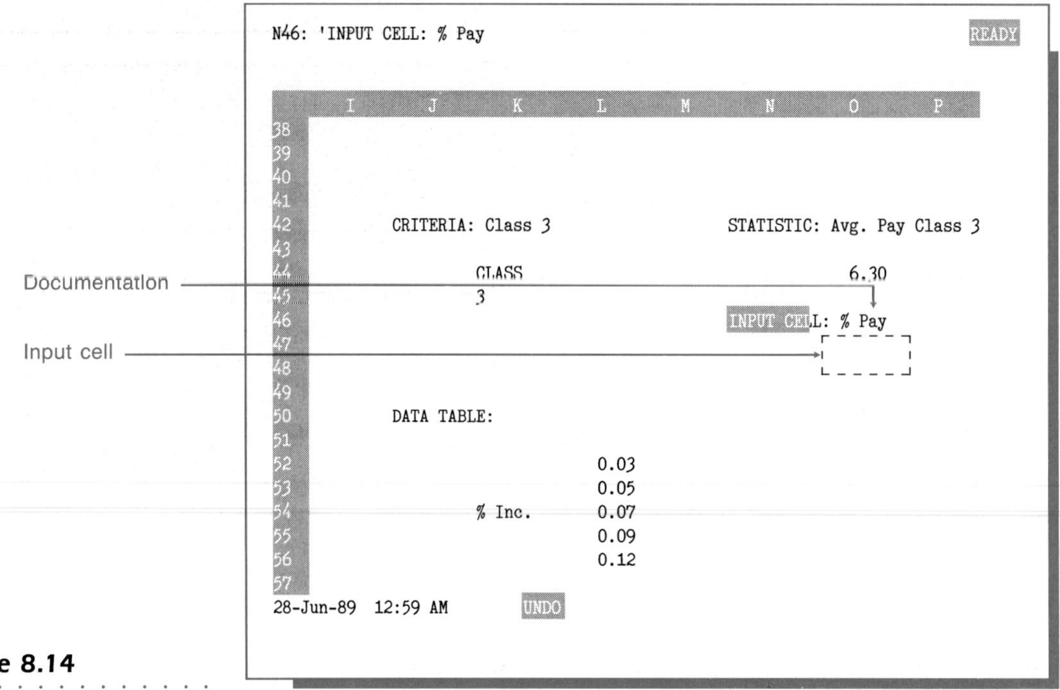

Figure 8.14

Next, you need to enter the formula to calculate the new pay rates based on a specific percent pay increase into the first cell of the second column of the data table (cell M51). The formula multiplies the current average pay rate (cell O44) by the sum of 1 plus the percent pay increase in the input cell (cell O48).

Move to: M51
Type: **+O44*(1+O48)**
Press: ↵

Your screen should look similar to Figure 8.15.

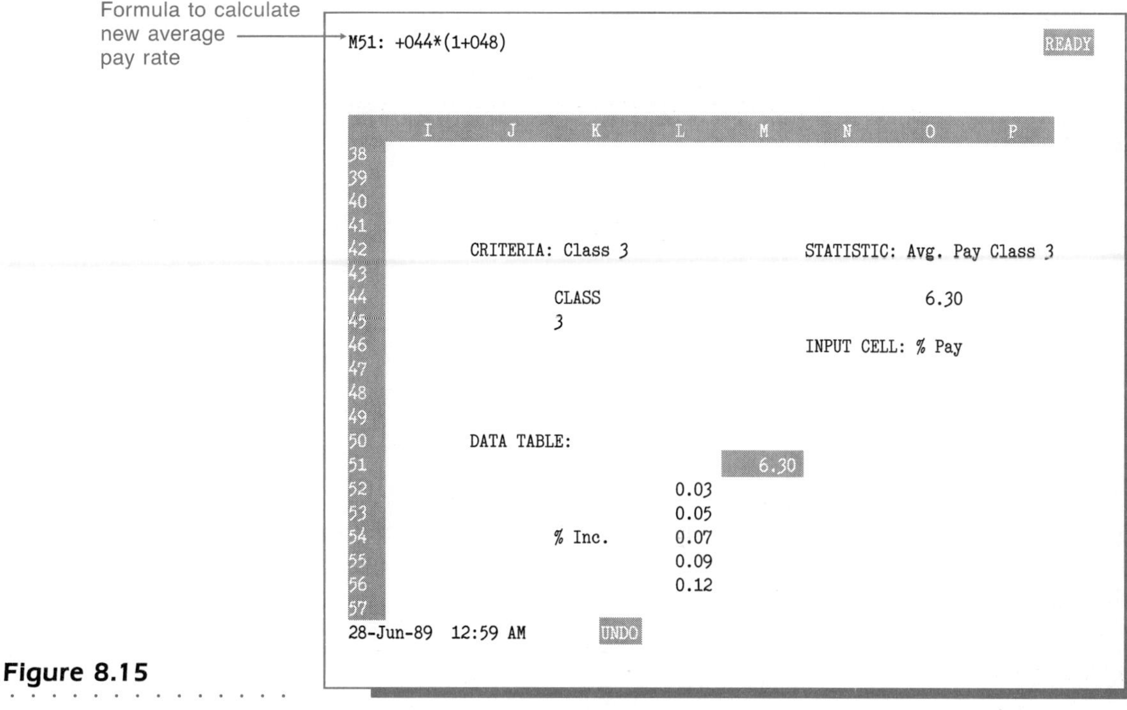

Figure 8.15

The value in M51 is the same as the current average pay rate in cell O44. This is because the current percent value in the input cell, O48, is 0 until you execute the Data Table command. Then each variable percent increase will be taken from the table, placed in O48, and used to calculate a new average pay rate to be displayed in the table.

Now you are ready to issue the command for Data Table 1:

/ **D**ata **T**able **1**

The first prompt asks you to specify the table range, which must include the percent values as well as the formula. Enter the table range as follows:

L51..M56 ↵

Next, specify the input cell location:

O48 ↵

After a few moments the table will be computed, and your screen should look similar to Figure 8.16.

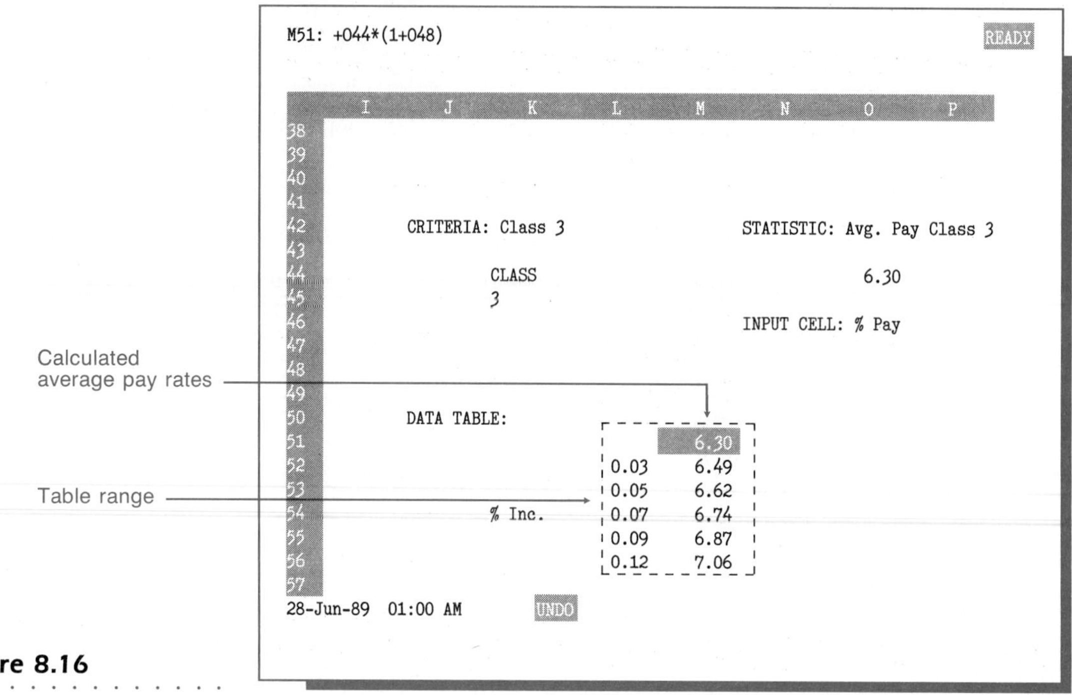

Figure 8.16

The data table displays the new average pay rate for employees in class 3 based on each variable's percent increase. For example, the union's proposed 12-percent wage increase would increase the average pay to $7.06 an hour.

Now, to improve the appearance of the table, set the format of the input values (L52..L56) to display as percentages with no decimal places.

Your screen should look similar to Figure 8.17.

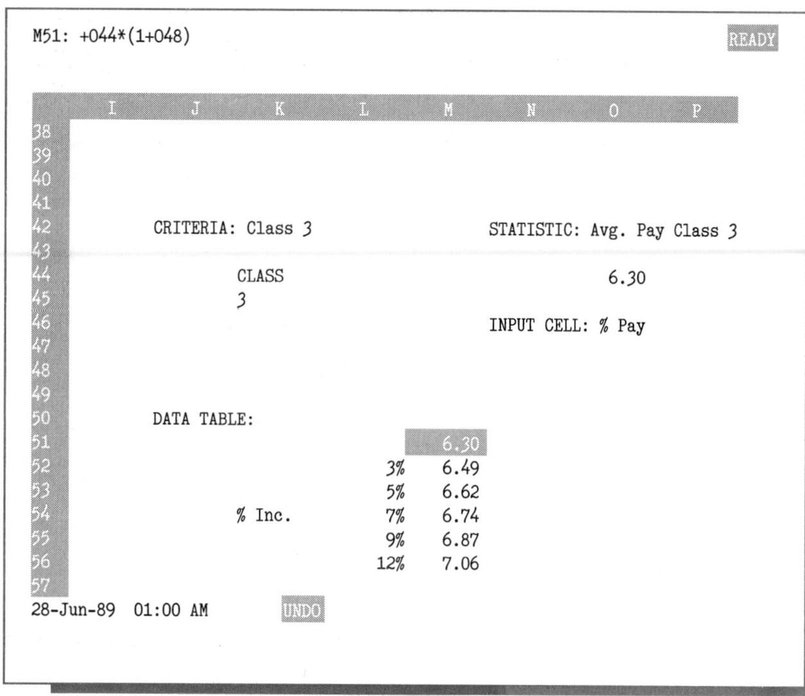

Figure 8.17

The data table clearly shows the effect of the variable percent on the average rate of pay. This information should help management in the negotiations.

Print a copy of the worksheet from cells A1 through P60.

Save the worksheet using the filename ANALYSIS.

When you are finished, exit 1-2-3.

Glossary of Key Terms

Bin range The range of values used in the Data Distribution command to determine the intervals for the count.

Data Table 1 A table that shows the different values generated by a formula each time a single variable is changed in the formula.

Frequency distribution table A table that tells you how many values in a specified range fall within defined numeric intervals.

Extract — Finds the records in a database that meet specified criteria and copies the specified fields of each located record to the output range.

Input cell — A cell used during the Data Table command that acts as a temporary storage area for the different values of the variable being tested.

Input value — The values substituted for a variable in a formula during calculation of a data table.

Offset number — A number assigned to the column in the input range required by the database @function field argument.

Output range — The area specified in the worksheet where the records meeting the criteria are copied during the Data Extract command.

Practice Problems

1. Matching

1. /RFP	______	**a.** the database @function field argument
2. Input cell	______	**b.** cell used for data table calculations
3. Count value	______	**c.** area of the worksheet to which extracted data are copied
4. /DQE	______	**d.** a database @function
5. Output range	______	**e.** series of values into which data are counted
6. Offset number	______	**f.** generates a data table
7. @DCOUNT	______	**g.** a command used to copy records meeting criteria to a separate area of the worksheet
8. Bin	______	**h.** value generated by the Data Distribution command
9. /DT1	______	**i.** generates a count of values falling within defined bin ranges
10. /DD	______	**j.** formats a range of cells to display as percents

2. Retrieve the file RECORDS.

   a. Extract the following fields: LAST, YEARS, and PAY for all employees whose YEARS equal 5 or whose PAY equals 9.25. Document your worksheet space.

   b. Calculate the number, average, minimum, and maximum YEARS for all employees in CLASS 2. Document your worksheet.

   c. Create a frequency distribution for all employees for YEARS, using the following bin ranges: 0–5, 6–10, 11–15, and 16–20. Document your worksheet.

   d. Put your name in cell A1 and the date in cell A2. Print the worksheet.

   e. Save this worksheet as RECORDS2.

3. Retrieve the file RECORDS.

   a. Use Data Table 1 to demonstrate the effects of pay increases of 2, 4, 6, 8, and 10 percent on the average pay for employees in CLASS 2. Document your worksheet.

   b. Put your name in cell A1 and the date in cell A2. Print the worksheet including the data table.

   c. Save the worksheet as RECORDS3.

9

Creating and Using Macros

Objectives

In Lab 9, you will learn how to:

- Create, edit, run, and debug macros
- Create interactive macros
- Use a repetition factor
- Use LEARN mode
- Use STEP mode

Case Study

Susan C. Smith is the sales manager for Entertainment Now, Inc., a retail store specializing in computer software programs, movie videos, and records. The district sales representative has just instructed Susan to give her salespeople a 10-percent commission this month on sales of specific products.

You will follow Susan as she creates a weekly sales report form. This report will specify the product name, price, number sold, total sales, and commission for each salesperson. Susan will use some basic macro commands to create the report and several other macro commands to help the salespeople enter the data.

Introducing Macros

A **macro** is a set of instructions for automating a 1-2-3 task, consisting of a sequence of keystrokes and commands that you type into a worksheet as cell entries. The commands are performed whenever you invoke (run) the macro.

You can use a macro to issue commands or to enter data into the worksheet. More complex macros can accept user entries from the keyboard, perform conditional tests, or display user-defined menus. Macros are particularly useful in automating frequently used 1-2-3 commands, performing repetitive procedures, and developing customized worksheets.

The simplest type of macro represents keys on the keyboard. The macro commands consist of **keystroke instructions**, which can be a single character key or key names enclosed in braces ({key name}). The single character keystroke instructions represent typewriter keys on the keyboard and are identical to the keys they represent. The only exception to this is the (↵) key. The single character key that represents (↵) is the ~ (tilde). Many of the keystroke instructions that consist of a key name enclosed in braces are shown in Table 9.1.

Table 9.1

Macro Key	Description
{U} or {UP}	Move pointer up (↑)
{D} or {DOWN}	Move pointer down (↓)
{R} or {RIGHT}	Move pointer right (→)
{L} or {LEFT}	Move pointer left (←)
{HOME}	Move pointer to cell A1 (HOME)
{END}	End key (END)

Table 9.1 Continued

Macro Key	Description
{PGUP}	Page Up key (PGUP)
{PGDN}	Page Down key (PGDN)
{BIGLEFT}	Move pointer one page left (CTRL-←)
{BIGRIGHT}	Move pointer one page right (CTRL-→)
{BACKSPACE} or {BS}	Backspace key (BACKSPACE)
{DELETE} or {DEL}	Delete key (DEL)
{ESCAPE} or {ESC}	Escape key (ESC)
{HELP}	F1
{EDIT}	F2
{NAME}	F3
{ABS}	F4
{GOTO}	F5
{WINDOW}	F6
{QUERY}	F7
{TABLE}	F8
{CALC}	F9
{GRAPH}	F10
{?}	Wait for keyboard entry (pause)
~ (tilde)	↵
{APP1}	ALT-F7
{APP2}	ALT-F8
{APP3}	ALT-F9
{APP4}	ALT-F10
/, <, or {MENU}	/ (slash) or < (less-than symbol)
{{}	{ (open brace)
{}}	} (close brace)

Susan Smith wants to create a weekly sales report form so her salespeople can record their sales and commissions on nine specific products.

Susan has decided to create this report in 1-2-3. To view the report she has started, load 1-2-3 and retrieve the file REPORT1.WK1.

Your screen should look similar to Figure 9.1.

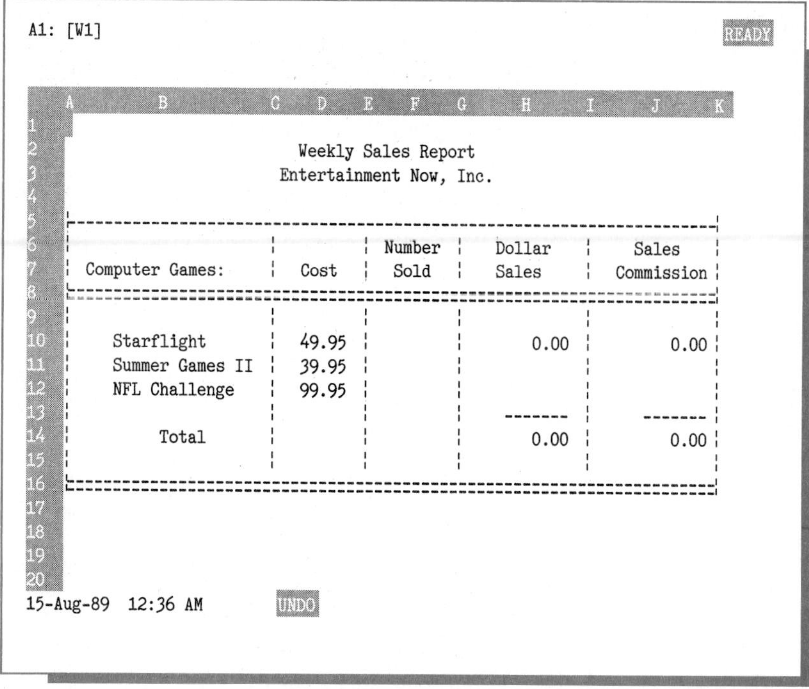

A1: [W1]
READY
Weekly Sales Report
Entertainment Now, Inc.
Computer Games:
Cost
Number Sold
Dollar Sales
Sales Commission
Starflight
Summer Games II
NFL Challenge
49.95
39.95
99.95
0.00
0.00
Total
0.00
0.00
15-Aug-89 12:36 AM
UNDO

Figure 9.1

The completed sales report will have three sections. Susan has created only the first section of the sales report, Computer Games. The cost of each item is listed next to the appropriate game name. The salespeople will enter their weekly sales in the Number Sold column.

The Dollar Sales column will be computed by taking the value in the Number Sold column and multiplying it by the figures in the Cost column. The Sales Commission column will be computed by multiplying the value in the Dollar Sales column by 10 percent, the sales commission rate.

Susan has entered the formulas to calculate the Dollar Sales and Sales Commission for Starflight. She has also entered the @functions to calculate the Total Dollar Sales and Total Sales Commission.

To see the formula used to calculate Dollar Sales for Starflight, use the pointer-movement keys.

Move to: H10

The first line in the control panel now displays the formula used to calculate Dollar Sales for Starflight.

Creating Macros

To complete this part of the report, you need to copy the formulas into the appropriate cells. The formula in cell H10 for the Dollar Sales must be copied into cells H11 and H12. Likewise, the formula in cell J10 for the Sales Commission needs to be copied into cells J11 and J12.

You will create a macro to perform this operation by following three basic steps: planning, entering, and naming the macro.

Step 1 Plan the macro. You must determine the exact steps necessary to copy a formula from one cell into two cells just below it.

With the cell pointer in H10, the command sequence that would copy the formula from cell H10 into the two cells below it would be / Copy [↵] H11..H12 [↵]

Alternatively, an equivalent command sequence using pointing would be / Copy [↵] [↓] . [↓] [↵]

By using only the first letter of the command and the macro keys shown in Table 9.1, this same command sequence using pointing expressed as a macro is /C~{D}.{D}~

The ~ is equivalent to [↵], {D} is equivalent to [↓], and a single period (.) anchors the range to copy to.

Step 2 Enter the macro. A macro is entered as a label. If the macro begins with a /, \, (, or one of the numeric symbols, you must begin the macro with a label-prefix character. In the macro you will enter, the first character you will type is a /. If you do not begin the macro with a label-prefix character, the 1-2-3 main menu will be displayed and you will be unable to enter the macro as a label in the cell.

The macro can be entered in either uppercase or lowercase characters. Be careful not to enter blank spaces in the macro instructions.

A macro is entered in any blank area of the worksheet. It can be entered in a single cell or a continuous range of vertical cells. You will enter this macro in a single cell.

To enter the macro instructions to copy the contents from one cell into the two cells immediately below it,

Move to: D18
Type: **'/C~{D}.{D}~**
Press: [↵]

Your screen should look similar to Figure 9.2.

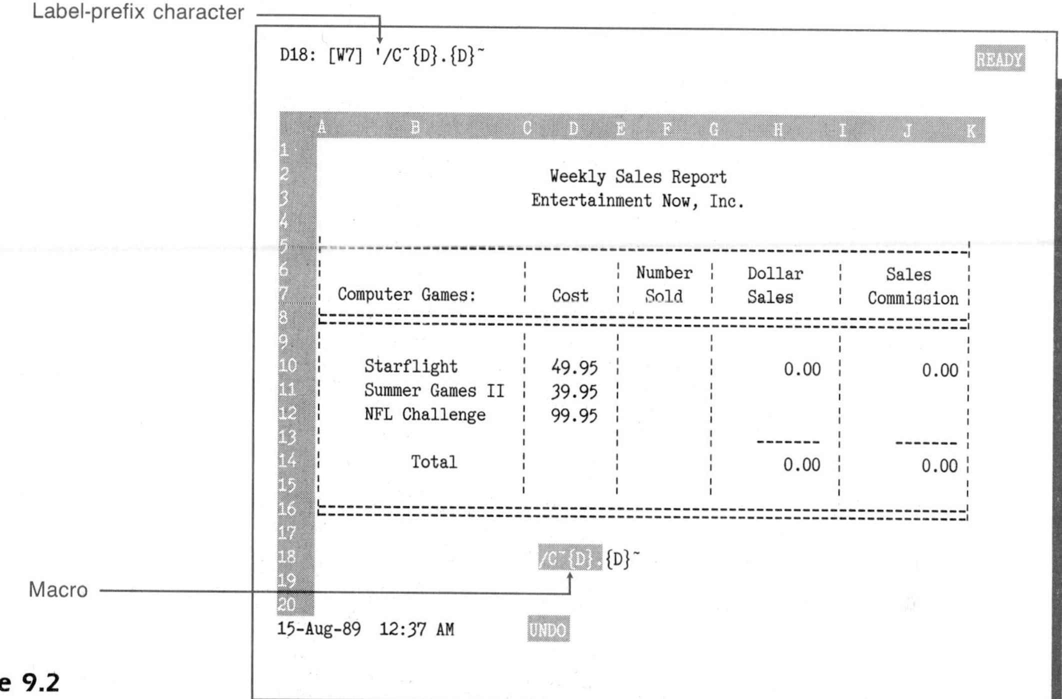

Figure 9.2

The commands written in cell D18 duplicate the keystrokes that you would use to copy the formula from cell H10 to cells H11 and H12 using pointing.

Be sure you have entered the macro into cell D18 exactly as it appears in Figure 9.2. If yours is not the same, correct the entry by editing the cell.

Step 3 Name the macro. To define cell D18 as a macro, it must be named. To do this, use the Range Name command. Select:

/ **R**ange **N**ame **C**reate

The prompt to enter a name is displayed in the control panel. There are two ways to name a macro. The first method consists of a backslash (\) followed by a single letter A to Z. The second method follows the same rules for naming a range. That is, it can consist of any combination of up to fifteen characters.

We will use the first method to name this macro. When assigning a macro a single-letter name, it is a good idea to use a letter that is descriptive of the action of the macro. For example, because this macro copies a formula down a worksheet, you will name the macro \D for Down.

In response to the prompt,

Type: \D
Press: ↵

To accept cell D18 as the range,

Press: ↵

Executing Macros

After a macro has been created, it should be run and tested. To run or execute a macro whose name consists of a \ and a single letter, hold down the ALT key and press the letter of the name of the macro (in this case, D).

First, position the cell pointer in the cell that contains the formula to be copied.

Move to: H10

Then, to run the macro,

Press: ALT-**D**

Your screen should look similar to Figure 9.3.

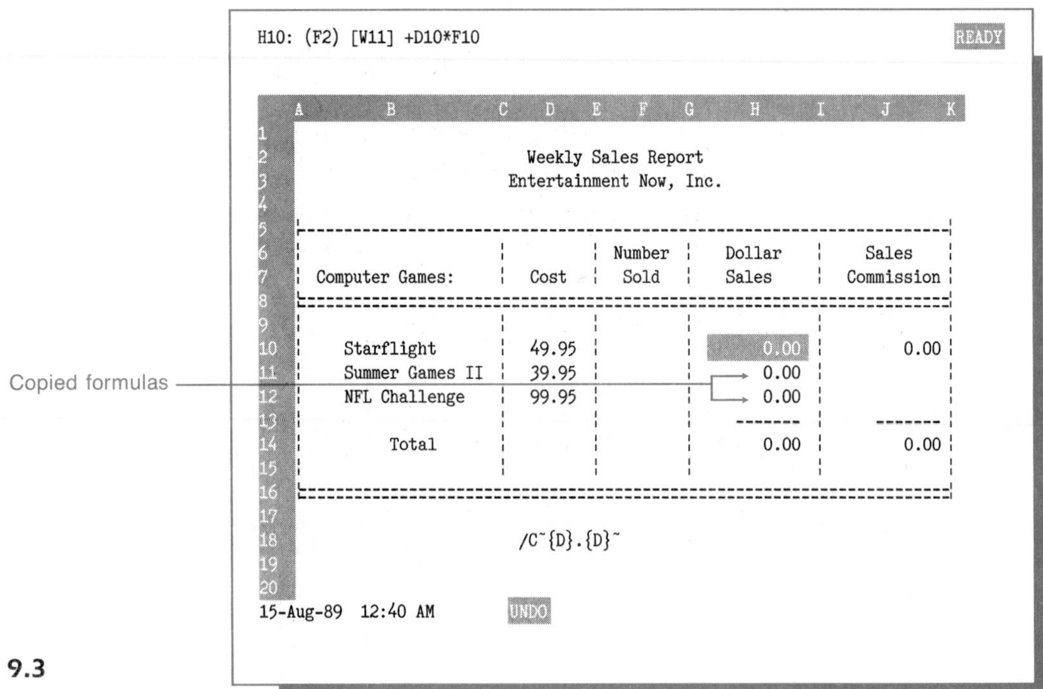

Figure 9.3

The macro you just executed should have copied the formula from cell H10 to cells H11 and H12, and the value 0.00 should be displayed in cells H11 and H12. If this did not happen, your macro probably contains an error. The next exercise will help you to **debug** or locate and correct errors in a macro.

Debugging Macros

Common errors to look for when you are debugging a macro are misspelled words, misplaced spaces and tildes, and missing commands.

To demonstrate, you will enter the same macro instructions in cell D20 with an intentional error. To do this,

Move to: D20
Type: **'/C~{DN}.{D}~**
Press: ↵

Note that the first key name, {D}, has been incorrectly entered as {DN}.

Name this macro \W (for wrong) using the following command sequence:

/ **R**ange **N**ame **C**reate \ **W** ↵ **D20** ↵

To test the macro, position the cell pointer and run this macro as follows:

Move to: J10
Press: ALT-**W**

Your screen should now look similar to Figure 9.4.

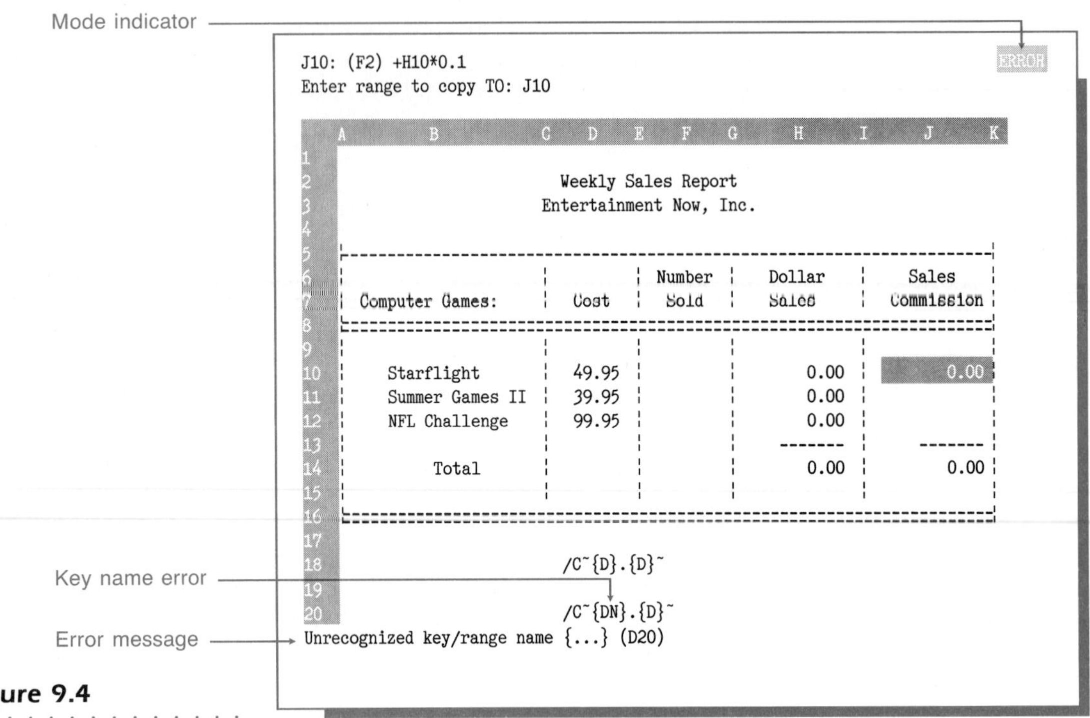

Figure 9.4

The mode indicator flashes ERROR, and the error message "Unrecognized key/range name {. . .} (D20)" is displayed on the bottom line of the screen. The message tells you the type and the location of the error.

To clear the error message and return to READY mode,

Press: ESC

You edit and correct macros just like any other cell entry. They can be edited in EDIT mode or READY mode.

Correct the entry in cell D20 by changing {DN} to {D}.

Because 1-2-3 records the range where the keystrokes are stored, not the actual keystrokes, it is not necessary to rename the macro.

Next, to position the cell pointer and invoke the \W macro again,

Move to: J10
Press: ALT-**W**

The formula in cell J10 should now be copied into cells J11 and J12, and the value 0.00 should be displayed in cells J11 and J12.

If your macro in cell D20 did not execute properly, go back and correct the macro, then execute the macro in cell J10 again.

Creating Interactive Macros

Next Susan wants to create a macro to help the salespeople insert data into the worksheet. During execution, this macro will temporarily pause to allow the user to enter data directly from the keyboard into the worksheet. This is called an **interactive macro**.

To create an interactive macro, the {?} (pause) macro keystroke instruction is used to stop macro execution temporarily to allow user entry. Execution continues when the user presses ↵.

Without a macro, the salespeople would begin by moving the cell pointer to cell F10. They would then enter the number of Starflight games sold, press ↓ once, enter the number of Summer Games II sold, press ↓ once, enter the number of NFL Challenge games sold, and press ↵.

You will enter the macro to perform this operation, beginning in cell H18 and continuing down the column.

Move to: H18

The first macro command will move the cell pointer to cell F10 using the GOTO feature. The macro key name for this feature is {GOTO}.

Type: **{GOTO}F10~**
Move to: H19

The next macro instruction tells 1-2-3 to pause execution to allow the entry of data, move down one cell, and pause again. The macro key name to pause execution is {?}.

Type: **{?}{D}{?}**
Move to: H20

The instructions in cell H20 will move the cell pointer down one row and then wait for user entry. The data is entered into the cell by the ~ (enter) macro instruction. Complete the macro instructions as follows:

Type: **{D}{?}~**
Press: ↵

Your screen should look similar to Figure 9.5.

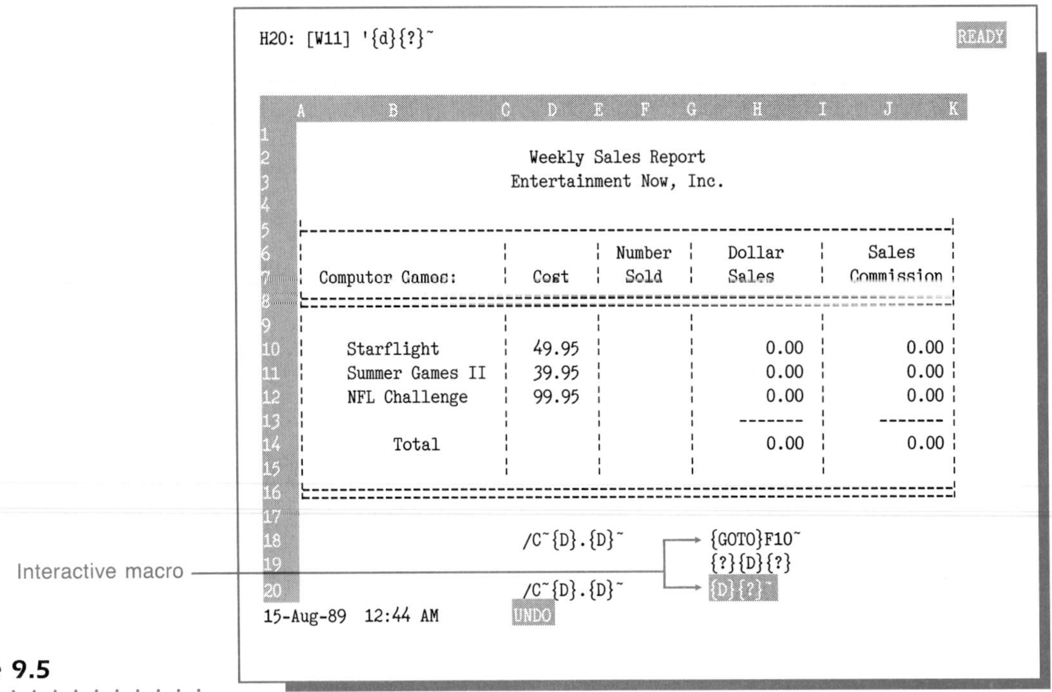

Figure 9.5

The macro instructions begin in cell H18 and continue through cell H20. When the macro is executed, 1-2-3 will read and perform the instructions in cell H18 from left to right. It will continue execution by performing the instructions in the next cell in the same column. Whenever it reads the {?} key name, it will pause execution to allow the user to enter data. To continue macro execution after a pause, you must press ↵. The macro will stop running when it encounters a blank cell, a numeric cell, or a Quit command.

Now you are ready to name the macro. The second method of naming a macro lets you assign a name up to fifteen characters long. Again, the name should be descriptive of the function of the macro. You will name the macro ENTRY. To do this, issue the following command sequence:

/ **R**ange **N**ame **C**reate **ENTRY** ↵

If the macro is longer than a single cell, it is necessary to specify only the cell beginning the macro as the range. To complete the command sequence,

Type: **H18**
Press: ↵

Now you are ready to run the macro. To run a macro that has been named using the second method, you must use the Run key (ALT-F3). You can use the Run key to run any macros, including those named with the backslash character.

Press: ALT-F3

The prompt "Select the macro to run:" is displayed in the second line of the control panel and the names of the macros are listed in the third line. The mode indicator displays NAMES. If there are other named ranges in the worksheet, they will be displayed along with the macro names. For this reason, you may want to begin all macro names in a worksheet with the same character, such as a backslash, to distinguish the macro names from the range names.

Since the highlight bar is already over the macro name we want to use (ENTRY), to select it:

Press: ↵

The cell pointer is positioned in cell F10. The status indicator, CMD, at the bottom of the screen indicates that the macro is executing. Macro execution is interrupted to accept the number of Starflight games sold. As soon as an entry is made and ↵ is pressed, the macro will continue execution. To enter 9 as the number of games sold,

Type: **9**
Press: ↵

The cell pointer has now moved down one cell to cell F11. The number 9 was entered in cell F10. The macro pauses again to accept the number of Summer Games II sold.

Type: **12**
Press: ↵

Again, the number 12 was entered in cell F11, the cell pointer moved down one cell, and the macro paused to accept the number of NFL Challenge games sold.

Type: **17**
Press: ↵

Your screen should look similar to Figure 9.6.

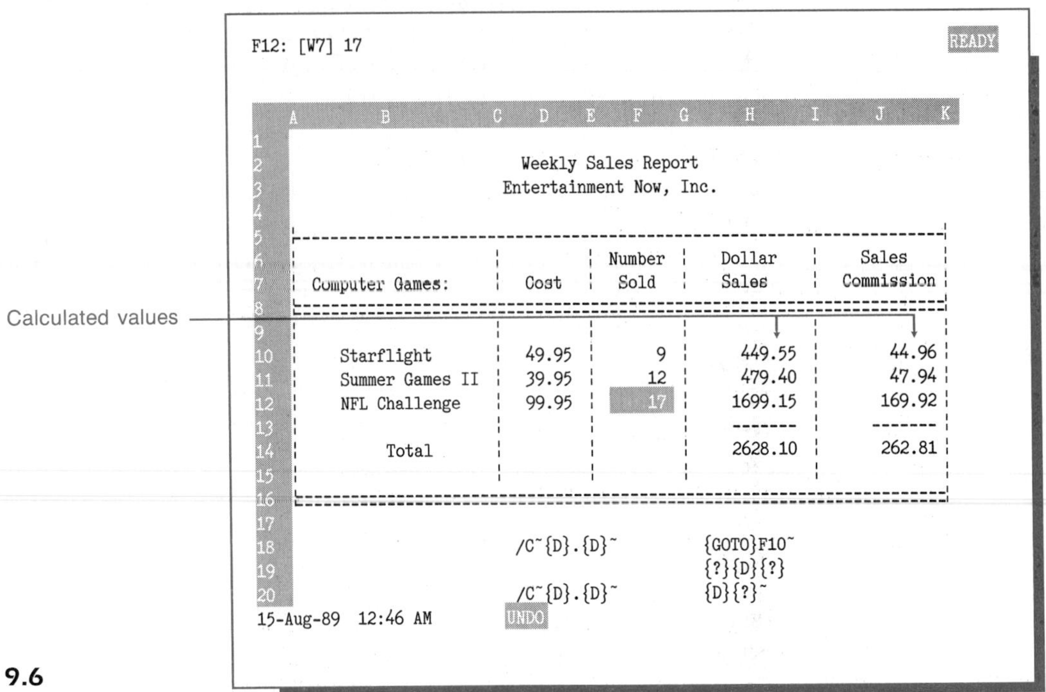

F12: [W7] 17
READY
Weekly Sales Report
Entertainment Now, Inc.
Computer Games:
Cost
Number Sold
Dollar Sales
Sales Commission
Calculated values
Starflight 49.95 9 449.55 44.96
Summer Games II 39.95 12 479.40 47.94
NFL Challenge 99.95 17 1699.15 169.92
Total 2628.10 262.81
/C~{D}.{D}~
{GOTO}F10~
{?}{D}{?}
/C~{D}.{D}~
{D}{?}~
15-Aug-89 12:46 AM
UNDO

Figure 9.6

The worksheet automatically calculated the Dollar Sales, Sales Commission, and Total Sales as the values were entered into the worksheet.

In summary, to develop a macro, follow these steps:

1. Plan the macro. Whenever you create a macro, you should actually perform and then write down the keystrokes that the macro will perform.
2. Enter the macro. The macro instructions are entered as a label in a single cell or in a series of continuous cells in a single column. You should enter the macro in a convenient and open area of the worksheet. The macro should not contain any blank spaces.
3. Name the macro. The Range Name Create command assigns a macro a name. A macro name can consist of a \ (backslash) followed by a single letter or any combination of up to fifteen characters.

4. Run the macro. If the macro name consists of a backslash and a single letter, you can use the ALT key followed by the letter name of the macro to run it. If the macro name consists of any other combination of up to fifteen characters, you must use the Run key (ALT-F3) to run the macro. The first time you execute a macro, it is a good idea to test it. Save your worksheet first so you don't lose any valuable data. Then, test the macro in an area of the worksheet that will not be affected if the macro performs incorrectly.

5. Edit the macro. Because a macro is interpreted exactly as it appears, any misspelled or misplaced commands will result in an error message. If an error message appears, use the ESC key to return to READY mode, then edit the macro. If during execution you notice that the macro is not performing its intended task, you can press CTRL-BREAK to stop macro execution, press ESC to return to READY mode, and correct the macro. Then repeat step 4.

Modifying Macros

Susan thought this macro would help the salespeople prepare their weekly reports. She modified and extended the worksheet to include the other two categories, movie videos and records. Retrieve the file REPORT2.WK1.

This file contains all the information from the previous worksheet plus two more product categories. To see the other two product categories, use ↓ to

Move to: A38

Your screen should look similar to Figure 9.7.

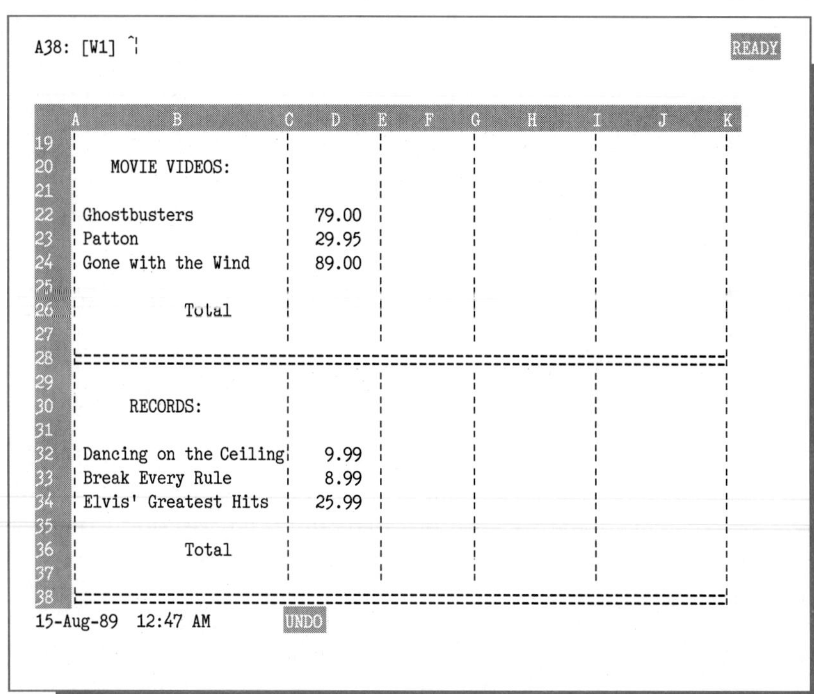

A38: [W1] ^|
READY
A B C D E F G H I J K
MOVIE VIDEOS:
Ghostbusters 79.00
Patton 29.95
Gone with the Wind 89.00
Total
RECORDS:
Dancing on the Ceiling 9.99
Break Every Rule 8.99
Elvis' Greatest Hits 25.99
Total
15-Aug-89 12:47 AM
UNDO

Figure 9.7

The prices for the movie videos and records are already entered in column D; however, columns H and J are empty.

Next, to see the macros,

Move to: A48

Your screen should look similar to Figure 9.8.

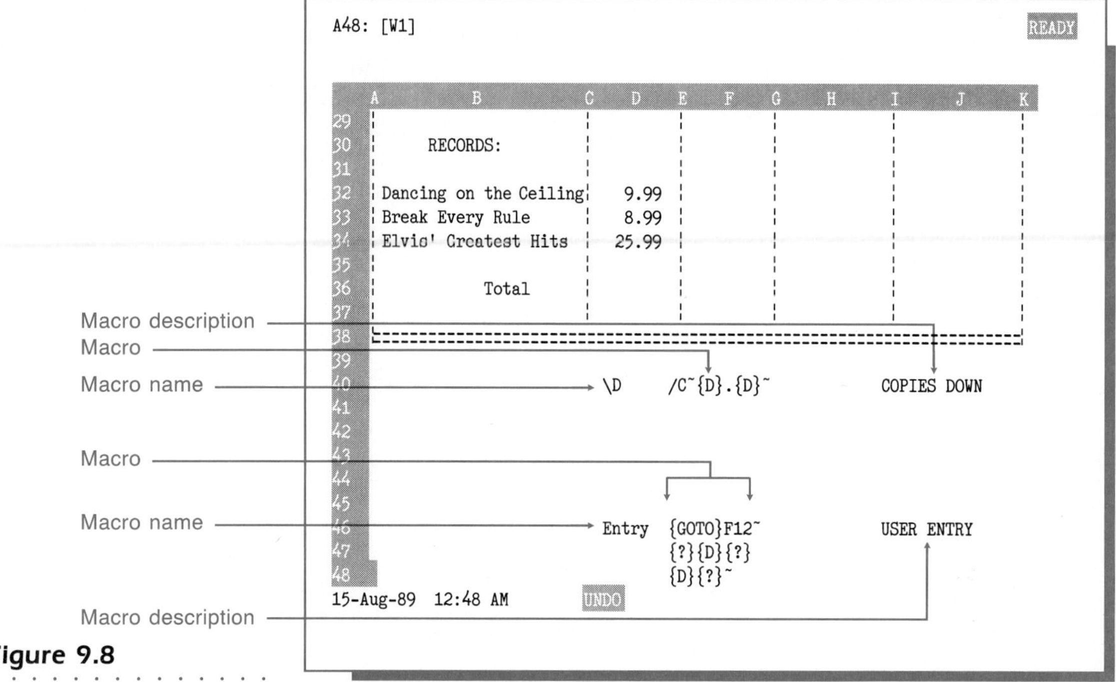

Figure 9.8

The two macros created earlier have been moved to the bottom of this new worksheet. Following good documentation procedures, Susan added some descriptive labels to document the worksheet.

She placed the name of the macros in the cells to the left of the macro commands and a brief description of the functions of the macros in the cells to the right.

Documenting macros is particularly important when several macros are used within one worksheet and when macros become more complex.

In the previous worksheet, the \D macro was used to copy the contents of one cell into two cells just below it. In this worksheet, all the formulas and labels have been inserted for the first product category, computer games, but not for the other two products.

You will modify the \D macro to copy the contents of a block of cells from one product category into another block of cells for the next product category.

Using a Repetition Factor

Specifically, the macro will copy from a range of five cells (H12 through H16), move down ten rows, and copy into another range of five cells (H22 through H26). To make it easier to enter consecutive uses of the same macro key name, 1-2-3 lets you enter a **repetition factor** within the key name. The repetition factor is a number that tells 1-2-3 how many times to repeat the key name. It is separated from the key name by a single space. For example, {D 4} is equivalent to {D}{D}{D}{D} or pressing ↓ four times. Using a repetition factor saves a lot of typing when you are entering macro instructions.

To enter this macro, edit the macro commands in cell E40 and continue the macro sequence in cell E41 as follows:

Move to: E40
Type: **'/C{D 4}~**
Move to: E41
Type: **{D 10}.{D 4}~**
Press: ↵

The \D macro has already been named. Your screen should look similar to Figure 9.9.

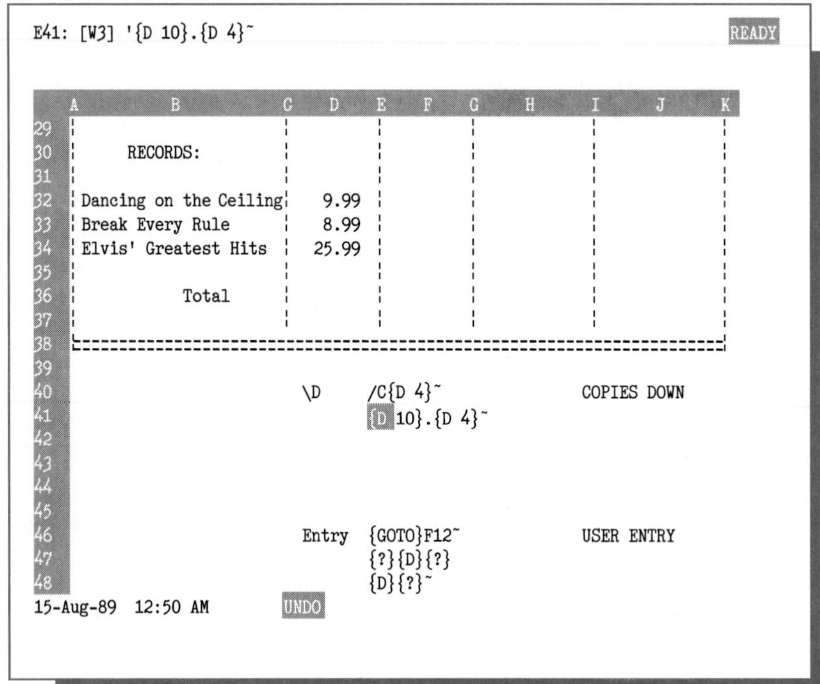

Figure 9.9

To test the macro, position the cell pointer at the beginning of the range to be copied and run the macro as follows.

Move to: H12
Press: ALT-**D**

The equations and dashed lines from cells H12 through H16 should have been copied correctly into cells H22 through H26. If they have not, correct your macro and try again.

Using LEARN Mode

To complete copying the formulas down the column, you could use the \D macro again by copying cells H22 through H26 into cells H32 through H36. However, Susan wants to use **LEARN mode** to modify the macro to copy the formulas down the entire column. LEARN mode is a 1-2-3 feature that records your keystrokes as a macro at the same time you are using the program to perform a task.

Before using this feature, you must define a range in the worksheet where the macro commands will be recorded. This is called the **learn range**. This range is a single column range that should be large enough to contain all the macro instructions. To continue the macro as part of the \D macro instructions, you will define the range as E42 through E44. To define the range, issue the following command sequence:

/ **W**orksheet **L**earn **R**ange **E42..E44** ↵

To have 1-2-3 record your keystrokes as a macro, you must turn on LEARN mode by pressing the Learn key (ALT-F5). First, be sure the cell pointer is in cell H12.

Press: ALT-F5

Your screen should look similar to Figure 9.10.

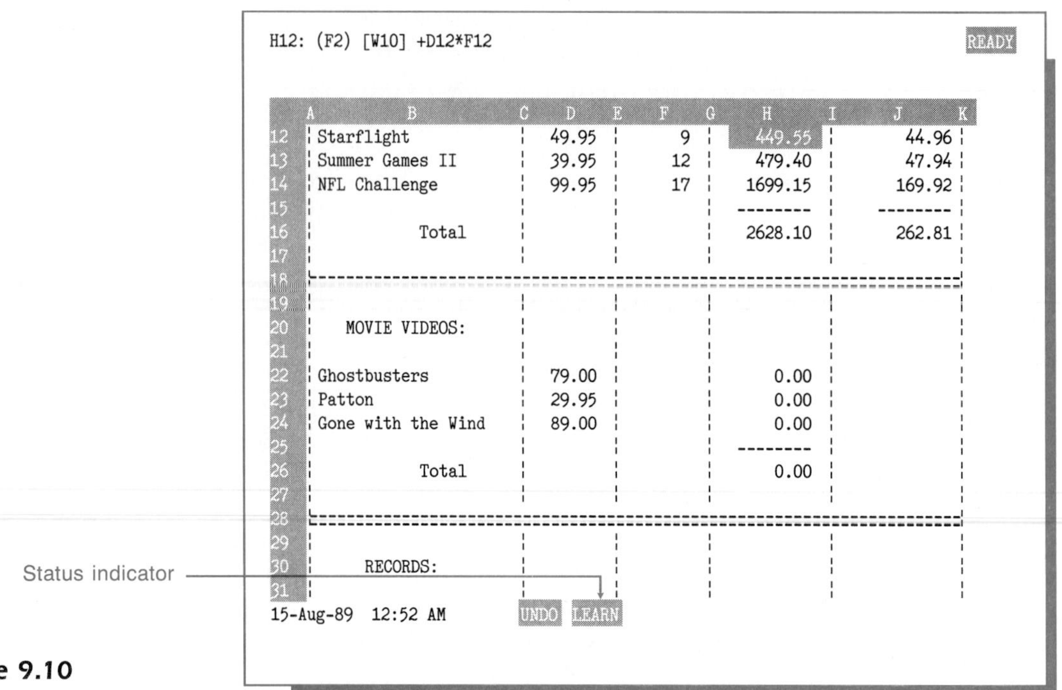

H12: (F2) [W10] +D12*F12
READY
A B C D E F G H I J K
12 Starflight 49.95 9 449.55 44.96
13 Summer Games II 39.95 12 479.40 47.94
14 NFL Challenge 99.95 17 1699.15 169.92
16 Total 2628.10 262.81
20 MOVIE VIDEOS:
22 Ghostbusters 79.00 0.00
23 Patton 29.95 0.00
24 Gone with the Wind 89.00 0.00
26 Total 0.00
30 RECORDS:
15-Aug-89 12:52 AM
UNDO LEARN
Status indicator

Figure 9.10

Notice the status indicator displays LEARN. Now anything you type or commands you enter will be recorded as a macro. To continue the macro to copy down the worksheet, select:

/ **C**opy

To define the range to copy from,

Press: ↓ four times
Press: ↵

To define the range to copy to,

Press: ↓ twenty times

(The cell pointer should be in cell H32.)

Press: . (period)
Press: ↓ four times
Press: ↵

The formulas have been copied down the column. The keystrokes to copy the formulas have also been recorded as a macro in the learn range. To turn off LEARN mode,

Press: ALT-F5

The LEARN indicator is no longer displayed. To see the macro instructions as they were recorded using LEARN mode,

Move to: H46

Your screen should look similar to Figure 9.11.

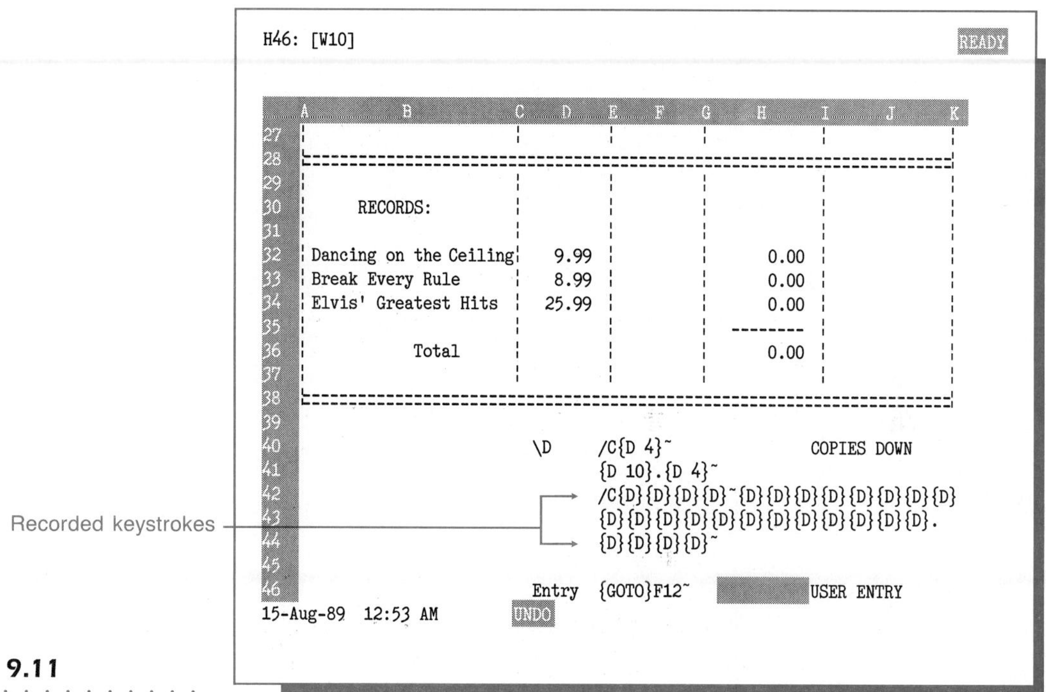

Figure 9.11

The macro commands are displayed in the learn range. Notice that it records each {D} key name individually. LEARN mode cannot use a repetition factor within key names. Consequently, the macro takes up much more worksheet space.

If you enter more characters than your learn range can hold, 1-2-3 will turn off LEARN mode and tell you that the learn range is full. The learn range will contain all the macro instructions entered up to that point. You can either erase the contents of the range, define a larger range and begin again, or define a larger range and start again where you left off.

Now you can use this macro to complete column J, Sales Commission. The macro does not have to be renamed, as the new instructions are a continuation of the \D macro.

To position the cell pointer at the beginning of the range to be copied and to run the macro,

Move to: J12
Press: ALT-**D**

Your screen should look similar to Figure 9.12.

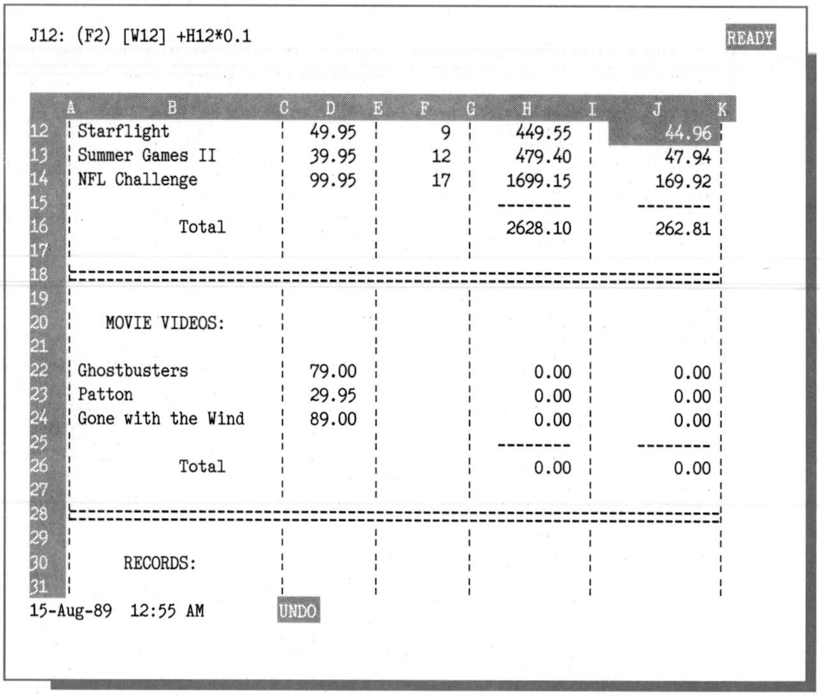

```
J12: (F2) [W12] +H12*0.1                                                    READY

   A          B            C    D     E    F   G      H       I       J       K
12 | Starflight              |  49.95 |     9 |    449.55 |           44.96 |
13 | Summer Games II         |  39.95 |    12 |    479.40 |           47.94 |
14 | NFL Challenge           |  99.95 |    17 |   1699.15 |          169.92 |
15 |                         |        |       |  -------- |        -------- |
16 |           Total         |        |       |   2628.10 |          262.81 |
17 |                         |        |       |           |                 |
18 |=================================================================================|
19 |                         |        |       |           |                 |
20 |    MOVIE VIDEOS:        |        |       |           |                 |
21 |                         |        |       |           |                 |
22 | Ghostbusters            |  79.00 |       |      0.00 |            0.00 |
23 | Patton                  |  29.95 |       |      0.00 |            0.00 |
24 | Gone with the Wind      |  89.00 |       |      0.00 |            0.00 |
25 |                         |        |       |  -------- |        -------- |
26 |           Total         |        |       |      0.00 |            0.00 |
27 |                         |        |       |           |                 |
28 |=================================================================================|
29 |                         |        |       |           |                 |
30 |      RECORDS:           |        |       |           |                 |
31 |                         |        |       |           |                 |
15-Aug-89  12:55 AM        UNDO
```

Figure 9.12

Confirm that cells J12 through J14 have been correctly copied down column J. If they have not, correct the macro and try again.

Using STEP Mode

Finding errors in a macro (especially a large one) can be difficult. **STEP mode** helps you locate errors by slowing down the macro execution to one keystroke at a time.

You will use STEP mode macro execution on the \D macro to demonstrate this procedure. To use STEP mode,

Press: ALT-F2

The STEP indicator appears at the bottom of the screen.

To run the macro,

Move to: H12
Press: ALT-**D**

The STEP indicator is no longer displayed. The status line now displays the cell address and the cell contents of the macro being executed. The macro instruction (/) to be executed next is highlighted. To execute the first macro instruction,

Press: any key (SPACEBAR is recommended)

Your screen should look similar to Figure 9.13.

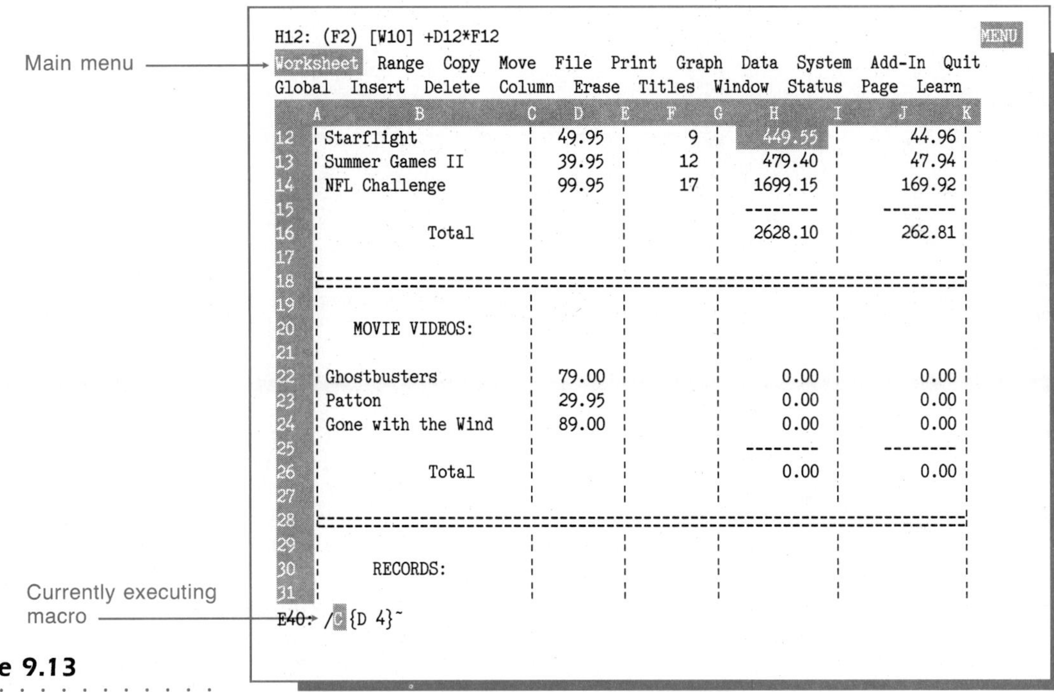

Figure 9.13

The first keystroke in the macro, /, has been executed, and the 1-2-3 main menu should be displayed in the control panel. The next macro instruction to be executed (C) is highlighted. To continue,

Press: SPACEBAR

Your screen should now look similar to Figure 9.14.

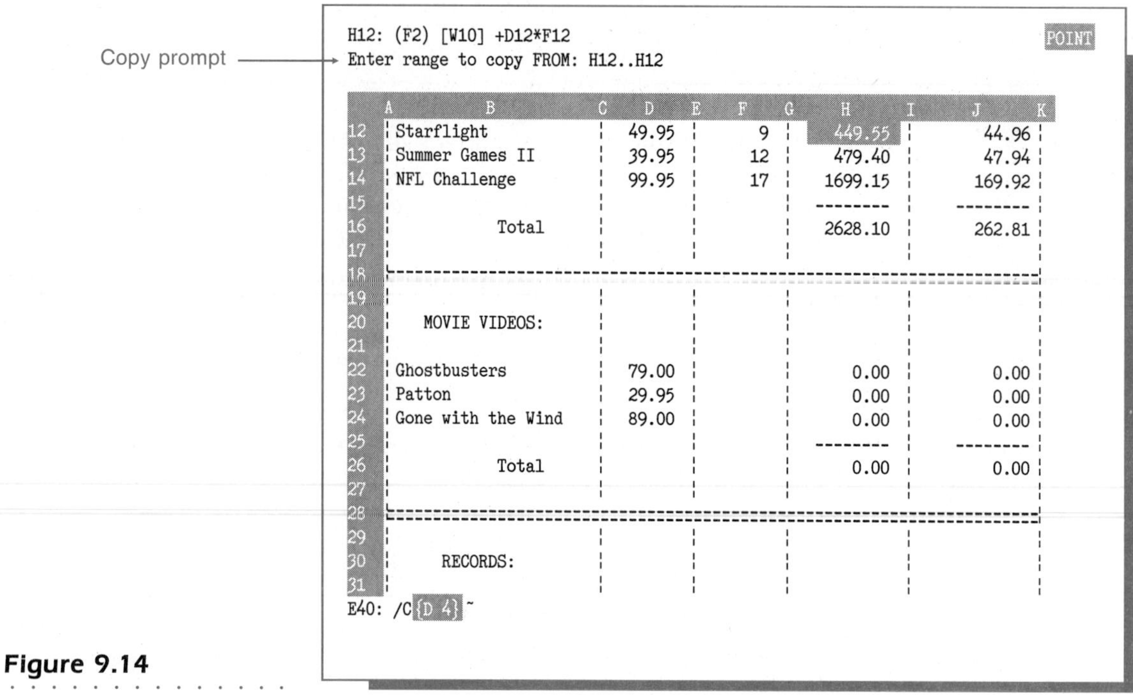

Figure 9.14

The macro has executed the Copy command, and the control panel now displays the prompt for the range to copy from. Each time you press a key, a command is executed and the macro advances one step to the next macro instruction.

Once you locate an error, you can stop the macro execution by pressing CTRL-BREAK followed by ESC, then edit and rerun the macro. STEP mode is still on when the macro runs again to let you continue testing your macro commands.

Continue to run the \D macro using STEP mode until the execution of the macro is complete and you return to READY mode. The STEP indicator is redisplayed to tell you that STEP mode is still on.

To turn off STEP mode,

Press: ALT-F2

Completing the Macro

The report is almost complete. However, Susan still needs to modify the ENTRY macro located in cell E46. After the numbers sold for the three computer games have been entered, the macro needs to skip down eight spaces to the next product category (movie videos), allow the user to enter the number sold in that category, move down eight more spaces to the next category (records), and allow the user to enter the number sold in that category.

To add these new instructions to the macro,

Move to: E49
Type: **{D 8}**{?}**{D}**{?}**{D}**{?}
Press: ↵

To continue the macro instructions to allow entry of data in the category for records, the same sequence of keys as in the macro instructions in cell E49 need to be used. A macro, like any other worksheet entry, can be copied.

Copy the macro instructions in cell E49 to cell E50. To enter the data in the last cell of that category, an enter (~) symbol needs to be added to this macro. Add a ~ as the last macro instruction in cell E50.

To execute your modified macro,

Press: ALT-F3

Select: ENTRY

Your screen should look similar to Figure 9.15.

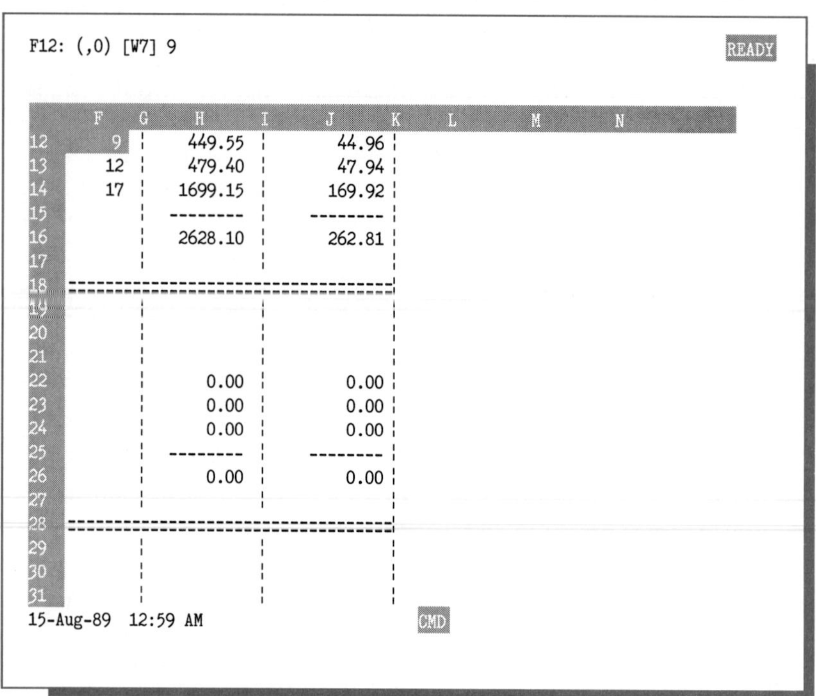

Figure 9.15

The macro should have moved the cell pointer to cell F12. However, the product categories and column labels are not visible in the current window. The window is not positioned properly over the worksheet.

Whenever {GOTO} references a cell outside the current window, the window is shifted to position the referenced cell in the upper left corner.

To correct this problem, you must interrupt execution of the ENTRY macro.

Press: CTRL-BREAK

Notice that the status line displays ''Break'' and that the mode indicator displays ERROR. To return to READY mode,

Press: ESC

To properly frame the worksheet in the window, modify the macro by entering {HOME} as the first instruction in the macro.

Your modified macro instruction in cell E46 should be {HOME}{GOTO}F12~.

Now, to see the entire macro,

Move to: E50

Your screen should look similar to Figure 9.16.

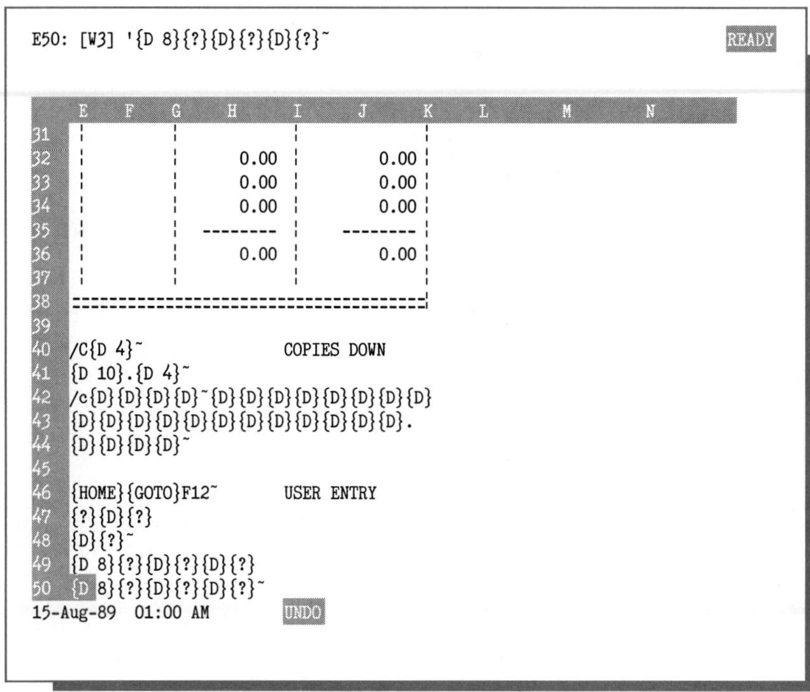

Figure 9.16

Run the macro again (ALT-F3, ENTRY).

Your screen should look similar to Figure 9.17.

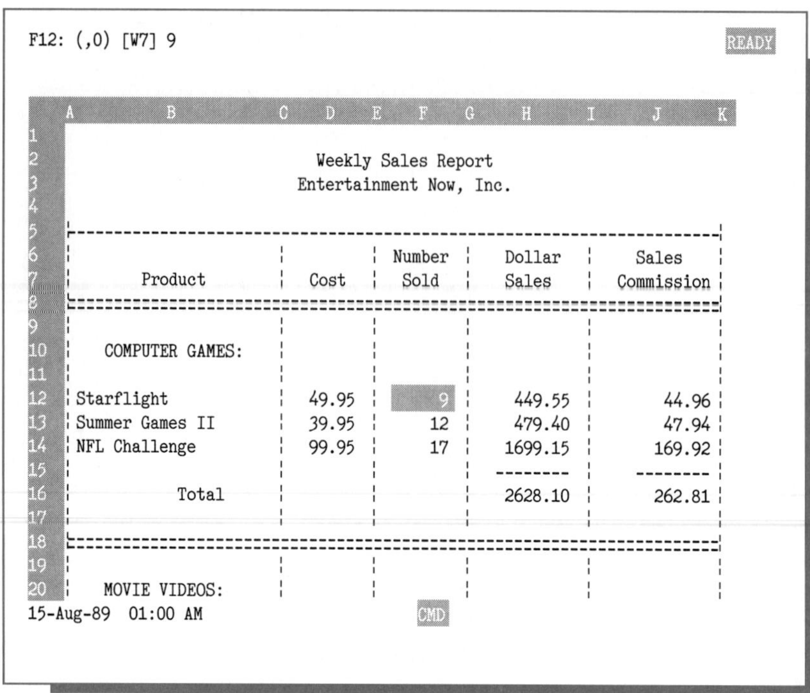
```
F12: (,0) [W7] 9                                                    READY

  A        B          C    D    E    F    G    H    I    J    K
1
2                        Weekly Sales Report
3                       Entertainment Now, Inc.
4
5  ------------------------------------------------------------------
6                                 | Number |  Dollar  |    Sales
7         Product        | Cost   | Sold   |  Sales   | Commission
8  ==================================================================
9
10   COMPUTER GAMES:
11
12 Starflight            | 49.95  |      9 |   449.55 |      44.96
13 Summer Games II       | 39.95  |     12 |   479.40 |      47.94
14 NFL Challenge         | 99.95  |     17 |  1699.15 |     169.92
15                                          --------    --------
16           Total                          2628.10      262.81
17
18 ==================================================================
19
20   MOVIE VIDEOS:
15-Aug-89  01:00 AM             CMD
```

Figure 9.17

The window now correctly frames the worksheet. If your screen is not similar to Figure 9.17, interrupt execution of the macro again and correct your macro before proceeding.

Enter some hypothetical data to test the macro. If your macro does not operate correctly, you may want to use STEP mode to locate the problem.

When your ENTRY macro operates correctly, run the macro again and enter the following values for the Number Sold column:

Starflight	12
Summer Games II	21
NFL Challenge	17
Ghostbusters	10
Patton	13
Gone with the Wind	8
Dancing on the Ceiling	5
Break Every Rule	9
Elvis' Greatest Hits	15

Your screen should look similar to Figure 9.18.

```
F34: (,0) [W7] 15                                                    READY

   A          B            C    D      E     F      G     H      I      J      K
15 |                       |           |            |  --------  |  --------  |
16 |          Total        |           |            |   3137.50  |    313.75  |
17 |                       |           |            |            |            |
18 |==================================================================|
19 |                       |           |            |            |            |
20 |   MOVIE VIDEOS:       |           |            |            |            |
21 |                       |           |            |            |            |
22 | Ghostbusters          |   79.00   |      10    |    790.00  |     79.00  |
23 | Patton                |   29.95   |      13    |    389.35  |     38.94  |
24 | Gone with the Wind    |   89.00   |       8    |    712.00  |     71.20  |
25 |                       |           |            |  --------  |  --------  |
26 |          Total        |           |            |   1891.35  |    189.14  |
27 |                       |           |            |            |            |
28 |==================================================================|
29 |                       |           |            |            |            |
30 |    RECORDS:           |           |            |            |            |
31 |                       |           |            |            |            |
32 | Dancing on the Ceiling|    9.99   |       5    |     49.95  |      5.00  |
33 | Break Every Rule      |    8.99   |       9    |     80.91  |      8.09  |
34 | Elvis' Greatest Hits  |   25.99   |      15    |    389.85  |     38.99  |
15-Aug-89  01:01 AM        UNDO
```

Figure 9.18

The values for the numbers sold have been entered into the appropriate cells, and the Total Dollar Sales and Sales Commission formulas have been recalculated. If your macro did not execute properly, correct it and try again.

The interactive macro should make it easy for Susan's salespeople to enter their weekly sales data into the worksheet.

Save the worksheet as REPORT3.WK1.

Print the worksheet including the macro commands, then exit from 1-2-3.

Glossary of Key Terms

Debug To locate and correct errors in a macro.

Interactive macro A macro that combines macro execution with manual entries by inserting a pause in the macro instruction sequence.

Keystroke instruction An instruction in a macro that represents a key on the keyboard.

LEARN mode A feature that will record your keystrokes as a macro while performing the task or command.

Learn range The area in a worksheet where 1-2-3 will record the macro instructions when LEARN mode is in use.

Macro A set of instructions that automates a 1-2-3 task. A macro consists of a sequence of keystrokes and commands that you type into a worksheet, name, and run to perform a task automatically.

Repetition factor A number used to specify two or more consecutive uses of the same key in a macro key symbol.

STEP mode A feature that helps you locate errors in a large macro by slowing down the macro execution to one keystroke at a time.

Practice Problems

1. Matching

1. ~	______	**a.**	activate LEARN mode
2. {?}	______	**b.**	the Run key
3. {L 4}	______	**c.**	illegal macro instruction
4. ALT-F5	______	**d.**	command to define a learn range
5. ALT-D	______	**e.**	macro instruction for ↵
6. {GOTO}	______	**f.**	invokes macro named \D
7. ALT-F2	______	**g.**	moves four cells to the left
8. /WLR	______	**h.**	turns STEP mode on and off
9. {4L}	______	**i.**	macro instruction to move to a particular cell
10. ALT-F3	______	**j.**	pauses macro execution

2. The pointer-movement area of the IBM PC keyboard doubles as a numeric keypad when you press the NUM LOCK key.

   This switching back and forth with the NUM LOCK key often frustrates those accustomed to numeric keypads. To help these people, you are to create macros that will control cell-pointer movements. These macros will allow the numeric keypad to enter data exclusively.

   a. In a blank worksheet, set the NUM LOCK key so that the numeric keypad can be used to enter data. Put your name in cell A1 and the date in cell A2.
   b. Create a macro that will move the cell pointer down one cell. Name this macro \D.
   c. Create three other macros that will move the cell pointer up, left, and right. Name these macros \U, \L, and \R, respectively.
   d. After you have created, executed, tested, and documented the macros, save the worksheet in a file named POINTER.
   e. Print the worksheet.

3. Susan Smith has decided to add a few more macros to the weekly sales report worksheet. Retrieve the file REPORT3.WK1.

   a. Create a macro that will go to cell A2 and erase the cell's contents. Then have the macro enter the function (@NOW) to calculate the current date and format the cell to display the date as mm/dd/yy. Name the macro DATE. Document the worksheet. Execute the macro, then edit it if necessary.
   b. Create and document a macro that will print only the sales report portion of the worksheet. Name this macro PRINT. Execute the macro, then edit it if necessary.
   c. Create and document a macro that will save the current worksheet file as REPORT4. Name the macro SAVE. Execute the macro, then edit it if necessary.
   d. Modify the SAVE macro to save and replace the filename. Execute the macro, then edit it if necessary.
   e. Modify the PRINT macro to print the entire worksheet, including the macro commands. Execute the macro.
   f. Save the current worksheet using your SAVE macro, then exit from 1-2-3.

Reference

1

Basic Skills

The 1-2-3 Screen

Figure 1.1 shows the 1-2-3 screen. 1-2-3 divides the screen into three areas: the worksheet area, the control panel, and the status line.

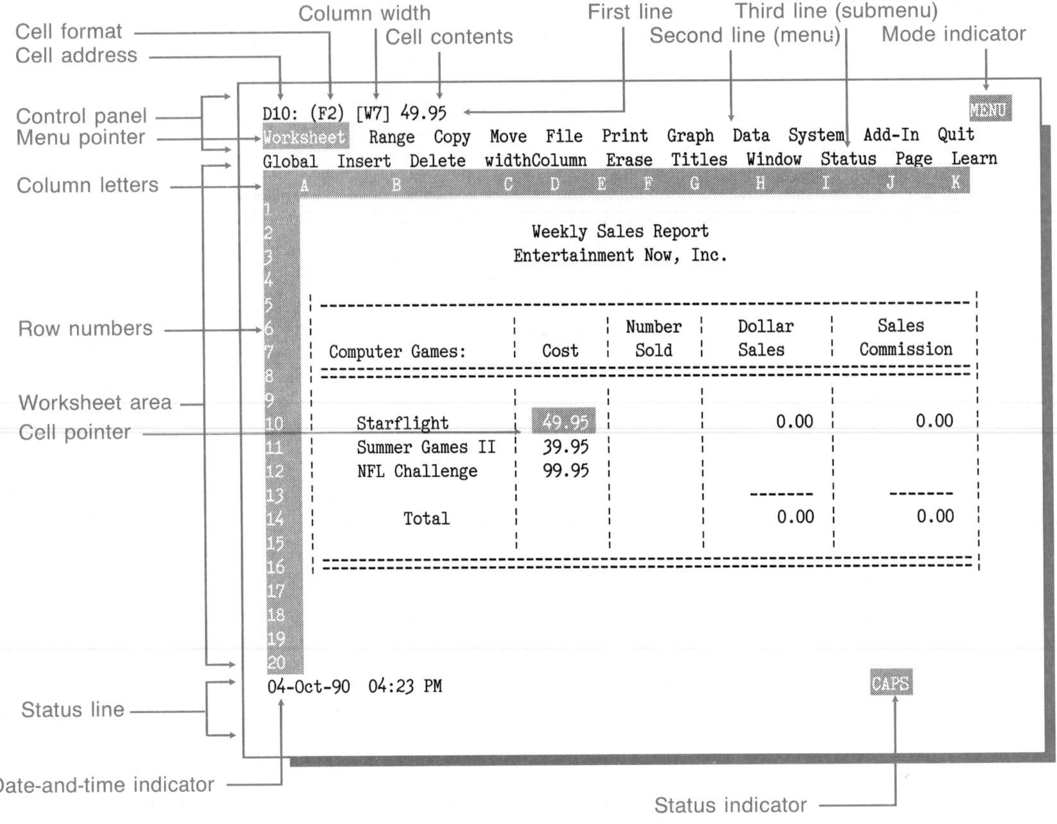

Figure 1.1

The worksheet area, which occupies the largest section of the screen, is where you enter and calculate data. It displays a section of the worksheet you are currently working on. The worksheet is a grid made up of rows and columns. The worksheet contains 8,192 rows and 256 columns. Each intersection of a row and column forms a cell, in which you can store data.

The control panel displays information about what 1-2-3 is doing and about your work. It contains three lines of information about the current cell and commands (actions you tell 1-2-3 to perform).

The status line is the last line of the screen. 1-2-3 uses the status line to display the date-and-time indicator, the status indicators, and error messages.

Table 1.1 describes the different parts of the 1-2-3 screen.

Table 1.1

Worksheet Item	Description
Control Panel	
First line	Contains information about the current cell, including the cell address, cell format, protection status, column width, and cell entry. It also contains the mode indicator. The cell address and the mode indicator always appear on the control panel; the other settings appear only when you establish them. The format setting determines the way in which an entry appears in the cell. The protection status tells you if you can change the cell contents. The mode indicator tells you in what state or condition 1-2-3 is currently operating. It often changes when you begin an action, such as executing a command or making an entry.
Second line	Displays the current entry when you are creating or editing an entry. It displays the main menu—a list of commands that appear when you press slash (/) in READY mode, as shown in Figure 1.1. It also displays submenus and prompts, or requests for information that 1-2-3 needs to complete a command you have selected.
Third line	Displays either a submenu or a one-line description of the command currently highlighted on the menu.
Worksheet	
Row number	Identifies a horizontal row in the worksheet. It appears in the left border of the worksheet. Rows are numbered from 1–8192.
Column letter	Identifies a vertical column in the worksheet. It appears on the top border of the worksheet. Columns are lettered A–Z, then AA–AZ, and then BA–BZ, and so on, to IV.
Cell	The unit of the worksheet that stores data. Each cell has a unique address that consists of its column letter and row number. For example, B14 identifies the cell in column B, row 14.
Cell pointer	A rectangular highlight that appears on one cell in the worksheet and identifies it as the current cell. You can move the cell pointer to any cell in the worksheet.
Current cell	The cell that contains the cell pointer, which indicates that your next entry or procedure affects this cell. For example, typing an entry or executing certain commands affects the current cell.

Table 1.1 Continued

Worksheet Item	Description
Status Line	
Date-and-time indicator	Tells you the current date and time.
Status indicator	Describes a particular program condition or key condition. For example, in Figure 1.1, CAPS indicates that the CAPS LOCK key has been pressed.
Error message	An error message appears in place of the date-and-time indicator when 1-2-3 detects a mistake or cannot perform a task.

(For more details about the worksheet, see Lab 1.)

Moving Around the Worksheet

You can use the pointer-movement keys, [↑], [↓], [←], [→], to move one cell at a time in the worksheet. You can move one screen at a time using PGUP, PGDN, CTRL-[→], or CTRL-[←]. You can move many screens at a time using the Goto function key ([F5]), HOME, or using END in combination with other pointer-movement keys.

Many of the pointer-movement keys move the menu pointer among the menu commands in addition to moving the cell pointer in the worksheet. Table 1.2 describes the effect of each key or key combination in several 1-2-3 modes.

Table 1.2

Key	READY and POINT Modes	MENU and HELP Modes
[←]	Moves left one cell	Moves left one item
[→]	Moves right one cell	Moves right one item
[↑]	Moves up one cell	Moves up one topic in HELP mode; beeps in MENU mode
[↓]	Moves down one cell	Moves down one topic in HELP mode; beeps in MENU mode
CTRL-[←] or SHIFT-TAB	Moves left one screen	
CTRL-[→] or TAB	Moves right one screen	
PGUP	Moves up one screen	
PGDN	Moves down one screen	
HOME	Moves to upper left corner	Moves to first item in MENU mode, first topic in HELP mode
END	(Must be used with another pointer-movement key)	Moves to last item in MENU mode, last topic in HELP mode

Table 1.2 Continued

Key	READY and POINT Modes	MENU and HELP Modes
END HOME	Moves to lower right corner of active area (area of worksheet where you have done work)	
END ↑	Moves up to intersection of a blank and non-blank cell.	
END ↓	Moves down to intersection of a blank and non-blank cell.	
END →	Moves right to intersection of a blank and non-blank cell.	
END ←	Moves left to intersection of a blank and non-blank cell.	

(For more details about pointer-movement keys, see Lab 1.)

Entering and Editing Data

You can enter any kind of data in a cell by typing. You can edit an entry as you type it or return to a completed entry and revise it.

Typing Entries

The simplest method of entering data in a cell is by typing. Move the cell pointer to a cell, type the entry, and press ↵. The entry appears in the cell after you press ↵.

Each character that you type appears on the second line of the control panel. A cursor, or underscore character, indicates where the next character you type will appear. A cell can hold up to 240 characters.

To complete an entry, press ↵ or one of the pointer-movement keys. When you press a pointer-movement key, 1-2-3 completes the entry and moves the cell pointer to another cell in the direction of the pointer-movement key.

When you press ↵ or a pointer-movement key to complete an entry, the following steps occur:

- 1-2-3 checks for errors in the entry. If it finds an error, 1-2-3 beeps, places the cursor at the problem location, and switches into EDIT mode.
- If 1-2-3 finds no error, it stores the entry in the current cell. The previous entry, if any, disappears from the cell.

- The entry disappears from the second line of the control panel. After you press ↵, the entry appears on the first line of the control panel. After you press a pointer-movement key, the entry disappears completely from the control panel.
- If the Recalculation setting is Automatic, 1-2-3 recalculates any formulas in the worksheet that are affected by the change. (See the section on the / **W**orksheet **G**lobal **R**ecalculation command in Chapter 2, "Commands.")
- 1-2-3 returns to READY mode.

(For more details about typing entries, see Lab 1.)

Editing Entries

Editing an entry means altering existing data rather than replacing it with entirely new data. You can edit an entry either as you type it or after you have entered it in a cell.

To edit an entry as you type it:

- To erase characters to the left of the cursor, press BACKSPACE.
- To erase everything you typed and start again, press ESC.
- To change part of what you typed, press the Edit function key (F2) to enter EDIT mode and use the editing keys described in Table 1.3.

Table 1.3

Key	Typing	Revising in EDIT Mode
←	Completes entry; moves cell pointer left one cell	Moves cursor left one character
→	Completes entry; moves cell pointer right one cell	Moves cursor right one character
↑	Completes entry; moves cell pointer up one cell	Completes entry; moves cell pointer up one cell
↓	Completes entry; moves cell pointer down one cell	Completes entry; moves cell pointer down one cell
↵	Completes entry	Completes entry
BACKSPACE	Erases character to left of cursor	Erases character to left of cursor
ESC	Cancels all characters on the second line of the control panel	Cancels all characters on the second line of the control panel
DEL		Deletes character at cursor

Table 1.3 Continued

Key	Typing	Revising in EDIT Mode
INS		Switches between inserting the text by moving existing text to the right and overwriting existing text
HOME	Completes entry; moves cell pointer to upper left cell of worksheet	Moves cursor to first character
CTRL-(→)	Completes entry; moves cell pointer right one screen	Moves cursor right five characters
CTRL-(←)	Completes entry; moves cell pointer left one screen	Moves cursor left five characters
PGUP	Completes entry; moves cell pointer up one screen	Completes entry; moves cell pointer up one screen
PGDN	Completes entry; moves cell pointer down one screen	Completes entry; moves cell pointer down one screen
END	Completes entry; turns END indicator on if it was off, and off if it was on	Moves cursor to last character

To edit a completed entry, follow these steps:

1. Move the cell pointer to the cell that contains the entry you want to revise.
2. Press the Edit function key, (F2). The mode indicator in the upper right corner of the screen changes to EDIT. Use the pointer-movement keys to move the cursor around in the entry.
3. Insert or delete characters at the cursor location.
4. Press (↵) to complete the entry. The cursor can be anywhere in the entry when you press (↵); it does not have to be at the end.

1-2-3 changes to EDIT mode automatically if you try to complete an entry that contains an error.

There is a difference between editing and erasing an entry. To erase an entry, use the / **R**ange **E**rase command described in Chapter 2, ''Commands.''

(For more details about editing entries, see Lab 1.)

Types of Data

A cell accepts two types of data: values and labels. Values are numbers or formula entries. Labels are text entries. When you type the first character of an entry, the mode indicator changes from READY to VALUE or LABEL to show which type of data you are entering. When you complete an entry, the mode indicator switches back to READY.

Values

Value entries conform to the following rules:

- Begin with a number (0–9) or one of the following numeric symbols: . + − $ (# @
- Cannot be longer than 240 characters
- Are between 10^{-99} and 10^{99}, inclusive; however, 1-2-3 can store a number as a result of calculations, ranging from 10^{-308} to 10^{308}
- Exclude spaces or commas; you can change the cell format later to include commas (see the section on the / **R**ange **F**ormat command in Chapter 2, "Commands")
- Contain no more than one decimal point
- Can end with a percent sign to indicate a percentage
- Can be entered in scientific format, as shown in Figure 1.2
- Can be a formula entry. A formula is an entry that performs a calculation.

When you enter the first character of a numeric or formula entry, the mode indicator changes from READY to LABEL.

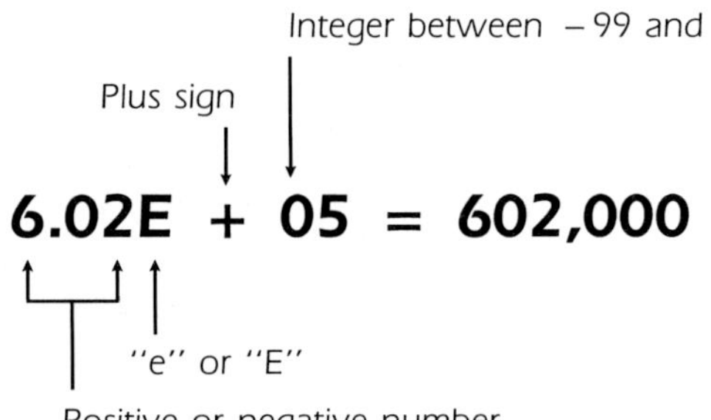

Figure 1.2

Alignment of a Value

A value aligns on the right edge of a cell. You cannot change the alignment of a value entry.

Format of a Value

You can change the format, or appearance, of a value entry in a cell without changing the way 1-2-3 stores the entry. For example, you can format the entry 65.3 so that it appears as $65.30, 65.3%, or 65. (See the section on the / **R**ange **F**ormat and / **W**orksheet **G**lobal **F**ormat commands in Chapter 2, "Commands.")

Long Values If a value contains too many characters to fit in a cell, 1-2-3 may display asterisks (*****) in the cell instead of the entry. This does not affect the way 1-2-3 stores the entry. When you make the column wide enough, the entire value appears in the cell space. The cell format determines if asterisks are displayed. (See the sections on the / **W**orksheet **C**olumn **S**et-Width or / **W**orksheet **G**lobal **C**olumn-Width commands in Chapter 2, "Commands.")

Decimal Places 1-2-3 can store a value with up to fifteen decimal places. The control panel, however, displays a maximum of nine decimal places. If you enter a value with twelve decimal places, for example, 1-2-3 calculates the entry using twelve decimal places, although you can see only nine decimal place numbers on the control panel. (For more details about numeric entries, see Lab 1.)

Labels

Any entry that 1-2-3 determines is not a number or a formula is a label. Often label entries are descriptive text, such as May Sales or Principal. A label can consist of any characters in the Lotus International Character Set (LICS). LICS is an extension of the ASCII character set.

Labels conform to the following rules:

- Begin with either a label-prefix character or any character that does not indicate the start of a number or a formula
- Cannot be longer than 240 characters
- Can contain numbers or numeric symbols as long as the first character is a label-prefix character

When you enter the first character of a label, the mode indicator changes from READY to LABEL. (For more details about labels, see Lab 1.)

Label-Prefix Characters Beginning an entry with a label-prefix character determines how the entry is aligned in the cell. There are three choices for labels: right-aligned, left-aligned, and centered. If you do not enter a label-prefix character, 1-2-3 automatically aligns the label entry according to the default worksheet alignment. Unless you change it, the label default alignment is left. (See the section on the / **W**orksheet **G**lobal **L**abel-Prefix command in Chapter 2, "Commands.")

A label-prefix character does not appear in the worksheet cell; it appears on the first line of the control panel when the cell pointer is on the cell.

The label-prefix characters are described below.

Prefix:	Example:	Result:	
'(single quote)	'TOTAL	left-aligned	[TOTAL]
''(double quote)	''TOTAL	right-aligned	[TOTAL]
^(caret)	^TOTAL	centered	[TOTAL]

You can also type the backslash (\) as the first character of a label entry. Characters you type after the backslash repeat across the worksheet cell. For example, * creates a cell filled with asterisks. If you enter a ¦ (split vertical bar) as the first character of a label entry, the label is displayed on the screen but does not print. (For more details about label-prefix characters, see Lab 1.)

Entering Numbers as Labels

To enter a label that starts with a number symbol, begin the entry with a label-prefix character. A label-prefix character identifies the entry as a label, no matter what characters the entry contains. For example, you would use a label-prefix character at the beginning of the entry 96 Lake St. If you omit the label-prefix character in such an entry, 1-2-3 beeps and changes to EDIT mode so that you can correct the entry.

Long Labels

If you enter a label entry that is too long to appear in one cell, the entry extends into the blank cells to the right. If the cells to the right are filled, 1-2-3 cuts off the entry at the right edge of the cell.

1-2-3 stores the entire entry even if it cannot display the entry in a worksheet cell. To make the complete entry appear in the worksheet cell, erase the cell entries to the right or widen the column that contains the entry.

Ranges

A range is a rectangular block of adjacent cells. It can be a single cell, a row, a column, or several rows and columns (see Lab 2, Figure 2.5). 1-2-3 prompts you to enter a range during many commands. For example, 1-2-3 prompts you to enter a range when you use the / **M**ove command to move a group of cells to another part of the worksheet. You can also enter a range in an @function.

Entering Ranges

You can enter or specify ranges in three ways:

- Typing the range address
- Highlighting the range
- Using a range name

Typing a Range Address

You can enter a range address by typing the addresses of any two diagonally opposite corners of the range, separated by one or two periods. For example, G5..H29 specifies the range whose corner cells are G5 and H29. Do not use spaces in the range address.

When you are entering a range during a command, press ↵ to complete the range address. For example,

Enter range to format: **A12..H19** ↵

1-2-3 displays range addresses in uppercase letters with the upper left and lower right corner cells separated by two periods. You can enter the range address in either uppercase or lowercase letters.

Highlighting a Range

When 1-2-3 is in POINT mode, you can specify a range by highlighting it. To highlight a range during a command, move the cell pointer to a cell that is one corner of the intended range and press . (period). This cell is now the anchor cell.

Once a corner of the range you want to highlight is anchored, use the pointer-movement keys to expand the highlight until it contains the range. To complete specifying the range address, press ↵. 1-2-3 displays the address of the highlighted area in the control panel with the anchor cell and the ending cell of the range separated by two periods.

Some commands, such as / **R**ange **F**ormat, make the current cell the anchor cell automatically. You can tell if the cell pointer is anchored by looking at the prompt in the control panel. A single cell address (such as B3) means the cell pointer is not anchored, while a range address (B3..B3) means it is anchored. If you want to make another cell the anchor cell, press ESC, move the pointer to the desired cell, and press . (period).

Table 1.4 shows the effect of three keys that you can use when you are highlighting a range.

Table 1.4

Key	Unanchored Range	Anchored Range
.(period)	Makes current cell the anchor cell; displays range address on the control panel	Moves anchor cell clockwise from one corner to next highlighted range
ESC	Returns you to previous menu	Returns range highlight to anchor cell; removes anchor
BACKSPACE	Returns cell pointer to original location	Removes range highlight; returns cell pointer to current cell

Note If you change your mind and want to highlight a different range, press BACKSPACE to remove highlighting from the range, unanchor the cell pointer, and return the cell pointer to wherever it was before 1-2-3 entered POINT mode; or, press ESC to remove highlighting and unanchor the cell pointer without moving it.

(For more details about entering ranges, see Lab 2.)

Using a Range Name

To refer more easily to a range, you can name it. For example, you can give the range A54 through B98 the name Sales. After you name a range, you can use the range name instead of typing the range address or highlighting the range in a command or formula. A range name is often easier to remember than a range address because the name can describe the contents of a range. (For details on naming a range, see the section on the / **R**ange **N**ame **C**reate command in Chapter 2, "Commands.")

Remembered Ranges

With most commands, 1-2-3 "remembers" the most recent range you specified. The next time you select the same command, 1-2-3 highlights the range you last specified and displays the range address in the control panel. Press ↵ to accept the range, or press ESC or BACKSPACE to clear the remembered range and specify a different range.

Entering Formulas

A formula is an entry that performs a calculation using numbers, other formulas, or strings. The calculation can be a simple mathematical operation, such as subtracting one number from another, or a more complicated operation, such as determining the net present value of a series of future cash flows. 1-2-3 allows you to enter three types of formulas:

1. Numeric formulas calculate numeric values using the arithmetic operators. For example, +H16/12 divides the number in cell H16 by 12 (see Table 1.5).

2. String formulas calculate string values using the string operator, the ampersand (&). A string is text enclosed in quotation marks or labels in a worksheet. For example, +B4&"Revenues" combines the label in B4 with the word Revenues.

3. Logical formulas compare values in two or more cells using the logical operators (=, <, >, <=, >=, <>, #AND#, #OR#, and #NOT#). A logical formula is a statement that produces a value that is either 0 (meaning false) or 1 (meaning true). For example, +BALANCE>=500 returns the value 1 (true) if the value in the cell named BALANCE is greater than or equal to 500; otherwise it returns the value 0 (false).

When you enter a formula, 1-2-3 displays the value that results from the calculation in the cell. For example, if you enter the formula 25+5, 1-2-3 displays the value 30 in the cell. When the cell pointer is on the cell, however, 1-2-3 displays 25+5 in the first line of the control panel.

Use the following guidelines when entering a formula:

- A formula can begin with a number or one of the numeric symbols + − . @ ($. In addition, the # (pound symbol) can be used to begin a logical formula.
- When the first element in a formula is a cell address, range name, or file reference, begin the formula with + − (or $. For example, +B7/B8, −B7*B8, $SALES/12, (SALES−EXPENSES), and +<<BUDGET.WK1>>B7 are all valid formulas.
- When a string formula starts with a literal string, begin the formula with + or (. For example, +“Ms. ”&LAST and (“Ms. ”&LAST) are both valid formulas.
- A formula can contain up to 240 characters.
- A formula cannot contain spaces, except within literal strings in string formulas.

You can use the following types of data in a formula:

- Numbers (for example, 450, −92, 7.1E12, date numbers, and time numbers)
- Literal strings (for example, “Budget for” or “TOTAL”)
- @Functions (for example, @SUM(A4..A8))
- Cell and range addresses (for example, B12, F23..H35)
- Range names (for example, JANSALES, BUDGET_90)

(For more details about entering formulas, see Lab 1 and Lab 2.)

Order of Precedence

Table 1.5 shows the operators you can use in formulas and their precedence numbers. These numbers represent the order in which 1-2-3 performs operations in a formula. 1-2-3 performs an operation with a lower precedence number before an operation with a higher precedence number. Operators with the same precedence are performed sequentially from left to right.

Table 1.5

Operator	Operation	Precedence Number
^	Exponentiation	1
− +	Negative, positive	2
* /	Multiplication, division	3
+ −	Addition, subtraction	4
= < >	Equal, not equal	5
< >	Less than, greater than	5
< =	Less than or equal	5
> =	Greater than or equal	5
#NOT#	Logical NOT	6
#AND#	Logical AND	7
#OR#	Logical OR	7
&	String combination	7

Overriding Precedence Numbers

You can override precedence numbers by putting parentheses around an operation. 1-2-3 performs operations in parentheses first. Within each set of parentheses, precedence numbers apply. You can include as many pairs of parentheses as you want within parentheses in a formula.

Figure 1.3 shows how 1-2-3 performs the operations in a formula according to precedence number.

Figure 1.3

450+((5000+A20)*.145)/12-J30

1-2-3 performs the operations in this order: 4th (+ after 450), 1st (+ A20), 2nd (*), 3rd (/), 5th (-)

Entering Addresses in Formulas

You can enter a cell or a range address in a formula by typing it or by moving to it. With the pointing method, you can use the pointer-movement keys to move the cell pointer to the cell or range whose address you want to enter.

Pointing to a Cell

To point to a cell in a formula, first type an operator. Then move the cell pointer to the cell whose address you want to include. The cell address appears on the control panel. Type the next operator or press (↵) to complete the formula. The pointer returns to the cell in which you are entering the formula.

Pointing to a Range

The only kind of formula that contains a range is an @function. To point to a range in an @function, first type the @function name and left parenthesis. Then highlight the range. Complete the range address by typing the next character of the @function. (For more details about pointing to a range, see Lab 2.)

Changing an Entry

When you point to a cell or a range in a formula, two keys let you change the cell or range you have selected: ESC and BACKSPACE. Table 1.6 describes the effect of these keys.

Table 1.6

Key	Single Cell	Range
ESC	Erases address; returns cell pointer to formula cell; mode indicator returns to VALUE	Erases free-cell address; returns cell pointer to anchor cell, unanchored; mode indicator remains POINT
BACKSPACE	Returns cell pointer to formula cell; mode indicator remains POINT	Returns cell pointer to formula cell, unanchored; mode indicator remains POINT

Using Cell and Range References in Formulas

Cell references in formulas can be relative, absolute, or mixed. The difference between relative, absolute, and mixed cell references is important when you copy formulas.

Use a relative reference to refer to a position of a cell in relation to the cell that contains the formula. A relative reference is not a permanent reference to a particular cell. To create a relative reference in a formula, you simply type the address or range name, such as B1, D25..D30, or PROFITS. For example,

Cell reference:	Meaning in a formula in H11:
G5	the cell one column left and six rows above this one

Use an absolute reference to refer to the same cell, no matter where you copy the formula to. An absolute reference is a permanent reference to a particular cell. To create an absolute reference, type a $ (dollar sign) in front of both the column letter and row number of the address (for example, $F$2 or $A$5..$B$10). To create an absolute range name, type a $ in front of the range name ($RATE). For example,

Cell reference:	Meaning in a formula in H11:
$G$5	cell G5

Use a mixed reference to make a cell reference that is part relative and part absolute—either the column letter or the row number remains constant. To create a mixed reference, precede the column letter or the row number with a $ (dollar sign)—for example, $C4 or C$4. For example,

Cell reference:	Meaning in a formula in H11:
$G5	the cell in column G, six rows above this one
G$5	the cell one column left of this one, in row 5

Cell references are relative by default. (For more details about cell references, see Lab 2.)

Using ABS (F4) to Change Reference Types

When entering or editing a formula, press ABS (F4) when the cursor is on or immediately to the right of a cell reference or range name. 1-2-3 cycles through the different reference types.

For example, Table 1.7 shows how pressing ABS (F4) changes the reference C5 after you type C5.

1-2-3 always cycles through the types of cell reference in the same order, regardless of whether the original reference type is relative, absolute, or mixed.

You can also indicate absolute, mixed, or relative references when pointing. After you point to a cell or a range and before you type the next character, press ABS (F4) repeatedly. The cell or range address on the control panel cycles through absolute, mixed, and relative.

You can edit an existing cell or range address. Move the cell pointer to the cell that contains the formula and press EDIT, F2. Move the cursor to the address you want to change and press ABS (F4) repeatedly to cycle through relative, absolute, and mixed. (For more details about indicating addresses, see Lab 2.)

Table 1.7

When Control Panel Displays	Press ABS (F4) to Get This
+C5	$C$5 (absolute address)
+$C$5	C$5 (mixed address with absolute row reference)
+C$5	$C5 (mixed address with absolute column reference)
+$C5	C5 (relative address)
+SALES	$SALES (absolute address)
+$SALES	SALES (relative address)

@Functions

1-2-3 has a special set of built-in formulas, called @functions. @Functions are different from regular formulas because you supply the values but not the operators.

Format of an @Function

An @function contains specific elements: the @function name and the values or data 1-2-3 needs to complete the @function calculation, which are enclosed in parentheses. Values in @functions are called arguments. An @function can have no arguments, one argument, or several arguments. (See Figure 1.4.)

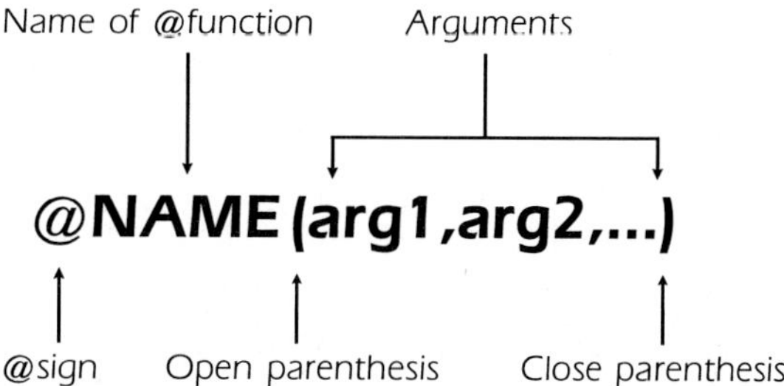

Figure 1.4

Many @functions allow you to perform common calculations more easily than standard formulas. For example, the @function @SUM(B4..B10) performs the same task as the formula +B4+B5+B6+B7+B8+B9+B10, but the @function is easier to enter.

Other @functions perform complex calculations efficiently. For example, the @function @PV calculates the present value of an annuity, which would otherwise require a complicated formula. (For more details about @functions, see Chapter 4, "@Functions.")

Indicators

An indicator is a highlighted word that 1-2-3 displays to provide you with information about the program or special keys. 1-2-3 has two kinds of indicators: mode and status.

Mode Indicators

During a 1-2-3 session, a mode indicator is always visible in the upper right corner of the control panel. This indicator tells you in what state or condition 1-2-3 is currently operating. Table 1.8 lists the mode indicators.

Table 1.8

Mode Indicator	Meaning
EDIT	An entry is being edited or needs to be edited.
ERROR	An error has occurred; press ESC or ↵ to clear it.
FILES	A menu of files is being displayed.
FIND	A / **D**ata **Q**uery **F**ind operation is in progress.

Table 1.8 Continued

Mode Indicator	Meaning
FRMT	A format line is being edited during a / **D**ata **P**arse operation.
HELP	The Help facility has been invoked.
LABEL	A label is being entered.
MENU	A 1-2-3 menu is being displayed.
NAMES	A menu of existing range names, graph names, or attached add-in names is being displayed.
POINT	The cell pointer is pointing to a cell or a range.
READY	1-2-3 is ready for the next entry or command.
STAT	Worksheet status information is being displayed.
VALUE	A number or a formula is being entered.
WAIT	A command or a process is being executed.

Status Indicators

Status indicators, which appear on the bottom of the screen in the status line, indicate a particular program condition exists or certain keys have been pressed. Table 1.9 lists the status indicators.

Table 1.9

Status Indicator	Meaning
CALC	The worksheet's formulas need to be recalculated; press the CALC key.
CAPS	The CAPS LOCK key is on.
CIRC	The worksheet contains a formula that refers to itself (occurs only when the recalculation order is Natural).
CMD	1-2-3 is pausing during a macro.
END	The END key is on.
LEARN	You pressed LEARN (ALT-F5) to turn on the Learn feature and 1-2-3 is recording your keystrokes in the learn range.
MEM	The amount of computer memory available for entering new data has fallen below 4096 bytes. If you continue to enter data without first increasing the amount of available memory, you may get a "memory-full" error.
NUM	The NUM LOCK key is on.
OVR	The INS key is on.
RO	The current file has read-only status, which means you cannot save any changes you make to the file unless you get the file reservation or save the worksheet with a new filename. The RO indicator appears when you are using 1-2-3 on a network or in another multiple-user environment and do not have the reservation for the current file.

Table 1.9 Continued

Status Indicator	Meaning
SCROLL	The SCROLL LOCK key is on.
SST	A macro in single-step mode is waiting for input.
STEP	Single-step mode has been turned on; once invoked, macros are processed one step at a time.
UNDO	The Undo feature is on.

1-2-3 Special Keys

Table 1.10 briefly describes the 1-2-3 special keys. To determine which keys on your computer's keyboard are equivalent to these keys, see the keyboard template.

Table 1.10

Key	Description
ALT	Invokes a macro when used in combination with a single-letter macro name.
BACKSPACE	Erases character to the left of the cursor in EDIT mode; if a range is selected, erases current range.
CAPS LOCK	Makes letter keys produce only uppercase letters; number and punctuation keys not affected.
CTRL	When used in combination with certain keys, changes the function of those keys.
CTRL-BREAK	Cancels current procedure.
DEL	Erases current character in EDIT mode.
ESC	Cancels current entry or range or returns to previous menu or command step.
INS	Switches between inserting the text by moving existing text to the right and writing over existing text.
< (less than symbol)	Displays 1-2-3 main menu in READY mode.
NUM LOCK	Switches between number keys and pointer-movement keys on the numeric keypad.
. (period)	When entering a range in POINT mode, anchors cell pointer if unanchored or cycles anchor cell and free cell in range.
↵ (ENTER)	Completes an entry, command, or part of a command.
SCROLL LOCK	Switches the pointer-movement keys between moving the cell pointer and moving the window.
SHIFT	When used in combination with another key on the typewriter section of the keyboard, produces the upper symbol of the key.
/ (slash)	In READY mode, displays the 1-2-3 main menu.
SPACEBAR	Inserts a space in LABEL, VALUE, and EDIT modes; moves the menu pointer right one item in MENU mode.
TAB	In READY mode, moves pointer one screen to the right; in EDIT mode, moves cursor five characters to the right.

1-2-3 Function Keys

You use the function keys on your keyboard to perform special operations. Each function key, except (F6), performs two operations: one when you press only the function key, and another when you hold down ALT and then press the function key. Table 1.11 briefly describes the 1-2-3 function keys. To determine which keys on your computer's keyboard are equivalent to these keys, see the keyboard template.

Table 1.11

Key	Description
ABS ((F4))	In POINT and EDIT modes, cycles a cell or range address between relative, absolute, and mixed.
APP1 (ALT-(F7))	Starts an add-in program assigned to the key.
APP2 (ALT-(F8))	Starts an add-in program assigned to the key.
APP3 (ALT-(F9))	Starts an add-in program assigned to the key.
APP4 (ALT-(F10))	If no add-in program is assigned to the key, displays the Add-In menu, which lets you attach, detach, invoke, or clear add-in programs.
CALC ((F9))	In READY mode, recalculates all worksheet formulas. In VALUE and EDIT modes, converts a formula to its current value.
COMPOSE (ALT-(F1))	Creates characters in 1-2-3 that you cannot enter directly from the keyboard.
EDIT ((F2))	Puts 1-2-3 in EDIT mode so you can edit the entry in the current cell.
GOTO ((F5))	Moves directly to a specified cell.
GRAPH ((F10))	Displays the current graph.
HELP ((F1))	Displays the 1-2-3 on-line Help screens.
LEARN (ALT-(F5))	Turns the Learn feature on or off.
NAME ((F3))	In POINT mode, displays a menu of named ranges in the current worksheet. In FILES and NAMES modes, displays a full-screen menu of names.
QUERY ((F7))	Repeats the last **/** **D**ata **Q**uery command you selected or, during a **/** **D**ata **Q**uery **F**ind command, switches 1-2-3 between FIND mode and READY mode.
RUN (ALT-(F3))	Selects a macro to run.
STEP (ALT-(F2))	Turns STEP mode on or off.
TABLE ((F8))	Repeats the last **/** **D**ata **T**able command you selected.
UNDO(ALT-(F4))	In READY mode, cancels any changes made to your worksheet since 1-2-3 was last in READY mode. Press UNDO (ALT-(F4)) again to restore those changes.
WINDOW ((F6))	In READY mode, moves the cell pointer between the two windows created with **/** **W**orksheet **W**indow. In MENU mode, turns off the display of settings sheets. Press WINDOW ((F6)) again to redisplay the settings sheets.

The Undo Feature

The Undo feature is an important safeguard against time-consuming mistakes. When the Undo feature is on, you can press UNDO (ALT-F4) almost any time 1-2-3 is in READY mode to cancel the most recent operation that changed worksheet data and/or settings. When you use UNDO (ALT-F4), 1-2-3 automatically restores whatever worksheet data and settings existed the last time 1-2-3 was in READY mode. In addition, if you change your mind about what you just undid, you can press UNDO (ALT-F4) again and 1-2-3 will undo the effect of the undo operation.

You can use the Undo feature if the UNDO indicator appears on the status line at the bottom of your screen. If the UNDO indicator is not displayed, pressing UNDO (ALT-F4) will have no effect.

Using Undo

Although the Undo feature is a valuable tool, you should not use it until you are familiar with how it works; otherwise you may get unexpected results.

- UNDO (ALT-F4) works only when you are using 1-2-3. You cannot use the Undo feature with any of the 1-2-3 utility programs (PrintGraph, Install, and Access) or while add-in programs (such as the Macro Library Manager) are invoked. You can, however, use UNDO while the add-ins are attached.
- Initially, the Undo feature is on, but you can turn it off with / **W**orksheet **G**lobal **D**efault **O**ther **U**ndo **D**isable. If you then use / **W**orksheet **G**lobal **D**efault **U**pdate to modify the 1-2-3 configuration file, Undo will automatically be turned off whenever you start 1-2-3.
- Any series of 1-2-3 commands performed after you press / (slash) to display the main menu and before 1-2-3 returns to READY mode is a single undoable operation (as long as some of those commands change worksheet data and/or settings). For example, if you select / **G**raph, complete a series of Graph commands without leaving the Graph menu, and then return 1-2-3 to READY mode, pressing UNDO (ALT-F4) cancels the entire series of Graph commands you completed.
- Any macro that changes worksheet data and/or settings is an undoable operation. If you use UNDO (ALT-F4) after running such a macro, 1-2-3 returns your worksheet data and settings to the state they were in prior to running the macro, regardless of how many individual changes the macro made.
- To undo your last operation, 1-2-3 must reserve a portion of memory to keep a copy of the worksheet. This reduces the amount of available memory.

When Does 1-2-3 Back Up the Worksheet?

1-2-3 creates a temporary backup copy of the worksheet when you press any key that might lead to a worksheet change. This allows 1-2-3 to restore your work to its previous state if you press UNDO (ALT-F4). For example, 1-2-3 backs up the worksheet when you press / (slash) to display the main menu, press a character that begins a label or value, or press the TABLE (F8) or QUERY (F9) keys. 1-2-3 does not wait for you to complete a command or cell entry before backing up the worksheet. Therefore, if you press / to select a new command but then press ESC because you decide you want to undo your previous operation, you will not be able to undo the previous operation because 1-2-3 backed up the worksheet again as soon as you pressed /.

1-2-3 does not back up the worksheet when the key you press cannot lead to worksheet changes. For example, 1-2-3 does not back up the worksheet when you press a pointer-movement key (such as ← or PGUP) or when you press a function key that cannot change the worksheet.

In addition to the pointer-movement keys, 1-2-3 does not back up the worksheet if you press any of the following keys in READY mode: ABS (F4); BACKSPACE; CTRL-BREAK; DEL; ↵; ESC; GOTO (F5); GRAPH (F10); HELP (F1); INS; LEARN (ALT-F5) (when pressed to turn off the Learn feature); NAME (F3); STEP (ALT-F2); WINDOW (F6).

What Operations Can't You Undo?

1-2-3 only backs up the state of the 1-2-3 worksheet. Therefore, you can only undo operations that change the 1-2-3 worksheet or modify a 1-2-3 setting. 1-2-3 cannot undo the following operations:

- 1-2-3 commands that create, modify, or delete disk files or that initiate printer activity
- 1-2-3 commands that change the default directory
- 1-2-3 commands that attach and detach add-in programs
- / **S**ystem, as well as any operating system commands you perform while using / **S**ystem
- / **W**orksheet **G**lobal **D**efault **O**ther **H**elp when you change the Help access method
- 1-2-3 macros that cause no changes to worksheet data or settings

(For more details about the Undo feature, see Lab 2.)

The Help Facility

1-2-3 provides a series of Help screens that you can view any time during a 1-2-3 session by pressing HELP (F1). When you press HELP (F1), 1-2-3 enters HELP mode and displays a series of screens that describe 1-2-3. The 1-2-3 Help system is context-sensitive, which means that when you press HELP (F1), 1-2-3 displays a screen that describes what you are currently doing in the program.

Each Help screen includes a menu of additional Help topics. Use the pointer-movement keys to highlight the topic about which you want additional help, and press ↵. You can select as many screens as you need. When you finish using Help, press ESC to return to the worksheet at the same place you left it. (For more details about the Help facility, see Chapter 5 in Section 1 and Lab 1.)

2

Commands

In this chapter, command sequences for each procedure are printed in color in the left margin. The first letter of each command option is in boldface type, indicating that the option can be selected by typing the boldface letter. Settings and options for a procedure (as they appear on the submenu) are printed to the right of the command sequences in black typeface outlined in a colored rectangle. The first letter of each submenu option is in boldface type, again indicating that it can be selected by typing the boldface letter.

This chapter is divided into eleven sections. At the beginning of each section, a functional summary describes the tasks you can perform with each command, and a menu tree shows the command and its submenus. Then each section describes the commands in the order in which they appear on the menu. The sections are **W**orksheet commands, **R**ange commands, the **C**opy command, the **M**ove command, **F**ile commands, **P**rint commands, **G**raph commands, **D**ata commands, the **S**ystem command, **A**dd-in commands, and the **Q**uit command.

Using 1-2-3 Menus

To tell 1-2-3 what you want to do, you select a series of commands from menus. You can select commands by highlighting or by typing.

When you press / (slash) or < (less-than symbol) to display the 1-2-3 main menu, a rectangular highlight, called the menu pointer, appears in the second line of the control panel. You can select a command by moving the menu pointer to the command you want (highlighting it) and then pressing ↵ to select the command.

Selecting a command by typing is faster than the highlighting method. You will find this method useful once you are familiar with the commands in each 1-2-3 menu. When you press / (slash) or < (less-than symbol) to display the 1-2-3 main menu, you'll notice that each item in the menu begins with a different letter or character. You can type the first letter (uppercase or lowercase) of the command you want to select.

When selecting commands, if you change your mind or realize that you have made a mistake, press ESC to back up one menu level or one command step at a time.

If you want to completely stop a procedure and return to READY mode, press CTRL-BREAK.

Responding to Prompts

Often when you select a command, 1-2-3 requires you to supply more information. Sometimes you provide this information through additional menu choices. In many cases, however, 1-2-3 displays a prompt, or message, asking you to enter specific information in the second line of the control panel. You may have to supply this information in one of several ways:

- If 1-2-3 displays a menu of names (for example, when you select / **F**ile **R**etrieve or / **R**ange **N**ame **C**reate), move the menu pointer to the name you want to select and press ↵. Alternatively, type your selection and press ↵.
- If 1-2-3 suggests a response to the prompt (for example, when you select / **F**ile **S**ave to save changes to an existing worksheet), press ↵ to accept the suggested response. Alternatively, type a new response and press ↵. However, you may need to press ESC one or more times to clear the suggested response before you can type a new one.
- If 1-2-3 does not display a menu or suggest a response (for example, when you select / **P**rint **P**rinter **O**ptions **H**eader), type the necessary information and press ↵.

Settings Sheets

Some 1-2-3 commands, such as Graph, Data Query, or Worksheet Global, require you to select lower-level commands to specify a number of settings. In such cases, 1-2-3 displays a settings sheet. A settings sheet is a special status screen that helps you keep track of the choices you are making. It shows you the current settings for all the options associated with a task. You cannot directly change settings in the settings sheet. You must change settings by selecting the appropriate commands from the menu that appears above the settings sheet.

Worksheet Commands

1-2-3 has two types of **W**orksheet commands:

- Commands that affect the entire worksheet, called global settings
- Commands that affect specific parts of the worksheet

Figure 2.1 shows the Worksheet menu tree.

Worksheet Global Commands

When you create a new worksheet, 1-2-3 automatically makes certain choices for you. These choices are called default settings. 1-2-3 comes with initial default settings. However, you can use 1-2-3 commands to change these settings and establish your own default settings. **W**orksheet **G**lobal commands change settings for the entire worksheet. (See the section on **R**ange commands for information on changing the default settings for only parts of the worksheet.)

When you select / **W**orksheet **G**lobal, 1-2-3 displays the Global settings sheet. It shows you the current global settings, such as the recalculation method and column width, as well as information about available memory and circular references. When you change settings by making selections from the Worksheet Global menu, the settings sheet reflects the changes.

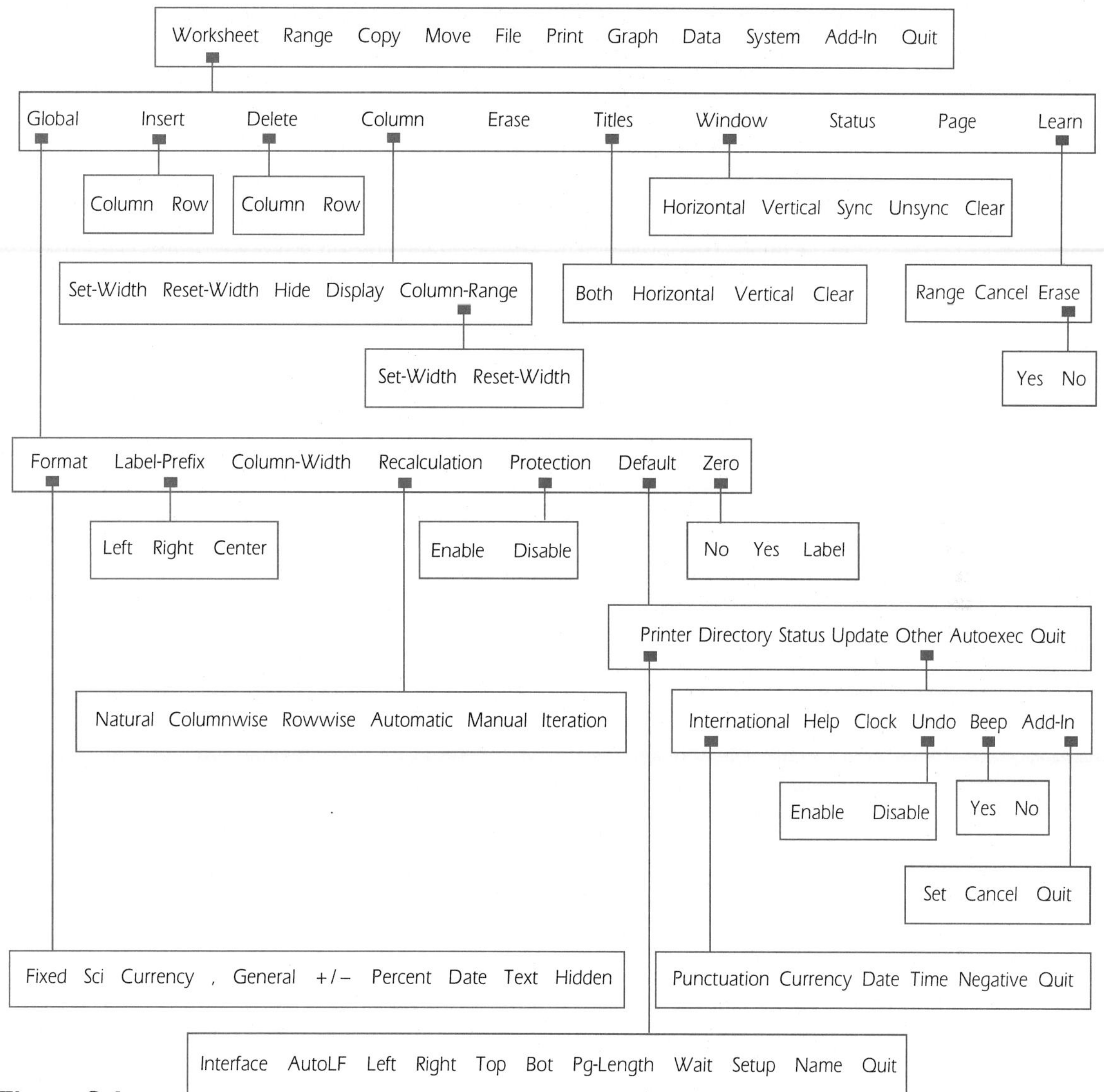

Figure 2.1

/ **W**orksheet **G**lobal **F**ormat

Fixed **S**ci **C**urrency **,** **G**eneral **+**/- **P**ercent **D**ate **T**ext **H**idden

/ **Worksheet Global Format** sets the way numeric values are displayed for the entire worksheet. It does not affect the data itself. Labels are unaffected by the command.

If you choose **Fixed**, **Sci**, **Currency**, **,** (comma), or **Percent**, you must specify the number of decimal places. Press ↵ to accept the default setting of 2 or type a different number (0–15) and press ↵.

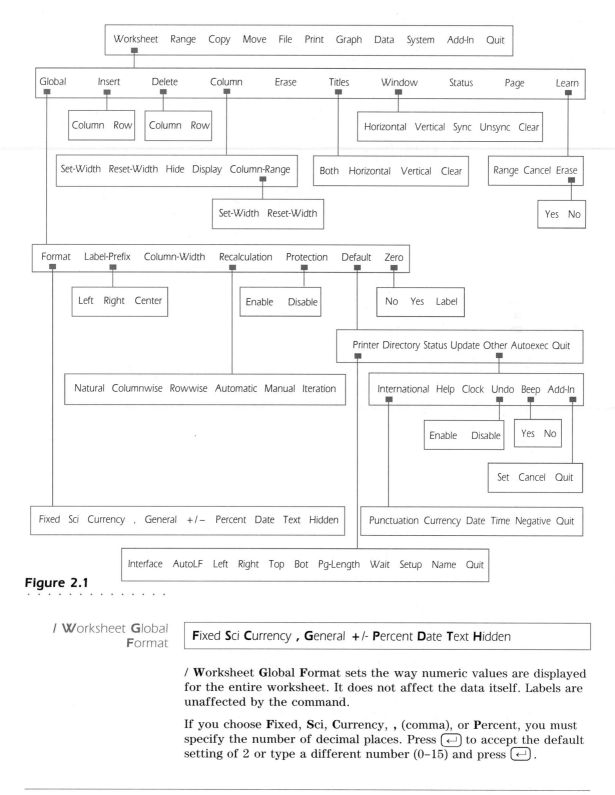

If you choose **D**ate, select one of the five date formats, or select **T**ime and one of the four time formats.

In date formats, a positive number (rounded off to an integer) is defined as the serial number of a date from 1 (1 January 1900) to 73050 (31 December 2099). Use the @DATE and @NOW functions to generate these serial numbers.

In time formats, fractional parts of serial numbers represent time (.000 = midnight, .5 = noon, 15/24 = 3:00 PM, and so on). Use @TIME and @NOW to generate these serial numbers.

See Table 2.7, in the Range Commands section in this chapter, for a description of each format.

If a value's formatted display does not fit within its column width, asterisks appear in the cell. 1-2-3 retains values with a precision of fifteen decimal places, regardless of format. (For more details about global formats, see Lab 5.)

/ **W**orksheet **G**lobal **L**abel-Prefix

Left **R**ight **C**enter

/ **W**orksheet **G**lobal **L**abel-Prefix sets the alignment of labels for the entire worksheet. Labels can be left-aligned, right-aligned, or centered.

The default label alignment is **L**eft. All labels subsequently entered into the worksheet without a label-prefix character are aligned according to the alignment set with this command. This command does not affect existing label entries.

You can override the global label alignment setting either by using / **R**ange **L**abel after you enter a label or by typing a label prefix as the first character in a label you are entering.

/ **W**orksheet **G**lobal **C**olumn-Width

/ **W**orksheet **G**lobal **C**olumn-Width sets the width for all worksheet columns, except those whose widths have been individually set with / **W**orksheet **C**olumn **S**et-Width or / **W**orksheet **C**olumn **C**olumn-Range **S**et-Width.

Column width can be from 1 to 240 characters. Initially, the default setting is 9. Use [→] or [←] to increase or decrease the width (the screen displays the effect of each change) or enter a number. (For more details about global column width settings, see Lab 2.)

/ **W**orksheet **G**lobal **R**ecalculation

Natural **C**olumnwise **R**owwise **A**utomatic **M**anual **I**teration

/ **W**orksheet **G**lobal **R**ecalculation controls when, in what order, and how many times formulas in the worksheet are recalculated. (See Table 2.1.)

Table 2.1

Menu Item	Description
To Change in What Order 1-2-3 Recalculates Formulas	
Natural	Before recalculating a particular formula, 1-2-3 recalculates any other formulas that it depends on. For example, if the formula in cell B7 depends on the formula in cell C28, 1-2-3 recalculates the formula in C28 before it calculates the one in B7. This is the initial default order of recalculation.
Columnwise	1-2-3 begins recalculating at the top of column A and proceeds to the bottom of the column. It then recalculates columns B, C, and so on.
Rowwise	1-2-3 begins recalculating at the beginning of row 1 and proceeds to the end of the row. It then recalculates rows 2, 3, and so on.
To Change When 1-2-3 Recalculates Formulas	
Automatic	1-2-3 recalculates any formulas that are affected each time you change the contents of a cell. Automatic is the default setting.
Manual	1-2-3 recalculates formulas only when you press CALC (F9). The CALC indicator appears in the lower right corner of the screen whenever any cell entries have changed since the last recalculation. Press CALC (F9) when you want to update the worksheet.
To Change How Many Times 1-2-3 Recalculates Formulas	
Iteration	Sets the number of times (1 through 50) 1-2-3 recalculates formulas when the recalculation method is set to Columnwise or Rowwise, or when recalculation is set to Natural and there is a circular reference. The default setting is 1. This setting has no effect if recalculation is set to Natural and there are no circular references.

Use **Manual** recalculation when 1-2-3 takes a long time to calculate a large or complex worksheet or to speed up macro execution. Use the **C**olumnwise or **R**owwise order only when you have constructed a worksheet in which you need to control the recalculation order explicitly. Whenever the recalculation is **N**atural, 1-2-3 calculates only formulas that are affected by a change in the worksheet. This is called minimal recalculation; there is no way to turn it on or off. If you change the recalculation order to a setting other than **N**atural, 1-2-3 does not use minimal recalculation and will recalculate all the formulas in the worksheet when you make a change. The initial default setting for recalculation order is **N**atural.

Note There are several @functions that 1-2-3 always recalculates—even when minimal recalculation is in effect—because their values may change even if you do not modify the worksheet: @@, @CELL, @CELLPOINTER, @DATEVALUE, @ISAAF, @ISAPP, @NOW, @RAND, @STRING, @TIMEVALUE, @VALUE.

/ **W**orksheet **G**lobal **P**rotection

Enable **D**isable

/ **W**orksheet **G**lobal **P**rotection works in conjunction with / **R**ange **P**rot and / **R**ange **U**nprot to prevent changes to particular cells.

When the protection facility is turned on with / **W**orksheet **G**lobal **P**rotection **E**nable, you cannot make changes to any cells in the worksheet. A PR appears on the control panel for protected cells when protection is enabled.

To make changes to cell entries after the protection facility has been turned on, use / **R**ange **U**nprot. A U appears in the control panel to identify unprotected cells when protection is enabled.

While protection is enabled, you cannot delete columns or rows that include protected cells. Protected cells whose contents you have hidden using / **R**ange **F**ormat **H**idden cannot be changed to make them visible. You can, however, erase the entire worksheet with the / **W**orksheet **E**rase command when protection is enabled. Choosing **D**isable turns off global protection and allows you to change any cell entry, even if it has been protected with / **R**ange **P**rot.

/ **W**orksheet **G**lobal **D**efault

Printer **D**irectory **S**tatus **U**pdate **O**ther **A**utoexec **Q**uit

The / **W**orksheet **G**lobal **D**efault commands allow you to specify certain settings for 1-2-3 to load when starting the program. Figure 2.2 shows the / **W**orksheet **G**lobal **D**efault menu tree.

With these commands, you can establish your own default settings for any of the following:

- Type of printer and its connection, as well as the printed page format
- Directory that 1-2-3 automatically uses when searching for files
- International and clock display formats
- Method of using the Help facility
- Auto-executed macros and auto-attached add-ins

These settings are preset in 1-2-3. You can change these settings and establish your own defaults for future sessions by using the / **W**orksheet **G**lobal **D**efault **U**pdate command.

When you select / **W**orksheet **G**lobal **D**efault, 1-2-3 displays the Default settings sheet, which shows the current default settings, such as the default directory and printer.

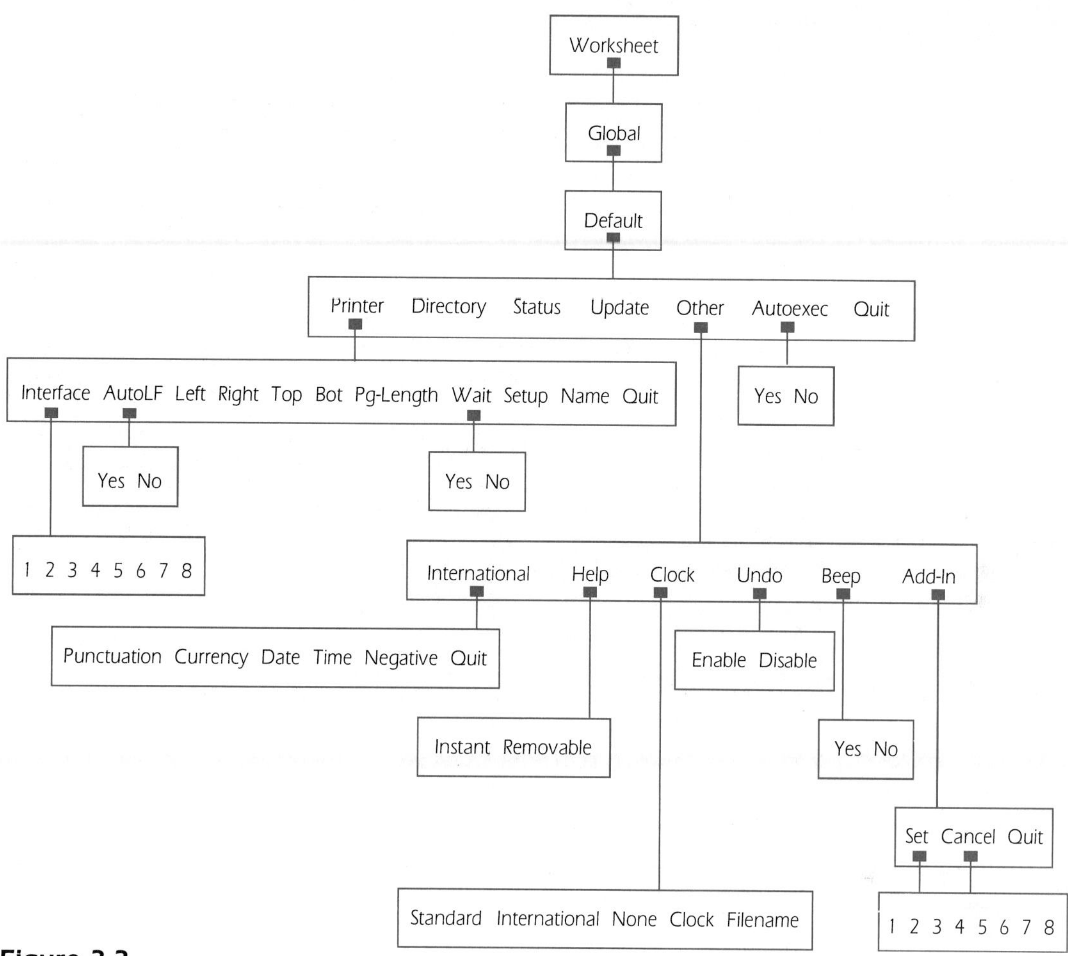

Figure 2.2

/ Worksheet Global Default Printer

Interface **A**utoLF **L**eft **R**ight **T**op **B**ot **P**g-Length **W**ait **S**etup **N**ame **Q**uit

/ **Worksheet Global Default Printer** specifies the default printer and interface settings and the default settings for printed pages.

The initial default settings supplied by 1-2-3 are shown in Table 2.2.

Table 2.2

Menu Item	Description	Choices
Interface	Specifies the connection between 1-2-3 and your printer. Computers send data to a printer through parallel or serial interfaces. You must configure 1-2-3 to work with your specific type of printer interface. If you select a serial interface, you must also supply a baud rate (speed of transmission) and set your printer to 8 bits, no parity, and 1 stop bit (except 2 stop bits at 110 baud). Choices 5 through 8 refer to devices accessed through DOS on a local area network.	(1) Parallel 1 (default) (2) Serial 1 (3) Parallel 2 (4) Serial 2 (5) DOS Device LPT1 (6) DOS Device LPT2 (7) DOS Device LPT3 (8) DOS Device LPT4
AutoLF	Specifies whether your printer automatically issues a linefeed after a carriage return. To test this for your printer, print a range of 2 or more rows. If the printing is double spaced, set AutoLF to Yes; if the paper does not advance, set AutoLF to No.	Yes No (default)
Left	Sets left margin (number of spaces) on printed page.	0–240 (default is 4)
Right	Sets right margin (number of spaces) on printed page.	0–240 (default is 76)
Top	Sets top margin (number of lines) on printed page.	0–32 (default is 2)
Bot	Sets bottom margin (number of lines) on printed page.	0–32 (default is 2)
Pg-Length	Sets length (number of lines) of printed page.	1–100 (default is 66)
Wait	Allows you to insert a pause at the end of each printed page to change paper in single-sheet feed printers.	Yes No (default)
Setup	Specifies a string of blank control characters to be sent to your printer before printing begins (some printers need to be initialized). The default setting is blank for no setup string. (See the printer control codes in your printer manual for a description of how to enter setup strings.)	
Name	Specifies which printer to use. If you selected more than one text printer when you installed 1-2-3, a list of the printers appears when you choose this menu item.	The default is the first printer you selected when installing 1-2-3.
Quit	Returns you to the **/ W**orksheet **G**lobal **D**efault menu.	

/ Worksheet Global Default Directory

/ **W**orksheet **G**lobal **D**efault **D**irectory specifies the directory that 1-2-3 will automatically search (when you retrieve a file) and write to (when you save a file) if you do not specify a directory.

1-2-3 initially uses the root directory in drive A as the default directory. If necessary, press ESC to clear the current directory before entering the new directory.

If you execute the command and clear the existing setting without providing a new directory, 1-2-3 uses the directory that was current when you started the program.

You can always override the default directory by typing in a directory when you specify a file with the **F**ile commands. See Section 1, ''Getting Started,'' for details on changing the default directory in 1-2-3 and PrintGraph.

/ Worksheet Global Default Status

/ **W**orksheet **G**lobal **D**efault **S**tatus displays the current settings established by the other **W**orksheet **G**lobal **D**efault commands.

The settings are only displayed in the status screen and cannot be changed here. Press any key to clear continue. To clear the status screen and to return to the worksheet, choose **Q**uit. Use the other **W**orksheet **G**lobal **D**efault commands to change the settings.

/ Worksheet Global Default Update

/ **W**orksheet **G**lobal **D**efault **U**pdate saves the current settings established by the other **W**orksheet **G**lobal **D**efault commands in a configuration file (123.CNF). This file is read by 1-2-3 each time you start a session, and the settings take effect automatically. If you have changed some settings and want to save them for future sessions, you must select / **W**orksheet **G**lobal **D**efault **U**pdate, which will save the changes in the 123.CNF file.

After starting 1-2-3 from a removable disk, verify that the disk containing the 1-2-3 program is in the drive and that the disk's write-protect tab is removed before you execute the **U**pdate command. When 1-2-3 cannot find the configuration file in the drive it was started from, it creates a new file on the disk currently in that drive.

/ Worksheet Global Default Other International

Punctuation **C**urrency **D**ate **T**ime **N**egative **Q**uit

/ **W**orksheet **G**lobal **D**efault **O**ther **I**nternational sets a variety of display formats for numeric punctuation, currency, date, time, and negative number display. Choose **Q**uit to return to the previous menu.

Table 2.3 describes the options for this command.

Table 2.3

Menu Item	Description	Choices
Punctuation	Specifies which characters 1-2-3 uses as the point and thousands separators on numbers and as the argument separator in @functions and macro keywords. The eight settings (A through H) provide fixed combinations of period, comma, and space separators and are listed in the order of decimal point separator, argument separator, and thousands separator.	(A)(.,,) (initial) (B) (,..) (C) (.;,) (D) (,;.) (E) (.,) (F) (,.) (G) (.;) (H) (,;)
Currency	Specifies the alphanumeric sequence to use as the currency sign. It also specifies whether the currency sign precedes or follows the value. You can use any Lotus International Character Set (LICS) character.	Alphanumeric sequence (initially $) preceding value
Date	Specifies the international date format setting (D4 and D5). The D4 format setting displays month, day, and year; D5 displays only month and day. 1-2-3 uses the D4 setting when it displays the date at the bottom of the screen if Clock is set to International. This setting affects how you enter the argument for @DATEVALUE. If you use this @function with either of the international formats, you must use the form specified here.	(A) MM/DD/YY (initial) (B) DD/MM/YY (C) DD.MM.YY (D) YY-MM-DD
Time	Specifies the international time format settings (D8 and D9). The D8 format setting includes hours, minutes, and seconds; D9 includes only hours and minutes. All the international time formats are 24-hour, instead of 12-hour. 1-2-3 uses the D9 setting when it displays the time at the bottom of the screen if Clock is set to International. This setting affects how you enter the argument for @TIMEVALUE. If you use this @function with either of the international formats, you must use the form specified here.	(A) HH:MM:SS (initial) (B) HH.MM.SS (C) HH,MM,SS (D) HHhMMmSSs
Negative	Specifies whether 1-2-3 uses parentheses (default) or a minus sign for negative values in cells formatted as Comma or Currency.	Parenthesis or Sign
Quit	Returns you to the Worksheet Global Default menu.	

/ **W**orksheet **G**lobal **D**efault **O**ther **H**elp

Instant **R**emovable

/ **W**orksheet **G**lobal **D**efault **O**ther **H**elp specifies the way 1-2-3 accesses the Help facility.

If you choose **I**nstant, 1-2-3 opens the Help file when you press the Help function key, (F1), and the file remains open throughout the session. When you press (F1) again, 1-2-3 reads the file instantly. Do *not* remove the disk that contains the Help facility. Use **I**nstant if the Help facility is on a fixed (hard) disk.

If you choose **R**emovable, 1-2-3 closes the Help file when you leave the Help facility. Use **R**emovable if the Help file is on a removable disk. This is the initial setting.

/ **W**orksheet **G**lobal **D**efault **O**ther **C**lock

Standard **I**nternational **N**one **C**lock **F**ilename

/ **W**orksheet **G**lobal **D**efault **O**ther **C**lock specifies the format in which the date and time are displayed in the lower left corner of the screen.

If you select **S**tandard, 1-2-3 displays the date in standard long format (DD-MM-YY) and the time in standard short format (HH:MM AM/PM). This is the initial setting.

If you select **I**nternational, 1-2-3 displays the date in the long international format (D4) and the time in the short international format (D9).

If you select **N**one, the date and time are not displayed on the screen.

If you select **C**lock, the date and time are displayed in the most recently selected format—Standard, International, or None.

If you select **F**ilename, the filename is displayed if the current worksheet has been retrieved from or saved in a file.

/ **W**orksheet **G**lobal **D**efault **O**ther **U**ndo

Enable **D**isable

/ **W**orksheet **G**lobal **D**efault **O**ther **U**ndo lets you turn the Undo feature on and off. When the Undo feature is on, you can press the Undo function key (ALT-(F4)) to cancel any changes made to the worksheet since 1-2-3 was last in READY mode.

Choosing **E**nable turns on the Undo feature. Choosing **D**isable turns off the Undo feature.

Note You may not be able to enable Undo if you have a very large worksheet or an add-in in memory.

/ Worksheet Global Default Other Beep

Yes **N**o

/ **W**orksheet **G**lobal **D**efault **O**ther **B**eep lets you control whether 1-2-3 sounds the computer bell when errors occur and when executing {BEEP} commands in a macro.

If you choose **Y**es, 1-2-3 will sound the bell. If you choose **N**o, 1-2-3 will not sound the bell.

/ Worksheet Global Default Other Add-In

Set **C**ancel **Q**uit

/ **W**orksheet **G**lobal **D**efault **O**ther **A**dd-In lets you configure 1-2-3 so that it automatically attaches an add-in program whenever you start 1-2-3. You can specify up to eight auto-attach add-ins. You can also specify whether you want 1-2-3 to automatically invoke an add-in as well.

Choosing **S**et sets an auto-attach add-in and attaches the add-in. 1-2-3 displays a menu of files with an .ADN extension in the directory from which you started 1-2-3. Choosing **C**ancel cancels an auto-attach add-in and detaches the add-in. Choosing **Q**uit returns you to the Worksheet Global Default menu.

/ Worksheet Global Default Autoexec

Yes **N**o

/ **W**orksheet **G**lobal **D**efault **A**utoexec lets you tell 1-2-3 whether to run autoexec macros, macros named \0 (zero), when it retrieves a file that contains one.

Choosing **Y**es automatically executes macros named \0 (zero). Choosing **N**o does not automatically execute macros named \0 (zero).

/ Worksheet Global Zero

No **Y**es **L**abel

/ **W**orksheet **G**lobal **Z**ero specifies whether values of zero are displayed on the screen.

Choosing **N**o displays zero values. The default is **N**o.

Choosing **Y**es suppresses the display of zero values whether they were entered as numbers or are the results of formulas. Though hidden, the values are still stored in the worksheet and displayed in the control panel.

Choosing **L**abel displays a label in cells whose value is zero. You must specify the label to be used in place of the zero. 1-2-3 displays the contents of those cells in the control panel.

CAUTION If you suppress the display of zeros, 1-2-3 can write over cells. To prevent writing over hidden data, enable **W**orksheet **G**lobal **P**rotection or **R**ange **P**rot.

Specific Worksheet Commands

/ **W**orksheet **I**nsert

Column **R**ow

/ **W**orksheet **I**nsert adds blank rows and columns in the worksheet. You will be prompted to specify the range, or else highlight the number of rows or columns you want to insert.

(For more details about inserting rows or columns, see Lab 2.)

When you insert rows or columns, existing rows or columns move down or over to make room for the new rows or columns, and 1-2-3 adjusts any formulas so that they continue to refer to the same data. If you insert rows or columns into a named range or a range that appears in a formula, the size of the range increases. Inserted rows or columns assume the global formats and column width of the worksheet.

/ **W**orksheet **D**elete

Column **R**ow

/ **W**orksheet **D**elete permanently removes entire rows or columns from the worksheet.

You will be prompted to specify the range of rows or columns you want to delete. (For more details about deleting rows or columns, see Lab 2.)

All columns to the right of a deleted column shift to the left, and all rows below a deleted row shift up. Deletions inside ranges make the range smaller. Deleting a corner of a range invalidates the range.

Formulas that refer to a deleted cell or to a range with a deleted corner now have the value ERR. 1-2-3 adjusts all other formulas and named ranges so that they continue to refer to the same data.

CAUTION / **W**orksheet **D**elete permanently deletes rows and columns from the worksheet. To avoid possible data loss, be sure these rows or columns do not contain important data. If you make a mistake and the Undo feature is on, press UNDO (ALT-F4) immediately to restore the worksheet to its original state.

/ Worksheet Column

Set-Width **R**eset-Width **H**ide **D**isplay **C**olumn-Range

/ **Worksheet Column** changes the width of one or more columns, hides and redisplays columns, or resets columns to the global column width. Table 2.4 describes the options for this command.

Table 2.4

Menu Item	Description
Set-Width	Changes the column width of the column that contains the cell pointer. The current column width appears on the control panel after the prompt. Use (←) or (→) to increase or decrease the width or type a number from 1 to 240 and then press (↵).
Reset-Width	Restores the global column width (initially nine spaces) for the column that contains the cell pointer.
Hide	Hides one or more columns without permanently erasing the data. Use (→) or (←) to highlight the column(s) you want to hide and press (↵). You can specify a range if you want to hide more than one adjacent column.
Display	Redisplays hidden columns. All the hidden columns appear with asterisks beside the column letter. Move the cell pointer to the column you want to redisplay and press (↵). You can specify a range if you want to redisplay more than one adjacent column.
Column-Range	Changes the column width of a range of adjacent columns (overriding the global default column width) or resets a range of columns to the global default column width (initially nine spaces).

Use / **W**orksheet **C**olumn **S**et-Width if a cell displays asterisks because it is too narrow for the values it contains.

(For more details about setting column widths, see Lab 2. For more details about hiding columns, see Lab 5.)

/ Worksheet Erase

No **Y**es

/ **Worksheet Erase** removes the current worksheet from the screen and memory and gives you a blank worksheet. If you want to keep the current worksheet, save it in a file before you use / **W**orksheet **E**rase.

If you choose **N**o, 1-2-3 returns to READY mode without erasing the worksheet. If you choose **Y**es, 1-2-3 erases the worksheet. (For more details about erasing a worksheet, see Lab 1.)

/ **W**orksheet **T**itles

Both **H**orizontal **V**ertical **C**lear

/ **W**orksheet **T**itles freezes rows or columns along the top or left edge of the screen so that they remain in view as you scroll the worksheet.

Before initiating the command sequence, position the cell pointer one row below the rows you want to freeze, one column to the right of the columns you want to freeze, or below and to the right of the rows and columns you want to freeze.

Both freezes the rows above and the columns to the left of the cell pointer. **H**orizontal freezes the rows above the cell pointer. **V**ertical freezes the columns to the left of the cell pointer. **C**lear unfreezes all existing titles. (For more details about freezing titles, see Lab 6.)

/ **W**orksheet **W**indow

Horizontal **V**ertical **S**ync **U**nsync **C**lear

/ **W**orksheet **W**indow divides the screen into two horizontal or vertical windows. You can use each window to see a different part of the worksheet.

If you are creating a window, move the cell pointer to the row you want to use as the top edge of the second window or to the column you want to use as the left edge of the second window, then initiate the command sequence. Table 2.5 describes the options for this command.

When you create a second window it displays the same part of the worksheet as the first window. Press WINDOW (F6) to move the cell pointer to the second window, and then use the pointer-movement keys to view a specific area of the worksheet. (For more details about creating and using windows, see Lab 6.)

Table 2.5

Menu Item	Description
Horizontal	Creates two windows with the screen split horizontally
Vertical	Creates two windows with the screen split vertically
Sync	For horizontal windows, if one window scrolls horizontally, the other also scrolls, keeping the same columns on the screen in both windows; for vertical windows, if one window scrolls vertically, the other also scrolls, keeping the same rows on the screen in both windows. This is the default setting.
Unsync	Windows scroll independently in all directions
Clear	Removes a second window from the screen

With horizontal or vertical windows, all commands that change the worksheet display affect both windows, except for / **W**orksheet **C**olumn, / **W**orksheet **G**lobal **C**olumn-Width, and / **W**orksheet **T**itles, which affect only the current window.

When you clear horizontal or vertical windows, 1-2-3 uses the titles, global and individual column width settings, and hidden or displayed columns of the top or left window.

/ **W**orksheet **S**tatus

/ **W**orksheet **S**tatus displays information about memory use, recalculation, global settings, circular references, and cell display formats.

When selected, the worksheet status information appears in a status screen, temporarily replacing the current worksheet. The mode indicator displays STAT. Press any key to return to your worksheet when you finish looking at the information in the status screen. (See Table 2.6.)

Circular reference displays the address of a cell where the formula refers to the cell itself. If you eliminate the circular reference in the cell, select / **W**orksheet **S**tatus again to see if another cell has a circular reference. The status screen can display only one circular reference at a time. (For more details about circular references and the status window, see Lab 5.)

Table 2.6

Status Display	Sample Settings
Conventional memory:	47994 of 350848 Bytes (13%)
Expanded memory:	(None)
Math coprocessor:	8087
Recalculation:	
Method	Automatic
Order	Natural
Iterations	1
Circular reference:	(None)
Cell display:	
Format	(G)
Label prefix	'
Column width	9
Zero suppression	No
Global protection	Disabled

/ **W**orksheet **P**age

/ **W**orksheet **P**age inserts a page break into a worksheet. When you print the worksheet, a new page begins at the page break.

Move the cell pointer to the leftmost column of the range you want to print and the row where you want the page to begin. Then initiate the command sequence. 1-2-3 inserts a row that contains :: (page-break symbol) in the current cell and moves the remaining rows down, adjusting cell and range addresses in formulas and redefining named ranges. To remove a page break symbol, use / **R**ange **E**rase or / **W**orksheet **D**elete **R**ow.

/ **W**orksheet **L**earn

Range **C**ancel **E**rase

/ **W**orksheet **L**earn provides an alternative method of entering macro instructions. Instead of typing the macro instructions, you perform the task that you want to automate.

Once you specify a learn range and turn on the Learn feature with the Learn key (ALT-F5), 1-2-3 translates your keystrokes into macro instructions and records them in the learn range. 1-2-3 continues recording the keystrokes you make until you turn off the Learn feature by pressing the Learn key (ALT-F5) again or until you fill the learn range. You then name the macro as you would any other macro. When you run the macro, 1-2-3 automatically executes the instructions recorded in the learn range.

For more information about the Learn feature, see Chapter 3, ''Macros'' and Lab 9.

Selecting **R**ange specifies the learn range where 1-2-3 will store macro instructions. Selecting **C**ancel cancels the currently specified learn range. Selecting **E**rase clears the contents of all cells in the currently specified learn range without cancelling the learn range.

Range Commands

The **R**ange commands manipulate ranges of cells. A range is any rectangular block of cells. It can be a single cell, a single row, a single column, or parts of several rows and columns. Figure 2.3 shows the Range menu tree.

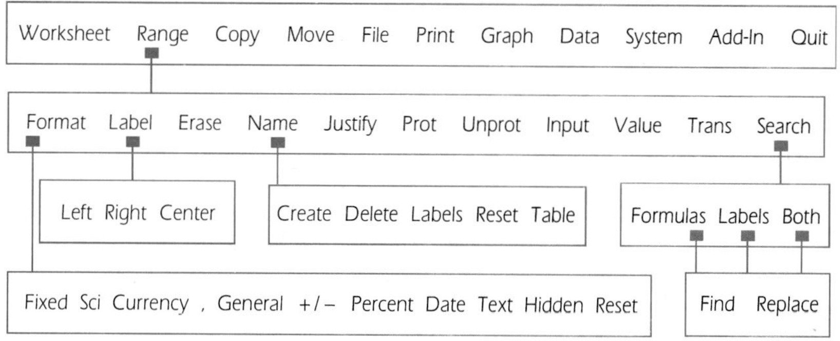

Figure 2.3

/ **R**ange **F**ormat

Fixed **S**ci **C**urrency **,** **G**eneral **+**/- **P**ercent **D**ate **T**ext **H**idden **R**eset

/ **R**ange **F**ormat sets the cell format for a range of cells, overriding the global cell format. The cell format determines the appearance of numbers but does not affect the display of labels.

- The cell format changes the appearance of numbers, not their actual value. You may, for example, choose to display a number without its decimal places. However, 1-2-3 still stores the number with its decimal places for calculations.
- A cell format you choose with / **R**ange **F**ormat overrides the global default cell format in which numbers automatically appear. (The default cell format is initially **G**eneral, but you can change the default with / **W**orksheet **G**lobal **F**ormat.) Changing the format has no effect on the way you enter numbers.
- A cell format affects the appearance of numbers and formula values but has no effect on labels unless you choose the **H**idden format. You can hide any kind of cell entry with the **H**idden format.
- To use date and time formats, you must first generate serial numbers that represent dates and times. You produce serial numbers with @functions (@DATE, @DATEVALUE, @TIME, @TIMEVALUE, and @NOW). (See Chapter 4, "@Functions.")
- Global default settings determine certain date and time formats. You can set these defaults with the / **W**orksheet **G**lobal **D**efault **O**ther **I**nternational command. Global default settings also determine the currency sign and its position and the separator used to separate thousands. You can set these defaults with the / **W**orksheet **G**lobal **D**efault **O**ther **I**nternational command.

Table 2.7 describes the command options.

Table 2.7

Menu Item	Description	Examples
Fixed	Constant number of decimal places (0 to 15). Displays a minus sign for negatives. Leading zero integers always appear.	12 −125.00 0.567
Sci	Scientific (exponential) notation with a specified number of decimal places (0 to 15) in the multiplier. Exponent of 10 from −99 to +99.	−4.3E+1.2E+01 1.245E+22 6.24E−24

Table 2.7 Continued

Menu Item	Description	Examples
Currency	Displays numbers with a currency symbol. Separator between thousands. Negative values displayed with a minus sign or in parentheses. Leading zero integers always appear. Decimal places (0 to 15).	$12.43 ($4.25) −.246 $8.999 $0.67
, (comma)	Separators between thousands. Negative values displayed with a minus sign or in parentheses. Leading zero integers always appear. Decimal places (0 to 15).	8,999.00 (15,000) −15,000 0.55
General	Trailing zeros suppressed (after decimal pointer). Leading zero integers always appear. No thousands separator. Negative values displayed with a minus sign. This is the default numeric format. Very large and very small numbers appear in scientific (exponent) format.	12.427 0.45 −4.25 1.3E+12 2E−07
+/−	Horizontal bar graph. Each symbol equals one integer. Symbols: + for positive values, − for negative values, . for zero and values between −1 and +1. Limited by column width.	+ + + − − −
Percent	Percentage, with specified number of decimal places (0 to 15). Displays the value times 100, followed by a percent sign.	1242.7% −4.25%
Date	1 DD-MMM-YY 2 DD-MMM 3 MMM-YY 4 MM/DD/YY (long international) 5 MM/DD (short international)	06-Jan-90 06-Jan Jan-90 01/06/90 01/06
Time	1 HH:MM:SS AM/PM 2 HH:MM AM/PM 3 HH:MM:SS 24-hour (long international) 4 HH:MM 24-hour (short international)	12:03:14 PM 04:23 AM 14:05:10 14:05
Text	Formulas (not their values) appear as entered; any numbers in the range appear in general format.	12.427 +C22/4
Hidden	Contents of the specified range do not appear on the screen although they still exist.	
Reset	Restores global cell format for specified range. Redisplays all or part of hidden range of cells.	

When the cell pointer is on a cell that you have formatted, the first letter of the format name and the number of decimal places you chose appear in parentheses before the cell contents on the control panel. For example, (C0) means Currency format with 0 decimal places.

If a formatted number has too many characters to fit in a cell, 1-2-3 displays asterisks in the cell space instead of the number. Asterisks indicate that the column width is too narrow for the number to be displayed. To remove the asterisks and redisplay the number, widen the column with / **W**orksheet **C**olumn **S**et-Width or / **W**orksheet **G**lobal **C**olumn-Width. However, if the format of the cell is General, 1-2-3 will display the number in scientific notation.

A cell retains the numeric format that you assign it with / **R**ange **F**ormat even if you subsequently erase its contents with / **R**ange **E**rase.

If you move the contents of a range that you have formatted, the moved data retain their numeric format. The area you moved the range from, however, reverts to the default numeric format.

If you copy formatted cells, 1-2-3 copies cell formats with the date.

(For more details about formatting ranges, see Lab 5.)

/ **R**ange **L**abel

Left **R**ight **C**enter

/ **R**ange **L**abel aligns existing labels in a range of cells. 1-2-3 can position labels at the left edge, the right edge, or in the center of cells in a range. You cannot "preformat" a range before entering labels in it; / **R**ange **L**abel affects only existing labels and has no effect on numbers, which are always right-aligned.

1-2-3 displays all the labels in the specified range according to the alignment you selected. Any labels you subsequently enter in this range, however, are unaffected by the alignment you chose.

/ **R**ange **E**rase

/ **R**ange **E**rase removes the contents of cells in a range. Before you use this command, be sure you do not need the data. If necessary, first save the worksheet with / **F**ile **S**ave.

1-2-3 erases the data from the specified range, leaving the cells blank. / **R**ange **E**rase does not affect the cell format and protection status of the cells in the range. (For more details about erasing ranges, see Lab 2.)

/ **R**ange **N**ame **C**reate

/ **R**ange **N**ame **C**reate names a range or redefines the cells that an existing range name refers to. Range names are useful when you frequently refer to the same range of data (or even to a single cell). Instead of constantly highlighting the range on the screen or typing its address, you can just type the name you have assigned to the range.

A range name can be up to fifteen characters long. To prevent confusion when using range names in formulas, avoid including spaces and arithmetic operators (+ or *) in a range name. Also avoid names that look like cell addresses, such as P12. Do not begin a range name with a number. 1-2-3 does not distinguish between uppercase and lowercase letters.

To change the cells an existing range name refers to or to view the current location of a named range, select a name from the menu of range names.

If you are just viewing the range, press (↵) to get back to READY mode; otherwise, specify the range you are naming or whose definition you are changing.

If you move data or insert or delete columns or rows so that either the upper left or lower right corner of a named range is affected, 1-2-3 modifies the named range.

If you are unsure of the name you assigned when 1-2-3 requests a range, press NAME ((F3)) to see a list of range names you have assigned and select the one you want.

When writing a macro, name the macro by assigning a range name to the first cell in the range that contains the macro.

1-2-3 saves range names as part of the worksheet when you save the worksheet with / **F**ile **S**ave. (For more details about naming ranges, see Lab 5.)

/ **R**ange **N**ame **D**elete

/ **R**ange **N**ame **D**elete removes a range name but leaves the contents of the range unchanged.

1-2-3 deletes the name that you type or select from the menu. You can no longer use this name in formulas or in commands requiring a range specification. If a formula previously used this name, however, it continues to refer to the same cells by cell address rather than by name.

/ **R**ange **N**ame **L**abels

Right **D**own **L**eft **U**p

/ **R**ange **N**ame **L**abels names single-cell ranges, using existing labels located in adjacent cells for the range names.

When you have labels that can serve as range names next to the cells you want to name, / **R**ange **N**ame **L**abels is useful. You can use / **R**ange **N**ame **L**abels to assign names to the fields of the first record of a database. 1-2-3 does not assign numbers as range names and uses only the first fifteen characters of a label for the range name.

Position the cell pointer on one of the corner cells in a range of labels you want to use, then initiate the command sequence. Choose **R**ight, **D**own, **L**eft, or **U**p, depending on the direction of the cells you are naming in relation to the labels, then specify the range of labels you are using to name the adjacent cells.

1-2-3 names each cell in the direction you indicated with the corresponding label in the cell in the range you specified.

If a label you used to name a range duplicates an existing range name, 1-2-3 erases the previous range address and uses the new cell address. 1-2-3 does not warn you of this change. If a formula referred to the named range as it was previously defined, refer to the new range.

/ **R**ange **N**ame **R**eset

/ **R**ange **N**ame **R**eset deletes all the range names in a worksheet but leaves the contents of the worksheet as they were. Formulas that used range names continue to refer to the same ranges but by range addresses rather than by range names.

CAUTION / **R**ange **N**ame **R**eset deletes all range names from the worksheet, also disabling named macros, so be sure you want to delete all of them before you use this command. To delete individual range names, use / **R**ange **N**ame **D**elete.

/ **R**ange **N**ame **T**able

/ **R**ange **N**ame **T**able lists alphabetically all the range names and their corresponding addresses in a two-column table in the worksheet.

When specifying the range for the table, only the upper left corner cell of the range needs to be entered. 1-2-3 will use as many rows as needed below this cell to display all the range names in the worksheet.

CAUTION Be sure you specify the range for the table in an empty part of the worksheet; otherwise, the table writes over any data in the range. If you make a mistake when creating a range name table and the Undo feature is on, press UNDO (ALT-F4) immediately to restore the worksheet to its original state.

If you name additional ranges or change the definition of existing ones, you must create another table with / **R**ange **N**ame **T**able to see the current status of range names.

/ **R**ange **J**ustify

/ **R**ange **J**ustify treats a continuous column of text as a paragraph, rearranging the words so that none of the lines is longer than a specified width.

You can use / **R**ange **J**ustify if you want the words in a series of long labels to appear on the screen at the same time or to be printed within specific margins. For / **R**ange **J**ustify to work, the long labels must all start in the same column and appear in consecutive rows. The first nonlabel cell in the column signifies the end of the "paragraph."

Position the cell pointer at the first cell in the column of labels you want to justify, then issue the command sequence. You will be prompted to specify a single-row or multiple-row range of the width you want the text to occupy.

When you specify a single-row range, 1-2-3 justifies the labels in consecutive rows of the first column of the range down to the first non-label cell in the column. If the justified labels occupy more rows than the original labels, 1-2-3 moves down any subsequent data in the column (data below the justified labels). If the justified labels occupy fewer rows than the original labels, 1-2-3 moves up any subsequent data. Use a single-row justify range only if all cells below the labels you are justifying are blank or if movement of data below the labels is acceptable.

If you specify a multiple-row range, 1-2-3 restricts the justification to the exact area you have specified. If you do not specify an area large enough for the labels you are trying to justify, you will get an error message.

After the justification, the width of the specified range becomes the new width for the labels in the first column. The maximum width is 240 characters.

You cannot use / **R**ange **J**ustify to justify text in more than one range at a time.

CAUTION Do not use / **R**ange **J**ustify if any cells in the range are protected, or you may get an error. Select / **W**orksheet **G**lobal **P**rotection **D**isable to turn off protection before using / **R**ange **J**ustify. (For more details about justifying a range, see Lab 6.)

/ **R**ange **P**rot

/ **R**ange **P**rot prevents changes and deletions to a range of cells that has been unprotected with / **R**ange **U**nprot when global protection for the worksheet is enabled.

Protecting cells is particularly useful when you create a worksheet for others to use, so they cannot change or delete data in specified ranges of cells.

/ **R**ange **P**rot has no effect unless you have first enabled global protection using / **W**orksheet **G**lobal **P**rotection **E**nable, or unless the protected cells are part of the range you are working with while using the / **R**ange **I**nput command.

Once global protection is enabled, to change or add data, unprotect specific cells with / **R**ange **U**nprot. Use / **R**ange **P**rot to specify the range you wish to protect again.

If you enabled global protection, a PR appears in the control panel to indicate protected cells.

/ **R**ange **U**nprot

/ **R**ange **U**nprot allows changes to a range of cells when global protection for the worksheet is enabled.

Specify the range to unprotect so you can make changes to its contents. 1-2-3 indicates unprotected cells with a U in the control panel.

If you are using the / **R**ange **I**nput command, you can move the cell pointer only to the unprotected cells in the specified range.

/ **R**ange **I**nput

/ **R**ange **I**nput limits the movement of the cell pointer to unprotected cells within a specified range.

/ **R**ange **I**nput helps you set up fill-in-the-blanks entry forms to facilitate data entry. With the cell pointer limited to unprotected cells, protected cells can contain information you do not want modified. The / **R**ange **I**nput command is especially useful in conjunction with macros.

Begin by entering labels or values into the worksheet to identify the information you will input. Then select / **R**ange **U**nprot to remove protection from the cells to be used to enter data. Select / **R**ange **I**nput and specify the range you want to serve as the entry form area. The entire data input range moves to the upper left corner of the screen. You can move the cell pointer only to unprotected cells in the range. You can now enter or edit the data in these cells using the following keys: ↵, F1, F2, BACKSPACE, HOME, END, →, ←, ↑, and ↓. To end the / **R**ange **I**nput command, press ↵ or ESC when 1-2-3 is in READY mode.

After you finish using / **R**ange **I**nput, the cell pointer returns to its initial position.

If you use / **R**ange **I**nput as part of a macro, 1-2-3 suspends all macro activity to process data input. When you end the / **R**ange **I**nput command, 1-2-3 returns control to the macro.

/ **R**ange **V**alue

/ **R**ange **V**alue converts formulas in a range to their values. / **R**ange **V**alue is useful if you want to copy only the displayed values of formulas, not the formulas themselves, to another part of the worksheet.

You need to specify the range of cells with the entries you want to convert as the FROM range and the location in the worksheet where you want the values displayed as the TO range.

1-2-3 copies cell values to the TO range. The copied entries include the cell format of the FROM range cells. Only the upper left corner cell of the TO range needs to be entered. 1-2-3 will use rows below this cell and columns to the right of this cell to display the values. Be sure you specify the TO range in an empty area of the worksheet since 1-2-3 will write over any data in the range.

To convert the formulas in a range to their values, specify the same range as the FROM and the TO ranges during the / **R**ange **V**alue command; however, by doing this, you lose the formulas.

/ Range Trans

/ **R**ange **T**rans reorders ranges from columns to rows or from rows to columns. Transposing a range leaves the original range as it was; the operation results in a rearranged copy of the original range. Any copied formulas are replaced with their current values.

The FROM range contains the cells you want to transpose (rearrange), and the TO range is the location where you want to place the transposed range. You need to specify only the upper left corner of the TO range. / **R**ange **T**rans may produce unexpected results if the FROM and TO ranges overlap.

CAUTION If you transpose a range to a location whose cells already contain data, 1-2-3 replaces their contents with the transposed range. Formulas that depend on the previous contents of the TO range will now refer to the transposed cell entries.

/ Range Search

Formulas **L**abels **B**oth

/ **R**ange **S**earch searches for character strings (letters or numbers in labels and/or formulas) within a specified range. You can also automatically replace the string with another string. 1-2-3 searches and replaces rightwards by column, starting with column A. The search string is not case sensitive. The replacement string is case sensitive.

To search for a string, specify the range to search and then enter the string. **F**ormulas looks only in formulas for the search string. **L**abels looks only in labels for the search string. **B**oth looks in both formulas and labels.

To find a string, select **F**ind to highlight the first occurrence of the search string. Then select **N**ext to highlight the next occurrence or **Q**uit to return to READY mode.

To replace a string, select **R**eplace, enter the replacement string, and then select **R**eplace (to replace the current string and search for the next occurrence), **A**ll (to replace all strings without confirmation), **N**ext (to search for the next occurrence without replacing the current string), or **Q**uit (to return to READY mode).

Copy Command

Figure 2.4 shows the Copy menu tree.

/ Copy

/ **C**opy creates copies of existing cell entries.

When you copy labels and numbers, 1-2-3 makes exact duplicates of the original entries in another location.

When you copy formulas, 1-2-3 may or may not adjust cell references in the formulas, depending on the type of cell references. (See the section on using cell and range references in formulas in Chapter 1, "Basic Skills," for more details.)

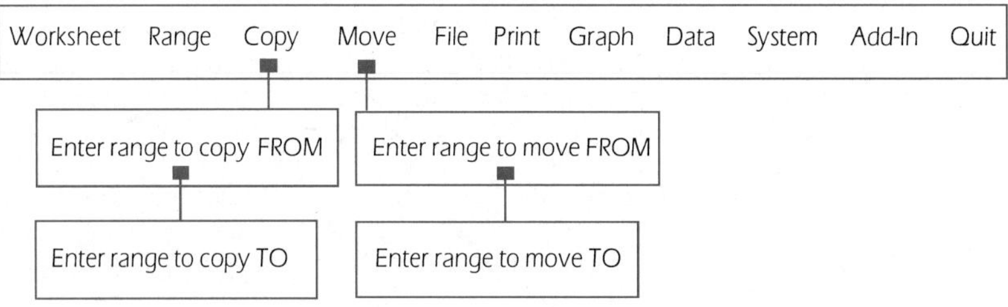

Figure 2.4

The FROM range contains the cells whose entries you want to copy, and the TO range contains the cells where you want the copies to appear. You need specify only the upper left corner cell of the TO range.

CAUTION Avoid specifying overlapping FROM and TO ranges. If they overlap, some of the original cell contents will be erased. If you copy data to an area of the worksheet that already contains data, 1-2-3 replaces the old data with the copied data. To avoid mistakenly erasing data, save the worksheet before using / **C**opy. If you make a mistake when copying data and the Undo feature is on, press UNDO (ALT-F4) immediately to restore the worksheet to its original state.

1-2-3 copies the data you specify to the area of the worksheet you specify and adjusts any relative references in formulas. (For more details about copying data, see Lab 2.)

Move Command

Figure 2.4 shows the Move menu tree.

/ **M**ove

/ **M**ove transfers a range of cell entries from one part of the worksheet to another.

/ **M**ove lets you rearrange data in the worksheet while maintaining all the functional relationships among the cells that contain the data. 1-2-3 automatically adjusts all formulas in the worksheet to account for moved data. As a result, / **M**ove is a powerful tool for redesigning the worksheet.

If you move a cell that contains a formula, the formula stays the same. If you move the contents of a cell to which a formula refers, 1-2-3 changes the formula to reflect the new location of the data.

The FROM range contains the cells whose entries you want to move, and the TO range contains the cells where you want the moved cell entries to appear. You need specify only the upper left corner cell of the TO range.

If you move a cell that is the upper left or lower right corner of a named range, 1-2-3 adjusts the definition of the named range. Moving any other cell in a named range effectively moves it out of the range but does not alter the range name definition.

CAUTION If you move data to an area of the worksheet that already contains data, 1-2-3 replaces the old data with the moved data. To avoid mistakenly erasing data, save the worksheet before using / **C**opy. If you make a mistake when moving data and the Undo feature is on, press UNDO (ALT-F4) immediately to restore the worksheet to its original state.

File Commands

The **F**ile commands save 1-2-3 worksheets in files stored on a disk. By saving your work in a file, you can retrieve your data after you leave 1-2-3 or turn off your computer. In addition, the File commands let you read files into 1-2-3 and help you organize and maintain the information you store in files. Figure 2.5 shows the File menu tree.

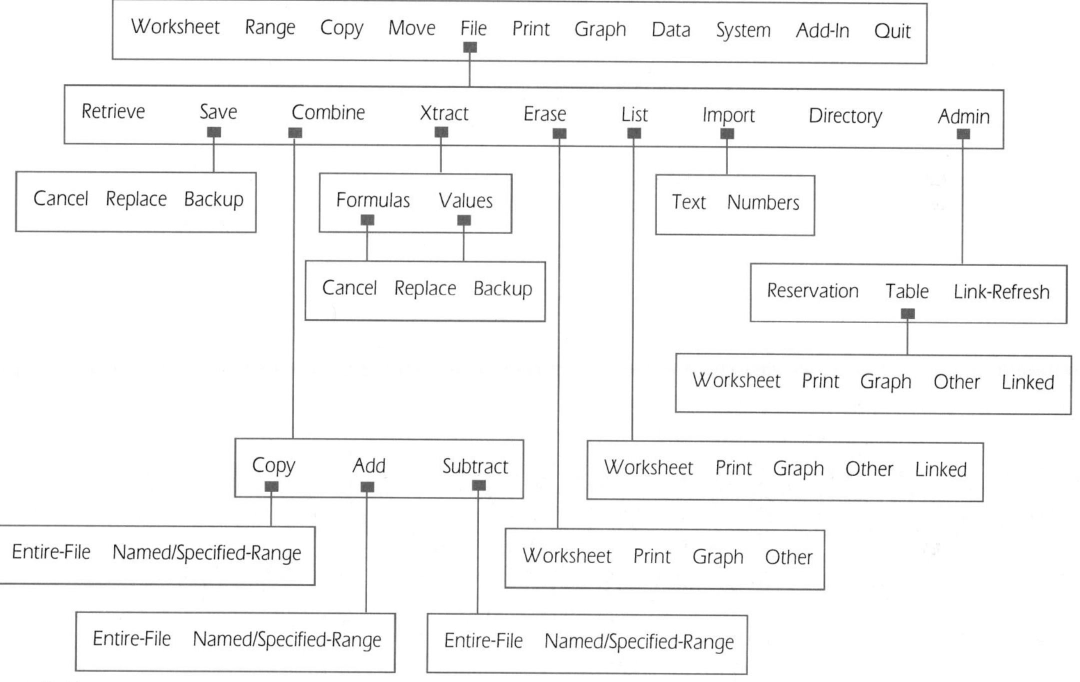

Figure 2.5

Filenames

When you save a file, 1-2-3 prompts you to type a filename. A filename can be up to eight characters long and can include uppercase and lowercase letters, numbers, hyphens (-) and underscores (__). Do not include spaces in a filename or use the name AUX, CON, COM1, COM2, LPT1, NUL, or PRN. Following are several examples of acceptable and unacceptable filenames:

If you type:	The result is:
STOCKS	1-2-3 accepts it.
1985_Rev	1-2-3 accepts it.
STOCKS 3	1-2-3 does not accept it because of the space.
CHECKBOOK	1-2-3 cuts the name off at the eighth letter.

Check your operating system manual to see if you can use any other special characters.

File Types and File Extensions

You can create four types of files in 1-2-3: worksheet files, print files, graph files, and backup files. 1-2-3 differentiates among these file types by adding a three-character file extension to each filename you enter: .WK1 to any worksheet file you save using the Student Edition of Lotus 1-2-3 Release 2.2, .PRN to any print file you save, .PIC to any graph file you save, or .BAK to any backup file.

With the Student Edition of Lotus 1-2-3 Release 2.2, if you save a worksheet as CLAS_AVG, 1-2-3 adds the extension .WK1. When you retrieve that file with the / **F**ile **R**etrieve command, 1-2-3 displays all the .WK1 files that you have saved, including the CLAS_AVG.WK1 file.

You can enter your own file extension when you save a file as long as it has no more than three characters. Previous releases of 1-2-3 save worksheet files with a .WKS and .WK1 extension, and 1-2-3 displays any of those files along with the .WK1 files when you retrieve a worksheet file. You can save the CLAS_AVG file as CLAS_AVG.WK1 or CLAS_AVG.LST. 1-2-3 automatically displays CLAS_AVG.WK1 when you retrieve a file. However, to retrieve CLAS_AVG.LST, you must type the filename and its extension after the prompt.

Filename Menus

1-2-3 keeps a list of all the files you have saved in 1-2-3 and all the directories you have created in DOS. When you retrieve a file, 1-2-3 displays a menu that shows the names of the files you have saved of the same file type. It also displays the directories you created when the directory on the screen was current. Directories appear with a backslash (\) after the directory name.

You can select a file or a directory from the menu. You can also select a file with a different extension by typing in the filename and the extension, or you can select a file from another directory by typing in the directory name first. Directories can contain many files. When you save a file, 1-2-3 stores it in the directory you see on your screen, called the current directory.

Drives and Directories

When you use the 1-2-3 File commands, you see certain characters after the prompt, such as B:\, that direct 1-2-3 to the right directory to locate a file. When you save a file, you see the prompt "Enter save filename: B:*.WK1." Each part of the name is a specification for 1-2-3.

The Drive Name

The B: tells 1-2-3 which drive to search. A drive name always consists of a single letter followed by a colon. 1-2-3 automatically searches the same disk drive when it saves and retrieves files. This drive is set in the configuration file. If you want 1-2-3 to retrieve a file from a different drive, begin the filename with the drive name to which you want 1-2-3 to go. For example, if you want to save a file named ACCT1 on drive C and drive C is not the drive 1-2-3 automatically searches, you must press ESC twice and then type C:\ACCT1 after the prompt. When you want to retrieve the file again, you also must type C:\ACCT1.

The Directory Specifier

The backslash (\) tells 1-2-3 which directory to search. A directory is a subdivision of a disk in which you group related files. Every 1-2-3 file exists in a directory. If you never create your own directory, the files exist in the main directory, called the root directory. The backslash (\) just after the disk drive specifier designates the root directory.

Consult your operating system manual for instructions on how to create directories and subdirectories.

In 1-2-3, you set one directory as the current directory. The current directory is the one 1-2-3 searches for files. The filenames listed in the menu when you retrieve a file are all in the current directory.

Using Wildcard Characters in Filenames and Extensions

The asterisk (*) in the filename is a wildcard character for any number of sequential characters. *.WK1 tells 1-2-3 to list the name of every file with a .WK1 extension in the current directory. *.PIC tells 1-2-3 to list the name of every file with a .PIC extension.

The question mark (?) is also a wildcard character, but it represents any single character in a filename or extension.

Directory Organization and Pathnames

You organize directories and subdirectories in a tree structure, beginning with the root directory.

When you want to save a file or retrieve a file, 1-2-3 always gives you the entire list of directories that mark the path to that file. This list, beginning with the root directory, is called a pathname. A complete pathname begins at the root directory. A partial pathname begins at the current directory and works its way down in levels.

File Protection

You can save any 1-2-3 file and protect it by typing a password during the / **F**ile **S**ave command. When you save a file with a password, you can retrieve it again only if you enter the correct password.

Automatic File Retrieval

When you start a 1-2-3 session, a blank worksheet appears on the screen. If you want to work on the same worksheet each time you start a session, name it AUTO123. 1-2-3 will automatically retrieve that worksheet every time you start a session.

Linking Files

You can use values from cells in other worksheets in the current worksheet. You create a link between two files by entering a linking formula in one file that refers to a cell in the other file; this way you don't have to manually update every worksheet affected by a change in another worksheet. The file in which you enter the formula is called the target file because it receives the data. The file that the formula refers to is called the source file because it supplies the data.

Once the two files are linked, 1-2-3 copies the value of the cell in the source file (the source cell) to the cell in the target file (the target cell). The value of the target cell is automatically updated whenever you retrieve the target file or select / **F**ile **A**dmin **L**ink-Refresh while you are working on the target file.

File linking saves you the effort of manually updating every worksheet affected by a change in another worksheet. One of the most useful applications of file linking is the consolidation of data from a number of worksheets in a summary worksheet.

You can also use the linking feature to create links to cells that depend on other linked cells.

It is important to be aware that if the data you are linking to depends on other linked cells, you can get incorrect results unless you update the files in an "upward" order. That is, if you think of the linked files being organized in a hierarchical structure, you must always start updating at the level where you are making changes and work to the top level.

Creating a Link

To create a linking formula, a formula that refers to a cell in another file, you must use the following format:

+<<*file reference*>>*cell reference*

The file and cell reference can be entered in uppercase or lowercase letters. However, 1-2-3 will always display the references in all uppercase letters.

Follow these steps when entering the formula:

1. Move the cell pointer to the target cell.
2. Type a + (plus sign) to begin the formula.
3. Enter a file reference enclosed in << >> (double angle brackets).

   A file reference must always include the name of the source file. In some cases, however, it may also be necessary for you to supply other information:

   - If the source file does not have the default file extension .WK1, you must include the appropriate file extension.
   - If the source file is not in the default directory (the directory specified with / **F**ile **D**irectory), you must include a directory name to tell 1-2-3 where to look for the file.
   - If the source file is not on the disk in the default drive (the drive specified with / **F**ile **D**irectory), you must include a drive name to tell 1-2-3 where to look for the file.

4. Enter a cell reference, either the address of the source cell or its range name.

   - If you enter a range address, 1-2-3 uses only the cell in the upper left corner of the range as the source cell.
   - If you enter a range name that represents a multiple-cell range in the source file, 1-2-3 uses only the cell in the upper left corner of the range as the source cell although it always displays the range name in the formula.

5. Press ↵ to complete the formula.

   When you press ↵ to complete the linking formula, 1-2-3 checks to make sure the source file you referenced exists. If any of the following conditions exist, 1-2-3 displays an error message and will not enter the formula in the worksheet:

   - The source file does not exist.
   - The specified directory does not exist so 1-2-3 cannot find the source file.
   - The specified drive is not ready (for example, you have not closed the door on a disk drive).
   - The specified range name does not exist in the source file.

- The source file is a password-protected worksheet.
- You are sharing files on a network and the source file is being retrieved or saved by another user.
- The data in the file cannot be read by 1-2-3.

  If 1-2-3 is able to locate the source file and cell, it copies the value of that cell into the target cell.

6. In order to make a link permanent, use / **F**ile **S**ave to save the worksheet.

(For more on linking files, see Lab 5.)

/ **F**ile **R**etrieve

/ **F**ile **R**etrieve loads a worksheet file from a disk into the computer's memory and displays it on the screen. 1-2-3 retrieves a file only from the current directory. Choose a file from the menu with the menu pointer or after the prompt type the name of a file not on the menu and its extension.

Because 1-2-3 erases the current worksheet when you use the / **F**ile **R**etrieve command, save the changes in the current worksheet before you retrieve a new file. If the Undo feature is on, however, you can press UNDO (ALT-F4) immediately to restore the worksheet that was in memory when you selected / **F**ile **R**etrieve. If you retrieve a protected worksheet file, 1-2-3 prompts you to enter the file's password. You must enter the exact combination of uppercase and lowercase letters in the password.

When you use / **F**ile **R**etrieve and the filenames appear on the menu, you can press the Name function key (F3) to see a list of current files and directories, when they were last used, and how large they are. Press F3 again to return to the File menu. (For more details about retrieving a file, see Lab 1.)

/ **F**ile **S**ave

Cancel **R**eplace **B**ackup

/ **F**ile **S**ave saves the current worksheet and the settings associated with it in a worksheet file.

At the prompt, select the current filename by pressing ↵ or type a new filename. If you choose **C**ancel, you return to the current worksheet in READY mode; nothing is saved. If you choose **R**eplace, you write over the existing file of the same name with the data from the current worksheet. If you choose **B**ackup, 1-2-3 copies the worksheet file on disk to a backup file with the same filename but the extension .BAK, and saves the current worksheet with the existing filename.

Save your files often, so an updated file of the changes in your worksheet is on the disk. If you try to save a file on a disk with inadequate available memory space, an error message appears. When this happens, press ESC, insert another data disk, and try again. (For more details about saving files, see Lab 1 and Lab 2.)

Saving a File with a Password

You can save and protect any 1-2-3 file by entering a password during the / **F**ile **S**ave command.

Type the filename, press SPACEBAR, and type **P**. You will be prompted to enter and then verify the password. You do not see your password on the screen. Your password can be up to fifteen characters long, and you can use any LICS characters except spaces.

To change or delete a password, begin the command sequence, / **F**ile **S**ave. The current filename is displayed, followed by the message "[PASSWORD PROTECTED]." To clear this message, press ESC or BACKSPACE, then press SPACEBAR and type **P** to display the password prompt. To change the password, enter and verify the new password. To delete the password, press ↵ at the password prompts. Select **R**eplace to save the worksheet.

CAUTION When you save a file with a password, you can retrieve it only if you enter the correct password. If you forget the password, there is no way to retrieve the file. (For more details about saving a file with a password, see Lab 6.)

/ **F**ile **C**ombine

Copy **A**dd **S**ubtract

/ **F**ile **C**ombine incorporates all or part of a worksheet file into the current worksheet at the location of the cell pointer. 1-2-3 uses the cell pointer as the upper left corner cell for the incoming data. All other entries fall into corresponding cells to the right and below the cell pointer.

Position the cell pointer in the upper left corner of the area of the worksheet where you want to incorporate the incoming data. Select **C**opy, **A**dd, or **S**ubtract from the menu (see Table 2.8 for a description of these options). You will be prompted to choose **E**ntire-File or **N**amed/Specified-Range from the menu. If you choose **E**ntire-File, select a name from the menu or enter a new filename. Include a disk drive name or a directory pathname if you want 1-2-3 to read files from another disk directory. If you choose **N**amed/Specified-Range, type the name of the range to extract from the worksheet. 1-2-3 does not display a menu of these names.

Table 2.8

Menu Item	Description
Copy	Replaces the entries in the current worksheet with incoming data.
Add	Adds incoming numeric data to the values in the current worksheet. If an incoming value overlays a cell that contains a number. 1-2-3 adds the two values. Incoming values replace blank cells. If an incoming value overlays a label or formula cell, 1-2-3 discards the incoming value and retains the label in the current worksheet.
Subtract	Subtracts incoming numeric data from values in the current worksheet file. A positive number subtracted from a blank cell produces a negative result. The incoming data has no effect on labels or formulas in the current worksheet.

1-2-3 combines only cell entries. No worksheet or print settings are incorporated into the current worksheet. Avoid any loss of data from combining a file incorrectly by saving the current worksheet before you use / **F**ile **C**ombine. If you make a mistake when combining files and the Undo feature is on, press UNDO (ALT-F4) immediately to restore the worksheet to its original state. (For more details about combining files, see Lab 6.)

/ **F**ile **X**tract

Formulas **V**alues

/ **F**ile **X**tract extracts and saves a portion of the current worksheet in a separate worksheet file. / **F**ile **X**tract does not change any data in the current worksheet.

Select **F**ormulas to copy labels, formulas, numbers, and all worksheet settings or **V**alues to copy labels, numbers, the value of formulas, and all worksheet settings. Then specify the range of cells to extract. Select a filename from the menu or enter a new filename at the prompt.

If you specified a filename that already exists, you can select one of the following: **C**ancel returns 1-2-3 to READY mode without extracting the range; **R**eplace writes over the file on disk with the extracted range; **B**ackup renames the previously extracted file on disk with the extension .BAK and saves the extracted range with the existing filename and the extension .WK1.

When you select a range to extract, it cannot contain formulas that reference cells outside the extracted range or range names that refer to ranges outside the extracted range.

The global settings in the current worksheet (such as named ranges, graphs, and formats) are saved in the new file with the extracted range.

Use / **File Xtract** to split a large worksheet into smaller parts or to use one part of a worksheet in another worksheet. (For more details about extracting files, see Lab 6.)

/ File Erase

Worksheet **P**rint **G**raph **O**ther

/ **File Erase** removes one or more files of a particular file type from the disk.

Worksheet displays all .WK1, .WKS, and .WK3 files. **P**rint displays all .PRN files. **G**raph displays all .PIC files. **O**ther displays all files in the current directory. Select the name of the file you want to erase and press (↵) or type in an explicit filename. In addition, / **File Erase** removes all files that match a description when you type in wildcard characters as part of a filename.

Consult your operating system manual for information on wildcard characters.

CAUTION Once you erase a file on disk, you cannot retrieve the data in that file or use UNDO (ALT-(F4)) to recover the file. Therefore, before using this command, make certain that you no longer need the data in the file you are erasing.

/ File List

Worksheet **P**rint **G**raph **O**ther **L**inked

/ **File List** displays the names of all files of a particular type stored in the current directory. When you highlight a filename in the list, 1-2-3 displays the date and time the file was last saved and the file size in bytes.

Worksheet displays all. WK1, .WKS, and .WK3 files. **P**rint displays all .PRN files. **G**raph displays all .PIC files. **O**ther displays all files in the current directory.

The list of filenames temporarily replaces the current worksheet on the screen. If no files of the specified file type are on the disk, 1-2-3 puts you in EDIT mode so that you can enter a new file extension. Use / **File List** after you erase a file to see if it is erased from the list of current files.

Linked displays all files on disk that are linked to the current worksheet by formula references. When you highlight a filename, 1-2-3 displays the full path in the control panel. Characters you typed when you linked the file are displayed in color or brighter intensity; 1-2-3 completes the path if necessary with characters displayed in normal color or intensity.

/ **F**ile **I**mport

Text **N**umbers

/ **File Import** copies a print file from the current directory into the current worksheet at the location of the cell pointer. You can import text or numbers. / **File Import** imports standard ASCII files.

There are two types of text files from which you can import data. A delimited text file contains characters (delimiters) that separate data. For 1-2-3 to import a delimited text file correctly, labels must be enclosed in quotation marks, and all labels and numbers must be separated by commas, spaces, colons, or semicolons. Numbers must not be formatted with commas because the commas will act as delimiters. A nondelimited text file does not separate data. For 1-2-3 to import a nondelimited text file correctly, each line in the file must end with a carriage return or a line feed and must not exceed 240 characters.

CAUTION Many word processors produce files that contain special characters. If you try to import these files with the / **File Import** command, you may get unpredictable results. Most word processors, however, produce standard ASCII files, which should be compatible with 1-2-3.

Before you initiate the command sequence, move the cell pointer to the top left corner of the range where you want the imported file to be displayed. Table 2.9 describes the command options.

Table 2.9

Menu Item	Action
Text	Imports labels and numbers from a nondelimited text file; do not use with a delimited text file. 1-2-3 imports each line of data as a long label, entering it in a single cell in the current worksheet beginning at the cell pointer location. 1-2-3 enters each successive line from the text file in the same column, one cell below the other.
Numbers	Imports only numbers from a nondelimited text file; imports numbers and labels from a delimited text file. In both cases, 1-2-3 places each entry in a separate cell in the current worksheet beginning at the cell pointer location.

/ **F**ile **D**irectory

/ **File Directory** replaces the current directory with a new one, making it the current directory for this 1-2-3 session. If you type a filename without a disk drive specifier, 1-2-3 automatically assigns the current disk drive and directory to the file.

/ **F**ile **A**dmin

Reservation **T**able **L**ink-Refresh

/ **File Admin** creates a table of information about files, updates file links in the current worksheet, and controls access to a worksheet file's reservation.

Selecting **R**eservation lets you get and release a file's reservation, or lock. You use this command when you share worksheet files on a network and want to save files or allow other people to save files. Selecting **T**able creates a table of information about files on disk. The table can be placed in any unprotected area of the worksheet. However, make sure that the worksheet location is blank or contains unimportant data, as 1-2-3 will write over existing data when it creates the table. Selecting **L**ink-Refresh recalculates formulas in the current worksheet that include references to files on disk by retrieving the current contents of the linked cells.

Print Commands

The **P**rint commands let you create printed copies of a worksheet. You can print a worksheet on a printer or print it to a file saved on a disk. Printing to a file lets you print the file later with an operating system command or use the file in another program, such as a word processing program. Figure 2.6 shows the Print menu tree.

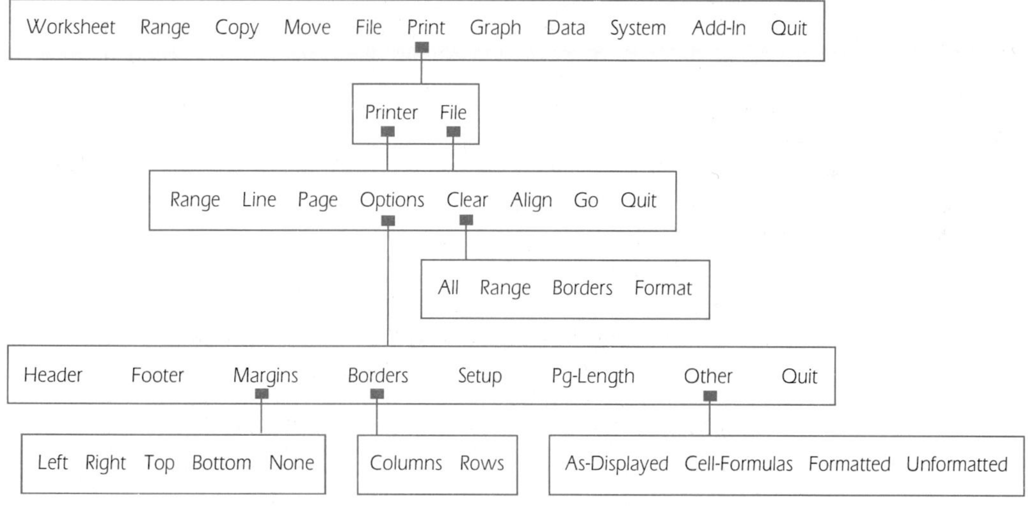

Figure 2.6

The basic steps for printing to a printer or to a file immediately follow. The rest of this section describes the printing options. Before you try to print a worksheet on a printer, be sure to use the Install program to indicate the printer you are using. (See Chapter 2, "Initializing and Installing 1-2-3" in Section 1, "Getting Started.") It is a good idea to save your file using / **F**ile **S**ave just before you print.

1. Select / **P**rint **P**rinter or / **P**rint **F**ile.
2. If you are printing to a file, type a filename or choose one from a list of existing filenames. If you choose an existing name, select **R**eplace to replace the file with the current worksheet or select **C**ancel and start the / **P**rint command again.
3. Select **R**ange.
4. Specify the range you want to print.
5. Select **O**ptions and make any changes.
6. Select **A**lign from the Print menu, turn your printer on, and adjust the paper so that it is at the top of a page.
7. Select **G**o to print the range.
8. Select **Q**uit to leave the menu.

(For more details about printing a worksheet, see Lab 2.)

If you are printing to a file, you will not see anything happen until you select **Q**uit.

When you select / **P**rint **P**rinter or / **P**rint **F**ile, the Print settings sheet will appear on your screen. This allows you to see the settings that will affect your printout.

If you do not make any changes in the individual or global page format, 1-2-3 uses the following settings when you print a worksheet on standard 8-½ × 11″ paper:

Left margin	4 spaces from the left edge of the paper
Right margin	76 spaces from the left edge of the paper
Top margin	2 lines from the top of the paper
Bottom margin	2 lines from the bottom of the paper
Page length	66 lines

You can change any of these settings for all worksheets with / **W**orksheet **G**lobal **D**efault **P**rinter. You can change them for a single worksheet with / **P**rint **P**rinter **O**ptions.

The default printer port is Parallel 1. If you are using a serial printer or a printer on a DOS network, select / **W**orksheet **G**lobal **D**efault **P**rinter **I**nterface and choose the appropriate port. Select **Q**uit and then **U**pdate to store this change for future 1-2-3 sessions.

When you print to a file, 1-2-3 automatically appends the extension .PRN to the filename so that you can easily identify print files on your disk.

A header that includes the student name entered during the Initialization program is automatically printed on the top of each page. (See Chapter 2, ''Initializing and Installing 1-2-3'' in Section 1, ''Getting Started.'')

/ **P**rint **P**rinter (or **F**ile) **R**ange

/ **P**rint **P**rinter (or **F**ile) **R**ange lets you specify the worksheet range you want to print or store in a file. (For more details about print range, see Lab 2.)

To indicate the print range, you can highlight it, type the corner address of the range, or use a range name created with / **R**ange **N**ame **C**reate.

When you specify the range, be sure that the highlight covers all the information you want to print. For instance, if column H has no filled cells, but long labels in column G extend into column H, you must highlight column H as well as column G, or the end of the labels will not be printed.

Because 1-2-3 remembers the last range you printed (it is displayed in the Print settings sheet), you do not need to use / **P**rint **P**rinter (or **F**ile) **R**ange if you want to print the same range again.

/ **P**rint **P**rinter (or **F**ile) **L**ine

/ **P**rint **P**rinter **L**ine advances the printer to the beginning of the next line on the page. If the printer reaches the bottom of a page, the paper advances to the top of the next page. / **P**rint **F**ile **L**ine inserts a blank line in a text file.

/ **P**rint **P**rinter (or **F**ile) **P**age

/ **P**rint **P**rinter **P**age advances the paper in the printer to the top of the next page. If you specified a footer, 1-2-3 prints the footer at the bottom of the current page and advances the paper to the next page. Using / **P**rint **P**rinter **P**age at the end of a document puts the footer on the last page and advances to the top of the next page. / **P**rint **F**ile **P**age inserts a footer and blank spaces in a print file.

/ **P**rint **P**rinter (or **F**ile) **O**ptions

Header **F**ooter **M**argins **B**orders **S**etup **P**g-Length **O**ther **Q**uit

/ **P**rint **P**rinter **O**ptions and / **P**rint **F**ile **O**ptions change the margins, borders, and page length of your printed documents, add headers and footers, and indicate font size and style. Table 2.10 describes the command options. The settings will appear in your Print settings sheet.

Table 2.10

Menu Item	Description
Header	Prints one line of text just below the top margin of every page. You can type up to 240 characters (limited by your paper width and margins). Use a number sign (#) to generate sequential page numbers, starting with 1. Use an at sign (@) to produce the current date. Use a backslash (\) followed by a cell address or range name to use the contents of a cell as a header (or footer).
Footer	Prints one line of text just above the bottom margin of every page. You can type up to 240 characters (limited by your paper width and margins). Use a number sign (#) to generate sequential page numbers, starting with 1. Use an at sign (@) to produce the current date. Use a backslash (\) followed by a cell address or range name to use the contents of a cell as a header (or footer).
Margins	Sets margins for the printed page. Select **L**eft, **R**ight, **T**op, **B**ottom or **N**one. 1-2-3 displays the current margin setting. To change the setting, type a number up to 240 (for left or right margin) or 32 (for top or bottom margin) and press ↵. To clear the current margins and reset the top, left, and bottom margins to 0 and the right margin to 240 in one step, select **N**one.
Borders	Prints specified rows or columns on every page, above or to the left of the range you are printing. Choose **R**ows or **C**olumns. If you have already specified that kind of border, 1-2-3 highlights it. To use that range, press ↵; otherwise, highlight or type a new range. Do not include the area specified for the borders in your print range, or you will get two copies of the same information.
Setup	Specifies font size and style for the printer. Type a setup string of up to 39 characters and press ↵. If 1-2-3 displays an existing setup string, press ESC first. Setup strings come from printer control codes, which you can find in your printer manual. You generally use a three-digit or four-digit code, prefaced with a backslash (\).
Pg-Length	Indicates the number of printed lines to be printed on a page. Press ↵ to use the current page length or type a number between 10 and 100 and press ↵.
Other	This command is described in the **/ P**rint **P**rinter **O**ptions **O**ther section.
Quit	Select **Q**uit to return to the Print menu.

(For more details about print options, see Lab 6.)

1-2-3 always leaves two blank lines between the text and the headers or footers. Headers and footers can have up to three parts: left-aligned, centered, and right-aligned segments. Use the split vertical bar (¦) to separate segments. The following examples illustrate page 15 of a document printed February 23, 1991.

Enter:	Result:
ABC Company	ABC Company
¦ABC Company	ABC Company (centered)
ABC Company¦¦Page #	ABC Company Page 15
@¦ABC Company¦Page #	2/23/91 ABC Company Page 15

The initial default page length is 66, which is appropriate for type that uses 6 lines per inch on 11-inch paper. With a page length of 66, you can print 56 lines from the worksheet.

To indicate a setup string, use your printer's control codes in the form *nnn* (refer to your printer's manual). If you change from one setup string to another, you usually have to turn your printer off and then on again for the change to take effect.

The following examples work for many printers.

Setup string:	Result:	Note:
\015	Turns on compressed print	Maximum right margin of 132
\018	Turns off compressed print	Maximum right margin of 80
\0270	Sets line spacing to 8 lines per inch	Set Pg-Length to 88
\0272	Sets line spacing to 6 lines per inch	Set Pg-Length to 66

You can enter certain setup strings in worksheet cells to switch from one print style to another within a single worksheet. Place two split vertical bars (¦¦) before the setup string. For example, on some printers, you can use ¦¦\015 to print a section of the worksheet in compressed print. Use ¦¦\018 at the point where you want to return to standard print.

/ **P**rint **P**rinter (or **F**ile) **O**ptions **O**ther

As-Displayed **C**ell-Formulas **F**ormatted **U**nformatted

/ **P**rint **P**rinter **O**ptions **O**ther and / **P**rint **F**ile **O**ptions **O**ther change the printing format and the information contained in the document. Table 2.11 describes the command options.

Table 2.11

Menu Item	Description
As-Displayed	1-2-3 prints the range as it appears on the screen. Use this option to restore standard output after you have chosen **C**ell-Formulas.
Cell-Formulas	1-2-3 prints the contents of each filled cell in the print range, one cell per line. Each line contains exactly what appears on the first line of the control panel when the cell pointer is on the cell: the cell address, the format, the protection status (P or U), and the value or formula in the cell.
Formatted	Restores any page breaks, headers, or footers after you have chosen **U**nformatted.
Unformatted	1-2-3 prints ranges without page breaks, headers, or footers. This is useful if you are printing a range to a file or if you are trying to print a very full page.

/ **P**rint **P**rinter (or **F**ile) **C**lear

All **R**ange **B**orders **F**ormat

/ **Print Printer** (or **File**) **Clear** clears the print range, headers, footers, and borders and resets other options. You may want to put these commands in macros to clear any preexisting print settings.

All cancels the current print range; clears all borders, headers, and footers; and resets all formats and options to their default settings. **R**ange cancels the current print range. **B**orders clears all borders (column and row ranges). **F**ormat resets margins, page length, and setup string to default settings.

/ **P**rint **P**rinter (or **F**ile) **A**lign

/ **Print Printer** (or **File**) **Align** tells the printer that you have positioned the paper at the top of a new page. You do not see any change on your screen.

Select **Align** each time you print a worksheet. If you do not use this command, you may get gaps in the middle of your printed page. (For more details about aligning the printer page, see Lab 2.)

/ **P**rint **P**rinter (or **F**ile) **G**o

/ **Print Printer** (or **File**) **Go** starts the process of printing the range you indicated with / **Print Printer Range** or / **Print File Range**. (For more details about starting the print process, see Lab 2.)

If your printer is off or disconnected when you select **Go**, 1-2-3 beeps and displays a printer error message on the bottom of the screen. Press ESC, check your printer, and try again. Select **Quit** to return to READY mode.

With some systems, you can interrupt printing and return to the Print menu by pressing BREAK and then ESC. The printer may not stop immediately because it still has characters in its memory. To clear the printer's memory, turn it off. When you turn it back on, reposition the paper and select / **P**rint **P**rinter **A**lign and then **G**o.

Graph Commands

You can represent numeric data you enter into a worksheet as a graph. The **G**raph commands can create five different types of graphs: line graphs, bar graphs, stacked bar graphs, XY (scatter) graphs, and pie charts.

Line graphs show changes in data over time; bar and stacked bar graphs emphasize differences between data items; XY graphs show relationships between two sets of data; and pie charts compare parts to the whole.

Figure 2.7 shows the Graph menu tree.

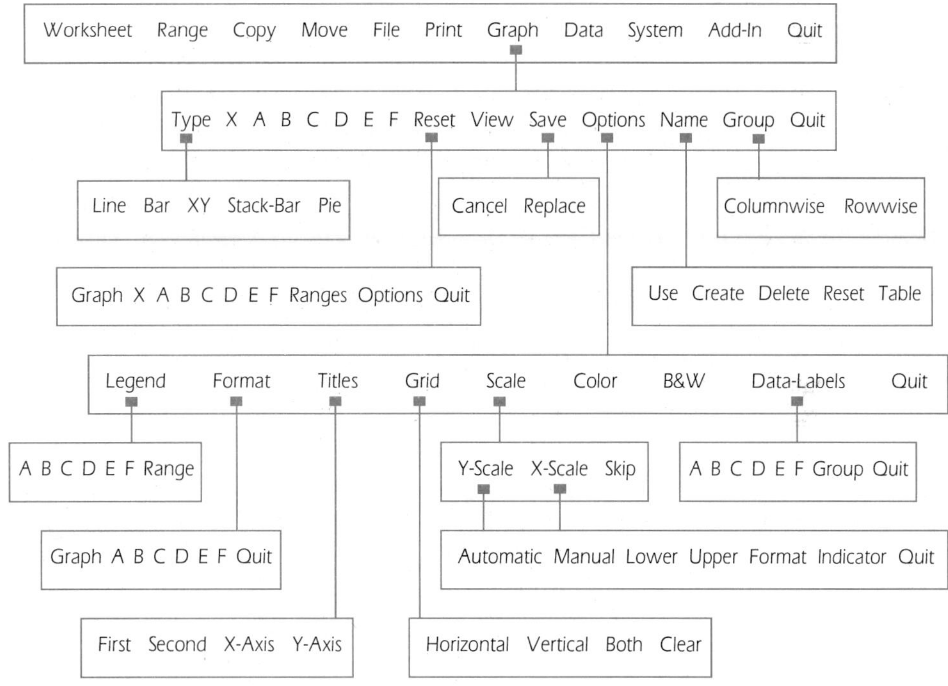

Figure 2.7

Creating a Graph

You can create graphs from worksheet data and view them on your computer's screen if your system has graphics capability. Even if you cannot view the graphs on your computer's screen, you can create a file to print graphs on a printer or plotter using the 1-2-3 PrintGraph program (see Chapter 5, "The PrintGraph Program").

When you select / **G**raph, 1-2-3 displays a Graph settings sheet, which lists the names of all the graph settings and the settings for the current graph (if any).

Graph Data Ranges

When you create a graph, you specify the data ranges you want 1-2-3 to represent in the graph. The different types of graphs display each data range in varying manners.

When displaying a graph, 1-2-3 matches up corresponding values or labels from each range based on their relative positions in the range. Therefore, when you specify data ranges, each range must be a column or a row that is the same size as all of your other specified data ranges.

To specify graph data ranges, you select the Graph menu option X and A through F. Use the following guidelines to determine the appropriate data range specification for your graph. You can also define all the data ranges (X, A, B, C, D, E, and F) at once, rather than specifying each data range separately, using the Graph Group command.

/ **G**raph **T**ype

Line **B**ar **X**Y **S**tack-Bar **P**ie

Line Graph

A line graph represents each value in a category as a point on a line. You can create up to six lines on a single graph. 1-2-3 uses different symbols to identify the points on each line.

Use the A range to indicate the set of values you want to represent with your first line or with one single line. Use the B through F ranges to indicate the sets of values you want to represent with each additional line. Use the X range to indicate labels for the points along the X (horizontal) axis.

1-2-3 automatically indicates a numerical scale along the Y (vertical) axis.

(For more details about line graphs, see Lab 3.)

Bar Graph

A bar graph represents the values in a range with bars of varying heights. You can create a single-range bar graph, which compares values in one set of data to each other, or a multiple-range bar graph, which displays comparable values for up to six sets of data at each point along the X axis. In a multiple-range bar graph, 1-2-3 uses a variety of shadings (hatch patterns) or colors to identify the bars for each data range.

For a single-range bar graph, use the A range to indicate the range of values you want each bar to represent. For a multiple-range bar graph, use the A through F ranges to indicate the ranges of values you want to represent simultaneously. You should use the X range to indicate labels for the points along the X axis. 1-2-3 automatically indicates a numerical scale along the Y axis.

(For more details about bar graphs, see Lab 4.)

XY Graph

In an XY graph (also called a scatter chart), 1-2-3 pairs each value from the X range with the corresponding value from each of the A through F ranges to plot points on the graph. You can create up to six lines on a single XY graph. 1-2-3 uses different symbols to identify the points on each line.

Use the X range to indicate the set of values you want to plot on the X axis. Use the A range to indicate the set of values you want to plot on the Y axis in your first line or in one single line. Use the B through F ranges to indicate the sets of values you want to plot on the Y axis in each additional line. 1-2-3 automatically indicates numerical scales along both the X and the Y axes.

(For more details about XY graphs, see Lab 4.)

Stacked Bar Graph

In a stacked bar graph, 1-2-3 displays the corresponding value from each data range stacked above the preceding value in each bar. You can create stacked bar graphs that show up to six corresponding values at each point along the X axis. 1-2-3 uses different shadings (hatch patterns) or colors to represent each data range.

You should use the A through F ranges to indicate each set of values you want to represent. The A range is the lowest portion of each bar. The B through F ranges are stacked successively above the A range. You should use the X range to indicate labels along the X axis. 1-2-3 automatically indicates a numerical scale along the Y axis.

(For more details about stacked bar graphs, see Lab 4.)

Pie Chart

A pie chart compares parts to the whole, so each value in the range is a slice of the pie.

Use the A range to indicate the set of values that 1-2-3 will represent as slices of the pie. You can indicate shadings or colors for the individual pie slices. In addition, you can explode (separate) one or more slices of the pie to emphasize a particular value or values. 1-2-3 displays the exploded sections slightly apart from the rest of the pie chart.

Use the B range to indicate the range where you enter shading or color and exploding codes for the pie slices. The B range can be any blank range of your worksheet that is the same size as the A range. Enter a number between 1 and 7 to indicate the desired shading (hatch pattern) or color for each corresponding pie slice. The number codes 0 and 8 indicate unshaded slices.

Indicate the section you want to explode by adding 100 to its corresponding shading or color code. For example, the code 106 in the seventh cell of the B range will explode a slice representing the seventh cell of the A range and display it with type 6 shading or color.

Use the X range to indicate labels for each pie slice. 1-2-3 automatically indicates the percentage value of each slice of the pie.

(For more details about pie charts, see Lab 4.)

/ Graph Reset

Graph **X A B C D E F R**anges **O**ptions **Q**uit

/ **Graph Reset** resets some or all graph or range settings. Use / **Graph Reset** to start over again on the current graph. Select **Graph** to cancel the settings for the current graph. This command does not affect named graphs.

Select **X**, **A**, **B**, **C**, **D**, **E**, or **F** to suppress the display of a particular range. Resetting a range also resets the corresponding data-label range. Resetting the X range removes the label entries, except on XY graphs. Select **Ranges** to cancel all graph data ranges but not graph options. Select **Options** to cancel all graph options but not graph data ranges. Select **Quit** to return to the previous menu.

(For more details about using / **Graph Reset**, see Lab 4.)

/ Graph View

You can select **View** to see the current graph any time you are in the top-level Graph menu.

You can view your current graph from READY mode by pressing the Graph function key, F10. Your most recently specified graph type and data ranges remain with the worksheet. The next time you create a graph, these specifications will appear if you saved the worksheet.

You can change the type of graph you create without altering the data ranges to see which type of graph displays your data most effectively. Select and specify the graph type and then view the graph.

(For more details about creating graphs, see Lab 3 and Lab 4.)

/ Graph Save

Cancel **R**eplace

/ **Graph Save** stores the current graph in a graph file (filename extension .PIC), so you can use the graph with other programs, such as PrintGraph.

Use / **G**raph **S**ave to generate a graph file that you print later with PrintGraph. This command saves the graph only for printing. You cannot bring the graph back to the screen to modify it. When you save a graph for printing, 1-2-3 stores the graph's image in the current directory unless you specify a different directory as part of the filename. If you save a graph under an existing graph filename, 1-2-3 writes over the contents in that file. Use the / **F**ile **S**ave command to save the graph settings and file before you end your work session. If you want to use a graph again or modify it later, you must create a name for it using the / **G**raph **N**ame **C**reate command. (For more details about saving a graph for printing, see Lab 4.)

Select **C**ancel to end the / **G**raph **S**ave command without saving the current graph. Select **R**eplace to complete the / **G**raph **S**ave command, replacing the graph file on disk with the current graph.

/ **G**raph **O**ptions

Legend **F**ormat **T**itles **G**rid **S**cale **C**olor **B**&W **D**ata-Labels **Q**uit

The Graph Options commands add enhancements such as titles, legends, colors, and grid lines to a graph, and determine the scaling method for the graph's axes.

/ **G**raph **O**ptions **L**egend

A B C D E F Range

/ **G**raph **O**ptions **L**egend adds a legend below the graph to identify what each symbol, color, or hatching represents in the graph.

Choose a data range, **A**, **B**, **C**, **D**, **E**, or **F**, to assign a legend to an individual data range. (1-2-3 displays the most recent legend, if any, for that range.) You can reselect that legend or press ESC to cancel it and specify a new legend. Choose **R**ange to assign legends to all data ranges at once.

To use the cell contents as a legend, type a backslash (\) followed by the cell address or range name. If you enter a range name, 1-2-3 uses the contents in the upper left cell as the legend.

To ensure that your legends will be displayed fully and print out completely, keep them each under nineteen characters. Legends will wrap to a second line if necessary. 1-2-3 truncates legends that extend beyond the graph frame and does not display legends that, because of their specified placement, would appear outside the graph frame.

When you use a cell address in a legend, 1-2-3 does not adjust the address if the referenced cells are relocated with the / **M**ove, / **W**orksheet **I**nsert, or / **W**orksheet **D**elete command.

(For more details about adding legends, see Lab 3.)

/ **G**raph **O**ptions **F**ormat

Graph **A B C D E F Q**uit

/ **G**raph **O**ptions **F**ormat controls data display for line and XY graphs.

Use / **G**raph **O**ptions **F**ormat to change the appearance of line and XY graphs.

- Select / **G**raph **O**ptions **F**ormat.
- Select **G**raph to change the format of the entire graph.
- Select **A** through **F** to format each data range individually.
- Choose **L**ines to connect each range data point with a straight line.
- Choose **S**ymbols to display each range data point with the same symbol (there is a different symbol for each range).
- Choose **B**oth to set lines and symbols. (This is the default.)
- Choose **N**either if you do not want symbols or lines to appear in the screen display. In this case, you must specify **D**ata-Labels to make the data points or lines visible.
- Select **Q**uit to return to the previous menu.

If you reset a data range, 1-2-3 saves the associated format settings and reuses them whenever you specify a new range.

/ **G**raph **O**ptions **T**itles

First **S**econd **X**-Axis **Y**-Axis

/ **G**raph **O**ptions **T**itles assigns a title to each axis or to an entire graph. Use this command in addition to the / **G**raph **O**ptions **L**egend and / **G**raph **O**ptions **D**ata-Labels commands to expand the descriptions of your graph data.

If you select **F**irst and **S**econd, lines in the graph titles appear centered at the top of the graph. First and second lines are independent of the names you use with / **G**raph **N**ame and / **G**raph **S**ave. With **X**-Axis, titles appear below the horizontal axis. With **Y**-Axis, titles appear on the side to the left of the vertical axis. A title can be up to thirty-nine characters in length.

To use the contents of a cell in the worksheet as a title, type a backslash (\) followed by the cell address or the range name. If you use a range name, 1-2-3 uses the contents from the upper left cell in the range as the title.

For printed graphs made with the PrintGraph program, the first title line is printed larger than the second. The second title line can be in a different font style. In some cases, the screen displays more characters than the printer can print, depending on the font you select and the total number of characters in the title.

(For more details about adding titles, see Lab 3.)

/ **G**raph **O**ptions **G**rid

Horizontal **V**ertical **B**oth **C**lear

/ **G**raph **O**ptions **G**rid adds or removes grid lines on your graph when the graph is viewed or printed.

You cannot use grid lines with pie charts.

If you use **H**orizontal, horizontal grid lines appear across the graph. With **V**ertical, vertical grid lines appear across the graph. With **B**oth, horizontal and vertical grid lines appear across the graph. **C**lear erases all grid lines. (For more details about adding grids, see Lab 3.)

/ **G**raph **O**ptions **S**cale

Y-Scale **X**-Scale **S**kip

/ **G**raph **O**ptions **S**cale sets the numeric scales for the Y axis and the X axis (for XY graphs) and specifies the skip factor for X-axis labels. It also controls the format of numbers used in the graph scale.

Use / **G**raph **O**ptions **S**cale to adjust the scale display on your graph. **Y**-Scale alters the scale of the Y axis. **X**-Scale alters the scale of the X axis. **S**kip determines which entries in the X range 1-2-3 displays along the X axis. Specify the skip factor. For a skip factor of n, 1-2-3 plots every nth entry from the X range on the horizontal axis in bar, stacked bar, and line graphs. For example, if $n = 10$, the first, eleventh, and twenty-first X-range entries appear on the X axis, and so on. The skip factor does not affect pie charts or XY graphs.

Select one of the options in Table 2.12 after you choose **Y**-Scale or **X**-Scale.

Table 2.12

Option	Description
Automatic	When you select **V**iew, 1-2-3 displays all the data points, using scale limits that let the graph fill the screen. 1-2-3 uses round numbers for the scale limits. This option overrides the other scale options and is the default setting.
Manual	When you select **V**iew, 1-2-3 displays the data points that fall within the limits you specify. You must specify upper and lower limits. Depending on the limits you choose, some data points may not be displayed. Also, when a data range includes values that vary widely (for instance, 10, 20, 30, 1,000,000, and 2,000,000), bars representing the larger values may not be displayed. If you set a scale to a limit smaller than the spread of data values, 1-2-3 expands the graph of the specified area to fill the screen.
Lower	Determines the lower scale limit 1-2-3 uses when displaying a graph. 1-2-3 adjusts the limit you set to a round number. This limit is used only after you select **/ G**raph **O**ptions **M**anual. Maximum values may be rounded off slightly. The default value is 0. 1-2-3 ignores a positive lower limit for bar and stacked bar graphs.
Upper	Determines the upper scale limit 1-2-3 uses when displaying a graph. 1-2-3 adjusts the limit you set to a round number. This limit is used only after you select **/ G**raph **O**ptions **M**anual. Maximum values may be rounded off slightly. The default value is 0. 1-2-3 ignores a positive upper limit for bar and stacked bar graphs.
Format	Lets you change the format of numbers in the graph scale. Select a format from the options in Table 2.7 in the Range Commands section of this chapter.
Indicator	Determines whether 1-2-3 displays scale indicators such as (thousands) or (millions) on a graph when you select **V**iew. Choose **Y**es to use indicators or **N**o not to use them. The default setting is **Y**es.
Quit	Returns you to **G**raph **O**ptions menu.

/ **G**raph **O**ptions **C**olor

/ **G**raph **O**ptions **C**olor displays data-range bars, pie slice hatches, graph lines, and symbols in contrasting colors if your monitor can display color graphs.

You can save a graph for printing with color settings even if your monitor cannot display colors. When you save a graph, 1-2-3 assigns a different color to each data range so that PrintGraph can draw each data range with a different color even if the graph was made with the / **G**raph **O**ptions **B**&W command. (However, do not use this command with a black and white printer, because the printer will print all ranges in solid blocks of black.) Bar and stacked bar graphs print out as solid bars of different colors. (For more details about viewing a graph in color, see Lab 4.)

/ Graph Options B&W

/ **G**raph **O**ptions **B**&W sets graph display to black and white (monochrome) if you previously selected / **G**raph **O**ptions **C**olor.

1-2-3 displays bars and pie slices (if you specified a B data range for the pie chart) in contrasting hatch patterns.

/ Graph Options Data-Labels

A B C D E F Group **Q**uit

/ **G**raph **O**ptions **D**ata-Labels labels the data points in data ranges A through F with the contents from a specified range of cells.

Use / **G**raph **O**ptions **D**ata-Labels to include detailed data value information in your graph.

You can select **A**, **B**, **C**, **D**, **E**, or **F** to assign a data-label range of the same size as the selected data range. You can select **G**roup to assign a data-label range of the same size to all data ranges at once. **G**roup also clears any settings previously set. If you select **G**roup and then specify a range, you can then select **C**olumnwise to divide the data-label range into individual ranges by columns, or **R**owwise to divide the data-label range into individual ranges by rows. **Q**uit returns you to the Graph Options menu.

In line and XY graphs, you must indicate how you want the data labels to align—centered, left, above, right, or below—in relation to their data points. For bar and stacked bar graphs, data labels are centered above positive bars and below negative bars. For pie charts, data labels are not displayed.

1-2-3 displays the specified range contents as data point labels the next time you view the graph. If a data-label cell contains a number or a formula, 1-2-3 displays the cell value as a label in the graph. If you reset a data range, 1-2-3 also resets the corresponding data-label range. (For more details about adding data labels, see Lab 3.)

/ Graph Name

Use **C**reate **D**elete **R**eset **T**able

/ **G**raph **N**ame lets you create or modify named graphs, delete a named graph or all named graphs in the worksheet, create a table of named graphs in the worksheet, or retrieve a named graph, making it the current graph.

/ **G**raph **N**ame **U**se makes a named set of graph settings current and draws the graph. You can use / **G**raph **N**ame **U**se only if you have created a graph and named it. (For more details about using named graphs, see Lab 4.)

CAUTION When you retrieve a named graph, you lose all of the previous graph settings. To preserve those settings for future use, assign them a name with / **G**raph **N**ame **C**reate before you use / **G**raph **N**ame **U**se.

/ **G**raph **N**ame **C**reate saves the current graph settings under a graph name. You can change the cell contents in a graph data range after you name it because the data range specifies only the location, or address, of a cell, not the cell contents.

Use / **G**raph **N**ame **C**reate to save more than one graph within a worksheet or to move quickly from one graph to another during a 1-2-3 session. A graph name can be up to fifteen characters long. If you use an existing graph filename, 1-2-3 replaces the previous specifications with the current graph settings. There is no Cancel or Replace step.

You must also use the / **F**ile **S**ave command to attach the named settings to the current worksheet. If you make any changes to the graph, select / **G**raph **N**ame **C**reate and then save the worksheet file. (For more details about naming graphs, see Lab 4.)

/ **G**raph **N**ame **D**elete erases one set of named graph specifications. Use / **G**raph **N**ame **D**elete to eliminate unwanted graphs or to free graph filenames for reuse.

CAUTION When you select / **G**raph **N**ame **D**elete, 1-2-3 erases the graph settings for the selected graph and automatically returns you to the Graph Options menu. There is no confirmation step. However, if the Undo feature is on, select **Q**uit to return to the worksheet, then press UNDO (ALT-F4) immediately to restore the named graph.

/ **G**raph **N**ame **R**eset erases all named graphs.

CAUTION When you select / **G**raph **N**ame **R**eset, 1-2-3 erases all named graphs and automatically returns you to the Graph Options menu. There is no confirmation step. The last graph created will remain with no name attached. However, if the Undo feature is on, select **Q**uit to return to the worksheet, then press UNDO (ALT-F4) immediately to restore the graphs.

/ **G**raph **N**ame **T**able creates a table that alphabetically lists all the named graphs in the worksheet. The table can be placed in any blank and unprotected area of the worksheet. It will occupy three columns and as many rows as there are named graphs plus one blank row. It will write over any existing worksheet data.

/ **G**raph **G**roup

Columnwise **R**owwise

/ **G**raph **G**roup specifies all graph data ranges (**X** and **A–F**) at once, when the X and A–F data ranges are in consecutive columns or rows of a range.

Columnwise divides the group range into data ranges by columns. **R**owwise divides the group range into data ranges by rows.

1-2-3 uses the first column or row of the group range as the X data range and subsequent columns or rows as the A–F data ranges. If the range includes more than seven columns or rows, 1-2-3 stops assigning data ranges after the seventh column or row.

Data Commands

The **D**ata commands let you analyze and manipulate data in ranges and in 1-2-3 databases. Figure 2.8 shows the Data menu tree.

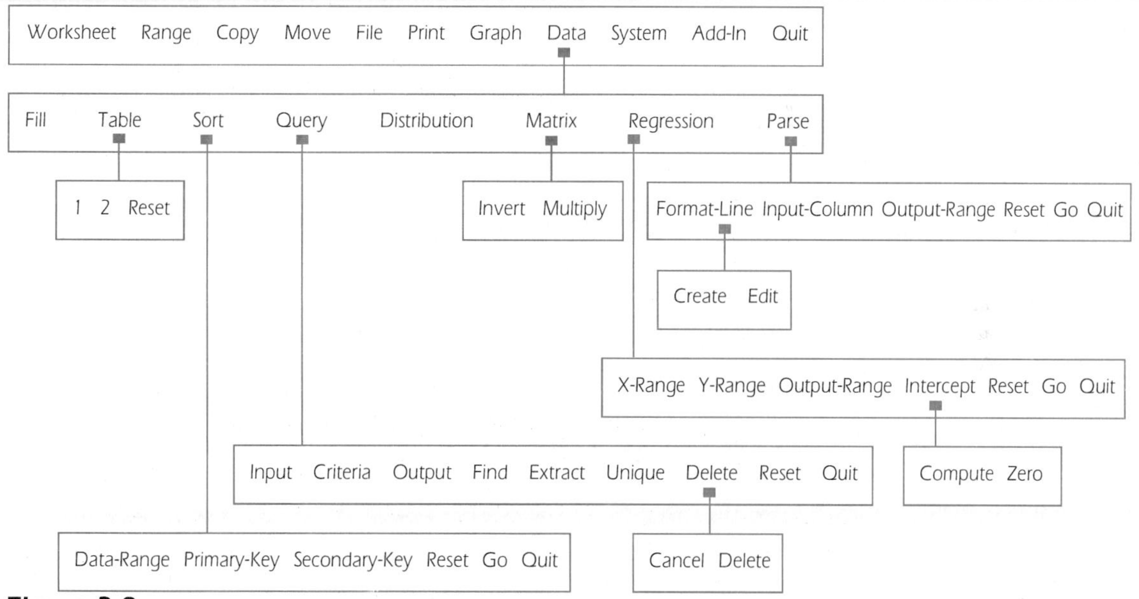

Figure 2.8

Database

A 1-2-3 database is a worksheet range that consists of data organized in a specific way. All entries in a single row constitute one record, which is a collection of information about one particular item in the database. Each record in a database consists of the same categories, called fields. Each column in the database comprises one field.

Each cell in the first row of a database contains a label, called a field name, that identifies the category of information in the column below. All subsequent rows contain records.

Any collection of data that you organize in records and fields can be a 1-2-3 database. When you create a database, do not leave any blank rows or divider lines below the field names or between records.

A 1-2-3 database can contain up to 256 fields and 8,191 records.

(For more details about databases, see Lab 7.)

/ Data Fill

/ **D**ata **F**ill enters an ascending or descending sequence of numbers into a specified range of cells.

Use / **D**ata **F**ill with a 1-2-3 worksheet or a 1-2-3 database. This command is often used to assign a unique record number to each record in a database.

Before you use this command, position the cell pointer in the upper left corner cell of the range you want to fill. After you initiate the command, 1-2-3 will prompt you to specify the fill range (the range of cells to fill), the Start value (the beginning number) of your sequence, the Step value (the increment between each of the numbers), and the Stop value (the final number) of the sequence. Stop value is an optional setting.

/ Data Table

1 **2** **R**eset

Data tables let you try out different values in formulas. You can perform sensitivity analysis, see the effects of a what-if test, prepare graphs, and quickly analyze data from a database.

/ **D**ata **T**able **1** produces a table that shows the different values a formula generates each time you change one value in that formula. When you create a Data Table 1, 1-2-3 places a single set of values into one or more formulas.

Before selecting / **D**ata **T**able **1**, you must set up the data table in a table range, which can be in any unused part of the worksheet. Use the following guidelines to set up a Data Table 1:

- Choose a blank area of the worksheet for your table range.
- Choose any cell outside the table range to use as input cell 1. You will use the cell address of this cell to represent the changing value in each of the formulas the data table will calculate.
- Leave the upper left cell of the table range blank.
- Enter formulas into the top cell of the second column of the data table. You can enter one or more formulas that contain values, strings, or cell addresses. You must use the cell address of input cell 1 as the variable in each of the formulas.
- Enter the variables (values) for the input cell address into the column of the table range directly below the blank cell.

Once the data table is set up, you can issue this command to generate the table.

- Position the cell pointer in the blank cell in the upper left corner of the table range.
- Select / **D**ata **T**able **1**.
- At the prompt, enter the table range. The table range contains the blank cell, all the formulas in the first row, and all the values in the column below the blank cell.
- At the prompt, enter the cell address of the input cell 1.

1-2-3 places each value from the first column into the input cell, one at a time, and uses that value to calculate the formulas in the first row. The result of each calculation appears in the data table in the cell below the appropriate formula and to the right of the appropriate value.

1-2-3 does not automatically recalculate the results area of a data table if you change any of the formulas or value entries in the table. You can recalculate your most recent data table from READY mode by pressing the Table function key, F8. 1-2-3 uses the most recently specified table range and input cell. To cancel the current table range and input cell specifications, use **R**eset.

If you are using / **D**ata **T**able **1** in conjunction with a database, you can use the database statistical @functions as formulas in the top row of the data table. These @functions let you perform calculations using data from only those records that meet your criteria. (See Chapter 4, "@Functions," for detailed information about @functions.)

(For more details about creating a data table, see Lab 8.)

/ **D**ata **T**able **2** produces a table that shows the different values a formula generates each time you change two values in that formula. When you create a Data Table 2, 1-2-3 places two sets of values into a single formula. Before selecting / **D**ata **T**able **2**, you must set up the data table in a table range, which can be in any unused part of the worksheet. Use the following guidelines to set up a Data Table 2:

- Choose a blank area of the worksheet for your table range.
- Choose any two cells outside the table range to use as input cell 1 and input cell 2. You will use the cell addresses of these cells to represent the two changing values in the formula that the data table will calculate.
- Enter the formula in the upper left cell of the table range. The formula can contain values, strings, or cell addresses. You must use the cell addresses of input cell 1 and input cell 2 as the two variables in the formula.

- Enter the first set of values into the column of the table range directly below the cell where you entered the formula. These are the values that 1-2-3 will use, one at a time, in place of the cell address of input cell 1 in the formula.
- Enter the second set of values into the top row of the table range to the right of the cell containing the formula. These are the values that 1-2-3 uses, one at a time, in place of the cell address of input cell 2 in the formula.

Once the data table is set up, you can issue the command to generate the table.

- Position the cell pointer in the cell containing the formula, the upper left cell of the table range.
- Select / **D**ata **T**able **2**.
- Enter the table range at the prompt. (The table range contains the cell with the formula, all the values in the column below that cell, and all the values in the top row to the right of that cell.)
- At the prompt, enter the cell address of input cell 1.
- At the prompt, enter the cell address of input cell 2.

The result of each calculation appears in the data table in the cell below the appropriate row value and to the right of the appropriate column value. The input cells themselves are unaffected.

1-2-3 does not automatically recalculate the results area of a data table if you change the formula or the value entries in the table. You can recalculate your most recent data table from READY mode by pressing the Table function key, (F8). 1-2-3 uses the most recently specified table range and input cells.

If you are using / **D**ata **T**able **2** in conjunction with a database, you can use any database statistical @function as your formula. These @functions let you perform calculations using data from only those records that meet your criteria. (See Chapter 4, "@Functions," for detailed information about @functions.)

/ **D**ata **T**able **R**eset clears all the table ranges and input cells you specified in the worksheet.

/ **D**ata **S**ort

Data-Range **P**rimary-Key **S**econdary-Key **R**eset **G**o **Q**uit

/ **D**ata **S**ort rearranges the records in a database in the order you specify. The **D**ata-Range and **P**rimary-Key are required settings. **D**ata-Range contains all the records you want to sort. You should include all fields. Do not include the row of field names.

When you select / **D**ata **S**ort, 1-2-3 displays a Sort settings sheet, which lists the location of the data range, primary sort key, and secondary sort key.

The **P**rimary-Key is the field that 1-2-3 uses to determine the new order for your records. Records are rearranged so that the values in the primary-key field appear in ascending or descending order. When prompted for the primary sort key, enter the cell address of any cell in the field you want 1-2-3 to use to determine the new order for your records. At the prompt for the primary sort order, select either **A** for ascending order or **D** for descending order. (See the section below on Sort Order for further information.)

The **S**econdary-Key is the field that 1-2-3 uses to break ties that occur when two or more records have the same entries in the primary-key field and you want these entries arranged in a specific order. **S**econdary-Key is an optional setting. Respond to the prompts for the secondary sort key and secondary sort order following the same procedure as for the **P**rimary-Key.

Reset cancels your current data-range, primary-key, and secondary-key settings. Select **G**o to begin the sort. **Q**uit returns you to READY mode before a sort is completed.

Avoid formulas with references to cells in different rows of the data range. Use relative cell references in formulas to refer to cells in other fields in the same record. Use absolute cell references in formulas to refer to any cells outside the data range.

Sort Order

Ascending sorts arrange data in the following order, using the collating sequence you choose during installation:

- Numbers last: blank cells, labels beginning with letters in alphabetical order, labels beginning with numbers in numerical order, labels beginning with other characters (ignores capitalization and most accent marks)
- Numbers first: blank cells, labels beginning with numbers in numerical order, labels beginning with letters in alphabetical order, labels beginning with other characters (ignores capitalization and most accent marks)
- ASCII blank cells: all labels using their ASCII values

Descending sorts reverse the above order. All sorts place numeric values or formulas after any label. The sort order of records whose primary- and secondary-key entries are equal is not predictable.

(For more details about sorting a database, see Lab 7.)

Data Query Commands

Data Query commands let you search a database for specific records, copy records from a database to a separate part of the worksheet, extract records with no duplication, and remove selected records.

When you select / **D**ata **Q**uery, 1-2-3 displays a settings sheet, which lists the location of the input range, the criteria range, and the output range. This helps you keep track of the choices you are making.

/ Data Query Find

/ **D**ata **Q**uery **F**ind locates the records in a database that match the criteria you specify. Use / **D**ata **Q**uery **F**ind only in conjunction with a 1-2-3 database. Before selecting / **D**ata **Q**uery **F**ind, set up an **I**nput range and a **C**riteria range.

Input Range

The input range is the range of a database that you want 1-2-3 to search when you select a / **D**ata **Q**uery command. The input range includes the database field names and all the records you want to search.

Setting Up a Criteria Range

The criteria range tells 1-2-3 which records to search for in the input range. To set up a criteria range, use the following guidelines:

- Choose a blank range in your worksheet, either several rows below your database or to the right of the database. This area will serve as your criteria range.
- In the first row of the criteria range, copy one, some, or all of the field names in the database. You must enter each field name exactly as it appears in the database.
- Enter your criteria in the second row (and subsequent rows) of the criteria range. Enter each criterion below the copy of the appropriate field name. You can enter a label or a value exactly as it appears in the database if you want 1-2-3 to search for records that match the criteria exactly. You can also enter formulas.
- Enter several criteria in the same row if you want 1-2-3 to search only for records that satisfy every criteria.
- Enter multiple criteria one per row if you want 1-2-3 to search for records that satisfy any of the criteria.

(See the section Writing Criteria in this chapter for information on creating single or multiple criteria to search for labels or values.)

Once the criteria range is set up, you can enter the command to find the matching records.

- Select / **D**ata **Q**uery.
- Specify the **I**nput and **C**riteria ranges.
- Select **F**ind.

1-2-3 highlights the first record that matches the criteria. To find other matching records in the database, use the following steps:

- Press (↓) or (↑) to move the cell pointer to other records that match the criteria. If there are no more matching records in those directions, 1-2-3 beeps.
- Press (←) or (→) to move the cell pointer from field to field within a highlighted record.
- Press HOME to move the highlight to the first record in the database or END to move the highlight to the last record in the database, even if the records do not match the criteria.
- Press (↵) or ESC to end the / **D**ata **Q**uery **F**ind command and return to the Query menu.
- Select **Q**uit to return to READY mode.

Use / **D**ata **Q**uery **F**ind to quickly locate records that you want to edit. Move the cursor to the cell you want to edit and press (F2) to turn on EDIT mode. The Query function key ((F7)) switches from FIND to READY mode. You can now use commands to alter your database. Use (F7) again to return to the most recently highlighted record in FIND mode or to repeat your most recent / **D**ata **Q**uery command from READY mode. Select **R**eset to clear the range specifications for the input and criteria ranges.

If there are no matching records, 1-2-3 beeps and returns to the Query menu.

(For more details about setting up a criteria range, see Lab 7.)

Writing Criteria

You can write criteria that match label or value entries, and you can use more than one criterion.

Searching for Labels

To search for exact matches, enter the label as the criterion. Two special characters allow you to search for similar label entries:

? matches any single character. For example, h?t matches hat, hot, and hut, but not huts; h??d matches head and hood, but not heel.
* matches all characters to the end of the label. For example, cat* matches cat, catsup, and catechism, but not cutthroat.

Precede a label with a tilde (~) to search for all labels except that one. (Empty cells, however, are never selected by any label-match criteria.) For example, ~Smith matches all records with an entry in that field other than Smith. ~S* matches all records with an entry in the field that do not begin with S.

Searching for Values

To search for exact matches, enter the value as the criterion.

To search for all values that meet a condition you set (such as all entries greater than 150), enter the condition as a logical expression, using the cell address of the appropriate field of the first record in the database. Use a logical operator (<, <=, >, >=, <>) in your formula to compare this cell entry to some value.

The logical formula generates a value of 1 if the condition is true or a value of 0 if it is false.

Using Multiple Criteria

Enter multiple criteria for different fields into the same row to search for only those records that match all these criteria at once. 1-2-3 treats criteria in the same row as if they are linked by the word AND.

Enter multiple criteria for different fields into separate rows to search for records that match any of the criteria. 1-2-3 treats criteria in separate rows as if they are linked by the word OR.

Use compound logical formulas if you want to create compound criteria that match more than one condition in the same field. Use #AND#, #NOT#, or #OR# in the formula to tie together the two conditions. For example, +D2>1500#AND#+D2<2200 will search for all records with entries greater than 1500.00 but less than 2200.00

/ **D**ata **Q**uery **E**xtract

/ **D**ata **Q**uery **E**xtract copies records that match criteria you specify from a database to a separate part of the worksheet. You can extract all or part of a record. Use / **D**ata **Q**uery **E**xtract only in conjunction with a 1-2-3 database. Before selecting / **D**ata **Q**uery **E**xtract, set up input, criteria, and output ranges. Set up the input and criteria ranges as you would for / **D**ata **Q**uery **F**ind.

Setting Up an Output Range

The output range is the area to which 1-2-3 copies the results of the / **D**ata **Q**uery **E**xtract command. To set up an output range, use the following guidelines:

- Choose a blank range that will not overlap your input or criteria ranges.
- Enter field names from the database in the first row of the output range. Include each field that you want listed when 1-2-3 copies records that match your criteria. Each field name must be identical to the corresponding field name in the input and criteria ranges, but it may appear in any order.

- The maximum width of an output range is 32 fields.

Once the criteria and output ranges are set, you can issue the command to extract the data.

- Select / **D**ata **Q**uery.
- Specify the input, criteria, and output ranges.

If you specify a multiple-row output range, include the top row of field names and enough additional rows to hold the records that 1-2-3 will copy in the range.

If you specify a single-row output range, include only the top row of field names. When you select / **D**ata **Q**uery **E**xtract, 1-2-3 will copy matching records and erase all other data in the columns below the output range. Specify a multiple-row output range if there are any data below the output range that you want to keep.

- Select **E**xtract. When you select **E**xtract, 1-2-3 copies the field from records that match your criteria into the appropriate columns below the field names in the output range.

1-2-3 beeps and an error message appears if you specified a multiple-row output range and the number of matching records cannot fit in the range. Press ESC and begin the procedure again, specifying a larger multiple-row range or, if it is safe to do so, a single-row range.

- Select **Q**uit to return to READY mode and then move the cell pointer to the output range.

To clear the range of specifications for the input, criteria, and output ranges, select **R**eset.

Press F7 to repeat your most recent / **D**ata **Q**uery command from READY mode. (For more details about using the **D**ata **Q**uery **E**xtract command, see Lab 8.)

/ **D**ata **Q**uery **U**nique

/ **D**ata **Q**uery **U**nique works exactly like / **D**ata **Q**uery **E**xtract, except that it eliminates any duplicate records from the records that 1-2-3 copies to the output range. It also eliminates any records that appear to be duplicates when you include only some of the database fields in the output range.

Follow the procedure for / **D**ata **Q**uery **E**xtract, but select **U**nique instead of **E**xtract as the final step.

/ **D**ata **Q**uery **D**elete

/ **D**ata **Q**uery **D**elete erases the records in the input range that match the criteria and deletes the rows from the database. As a safety precaution, 1-2-3 prompts you for confirmation before the deletion.

Follow the procedure for / **D**ata **Q**uery **F**ind, but select **D**elete instead of **F**ind as the final step. Then select **D**elete again if you actually want to delete these records or **C**ancel if you chose this accidentally and want to return to the Data Query menu.

/ Data Distribution

/ **D**ata **D**istribution creates a frequency distribution of the values in a range. A frequency distribution tells you how many values in a specified range (values range) fall within specified numeric intervals (bin range).

Before you begin the command, choose two adjacent blank columns. The left column serves as the bin range. The right column serves as the output range. Enter the values you want to use as intervals into the bin range column in ascending order with the smallest value at the top.

Initiate the command sequence and enter the values range at the prompt (the range that contains the values you want to analyze). Next, enter the bin range at the prompt (the range that contains the intervals for the distribution).

The frequency values appear in the output-range column to the right of the bin range. The numbers in the output range represent how many values in the value range are less than or equal to the adjacent value in the bin range but greater than the preceding value in the bin column. Blank and label cells have a count value of 0.

The output range always contains a value one row beyond the end of the bin column. This last value is the frequency of values that are greater than the last bin value.

(For more details about creating a frequency distribution, see Lab 8.)

/ Data Matrix

Invert **M**ultiply

/ **D**ata **M**atrix multiplies and inverts matrices formed by rows and columns of cell entries.

- Select / **D**ata **M**atrix.

To invert a matrix:

- Select **I**nvert. Enter the range to invert at the prompt (up to 80 columns and 80 rows). You can invert only square matrices. Next, enter the output range at the prompt. You need enter only the address of the upper left corner of the output range where you want the inverted matrix to appear.

To multiply matrices:

- Select **M**ultiply. Enter the first and second ranges to multiply at the prompts. When you are multiplying matrices, there must be the same number of columns in the first range of numbers as there are rows in the second range of numbers. Next, enter the output range. You can enter the range address where you want the product of the multiplication to appear. You can choose values up to 256 rows and 256 columns.

/ **D**ata **R**egression

X-Range **Y**-Range **O**utput-Range **I**ntercept **R**eset **G**o **Q**uit

/ **D**ata **R**egression computes the coefficient values and constant for a formula that ties one or more ranges of independent variables to a range of dependent variables. It also indicates the statistical accuracy of these values.

When you select / **D**ata **R**egression, 1-2-3 displays a Regression settings sheet that lists by cell address the location of the X range, Y range, output range, and Y-axis intercept.

Use / **D**ata **R**egression if you have several sets of values and you want to see how and whether one set is dependent on the other(s). You can also use / **D**ata **R**egression to determine the slope(s) and the Y intercept(s) of the best fitting line(s) for a set of data points.

Regression analysis allows you to predict a value for a dependent variable based on other values for one or more independent variables. In the results, the Y-axis intercept appears as the constant, and the X coefficient(s) are the slopes.

The **X**-Range is the range that contains all the columns of data to be analyzed as independent variables. You can specify up to sixteen independent variables for multiple regression.

The **Y**-Range is the range that contains the column of data to be analyzed as dependent variables. The X range and the Y range must have the same number of rows.

When entering the **O**utput-Range, you can specify a single cell (the upper left cell of the range), the entire range, or the range name. The range must be at least nine rows long and two columns wider than the number of independent variables. It must be at least four columns wide.

The **I**ntercept option allows you to choose between **C**ompute, computing the Y intercept, and forcing it to be **Z**ero. The default is to compute the Y intercept.

1-2-3 enters the following information into the output range: the constant, the standard error of the Y estimate, the r-squared value, the number of observations, the degrees of freedom, the X coefficients (for each of the independent variables), and the standard error of each of these coefficients.

Reset cancels all the current regression settings.

Go begins the analysis.

Use **Q**uit to return to READY mode before completing the **D**ata **R**egression.

To graph a regression line of estimated Y values against actual Y values, select the XY graph type. Then assign the range of estimated Y values to both the X and A ranges of the graph. Assign the actual Y values to the B range of the graph. Set the format for the B range of the graph to symbols only. The resulting graph shows the regression line with real Y values as points.

/ **D**ata **P**arse

Format-Line **I**nput-Column **O**utput-Range **R**eset **G**o **Q**uit

/ **D**ata **P**arse converts a column of long labels into several columns of labels or numbers.

When you select / **D**ata **P**arse, 1-2-3 displays a Parse settings sheet that lists the location of the input column and the output range.

Use / **D**ata **P**arse to convert an ASCII text file you have imported into your worksheet with / **F**ile **I**mport **T**ext into a standard 1-2-3 worksheet or database.

1-2-3 treats data imported with / **F**ile **I**mport **T**ext as long labels of text contained in a single column. You must parse this data, breaking up the long labels into individual cell entries that 1-2-3 can use, if you want to perform any other 1-2-3 task, such as numeric analysis or graphing, with the data.

- Before you initiate this command, position the cell pointer in the top cell of the column you want to parse. Initiate the command sequence, then select **F**ormat-Line **C**reate. Format lines control the manner in which a long label is divided into blocks of data that will become individual cell entries, one per column.

1-2-3 analyzes the label at the current position of the cell pointer and inserts a format line of the same length above it in a new row. The format line that is created is 1-2-3's best guess of how the label should be parsed.

The format line is a label preceded by a split vertical bar (¦). 1-2-3 inserts a format line in the cell above the previous position of the cell pointer. The characters in the format line reflect the data type and the width of each block of data in the cell below.

Format lines can contain the following symbols:

L	The first character of a label block
V	The first character of a value block
D	The first character of a date block
T	The first character of a time block
S	Skip the character below when parsing
>	Characters in a data block
*	Blank space immediately below, currently undefined, but can become part of a block of data in following cells

1-2-3 creates the following format line for the long label in the cell below it:

```
¦L>> >>*********************V >>>*********V>>****V>>>
'C o s t s                   1 5 0 0       9 5 0    1 2 0 0
```

/ **D**ata **P**arse will enter Costs as a label in one column, 1500 as a value in a second column, 950 as a value in a third column, and 1200 as a value in a fourth column.

- An optional step is to edit the format line. Edit format lines if any block (including adjacent * characters) is not wide enough to accommodate any of the data that will be parsed in the rows beneath it, if any of the block widths or data type characters are incorrect, or if any single block contains a space, since the format line treats it as two shorter blocks. (See the next section, ''Editing a Format Line,'' for more information.)

The Skip symbol (S) can be entered only manually. You can replace a symbol with an S when you edit the format line. If you begin a block with an S, 1-2-3 does not copy that block into the output range when it passes the line below.

- Another optional step is to create one or more additional format lines. Create an additional format line if any cell below the format line contains a block whose data type does not match that indicated in the format line, or if any cell below the format line contains a block whose width should be different from that indicated in the format line.

To create each additional format line, select **Q**uit to return to READY mode, position the cell pointer in the next cell in the column requiring a new format line, and select / **D**ata **P**arse **F**ormat-Line **C**reate. Edit each new line if necessary.

- Select **I**nput-Column to enter the range that contains the column of format lines and the cells you want to parse at the prompt. Be sure to include the format lines. Remember that the range includes only one column.
- Select **O**utput-Range to enter the cell address of the upper left corner of a blank range in the worksheet large enough to hold your rows and columns of parsed data.
- After specifying **F**ormat-Line, **I**nput-Column, and **O**utput-Range, select **G**o.

1-2-3 produces a parsed copy of the imported data in the output range. Each block of data has been entered in an individual cell as a value, a date, a time, or a label.

Editing a Format Line

To edit a format line, position the cell pointer in the cell containing the format line you want to edit. Select / **D**ata **P**arse **F**ormat-Line **E**dit.

The cell pointer disappears. You can edit the format line on the worksheet itself. The cursor is below the first character of the format line, and the status indicator reads OVR. This tells you that the overstrike editing feature is activated. Use [→] or [←] to move through the format line to the characters you want to edit. Then type new characters in place of the incorrect ones. You can also use DEL, BACKSPACE, CTRL-[→], CTRL-[←], and INS as you would in EDIT mode.

Press [↓], [↑], PGDN, or PGUP to scroll the rows below the format line to see rows not currently visible on your screen. You can also move a row directly below the format line temporarily so you can check the format of that row more easily. You do not have to undo scrolling before you press [↵] to finish editing the format line.

Press ESC to erase the entire format line. This does not delete the row. Press HOME to return the cursor to its initial position in the format line and to undo any scrolling. Press BREAK to cancel the format line edit and to return to READY mode with the format line as it was before you began to edit it. Press [↵] when you have completed editing the format line.

After you have edited the format line, the new format line appears in your worksheet, and 1-2-3 returns you to the Data Parse menu so that you can continue with the parse procedure.

System Command

/ System

/ **S**ystem lets you leave 1-2-3 temporarily, use a DOS command, and then return to your 1-2-3 session.

CAUTION Before you use the System command, it is recommended that you use / **F**ile **S**ave to save your work.

You can use any DOS command except commands that load another program into memory, such as PRINT and SET-CLOCK. If you load another program into memory, you will not be able to return to the 1-2-3 program.

To return to the 1-2-3 session, type **EXIT** and press (↵) at the operating system prompt.

If you have inserted a DOS disk, remove it from the drive, return the 1-2-3 System disk to the drive, type **EXIT**, then press (↵).

Add-In Commands

The **A**dd-In commands let you use 1-2-3 add-in applications. Add-ins are programs, created by Lotus and other software developers, that you can run while you are using 1-2-3 and that provide 1-2-3 with additional capabilities. You never have to leave the worksheet to use an add-in. The program actually becomes part of 1-2-3. Figure 2.9 shows the Add-In menu tree.

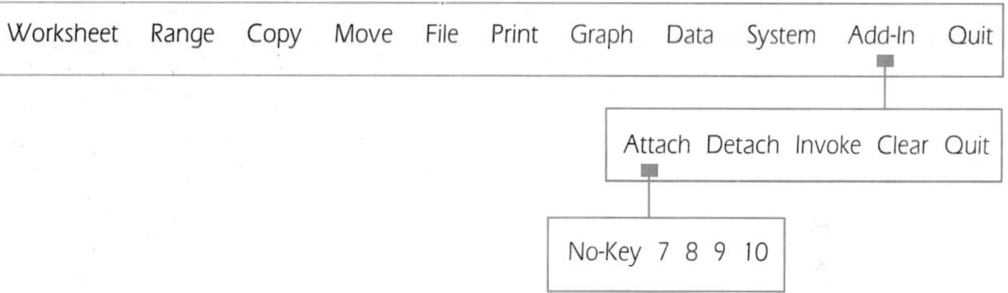

Figure 2.9

A variety of add-ins are available for 1-2-3, including programs that allow you to audit and annotate 1-2-3 worksheets, create three-dimensional graphs with your 1-2-3 data, perform word processing tasks in the worksheet, link 1-2-3 with database programs, create index files and relational databases in 1-2-3, print your 1-2-3 data sideways or in a specified report format, and change the size or color of the worksheet.

Your 1-2-3 package includes one add-in:

- The Macro Library Manager add-in, which lets you store macros, formulas, and ranges of data in a library that you can use with any worksheet. (See Chapter 3, "Macros," for more on the Macro Library Manager add-in.)

You can use the Add-In commands by selecting / **A**dd-In from the 1-2-3 main menu, or by pressing APP4 (ALT-F10) if you have not assigned that key to an add-in program.

/ Add-In Attach

No-Key **7 8 9 10**

/ **A**dd-In **A**ttach loads an add-in program into memory. Add-ins remain in memory until you detach them with / **A**dd-In **D**etach, / **A**dd-In **C**lear, / **W**orksheet **G**lobal **D**efault **O**ther **A**dd-In **C**ancel, or until you end the current 1-2-3 session. An attached add-in is not activated until you select / **A**dd-In **I**nvoke or press the key you have assigned to the add-in.

If you have a two-disk system, make sure the disk that contains the add-in program you want to attach is in one of the disk drives. Select / **A**dd-In **A**ttach. 1-2-3 displays a menu of files with an .ADN extension in the directory from which you started 1-2-3. If you want to display files in a different drive and/or directory, press ESC to clear the filenames, edit the drive and/or directory name, and then press ↵. Specify the filename of the add-in you want to attach and press ↵.

Selecting **N**o-Key does not assign the add-in to any specific key. Selecting **7** assigns the add-in to APP1 (ALT-F7). Selecting **8** assigns the add-in to APP2 (ALT-F8). Selecting **9** assigns the add-in to APP3 (ALT-F9). Selecting **10** assigns the add-in to APP4 (ALT-F10).

Note Once you assign an add-in to a key, that key will no longer appear in the menu during the current 1-2-3 session, unless you detach the add-in.

If you do not assign the add-in to a key, you will have to invoke it using / **A**dd-In **I**nvoke.

/ Add-In Detach

/ **A**dd-In **D**etach removes an attached add-in program from memory, freeing the memory it occupied.

Note You cannot detach add-in @functions. Once attached, they remain in memory until you end the 1-2-3 session.

/ Add-In Invoke

/ **A**dd-In **I**nvoke activates an add-in program that you have attached with / **A**dd-In **A**ttach. If you assigned the add-in to a key, you can use that key to invoke the add-in.

/ Add-In Clear

/ **A**dd-In **C**lear removes all attached add-in programs from memory, freeing the memory they occupied.

Quit Command

/ Quit

/ **Q**uit lets you leave 1-2-3.

CAUTION 1-2-3 does not automatically save your work when you leave the program. You must save your work first.

You must select either **Y**es to leave 1-2-3 or **N**o to cancel the / **Q**uit command and return to READY mode. (For more details about leaving 1-2-3, see Lab 1.)

3

Macros

Macros help you automate your work during a 1-2-3 work session. A macro is a set of instructions made up of a sequence of keystrokes and commands that you type into a worksheet as cell entries. After you have entered and named the macro, you can invoke it. Whenever you type the macro name, 1-2-3 reads the instructions and performs the specified tasks. When 1-2-3 finishes executing the macro, you can continue with your work.

A macro can automate any 1-2-3 task that you perform manually. Macros save you time and simplify worksheet operations by letting you use fewer keystrokes to execute a complex or repetitive task.

Macros are most useful for the following purposes:

- Automating frequently used 1-2-3 commands
- Typing the same label many times in a worksheet
- Performing a repetitive procedure that requires a series of sequential commands
- Developing a customized worksheet for someone not familiar with 1-2-3

The information in this chapter is divided into four sections. The section on Macro Basics presents the basic concepts and procedures for creating and using 1-2-3 macros. The section on the Learn Feature describes this alternate method of entering macro instructions. The third section, on Advanced Macro Commands, introduces a more advanced way of automating 1-2-3. You should not attempt to use these advanced macro capabilities unless you are an experienced 1-2-3 user or familiar with programming concepts and techniques. The last section, on the Macro Library Manager, describes basic information on this add-in program.

Macro Basics

A macro is a series of cell entries typed in one or more cells in a single column. A macro cell entry must appear in the form of a label, whether it is a command, a number, or a formula.

A macro can include advanced macro commands and keystroke instructions. Advanced macro commands cause 1-2-3 to perform built-in programming functions. (See ''Advanced Macro Commands'' later in this chapter.) Keystroke instructions represent keys on the keyboard and cause 1-2-3 to perform as it does when you press those keys. They can be divided into two groups: instructions that consist of a single character, such as / (slash), w, and ~ (tilde); and instructions that consist of a key name within {} (braces), such as {RIGHT}.

The single-character keystroke instructions represent the typewriter keys on your keyboard. Most of these instructions duplicate the character on the key they represent. For example, the keystroke instruction that displays the 1-2-3 main menu is / (slash); the keystroke instruction that selects **W**orksheet from the main menu is w, and so on.

The keystroke instructions that consist of a key name within {} (braces) represent the pointer-movement keys, function keys, and a few other keys. (See "Keystroke Instructions" later in this section.)

Creating a Macro

You can create a macro in five steps:

1. Plan your macro and go through the steps of your task manually.
2. Enter the macro as one or more labels.
3. Name the macro.
4. Document the macro.
5. Run the macro.

(For more details about creating a macro, see Lab 9.)

Planning a Macro

Before you write a macro, plan the steps necessary to accomplish the desired task. When you have a good grasp of the required steps, go through each keystroke manually, carefully noting each key that you press. After confirming that the sequence of keystrokes is correct, you are ready to enter the macro.

Entering a Macro

Some guidelines for entering a macro, as well as some rules on macro structure, follow:

- If you enter macros in the same worksheet as data, use a blank area of the worksheet so that the macro does not affect any data that already exist.
- Type the entries for a macro in any column of cells. You can type more than one instruction or command sequence in the same cell.
- The instructions you type in a macro can include any of the standard keyboard characters (for example, h, 9, +), keystroke instructions, and advanced macro commands.
- The instructions in each cell can be as short as a single keystroke or as long as 240 characters. If the keystroke sequence is very long, divide it into more than one cell in a column for easier reading and editing.

- Type all cell entries for a macro in the form of labels. When entering commands (beginning with a /), numbers, or formulas, you must begin the macro entry with a label-prefix character, such as a single quote (').
- Leave the cell below the macro instructions blank so that 1-2-3 does not include any information immediately below the macro as part of the macro's instructions.
- You can use the Learn feature to create macros by entering the keystroke instructions and testing them at the same time. (See "Using the Learn Feature to Create Macros" later in this section.)
- You can also save the macros in a macro library, a special file that contains only macros. (See "Creating and Using the Macro Library Manager" in this chapter.)

Keystroke Instructions

You can enter most keystrokes in a macro simply by typing the appropriate key; however, you must type the keystroke instructions, which represent keys on the keyboard, as they appear in Table 3.1.

Table 3.1

Keystroke Instruction	1-2-3 Key
~ (a tilde)	↵
{D} or {DOWN}	↓
{U} or {UP}	↑
{L} or {LEFT}	←
{R} or {RIGHT}	→
{APP1}	APP1 (ALT-F7)
{APP2}	APP2 (ALT-F8)
{APP3}	APP3 (ALT-F9)
{APP4}	APP4 (ALT-F10)
{HOME}	HOME
{END}	END
{PGUP}	PGUP (move up one screen)
{PGDN}	PGDN (move down one screen)
{BIGLEFT}	CTRL-← (move left one screen)
{BIGRIGHT}	CTRL-→ (move right one screen)
{HELP}	HELP, F1
{EDIT}	EDIT, F2
{NAME}	NAME, F3
{ABS}	ABS, F4
{GOTO}	GOTO, F5
{WINDOW}	WINDOW, F6
{QUERY}	QUERY, F7
{TABLE}	TABLE, F8
{CALC}	CALC, F9

Table 3.1 Continued

Keystroke Instruction	1-2-3 Key
{GRAPH}	GRAPH, F10
{INSERT} or {INS}	INS
{ESCAPE} or {ESC}	ESC
{BACKSPACE} or {BS}	BACKSPACE
{DELETE} or {DEL}	DEL (use only in EDIT mode)
/ <, or {menu}	/ (slash) or < (less than symbol)
{~}	to have tilde appear as ~
{{} and {}}	to have braces appear as { and }

You must enclose all the keystroke instructions (with the exception of the ↵ symbol) in braces ({ and }). You can type uppercase or lowercase letters interchangeably when entering the key names.

Note To specify two or more consecutive uses of the same key, you can enter a number following the key name. Separate the number from the keyname with a space.

(For more details about special key indicators, see Lab 9.)

Naming a Macro

After you enter a macro, you must name the range that contains the macro. 1-2-3 executes a macro when you invoke its name. To name the macro range, follow these steps:

1. Move the cell pointer to the first cell of the macro.
2. Select / **R**ange **N**ame **C**reate.
3. At the prompt, enter the macro name. There are two ways to name a macro. The first consists of a backslash and a single letter, such as \N. The second consists of any combination of up to fifteen characters, like any other range name.
4. At the next prompt, press ↵ to accept the first cell of the macro as the range. (You do not need to specify the entire range of the macro; 1-2-3 needs to know only the starting location, or first cell, of the macro instructions.)

(For more details about naming a macro, see the discussion of / **R**ange **N**ame in Chapter 2, ''Commands,'' and in Lab 9.)

Documenting a Macro

After writing a macro, you may want to write a description of the step-by-step instructions for the macro to the right of the cell or cells containing the macro and the macro's range name as a label to the left of the first cell of macro instruction. Make sure that the descriptions are not in the same cells as the macro, so 1-2-3 does not confuse your notes with the macro instructions. Documenting a macro clarifies the macro's purpose, describes the steps of the macro procedure, and identifies the range name that belongs to the macro. (For more details about documenting a macro, see Lab 9.)

Running a Macro

After you name the macro, you can run it in one of two ways. If the macro's name consists of a backslash (\) and a single letter, you can press ALT and the letter name simultaneously. Do not type a backslash before the macro name when you invoke it. If you try to execute a macro you have not named, 1-2-3 will beep. If the macro's name consists of any other combination of characters, you must use RUN (ALT-F3) to run the macro. 1-2-3 displays a list of range names in the worksheet. If you have a lot of range names press F3 (NAME) to see a full-screen list. In this case, 1-2-3 will also display the range address of the highlighted range name. Select the macro name you want to run from the list.

When you run the macro, 1-2-3 carries out the keystroke sequence automatically. It executes the keystrokes of the macro beginning with the first cell in the instructions and continuing downward until the macro ends.

You can run a macro when 1-2-3 is in READY mode or during a command procedure. In the latter case, you can start a 1-2-3 command manually, use the macro to continue, and finish the command manually. (For more details about running a macro, see Lab 9.)

Interrupting a Macro

To interrupt a macro at any time during execution, press CTRL-BREAK then press ESC to cancel the error. 1-2-3 returns immediately to READY mode and lets you resume your work session. CTRL-BREAK is useful for halting a lengthy macro sequence that you want to end early or for ending a macro in an infinite loop. See the discussion of {BRANCH} in the section ''Advanced Macro Commands.''

Interactive Macros

You can combine macro execution with manual entries by inserting a pause in the macro instruction sequence.

The {?} keystroke instruction causes the macro to pause for manual entries. You can enter {?} anywhere in the macro instruction sequence. When 1-2-3 reads a {?} keystroke instruction in the macro, it stops executing the macro until you type something and press ↵.

When you enter {?} in the macro instruction sequence, you must complete the cell entry with a ~ character, which instructs 1-2-3 to continue macro execution after you press ↵.

(For more details about interactive macros, see Lab 9.)

Autoexecute Macro

An autoexecute macro is a special macro that specifies a task that 1-2-3 implements automatically when you first load the worksheet using the / **F**ile **R**etrieve command. Autoexecute macros are useful for worksheets you use often or are preparing for others to use.

You create an autoexecute macro the same way that you create any other macro. However, you give it a special name: \0 (zero). Do not use this name when naming any other macro. A worksheet can contain only one autoexecute macro.

1-2-3 automatically invokes a macro named \0 when you retrieve a worksheet that contains it. To use an autoexecute macro during a 1-2-3 work session, you must assign it an additional macro name, for example, \E.

Debugging a Macro

If, when you run a macro, it does not perform as you expected it to, or if 1-2-3 does not finish running it because of an error, you need to debug the macro—find out which macro instructions are causing the problem and edit them.

Some cases in which you would edit a macro are as follows:

- You observe a typing error or an omission of a keystroke. A common missing keystroke is the tilde (~) symbol representing [↵].
- While the macro is executing, 1-2-3 encounters an error in your keystroke sequence and displays an error message. You need to find and correct the error before you can successfully execute your macro.
- The existing macro, if altered slightly, could be used to perform a similar worksheet procedure, saving you the task of rewriting the entire macro.

To edit a macro, go to the range that contains the macro keystroke sequence and edit the cells as you would any label. As long as the macro begins in the same place as it did previously, you can invoke it using its original name. (For more details about editing a macro, see Lab 9.)

Debugging a Macro in STEP Mode

The keystrokes that are causing an error in a lengthy and complicated macro may not be easy to find. To help you diagnose problems in a macro, 1-2-3 has a feature called STEP mode. This feature allows you to examine a macro one keystroke at a time, so you can locate the error.

To turn on STEP mode, hold down ALT and press [F2]. A STEP indicator appears in the status line. Then invoke the macro as usual.

To proceed through the macro in STEP mode, press any key to execute the macro one step at a time. Each time you press a key to execute another step, 1-2-3 replaces the STEP indicator at the bottom of the screen with the cell address of the cell that contains the macro instructions and the contents of that cell. Keep pressing any key to proceed to the next step.

Note If you have a {?} command, indicating a pause in the macro, you must press ↵ to continue STEP mode macro execution.

Once you have found the error, end the macro by pressing CTRL-BREAK and then you can edit it. If you encounter an error that produces an error message, press ↵ or ESC both to clear the error and to exit the macro.

You do not need to leave STEP mode to edit a macro. When you exit a macro to edit it, 1-2-3 redisplays the STEP indicator to remind you that STEP mode is still on.

After editing the macro, you can invoke the macro again, remaining in STEP mode. You can then repeat the debugging procedure from the beginning of the macro, if necessary.

To leave STEP mode, press STEP (ALT-F2) again and then press any key. (For more details about STEP, see Lab 9.)

Using the Learn Feature to Create Macros

When you use the Learn feature to create a macro, 1-2-3 automatically records all your keystrokes in a learn range, a single-column range that you define. To create a macro with the Learn feature, you first specify a learn range for the macro in an empty part of your worksheet. To specify the single-column range, select / **W**orksheet **L**earn **R**ange and specify a single-column range when prompted. When determining a size for the learn range, it's always better to make it larger than you think you might need so 1-2-3 doesn't run out of space when recording your keystrokes.

Next, you turn on the Learn feature by pressing LEARN (ALT-F5). The LEARN indicator appears in the status line. You then perform the task(s) you want to record. As you do so, 1-2-3 records all your keystrokes in the learn range; you do not enter anything into the learn range directly. 1-2-3 records keystrokes in macro instruction format. For example, when you press GOTO (F5), type A5, and press ↵, 1-2-3 records {GOTO}A5~.

After you finish, press LEARN (ALT-F5) again to stop 1-2-3 from recording more keystrokes. Move the cell pointer to the learn range and examine the recorded keystrokes. If you made any mistakes, edit them before you go any further. If you made many mistakes and want to start over, erase the learn range with / **W**orksheet **L**earn **E**rase and start again.

If the macro looks correct, assign it a range name (see "Naming a Macro" earlier in this section). Depending on how you named the macro, run it by using either ALT or RUN (ALT-F3) (see "Running a Macro" earlier in this section).

If the macro isn't working as you expected, debug and edit it as explained in "Debugging a Macro in STEP Mode" earlier in this section.

Advanced Macro Commands

Besides its keystroke instruction feature, 1-2-3 includes advanced macro commands that cause 1-2-3 to perform a built-in programming function. You implement each of these special macro commands with a 1-2-3 advanced macro keyword, such as {IF}, {BRANCH}, and {QUIT}.

This section contains a general explanation of advanced macro commands, including grammar (syntax), arguments, and subroutines; a summary of advanced macro commands by category; and a description of each macro command.

Note This section contains advanced 1-2-3 material. Do not attempt to use the information presented here unless you are an experienced user of 1-2-3 macros or are familiar with programming concepts and techniques.

Advanced Macro Grammar

Each advanced macro command you create must have the correct syntax or grammatical structure. The first word in an advanced macro command is the keyword. You must type the keyword exactly as it appears in this chapter. Uppercase and lowercase letters are interchangeable.

Most of the advanced macro commands require an additional word or two, called arguments. Grammatically speaking, macro keywords are like verbs in a sentence; they tell 1-2-3 what action to perform. Arguments are like direct objects; they complete the command by indicating the what, where, or when of the particular action.

You supply the arguments for advanced macro commands. For example, if you want 1-2-3 to place the number 96.5 in cell B10, use the {LET} command, which has this format:

{LET *location,entry*}

You fill in the arguments as follows:

{LET B10,96.5}

1-2-3 includes several rules of grammar for advanced macro commands. You must create advanced macro commands as label entries or string-valued formulas (a formula that generates a label). Each command must begin with a left brace ({) character followed by a macro command keyword.

After the keyword, type a single-space character, then one or more arguments. Each argument must be the correct type—number, string, or location (cell address or range). Some macro commands require more than one type of argument. Others require no arguments at all. Multiple arguments are separated from one another with argument separators.

The two valid argument separators are the comma (,) and the semicolon (;). The comma is the default configuration for the argument separator; however, the semicolon is always valid regardless of the default configuration. Do not leave any space characters before or after an argument separator.

Each advanced macro command must end with a right brace (}), and the entire macro command must be within a single cell. You cannot have the beginning brace in one cell and the ending brace in another. The format for writing advanced macro commands is as follows:

{*Keyword Arg1,Arg2,...,Argn*}

You can store any number of macro commands in a single cell, as long as you do not enter more than 240 characters. You can mix advanced macro commands with individual keystrokes in the same cell.

The following advanced macro commands show the correct syntax, using the {BLANK *location*} command as an example. The {BLANK} command erases the contents of a specified cell or range.

{BLANK A1..G45}	A range as the location argument
{blank G45}	A single-cell address as the location argument

The following commands are incorrect:

{BLANKB45..H56}	Space missing after keyword
{BLANKE A 100}	Keyword misspelled, cell address error

Argument Types

Table 3.2 describes the four types of advanced macro command arguments.

Table 3.2

Argument	Description
Number	A number, a numeric formula, or the range name or address of a cell that contains a number or numeric formula.
String	Any sequence of characters up to 240. With a few exceptions, you cannot use a string-valued expression (formula) in a command that calls for a string argument. Exceptions are noted individually in this chapter.
Location	Any range of one or more cells. You can specify a range with cell addresses or a range name.
Condition	Any logical formula. The macro proceeds depending on the result of a true-false test specified in the condition. It compares the values in two cells to determine if one is less than, greater than, or equal to another or checks the result of a specified formula. The expression can contain any entry, a number, or a string-valued formula.

Note In many cases, you must enclose a string argument in quotation marks. Enclose in quotation marks any string or range name that contains a colon, a semicolon, or a comma.

For example,

string: {LET A25,"Type a letter; then a number"}

range name: {BLANK "TOTAL, 5 YEARS"}

In addition, enclose in quotation marks any formula you want to appear as a label or any string argument that may be confused with a range name.

CAUTION 1-2-3 does not adjust cell addresses in macros when you use / **M**ove, / **W**orksheet **I**nsert, and / **W**orksheet **D**elete commands. Therefore, use range names to refer to all individual cells, as well as ranges, in the worksheet. In addition, if the macro contains instructions to insert or delete a row, the results may affect macro execution following those instructions.

Declaring Argument Types

Some commands can process more than one type of argument. For example, a {LET} command can store either a label or a number in a cell. You can use the suffixes :string and :value to explicitly define the argument type.

For example,

{LET A1,12+13} or	
{LET A1,12+13:value}	enters the number 25 into cell A1
{LET A1,"12+13"} or	
{LET A1,12+13:string}	enters the label '12+13 into cell A1

Macro Subroutines

The section on invoking a macro described the process of starting a macro with the Macro key, ALT. One macro can also invoke another macro. One way to do this is to use a {BRANCH} command.

When 1-2-3 reads a {BRANCH} command, it continues reading macro keystrokes and advanced macro commands at the specified location. In effect, one macro passes control of the 1-2-3 session to another macro.

If you want to use a sequence of macro instructions in several different places in a macro program, you can create a subroutine. Instead of typing the entire macro sequence each time or using a {BRANCH} command to send 1-2-3 somewhere else to get its instructions, you simply put the range name assigned to the sequence in braces at the appropriate location in the macro instructions. This is the subroutine call. When 1-2-3 encounters this subroutine call command, it executes the sequence of instructions you named. When the sequence is finished or it reads a {RETURN} command, 1-2-3 returns to the original routine immediately after the subroutine call.

For example, the macro named MASTER (see below) contains the subroutine call command {CLEANUP}. As 1-2-3 executes the commands in MASTER, it will encounter this subroutine call command. This command tells 1-2-3 to stop executing MASTER and begin executing the commands in the macro named CLEANUP. This is known as calling a subroutine. When 1-2-3 comes to the end of CLEANUP, or reads a {RETURN} command, it returns to the macro instructions in MASTER located immediately below the {CLEANUP} command. This is known as returning from a subroutine.

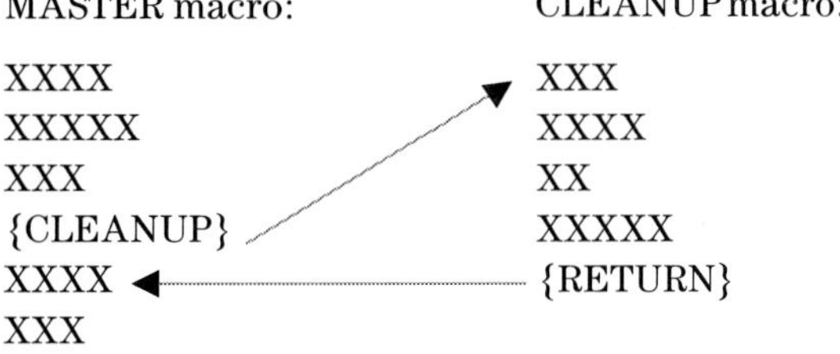

One macro can call another at any time—in the middle of a range specification, at a filename menu, and so on.

CAUTION Do not use a subroutine name that is the same as one of the special macro keys in Table 3.1. If a duplication occurs, 1-2-3 performs the subroutine, not the keystroke.

Passing Arguments to Subroutines

In most 1-2-3 advanced macro commands, you specify a keyword followed by one or more arguments. For instance, the command {LET A1,999.5} assigns 999.5 to the location A1. You can also give values to the macro program subroutines that you create. This process is called passing arguments to a subroutine. If you create a subroutine called COMPUTE, you can pass its values by enclosing both the subroutine name and the arguments in braces {COMPUTE 52,G1}. The command is a subroutine call in which two arguments are passed. You may want 1-2-3 to interpret 52 as a number and the argument G1 as a cell address. For each argument you specify in a subroutine, you must also specify a cell in which to store the value being passed. You may also need to tell 1-2-3 how to interpret the arguments in the subroutine call. To do this, begin a subroutine with a {DEFINE} command.

For more information about the {subroutine} command, see the command description later in this chapter.

Updating Results of Advanced Macro Commands

When you run a macro with the worksheet recalculation method set to Automatic (see / **W**orksheet **G**lobal **R**ecalculation **A**utomatic in Chapter 2), 1-2-3 does not recalculate all data continuously. Automatic recalculation of advanced macro commands occurs if the user enters data in the worksheet in response to a {?} command or if you have followed a command such as {LET} or {GET} with a ~ (tilde) to represent [↵] (which 1-2-3 interprets as user input). Suppose you have a series of {LET} commands, but no user data entry in response to a {?} command. If any other commands in the macro depend on the results of the {LET} command, you'll need to recalculate the worksheet, either by following the last {LET} command with a ~ (tilde) or by including a {RECALC} or {RECALCOL} command.

Types of Advanced Macro Commands

The advanced macro commands can be grouped in five command categories: screen control, interactive, flow-of-control, data manipulation, and file manipulation.

- Screen control commands control different parts of the screen display, change the contents of the mode indicator, and sound your computer's bell.
- Interactive commands suspend macro execution for keyboard input, control the timing of macro execution, and prevent undesired changes to a worksheet while a macro is running.
- Flow-of-control commands direct the path of macro execution so you can create a macro that includes for loops, branches, subroutine calls, and conditional processing.

- Data manipulation commands enter data, edit existing entries, erase entries, and clear control panel prompts.
- File manipulation commands work with text files. Text files, also called print files, are files on disk in ASCII format. You can use the file manipulation commands to create a new text file, copy data from a text file to a worksheet, or copy data from a worksheet to a text file.

The following is a description of each advanced macro command by category. Throughout the remainder of this chapter, uppercase words indicate macro keywords. Lowercase *italic* words indicate the type of argument required by a macro keyword. Arguments enclosed by < > are optional. When you enter a macro, you can use either uppercase or lowercase characters. In the examples, range names also appear in uppercase.

Screen Control Commands

The following commands are used to control the screen:

{BEEP}	{GRAPHON}
{BORDERSOFF}	{INDICATE}
{BORDERSON}	{PANELOFF}
{FRAMEOFF}	{PANELON}
{FRAMEON}	{WINDOWSOFF}
{GRAPHOFF}	{WINDOWSON}

BEEP

{BEEP <*tone-number*>} sounds the bell or tone. The *tone-number* argument is optional.

{BEEP} causes 1-2-3 to sound the computer's bell. This command is normally used to signal the end of a macro, to alert you to an error (see {ONERROR}), and to signal the end of a time period (see {WAIT}).

The *tone-number* argument specifies the tone of the bell. There are four different beeps, invoked with the arguments 1, 2, 3, and 4. If you do not specify a number argument, 1-2-3 uses the beep invoked by number 1.

BORDERSOFF

{BORDERSOFF} suppresses display of the worksheet frame (column letters and row numbers). The worksheet frame remains hidden until 1-2-3 reaches a {BORDERSON} command or the macro ends. When the macro ends, the borders return to their default state of being displayed.

BORDERSON {BORDERSON} restores standard display of the worksheet frame.

FRAMEOFF Identical to {BORDERSOFF}.

FRAMEON Identical to {BORDERSON}.

GRAPHOFF {GRAPHOFF} removes a graph display by {GRAPHON} and redisplays the worksheet.

GRAPHON {GRAPHON} [*named-graph*],[nodisplay] has three possible results, depending on the syntax you use.

{GRAPHON} displays a full-screen view of the current graph while the macro continues to run. {GRAPHON *named-graph*] makes the named-graph settings the current graph settings and displays a full-screen view of *named-graph* while the macro continues to run. {GRAPHON *named-graph*,[nodisplay] makes the named-graph settings the current graph settings without displaying the graph.

INDICATE {INDICATE <*string*>} changes the mode indicator in the upper right corner of the screen. The string argument is optional. 1-2-3 replaces the mode indicator with the indicator string you specify. The new indicator remains on the screen even if the mode subsequently changes when you execute a command or type an entry. The only way to clear the indicator is to execute another {INDICATE} command.

{INDICATE} with no argument restores the READY mode indicator. To remove the mode indicator from the control panel entirely, use the command {INDICATE " "}.

1-2-3 uses only the first five characters of the string. You must type the string into the {INDICATE} command. You cannot use the address of a string-valued cell.

PANELOFF {PANELOFF [clear]} freezes the control panel and status line until 1-2-3 encounters a {PANELON} command or the macro ends. If you include the optional clear argument, 1-2-3 clears the control panel and status line before freezing them. Use {PANELOFF} in interactive macros to suppress activity in the control panel and status line that might be distracting to users.

PANELON {PANELON} restores standard control panel redrawing. It does not take an argument.

WINDOWSOFF {WINDOWSOFF} freezes the screen display, except for the control panel. It also turns off the display of settings sheets. It does not take an argument.

{WINDOWSOFF} allows you to manipulate data without having the changes flash on the screen. During normal macro execution, you can see each stage that the macro goes through during its operation. Use this command to suppress macro activity, especially during a long macro. {WINDOWSOFF} also speeds up macro execution, since 1-2-3 does not have to keep redrawing the screen.

WINDOWSON

{WINDOWSON} restores normal updating of the screen display, undoing a {WINDOWSOFF} command. It also turns on the display of settings sheets during macro execution. It does not take an argument.

Note If {WINDOWSOFF} is in effect, you must use two consecutive {WINDOWSON} commands to turn on the settings sheets display.

Interactive Commands

The following commands are used for keyboard interaction:

{?}	{GETNUMBER}
{BREAK}	{LOOK}
{BREAKOFF}	{MENUBRANCH}
{BREAKON}	{MENUCALL}
{GET}	{WAIT}
{GETLABEL}	

?

{?} halts macro execution temporarily, allowing you to type and move around the worksheet; macro execution continues when you press ↵. {?} does not take an argument. When you press ↵, it indicates only that 1-2-3 should resume execution of the macro. If you want 1-2-3 to execute a ↵, you must include a ~ in the macro. (For more details about {?}, see Lab 9.)

BREAK

{BREAK} returns 1-2-3 to READY mode; it does not interrupt a macro.

BREAKOFF

{BREAKOFF} disables the BREAK key during macro execution. It does not take an argument. Unless a macro executes a {BREAKOFF} command, you can always stop the execution of a macro by pressing BREAK. If you are preparing an application for others to use but not change, you can make sure they stay under macro control with {BREAKOFF}. When BREAK is disabled, they cannot discontinue or interfere with the macro, either inadvertently or deliberately. {BREAKOFF} stays active until it is canceled with {BREAKON} or until the macro ends.

CAUTION If {BREAKOFF} is active and the macro goes into an infinite loop, you cannot return to 1-2-3. The only way to stop the macro is to stop and then restart the computer.

BREAKON {BREAKON} restores the BREAK key, undoing a {BREAKOFF} command. It does not take an argument.

GET {GET *location*} pauses for you to type a single character and then stores it at the specified location. The single character you type can be a standard typewriter key or a 1-2-3 standard key (for instance, CALC). The character or standard key is stored as a left-aligned label entry at the upper left corner cell of the location. {GET} makes no provision for a prompt on the control panel. Use {GETLABEL} or {GETNUMBER} when such a prompt is required.

GETLABEL {GETLABEL *prompt,location*} displays *prompt* in the control panel and pauses for you to type a character string and then stores it as a left-aligned label entry at the *location* cell. {GETLABEL} overrides a current {PANELOFF} condition.

You can use any literal string, with as many characters as fit within the control panel edit line, as *prompt*. (The maximum number of characters 1-2-3 displays is a few characters less than the full screen width.) *Prompt* can also be the range name or address of a cell that contains the prompt string, or a string formula that evaluates to the prompt string.

You can specify a cell or a range as *location*. If you specify a range, 1-2-3 stores your response in the first cell of the range. You can also precede *location* with a + (plus) to indicate it contains the address of a cell where you want to store the label.

The response to the prompt can include up to 240 characters. If you press ↵ without typing anything, 1-2-3 enters an ' (apostrophe) label prefix in *location*. If you enter a numeric value, it's converted to a label in *location*.

GETNUMBER {GETNUMBER *prompt,location*} pauses for you to type a number and then stores it as a number entry at the location. See {GETLABEL} for *prompt* and *location* argument details.

When 1-2-3 encounters a {GETLABEL} or {GETNUMBER} command, it displays the prompt string on the control panel and then pauses.

The response to the prompt must be a number, a numeric formula, or a reference to a cell containing a number or numeric formula. The response can include up to 240 characters. If you enter a label, string formula, or reference to a cell containing a label or string formula as the response, 1-2-3 enters ERR in *location*. 1-2-3 also enters ERR if you press ↵ without typing anything.

{GETNUMBER} overrides a current {PANELOFF} condition.

LOOK {LOOK *location*} checks to see if you have typed a character. If you have typed a character since the macro began executing, 1-2-3 stores the first character typed at the specified location. If no characters have been typed, 1-2-3 enters an apostrophe label prefix in the location cell.

While a macro is running, 1-2-3 does not pay attention to the keyboard. If you type something while a macro is running, the operating system stores the characters in its keyboard buffer until 1-2-3 requests them. The keyboard buffer is usually small (for instance, ten characters). When you fill this buffer, the computer beeps each time you press another key.

{LOOK} is similar to {GET}, except that {LOOK} does not suspend macro execution. {LOOK} leaves the character in the keyboard buffer for use by a {?}, {GET}, {GETNUMBER}, or {GETLABEL} command.

MENUBRANCH {MENUBRANCH *location*} halts execution temporarily to let you select a menu item and then branches accordingly.

MENUCALL {MENUCALL *location*} halts execution temporarily to let you select a menu item and then executes the corresponding macro as a subroutine. When 1-2-3 encounters a {MENUBRANCH} or {MENUCALL} command, it displays a menu on the control panel, based on the contents of the range whose upper left corner is the location. When you choose a menu item, 1-2-3 continues reading macro keystrokes in the column that contains the menu item you select.

{MENUBRANCH} and {MENUCALL} differ in what happens after 1-2-3 executes the last command in the column containing the menu item. Following a {MENUBRANCH} command, 1-2-3 ends the macro after the last command in the column. Following a {MENUCALL} command, 1-2-3 continues macro execution immediately.

To construct a macro menu, follow these steps:

1. Place each menu item in a separate cell in the first row of the menu range. Blank cells are not allowed between menu items. You can include up to eight items in the menu. Keep the total number of characters small to avoid extending beyond the screen. The cell to the right of the final menu item must be blank.
2. Supply brief descriptions (they must be labels) for each item in the second row of the menu range. To create a blank label as a description, use a label that consists only of spaces.
3. Enter the macro instructions for each menu item in the cells immediately below the menu descriptions.

Begin each macro item with a different character so you can select items by typing the first character. Otherwise, 1-2-3 will select the first entry (reading from left to right) whose first character matches the character you type.

Uppercase and lowercase letters are equivalent when you make a menu selection. For example, you can select **Q**uit by typing **q** or **Q**. You can always select a menu item by moving the highlight bar and pressing (↵).

If you press ESC at a {MENUBRANCH} or {MENUCALL} menu, 1-2-3 cancels the menu selection process. Execution continues just after the macro command. This is the same point to which control returns after a {MENUCALL}.

{MENUBRANCH} and {MENUCALL} override a current {PANELOFF} condition.

WAIT

{WAIT *time-number*} suspends macro execution until the time specified by *time-number*. {WAIT} causes 1-2-3 to halt execution and to display WAIT in the mode indicator. During this time, 1-2-3 will not respond to keystrokes. When the time specified by *time-number* is reached, execution continues. You can interrupt a {WAIT} command by pressing CTRL-BREAK, unless you have executed a {BREAKOFF} command.

Time-number can be a number, numeric formula, or reference to a cell that contains a number or numeric formula. The number must represent a future moment in time. If the number represents a nonexistent time or a time that has already passed, 1-2-3 ignores the {WAIT} command and continues to the next macro instruction. In most cases you will use date and time @functions to specify *time-number*.

Flow-of-Control Commands

The following commands control program flow:

{BRANCH}	{ONERROR}
{DEFINE}	{QUIT}
{DISPATCH}	{RESTART}
{FOR}	{RETURN}
{FORBREAK}	{subroutine}
{IF}	{SYSTEM}

BRANCH

{BRANCH *location*} continues macro execution at a different cell. 1-2-3 immediately begins reading keystrokes at the new location. You can specify a single cell or a range name as the location. Execution continues at the upper left corner cell of the location.

Note {BRANCH} produces different results from a subroutine call. With {BRANCH}, you cannot return to the original routine except with another {BRANCH} command. A subroutine call returns macro control to the original routine immediately after the subroutine call.

CAUTION Do not confuse {BRANCH} with {GOTO}. {GOTO} moves the cell pointer. {BRANCH} transfers macro execution to the location you specify.

DEFINE

{DEFINE *location1,location2,...locationn*} allocates storage locations and declares argument types for arguments to be passed to a subroutine. Use {DEFINE} in subroutines to specify where variables passed to that subroutine are to be stored. It must come before the point in the subroutine where the arguments are used.

The number of arguments in a {DEFINE} command must be the same as in the subroutine call command. Otherwise, 1-2-3 displays an error message when the subroutine is called.

Each location specification can be a single cell, a range, or a range name. If you specify a range, 1-2-3 uses the first cell of the range as the storage location.

1-2-3 has a simple scheme for passing arguments to subroutines. It checks each argument in a subroutine call against the type specified by the {DEFINE} command in the subroutine and then stores the argument in the cell specified by the {DEFINE} command either as a string or as a value.

This is a typical subroutine call:

```
{SUBR1 45*10,+''Dow''&''Jones'',F10}
```

When the {DEFINE} command in SUBR1 is executed, 1-2-3 checks each argument to see if it should be stored literally as a string or evaluated first. String arguments are always stored as left-aligned labels, regardless of the worksheet's current default label prefix. Value arguments can be stored as numbers or as left-aligned labels, depending on the argument itself.

Declaring a String Argument Type

1-2-3 stores the arguments specified in a {DEFINE} command just as they appear in the command. Thus, 1-2-3 interprets the following {DEFINE} command as a string declaration:

```
{DEFINE X1,X2,X3}
```

If this command is the first item in SUBR1, 1-2-3 stores the label 45*10 in cell X1, the label +''Dow''&''Jones'' in cell X2, and the label F10 in cell X3.

Declaring a Value Argument Type

As an alternative to the process just described, you can instruct 1-2-3 to evaluate an argument before storing it by typing :value after the cell address in the {DEFINE} command. For example,

```
{DEFINE X1:value,X2:value,X3:value}
```

If this command is the first item in SUBR1, 1-2-3 evaluates all three arguments before storing them. Thus, it stores the value of the first argument, 450, as a number in cell X1, the value of the second argument, the string Dow Jones, as a label in cell X2; and the value of the third argument, the contents of cell F10, as either a number or a label in cell X3.

DISPATCH

{DISPATCH *location*} branches to a destination specified in the location cell. The location cell should contain the cell address or the range name of another cell, the branch destination. If the location cell is blank or contains a numeric value, 1-2-3 ends macro execution and returns control to the user.

A typical use of {DISPATCH} would involve setting up the location cell as a variable cell, dependent on continually varying conditions in the worksheet. {DISPATCH} then allows you to branch conditionally to one of many alternative destinations, based on the current contents of the location cell.

Note {DISPATCH} differs from {BRANCH} in that {BRANCH} can execute instructions only in the location cell; it cannot continue to execute instructions at another destination specified in the location cell.

If you use a range name to specify the location cell, make sure the range you name contains only one cell. Specifying a range that contains more than one cell as the location makes {DISPATCH} equivalent to {BRANCH}.

FOR

{FOR *counter,start-number,stop-number,step-number,subroutine*} repeatedly executes the macro that begins at a particular location. {FOR} provides a loop capability (often called FOR-NEXT) similar to that provided by many other programming languages.

The *counter* is a cell in which 1-2-3 keeps track of the repetition of the macro routine it is executing. You do not need to enter anything at the counter location. Initially, the value of the counter cell is the start-number value.

The start-number is the beginning value of the counter. The stop-number indicates the end of the counter. The step-number is the value by which the counter increases each time 1-2-3 executes the subroutine. The subroutine is the first cell or range name of the subroutine to be executed.

Processing the Loop

To execute a {FOR} command, 1-2-3 first evaluates the start-number, stop-number, and step-number values. Then (and each subsequent time a repetition is about to begin) 1-2-3 does the following:

1. Enters the start-number in counter.
2. Compares the stop-number and counter values. If the counter value does not exceed the stop-number value, 1-2-3 executes the routine at the subroutine and goes to step 3. Otherwise, 1-2-3 continues reading keystrokes at the cell below the {FOR} command and does not perform the subroutine.
3. Increases the value in the counter cell by the step-number value and returns to step 2.

It is possible that 1-2-3 will not perform the routine at all (see the fourth case in Table 3.3) or that the routine will fall into an infinite loop (see the fifth case). In the latter case, you must press CTRL-BREAK to stop the {FOR} loop.

Some typical combinations of start-number, stop-number, and step-number actions are listed in Table 3.3.

Table 3.3

Start	Stop	Step	Repetition Count
1	10	1	10
2	10	2	5
2	9	2	
2	1	1	0 (start value exceeds stop value at beginning)
4	5	0	Infinite (counter never exceeds stop value)

Note Ending the routine with {RETURN} is acceptable but not necessary. Do not use {QUIT} to end the routine. If you do, the loop will always terminate after the first pass.

1-2-3 stores the start-number, stop-number, and step-number values internally. You cannot have the routine modify these values once it starts.

FORBREAK

{FORBREAK} cancels execution of a {FOR} loop and continues processing at the first character after that {FOR} command.

CAUTION Use {FORBREAK} only within a subroutine called by a {FOR} command. Using {FORBREAK} anywhere else will result in an error.

{FORBREAK} does not take an argument. {FORBREAK} immediately ends a subroutine called by a {FOR} command and returns processing to the point immediately following the {FOR} command.

IF {IF *condition*} conditionally executes the command that follows the {IF} command. {IF} allows a macro program to branch depending on the result of a true/false test. 1-2-3 evaluates the condition argument, which can be numeric, string-value, or formula.

If the formula does not have the numeric value zero, 1-2-3 considers it to be true. Execution of the macro continues in the same cell immediately after the {IF} command.

If the formula has the numeric value zero, 1-2-3 considers it to be false. Execution of the macro continues in the cell below the one with the {IF} command. A blank cell (but not a cell that contains a blank string), string values, ERR, and NA are zero or false.

The {IF} command implements an if-then-else capability, similar to that in many other programming languages. The instructions in the cell after the {IF} command are the then clause. The instructions in the cell below the {IF} command are the else clause.

Be careful when you compose the then clause. In most instances, you should include a {BRANCH} or {QUIT} command to prevent the else clause from being executed directly after the then clause.

ONERROR {ONERROR *branch-location*,<*message-location*>} branches to the branch location if a 1-2-3 error message occurs during macro execution. It optionally records the error message that 1-2-3 would have displayed at the message location.

The message-location argument is optional. If you include this argument, 1-2-3 stores the error message it would have displayed in the status line in that cell. If you omit the argument, you will not know the type of error that occurred, because 1-2-3 does not display the message on the screen.

You should structure your macro so that there is no possibility of an error occurring before 1-2-3 encounters the {ONERROR} command.

1-2-3 can use each {ONERROR} command only once. An {ONERROR} condition remains in effect until another {ONERROR} command supersedes it, an error occurs, or macro execution ends. Once an error has occurred, the {ONERROR} condition is canceled. To continue trapping errors, include another {ONERROR} command in the branch-location routine.

CAUTION Pressing CTRL-BREAK causes an error. {ONERROR} takes effect if you press CTRL-BREAK unless you have executed a {BREAKOFF} command.

QUIT {QUIT} terminates macro execution, returning control to the keyboard. {QUIT} does not take an argument. {QUIT} is often most useful at the end of an {IF} command or as a result of a {MENUCALL} choice. {QUIT} ends all macro execution, not just the subroutine that may contain it.

RESTART {RESTART} cancels a subroutine and clears the subroutine stack. {RESTART} does not take an argument. {RESTART} is useful only in a subroutine that has been called from at least one other macro or subroutine. Use {RESTART} if your subroutine is nested below the calling routines (the stack) to which you will no longer return. When 1-2-3 encounters a {RESTART}, it continues executing instructions that follow in the subroutine. The macro stops when it encounters a {RETURN} command or a blank cell. It will not return to any of the routines that called it.

RETURN {RETURN} affects flow of control in subroutines. {RETURN} does not take an argument. Use {RETURN} in conjunction with {subroutine} or {MENUCALL} to cause 1-2-3 to immediately return to the calling routine. {RETURN} is not required if a subroutine ends because 1-2-3 encounters a blank or numeric cell. In such cases, control returns automatically to the calling routine.

{RETURN} is not equivalent to {QUIT} in a subroutine. {QUIT} ends macro execution and returns control of the 1-2-3 session to you. {RETURN} causes macro execution to continue just after the location of the last {subroutine} or {MENUCALL} command.

{subroutine} The {*subroutine*<*arg1*>,<*arg2*>,...<*argn*>} command calls a subroutine, optionally with one or more arguments. Using subroutines allows you to assemble a macro out of a series of modules, each of which can be individually tested and then called from a master routine.

To call a macro subroutine, you enclose the range name assigned to the subroutine's starting cell in braces. For example:

```
{SUBR1}
```

1-2-3 immediately begins reading keystrokes and macro commands at the location specified by the range name {SUBR1}.

When 1-2-3 encounters a {RETURN} command or a cell that is not a label or a string formula, macro execution continues at the point just after the subroutine call. A {QUIT} command also terminates the subroutine and the entire macro program. Control of the 1-2-3 session returns to the keyboard.

You must follow certain guidelines for the {subroutine} command. The {subroutine} location must be a range name assigned to a single cell or a range. Specifying a range does not restrict the size of the subroutine to the size of the range. Only a {RETURN} command, a blank cell, or a nonstring-valued cell (a cell that does not contain a label or a string-valued formula) can indicate the end of a subroutine. Do not use a {subroutine} that is the same as one of the key names in Table 3.1 (for example, NAME). If a duplication occurs, 1-2-3 performs the subroutine, not the keystrokes. Also, do not use a cell address at the {subroutine} location.

You can specify one or more arguments, which 1-2-3 evaluates and stores in separate cells before executing the subroutine. If you include arguments, you must include a {DEFINE} command in the subroutine.

SYSTEM

{SYSTEM *command*} temporarily suspends the 1-2-3 session and executes the specified operating system command. When the command is completed, the 1-2-3 session automatically resumes and the macro continues. *Command* can be any operating system command, including batch commands or commands to run another program such as an editor, to a maximum of 125 characters. The command must be enclosed in quotes.

CAUTION If you are running 1-2-3 under DOS, do not use {SYSTEM} to load memory-resident programs such as terminate-and-stay-resident programs. If you do so, you may not be able to resume 1-2-3.

Note To temporarily suspend the 1-2-3 session without specifying an operating system command, use the System command (/S) in the macro instead of {SYSTEM}.

Data-Manipulation Commands

The following macro commands manipulate data:

{BLANK}	{PUT}
{CONTENTS}	{RECALC}
{LET}	{RECALCCOL}

BLANK

{BLANK *location*} erases the contents of cells in a range (location). {BLANK} produces the same results as the / **R**ange **E**rase command. 1-2-3 erases the entry from every cell in the specified range. {BLANK} does not affect numeric format and protection settings.

{BLANK} is often more convenient to use than the / **R**ange **E**rase command. For example, use {BLANK} to erase a cell or a range in the middle of a menu command sequence in a macro.

CONTENTS

{CONTENTS *target-location*,*source-location*,[*width*],[*cell-format*]} copies the contents of *source-location* to *target-location* as a label. Use {CONTENTS} to store a numeric value as a string so you can use it in a string formula.

Although the {CONTENTS} command is similar to the {LET} command, {LET} stores either a number or a label in a specified cell, and {CONTENTS} stores a label that looks like a number in a cell.

When it executes a {CONTENTS} command, 1-2-3 evaluates the contents of the source-location. If you specify a range, 1-2-3 uses the first cell of the range. 1-2-3 then stores this value in the target-location as a label.

If you do not specify the optional arguments, 1-2-3 uses the current column width and numeric format of the source-location cell.

Optional Arguments

If you specify the optional width argument, 1-2-3 treats the source-location cell as having that column width; it does not actually change its column width. *Width* can be a number, numeric formula, or reference to a cell that contains a number or formula whose value is from 1 to 240. If you specify the optional cell-format, 1-2-3 treats the source-location cell as having the corresponding numeric format. *Cell-format* must be one of the code numbers shown in Table 3.4, a formula that evaluates to a code number, or a cell reference that contains a code number. The resulting display (incorporating a number, a width, and a format) is stored as a left-aligned label in the target-location cell.

Table 3.4

Code	Corresponding Numeric Format
0 to 15	Fixed, 0 to 15 decimal places
16 to 31	Scientific, 0 to 15 decimal places
32 to 47	Currency, 0 to 15 decimal places
48 to 63	%, 0 to 15 decimal places
64 to 79	, (comma), 0 to 15 decimal places
112	+/− (horizontal bar graph)
113	General
114	D1 (DD-MMM-YY)
115	D2 (DD-MMM)
116	D3 (MMM-YY)
121	D4 (full international; varies with configuration settings)
122	D5 (partial international; varies with configuration settings)
119	D6 (HH:MM:SS AM/PM)
120	D7 (HH:MM AM/PM)
123	D8 (full international; varies with configuration settings)
124	D9 (partial international; varies with configuration settings)
117	Text display (formulas shown as entered)
118	Hidden (prevents the cell's contents from appearing on the screen)
127	Worksheet's global cell format

Using {CONTENTS} with the text display format number 117 provides a quick way to retrieve the text of a formula.

LET

{LET *location*,*entry*} enters a number or label entry at the cell location. {LET} stores an entry in a specified cell location. *Entry* can be a number, literal string, formula, or reference to a cell that contains a number, label, or formula. If you specify a range as the location, 1-2-3 stores the entry in the first cell of the range.

{LET} can create either a label entry or a number entry. This is one of the few commands in which you can specify a string-valued expression. For example,

{LET G34,15*14:string} stores the label 15*14 in cell G34.

{LET G34,15*14:value} stores the number 210 in cell G34.

{LET G34,+Hello, "&X22:value} stores the label Hello, Denise in cell G34 if cell X22 contains the label Denise.

If you do not specify the :string or the :value suffix, 1-2-3 attempts to evaluate the argument as a numeric or string expression. If successful, 1-2-3 creates a number or label entry at the location. Otherwise, 1-2-3 creates a label entry that contains the characters in the argument.

PUT {PUT *location,column-offset,row-offset,entry*} stores the number or label at a cell within a location.

{PUT} is a variant of {LET}. {LET} stores a label or number in a specified cell. {PUT} processes a label or a number in exactly the same way. However, instead of storing the result in a particular cell, it stores the result at a particular column and row of a specified location.

You should specify a range as the location which includes the cell in which you are entering data. If you specify a single cell, an error results unless both the column number and the row number equal zero. The first column of the location range is numbered 0, as is the first row.

Note Specifying a row or column location outside the location causes an error, which you cannot trap with the {ONERROR} command.

RECALC {RECALC *location,<condition>,<iterations>*} recalculates the formulas in a specified location, proceeding row by row. Use {RECALC} to recalculate formulas located below and to the left of cells on which they depend.

RECALCCOL {RECALCCOL *location,<condition>,<iterations>*} recalculates the formulas in a specified location, proceeding column by column. Use {RECALCCOL} to recalculate formulas above and to the right of cells on which they depend.

{RECALC} and {RECALCCOL} are helpful for recalculating sections of a large worksheet. They save you time by recalculating only a small, specified region of the worksheet.

1-2-3 evaluates the condition after it executes the range-location calculation. If the condition is false, it calculates the range again. The iteration argument specifies the number of times 1-2-3 recalculates the range. This argument is reduced and compared once each time the range is calculated. Recalculation will continue until the condition is true or until the iteration count is false, whichever comes first. You need to include both optional arguments.

Location can be any cell or range.You can also precede *location* with a + (plus) to indicate it contains the address of a cell or range where you want recalculation to take place. *Condition* is typically a logical formula or reference to a cell containing a logical formula, but it can be any formula, number, literal string, or cell reference. 1-2-3 evaluates any *condition* that does not equal zero as true and any *condition* that does equal zero as false. Blank cells, strings, and ERR and NA values all equal zero when used as *condition*. *Iterations* can be a number, numeric formula, or reference to a cell that contains a number or numeric formula. You cannot use the *iterations* argument without the *condition* argument.

You may need to use {RECALC} or {RECALCCOL} after macro commands that change the data in the worksheet, such as {LET} and {GETNUMBER}. You do not need to use these commands after invoking 1-2-3 commands, such as / **C**opy and / **M**ove. 1-2-3 automatically recalculates the worksheet after such commands, even during macro execution.

To redraw the screen to reflect the recalculation, include {WINDOWSOFF} and {WINDOWSON} following {RECALC} or {RECALCCOL} in a macro. Otherwise, any subsequent cell entry will redraw the screen.

CAUTION Recalculating a portion of the worksheet can cause some formulas—the ones you do not process with {RECALC} or {RECALCCOL}—to fail to reflect the current data. Be sure to perform a general recalculation at the end of the macro routine that uses {RECALC} or {RECALCCOL} by including a {CALC} instruction in the macro.

File-Manipulation Commands

The following commands are used for working with files:

{CLOSE}	{READLN}
{FILESIZE}	{SETPOS}
{GETPOS}	{WRITE}
{OPEN}	{WRITELN}
{READ}	

Note Use these commands only when you are working with ASCII (text) files.

CLOSE {CLOSE} closes the text file that was opened with the {OPEN} command. {CLOSE} does not take an argument. Read and write access to the currently open file is terminated. Any macro instruction that follows {CLOSE} in the same cell is not executed, so you should keep {CLOSE} on a separate line.

Note If no file is open, {CLOSE} has no effect. 1-2-3 continues executing the macro as though the command is not there.

FILESIZE {FILESIZE *location*} determines the number of bytes in a currently open text file and then records the number of bytes in the cell specified by the location. You must {OPEN} a text file first.

The location is a cell address or a range name where 1-2-3 should display the file size. The total size of the currently open file is placed as a numeric value in the specified cell location.

Macro execution continues after completion of the {FILESIZE} command in the next cell of the macro. If no file is currently open, 1-2-3 ignores {FILESIZE}, and macro execution continues in the current cell.

GETPOS {GETPOS *location*} determines the current position of the byte pointer in an open file and displays it in the location cell. You must {OPEN} a text file first. The location can be a cell address or a range name. The current position of the byte pointer in the open file appears as a number in the location. (The first position in a file is 0, not 1.)

Macro execution continues after completion of the {GETPOS} command in the next cell of the macro. If a file is not currently open, 1-2-3 ignores {GETPOS}, and macro execution continues in the current cell.

OPEN {OPEN *file-name*, *access-type*} opens a specified text file for reading, writing, or both. You must open a file with {OPEN} before you can use any of the other file-manipulation commands. *File-name* is a full name (including the extension) of a text file, or a range name that refers to a single cell containing the full filename. The string cannot exceed 64 characters. If the file you want to open is not in the current directory, the filename should specify a drive location and a subdirectory path and enclose the argument in quotation marks.

The access-type is a single-character string that indicates the type of file access you want:

- R (Read access) opens an existing file with the specified name and allows access with the {READ} and {READLN} commands. You cannot write to a file opened with a Read access mode.

- W (Write access) opens a new file, assigns it the specified name, and allows access with the {WRITE} and {WRITELN} commands, as well as the {READ} and {READLN} commands. 1-2-3 erases and replaces any existing file with the specified name with the new file.
- M (Modify access) opens an existing file with the specified name and allows access with both read ({READ}, {READLN}) and write ({WRITE}, {WRITELN}) commands.
- A (Append access) opens an existing file for reading and writing, placing the byte pointer at the end of the file. You can use {READ}, {READLN}, {GETPOS}, {SETPOS}, {WRITE}, and {WRITELN} with a file opened with Append access.

{OPEN} succeeds if the correct conditions for the desired access mode exist. When successful, if you try to open a file with read or modify access and the file does not exist, the {OPEN} command fails, and macro execution continues in the current cell. If you try to open a read-only file for writing, an error may occur.

{OPEN} with write access always succeeds (unless you specify a non-existent drive or directory) because it opens a new file. When successful, macro execution continues in the cell immediately following the {OPEN} command.

Note Only one text file can be open at a time. If a text file is open when 1-2-3 performs an {OPEN} command, 1-2-3 automatically closes that text file before opening the new one. If a text file is open when a macro ends, 1-2-3 does not automatically close the text file. You must include a {CLOSE} command in the macro to close the file.

READ

{READ *byte-count,location*} reads the characters from a file into the cell specified as the location. Beginning at the current position of the byte pointer in the file, {READ} copies the specified number of characters (*byte-count*) from the file to the worksheet, placing them into a left-aligned label at the specified cell location. If the byte-count is larger than the number of characters left in the file, 1-2-3 reads the remaining characters.

The *byte-count* must be a number or a formula that results in a number. The number must be between 0 and 240. A negative byte count is equivalent to the maximum positive byte-count of 240.

The location can be a cell address or a range name. Using a range name is equivalent to specifying the first cell of the range.

The byte pointer advances by the number specified as the byte-count, so a subsequent {READ} command begins at the next character.

If the file is not currently open, {READ} is ignored, and macro execution continues in the same cell. Otherwise, when {READ} is completed, macro execution continues in the next cell.

READLN {READLN *location*} copies a line of characters from the currently open file into the specified location.

{READLN} works the same way {READ} does, except that instead of reading a specified number of characters, {READLN} reads a whole line beginning with the current position of the byte pointer and ending with a carriage-return line feed. Thus, a byte-count argument is not needed for this command.

Because the file pointer advances to the beginning of the next line, a subsequent {READLN} command begins there. The carriage return is not copied with the line of text.

SETPOS {SETPOS *offset-number*} sets a new position for the file pointer in the currently open text file. The offset number is a number or a formula that results in a number that specifies the character at which you want to position the pointer. The first character in the file is at position 0, the second at position 1, and so on.

If a file is not currently open, {SETPOS} is ignored, and macro execution continues in the same cell. Otherwise, when {SETPOS} is completed, macro execution continues in the next cell.

CAUTION 1-2-3 does not prevent you from placing the byte pointer past the end of the file. Use the {FILESIZE} command to determine the number of the last character in your file.

WRITE {WRITE *string*} copies characters into an open file.

{WRITE} copies a string from the worksheet into the current position of the byte pointer in a file that was opened with either the write, append, or the modify access type. The string can be a literal string, a range name assigned to a single cell, or a string-valued expression.

1-2-3 evaluates the argument to produce a character string and then converts each character to a DOS code before sending it to the open file. If necessary, 1-2-3 extends the length of the file to accommodate the incoming string. The byte pointer advances to just beyond the last character written. A subsequent {WRITE} command picks up where this one leaves off, unless you reset the pointer with the {SETPOS} command.

WRITELN {WRITELN *string*} adds a carriage-return line-feed (CR-LF) sequence to a string of characters and writes the string to a file. {WRITELN} works the same as {WRITE}, except that it adds a CR-LF sequence to the end of the string in the file.

As with {WRITE}, the string can be a literal string, a range name assigned to a single cell, or a string-valued expression. You can use {WRITELN} with an empty string ("") argument to add a CR-LF sequence to the end of a line: {WRITELN ""}.

Creating and Using the Macro Library Manager

The Macro Library Manager add-in lets you create and use macro libraries. A macro library is a range taken from a 1-2-3 worksheet and stored in memory (in an area that is separate from the worksheet) and in a file on disk called a library file (with an .MLB extension). The range can contain a single macro, several macros, a combination of macros and data (including formulas), or just data. Because Macro Library Manager is an add-in, it does not have to be stored in memory all the time. You can attach it (load it into memory) when you need to use it, and detach it (remove it from memory) when you need more memory for completing other tasks.

Using the Macro Library Manager allows you to:

- Use macros, formulas, and ranges of data in a different worksheet from the worksheet in which you created them.
- Leave some data in memory when you clear the worksheet and retrieve a new worksheet file.
- Build sophisticated applications to use with more than one worksheet.

The Macro Library Manager is in a file called MACROMGR.ADN on the Utilities disk. To start the 1-2-3 Macro Library Manager:

1. If you are running 1-2-3 from a hard disk, make the directory where you copy the program files the current directory. If you are running 1-2-3 on a two-disk system, insert the Utilities disk in the disk drive.
2. Select / **A**dd-In **A**ttach

   If MACROMGR.ADN is not an option in the menu that appears, you must change the specified directory. Press ESC to clear the currently displayed filenames, edit the directory or drive name, and then press (↵).
3. Select MACROMGR.ADN.
4. Select the key you want to use to invoke (activate) the Macro Library Manager: **N**o-Key does not assign Macro Library Manager to any key. **7** assigns it to APP1 (ALT-(F7)). **8** assigns it to APP2 (ALT-(F8)). **9** assigns it to APP3 (ALT-(F9)). **10** assigns it to APP4 (ALT-(F10)).

   Macro Library Manager is now attached (in memory). To use it, you must still invoke it. The step you use to invoke Macro Library Manager depends on whether you assigned it to a key when you attached the add-in. If you selected a key when you attached Macro Library Manager, press that key to invoke it. If you selected **N**o-Key, select / **A**dd-In **I**nvoke, and then select MACROMGR.ADN from the menu of attached add-ins that appears.

5. The Macro Library Manager menu appears. A brief description of the commands follows.

Load lets you copy data from a library file (a file with an .MLB extension) on disk into a library in memory. The library is stored separately from the worksheet.

Save lets you move the contents of a worksheet range and its range names into both a macro library in memory and a library file on disk. Range names associated with the cells no longer refer to the worksheet; they now refer to library locations.

Note Be sure to test your macros in the worksheet before you save them in a library.

Edit lets you copy a macro library from memory into the worksheet so you can make changes to the contents of the library or use it in the worksheet.

CAUTION The library can be placed in any unprotected area of the worksheet. Make sure that the worksheet location is blank or contains unimportant data because Macro Library Manager writes over existing data when it copies the library into the worksheet.

Remove lets you erase a macro library from memory but leaves a copy of the library intact on disk. (To erase a library file from disk, select / **F**ile **E**rase **O**ther, press ESC, type ***.MLB**, and select the library you want to delete.)

Name-List lets you create a list in the worksheet of the range names contained in a library. The list consists of a column of labels. The list will occupy a single column and as many rows as there are range names in the library.

CAUTION The range name list can be placed in any unprotected area of the worksheet. Make sure that the location is blank or contains unimportant data because Macro Library Manager writes over existing data when it creates the list.

Quit lets you leave the Macro Library Manager menu, but keeps Macro Library Manager attached. The data in the macro libraries that you have loaded or saved are still available.

Basic Macro Library Manager Rules

- You must attach Macro Library Manager before you attempt to save data in a library or load a library file into memory. If you detach Macro Library Manager during a work session, the macro libraries you have saved or loaded disappear from memory. The library files already on disk are not affected.
- A macro library can contain up to 16,376 cells.

- Macro Library Manager places a library in memory when you select either the **L**oad or **S**ave command from the Macro Library Manager menu. You can have up to ten libraries in memory simultaneously.

- When you specify the range you want to save in a library, Macro Library Manager allocates a cell in conventional memory for each cell in the range, even if it is empty. To save memory, try to make your macros as compact as possible and specify ranges with as few empty cells as possible.

- Macro libraries are stored in an area of memory separate from the worksheet. Because a library has no cell coordinates, you cannot refer to data in a library with a cell or range address such as B3..B12. If you want to create a macro in the worksheet that uses data in a macro library, the data in the library must be contained in a named range (such as SALES89) and you must use the range name in the marco.

- / **W**orksheet **E**rase and / **F**ile **R**etrieve do not erase macro libraries from memory so you can erase all data from a worksheet or retrieve a new worksheet without affecting the libraries.

- You use the same techniques to run a macro stored in a library as you would use with a macro in a worksheet.

- You can specify a password when you save data in a macro library. The password can be up to 80 characters long. Passwords protect libraries you created from being edited by others or from being viewed in STEP mode.

- You cannot have two or more libraries in memory with the same name.

- Try to assign unique names to each range you save in the library.

- Macro Library Manager will not let you save a range in a library if the range includes a reference, or link, to data in another file.

4

@Functions

1-2-3's @functions are built-in formulas that perform specialized calculations. For example, instead of adding a range of numbers (+A5+A6+A7+A8+A9+A10+A11), you can use the function @SUM(A5..A11) to do the work for you. You can use an @function by itself in a cell or combine it with other functions and formulas.

Most of 1-2-3's @functions calculate numeric values. Some @functions, however, manipulate sequences of text, called strings. For example, @LENGTH(B9) counts the number of characters in cell B9 when B9 contains text.

The first section of this chapter presents general information about @functions and their arguments. The remainder of the chapter is divided into sections containing descriptions and examples of each @function. Each section begins with a list of specific rules and procedures for that group of @functions. The @functions within each section are organized alphabetically.

@Function Format

The general format of an @function is as follows:

@function name(*argument1*,*argument2*,...)

The @function name begins with the ''at'' character (@) and tells 1-2-3 which calculation to perform. The arguments you enter are the values 1-2-3 uses in the function's calculations. In the @function @SUM(A5..A11), @SUM is the @function name, and A5..A11 is the @function's argument. Every @function produces, or returns, a single value, depending on the arguments you give it to evaluate. In this chapter, @function names are in uppercase letters, and argument names are in lowercase *italic* letters. You can type an @function name in uppercase or lowercase letters. 1-2-3 automatically converts @function names to uppercase.

Arguments

There are four argument types: values, strings, locations (cells or ranges), and conditions. Different @functions require different types of data as arguments. The @function @INT(*x*) asks you to substitute a numeric value for *x*. The @function @SUM(*list*) asks you to substitute one or more ranges of numeric values for *list*. The @function @LENGTH(*string*) asks you to substitute a text string value for *string*. The @function @IF (*condition*,*x*,*y*) evaluates a condition (usually a logical formula).

You can enter arguments as actual numeric or string values or as cells or ranges that contain the values you want to use. Table 4.1 gives examples of the ways you can enter arguments in @functions.

Table 4.1

Types of Arguments	Examples
Numeric values by	
Actual value	@INT(375.68)
Cell address	@INT(D6)
Cell range name	@INT(TOTAL)
Formula	@INT((25+47)/5)
@Function	@INT(@SUM(A5..A11))
Combination	@INT(@SUM(D2..D*)+TOTAL+33.5)
Range values by	
Range address	@SUM(A5..A11)
Range name	@SUM(RANGE2)
Combination	@SUM(RANGE2,D2..D8,TOTAL)
String values by	
Actual value	@LENGTH("Monthly Profits")
Cell address	@LENGTH(B9)
Cell name	@LENGTH(TITLE)
Formula	@LENGTH("Monthly"&"Profits")

Entering Arguments in @Functions

Use the following guidelines when you write @functions:

- Begin every @function with the @ sign.
- Enclose an @function's argument in parentheses.
- Do not include any spaces between the @function's name and its arguments.
- Separate multiple arguments in an @function with argument separators. A comma (,) or a semicolon (;) are the default valid argument separators. Do not use spaces between arguments.
- When you use an @function as an argument, enclose its arguments in parentheses and enclose the @function, including its arguments, in another set of parentheses. For example, in @INT(@SUM(A5..A11)), the range A5..A11 is the argument for the @SUM function, and the @function @SUM(A5..A11) is the argument for the @INT function.
- Use a pair of double quotes (" ") around the actual string values you use as arguments.
- Seven @functions do not require arguments: @RAND, @PI, @FALSE, @TRUE, @ERR, @NA, and @NOW. Write them without parentheses.

- The @functions @CELL, @N, and @S take single-cell values as arguments but require you to enter these values as ranges. You can enter single-cell ranges in two ways: with the range address format @N(G5..G5) or with the cell address preceded by an exclamation point, such as @N(!G5).
- Use only the required argument type in an @function. For example, you cannot use a string value in an @function that requires a numeric value.
- If you make an error in entering any @function argument, 1-2-3 returns the value ERR in the cell in which you entered the @function.
- If you type an @function name incorrectly or enter an @function in an incorrect format, 1-2-3 beeps and puts you in EDIT mode.

Mathematical @Functions

1-2-3's mathematical @functions perform a variety of calculations with numeric values, including the trigonometric functions. Single numeric arguments can be in the form of numbers, cell addresses, formulas, or other @functions. Each mathematical @function produces (or returns) a numeric value, and all except @PI take numeric values as arguments.

All angles that you enter for the sine, cosine, and tangent @functions must be expressed in radians. To convert degrees to radians, multiply the number of degrees by @PI/180.

The arc sine, arc cosine, and arc tangent @functions return all angles in radians. To convert radians to degrees, multiply the number of radians by 180/@PI.

@ABS

@ABS(x) returns the absolute, or positive, value of x.

Example: @ABS(−6.2) = 6.2

@ACOS

@ACOS(x) computes the arc cosine of a value. It returns the angle, in radians, whose cosine is x. The result always lies between 0 and π, representing a quadrant I or II angle.

Argument x must be between −1 and 1, inclusive.

Example: @ACOS(.5) = 1.047197 (radians)

@ASIN

@ASIN(x) computes the arc sine of a value. It returns the angle, in radians, whose sine is x. The result always lies between $\pi/2$ and $-\pi/2$, representing a quadrant I or IV angle.

Argument x must be between −1 and 1, inclusive.

Example: @ASIN(1) = 1.570796 (radians)

@ATAN @ATAN(x) computes the second-quadrant arc tangent of an angle. It returns the angle, in radians, whose tangent is x. The result always lies between $\pi/2$ and $-\pi/2$, representing a quadrant I or IV angle.

There is no restriction on the value of argument x.

Example: @ATAN(1) = 0.785398 (radians)

@ATAN2 @ATAN2(x,y) computes the fourth-quadrant arc tangent of an angle. It returns the angle, in radians, whose tangent is y/x.

Arguments x and y can be any numeric value. If y is 0, the @function returns 0. If both x and y are 0, the result is ERR.

@ATAN2 differs from @ATAN in that its result lies anywhere between $-\pi$ and π, representing any quadrant. The possible ranges of values of @ATAN2 are the following:

If x is:	And y is:	@ATAN2(x,y)returns:
Positive	Positive	Between 0 and $\pi/2$
Negative	Positive	Between $\pi/2$ and π
Negative	Negative	Between $-\pi$ and $-\pi/2$
Positive	Negative	Between $-\pi/2$ and 0

Example: ATAN(1.5,2) = 0.927295 (radians)

@COS @COS(x) returns the cosine of angle x. The result lies between -1 and 1, inclusive.

Angle x must be expressed in radians.

Example: @COS(45*@PI/180) = 0.707106

@EXP @EXP(x) returns the value of e, approximately 2.718282, raised to the xth power. To incorporate the value e in any calculation, use the function @EXP(1) in that calculation. @EXP is the inverse function of @LN.

Argument x cannot be larger than 709, because the result would be too large for 1-2-3 to store. If x is larger than 230, 1-2-3 can calculate and store the value of @EXP but cannot display it. 1-2-3 cannot display a number greater than 9.9E99.

Example: @EXP(1.25) = 3.490342

@INT @INT(x) returns the integer part of x. It ends x at the decimal point but does not round it. To round a number, use @ROUND. X can be any value.

Example: @INT(35.45) = 35

@LN $@LN(x)$ computes the natural logarithm (base e) of x. Natural logarithms use the value of e (approximately 2.718282) as a base. @LN is the inverse function of @EXP. To incorporate the value e in any calculation, use the function @EXP(1) in that calculation.

Argument x must be greater than 0.

Example: @LN(2) = 0.693147

@LOG @LOG(x) computes the common logarithm (base 10) of x. @LOG is the base 10 exponent of a number.

Argument x must be greater than 0.

Example: @LOG(100) = 2

@MOD @MOD(x,y) returns the remainder (modulus) of x/y.

Argument x can be any number. Argument y must be a number other than 0. The sign (+ or −) of the result is always the same as the sign of x.

Example: @MOD(4,3) = 1

@PI @PI returns the number π (approximately 3.1415926). π is the ratio of the circumference of a circle to its diameter.

Example: @PI*4^2 = 50.26548, the area of the circle whose radius is 4

@RAND @RAND generates a random number between 0 and 1. 1-2-3 calculates the same random values, in the same order, during every work session.

Each time 1-2-3 recalculates the worksheet, the value of @RAND changes. To generate random numbers in larger numeric intervals, multiply @RAND by the size of the interval.

Example: @RAND*10+1 = any integer between 1 and 10

@ROUND @ROUND(x,n) rounds number x to n places. 1-2-3 can round on either side of the decimal point; n specifies the power of 10 to which 1-2-3 rounds x.

Argument n must be any integer between −15 and 15, inclusive. Argument x can be any value.

If n is positive, 1-2-3 rounds x to n digits to the right of the decimal point. If n is negative, 1-2-3 rounds x to the positive nth power of 10. For example, if n is -2, 1-2-3 rounds x to the nearest hundred. If n is zero, 1-2-3 rounds x to an integer. If n is not an integer, 1-2-3 uses only its integer part.

Example: @ROUND(134.578,1) = 134.6

@SIN

@SIN(x) returns the sine of angle x.

Angle x must be expressed in radians.

Example: @SIN(.883) = 0.772646

@SQRT

@SQRT(x) returns the positive square root of x.

Argument x must be a positive number or 0.

Example: @SQRT(100) = 10

@TAN

@TAN(x) returns the tangent of angle x.

Angle x must be expressed in radians.

Example: @TAN(.52) = 0.572561

Logical @Functions

1-2-3's logical @functions produce values based on the results of conditional (logical) formulas.

A conditional formula evaluates a condition in the form of an equation. The condition is either true or false. For example, the @ISNUMBER function tests to see if a value in a cell is numeric. If the value is numeric or the cell is blank, @ISNUMBER returns the logical value 1 (true). If the value is not numeric, @ISNUMBER returns the logical value 0 (false).

ERR and NA are special values in 1-2-3, generated either by 1-2-3 or by you when you use the @ERR or @NA function. ERR denotes an error in a formula, and NA denotes that the number needed to complete a formula is not available. Both ERR and NA have a ripple-through effect on formulas, meaning that any formula dependent on a formula containing ERR or NA will also result in ERR or NA. It also means that when you correct the formula containing ERR or provide the unavailable number to the formula containing NA, the results of dependent formulas will become correct.

The @ISERR, @ISNA, @ISNUMBER, and @ISSTRING functions stop this ripple-through effect because they can test for these values before you perform a calculation. The arguments for @ISERR, @ISNA,

@ISNUMBER, and @ISSTRING are generally cell addresses or range names. If you use a range name that represents a multiple-cell range, 1-2-3 tests the upper left corner cell.

ERR and NA are both numeric values. A blank cell has the value 0.

@FALSE @FALSE returns the logical value 0. You can use @FALSE with other @functions to create logical arithmetic formulas that are easy to read.

Example: @IF(PASSWORD = ''music'',@TRUE,@FALSE) = 0, when the value in the cell named PASSWORD is not music

@IF @IF(*condition*,*x*,*y*) returns the value *x* if the condition is true or the value *y* if the condition is false.

The condition must be a numeric value or any type of formula that results in a numeric value. It is usually a logical formula. Arguments *x* and *y* can be either numeric or string values.

Example: @IF(9>8,C3,D3) = the value in C3

@ISAAF @ISAAF (*name*) returns 1 (true) for a defined add-in @function and 0 (false) for any other entry. *Name* is the name of the add-in @function you want to test.

Example: @ISAAF(''DSUM'') = 0 (because @DSUM is a built-in 1-2-3 @function, not an add-in @function)

@ISAPP @ISAPP(*name*) returns 1 (true) for a currently attached add-in and 0 (false) for any other entry. *Name* is the name of the add-in you want to test.

Example: @ISAPP (''FINANCE'') = 1 (if an add-in called FINANCE is currently attached)

@ISERR @ISERR(*x*) tests to see if *x* contains the value ERR. @ISERR returns 1 if *x* is the value ERR; otherwise, it returns 0. This function stops the ripple-through effect of the value ERR. *X* can be any string, value, location, or condition.

Example: @ISERR(45/0) = 1

@ISNA @ISNA(x) tests to see if x contains the value NA. @ISNA returns 1 if x is the value NA; otherwise, it returns 0. This function stops the ripple-through effect of the value ERR. X can be any string, value, location, or condition.

Example: @ISNA(B1) = 1 if B1 contains the value NA,
@ISNA(B1) = 0 if B1 contains any other entry

@ISNUMBER @ISNUMBER(x) tests to see if x contains a numeric value. @ISNUMBER returns 1 if x is a number, a formula that results in a numeric value, or a blank cell; otherwise, it returns 0. X can be any string, value, location, or condition.

Example: @ISNUMBER(745) = 1

@ISSTRING @ISSTRING(x) tests to see if x contains a string value. @ISSTRING returns 1 if x is a string, even if the string contains only a space character or an empty string. If x contains any other value or a blank cell, @ISSTRING returns 0. X can be any string, value, location, or condition.

Example: @ISSTRING(745) = 0

@TRUE @TRUE returns the logical value 1.

1-2-3 sees the value TRUE as a condition that produces a positive result. For example, the formula @IF(25=5*5, ''yes'', ''no'') returns yes, because 25=5*5 is a true condition.

When you use the value TRUE in a formula, you can use either @TRUE or the number 1. Using the number 1 may make the meaning of the formula unclear. Using @TRUE prevents any ambiguity.

Example: @IF(PASSWORD= ''music'',@TRUE,@FALSE) = 1, when PASSWORD contains the string music

Special @Functions

Special @functions perform a variety of advanced tasks, primarily the ability to look up a value in a table.

The @function acts as a pointer by referencing a specific cell whose contents are another address. The @CELL and @CELLPOINTER functions provide information on a cell's contents, format, and location in a worksheet.

The @CHOOSE function returns a specific numeric or string value from an argument list. The @COLS, @HLOOKUP, @INDEX, @ROWS, and @VLOOKUP functions locate values in specific cells in a table.

The @ERR and @NA functions mark cells that contain formulas with errors (@ERR) or unavailable values (@NA). They also cause every cell that depends on formulas containing ERR or NA to have those values. This is called a ripple-through effect on the worksheet.

An empty string has a length of 0. An empty string is one that you enter into a cell by typing the label-prefix character '', ^, or '. The cell looks blank, but it has a string value.

@@ @@(*location*) returns the contents of the cell whose name or address is specified by *location*.

The location must be the name or cell address of a single cell range that contains a valid cell reference.

Contents of cell address:	Examples:
A cell address written as a label	A33
A range name assigned to a cell	INPUT, where INPUT is the cell name of cell A33

Examples: @@(D4) = 37, when cell D4 contains the label F5, and cell F5 contains the value 37

@@(D4) = Balance, when D4 contains the label INPUT, INPUT is the name of cell F6, and cell F6 contains the string Balance

@CELL @CELL(*attribute,range*) returns a particular piece of information, called an attribute, about a given cell after you enter a range name or address for the cell and an attribute string from the attribute table (Table 4.2).

The attribute must be enclosed in quotation marks ('' '') and can be in either uppercase or lowercase letters, for example, ''width'', ''WIDTH'', and ''Width''. You can also enter an attribute by typing a cell address that contains one of the attribute strings. You can enter B2 as the attribute if B2 contains the label WIDTH (or Format, TYPE, contents, and so on).

The range can be a range name or address. If *range* consists of more than one cell (for example, H7..K14), 1-2-3 uses the first cell in the range.

@CELL returns a result for the cell attribute you request about the specified cell. You must press the Calc function key, F9, to update cell attributes.

Table 4.2 lists attributes and results.

Example: @CELL(''row'',J5..J5) = 5

Table 4.2

Attribute	Result
"address"	The absolute cell address (for example $B$7 or B7)
"row"	The row number (between 1 and 8192)
"col"	The column letter as a number (between 1 and 256)
"contents"	The cell contents
"type"	The type of data in the cell: b if the cell is blank (it has no cell entry) v if the cell contains a numeric value or formula or a string-valued formula l if the cell contains a label
"prefix"	The label prefix: ' if the cell contains a left-aligned label " if the cell contains a right-aligned label ^ if the cell contains a centered label \ if the cell contains a repeating label ¦ if the cell contains a nonprinting label a blank, if the cell is empty or contains a number or any kind of formula
"protect"	The protection status: 1 if the cell is protected 0 if the cell is not protected
"filename"	The name of the current file including the path
"width"	The column width (between 1 and 240 in the current window)
"format"	The numeric format: F0 to F15, if fixed; 0 to 15 decimal places S0 to S15, if scientific; 0 to 15 decimal places C0 to C15, if currency; 0 to 15 decimal places G, if general P0 to P15, if percent; 0 to 15 decimal places D1, if DD-MMM-YY D2, if DD-MMM D3, if MMM-YY D4, if MM/DD/YY, DD/MM/YY, DD.MM.YY, YY-MM-DD D5, if MM/DD, DD/MM, DD.MM, MM-DD D6, if HH:MM:SS AM/PM D7, if HH:MM AM/PM D8, if HH:MM:SS 24hr, hh.MM.SS 24hr, HH,MM,SS 24hr, or HHhMMmSSs D9, if HH:MM 24hr, HH.MM 24hr, HH.MM or HHhMMm T, if text format (cell formula appears in cell) H, if hidden format a blank, if the cell contains an empty string

If cell B2 contains the label WIDTH, @CELL(B2,G12) = 14, because the column width for cell G12 is 14, and B2 contains the word WIDTH.

@CELLPOINTER

@CELLPOINTER(*attribute*) returns information, called an attribute, about the current cell and is useful when you are testing cell values in a macro.

This function is similar to the @CELL function. @CELL yields information about a cell whose address or range name you specify. @CELLPOINTER yields information about the current cell, the cell that the cell pointer is currently highlighting. The value of this function changes to reflect the attribute of the cell that the cell pointer was on during the most recent recalculation.

Use Table 4.2 to enter a cell attribute.

Examples: @CELLPOINTER(''row'') = 4, if the cell pointer was in row 4 at the time of the last recalculation

@CELLPOINTER(''col'') = 26, if the cell pointer was in column Z at the time of the last recalculation

@CHOOSE

@CHOOSE(*offset*,*list*) finds the value or string in *list* that is specified by *offset*.

Offset represents an offset number. An offset number corresponds to the position an item occupies in *list*. The first item has an offset number of 0, the second item has an offset number of 1, and so on. *Offset* can be 0 or any positive integer that is less than or equal to the number of items in *list* minus 1. *List* can contain one or more values, strings, references to ranges that contain values or strings, or any combination of values, strings, and range references.

Use @CHOOSE to enter a list of lookup values without setting a lookup table.

Examples: @CHOOSE(1, ''Profit'', ''Loss'', ''Bankruptcy'') = Loss

@CHOOSE(H5,B1,B2,B3) = the value in cell B2 if H5 contains the value 1.3

@COLS @COLS(*range*) returns the number of columns in *range*. This @function is helpful when used with range names. *Range* can be any range name or address.

Examples: @COLS(A3..F7) = 6

@COLS(SCORES) = 6 if the range A3..F7 is named SCORES

@COLS(A3) = 1

@ERR @ERR returns the numeric value ERR.

Use @ERR to force a cell to have the value ERR. All cells containing formulas that depend on this cell's value also assume the value ERR, causing a ripple-through effect on the worksheet.

You cannot substitute the label ERR for the value ERR.

The @functions @COUNT, @ISERR, @ISNA, @ISNUMBER, @ISSTRING, @CELL, and @CELLPOINTER stop the ripple-through effect of ERR values.

Example: IF(B14>3.2,@ERR,B14) returns ERR if the value in cell B14 is greater than 3.2; otherwise, the value in B14 is returned

@HLOOKUP @HLOOKUP(x,*range*,*row-offset*) performs a horizontal table lookup. A horizontal table lookup compares the value x to each cell in the top, or index, row in the range. When it locates a cell containing a value that matches x, it stops moving horizontally across the index row. @HLOOKUP then moves down the column the number of rows specified by *row-offset* to return the answer. If you include formulas in a lookup table, make sure the lookup range includes the row specified by *row-offset*.

@HLOOKUP searches an index row of *range* until it finds a cell containing a numeric value that is larger than the value x. It then moves back one cell so that it stops at the cell whose value is the highest number that is less than or equal to the value x. For example, if the index row contains the values 10, 20, 30, 40, and 50, and x is 33, @HLOOKUP stops at the cell containing 40 and then backs up to the cell containing 30. At this point, @HLOOKUP moves the number of rows specified by the row offset.

Example: @HLOOKUP(2,A1..C5,3) returns the second value in row 3 from the table located in cells A1..C5

@INDEX @INDEX(*range*,*column-offset*,*row-offset*) returns the value of the cell in *range* at the intersection of *column-offset* and *row-offset*.

@INDEX uses *range* as its table range; *column-offset* and *row-offset* specify the number of columns to count over from the first column and how many rows to count down from the top row. The first column is column 0, and the top row is row 0.

Column-offset and *row-offset* represent offset numbers and can be zero or any positive integer that is less than or equal to the number of columns or rows in *range* minus 1.

Example: @INDEX(A3..G7,0,2) returns the value in the first column in row 3 of the range A3..G7

@NA @NA returns the numeric value NA (not available) when a number is not available to complete a formula. This @function enters NA in the current cell and in all other cells that depend on the formula in the cell.

@NA is useful when you are building a worksheet that will contain data that have not been specified. You can use @NA in cells where the data are to be entered. Formulas that reference those cells will have the value NA until you supply the correct data. Because NA appears in every cell that depends on the cell containing NA, this @function ripples through the worksheet. You cannot substitute the label NA for the value NA.

The @functions @COUNT, @ISERR, @ISNA, @ISNUMBER, @ISSTRING, @CELL, and @CELLPOINTER stop the ripple-through effect of NA values.

Example: @IF(B14>3.2,@NA,B14) returns NA if the value in cell B14 is greater than 3.2; otherwise, the value in B14 is returned

@ROWS @ROWS(*range*) returns the number of rows in *range*. This function is helpful when used with named ranges. *Range* can be any range name or address.

Examples: @ROWS(A3..F7) = 5

@ROWS(SCORES1) = 5 if SCORES1 names the range A3..F7

@VLOOKUP @VLOOKUP(*x*,*range*,*column-offset*) performs a vertical table lookup. A vertical table lookup compares the value *x* to each cell in the top, or index, column in *range*. When it locates a cell containing a value that matches *x*, it stops moving vertically down the index column. @VLOOKUP then moves across that row the number of columns specified by *column-offset* to return the answer. *Column-offset* represents an offset number, which corresponds to the position the column occupies in *range*. *Column-offset* can be zero or any positive integer that is less than or equal to the number of columns in *range* minus 1.

@VLOOKUP searches an index column *range* until it finds a cell containing a numeric value larger than the value *x*. It then moves up one cell so that it stops at the cell whose value is the highest number that is less than or equal to the value *x*. For example, if the index column contains the values 10, 20, 30, 40, and 50, and *x* is 33, @VLOOKUP stops at the cell containing 40 and then moves up to the cell containing 30. At this point, @VLOOKUP moves the number of columns specified by *column-offset*.

Example: @VLOOKUP(3,B2..E5,2) returns the second value in row 3 from the table located in cells B2..E5

String @Functions

String @functions manipulate a series of characters called strings, make calculations using strings, and produce string values. Strings can be letters, numbers, and special characters, as long as they are label data types.

The string argument can be a literal string, range names, or addresses of cells that contain labels or formulas or @functions that evaluate to a string.

When you enter actual string values as arguments, enclose them in a pair of quotation marks (“ ”). When you enter string values by cell address or range name, you do not need to use quotation marks. For example, @LEFT(“Monthly Expenses”,5) returns the word Month. If the string Monthly Expenses was in cell G8, you could also write @LEFT(G8,5).

Many string @functions use offset numbers to locate the characters in a string. Offset numbers always start at position 0. The string Red Shoes contains nine characters. The R is at position 0, the e is at position 1, the d is at position 2, the space is at position 3, and the last s is at position 8. The last position number is always one less than the length of the string.

Use positive integers to indicate an offset number. 1-2-3 interprets an entry with a negative position number as invalid and returns ERR. If you type 4.5 as a position number, 1-2-3 abbreviates it to 4.

The argument start number is an offset number of a character in a string from which you want to begin the calculation.

@Functions can read 240 characters in one string. Therefore, offset numbers can be from 0 to 239 for each string value.

You can create a string that has no letters, numbers, spaces, or special characters by typing a label-prefix character in a cell. This is called an empty string and has a length of 0. An empty string has an LICS code of 0, which differs from a blank cell, which has no LICS code value.

@CHAR @CHAR(x) returns the LICS character that corresponds to the code number x. 1-2-3 stores each character displayed on the screen as one of the numeric character codes in LICS. LICS is an extension of the ASCII character set.

Argument x can be any numeric value between 1 and 255. Values outside the range yield ERR. 1-2-3 abbreviates any fractional numbers to integers.

If your computer does not have a display character for x, @CHAR returns either a character that resembles the desired character or a blank. For characters outside the printable ASCII character set (codes below 32), the LICS code may not correspond to the codes used by your computer. The display driver you include in the 1-2-3 driver set takes care of any required translation.

Examples: @CHAR(52) = 4

@CHAR(65) = A

@CHAR(97) = a

@CLEAN @CLEAN(*string*) removes certain control characters from *string*. @CLEAN removes control characters with ASCII codes below 32, the begin and end attribute characters, as well as the attribute character itself, the merge character (LICS 155) and the character following.

@CODE @CODE(*string*) returns the LICS code number of the first character in *string*.

The @CHAR and @CODE functions let you switch between the displayed characters and the LICS character codes that identify them.

Examples: @CODE(''4.2'') = 52

@CODE(''A'') = 65

@CODE(''Anyone'') = 65

@EXACT @EXACT(*string1*,*string2*) tests whether two strings are exactly the same. If *string1* is exactly the same as *string2*, @EXACT returns 1; otherwise, it returns 0.

This function provides a more precise alternative to the equal operator (=) in a formula, because unlike the equal operator, @EXACT distinguishes between uppercase and lowercase letters and between letters with and without accent marks.

Examples: @EXACT(''LONDON'', ''London'') = 0 (false)

+ ''LONDON'' = ''London'' = 1 (true), because this formula is not sensitive to uppercase and lowercase letters

@FIND @FIND(*search-string*,*string*,*start-number*) finds the position at which the first occurrence of *search-string* begins in *string*.

The @FIND function begins searching *string* at *start-number*. If the search fails, the result is ERR. @FIND is case sensitive.

To extract a substring after locating its starting position with @FIND, use the @MID function.

Examples: @FIND(“even”, “Seven is not even”,0) = 1

@FIND(“even”, “Seven is not even”,2) = 13

@FIND(“e”, “THE”,0) = ERR

@LEFT @LEFT(*string*,*n*) returns the first *n* characters in *string*. 1-2-3 counts punctuation and spaces as characters.

Example: @LEFT(“This is a test”,4) = This

@LENGTH @LENGTH(*string*) returns the number of characters found in *string*. 1-2-3 counts punctuation and spaces as characters.

Examples: @LENGTH(“computer”) = 8

@LENGTH(“”) = 0

@LENGTH(A5&G12) = the total number of characters found in cells A5 and G12

@LOWER @LOWER(*string*) converts all the uppercase characters in *string* to lowercase.

Example: @LOWER(“A FinE THINg”) = a fine thing

@MID @MID(*string*,*start-number*,*n*) extracts *n* characters from *string* beginning with the character at *start-number*.

The @LEFT and @RIGHT functions are special cases of @MID. They extract a substring from either end of the string value.

If *start-number* is beyond the end of *string*, the result is an empty string, consisting of no characters. If *n* is 0, the result is an empty string. *N* can be any positive number or 0. If *n* is 0, the result of @MID is an empty string.

You can use a large number for *n* if you do not know the length of the string and want to make sure you get all of it. The extra length has no effect on the result.

Examples: @MID(“Our finest hour”,4,6) = finest

@MID(“Our finest hour”,25,6) = empty string

@MID(“data” & “base”,0,4) = data

@N @N(*range*) returns the value in the first cell in *range* as a numeric value. If the cell contains a value, @N returns that value. If the cell contains a label, @N returns the value 0.

Range can be any range name or address.

Examples: @N(!A3) = 0, if cell A3 was empty

@N(B3..B7) = 1981, if cell B3 contained 1981

@PROPER @PROPER(*string*) converts the letters in *string* to proper capitalization, that is, the first letter of each word in uppercase and all others in lowercase.

Examples: @PROPER(“A FINE THING”) = A Fine Thing

@PROPER(“354 – a babcock”) = 354 – A Babcock

@REPEAT @REPEAT(*string*,*n*) duplicates *string* the number of times specified by *n*. *N* can be any positive integer.

@REPEAT differs from a repeating label (a cell entry that begins with a label-prefix backslash) in that the repeating label repeats the label only to fill the current column width. @REPEAT duplicates the string the number of times you specify; it is not limited by the current column width.

Example: @REPEAT(“Hello ”,3) = Hello Hello Hello

@REPLACE @REPLACE(*original-string*,*start-number*,*n* ,*new-string*) removes *n* characters from the original string beginning at *start-number* and then inserts *new-string* in the same place. *N* can be any positive integer or 0.

There are several procedures you can perform with @REPLACE:

- By making *n* equal to the number of characters in *original-string*, you can replace the entire original string with *new-string*.
- By specifying a position immediately beyond the end of *original-string* as *start-number*, you can add *new-string* to *original-string*.

- By making *n* equal to 0, you can insert a new string.
- By making *new-string* an empty string, you can delete a string.

Example: @REPLACE(“This is the only one”,12,4,“first”) = This is the first one

@RIGHT @RIGHT(*string*,*n*) returns the last *n* characters in *string*.

Example: @RIGHT(“Allons enfants de la”,5) = de la

@S @S(*range*) returns the entry in the first cell in *range* as a label if the cell contains a label; if it contains a value, @S returns an empty string.

Example: @S(A4..A7) = Rent, if A4 contains the label “Rent”

@STRING @STRING(*x*,*n*) converts a numeric value *x* to a string with *n* decimal places. This @function formats the string as if it were a number, using the fixed numeric format. @STRING also rounds the formatted string value to the number of specified decimal places, just as it would when formatting a number.

To convert a string to its numeric equivalent, use @VALUE; *n* specifies the number of decimal places (0 to 15). *X* can be any value.

Example: @STRING(1234,3) = the string value 1234.000

@TRIM @TRIM(*string*) removes excess space characters from *string*. It removes all spaces that precede the first nonspace character and that follow the last nonspace character. It also replaces all consecutive spaces within the string with single spaces.

Example: @TRIM(“too   much   space”) = too much space

@UPPER @UPPER(*string*) converts all lowercase letters in *string* to uppercase.

Example: @UPPER(“A Fine Thing”) = A FINE THING

@VALUE @VALUE(*string*) converts a number entered as a *string* to its corresponding numeric value. The string may appear as a standard number (456.7), a number in scientific format (4.567E2), or a mixed number (45 7/8).

1-2-3 ignores numeric values and returns 0 for blank cells and empty strings. Leading and trailing space characters do not affect the result. In some cases, however, a string that contains editing symbols (for instance, a two-character trailing currency sign) yields ERR.

Example: @VALUE(“543”) = the numeric value 543

Date and Time @Functions

Date and time @functions generate and use serial numbers to represent dates and times. As a result, you can use dates and times in calculations.

Each date between January 1, 1900 and December 31, 2099 has an integer serial number called a date number. The first serial date number is 1, and the last date number is 73050. January 1, 1900 corresponds to 1, and December 31, 2099 corresponds to 73050.

Each moment during the day corresponds to a fractional serial number called a time number. For example, 0.000 is midnight, .5 (or 1/) is noon, and 0.99999 is just before midnight. You can enter a time number as a fraction or as a decimal.

Even though 1-2-3 stores dates and times as serial numbers for calculations, you can format them on the screen to appear as actual dates and times. For example, @DATE(86,10,12) generates the date number 31697. You can format this number to appear on the screen as 12-Oct-86. @TIME(23,59,59) generates the serial time number 0.99999. You can format this number to appear as 23:59:59.

To format dates and times, use the / **R**ange **F**ormat command. 1-2-3 has five possible date formats. The first three formats are permanent, but you can reset the last two formats using the / **W**orksheet **G**lobal **D**efault **O**ther **I**nternational **D**ate command. The first two of the four time formats are permanent 1-2-3 formats. You can reset the last two formats using the / **W**orksheet **G**lobal **D**efault **O**ther **I**nternational **T**ime command.

The date and time @functions that generate serial numbers are @DATE, @DATEVALUE, @NOW, @TIME, and @TIMEVALUE. The date @functions that use serial numbers are @DATE, @MONTH, and @YEAR. The time @functions that use serial numbers are @HOUR, @MINUTE, and @SECOND.

If you enter mixed numbers as date numbers in arguments, 1-2-3 uses their integer part. For example, if you enter 31790.45 as a date number, 1-2-3 uses 31790.

If you enter integers as arguments for time numbers, 1-2-3 interprets the fractional part as 0. For example, if you enter 31795 as a time number, 1-2-3 sees it as 31795.0 and uses .0 as the time number.

@DATE

@DATE(*year*,*month*,*day*) returns the serial date number of the year, month, and day.

You can extract the year, month, and day from a date number with @YEAR, @MONTH, and @DAY. You can use @MOD to determine the day of the week for a given date. (See p. R-151 for a discussion of @MOD.)

The year must be a number between 0 (1900) and 199 (2099), inclusive. The month must be a number between 1 and 12, inclusive. The day must be a number between 1 and 31, inclusive, and it must be a valid date for the given month. For example, you cannot use 31 for April. If the year, month, and day are not valid numbers, 1-2-3 returns the value ERR.

Note Even though there was no February 29, 1900 (it was not a leap year), 1-2-3 assigns a date number to this "day." This does not invalidate any of your date calculations unless you use dates between January 1, 1900 and March 1, 1900.

Example: @DATE(82,9,27) = 30221 (for 27-Sep-82 in D1 format)

@DATEVALUE

@DATEVALUE(*string*) returns the serial date number of the string value stating the year, month, and day.

@DATEVALUE is similar to @DATE in that it generates the serial date number for a particular date between January 1, 1900 and December 31, 2099. The difference is that @DATE uses three numeric values as arguments, and @DATEVALUE uses a single string value as its argument. Use @DATEVALUE when you want to convert data entered as labels to date numbers so you can use the dates in calculations.

The *string* must be in one of the five 1-2-3 date formats and must be enclosed in double quotes. 1-2-3's three permanent date formats are D1, DD-MMM-YY; D2, DD-MMM, with the current year automatically included; and D3, MMM-YY, with the date stored as the first of the month.

The two other formats in which you can enter a date are D4 and D5, which have more than one option in each format.

Examples: If you set the D4 format as DD.MM.YY, @DATEVALUE("23.12.85") = 31404

If you set the D4 format as MM/DD/YY, @DATEVALUE("12/23/85") = 31404

You need to press the Calc function key, (F9), to see the results when you change a date format.

Example: @DATEVALUE("23-Aug-86") = 31647

@DAY

@DAY(*date-number*) returns the day of the month (1 to 31) of *date-number*.

The date number must be the serial number of the desired date generated by the @DATE, @DATEVALUE, or @NOW function.

Example: @DAY(@DATE(85,3,27)) = 27

@MONTH @MONTH(*date-number*) returns the month (1 to 12) of the year of *date-number*.

The date number must be the serial number of the desired date generated by the @DATE, @DATEVALUE, or @NOW function.

Example: @MONTH(@DATE(85,3,27)) = 3

@YEAR @YEAR(*date-number*) returns the year (0 to 199) of *date-number*.

The date number must be the serial number of the desired date generated by the @DATE, @DATEVALUE, or @NOW function.

Example: @YEAR(@DATEVALUE("14-Feb-2019")) = 119

@NOW @NOW returns the serial number for the current date and time on the computer's clock. This includes both a date number (integer part) and a time number (fractional part). Every time 1-2-3 recalculates, it updates the value of @NOW.

You can format the value of @NOW in one of the date formats or one of the time formats. With a date format, 1-2-3 ignores the fractional part of the number; with a time format, 1-2-3 ignores the integer part of the number. In both cases, 1-2-3 records the date and time.

Examples: @NOW = 31048.5 at noon on January 25, 1985

@MOD(@NOW,7) = a value between 0 and 6, from which you can determine the day of the week

@MOD produces the remainder of the serial number generated by @NOW/7. 1-2-3 sees Sunday as the first day of the week and Saturday as the seventh day. If the result of this @function is 1, the day is Sunday; if the result is 2, the day is Monday; if the result is 0, the day is Saturday.

@TIME @TIME(*hour,minutes,seconds*) returns the serial time number of the specified hour, minute, and second. You can extract the hour, minute, and second from a time number with the @HOUR, @MINUTE, and @SECOND functions.

The hour must be any integer between 0 and 23, the minute must be between 0 and 59, and the second must be between 0 and 59. If *hour*, *minutes*, and *seconds* are not valid numbers, 1-2-3 returns the value ERR.

Example: @TIME(8,19,27) = 0.246840 (or 8:19:27 PM in D6 format)

@TIMEVALUE

@TIMEVALUE(*string*) returns the serial time number for a string stating the hour, minute, and second. Use @TIMEVALUE when you want to convert time entered as labels to time numbers so they can be used in calculations.

@TIMEVALUE is similar to @TIME in that it generates the serial number fraction that corresponds to a particular time of day. The difference is that @TIME uses three numeric values as arguments, and @TIMEVALUE uses a single string value as its argument.

The string must be in one of the four 1-2-3 time formats and must be enclosed in double quotes. 1-2-3's two permanent time formats are D6, HH:MM:SS AM/PM; and D7, HH:MM AM/PM. The two other formats in which you can enter a time are D8 and D9, which have more than one option in each format.

Examples: If you set the D8 format as HH:MM:SS 24 hr, @TIMEVALUE("15:12:00") = 0.6333

If you set the D8 format as HH.MM.SS 24hr, @TIMEVALUE("15.12.00") = 0.6333

You need to press CALC, F9, to see the results when you change a time format.

Example: @TIMEVALUE("3:12:00 PM") = 0.6333 (D6 format)

@HOUR

@HOUR(*time-number*) extracts the hour value from a *time-number* and returns a value between 0 (midnight) and 23 (23:00, or 11:00 PM).

The time number can be any fraction or a fractional serial number generated by @TIME, @TIMEVALUE, or @NOW.

Example: @HOUR(31774.5) = 12 (noon)

@MINUTE

@MINUTE(*time-number*) extracts the minute value from *time-number* and returns a value between 0 and 59.

The time number can be any fraction or a fractional serial number generated by @TIME, @TIMEVALUE, or @NOW.

Example: @MINUTE(0.333) = 59

@SECOND

@SECOND(*time-number*) extracts the second value from *time-number* and returns a value between 0 and 59.

The time number can be any fraction or a fractional serial number generated by @TIME, @TIMEVALUE, or @NOW.

Example: @SECOND(0.333) = 31

Financial @Functions

The 1-2-3 financial @functions make calculations relating to loans, annuities, and cash flows that occur over a term or a period of time.

Interest rates are entered as either percents or decimal fractions. You can type 15.5 percent as 15.5% or as .155. 1-2-3 automatically converts all percentages to decimal values.

You should express the term and the interest rate in the same units of time. To calculate a monthly payment when the interest and term are given in years, divide the annual interest rate by 12 to find the monthly interest rate, and multiply the term by 12 to obtain the number of monthly payment periods.

An annuity is an investment of a series of equal payments. An ordinary annuity is an annuity in which a payment is made at the end of each period. An annuity due is an annuity where each payment is made at the beginning of each period. The financial @functions make calculations by assuming that investments are ordinary annuities.

In the financial examples, monetary results are in cells formatted as Currency, and percentage results are in cells formatted as Percent.

@CTERM

@CTERM(*interest*,*future-value*,*present-value*) computes the number of compounding periods it will take an investment (*present-value*) to grow to a *future-value*, earning a fixed *interest* rate per compounding period.

@CTERM uses the following formula to compute the term:

$$\frac{\ln(fv/pv)}{\ln(1+int)}$$

where:
fv = future-value
pv = present-value
int = periodic interest rate
ln = natural logarithm

Example: You have just deposited $10,000 in an account that pays an annual interest rate of 10%, compounded monthly. You want to determine how long it will take to double your investment.

@CTERM(10%/12,20000,10000) returns 83.52, which tells you that it will take 83.52 months, or about seven years, to double your $10,000.

@DDB @DDB(*cost*,*salvage*,*life*,*period*) computes the depreciation allowance on an asset for a specified period, using the double-declining balance method.

The double-declining balance method accelerates the rate of depreciation, so that more depreciation expense occurs (and can be written off) in earlier periods than in later ones. Depreciation stops when the book value of the asset reaches the salvage value. The book value in any period is the total cost minus the total depreciation over all prior periods.

@DDB uses the following formula to compute the double-declining balance depreciation for any period:

$$\frac{(bv*2)}{n}$$

where: bv = book value in that period
n = life of the asset

1-2-3 adjusts the result of the formula when necessary to ensure that total depreciation taken over the life of the asset equals the asset's cost minus its salvage value.

You give @DDB this information as arguments:

cost	The amount you paid for the asset
salvage	The value of the asset at the end of its life
life	The number of periods it will take to depreciate to salvage value
period	The period you want to find the depreciation allowance for

Example: You have just purchased an office machine for $10,000. The useful life of the machine is considered to be eight years, and the salvage value after eight years is $1,200. You want to compute the depreciation expense for the fifth year, using the double-declining balance method.

@DDB(10000,1200,8,5) returns $791, which tells you that the depreciation expense for the fifth year will be $791.

@FV

@FV(*payments*,*interest*,*term*) determines the future value of an investment. It computes the future value based on a series of equal *payments*, each of a specific amount earning a periodic *interest* rate over the number of payment periods in the *term*.

@FV uses the following formula to compute future value:

$$pmt\frac{(1+int)^n-1}{int},$$

where: *pmt* = periodic payment
int = periodic interest rate
n = number of periods

@FV makes its calculations by assuming that the investment is an ordinary annuity.

Example: You plan to deposit $2,000 each year for the next 20 years into a bank account. The account is paying 10% interest, compounded annually. Interest is paid on the last day of each year. You want to compute the value of your account in 20 years. You make each year's contribution on the last day of the year.

@FV(2000,10%,20) returns $114,550, the value of your account at the end of 20 years.

To compute the future value of an annuity due, use the formula @FV(*payments*,*interest*,*term*)*(1+*interest*).

Example: If you make each year's contribution on the first day of the year, you would compute the amount for an annuity due.

@FV(2000,10%,20)*(1+10%) would return $126,005, the value of your account in 20 years, an additional $11,455 over the ordinary annuity.

@IRR

@IRR(*guess*,*range*) computes the internal rate of return for a series of cash flow values generated by an investment. In general, the IRR is the rate that equates the present value of an expected future series of even or uneven cash flows to the initial investment. 1-2-3 assumes that the cash flows are received at regular intervals.

1-2-3 bases its calculations on a series of approximations for the internal rate of return. Because this @function uses approximations, you enter a guess as the first argument. Enter a guess you feel is reasonable for the IRR. Because there may be more than one solution, try another guess if the result does not seem correct. If you get unexpected results with @IRR, you may want to use @NPV to analyze the cash flow.

Guess is a percentage that represents your estimate of the internal rate of return. In general, specify a guess between 0 and 1. If the iteration cannot approximate the result to within 0.0000001 after twenty tries, the result will be the value ERR.

Range is the cell range that contains the cash flow amounts. 1-2-3 considers negative numbers as cash outflows and positive numbers as cash inflows. The first cash flow in *range* must be a negative number.

Example: @IRR(A2,B2..B14) returns 6.11% over a 12-month term if the initial payment is $1000 and the twelve periodic receipts are each $120. Cell A2 contains the guess. In range B2 through B14, B2 contains the value −1000, and B3 through B14 each contain the value 120.

@NPV

@NPV(*interest,range*) computes the net present value of a series of future cash flows, discounted at a fixed periodic interest rate. 1-2-3 assumes that the cash flows occur at equal time intervals, that the first cash outflow occurs at the end of the first period, and that subsequent cash outflows occur at the end of subsequent periods.

@NPV uses this formula to compute net present value:

$$\sum \frac{V_i}{(1+int)^i}$$

where: $V_i \ldots V_n$ = series of cash flows in range
int = interest rate
n = number of cash flows
i = the current iteration (1 through n)

Example: @NPV(10%,D2..D13) = $340.69 if the assumed interest rate is 10 and D2..D13 contains twelve future cash flows, each of which is $50.

To find the net present value of an investment where you make an initial cash outflow immediately and follow it by a series of future inflows, you must factor the initial outflow separately because it is not affected by the interest.

If INITIAL is your initial outflow, SERIES is a range of future cash flows, and RATE is the periodic interest rate, the overall net present value is calculated by +INITIAL+ @NPV(RATE,SERIES).

Example: +INITIAL+@NPV(RATE,SERIES) = $904.07 when

INITIAL = ($4,700.00)
RATE = 14%
SERIES = $1,600.00
$1,600.00
$1,600.00
$1,700.00
$1,700.00

@PMT @PMT(*principal,interest,term*) computes the amount of the periodic payment on a loan. Most installment loans are computed like ordinary annuities in that payments are made at the end of each payment period.

@PMT uses the following formula to compute the payment:

$$prin * \frac{int}{1-(int+1)^{-n}}$$

where: *prin* = principal
int = periodic interest rate
n = term

Example: You are considering taking out a $50,000 mortgage for 30 years at an annual interest rate of 12.5%. You want to determine your monthly payment.

@PMT(50000,12.5%/12,30*12) returns your monthly payment, $533.63.

To compute the periodic payment of an annuity due, use the formula @PMT(*principal,interest,term*)/(1+*interest*).

@PV @PV(*payments,interest,term*) determines the present value of an investment. It computes the present value based on a series of equal *payments*, each of a specific amount, discounted at a periodic *interest* rate, over the number of periods in the *term*.

@PV uses the following formula to compute the present value:

$$pmt * \frac{1-(1+int)^{-n}}{int}$$

where: *pmt* = periodic payment
int = periodic interest rate
n = term

Example: You have just won a million dollars. The prize is awarded in 20 annual payments of $50,000 each (a total of $1,000,000 over 20 years). Annual payments are received at the end of each year.

You are given the option of receiving a single lump-sum payment of $400,000 instead of the million-dollar annuity. You want to find out which option is worth more in today's dollars.

If you were to accept the annual payments of $50,000, you assume that you would invest the money at a rate of 12%, compounded annually. @PV(50000,12%,20) returns $373,472, which tells you that the $1,000,000 paid over 20 years is worth $373,472 in present dollars.

Based on your assumptions, the lump-sum payment of $400,000 is worth more than the million-dollar ordinary annuity in present dollars (before taxes).

To compute the present value of an annuity due, use the formula @PV(*payments*,*interest*,*term*)*(1+*interest*).

Example: If the annual payments of $50,000 were made at the beginning (rather than at the end) of each year, you could use the annuity due formula.

@PV(50000,12%,20)*(1+12%) returns $418,289. Using the same assumptions, if the annual payments were made at the beginning of each year, the million-dollar annuity would be worth more than the lump-sum payment in present dollars (before taxes).

@RATE

@RATE(*future-value*,*present-value*,*term*) returns the periodic interest necessary for a *present-value* to grow to a *future-value* over the number of compounding periods in the *term*. If the investment is compounded monthly, for example, you multiply the value of @RATE by 12 to compute the annual rate.

@RATE uses the following formula to compute the periodic interest rate:

$$\left(\frac{fv}{pv}\right)^{1-n} - 1$$

where: fv = future-value
pv = present-value
n = term

Example: You have invested $10,000 in a bond. The bond matures in five years and has a maturity value of $18,000. Interest is compounded monthly. You want to determine the periodic interest rate for this investment.

@RATE(18000,10000,5*12) returns .00984, which tells you that the periodic (monthly) interest rate is 0.984%, just under 1% a month.

To determine the annual rate, multiply the above formula by 12, which yields a result of 11.8%.

@SLN @SLN(*cost*,*salvage*,*life*) computes the straight-line depreciation of an asset for one period.

The straight-line method of depreciation divides the depreciable cost (*cost – salvage*) evenly over the useful life of an asset. The useful life is the number of periods (typically years) over which an asset is depreciated.

@SLN uses the following formula to compute depreciation:

$$\frac{(c-s)}{n}$$

where:
- c = cost of the asset
- s = salvage value of the asset
- n = useful life of the asset

You give @SLN this information as arguments:

cost	The amount you paid for the asset
salvage	The value of the asset at the end of its life
life	The number of years it will take to depreciate to the salvage value

Example: You have purchased an office machine for $10,000. The useful life of this machine is eight years, and the salvage value in any year will be $1,200. You want to compute yearly depreciation expense, using the straight-line method.

@SLN(10000,1200,8) returns $1100, the annual depreciation allowance.

@SYD @SYD(*cost*,*salvage*,*life*,*period*) returns the sum-of-the-years'-digits depreciation for a specified period.

The sum-of-the-years'-digits method of depreciation accelerates the rate of depreciation so that more depreciation expense occurs in earlier periods than in later ones. The depreciable cost is the actual cost minus salvage value. The useful life is the number of periods (typically years) over which an asset is depreciated.

@SYD uses the following formula to compute depreciation:

$$\frac{(c-s)^*(n-p+1)}{(n^*(n+1)/2)}$$

where:
- c = cost of the asset
- s = salvage value of the asset
- n = useful life of the asset
- p = period for which depreciation is being computed

You give @SYD this information as arguments:

cost	The amount you paid for asset
salvage	The value of asset at the end of its life
life	The number of periods it will take to depreciate to salvage value
period	The period for which you want to find the depreciation allowance

Example: You have just purchased an office machine for $10,000. The useful life of this machine is eight years, and the salvage value after eight years will be $1,200. You want to compute depreciation expense for the fifth year, using the sum-of-the-years'-digits method.

@SYD(10000,1200,8,5) returns $978, the depreciation allowance for the fifth year.

@TERM

@TERM(*payments,interest,future-value*) returns the number of *payments* in the term of an ordinary annuity necessary to accumulate a *future-value*, earning a periodic *interest* rate. Each payment is equal to a specific amount.

@TERM uses the following formula to compute the term:

$$\frac{\ln(1+(fv*int/pmt))}{\ln(1+int)}$$

where: *pmt* = periodic payment
fv = future-value
int = periodic interest rate
ln = natural logarithm

Example: You deposit $2,000 at the end of each year into a bank account. Your account earns 10% a year, compounded annually. You want to determine how long it will take to accumulate $100,000.

@TERM(2000,10%,100000) returns 19 (when the cell format is fixed, 0), the number of years it will take to accumulate $100,000 in your account.

You want to know how long it will take to pay back a $10,000 loan at 10% annual interest, making payments of $1,175.60 a year. You can calculate the term necessary to pay back a loan by entering the future value as a negative number.

To compute the term of an annuity due, use the following formula @TERM(*payments,interest,future-value*/(1 + *interest*)).

Statistical @Functions

1-2-3's statistical @functions perform calculations on lists of values.

Every @function in this group except @COUNT accepts only numeric values as single arguments. @COUNT accepts numeric and string values as single arguments.

Numeric arguments can be numbers, cell addresses, cell names, range addresses, and range names. String arguments can be strings enclosed in quotation marks, cell addresses, cell names, range addresses, and range names.

A list contains one or more arguments. Each argument in a list can be a single value or a range. A list can contain both single values and ranges. For example, the argument list in the function @COUNT (B3..B8,C3..C8,D9,J3) is a valid argument list.

A list can include some blank ranges, but not all ranges can be blank. 1-2-3 ignores blank cells in multiple-cell ranges. For example, if you use @AVG to average the values in a range that spans eight cells and there is a blank cell in that range, 1-2-3 divides the sum by 7 to find the correct average. 1-2-3 sees a blank cell used as a single argument in a list as the value 0.

CAUTION When you use a range to calculate with the statistical @functions, 1-2-3 assigns the value 0 to all labels within that range and includes them in calculations.

All examples are based on the Weekly Sales worksheet in Figure 4.1. All monetary results are returned in Currency format. All dates are returned in D1 format.

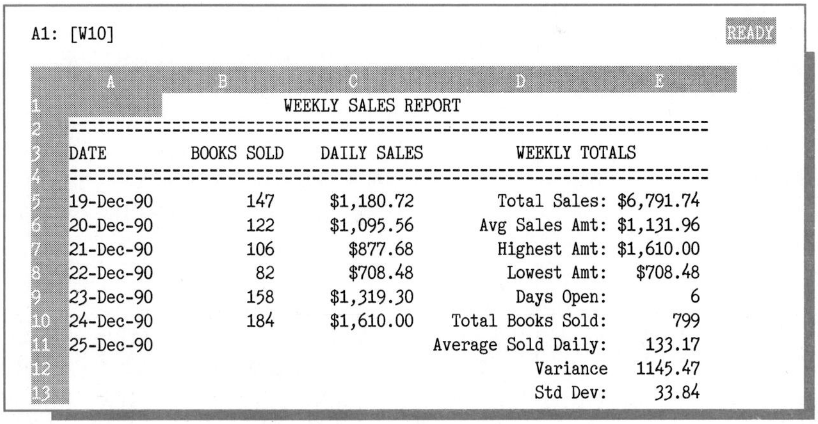

```
A1: [W10]                                                        READY

      A          B             C                  D              E
 1                          WEEKLY SALES REPORT
 2   ====================================================================
 3   DATE      BOOKS SOLD   DAILY SALES          WEEKLY TOTALS
 4   ====================================================================
 5   19-Dec-90        147    $1,180.72          Total Sales: $6,791.74
 6   20-Dec-90        122    $1,095.56        Avg Sales Amt: $1,131.96
 7   21-Dec-90        106      $877.68        Highest Amt: $1,610.00
 8   22-Dec-90         82      $708.48          Lowest Amt:   $708.48
 9   23-Dec-90        158    $1,319.30           Days Open:         6
10   24-Dec-90        184    $1,610.00    Total Books Sold:       799
11   25-Dec-90                          Average Sold Daily:    133.17
12                                                Variance    1145.47
13                                                 Std Dev:     33.84
```

Figure 4.1

@AVG @AVG(*list*) computes the average of all values in *list*. @AVG(*list*) is equivalent to the formula @SUM(*list*)/@COUNT(*list*).

Example: @AVG(C5..C11) = $1,131.96, the average sales amount for the week

(For more details about @AVG, see Lab 5.)

@COUNT @COUNT(*list*) counts the number of cells in *list*. @COUNT is one of the @functions that stops the ripple-through effect of the values NA and ERR, explained in the section on Special @Functions in this chapter.

If the list includes only blank ranges, the result is 0. @COUNT(A1..A4) = a value between 0 and 4. If every cell in range A1 through A4 is blank, @COUNT returns 0. If cells A1 through A4 contain one filled cell, it returns 1, and so on.

Each single value in the list adds 1 to the count, even if it is blank; therefore, you should use @COUNT with range arguments. For example, @COUNT(H54) = 1 even if cell H54 is blank.

Example: @COUNT(B5..B11) = 6, the number of days open that week

@MAX @MAX(*list*) returns the maximum value in *list*.

Example: @MAX(C5..C11) = $1,610.00, the highest daily amount taken in that week

(For more details about @MAX, see Lab 5.)

@MIN @MIN(*list*) returns the minimum value in *list*.

Example: @MIN(C5..C11) = $708.48, the lowest daily amount taken in that week

(For more details about @MIN, see Lab 5.)

@STD @STD(*list*) computes the population standard deviation of the values in *list*. The standard deviation is the square root of the variance.

The standard deviation measures the degree to which individual values in a list vary from the mean (average) of all values in the list. The lower the standard deviation, the less individual values vary from the mean and the more reliable the mean. A standard deviation of 0 indicates that all values in the list are equal.

@STD uses the n method (biased) to compute the standard deviation of population data, which uses the following formula:

$$\sqrt{\frac{\Sigma(V_i - AVG)^2}{n}}$$

where: n = number of items in *list*
V_i = the ith item in *list*
AVG = average of values in *list*

Example: @STD(B5..B11) = 33.84, the standard deviation for the daily average of books sold that week

If you want to compute the standard deviation of sample data, use the $n-1$ method (unbiased) by entering the following formula:

@SQRT(@COUNT(*list*)/@COUNT(*list*) – 1)*@STD(*list*)

@SUM @SUM(*list*) adds the values in *list*.

Example: @SUM(C5..C11) = $6,791.74, the total sales for that week

@SUM(B5..B11) = 799, the total number of books sold that week

(For more details about @SUM, see Lab 2.)

@VAR @VAR(*list*) computes the population variance of the values in *list*. Variance is a measure of the degree to which individual values in a list vary from the mean (average) of all values in the list. The lower the variance, the less individual values vary from the mean, and the more reliable the mean. A variance of 0 indicates that all values in the list are equal.

@VAR uses the n method (biased) to compute the variance of population data with the following formula:

$$\frac{\Sigma(V_i - AVG)^2}{n}$$

where: n = number of items in *list*
V_i = the ith item in list
AVG = average of values in list

@VAR(SAT_SCORES) computes the variance in SAT scores for the entire freshman class.

If you want to compute the variance for sample data, use the $n-1$ method (unbiased) by entering the following formula:

@COUNT(*list*)/(@COUNT(*list*) – 1)*@VAR(*list*)

In this example, @COUNT/(COUNT – 1)*@VAR(SAT_SCORES) computes the variances for the whole freshman class when SAT_SCORES includes a random sample of all scores.

Database Statistical @Functions

The database statistical @functions perform the same calculations on a field of a database as the statistical @functions perform on a list. Therefore, to use database statistical @functions, you must set up a database in a worksheet and establish a criteria range. If you have not yet created a database in 1-2-3, read the section on Data Commands in Chapter 2.

Each database statistical @function scans the database, selects the records that match the criteria range, and then performs the calculation on the selected values in the field you specify.

Each database statistical @function has three arguments: *input*, *field*, and *criteria*.

1. *Input* is the range. This range must include all the database records and their field names.
2. *Field* is the number containing the field. The first column of the input range is field 0, the second column is field 1, the third column is field 2, and so on.
3. *Criteria* is the criteria range you set up. The criteria range must contain the same field names as the input range and must include the criteria directly below each field name.

The first row in both the input and criteria ranges must contain the field names of each column. You can set up as many criteria ranges as you want to select values.

@DAVG @DAVG(*input*,*field*,*criteria*) averages the values in a *field* of the *input* range that meet the criteria in the *criteria* range. (For more details about @DAVG, see Lab 8.)

@DCOUNT @DCOUNT(*input*,*field*,*criteria*) counts the nonblank cells in a *field* of the *input* range that meet the criteria in the *criteria* range. (For more details about @DCOUNT, see Lab 8.)

@DMAX @DMAX(*input*,*field*,*criteria*) finds the maximum value in a *field* of the *input* range that meets the criteria in the *criteria* range. (For more details about @DMAX, see Lab 8.)

@DMIN @DMIN(*input*,*field*,*criteria*) finds the minimum value in a *field* of the *input* range that meets the criteria in the *criteria* range. (For more details about @DMIN, see Lab 8.)

@DSTD @DSTD(*input*,*field*,*criteria*) computes the population standard deviation for values in a *field* of the *input* range that meet the criteria in the *criteria* range.

@DSUM @DSUM(*input*,*field*,*criteria*) adds the values in a *field* of the *input* range that meet the criteria in the *criteria* range.

@DVAR @DVAR(*input*,*field*,*criteria*) computes the population variance for values in a *field* of the *input* range that meet the criteria in the *criteria* range.

Add-In @Functions

Add-in @functions that perform a variety of tasks are available from many software developers who create 1-2-3 add-in programs. These add-ins increase the number of @functions you can use to work with data in 1-2-3.

Once you attach add-in @functions, they remain in memory until you end the 1-2-3 session. If you want to retrieve a worksheet that contains add-in @functions, you should attach the appropriate add-in @function before retrieving the file.

5

The PrintGraph Program

The PrintGraph program lets you print graphs from files you create with the / **G**raph **S**ave command. / **G**raph **S**ave stores a description of the current graph file and adds the extension .PIC to the file's name. These are the only files PrintGraph can print.

PrintGraph does not work with all printers. PrintGraph can print graphs only on a graphics printer or plotter. You can use your printer with PrintGraph only if you specify an appropriate driver for it in the driver set that you build during the Install program. Your printer may appear as one of the choices in the Install program. If you have acquired a driver for your printer, you can add it as a single driver. (See Chapter 2, "Initializing and Installing 1-2-3," in Section 1, "Getting Started," for more information on using the Install program.)

See Chapter 4, "Starting and Ending PrintGraph," in Section 1, "Getting Started," for instructions on how to start PrintGraph on your computer system and for a description of the requirements for your particular hardware.

PrintGraph Commands

Before you print the graph, you must choose settings in PrintGraph. Your choice of settings determines layout, proportions, angle, typeface styles, and colors. You also use the settings to configure PrintGraph to your particular graphics printer and to specify the order in which you want to print a series of graphs. Table 5.1 summarizes the PrintGraph commands.

Table 5.1

Command	Description
Image-Select	Lets you specify one or more graph files (file extension .PIC) to be printed
Settings	Controls all PrintGraph settings, including the size and proportion of the graph, fonts, colors (if any), and the hardware you want to use
Go	Starts printing
Align	Tells PrintGraph that the paper is positioned at the top of the page
Page	Advances the paper to the top of the next page
Exit	Ends the PrintGraph session

When PrintGraph starts, the PrintGraph settings appear on your screen, and the PrintGraph menu appears on the control panel. You do not need to press slash (/) to make the menu appear. Figure 5.1 shows the PrintGraph menu tree.

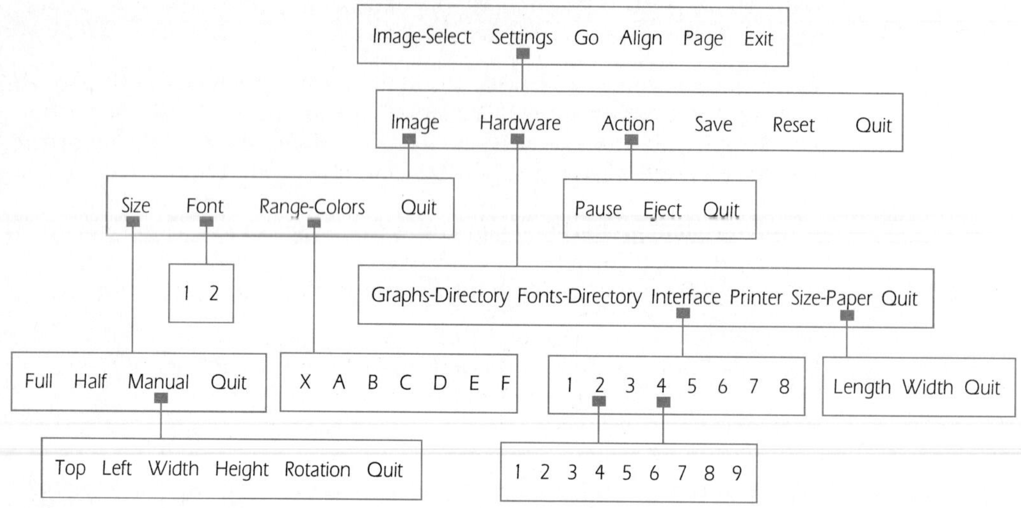

Figure 5.1

You issue a command by making a selection from the PrintGraph menu. To move the menu pointer to your selection, use →, ←, or SPACEBAR to select the option. You can also type the first letter of the option to select it. If you forget what a command or setting does, press F1 to display the corresponding Help screen.

The following steps summarize the procedure for printing a graph that you created and saved in 1-2-3:

1. Enter PrintGraph from DOS by typing **PGRAPH** at the operating system prompt. (Or, start PrintGraph from the Access system by choosing PrintGraph from the Access menu.)
2. Select **S**ettings from the PrintGraph menu to make any necessary changes. The default PrintGraph directory is drive A.
3. Select **I**mage-Select to indicate the graphs you want to print.
4. Make sure the printer is correctly set up and that the paper is in the right position, then select **A**lign.
5. Select **G**o to begin printing.
6. Select **P**age to advance the page when printing is complete.
7. Repeat any of steps 1–6 or end PrintGraph by selecting **E**xit. When you end PrintGraph, you return to DOS.

Note You cannot make changes to a graph file when you are in PrintGraph. You must return to 1-2-3 and re-create the graph (you cannot retrieve a .PIC file in 1-2-3). After you re-create the graph, you must save it before returning to PrintGraph.

The following sections describe the PrintGraph commands in the order in which they appear in the PrintGraph menu.

Image-Select Command

The **I**mage-Select command lets you specify the graph files that you want to print. When you select **G**o, the selected graphs print in the order in which you choose them. You can also use this command to look at a graph while in PrintGraph.

After selecting **I**mage-Select, an alphabetical menu of graph files in the specified directory is displayed. The menu shows when you created each file and the file's size in bytes. Use ↑ and ↓ to highlight a graph filename.

While the list of graph files is on the screen, you can press the Graph function key, F10, to preview a highlighted graph (if your monitor can display graphs).

A previewed graph in PrintGraph may look clearer than, and be scaled differently from, a graph that 1-2-3 displays. The printed graph prints the correct scaling and the clearer picture. The graph that appears on screen may not reflect the PrintGraph settings you have chosen; PrintGraph always uses the Block1 font for titles, legends, and scale numbers. (See the section on **S**ettings **I**mage **F**ont in this chapter.)

To select the graph files you want to print, highlight the filename and press SPACEBAR. PrintGraph marks a file you select for printing with a # symbol. To unmark a graph file, press SPACEBAR again when the filename is highlighted. To leave the graph file menu, press ↵.

The graphs you have selected will be printed using the print settings you have specified with the Settings command.

The next time you select **G**o, PrintGraph will print the graph files marked with a # symbol in the order in which you selected them. The names of the graph files you selected appear on the **I**mage-Select screen.

Settings Commands

The PrintGraph settings specify the graphics printer and interface that you are using, how you want your graph to look, when PrintGraph should do certain things such as eject paper, and whether PrintGraph should save or reset the current settings. Figure 5.2 shows the PrintGraph settings screen with the settings that 1-2-3 supplies. (Your system's default settings may be different.)

```
Copyright 1986, 1989 Lotus Development Corp.  All Rights Reserved. V2.2    MENU

Select graphs to print or preview
Image-Select  Settings  Go  Align  Page  Exit

   GRAPHS     IMAGE SETTINGS                      HARDWARE SETTINGS
  TO PRINT     Size               Range colors     Graphs directory
                Top        .395  X                   A:\
                Left       .750  A                 Fonts directory
                Width     6.500  B                   A:\
                Height    4.691  C                 Interface
                Rotation   .000  D                   Parallel 1
                                 E                 Printer
               Font              F                   Eps FX,RX/lo
                1  BLOCK1                          Paper size
                2  BLOCK1                            Width      8.500
                                                     Length    11.000

                                                  ACTION SETTINGS
                                                   Pause  No   Eject  No
```

Figure 5.2

When you change one of the settings, PrintGraph updates the screen display. Use BACKSPACE to erase characters and use (→) and (←) to move between existing characters. Use ESC to clear the entry and start again. When you select **G**o, PrintGraph prints the selected graph images using the current settings. The settings remain current until you change them or end the PrintGraph session.

Quit appears on several menus. Like ESC, **Q**uit returns you to the previous menu.

The following sections describe each **S**ettings command. The commands are listed in the order in which they appear in the Settings menu.

Settings Image

Size **F**ont **R**ange-Colors **Q**uit

Settings **I**mage controls the appearance of a graph.

The **I**mage settings control the way PrintGraph prints the graph: size, font (typeface), color, angle of rotation, and top and left margins.

Settings **I**mage **S**ize

Full **H**alf **M**anual **Q**uit

Settings **I**mage **S**ize determines the size and proportions of the graph on the paper.

Each setting controls the values (in inches) for margins, height and width, and (in degrees) rotation. If you use **F**ull or **H**alf, PrintGraph sets the **H**eight and **W**idth automatically. PrintGraph optimizes these settings for use with 8½ × 11-inch paper. The height and width settings do not change when you change the **H**ardware **S**ize-Paper setting. When you set the values with **S**ettings **S**ize **M**anual, PrintGraph may display settings slightly different from those you entered. Differences on the printed graph, however, will not be noticeable. Table 5.2 describes the settings you need to specify.

The **H**eight setting always measures the graph vertically (from top to bottom, as the paper feeds into the printer). The **W**idth setting always measures the graph horizontally (across the page, as it feeds into the printer).

Table 5.2

Setting	Meaning
Full	Sets rotation to 90 degrees to print the graph sideways on the page. (The X axis is drawn along the height of the page.) Proportions are close to those you see displayed on the screen. With 8½ × 11-inch paper, this setting prints one graph on a page.
Half	Sets rotation to 0 degrees. (The X axis spans the width of the page.) Proportions are close to those you see displayed on the screen. With 8½ × 11-inch paper, this setting lets you print two graphs on a page. This is the default setting.
Manual	Sets all variables as shown below. Proportions depend on your settings.
Top	Sets the size of the top margin in inches.
Left	Sets the size of the left margin in inches.
Width	Sets the width of the graph (horizontal distance) in inches.
Height	Sets the height of the graph (vertical distance) in inches.
Rotation	Sets the number of degrees the graph is turned counterclockwise (90 degrees produces a quarter turn to the left).

Three of these settings affect the proportions of your graph: width, height, and rotation. If you set these manually and want to retain the standard proportions of the graph, you must consider several things:

When PrintGraph sets a graph's size automatically, it preserves the aspect ratio, or the ratio of the graph's width to its height: approximately 1.385 (X axis) to 1 (Y axis). If you want to maintain these proportions, you must calculate this ratio. For instance, if X = 3.0, then Y = 2.165 (because Y = X/1.385). If Y = 4.5, then X = 6.237 (because X = Y*1.385).

If, however, you change the rotation to anything except 0, you must calculate the aspect ratio again to retain the standard proportions. Height and width are always measured in relation to the page, not in relation to the graph's axes. Thus, if rotation is set to 0 degrees, the height setting refers to the Y axis. If rotation is set to 90 degrees, the height setting refers to the X axis. To maintain the same proportions when setting rotation from 0 to 90 degrees, you must invert the width and height settings.

Rotation settings that turn rectangular graphs along vertical or horizontal axes (0, 90, 180, or 270 degrees) always create right-angled corners. If you select other rotations, you must make another calculation to preserve right-angled corners. Without this calculation, your graphs will be drawn as rhomboids and your pie charts as ellipses.

Pie charts must always retain the standard aspect ratio of 1 (Y axis) to 1.385 (X axis) to preserve their circular shape. The first radial line drawn always runs from the center of the pie toward the title line at the top of the graph. PrintGraph interprets this line as the Y axis when rotating the pie chart.

Settings **I**mage **F**ont

1 2

Settings **I**mage **F**ont determines which font (typeface) PrintGraph uses in printing the graph's text portions.

Follow these steps to establish which typeface PrintGraph uses when printing your graphs:

1. Select **1** or **2** to see the list of available fonts. PrintGraph uses Font 1 for the first line of the graph's title and Font 2 for all other alphanumeric characters in the graph, including the other titles, legends, and scale numbers. If you do not select Font 2, PrintGraph uses Font 1 for the entire graph.

   The available fonts are, Block1, Block2, Bold, Forum, Italic1, Italic2, Lotus, Roman1, Roman2, Script1, and Script2.

The numbers at the end of similar font names indicate how heavy (dark) each font is; for example, Script2 is heavier than Script1. The heavier font produces high-quality graphs only with high-resolution printers and plotters.

Note Some PrintGraph fonts are designed for plotters, not raster graphics printers such as dot matrix and inkjet printers. In particular, the Italic and Script fonts will probably be unsatisfactory if you use them with a dot matrix printer. The Bold, Forum, and Roman fonts work well on raster printers if you choose a high enough density. The Block fonts provide the best results with a raster printer.

2. Highlight your choice using (↑) and (↓). Mark it by pressing SPACEBAR. The # symbol appears to the left of your choice. To remove the # symbol from a selection, highlight the selection and press SPACEBAR again.

3. Press (↵) to enter your selection and return to the previous menu. Use ESC to return from the font listings without making any changes.

Before you print a graph, make sure the fonts directory setting is correct. If you need to change it, select **S**ettings **H**ardware **F**onts-Directory and specify the correct directory.

CAUTION If the fonts PrintGraph uses are stored on a removable disk (for instance, in a two-disk system), do not remove the disk from the drive during the PrintGraph session.

Settings Image Range-Colors

X A B C D E F Quit

Settings **I**mage **R**ange-Colors assigns colors to graph ranges.

When you select **R**ange-Colors, PrintGraph displays a menu that lists the graph ranges (X, A through F). Each range is associated with an available color. Depending on the type of printer you are using, this menu may offer several colors or only black. Use (→) and (←) to move through the menu and see what colors your system offers.

The color you assign to the X range determines the color of the grid (the box that contains the graphed data and everything, except legends, outside the box). The grid includes scale numbers, titles, and exponents. PrintGraph uses the colors you assign to ranges A through F to draw the graphed data and the legends.

You cannot select **R**ange-Colors until you have specified a printer or plotter.

Pie Charts

When you print a pie chart, two things determine the colors of slices: the values in the B data range when you saved the graph in 1-2-3 (/ **G**raph **S**ave) and the colors assigned in PrintGraph (**R**ange-Colors). Each B data range value in 1-2-3 corresponds to a range in PrintGraph, as follows:

B data range values in 1-2-3:	Range in PrintGraph:
1	X
2	A
3	B
4	C
5	D
6	E
7	F

PrintGraph uses the color you assign to a range in each slice that has the corresponding B-range value. For example, if the B-range slice is 4 (or 104, exploded), PrintGraph prints the slice in the color you assigned to range C using **R**ange-Colors; if the B-range value of a slice is 6, PrintGraph prints it in the color you assigned to range E; and so on.

PrintGraph uses the color you assigned to the X range for labels and titles. It uses the color you assigned to the A range for the pie's border.

Plotter Pens

If you are using a plotter, 1-2-3 prompts you to load the pens in a specific order when you select **G**o. Depending on the plotter, PrintGraph beeps when it is time to change the color of a pen and prompts you to do so. Refer to your plotter's documentation for information on using different pens.

Note When you print a graph on a remote plotter, the number of pens in the plotter limits the number of colors you can use. In addition, the number of colors you specify when you are using a remote plotter cannot exceed the number of pen stalls in the plotter.

Settings **I**mage **Q**uit

Settings **I**mage **Q**uit returns you to the Settings menu.

Settings **H**ardware

Graphs-Directory **F**onts-Directory **I**nterface **P**rinter **S**ize-Paper **Q**uit

Settings **H**ardware tells PrintGraph how to find and print a graph. These settings tell PrintGraph the type of printer you are using, where your files are located, which interface you require, and what size paper you are using. Unless you change printers, you can usually leave these settings unchanged.

The next sections describe each selection in the Settings Hardware menu.

Settings Hardware Graphs-Directory

Settings **H**ardware **G**raphs-Directory specifies the directory, including the drive, that PrintGraph searches for graph files (file extension .PIC). The default drive is A. If you plan to use graph files stored on the disk in drive B, enter the specification B:\. See Chapter 4, ''Starting and Ending PrintGraph,'' in Section 1, ''Getting Started,'' for details on establishing your PrintGraph hardware setup.

Settings Hardware Fonts-Directory

Settings **H**ardware **F**onts-Directory specifies the directory, including the drive, that PrintGraph searches for font (.FNT) files. The default drive is A. PrintGraph searches the directory you specify here before it prints or displays a graph.

Settings Hardware Interface

1 2 3 4 5 6 7 8

Settings **H**ardware **I**nterface sets the communication channel between PrintGraph and your printer. Your choice for a setting depends on your computer. Some sample settings follow:

Setting:	Meaning:
1	Parallel 1 (standard interface for personal computers)
2	Serial 1
3	Parallel 2
4	Serial 2
5	DOS device LPT1
6	DOS device LPT2
7	DOS device LPT3
8	DOS device LPT4

Note These are sample settings only. PrintGraph needs to know the correct settings for your hardware. If you are unsure about interface types, ports, and baud rates, consult your printer's manual or your dealer. Settings 1 through 4 are for printers physically linked to your system. The rest are for logical devices and are generally used to connect printers over a local area network.

CAUTION If you use a logical device to print a graph file on a raster printer, you may use substantial disk space on the machine to which the printer is attached. A low-density raster printer used this way requires about 40K of disk space; a high-density printer requires about 500K.

Baud Rates for a Serial Printer

If you specify a serial interface for this setting, you must also tell PrintGraph your printer's baud rate. Baud rate is the speed at which PrintGraph transfers data. You can probably adjust the baud rate your printer uses. If so, select the fastest baud rate that will correctly transmit data without losing it. See your printer's manual for details. Baud rates in order of increasing speed are as follows:

Setting:	Baud Rate:
1	110
2	150
3	300
4	600
5	1200
6	2400
7	4800
8	9600
9	19200

Before you use a serial port to print 1-2-3 graphs, you must also configure it to the following settings:

Setting:	Value:
Data bits	8
Stop bits	If 110 baud, 2; otherwise, 1
Parity	None
Handshaking (XON/XOFF)	Enabled

You must change these settings on your printer, not in PrintGraph. See your printer's manual for details.

Settings Hardware Printer

Settings **H**ardware **P**rinter tells PrintGraph which printer you are using and, in some cases, how densely to print the graph.

When you select **P**rinter, PrintGraph displays a list of graphics printers that you selected with the Install program. Select the type of printer you are currently using. (See Chapter 4, "Starting and Ending PrintGraph," in Section 1, "Getting Started," for more information about creating and updating your list of printers.) Follow these steps to select the printer from the list PrintGraph displays on your screen:

1. Highlight your choice using ↑ and ↓.
2. Mark your selection by pressing SPACEBAR.

3. The # symbol appears to the left of your choice. To remove the # symbol from a selection, highlight the selection and press SPACEBAR again.

4. Press ↵ to enter your selection and return to the previous menu.

Some printer names on the list are described as low or high density, indicating the relative density, or resolution, of the printing. Denser printing means finer detail in your graphs, but it also means much slower printing. If you are using a dot matrix printer, some fonts will work only if you use high density. (See the section on **S**ettings **I**mage **F**onts, earlier in this chapter, for details.)

Settings **H**ardware **S**ize-Paper

Length **W**idth **Q**uit

Settings **H**ardware **S**ize-Paper identifies the size of paper you are using with your graphics printer. The default is 8½ × 11 inches.

To specify a length of printer paper different from the default length of 11 inches, change the **L**ength setting in PrintGraph. Manually adjust the settings for paper length (sometimes called form length) on your printer. See your printer's manual for information on changing the paper length setting.

If you cannot adjust the paper length setting on your printer manually, leave the PrintGraph default setting of 11 inches.

To adjust the paper's width, change the **W**idth setting in PrintGraph.

Settings **A**ction

Pause **E**ject **Q**uit

Settings **A**ction controls what PrintGraph does between printing graphs.

Pause controls whether PrintGraph pauses before printing each graph.

Setting:	Meaning:
Yes	PrintGraph pauses before printing each graph and signals the pause by beeping continuously. Use this setting when you need to change paper or switch settings on a printer between graphs. Press SPACEBAR to continue.
No	PrintGraph does not pause before printing each graph.

Note When you are printing on a network device, **S**ettings **A**ction **P**ause has no effect on the printer. PrintGraph pauses but does not let you know what is happening at the network device.

Eject controls whether PrintGraph automatically advances the paper to the next page after printing a graph.

Setting:	Meaning:
Yes	Paper advances to the next page after each graph is printed. Use this setting to print one graph per page. On continuous formfeed paper, the paper advances to the top of a new page before printing resumes. On a plotter, PrintGraph prompts you to insert a new sheet of paper before printing resumes.
No	Paper does not advance after each graph is printed. If PrintGraph determines that the next graph is too long for the current page, the paper advances to the top of the next page. This depends on the **S**ize-Paper setting.

Quit returns you to the previous menu.

Settings **S**ave

Settings **S**ave stores PrintGraph settings (except graph images).

Each time you start a session, PrintGraph reads settings from PGRAPH.CNF. You can change these settings any time during the current session. Use **S**ave to copy your changes to PGRAPH.CNF so that they become the new standard for your PrintGraph sessions. 1-2-3 stores the settings, except for the selected graph images, in the file PGRAPH.CNF.

PrintGraph does not remember the settings you change during a session unless you use **S**ettings **S**ave. Each time you start a session or select **R**eset, PrintGraph reads the more recently saved settings.

If you use PrintGraph directly from the disk that contains the PrintGraph program, make sure it is in the disk drive with its write-protect tab removed before you select **S**ave.

Settings **R**eset

Settings **R**eset replaces the current settings with those in PGRAPH.CNF.

Use **R**eset if you have changed, but not saved, the settings during the current session and you want to restore the settings you had when you started the session.

Settings **Q**uit

Settings **Q**uit lets you return to the PrintGraph main menu after changing any setting.

Go Command

Go tells PrintGraph to print the graphs you choose. Before you select **G**o, make sure you have established the right settings and selected all the graphs you want to print. There is no confirmation step.

If you are using a plotter, PrintGraph prompts you to load the pens in the order of the list PrintGraph displays. When you finish loading the pens, press SPACEBAR.

There may be a brief pause before printing actually begins. PrintGraph uses the settings you selected to format and print the selected graphs on your printer or plotter. As PrintGraph works, the control panel displays messages about PrintGraph's activities. During printing, your printer or plotter may pause for several seconds. When PrintGraph finishes printing, the control panel returns to the main PrintGraph menu.

To stop printing a graph, press BREAK. If you are on a network and PrintGraph returns to the 1-2-3 main menu before printing begins, you can select **P**age to start printing the graph.

Align Command

PrintGraph automatically assumes that the paper is aligned at the top of the print page only at the beginning of a PrintGraph session. If you adjust the paper's position manually after the start of the session so that the top of the page is at the right place to start printing, use **A**lign to tell PrintGraph that the current paper position is the top of the page.

No paper movement takes place, but PrintGraph now assumes that the paper is correctly positioned at the top of the page in the printer. If you are using a plotter, PrintGraph prompts you to set up the plotter and to press SPACEBAR.

With some printers, you must also set the printer's Top of Page or Home position. See your printer's manual.

Page Command

Page advances the paper one page in your printer or plotter. Use it to separate batches of graphs or whenever you want a blank page.

Exit Command

Select **E**xit to end the PrintGraph session.

CAUTION PrintGraph does not automatically save your current settings. If you want to use them in future sessions, save them before you select this command.

If you select **Y**es, PrintGraph ends, returning you to DOS (or to the Access system if you began PrintGraph from the Access menu). If you select **N**o, the PrintGraph session continues.

Appendix A Removing 1-2-3 Release 2.01 from Your Hard Disk

Follow the instructions below to use your previous 1-2-3 program directory for the Release 2.2 program files.

1. If your previous 1-2-3 program directory contains data files (such as .WKS, .WK1, .PRN, or .PIC files), create a data directory and copy your data files to it. You can read the files from this directory when you use them with Release 2.2. To do this, follow these steps:
   - Type **C**: and press (↵) to make drive C the current drive.
   - Type **CD**\ and press (↵) to make the root directory of your hard disk the current directory.
   - Type **MD\123DATA** and press (↵) to create a new directory for your data files.
   - Type **CD**\ followed by the name of your previous 1-2-3 program directory (e.g., CD\123) and press (↵) to make it the current directory.
   - Type **COPY *.W?? C:\123DATA** and press (↵) to copy any worksheet files to your data directory. Repeat this step for text files and graph files; substitute the extensions .PRN and .PIC for .W??.
2. Remove copy protection from your Release 2.01 files.
   a. *If you have your original System Disk*, follow one of these procedures:
      - Start the 1-2-3 Release 2.01 Install program, select Advanced Options, and then select Remove 1-2-3 from a Hard Disk.

      OR
      - Follow the COPYHARD/U directions in the chapter entitled "Installing 1-2-3" in your Release 2.01 manual.

   b. *If you do not have your original System Disk*, follow these steps:
      - Make your Release 2.01 program directory the current directory.
      - Insert the 1-2-3 Release 2.2 Install Disk in drive A.
      - Type **A:ZAP 2.01** and press (↵).

Note If you are using a version of DOS 2, you will not be able to run ZAP from drive A. In this case, you must copy ZAP.EXE from the 1-2-3 Release 2.2 Install Disk into your 1-2-3 program directory. Once you have done this, type **DIR ZAP.COM** and press (↵). If the message 'File not found' appears, type **ZAP 2.01** and press (↵). Otherwise, type **DEL ZAP.COM** and press (↵) to delete the ZAP.COM file. You can then run ZAP by typing **ZAP 2.01** and pressing (↵).

3. Use the **DEL *.*** or **ERASE *.*** command to erase the contents of your previous 1-2-3 program directory.
4. Continue your installation procedure as outlined in "Initializing and Installing 1-2-3."

Appendix B Printer and Display Drivers

Video Drivers

AT&T 6300, single-color monitor
AT&T 6300, color monitor
AT&T Hi-Res B&W
Compaq CGA with Color Monitor
Compaq Display
GRiDCase Series
Hercules Card (80x25) Mono
Hercules Card (90x38) Mono
Hercules RamFont — Combined (90×25)
Hercules RamFont — Combined (90×38)
IBM 3270, Mono — Separate
IBM 3270-PC/GX Hi-Res
IBM 3270-PC/GX Med-Res
IBM 3270-PC Hi-Res
IBM 3270-PC Med-Res
IBM Color Monitor Med-Res
IBM/Compaq CGA with B&W Monitor
IBM/Compaq Enhanced Graphics (80×25)
IBM/Compaq Enhanced Graphics (80×43)
IBM/Compaq Enhanced Graphics (EGA)
IBM/Compaq Enhanced Graphics — Dual
IBM/Compaq Hi-Res
IBM/Compaq Hi-Res — Dual
IBM/Compaq Med-Res — Dual
IBM/Compaq Video Graphics (VGA 80×43)
IBM/Compaq Video Graphics (VGA 80×25)
IBM/Compaq Video Graphics (VGA 80×50)
IBM/Compaq Video Graphics (VGA) — Dual
IBM/Compaq Video Graphics (VGA)
IBM Monochrome Display
IBM Multi-Color Graphics (MCGA) Color
IBM Multi-Color Graphics (MCGA) Mono
IBM PC Convertible & Color Monitor
IBM PC Convertible & One-color Monitor
IBM PC Convertible LCD screen
IBM PC or Compatible
Toshiba T1100 Plus
Toshiba T1100 Plus and T1200
Toshiba T3100/T3200/T5100 (80×50)
Toshiba T3100/T3200/T5100 (80×25)
Universal Text Display
Universal Text Display ASCII No LICS

Non-Video and Non-Printer Drivers

Math Coprocessor Floating Point Driver
IBM Keyboard
IBM Port Interface
Numbers first
Numbers last
Software Floating Point Driver

Printer Drivers

Amdek Amplot II Plotter
Anadex DP-9620A Silent Scribe
ASCII
CalComp Model 84 Plotter
Canon A-1210
Canon PJ-1080A Color Ink Jet Printer
C. Itoh Prowriter 8510
C. Itoh Prowriter 8510A
Diablo 630
Epson FX and RX series High density
Epson FX and RX series Low density
Epson FX, RX and JX/LQ-800, 1000, and 1500
Epson GQ-3500 Hi density
Epson GQ-3500 Low density
Epson GQ-3500
Epson HI-80 Plotter
Epson JX series High density
Epson JX series Low density
Epson LQ-2500 Hi density
Epson LQ-2500 Low density
Epson LQ-800, 1000 and 1500 Hi density
Epson LQ-800, 1000 and 1500 Low density
Epson MX series
Epson MX series High density
Epson MX series Low density
Epson LQ 2500 and 2550
Epson LQ 2550 High density 180 dpi Color
Epson LQ 2550 High density 180 dpi B&W
Epson LQ 2550 Lo density 60 dpi Color
Epson LQ-2550 Lo density 60 dpi B&W
GE/Genicom 3000 B&W or Color Low density
GE/Genicom 3000 B&W or Color High density
GE/Genicom 3000 B&W or Color
Houston Instrument DMP-29 Plotter
HP 2225 series and 2930 series
HP 2225 ThinkJet
HP 2686 LaserJet series
HP 2930 series — PaintJet paper
HP 3630 PaintJet — paper
HP 3630 PaintJet — transparency
HP 7440A Plotter — 8½×11 paper

HP 7440A Plotter — 8½×11 transparency
HP 7470A Plotter — 8½×11 paper
HP 7470A Plotter — 8½×11 transparency
HP 7475A Plotter — 8½×11 paper
HP 7475A Plotter — 8½×11 transparency
HP 7475A Plotter — A3 paper
HP 7550A Plotter — 8½×11 paper
HP 7550A Plotter — A3 paper
HP DeskJet Hi density
HP DeskJet Low density
HP LaserJet Low density
HP LaserJet+ or LaserJet II Med density
HP LaserJet+ or LaserJet II High density
HP DeskJet and DeskJet Plus portrait
HP DeskJet Plus Hi density 300 dpi
HP DeskJet Plus landscape
HP DeskJet Plus Lo density 150 dpi
IBM Graphics Printer High density
IBM Graphics Printer Low density
IBM Graphics, Quietwrt, PC Convertible
IBM Jetprinter Hi-Res
IBM Jetprinter High density
IBM Jetprinter Low density
IBM Jetprinter Low-Res
IBM PC Color Printer
IBM PC Color Printer High density
IBM PC Color Printer Low density
IBM PC Convertible Printer High density
IBM PC Convertible Printer Low density
IBM 3812 Pageprinter
IBM 3852 Color Printer
IBM Proprinter High density
IBM Proprinter Low density
IBM Proprinter or Proprinter XL
IBM Proprinter XL High density
IBM Proprinter XL Low density
IBM Quickwriter
IBM Quickwriter High density
IBM Quickwriter Low density
IBM Quietwriter II and III High density
IBM Quietwriter II and III Low density
IBM XY/749 Plotter
IDS Prism 80, 132
IDS Prism 80, 132 High density
IDS Prism 80, 132 Low density
Inforunner Riteman 280 High density
Inforunner Riteman 280
Inforunner Riteman 280 Low density
Infoscribe 1200 High density
Infoscribe 1200 Low density
MPI Printmate 150
NEC 3550 Spinwriter
NEC 8023
NEC Pinwriter P5
NEC Pinwriter P5 High
NEC Pinwriter P5 Low
NEC Pinwriter P5XL
NEC Pinwriter P5XL High
NEC Pinwriter P5XL Low
NEC Pinwriter P6
NEC Pinwriter P6 High
NEC Pinwriter P6 Low
NEC Pinwriter P7
NEC Pinwriter P7 High
NEC Pinwriter P7 Low
Okidata Microline 82A, 83A
Okidata Microline 84, 92, 93
Okidata Pacemark 2410
Okidata 391, 393 and 393C
Okidata 391 Hi density 180 dpi B&W
Okidata 391 Lo density 60 dpi B&W
Okidata 393C Hi density 180 dpi Color
Okidata 393C Lo density 60 dpi Color
Printek 920
Printronix MVP 150
Printronix MVP 150B High density
Printronix MVP 150B Low density
Qume Sprint 11/40
Star Gemini 10x, 15x
Star Gemini 10x, 15x High density
Star Gemini 10x, 15x Low density
TI 850, 855
TI 850, 855 High density
TI 850, 855 Low density
Toshiba P351 series
Toshiba P351C
Toshiba P351C High
Toshiba P351C Low
Toshiba P1350 series
Transtar 315 Color Printer
Unlisted Complete Capability
Unlisted Forced Auto-LF
Unlisted No Backspace
Unlisted No Backspace, Forced Auto-LF
Xerox 4020
Xerox 4020 Enhanced Color
Xerox 4020 Hi density Color
Xerox 4020 Lo density Color
Xerox 4045 CP
Xerox 4045 CP Bold High Res
Xerox 4045 CP Bold Medium Res
Xerox 4045 CP High Res (300 dpi)
Xerox 4045 CP Low Res (75 dpi)
Xerox 4045 CP Medium Res (150 dpi)

Index